VISITATIONS
OF THE
ARCHDEACONRY
OF STAFFORD
1829–1841

The Venerable Archdeacon GEORGE HODSON MA
From an engraved portrait (*Staffordshire Record Office* D 1274/8/27)

ROYAL COMMISSION ON HISTORICAL MANUSCRIPTS

Joint Publications Series Number 25

VISITATIONS OF THE ARCHDEACONRY OF STAFFORD

1829-1841

EDITED BY

DAVID ROBINSON

MA, Ph D

LONDON

HER MAJESTY'S STATIONERY OFFICE

© Crown copyright 1980
First published 1980

This volume has been prepared by the
Staffordshire Record Society.
It is published as that Society's
Collections for a History of Staffordshire,
4th series, Vol X, and
No 25 in the
Joint Publications
series of the Royal Commission on
Historical Manuscripts

ISBN 0 11 440066 0*

FOREWORD

The manuscript of Archdeacon Hodson's visitations is printed by courtesy of the Bishop and Dean and Chapter of Lichfield and of Mr MBS Exham, Diocesan Registrar and Chapter Clerk.

I owe to Mr MW Greenslade, Hon Editor of the Staffordshire Record Society, a considerable debt for his advice and assistance during the preparation of this edition. Mr DA Johnson and Mr RJ Sherlock have made helpful comments on the Introduction.

I am also indebted to the Staffordshire Record Society and the Royal Commission on Historical Manuscripts for publishing this book as a Joint Publication and to the staff of the Commission for seeing it through the press.

Although Hodson's visitations throw light on the clergy and their houses, the strength of Dissent and educational provision in his archdeaconry as well as on fabric and furnishing of the churches, I have concentrated in my introduction on the two last subjects. A study of the visitations as evidence of the state of the clergy in 1829–30 which originally formed part of my introduction will, it is hoped, be published in the Transactions of the South Staffordshire Archaeological and Historical Society. It may suffice to comment that the 1830s mark the beginning of a change in the nature and attitudes of the clergy as significant as, and in some respects parallel with, the change in attitudes to churchbuilding.

In 1974 Derbyshire Archaeological Society published *The Church in Derbyshire in 1823–24* (Record Series V, for 1969–70), an edition by Dr MR Austin of Archdeacon Butler's visitation of the archdeaconry of Derby. Dr Austin's volume appeared after the completion of my own edition and I have therefore not been able to make use of his conclusions in my Introduction.

David Robinson

CONTENTS

FOREWORD   iii

ABBREVIATIONS   vii

ORIGINAL DOCUMENTS CITED   viii

INTRODUCTION   ix

   GEORGE HODSON   ix

   THE ARCHDEACONRY   x

   THE VISITATIONS   xi

ARCHITECTURE AND STRUCTURE OF THE CHURCHES

   MEDIAEVAL   xiii

   CLASSICAL   xiv

   GOTHIC REVIVAL   xv

   CHURCH EXTENSION   xvi

   SITES OF CHURCHES   xvii

   ACCOMMODATION   xviii

   FREE SEATING   xviii

STATE OF THE CHURCHES

   FABRIC   xx

   FITTINGS   xxi

   VESTRIES   xxii

   SURPLICES   xxiii

   CHURCHYARDS   xxiii

   CONCLUSIONS   xxiv

CHURCHWARDENS, PARISH CLERKS AND INCUMBENTS

CHURCHWARDENS	xxiv
PARISH CLERKS	xxv
INCUMBENTS	xxvi

WORSHIP	xxvi
RESULTS OF HODSON'S VISITATIONS	xxvii
THE VOLUMES AND THEIR PROVENANCE	xxx
THE TEXT AS PRINTED	xxxi
NOTES TO THE INTRODUCTION	xxxiii
VISITATIONS	1

APPENDIXES

I. CHURCHWARDENS' EXPENDITURE ON CHURCH FABRICS	137
II. EXAMPLES OF HODSON'S ORDERS AND THE RESPONSE TO THEM	144
III. THE VISITATION OF ALREWAS	147
INDEX OF VISITATION RETURNS	149

ILLUSTRATIONS

THE VEN ARCHDEACON GEORGE HODSON MA	facing title page
MAP OF THE ARCHDEACONRY OF STAFFORD IN 1830	facing page 1

ABBREVIATIONS

Colvin
HM Colvin, *Biographical Dictionary of English Architects, 1660–1840* (London, 1954)

Eccles. Revs.
Report of the Commissioners appointed by his Majesty to inquire into the Ecclesiastical Revenues of England and Wales (London, 1835)

LJRO
Lichfield Joint Record Office

Scott, *Recollections*
GG Scott, *Personal and Professional Recollections* (London, 1879)

SRO
County Record Office, Stafford

VCH Staffs
Victoria History of the County of Stafford

WSL
William Salt Library, Stafford

White, *Dir. Staffs.* **(1834)**
W White, *History, Gazetteer, and Directory of Staffordshire* (Sheffield, 1834)

ORIGINAL DOCUMENTS CITED

LICHFIELD JOINT RECORD OFFICE

A/V/1/1	Archdeaconry of Derby: archdeacon's visitation book, 1823–1824
A/V/1/2–4	Archdeaconry of Stafford: archdeacon's visitation books, 1829–1841
B/A/1	Bishops' registers
B/A/3	Presentation deeds
B/A/11A	Curates' nominations and licences
B/A/19	Registrars' correspondence (including correspondence of proctors)
B/C/2	Consistory court books: instance and office promoted cases
B/C/5	Consistory court cause papers
B/V/5	Episcopal primary visitation returns

STAFFORDSHIRE RECORD OFFICE

D14/A/PC/2	Stowe parish records: churchwardens' account book, 1828–1887
D24/A/PC	Colwich parish records: churchwardens' vouchers and receipts, 1753–1855
D/120/A/PC	Aldridge parish records: churchwardens' vouchers and receipts, 1754–1849
D233/S/PV/1	Cheadle parish records: vestry minute-book, 1761–1839
D568/A/PC/1	Great Barr parish records: chapelwardens' account book, 1781–1899
D731/11	Seighford parish records: churchwardens' account book, 1805–1900
D795/16	Leigh parish records: parish officers' account book, 1811–1864
D874/3/7	Colwich parish records: printed circular on repewing of church, 1852
D922/36	Alstonefield parish records: churchwardens' account book, 1801–1901
D1016/2	Shenstone parish records: churchwardens' account book, 1823–1882
D1016/3	Shenstone parish records: vestry minute-book, 1821–1852
D1048/6/2	Sandon parish records: diaries of Edward Thomas, schoolmaster and parish clerk, 1829–1862
D1137/4/1	Barton under Needwood parish records: churchwardens' accounts, 1774–1895

INTRODUCTION

In 1841 the Hon and Revd FE Paget, rector of Elford, described in his novel *St. Antholin's* the inspection of a village church by a newly appointed archdeacon 'Dr Sharpe'.[1] The archdeacon is already on the roof of the nave when the churchwarden arrives, and proceeds to make a detailed survey of the church. He criticizes the dilapidated state of the east and south walls and observes that some of the roof beams need attention. Despite the churchwarden's attempts at dissuasion, he climbs a 'rude oak ladder the rounds of which were about two feet apart', to inspect the tower, saying 'nobody is fit for my office, who does not examine with his own eyes'. He finds the belfry choked with the remains of jackdaws' nests and the spire in a dangerous state. On his departure he promises to send within a day or two a list of repairs needed, leaving the churchwarden indignant at their probable scale and cost.

In the same year the Revd George Hodson, in discharge of his duties as archdeacon of Stafford, made his third tour of inspection of the fabrics of churches under his jurisdiction. He visited Elford and found the church undergoing the repair and restoration to which the profits of *St. Antholin's* were devoted. Hodson may indeed in some respects have been Paget's model for 'Dr Sharpe'. Within two months of his appointment as archdeacon on 9 May 1829 he had begun a careful and detailed inspection of the churches in his archdeaconry, issuing orders to those responsible – clergy, wardens and lay impropriators – to repair the fabrics in their care. The fictional archdeacon's recommendation of an experienced builder's opinion on the state of the steeple of St. Antholin's may be compared with Hodson's order at Elford in 1829 for a surveyor to report on the state of the walls and roof. The succession in which Paget lists the objects of Dr Sharpe's 'careful but rapid survey; roof, walls, windows, doors, each in turn were submitted to his scrutiny', follows the precise order of certain of Hodson's articles. Furthermore the schoolmaster and parish clerk of Sandon, another church visited by Hodson, recorded in his diary that Hodson was sufficiently active to climb the church tower.[2] Hodson's frequent orders for the repair of bells and bell chamber show that this was no isolated case.

There are, however, also notable points of difference. 'Dr Sharpe' was created by Paget in his own image as an ecclesiologist, who removed successive coats of whitewash with his clasp-knife to reveal carved foliage in Caen stone whereas Hodson, eighteen years Paget's senior, reflected the architectural taste and religious enthusiasm of Simeon's Cambridge rather than the Oxford of Keble. Much of the interest of Hodson's descriptions and orders here published lies in the fact that his inspections were made shortly before Paget and those who shared his views had started on their work of 'restoration'.

GEORGE HODSON

George Hodson was born in 1788, the youngest son of a Carlisle merchant. From Carlisle Grammar School he went to Trinity College, Cambridge, in 1805. He read mathematics and in 1810, the year of his graduation, migrated to Magdalene. As a schoolboy in Carlisle, he had heard Charles Simeon preach, and at Cambridge he came under his influence. Throughout his life he retained close links with Simeon, to whose influence he paid tribute in a memorial sermon preached in 1836 in Simeon's own church.[3] In 1811 he was ordained deacon and in the following year priest. Four years later he became curate of Clifton Old Church and married Mary Stephen: dual testimony to his membership of the closely-knit family of Evangelicals. He became chaplain to Lewis Way of Stanstead Park, Sussex, and tutor to Way's son Albert, the noted antiquary, and to the sons of friends of Way. Most notable among these pupils were Samuel Wilberforce, son of the Emancipator and later bishop of Oxford and of Winchester, and James Thomason, the Indian civil servant.[4]

In 1820 Hodson returned to Gloucestershire, having obtained a curacy at Maisemore near Gloucester, and took his pupils with him. His bishop, Henry Ryder, 'the first Evangelical on the Bench', was also patron of the benefice. When Ryder was translated from Gloucester to Lichfield and Coventry, one of his first acts of episcopal patronage was to collate to Hodson, on 2 October 1824, the perpetual curacy of Christ Church, Birmingham. In 1828 he collated to him the vicarage of Colwich and in 1829 the archdeaconry of Stafford.[5] Hodson remained archdeacon until his death in 1855, and vicar of Colwich until 1851 when he moved to St. Mary's, Lichfield. In 1833 he became chancellor of Lichfield Cathedral. In 1837 he was appointed one of Simeon's Trustees, but in his later years he became less markedly a party Evangelical.

THE ARCHDEACONRY

The archdeaconry of Stafford to which Hodson was appointed in 1829 was approximately coterminous with the county. It included three parishes – Cheswardine, Quatt and Worfield – which had been in the county at the time of the Domesday survey but had passed into Shropshire before 1100.[6] It excluded two detached Staffordshire parishes, Clent (with its chapelry of Rowley Regis) and Broome,[7] and the Staffordshire parts of three other parishes.[8] More recent alterations in boundaries have taken Handsworth, Harborne and Upper Arley out of Staffordshire, but of these only Handsworth came under the archdeacon's control. Harborne and Upper Arley, like thirty other ancient parishes, containing more than a quarter of the county's population, lay within peculiar jurisdictions. The main peculiars were those of the dean and chapter of Lichfield, of individual dignitaries and prebendaries of the cathedral, and of the royal free chapels of Wolverhampton, Tettenhall and Penkridge. The Lichfield peculiars covered a broad swathe of central Staffordshire from Lichfield north-west to Baswich, on the outskirts of Stafford, including Hodson's own parish of Colwich. They also covered certain parishes in the rural west of the county (Brewood, Adbaston and Ecceleshall) and the industrial south (Harborne, including Smethwick, and Tipton). The royal peculiars of Wolverhampton, Tettenhall and Penkridge formed a *bloc* in the west of the county, the ancient parish of Wolverhampton covering a large part of the Black Country.

The parishes under Hodson's jurisdiction covered a wide range of social and economic conditions. They included extensive, remote moorland parishes such as Alstonefield and Leek, lowland agrarian parishes (Hamstall Ridware, Clifton Campville), small parishes dominated by one landowner (Thorpe Constantine, Patshull), old-established towns such as Stafford[9] or Newcastle-under-Lyme, and parishes transformed by mining and industry such as West Bromwich and Stoke-upon-Trent. The main problem for the Church lay in the industrial areas. Already seventeen parishes – twelve of them ancient – contained more than half the population of the archdeaconry. The parochial structure had scarcely begun to respond to their needs.

THE VISITATIONS

Hodson made his first visit of inspection on 13 July 1829. The church was Tatenhill, annexed to the deanery of Lichfield, but neither the seniority in age and status of its incumbent nor the recent date of his own appointment prevented him from looking critically at it. On the following day he visited the neighbouring church of Barton-under-Needwood. The printed questionnaire he used was identical with those used by Hugh Owen as archdeacon of Salop in 1824 and by Samuel Butler as archdeacon of Derby in 1823-4.[10] Its eighty-five articles were derived from three sources. From eighteenth-century episcopal primary visitations it inherited questions about worship (the number of Sunday services, the frequency of administration of Holy Communion and the average number of communicants), the clergy (non-residence and the provision of curates), the benefice, and the strength of Dissent.[11] From early nineteenth-century reforming zeal came the concern for education and church accommodation, a concern also found in Bishop Ryder's primary visitation articles.[12] The third element, comprising almost half the articles, was the ancient legal responsibility of the archdeacon to inspect the fabric and furnishings of churches under his jurisdiction,[13] and these were virtually the sole subjects of the orders subsequently sent to the clergy and churchwardens of each church inspected.

Hodson's further visits of inspection in 1829 were spasmodic and depended probably on his presence in the areas visited for other reasons. Most of the churches were in the east of the county, near Lichfield; a few, such as Colton, Tixall, Weston and Stowe, were near Colwich. By the end of 1829 he had visited a total of nineteen churches on fifteen different days.

The visits of inspection made in 1830 were undertaken more systematically. Hodson began with the Black Country. On Monday, 19 April, he visited the two churches at Walsall and those at Darlaston and Wednesbury; on the following day All Saints' and Christ Church at West Bromwich, and Handsworth. On the Wednesday he turned his attention to the south-west of the county, inspecting the new church at Sedgley, a large industrial parish, and those of four other parishes lying beyond the industrial belt: Himley, Wombourn, Trysull and Penn. A month later, in mid-May, he visited four more churches in the Walsall area followed by seven in the south-west of the county and two (Worfield and Quatt) in adjacent parts of Shropshire. On Monday and Tuesday of the following week he turned his attention to the extreme east of the county, where he visited Tamworth and six neighbouring churches. Between Monday and Thursday, 7-10 June, he inspected eleven churches in central and western Staffordshire, and in the following week he set off northwards from Colwich in heavy rain[14] and visited fourteen churches in the Trent Valley and the Potteries in the course of four days. After inspecting a number of churches in mid-Staffordshire during the next three weeks, he began on 13 July an extensive tour of the north-east of the county – roughly the deanery of Leek and Alton[15] – where he visited forty churches in two weeks. Although most of these churches were in limestone dales or remote gritstone moors, he seems to have averaged distances of more than fifteen miles a day. After this strenuous tour the main area still to be visited was the north-west of the county, and in the week beginning 4 October he inspected fourteen churches there. On Friday 8 October 1830 he completed his first visitation by going to Cheswardine and Ellenhall.

Hodson's orders appear to have been written on the evening of each visit or the following morning. His letter to the churchwardens of Cheadle, for instance, is dated 16 July and headed 'Rectory'. His inspection is dated the previous day. Presumably he stayed at Cheadle rectory overnight and wrote the letter the following morning.

From 1831 to 1836 Hodson's annual visitations were not accompanied by inspection of individual churches, although on his appointment as cathedral chancellor in 1833 he at once visited Alrewas church, which came within the peculiar jurisdiction of that office. In 1837 and 1838 he made his second general tour of inspection of the archdeaconry, recording his orders in a copy of the original printed questionnaire.

This second inspection was undertaken at greater speed than that of 1829-30. Hodson began with a two-day tour through Lower Dovedale to Burton, inspecting the churches at Marchington, Hanbury, Tutbury and Rolleston, with the two Burton churches, on Friday, 25 August, and four other churches on the return journey through Needwood Forest the next day. On Thursday and Friday of the following week he inspected eleven churches in the area between Lichfield, Tamworth and the Leicestershire border. On Tuesday 6 September he completed his coverage of the eastern part of the county by visiting the church at Wychnor. On Friday and Saturday of the same week he visited ten churches north of Colwich and around Stafford. There followed ten days of unbroken activity, 11-21 September (excluding Sunday), when a total of forty-nine churches were seen. He travelled eastwards to Uttoxeter, and then north through the moorlands to Longnor. From there he went on through Leek to Audley and, on 20 and 21 September, to the Potteries and Newcastle-under-Lyme. Between the Monday and the Thursday of the following week he inspected a further eighteen churches around Trentham and Cheadle. A week later he went north-west to Mucklestone and Woore, south to Weston-under-Lizard, and thence east to the Black Country, where he inspected the two Walsall churches, Darlaston, Wednesbury, the two West Bromwich churches, Handsworth and the new chapel of Perry Barr on a single day, 13 October. On the following day he returned through Great Barr, Aldridge and Rushall. After two further isolated visits to Stowe and Tatenhill in 1837, and to two nearby churches, Colton and Blithfield, early in 1838, only the south-west of the county remained unvisited. In July 1838 he inspected, in four days, the eighteen churches in that area: Sedgley and Kingswinford in the western Black Country, the rural parishes and the adjacent parishes in Shropshire.

Three years later, in 1841, Hodson again preceded his visitation by a tour of inspection of the churches in his archdeaconry. He again entered his orders in a copy of his 1829-30 printed questionnaire. This visitation was yet more concentrated than its predecessors. A few churches were not visited or the orders have not survived, but most of the churches in the archdeaconry – and the number had again increased – were inspected during a single fortnight, 6-18 September, when sixty-six were seen, and during the four days 18-21 October, when a further twenty-six were visited.

In 1847 Hodson undertook a fourth tour of inspection, covering two-thirds of the archdeaconry.[16] For this his orders do not appear to have survived *en bloc*. A letter, however, containing his report on Kinver is preserved among its parish records.[17]

ARCHITECTURE AND STRUCTURE OF THE CHURCHES

MEDIAEVAL

Of the churches Hodson visited, rather more than half were essentially mediaeval in structure. Few of these were fine. St. Mary's, Stafford, had before the Reformation been a collegiate church with dean and chapter, and Tutbury the church of a Benedictine monastery. There were no substantial remains of Anglo-Saxon churches although, owing to continuing poverty, a comparatively high proportion of Norman buildings survived. Gothic church building continued late, especially in the north of the county, several Perpendicular churches being built in the seventeenth century.

Gothic work had been least subject to major alteration in medium-sized villages, wealthy for reasons either of agriculture or of parochial geography. The town churches had in most cases been rebuilt in the eighteenth century, as at Burton-upon-Trent, Newcastle-under-Lyme and Stone, or during the first three decades of the nineteenth century, as at Stoke-upon-Trent, Darlaston, Sedgley and Walsall. Some, such as Handsworth, West Bromwich, Wednesbury and Kingswinford, had been considerably altered in the 1820s. Four Gothic town churches survived comparatively unaltered in Hodson's day: Tamworth, Leek, Cheadle and Stafford, but of these Cheadle was rebuilt in the 1830s and Stafford heavily restored in the 1840s.

Hodson's descriptive vocabulary for Gothic buildings is purely eighteenth-century. He uses the adjectives 'neat', 'regular' and 'handsome', and his architectural judgments show a liberal acceptance of both Gothic and classical, such as was possible in the period after the rediscovery of Gothic and before its canonization. The counterpart, however, of this liberalism is imprecision and occasional inaccuracy. Writing eleven years after Thomas Rickman's *Attempt to Discriminate the Styles of English Architecture* he is still able to describe Norman buildings as Saxon, recognizing them by their 'massy pillars and circular arches'. He rarely attempts to describe other mediaeval buildings more precisely than as 'Gothic'. Blore, a largely fifteenth-century church with fourteenth-century tower, he describes as 'ancient Gothic . . . said to be eight hundred years old' and Alstonefield, mostly Decorated and Perpendicular, as 'early Gothic'. Blithfield, which was a mixture of Early English nave and chancel, Decorated tower and Perpendicular windows, he describes as 'regular'.

In contrast to Hodson's lack of antiquarian accuracy his aesthetic judgments were sound and vigorously expressed. Tutbury was 'a remarkably fine, noble Saxon structure, tho' mutilated and otherwise injured by time'. St. Mary's, Stafford, despite its poor state of repair, was 'very handsome . . . resembling a Cathedral in its structure'. Enville, Worfield and Blithfield were all 'very handsome', and Audley and Madeley were 'remarkably handsome'. The small seventeenth-century churches and chapels with square-headed windows were not described as Gothic but simply as 'ancient, low' (Maer), 'small, old' (Whitmore, Meerbrook) or 'very old, low' (Rushton Spencer).

Hodson was critical of cheap and tasteless repairs, alterations and additions. He frequently described churches as 'Gothic, but disfigured by modern alterations' (West Bromwich, Penn), 'spoilt by modern alterations' (Trysull) or 'the style and symmetry injured by successive alterations and additions' (Handsworth). In these instances the alterations appear to have been Gothic. At Forton the modern alterations which 'much spoilt' the church comprised the addition of a simple classical nave which by itself would probably have qualified for praise as neat.[18] At Draycott-in-the-Moors Hodson's objection, expressed in the comment 'rebuilt 100 years ago, without any regard to ancient style of structure', referred to the rebuilding of the church in a simple classical idiom. A similarly ecclesiological spirit may be detected in his comments on the church at Keele, where he described the simple Churchwarden Gothic, with pointed arches but Georgian proportions and no tracery, as 'by no means ecclesiastical'.

CLASSICAL

The first church built in Staffordshire in the classical style was the impressive and important one at Ingestre, 'incomparably the most elaborate country church of its time', in the style of Wren and perhaps designed by him.[19] The only other major classical architect represented in the county was James Gibbs, who built Patshull church and hall for Sir John Astley in the 1740s. Both these churches were built for squires who were the lords and virtually sole landowners of small parishes, and were quasi-private chapels.[20] At the other extreme of size and social organization three large town churches were also rebuilt in the eighteenth century. St. Modwen's at Burton-upon-Trent and St. Giles' at Newcastle-under-Lyme were rebuilt early in the century to provincial Baroque designs by the Smith family, local builder-architects of Tettenhall. Stone was rebuilt in 1754 to the design of William Robinson, the first Gothicizer of Strawberry Hill. Although classical in its proportions it was Gothic in detail, like an increasing proportion of churches built during the second half of the eighteenth century. In the Potteries three churches were built or rebuilt during the late eighteenth century. At Burslem a mediaeval chapel was rebuilt as a plain oblong building with round-headed windows,[21] and the chapels at Hanley and Lane End were similar to this in general structure but had pointed windows, set in two tiers to light the galleries.[22] In the industrial south a chapel was built at Brierley Hill in Kingswinford parish[23] during the 1760s. Darlaston church was rebuilt as a large simple structure in the first decade of the nineteenth century. These churches were perhaps a more satisfactory solution to the need for inexpensive churches in industrial areas than the 'cheap churches' of the 1820s and 1830s.

Another group of eighteenth-century churches comprised the chapels built or rebuilt in the remote hamlets of the Pennine moors, where small-scale mining and industrial development and agricultural encroachment on the waste had led to increases in population.[24] These chapels were mostly small and possessed very little architectural character beyond such features as projecting keystones to the windows, as at Quarnford, Elkstone and Endon, a Venetian east window as at Elkstone, Onecote and Longnor, a rusticated doorway as at Warslow or the symmetry produced by setting the doorway centrally in the south wall as at Longnor and Elkstone.[25] Several of them had broad, squat, crenellated towers. A local family of builder-architects, the Billinges, was associated with work at Longnor, Warslow and Quarnford, as well as carrying out repairs in Alstonefield, the mother-church of all three.[26]

To the south of these chapels, on the skirts of the Pennines, were three eighteenth-century churches of greater architectural pretensions. These were Rocester, with an apsidal east end and a south doorway over which a broken pediment enclosed a semi-circular window; Bradley-in-the-Moors, with a heavy string course at the level of the springers of the windows; and Draycott-in-the-Moors, with two string courses and a broken pediment to the doorway. At Marchington rusticated windows and doorways, *oculi* over the east window and west door, and a cupola crowning the tower bore witness to greater agricultural prosperity. This church was the work of Richard Trubshaw, a member of a family of builder-architects at Great Haywood[27] which was involved in much repair and rebuilding of churches elsewhere in mid-Staffordshire.

For classical churches, as for Gothic, Hodson's descriptive terminology is imprecise. Any building which employs the orders may be described as 'Grecian', a term he uses to cover Ingestre, Patshull, Burton-upon-Trent and Newcastle-under-Lyme. The two latter churches, built in the 1720s, he also describes as 'modern'. He offers no critical comment on the more architecturally notable churches. That at Weston-under-Lizard is described as 'very neat, plain'; elsewhere his greatest praise is 'neat'. Criticism is similarly rare, although Drayton Bassett church was found to be 'very plain and inelegant'. In contemporary prints, however, Drayton looks little different from the 'neat and Grecian' church at Great Barr. The large urban churches of Darlaston and Lane End are also described as 'plain', as is the greater sophistication of the church at Marchington. The moorland churches were almost invariably 'small'. In some cases they are also 'plain' as at Elkstone and Quarnford, or 'very plain' as at Onecote and Talke.

GOTHIC REVIVAL

From the mid-eighteenth century some Staffordshire churches had been built or rebuilt in a simple Gothic style, either with broad pointed windows of classical proportions as at Seighford (south wall), Trentham (nave) and Ellenhall, or with simple Y-tracery as at Stone and Wetton. By the late 1780s and the 1790s, the style of rebuilding of such churches as Ipstones, Mucklestone and Milwich was more obviously Gothic, although the thin Y-tracery persisted. In the 1820s Gothic detail of an increasingly convincing and rather more accurate kind began to appear, particularly in the towns, although the churches remained classical in plan. Other churches and chapels such as those at Sheen,[28] Fulford, Stonnall and Wilnecote continued to be built with Y-tracery and thin, pinched towers hardly more 'correct' than those of the late eighteenth century.

The architects responsible for the nineteenth-century churches included both local and London-based men. Although non-Staffordshire architects were still in a minority they were, for the first time, not rare exceptions. Lewis Vulliamy designed St. Paul's, Burslem (1828-30), Wordsley (1832) and Cobridge (1837-40). Francis Bedford built St. George's, Newcastle-under-Lyme, and Christ Church, Tunstall. Both were London men with predominantly London practices.[29] Thomas Lee, who built Sedgley and Coseley, was described as 'an architect from London', and seems to have been employed because of a connexion with Lord Dudley, the patron and benefactor of both churches.[30] JP Pritchett of York, who in 1832 built a new chapel recommended by Hodson at Oakamoor in the parish of Cheadle and in 1837 rebuilt the parish church, was a brother of the rector of Cheadle.[31] Francis Goodwin, the most prolific of the non-Staffordshire architects, plied a flourishing trade in 'Commissioners'' churches in the Midlands and Lancashire. After rebuilding the nave of St. Matthew's, Walsall (1820-1), he built Christ Church, West Bromwich (1821-8), Holy Trinity, Burton-upon-Trent (1823-4), and St. Paul's, Walsall (1826). In the Wolverhampton peculiar jurisdiction he rebuilt St. Leonard's, Bilston (classical), and built St. Paul's, Bilston (Gothic).[32] Most of these churches – those of Pritchett excepted – are to the pattern of the 'Commissioners' ' churches: lancets or Perpendicular tracery, high, pinnacled buttresses, a flat roof, and a shallow chancel.

The best of the local architects of this period were James Trubshaw and Thomas Johnson. Stoke-upon-Trent parish church, which they rebuilt, was the first new church in the Potteries in the nineteenth century. It was also distinguished in plan by a comparatively long chancel and a stone chancel arch 'unlike the mimick chancels of most modern churches'.[33] Their other church was at Uttoxeter.[34] The most prolific local architect was Robert Ebbels of Trysull, and later of Tettenhall Wood.[35] At Upper Gornal he concentrated display on a somewhat pretentious west end. At St. James's, Handsworth, he built a church 'of the thinnest Gothick'.[36] His church at Ettingshall was half-timbered. Although, like St. Paul's, Wolverhampton, another of his churches, the walls were thin and let in the damp, it seated 928 people at a cost of only £1,230.[37] For the dampness Hodson recommended in his report the effective if unattractive remedy of covering the south and west walls with slate. Among other local architects CH Winks, a Trentham builder, designed Hanford, with its curious spire, and the simple chapel at Fulford.[38] The north aisle of Tutbury was rebuilt by JBH Bennett, a local land-surveyor.[39]

Hodson rarely described eighteenth- or early nineteenth-century buildings as Gothic. Ipstones, Georgian in plan with simple Y-tracery, he described merely as having pointed windows; Fulford and Stonnall he described similarly. Woodcote had 'Gothic windows'. Other churches, such as Stone, Ellenhall, Milwich and Lower Gornal, all, in varying degrees, classical in plan with pointed windows, when any description was given, were simply 'modern'. Milwich had a 'low, ugly' chancel arch, Ellenhall a 'very ugly' one. The most recent churches offered him the greatest scope for praise and blame. He agreed with contemporaries in praising Stoke as 'handsome' and praised the same architects' church at Uttoxeter. Vulliamy's Wordsley was described as 'remarkably handsome' with a 'handsome' tower; his church at Cobridge was 'neat'. Perry Barr chapel, another small and simple lancet church of the same date, was also 'neat'. Lee's simple church at Coseley ('handsome') was preferred to that at Sedgley ('plain and substantial tho' somewhat heavy'). Both of Bedford's churches were criticized on structural grounds.[40] Goodwin's rebuilding of Walsall parish church, which he criticized both internally and externally, was 'modern pseudo-Gothic'. Among less pretentious buildings, Christ Church, Needwood, in brick with simple Perpendicular detail, was 'modern, in imitation of Gothic'. Hanford, 'a small, neat building', had 'some *imitation* of Gothic Architecture in windows, etc.' His praise of Hilderstone as 'very elegant Gothic' is perhaps a comment on its architectural pretensions rather than its good taste. His main criticism of modern churches was also that of Paget in *St. Antholin's*: lack of strength, and windows and roofs that let in the wet. Walsall Wood, described in 1837 as a 'neat' plain brick church, had by 1841 been so ravaged by damp that the ceiling was falling down at the west end. Dry rot was present at Longton and feared at Goodwin's St. Paul's, Walsall. The 'florid Gothic' Christ Church, West Bromwich, let in the wet; the stability of the tower was also questioned. Even at Wordsley, which he praised in most respects, the pipes did not adequately take the rain off the roof. In his 1838 *Charge* he pointed to the inadequacy of down-spouts as 'one reason why we so often see in our handsome new churches the walls damp and discoloured under the wall-plate', and cited Rickman on the further need to clear the ground around the walls.[41] In 1847 he described some of the new churches as already showing signs of superficial and unsound construction, only partly from lack of funds.[42]

CHURCH EXTENSION

For Hodson, however, as for many others of his day, style was less important than the need to provide adequate church seating for a rapidly increasing population, and in particular free seats for the urban poor.

In 1810, Dudley Ryder, 1st Earl of Harrowby, a devout Evangelical whose seat was at Sandon in Staffordshire, had drawn the attention of the House of Lords to the shortage of church accommodation in manufacturing towns. He had suggested that, following the precedent of the Fifty New Churches Act of 1710, legislation was required to allow new churches to be built in large numbers.[43] In 1818 such an Act was passed by Parliament, which voted £1,000,000 for the purpose, to be administered by Commissioners to supply 'a proper accommodation for the largest number of persons at the least expense'. Of these Commissioners Lord Harrowby was one of the first.[44] In the same year the Society for Promoting the Enlargement, Building and Repairing of Churches and Chapels in England and Wales was also established. In 1824 Parliament voted a further £500,000 for church building.

Lord Harrowby's interests were shared by his brother Bishop Ryder, Hodson's patron, and by Hodson himself. In 1835, at a meeting held in Birmingham to found the Lichfield Diocesan Church Building Society, he stated that new churches could be built for £2 a sitting or for £3 including the purchase of the site, the furnishing of the church and the legal expenses of consecration. 'Of course,' he said, 'useless decorations must be excluded; nor does the estimate allow for towers or spires: but these, however ornamental, are not necessary.'[45] In this opinion he was by no means a Philistine: six years later it was reiterated in the first issue of *The Ecclesiologist,* and by Paget in *St. Antholin's*. Unfortunately the priorities of churchwardens and vestries were often different. Thus in 1841 Hodson was obliged to comment that in the enlargement of Aldridge church more care had been spent 'on the ornamental than the useful'.

SITES OF CHURCHES

In 1830 the archdeaconry of Stafford contained 116 parishes.[46] The areas and boundaries of these parishes reflected the physical and tenurial geography of the early Middle Ages when population was sparse. They were generally large: their average size, at 8 square miles, was almost double the national average. In the Pennine moorlands of the north-east, the parish of Leek covered 51 square miles and that of Alstonefield 36 square miles. Stoke-upon-Trent, another large northern parish, which had increased rapidly in population with the growth of the pottery and mining industries, had been divided into six independent parishes by Act of Parliament in 1807.[47] This was exceptional: elsewhere, tampering with vested interests had begun only with the New Churches Acts and had as yet made little progress. In the south of the county also the poor quality of the soil had only supported small mediaeval populations in large ancient parishes such as Sedgley (12 square miles) and Kingswinford (11 square miles), but the recent exploitation of mineral wealth had led to a rapid growth in population. Between 1801 and 1831 the populations of Sedgley, Kingswinford and West Bromwich all increased two- to threefold and by 1831 each contained more than 15,000 people, as did Walsall, an old-established borough which had grown less dramatically. These increases did not necessarily centre on the mother-village and parish church. In Kingswinford industrial development was concentrated at Brierley Hill, where a chapel was built in the 1760s, and at Wordsley. In Sedgley mining and manufacturing developed in the villages of Upper and Lower Gornal and the small hamlets east of the limestone ridge which divided the parish. At West Bromwich the church was more than a mile from the new centre of population along the Holyhead Road. At Walsall the growth of the 'Foreign', the part of the parish outside the borough, outstripped that of the borough itself. In the case of Kingswinford, a new church built at Wordsley was designated the parish church and the existing parish church became a chapel of ease. At Sedgley a new chapel was built in 1817 in Lower Gornal, and another in 1830 at Coseley.[48] At West Bromwich and Walsall additional churches were built during the 1820s. In the north of the county mining villages had often similarly grown up several miles from the original centre of the parish, as at Talke in the parish of Audley and Newchapel in the parish of Wolstanton, where chapels of mediaeval foundation were rebuilt in the eighteenth century. In the pottery town of Tunstall, also in Wolstanton, no Anglican church was built until 1832.[49] At Checkley in the east of the county there were a few houses clustered around the church, but the tape mills of Tean lay over a mile to the north-west and the quarries of Hollington two miles to the north-east. Neither Tean nor Hollington had churches by 1841. In two cases Hodson recommended that churches should be rebuilt more centrally for the population, namely at West Bromwich and Rushton Spencer, a moorland chapelry. In neither case was he successful, although at Rushton Spencer he was apparently supported by the 'more respectable' parishioners. At West Bromwich, the patron and chief landowner, Lord Dartmouth, opposed the move.[50]

ACCOMMODATION

On the basis of the answers to Hodson's questionnaire, there were church places for only 71,000 out of a population of 267,000. In the seventeen parishes which contained more than half this total there were seats for only one person in six. A decade earlier this proportion would have been much smaller. In the parishes of Kingswinford, Newcastle-under-Lyme, Sedgley and West Bromwich the building of new churches had almost trebled church seating, while at Walsall, Stoke-upon-Trent and Handsworth the extension of old churches had considerably increased accommodation. This increase in church building became more rapid in succeeding decades. The dates of foundation of Anglican churches in Staffordshire as recorded in the 1851 religious census[51] were as follows:

pre-1801	172
1801-1811	1
1811-1821	2
1821-1831	8
1831-1841	36
1841-1851	82
not stated	16
Total	317

These figures take no account of churches rebuilt or refitted. The increase in church building, as elsewhere in industrial England, scarcely kept pace with increases in population. In 1831 there was church accommodation in Hodson's archdeaconry for 26 per cent of the population. By 1851 the county as a whole had church accommodation for 27 per cent, but by 1881 the percentage had declined to 19 and by 1901 to 15.[52]

FREE SEATING

In addition to providing more church accommodation and ensuring that it was provided where it was most needed, there was the problem of providing sufficient free seats for the poor. In his 1847 *Charge* Hodson commented on the waste of space in churches caused by 'large double pews, many of them perhaps more than half empty; whilst the poor are either excluded, or thrust into back seats, or damp, cold corners where they can neither sit nor kneel comfortably, and can neither see nor hear the clergyman.'[53] A precise total of free seats is given in only eighty of his returns. The others usually state merely that they were 'sufficient', 'insufficient' or 'very insufficient'.⁵⁴ In the very populous industrial parishes, the comparatively large numbers of free seats, although still only sufficient for 7 per cent of the population, reflected the building work of the previous decade. The new churches at West Bromwich, Newcastle-under-Lyme and Coseley had added 2,500 free seats. The rebuilt churches of Sedgley, Walsall and Stoke, together with that of Wednesbury which was heavily restored, contained 2,500 more, a considerable increase on the capacity of the buildings they replaced. In contrast All Saints' at West Bromwich, Darlaston, St. Giles' at Newcastle-under-Lyme, Leek, and St. Mary's at Stafford, all older churches in populous industrial parishes, had only 1,200 free seats between them. Some eighteenth-century chapels in industrial towns also lacked places for the poor.

In certain parishes, such as Biddulph and Caverswall, private pews irregularly arranged had gradually taken up an increased proportion of the floor of the church. The shortage of free seating, however, was probably worst in those churches where a single, planned repewing had been carried out. Contributors to the cost of this naturally expected appropriated pews, and the repayment of any debt incurred might necessitate the sale or letting of others, and leave little or no space for open benches. The pews at Stowe were 'regular and good' but only four, with seats for thirty people, were free. Of these, three had been purchased for the poor with money from a bequest. At Cheadle, with 4,000 parishioners, the pews were 'neat and uniform' but only one, with five sittings, was unappropriated. At Bloxwich, a large urban chapel with uniform pewing, there were free seats only for schoolchildren, the singers and the workhouse poor. Burslem, Keele, Milwich, Ranton, Church Eaton and Mucklestone all had churches rebuilt, modernized or repewed between 1780 and the early nineteenth century in which the seating for the poor remained inadequate or badly sited. Of these Burslem, with free accommodation for schoolchildren only, was the worst. There was a significant change in attitude between the first decade of the nineteenth century, when Darlaston church was rebuilt without any free seats, and the 1820s, but even in churches rebuilt as late as Shelton (1831-4), 1,600 pews were appropriated out of 2,100, and at Tunstall (1832), 639 pews out of 1,000. The incumbent's stipend in both places derived from pew-rents.⁵⁵ At Cotton, built in the 1790s at the expense of the local squire Thomas Gilbert, the promoter of 'Gilbert's Acts', almost all the sittings were unappropriated open benches.

In all but the smallest churches galleries were usual. Of seventeen churches without galleries, only Biddulph served a population of more than 1,000 and only those at Forton and Swynnerton served populations of more than 500. In a speech at Birmingham in 1835 Hodson described the three ways to increase accommodation in existing churches as being to extend the building, to erect additional galleries, and to rearrange the sittings in the area already occupied. Of these he considered that the erection of galleries was probably the least expensive.⁵⁶ He observed, however, that repewing might sometimes be preferable, especially in some of the older churches 'which do not so well admit of galleries, but where there is a great waste of room on the ground floor from the inordinate size of some of the pews, and the awkward construction of the open benches'.⁵⁷ At Norton-in-the-Moors, Worfield and Wetton he recommended that galleries be provided, and at Checkley and Draycott that existing ones should be extended.

SUMMARY OF SEATS, FREE SEATS AND COMMUNICANTS 1829-30

Population Range	No. of Parishes	Population in Parishes	Seats		Free Seats	Communicants	
up to 500	48	16,024	8,825	(55%)	1,374[a]	1,062	(6.6%)
501–1,000	42	32,559	14,989	(46%)	2,973[b]	1,360	(4.1%)
1,001–2,000	24	37,390	12,347	(33%)	2,205[c]	826	(2.3%)
2,001–5,000	11	35,800	11,259	(31%)	1,520[d]	476	(1.3%)
over 5,000	17	144,770	23,906	(17%)	7,864[e]	1,292	(0.9%)

a Based on 19 returns. Free sittings in 19 other parishes were described as sufficient, in 3 as insufficient, and in 5 were not described in either quantitative or qualitative terms. In 2 cases Hodson stated that no free sittings were required.
b 22 returns; also 12 'sufficient', 5 'insufficient'.
c 16 returns; also 2 'sufficient', 5 'insufficient'.
d 9 returns; also 1 'sufficient'.
e 15 returns; also 1 'sufficient'.

AVERAGE NUMBERS OF SITTINGS AND COMMUNICANTS 1829-30

Population Range	Average Population of Parish	Average Number of Seats per Parish	Average Number of Free Seats	Average Number of Communicants
up to 500	334	188	72	23
501–1,000	775	357	135	35
1,001–2,000	1,558	514	138	38
2,001–5,000	3,345	1,024	190	43
over 5,000	8,516	1,406	591	81

STATE OF THE CHURCHES

FABRIC

Most of Hodson's orders concerned the fabric of the churches. Only a few churches seem to have been in a really bad state of repair, but it is clear that those which failed to reach his standards did so because they fell below a basic minimum of stability and comfort rather than an ideal.[58] Windows, doors, floors, walls and roofs were criticized in only a small number of cases, but the inadequacies to which he drew attention were often serious.

In three-quarters of the churches, doors and windows were described as good or otherwise praised. In about ten cases they were described as bad or otherwise severely criticized. A few doors needed painting (St. Mary's, Stafford, Butterton), lining (Bramshall) or easing (Milwich). At Wolstanton they let in the wind. Windows were sometimes dirty (Marston, Cotton) or needed painting (Grindon) but were most frequently criticized as lacking casements to air the church in fine weather.

The floors of twenty churches were criticized, three of them – at Bucknall, Waterfall and Alton – severely. Many floors were uneven, the digging of graves and vaults being the usual cause, but at Lane End on account of mining subsidence. Frequently they were also damp, especially when the floors of the pews were of brick rather than of wood, as at Tamworth and Church Eaton.

Walls were only occasionally criticized but included some which were 'very insecure' (Worfield, Trentham), 'very unsound' (Elford), 'very infirm' (Ellastone), 'not solid' (Hanbury), 'much out of the perpendicular' (Trentham, Biddulph, Leigh), 'far from upright' (Swynnerton) or 'not quite upright' (Meerbrook). In several cases Hodson ordered walls to be examined by an architect, surveyor or workman as at Chebsey, Meerbrook and Tixall. Swynnerton and St. Mary's, Stafford, were in poor state externally, Blore was very dirty, and Marston, Butterton and Dilhorne needed whitewashing.

Roofs were in the worst condition. Only sixty were praised and thirty were criticized. Cracks were visible at Cauldon, Hanley and Milwich. The roof of Lapley parish church had 'tumbled down' in the previous year. At Himley the rain came in, at Bucknall the tiles were bad, and at Rocester the slate roof, although only seven years old, was 'not very good'. Slate was increasingly being used in place of lead and tile as a roofing material, as at Ipstones, on the new church at Sheen (specifically Welsh slate), on the new part of the roof at Ellastone, and at Bradley where the lead had been sold a few years before.

One-third of the churches were described as badly affected by damp, and another third as affected to a lesser extent. The causes included the absence of gutters and drains, lack of clear space at the foot of the walls and inadequate airing. Very few churches were described as having good drainage. They included Handsworth, with surface drains, Stone, with underground drainage, Haughton and Thorpe Constantine, where the drains had been laid recently, Sedgley, Bloxwich, Elford, Wednesbury, Uttoxeter, Lane End, Newchapel and Norton-in-the-Moors. Of these, only Uttoxeter was seriously affected by damp. At Tatenhill, Hodson noted that the making of a surf had 'much diminished' the dampness. At Abbots Bromley he found that the drains were not in good order and at Blurton, Sandon and Hanbury they were not kept clean. In most other places they were non-existent. Orders for roof gutters, downpipes, surfs, and soughs were, with orders for casements, the most common of Hodson's orders. Other causes of dampness included ivy on the walls (Ingestre, Kinver), faults in the roof (St. Matthew's, Walsall), rain at the windows (Wilnecote, Wigginton, Burslem) and 'the late excessive rains' (Newborough). At Colton, sited on low-lying ground by a brook, the problem of dampness was aggravated by the absence of land drainage so that graves were full of water. At two new churches, Hanford and St. George's, Newcastle-under-Lyme, the walls had not yet dried out.

Lack of cleanliness Hodson found a less common fault. The cleanliness of two-thirds of the churches he described as 'good' and of only about one-fifth as 'bad'. The latter included some large village churches such as those at Clifton Campville and Abbots Bromley, the modern church at Lower Gornal and town churches such as those at Tamworth, West Bromwich and Stafford. At two small chapels, Marston and Cotton, no one was paid for cleaning. At Bradley, coals were kept in a pew.

FITTINGS

Fonts: A number of fonts were in an unsatisfactory condition. At Clifton Campville the font was dirty. At Church Eaton, it lacked a basin. A number of fonts described as ancient, very ancient or old-fashioned, were praised, such as those at Croxden, Blore, Wychnor and Walsall.[59] Hodson also praised the small, seventeenth-century marble font at Ingestre. Some mediaeval fonts were found to have been thrown out into the churchyard as at Sheen. The font at Lapley was being used to feed calves, the one at Longnor was about to be replaced.

Pulpits and reading-desks: For normal Sunday worship the congregation needed to see the pulpit and reading-desk. In thirty-nine churches Hodson commented that these were well placed and in eleven that their siting was bad. In general he praised the positions of those which did not interrupt the view of the altar, as at Mayfield where the pulpit was against the north chancel arch and at Newborough where it was a three-decker against the north wall.[60] But in some cases he does not seem to have objected to such interruption, for instance at Dilhorne and Trysull, where the pulpits appear to have projected well to the centre of the chancel arch, and Kingsley where the three-decker pulpit was directly in front of the altar.[61] Other churches criticized included Checkley where he thought the pulpit too high for the south aisle pews, and Uttoxeter where he thought it too low. At Abbots Bromley the pulpit, which had not been moved when the church was repewed in 1825, was in the middle of the south arcade.[62] The 'strangely placed' pulpit at Wilnecote was at the south-east angle of the church. At Alstonefield Hodson noted, with exclamation marks, that the pulpit and reading-desk, which were a gift of Izaak Walton's fishing companion, Charles Cotton, were painted blue.[63] At Trentham the pulpit and desk were decked with 'the trappings of a Mameluke saddle', apparently presented by the Emperor of Morocco to George II, who had in turn given it to one of the Leveson-Gowers.[64]

Books: The state of bibles and prayer-books was often found by Hodson to be unsatisfactory. The condition of scarcely more than one-third was described as good, and there were limited criticisms of the condition of another third, while in forty-three parishes the books were described as 'not in good repair', 'bad' or 'very bad'. In the poor moorland parishes and chapelries (for example those at Butterton, Cotton, Elkstone, Ilam, Kingsley, Longnor, Onecote, Quarnford and Sheen) their condition was particularly unsatisfactory. At Colton, low-lying by a stream, at Quarnford, high and exposed on the ill-drained gritstone moorlands, and at Hanford, where the church walls were not yet dry, they had been affected by the prevailing dampness.

Organs: Only in the larger parishes was an organ the rule. Of the forty-nine organs recorded by Hodson twenty-three were in parishes and chapelries with a population of more than 2,000. The only large parishes without an organ were Wolstanton and Norton-in-the-Moors. The newly erected chapels at Coseley and St. Paul's, Walsall, and four older chapels serving large populations (Brierley Hill, Bloxwich, Lower Gornal and Newchapel) also lacked them. Three organs, at Stonnall, Ellastone and Tatenhill, were described as small. Ilam church and the chapels at Great Barr and Cotton had barrel organs.[65]

VESTRIES

Eighty-three churches had vestries. Of the larger churches only eleven had none, and of these only Cheadle served a population of more than 2,000. Of the forty-eight parishes containing fewer than 500 souls thirty-three were without a vestry, and of forty-two with populations between 500 and 1,000, fifteen lacked one. Some of the smallest parishes had no need of a vestry, since the incumbent lived near at hand and could robe in his own house, as at Thorpe Constantine. Several vestries were inadequate through damp as at Ranton, Wombourn, Alton and Rolleston. In many cases they were too small: the vestry at Wetton was a single pew. A few parishes (Bloxwich, Penn, Tamworth) had vestries described as 'handsome'; the 'very handsome' one at Madeley had formerly been a private chapel. At Swynnerton the rector claimed the right to use the south chancel as his vestry.

SURPLICES

Most churches had two surplices. Where there was only one Hodson usually ordered another to be obtained, as at Wombourn, Chebsey and Christ Church, West Bromwich. Kingswinford, Sedgley and St. Matthew's, Walsall, all with assistant curates, had four surplices. Fifteen other churches had three. At twelve churches the condition of the only surplice, or of both surplices, was described as 'bad'. The surplice at Drayton Bassett had recently been stolen, together with a black cloth surviving from Sir Robert Peel's funeral.

CHURCHYARDS

The state of churchyards was another common subject of Hodson's critical comment. Several suffered from use as thoroughfares. In 1839 he commented in his *Charge* that 'it is undesirable, to say the least, even in villages, that Churchyards should be converted into playgrounds for children, and places of traffic and thorough-fare for passengers; but in *towns* it is a *foul abomination*.'[66] At Rocester the thoroughfare led to a mill, at Tutbury to the clerk's house. At Cheadle, owing partly to the proximity of the main road, the churchyard was 'made a complete thoroughfare'. At Rolleston schoolboys made a playground of the churchyard, and at Haughton and Church Eaton the school privy was in or adjoining it. The problems created by the existence of thoroughfares included disturbance at funerals (Newcastle-under-Lyme) and lack of room for graves (Mucklestone). A path at Barton-under-Needwood went across the graves. At St. Matthew's, Walsall, the churchyard was a place of common resort for children and the 'worst characters of the town'. At Worfield, in 1841, 'idle persons' misbehaved in the churchyard during service time.

Probably the best means of keeping the grass short was to graze sheep, and these are found even in the churchyards of such Black Country industrial towns as Darlaston, Handsworth, Wednesbury and West Bromwich. Cows were less effective and liable to cause damage, as at Clifton Campville where the late rector's cows had damaged the church windows. At Wigginton, Butterton and Checkley the clerks' cows were held responsible for damage. At Stowe the vicar rented the herbage to the landlord of a local public house. At Ranton the impropriator leased it out. In only a few instances was any reference made to mowing.[67]

In over twenty cases, excluding those where repairs and rebuilding were responsible, Hodson reported churchyards in really bad condition. At Seighford, Stafford, Whitmore, Ranton and Colton there was rubbish. At Rushall there were heaps of stones, and at Walsall 'sad nuisances'. In many churchyards there were weeds and on a number of churches ivy. The latter included Lapley where the church was almost buried in 'soil and herbage and bushes etc. of all kinds', and Quatt where trees grew on the buttresses. Ivy was a particular fault of churches that also served as visual adjuncts to the houses or grounds of local landowners. Ilam, Ingestre, Patshull and Weston-under-Lizard suffered in this way. The squires were tenacious of their views. Only at Weston was an order to remove the ivy made in 1829-30 not repeated in 1837-8. At Patshull and Ilam the ivy had not been cleared by 1841. In only about a third of the returns was the question about rubbish in churchyards answered satisfactorily.

The walls, fences and hedges of churchyards were also often inadequate. Their maintenance was usually a parochial responsibility. Occasionally it was carried out in doles, an inefficient method which resulted in neglect, as at Ranton. Hedges maintained privately, as at Haughton and Wombourn, were criticized when those maintained by the parish or the incumbent were not. At Ilam and Barlaston the boundary between the churchyard and the squire's pleasure grounds was not marked. Elsewhere, as at St. Matthew's, Walsall, and Caverswall, part of the boundary was uncertain.

CONCLUSIONS

Six churches and chapels stand out from Hodson's reports as being in a particularly bad state: the parish churches at Biddulph, Wolstanton and Bramshall and the chapels at Lower Gornal, Rushton Spencer and Chilcote. At Wolstanton, the 'remains of a handsome church', he found the stone dilapidated externally, the roof out of repair, the walls not upright, the doors unable to be closed and so letting in the wind, the seats out of repair, the books not good, and much damp in all parts of the church. His list of orders, however, was not exceptionally long and concentrated on major faults. In 1837 when he found the church still 'in a very damp, uncomfortable and dilapidated state', he made a longer one. By 1841 repairs appear to have been carried out as his list was then short and referred only to minor points. Biddulph and Bramshall churches, which he found in a very bad state in 1830, had been rebuilt before his next visit in 1837. But both the new churches were inadequately ventilated and at Bramshall there was 'much appearance of *damp*'. By 1841 Biddulph church was once more showing signs of neglect.

In the case of the chapels, the absence of any legal compulsion to provide for their upkeep through the parish rates presented a major problem. Chilcote was a *locus classicus* of ill-repair, the ceiling bad, the walls damp and 'very much out of the perpendicular', the floor uneven. In the absence of a pulpit, the lessons and sermon were delivered from a single 'very unsteady' reading-desk, in which the books were 'imperfect'. There was no porch and the steeple was indifferent. Of the two bells one was cracked and had no rope; the other had only half a wheel. The inhabitants, wrote Hodson, 'complain, as usual of the hardship of having to repair their own Chapel, and *also* to contribute to the repairs of the Mother Church'. Similarly at Quarnford, in 1841, he recognised the justice of the inhabitants' claim that while they paid rates both to Alstonefield and to Longnor, they had to maintain their own chapel by voluntary subscriptions alone.[68] After making directions aimed at curing the dampness there, he added: 'I really could not enjoin much upon them – they would, I believe, gladly rebuild their Chapel, if they might be freed from their other obligations'. At Lower Gornal, in the industrial south-west, as at Quarnford, there was no provision for the upkeep of the chapel by rates, and Hodson 'judged it superfluous to leave any orders'.

CHURCHWARDENS, PARISH CLERKS AND INCUMBENTS

CHURCHWARDENS

The main responsibility for the upkeep of the church fabric rested on the churchwardens. In his 1847 *Charge* Hodson acknowledged their 'kind attentions, unwearied zeal, and disinterested exertions' and their work 'not seldom at much personal sacrifice both of time and money'.[69] In rural parishes the churchwardens were drawn from the leading farmers, often those described as 'yeoman farmers'.[70] In general the office was below the notice of the gentry. AJB Beresford Hope, who became patron of Sheen in the 1840s, installed a leading Tractarian as perpetual curate and planned to make the village an Anglo-Catholic watering-place. He could not be accused of neglecting his religious duties, but he wrote to the curate, Benjamin Webb: 'I know that my own moral deficiency is a somewhat too great contempt for and impatience of parochial constitutionalism. No doubt you felt that this came out in the way I have neglected the Churchwardenship of Sheen, never even qualifying . . . I can do a little local autocracy pretty well, or legislation, or speechifying, but I am not the man for quiet, horse-in-harness work.'[71]

A few gentlemen in fact held office as churchwardens in 1830. They included William Derrington at Norbury, John Bott of Coton Hall, Hamstall Ridware, John Owen of Field House, Marchington, and Charles Philip Johnstone of Newbold Manor, Barton-under-Needwood. In addition to the farmers, there was an occasional land-surveyor such as Charles Smith at Alton or land-agent such as Zachary Bradbury at Dilhorne and Richard Ford at Swynnerton. There were also several millers such as Thomas Parton at Pattingham, TA Smith at Lapley and Joshua Braddock at Cheddleton. In the moorland chapelries the social level of the wardens seems to have been lower. They included two joiners (Thomas Darbyshire at Grindon and John Barker at Warslow), a blacksmith (George Beardmore at Wetton) and an innkeeper (Thomas Slack at Quarnford). In the smallest parishes there was little choice: at Wychnor the four principal farmers took the office in turn. The warden at Thorpe Constantine, William Dennett, was one of two farmers who, with the Inge family, were the principal residents.

In the towns the office perhaps conveyed social status on newly rich manufacturers, and as a result the principal local industries were represented. In his 1839 visitation *Charge* Hodson observed, when recommending gentlemen of rank and property to become churchwardens, that this was more generally the case in town than in country parishes.[72] Hanley, Lane End and Stoke had each a pottery manufacturer as warden. At Stoke this was Herbert Minton, a devout churchman whose encaustic tiles were to become an essential part of Victorian ecclesiastical décor. The brewing trade was represented at Burton by a Worthington, who was partnered by an iron-founder, and at Stone by a Joule, partnered by Mr Vaughan of the Trent and Mersey Canal Office. The main industries of the Black Country were well represented, the saddlery of Walsall by Thomas Franklin, a bridle-cutter, the fireclay industry of Brierley Hill by John Eades at Kingswinford, and iron manufacture by a Parkes at Wednesbury, and an Izon and a Dawes at Christ Church, West Bromwich. The retail trades were represented by Richard Barrett at Tamworth and Joseph Cotterill at Walsall, both drapers, EE Stanley, a grocer, at Bloxwich, and John Malkin at Cheadle. Thomas Brindley, at Burslem, was a colliery agent. Among the professions, banking was represented by John Addison at Wednesbury and teaching by Stephen Hawksworth, who kept an 'academy' at Barton-under-Needwood.[73]

The churchwardens of Ranton in 1830 and the churchwardens of Weston-under-Lizard in 1841 were found to have failed to submit their accounts. At Ranton, the warden had not done so for several years. At Leek disputes between the mother-church and the chapelries over the apportionment of church rates had resulted in the election of only one churchwarden, instead of four.

PARISH CLERKS

The parish clerk had varied responsibilities. To such duties as writing up the registers and leading the music in worship might be added those of sexton or schoolmaster, cleaning the church and washing the surplice. Salaries ranged from 15s. at Kingsley to £20 at Tamworth and over £10 at fifteen other places. Strict comparisons, however, are difficult, because the clerk's income from fees varied enormously from one parish to another. Fees were the main or only income of the clerks of St. Modwen's, Burton and Lane End. At Hanley the clerk added 'large' fees to his £10–£15 salary. It was presumably for this reason that at Burton-upon-Trent, with 4,000 parishioners and at Dilhorne, with 1,500, the clerk received no fixed salary. Similarly the clerks of other large parishes, such as Cheadle, Handsworth, Wednesbury and Walsall, received only between £1 8s. and £3 10s. apiece. Voluntary subscriptions were the sole source of the clerk's income at Wigginton and Wilnecote. At Chilcote and Cheswardine his payment took the form of Easter dues, at Draycott that of a Christmas collection, and at Stowe the clerk was paid 3d. per sitting at Christmas. The clerks at Betley and Colton received their main salary from teaching. At All Saints', West Bromwich, he received seven guineas for cleaning the church 'which he neglects'. Occasionally Hodson described the clerk's income as too small, as at Cotton (30s.) and Mayfield (£2 2s.). At Walsall, where it was 'only £3' he recommended an increase.

INCUMBENTS

The physical well-being of a church owed much to the care of the incumbent or his *locum tenens*. At Bushbury, Hodson noted that the church suffered from the incumbent's 'non-residence, or inattention'. At Christ Church, Needwood, the incumbent was the romantic Evangelical and Radical Humphrey Price, whose participation in political and religious controversies[74] left him little time for the upkeep of his church or parsonage – when Hodson visited his church in 1830 Price had just emerged from gaol, having slandered the carpet manufacturers of Kidderminster. In this case the problem was exacerbated by the near-impossibility of raising a church-rate. At Checkley the rector, Samuel Langley, was old and the son and grandson of successive rectors. His church was in poor state, and although by 1837 the nave had been repaired so that it was 'as satisfactory as formerly it was disgraceful', the chancel remained untouched 'owing to the impracticable temper of the Rector' until his death in 1839. Hodson makes no mention in his returns of the behaviour of Richard Thursfield, vicar of Patshull and Pattingham. But on 20 July 1838, two days after inspecting these churches, he wrote to Bishop Butler:[75] 'The wretched incumbent was brought home drunk in a cart last Saturday night – is frequently seen lying in the roads in a state of intoxication – lives like a pig, in a poor house, with a pauper as his companion, in one room of a large vicarage house which is sadly out of repairs, and which if not speedily repaired will soon be in a ruinous condition. The parish registers have not been filled up for the last two or three years, and are lying about in all directions.' As for the services, 'Your Lordship will judge how these duties are performed by a drunkard of sixty-seven'.

WORSHIP

Hodson's returns show that two Sunday services, Morning and Evening Prayer, were held in most churches in his archdeaconry, but that in many cases, especially in winter, there was no sermon at the second.[76] Three churches, St. Mary's, Stafford, Tamworth and Fazeley (a small industrial curacy in Tamworth parish), had three services. Of forty-seven churches which had only one service, many were chapelries or perpetual curacies sharing a curate. At Sheen the rebuilding of the church was made an excuse for the total neglect of services.

Only in urban parishes[77] were weekday services recorded by Hodson, except before Sacrament Sundays and during Lent. A number of parish churches and chapels held evening lectures on Wednesdays (Alstonefield, Darlaston, Lower Gornal, St. Mary's, Stafford, St. Paul's, Walsall) or Thursdays (Tamworth and St. Modwen's, Burton).[78] Prayers were said publicly on Wednesdays, Fridays and saints' days at St. Matthew's, Walsall, and Cheadle, on Wednesdays and Fridays at Stone, Leek and Uttoxeter, on Tuesdays at Burslem and on Wednesdays at Newcastle. They were also read on Fridays at Shenstone but the parishioners did not attend.

But at least in some parishes, Hodson's returns clearly do not record services or meetings of a less formal kind than Holy Communion and the Offices. Throughout 1830 for example the curate of Sandon, Philip Seckerson, is known from other sources to have held Sunday evening meetings or lectures,[79] at which he preached. In addition he held regular Thursday evening services alternately in the hamlets of Enson, in the parish of St. Mary's, Stafford, and Burston, in Stone, and he also held occasional services at Sandon Bank and Salt.[80]

Holy Communion was normally celebrated four times a year, at Christmas, Easter, Whitsun and at Michaelmas. Only eight churches held fewer celebrations than this. Forty-eight churches held between five and eight celebrations, which may, however, have been concentrated about the four feasts, in the way that the Primary Visitations of 1772-3 record for Shenstone (seven celebrations, two each at Christmas, Easter and Whitsun, one at Michaelmas), Caverswall (six celebrations, of which three were at Easter) and Cheadle (six celebrations, including two at Christmas and two at Easter). Nineteen churches, mainly in large towns, held more than eight celebrations, in most cases monthly.[81] The proportion of churches where frequent celebrations were held was higher than in most dioceses for which figures have been published, which reflects the more urban nature of Staffordshire.[82] There seems to have been little change in the frequency of celebration since the mid-eighteenth century.[83]

The communicant proportion of the population was less than 2 per cent, and was lowest in the most populous towns. Stafford and Walsall, where about 2½ per cent of the population communicated, were unusual among the towns. Each was an established borough which had not grown up with exceptional speed. Communicants were fewest in parishes made up of scattered mining and manufacturing villages, and in the north where Methodism had made its greatest impact. At Kingswinford, with its chapelry of Brierley Hill, in the south and at Wolstanton, Hanley and Leek in the north, only one person in 200 communicated. Some small parishes like Sheen and Ranton had only six communicants each, and Onecot had nine. On the other hand, in a few small parishes, usually inhabited by the tenants and servants of a single landowner, the proportion reached over 25 per cent, as at Thorpe Constantine (15 out of 55), Wychnor (27 out of 100), and Ingestre (55 out of 200). In three larger parishes, Himley (70 out of 435), Haughton (78 out of 500) and Blithfield (75 out of 475), it exceeded 15 per cent. In the southern half of the archdeaconry, in 1882, when Archdeacon Iles prepared a report, the percentage of communicants still remained higher in the small parishes than in the large ones. In parishes of 500 or less the highest percentage of communicants was 27 and the fifth highest, 21; in parishes of 5,001–6,000 the corresponding percentages were 7 and 4.[84]

RESULTS OF HODSON'S VISITATIONS

In his 1839 *Charge* Hodson commented that there were then 'comparatively few cases of sordid neglect or serious dilapidation' in the churches of his archdeaconry.[85] The period covered by Hodson's visitations saw a marked increase in general concern for church repair. In many cases, as at Elford, this was completely independent of his activity. In some, as at St. Mary's, Stafford, Hodson's was only one of many voices advocating repair. In only a few cases, and these comparatively minor, is there clear documentary evidence that work was undertaken as a direct result of his orders.

Among the minor pieces of direct evidence is the expenditure of £2 15s. by the churchwardens of Aldridge 'in removing soil round Church by order of Archdeacon'.[86] In addition, on 19 June 1831 the churchwardens called a meeting for ten days' time 'for the purpose of taking into consideration, and deciding on the most eligible plan, for repairing the outside of the Church Walls, and of doing other necessary repairs to the Church, according to an Order from the Archdeacon'.[87] An estimate of £24 had already been submitted for cementing the exterior of the church to correspond with the chancel and of £6 for the repair of the stone turrets and their restoration to their original state in cement.[88] Most of this money was in fact raised by the subscriptions of the rector and leading parishioners.[89] The parish also incurred in 1830 and 1831 expenditure which clearly resulted from Hodson's orders: 113 feet of nine-inch spouting, 26 feet of wall piping, eleven feet of two-inch wall piping, two large 'receivers' and a small one, three sough grates and frames, fourteen 'plough points' and stays for spouts were purchased, for £9, and a casement and two hooks for 3s. 10d.[90] At the chapelry of Great Barr, within two months of Hodson's orders, an account had been settled for £6 12s. for bricks, lime and sand for an open drain around the chapel, and on the following 1 January were entered payments of £4 7s. 8d. for brick-laying for the drain and £8 18s. for spouting. In 1842 the chapelwardens spent £7 on painting and colouring, in accordance with Hodson's orders.[91]

At Leigh[92] the churchwardens' total annual expenditure was usually in the region of £40–£60. In 1830 they spent £142 9s. 1d. This included the purchase of 2,500 floor bricks for £7 18s. 4d., £1 11s. 8d. spent on soughing the churchyard, £37 11s. 4d. paid to a local joiner for 'Sundries at the Church and Vestry' and £19 8s. to a plumber and glazier. In addition work costing at least £2 13s. 4d. was carried out on the buttresses. In 1831 £68 0s. 4d. was spent, including £16 16s. 6d. for new doors and other woodwork, and £14 5s. 11d. for plumbing and glazing, and in the following year iron gates were put up in the porch as Hodson had ordered, and spouts were provided. In 1838 expenditure was again above average, including £22 17s. for glazing.

Similar evidence survives for Seighford, Stowe, Alstonefield and Shenstone.[93] In most cases the work was carried out by local tradesmen and the money spent remained almost entirely within the parish.

A precise record of the response of a parish to Hodson's orders is supplied by the minute-book of Cheadle vestry meeting.[94] His letter to the churchwardens was read at a meeting held on 12 August 1830, one month after his inspection. His orders for repairing and whitewashing the belfry and for repairing the pews were put into effect. Instead of repairing or renewing the covering of the communion table the vestry decided to dye it blue and instead of removing the earth from the north side of the church, it ordered that that side of the church be spouted, 'it appearing that the soil on the North side of the Church cannot with propriety be removed'. Only one casement was inserted in each side instead of two. Hodson's recommendation for the provision of a suitable vestry was met by a resolution to widen the existing one, which he had described as a 'small closet, enclosed in the Belfry – very unsuitable'. The order for the replacement of the outer door by a light gate was unanimously rejected. The trespass footpaths were 'considered absolutely necessary for the safety of the Publick' – as perhaps they were, because a faculty of 1840 subsequently removed a corner of the churchyard for road-widening.[95]

In some cases, the repetition by Hodson at subsequent visitations of orders that he had first made in 1829–30 shows that no action had been taken upon them. Marchington in 1837 displayed 'the very same defects, increased by lapse of time', and was 'disgracefully dirty, damp and bearing every appearance of neglect'. Blore was 'still in a sad state of dilapidation and disorder: Scarcely anything done to it since my former visit'. By 1841, however, Marchington was 'much improved internally' and Blore was undergoing repair. At Bucknall, even in 1841 the church was 'still in the same disgraceful state'. At Needwood and Checkley the incumbents were to blame, a change of incumbent at Checkley in 1839 bringing immediate improvement. At Himley repairs had been neglected under the impression that Lord Dudley would carry them out. At All Saints', West Bromwich, orders were not carried out for want of funds. Hodson judged by higher standards at his later Visitations. Patshull was described in 1838 as 'still shamefully neglected' and Audley in 1837 as 'still *very* unsatisfactory' even though neither had been criticized severely in 1830. Rushall, at which Hodson issued very few orders in 1830 and 1837, was described in 1841 as 'very much improved'.

In most cases, however, Hodson indicates by a short list of orders or specific comment on improvements that progress had been made. The county town provided a significant sign of change. In 1837 Hodson ordered the churchwardens of St. Mary's to employ an architect to examine the fabric and estimate the cost of repairs. Contemporary visitors were equally critical of the state of the church. A major restoration was then entrusted to Messrs Scott and Moffatt, which meant that in practice it was in the hands of the thirty-year-old George Gilbert Scott. Scott had seven churches behind him[96] and was in the throes of discovering Gothic revivalism from the Cambridge Camden Society and the writings of Pugin. He found that major structural repair, including the underpinning of the central tower, was needed. Like Hodson he objected to the pewing of the church and the position of the pulpit. He also objected, on aesthetic grounds, to the Perpendicular south transept window, and replaced it by an Early English one, considering himself justified when he discovered remains of an Early English window *in situ*, and made other drastic alterations. His ruthlessness was criticized but his proposals, with the exception of his intended central spire, were carried out. This work, together with concurrent restorations at Castle Church and Betley, covered the period from his 'awakening' to Gothic to the break with Moffatt which marked the beginning of 'a new era in my professional life'. Hodson was present at the reopening of St. Mary's in 1844. How far beyond his intentions the restoration had gone – its cost of £8,000 would have built several new churches – can only be guessed. Pugin pronounced it the best restoration of modern times and the *Ecclesiologist*, which had praised its inception in its first issue (1841), praised its near-completion in the first volume of its new series (1845).[97] Scott, for his part, when his practice as a restorer was under attack more than thirty years later, looked back to Stafford and described his work there in detail. It was his first major restoration and the pattern for the future.[98] The change in ethos is also marked by the foundation, in 1841, of the Lichfield Society for the Encouragement of Ecclesiastical Architecture. Although Hodson, as archdeacon, was a vice-president, the society was the creation of FE Paget and William Gresley. This society differed from Ryder and Hodson's Diocesan Church Building Society as the Cambridge Camden Society differed from the Incorporated Church Building Society.[99]

The practical difficulties faced by vestries in carrying out the archdeacon's orders for alterations and repairs are perhaps best illustrated by Hodson's own difficulties in his parish of Colwich. In 1852, the year following his resignation as vicar, Colwich church was restored. The faculty citation gave as the reason its 'inadequate accommodation and very inconvenient arrangement'. These are described in greater detail in a contemporary *Report on the Church Accommodation in the Parish of Colwich,*[100] from which it appears that there were 372 houses in the parish, and that 91 of the pews in the parish church were appropriated to families. This left only 213 free seats, 93 for adults and 120 for children, to accommodate the 1,405 other inhabitants. The *Report* continued: 'If the accommodation for the poor is deficient in quantity, it is still more deficient in kind – if they have been discouraged from coming to Church by want of room, they have been still more alienated from the Church by the lamentable fact that the little space allowed them is to be found only in the dark and damp and distant corners of the building, which, when the pews were sold, no one else would occupy; whilst the seats for the children are situated where no seats were ever intended or ought to have been placed – down the middle aisle and round the communion rails, the latter at such a distance from the desk and pulpit, and so shut in by the high pews in the chancel, that considering their age, they cannot be expected either to see or hear, or take any intelligent part in the service.' These defects were the result of the repewing of the church in 1813, for which the architect's bill had still not been paid when Hodson became vicar in 1829.[101] In his first two years the church was thoroughly examined, the roof was tiled, the walls spouted and a new casement inserted. The walls were coloured. The churchyard was drained.[102] The expense of these repairs,[103] together perhaps with the psychological impossibility of repewing the church so soon after the earlier expensive fitting-out, presumably deterred Hodson. The *Report* went on to say that Hodson 'had long wished to have the Parish Church made more commodious for all classes of his Parishioners, especially the poor; other objects, however, of equal or greater importance to the Parish, successively demanding attention, the opportunity for this never came'.

A second irony is that in 1853 the tower of Hodson's new church, St. Mary's, Lichfield, was rebuilt as a memorial to Hodson's predecessor, FG Lonsdale. St. Mary's was a plain classical eighteenth-century church, but the tower was rebuilt with a spire in a serious and archaeologically correct Decorated style by GE Street. The contrast between Hodson's concern for the essential and this purely ornamental addition is as great as the contrast between the architect who 'delighted to call himself Goth' and the archdeacon who could praise indifferently 'neat classical' and 'handsome Gothic'. After Hodson's death a monument to him was set up in the cathedral: the design was that of a mediaeval tomb-chest; the designer, Street.

THE VOLUMES AND THEIR PROVENANCE

The articles of enquiry of Hodson's visitations are now bound in three volumes transferred in 1964 from Lichfield Cathedral Library to Lichfield Joint Record Office. The first of the volumes, with the Record Office call-number A/V/1/2, contains the original text of the 1829–30 visitation. The two others, A/V/1/3 and 4, contain a copy of this text, sometimes slightly abbreviated, with pages left blank between each of the parish questionnaires on which the orders of 1837–8 and 1841 were entered. Curacies and chapelries visited for the first time in one of the two later tours of inspection are accordingly to be found only in A/V/1/3 and 4. It is clear from the order of the entries (in particular Coseley and Perry Barr in A/V/1/3 and Wetley Rocks, Tunstall, Shelton and Longton in A/V/1/4) that neither of the two latter volumes was copied before 1837. The position of the entry for Cobridge, consecrated in 1841, in A/V/1/4 suggests that they may not have been copied until later still, but the Cobridge entry is possibly a later insertion. Other parishes first visited in 1838 and 1841 were entered on blank leaves in the front of A/V/1/3. The visitation orders made for a number of parishes, mostly near Colwich, in 1841, were not entered in A/V/1/3–4 but left on loose sheets of paper in A/V/1/3.

The volumes passed into the Cathedral Library in 1895. On 24 June in that year, FT Beck, a Wolverhampton architect and active Anglo-Catholic churchman, wrote to Canon Bodington at Lichfield informing him that *two* books had come into his possession 'on Friday' (21 June) at a sale of books at The Woodhouse, Tettenhall. The late owner had been preceded in the house by Henry Moore, Hodson's successor as archdeacon of Stafford, to whom he had presumably transferred them. Beck asked Bodington for advice, wishing to preserve the volumes 'with other documents, etc. of the Diocese'. On 28 June Beck again wrote stating that he was sending the volumes by passenger train to Lichfield for preservation 'in the Library to which I consider they belong'. On 6 July he also wrote to the bishop, placing the volumes 'unreservedly at Your Lordship's disposal to be preserved where, and in such a manner as you may deem most desirable for the good of the Church in the Diocese of Lichfield'.

THE TEXT AS PRINTED

The text here presented of the 1829–30 visitation is taken from the original version (A/V/1/2). Where that of the A/V/1/3–4 text is fuller, it has been inserted in square brackets. Alterations and clarifications in A/V/1/3–4 together with editorial notes are given in footnotes. Each parish entry is therefore a conflation of the 1829–30 text from A/V/1/2 and the results of later visits from A/V/1/3–4. In some cases, Hodson made further notes in pencil. These mostly relate to reports from rural deans about the execution of his orders but occasionally they record other information, for instance the names of new clergy. These pencil additions have been distinguished in the printed text by the use of quotation marks.

Hodson's printed form of questionnaire is divided into fourteen sections, each with a general heading and containing between three and twenty-eight articles. The articles themselves are numbered consecutively from one to eighty-six.

In printing the questionnaire for each parish general headings have been given in capitals and the articles in bold lower case. The first article in a section has not been printed where the general heading would serve, that is, articles 1, 6, 34, 38, 62 and 82. It has also not been given where no return was made. Where Hodson makes a single return serve for more than one answer the headings have been grouped together. In general, Hodson's own spelling, punctuation and capitalization have been adopted, but some modernization has taken place in the course of printing.

THE QUESTIONNAIRE

BENEFICE
1 Name
2 Nature
3 Ecton*
4 Patron
5 Impropriator

CHURCH
6 General Description
7 Number it will contain
8 Accommodation for Poor
9 Roof
10 Walls
11 Floor

* Article 3 gives the valuation of the benefice as given in John Ecton's 'Liber Valorum et Decimarum; being an Account of the Valuations and Yearly Tenths of all such Ecclesiastical Benefices in England and Wales as now stand chargeable with the Payment of First-Fruits and Tenths ... (Some Things necessary to be ... performed by a Clergyman upon his admission to any Benefice)' (1711), republished in 1786 as 'Liber Regis' by John Bacon (hence Hodson's 'King's Book').

	12	Windows
	13	Doors
	14	Pulpit and Desk
	15	Books
	16	Seats
	17	Galleries
	18	Organ
	19	Font
	20	Chapels
	21	Benefaction Tables
	22	Vestry
	23	Surplices
	24	Linen
	25	Plate
	26	Chest for Papers
	27	Iron Chest for Register
	28	Register
	29	Porch
	30	Vaults
	31	Cleanliness
	32	Damp
	33	Dimensions
CHANCEL	34	Dimensions
	35	Table
	36	Ornaments
	37	Repaired by whom
STEEPLE	38	Description
	39	State of
	40	Bells
	41	Clock
CHURCHYARD	42	Fence
	43	Gates
	44	Drains
	45	Graves
	46	Rubbish
	47	Footpaths
	48	Cattle
DIVINE SERVICE	49	On Sundays
	50	On other Days
	51	Sacrament
	52	Communicants
	53	Catechism
INCUMBENT	54	Name and Residence
	55	If not resident
	56	What Duty he performs
CURATE	57	Name and Residence
	58	If not resident
	59	Licensed
	60	Salary
	61	If serving another Church

PARSONAGE	62	Description of
	63	State of
	64	Outbuildings
INCOME	65	Gross Value
	66	Tithes
	67	Glebe
	68	Surplice Fees
	69	Easter Dues and small Payments
	70	Queen Anne's Bounty
	71	Terrier
SCHOOLS	72	Endowed School
	73	Subscription Day School
	74	Sunday School
	75	Lancaster School
DISSENTERS	76	Dissenters' School
	77	Dissenting Chapels
	78	Population*
MISCELLANEOUS	79	Monuments
	80	Chandeliers, &c.
	81	Parochial Library
PARISH CLERK	82	Name
	83	Appointed by
	84	Salary
	85	Churchwardens†
	86	Orders made†

* Article 78 refers to the *total* population of the parish or chapelry, and not to the number of dissenters.

† Articles 85 and 86 appear, in the original format, to be included in the section relating to the 'parish clerk'.

NOTES TO THE INTRODUCTION

1 FE Paget, *St. Antholin's; or, Old Churches and New. A Tale for the Times* (London, 1841), 11–16.

2 SRO, D1048/6/2, 14 June 1830. The Thomas diaries were preserved with Sandon parish records.

3 'I can truly say, that if I ever loved and honoured any human being, your revered and lamented pastor was that man': *A Sermon preached in Trinity Church, Cambridge, on the evening of Sunday, November 20, 1836, on occasion of the death of the Revd Charles Simeon, MA* (Cambridge, 1836), 8–9.

4 JA Venn, *Alumni Cantabrigienses,* ii (3) (Cambridge, 1947), 402; D Newsome, *The Parting of Friends* (London, 1966), 39–41.

5 LJRO, B/A/3; B/A/1/29, p.163.

6 Most of the parish of Sheriff Hales had also passed into Shropshire. Mucklestone and Pattingham were partly in Shropshire but wholly in the archdeaconry of Stafford, and Tamworth was partly in Warwickshire but wholly within the archdeaconry. The peculiar jurisdiction of Bridgnorth was territorially within Hodson's archdeaconry, but this conveyed no rights on the archdeacon. *VCH Staffs*. iii, 92–8, describes the extent of the archdeaconry, peculiar jurisdictions and rural deaneries.

7 Clent and Broome (but not Rowley Regis) are now in Worcestershire.

8   Amblecote was part of Old Swinford parish (diocese of Worcester); Tyrley part of Market Drayton (archdeaconry of Salop); Balterley part of Barthomley (diocese of Chester).

9   A small island in Stafford – probably the former episcopal estate – formed the parish of St. Chad, in a prebendal peculiar. It contained only about thirty-five houses in 1834 (W White, *Dir. Staffs.* (1834), 110), and for most purposes St. Mary's parish can be equated with the town together with several townships in the surrounding countryside.

10 The same forms were used by Owen's successor, Edward Bather, in 1843. The archdeaconry of Derby volume is LJRO, A/V/1/1; the Salop returns are in the possession of the Ven. Archdeacon of Salop. See also pp. xxxi–xxxiii.

11 For the diocese of Lichfield and Coventry see the articles of Bishops Chandler (1718), Frederick Cornwallis (1751) and North (1772–73), for each of which incomplete returns survive (LJRO, B/V/5).

12 For these only a solitary return, for Ashbourne (Derbs.), survives among the diocesan records (LJRO, B/V/5). The two first questions were: 'What is the number of persons which your Church can contain *in its present state*, allowing eighteen inches to each adult, side by side, and fifteen inches to each child?' and 'If the above number be less than one-third of your population, in what way can the capacity of your church be increased; and what prospect have you of raising funds for that purpose?' A further questionnaire issued by Ryder in 1832 also concentrated on education and accommodation, and for this returns survive covering parishes in the archdeaconry of Salop (LJRO, B/V/5).

13 Perhaps most comprehensively summarised in the *Constitutiones Cuiusdam Episcopi*, probably of 1225 × 1230 and largely deriving from earlier decrees: *Councils and Synods*, ed. FM Powicke and CR Cheney, ii(1) (Oxford, 1964), 195.

14 SRO, D1048/6/2, 14 June 1830.

15 The rural deaneries were merely convenient units, with little administrative significance, and the revival of the office of rural dean in 1837 was carried out without regard for the ancient boundaries, with thirteen deaneries in place of the previous four. Hodson was active in encouraging the revival and the deans commented on the fulfilment of his orders after the 1837–8 visitation. See *VCH Staffs*. iii, 74; below, p. xxxi.

16 Hodson, *Diocesan Union the Strength and Ornament of the Church* (London, 1847), 24.

17 See below, pp. 145–6.

18 Contemporary prints show no signs of the alterations at Wychnor and Bradley to which Hodson objected. At Wednesbury the 'remarkably handsome modern structure' was in fact a heavy restoration of a mediaeval structure rather than a totally modern building.

19 M Whiffen, *Stuart and Georgian Churches* (London, 1947–48) 14–15; M Whinney, *Wren* (London, 1971), 195.

20 Walter Chetwynd's name and arms appear prominently over the west door at Ingestre.

21 Originally rebuilt in 1717 and enlarged 1788: *VCH Staffs*. viii, 122.

22 Hanley, originally built in 1738, rebuilt 1790; Lane End, built in 1762, rebuilt 1795 and enlarged 1827 (*VCH Staffs*. viii, 154, 233). The doorways of both churches were classical, those at Hanley being set symmetrically at each end of the north and south sides.

23 FW Hackwood, *A History of Darlaston* (Wednesbury, 1887), 60; White, *Dir. Staffs*. (1834), 267.

24 FJ Johnson, 'The Settlement Pattern of North-East Staffordshire: a Study in Historical Geography' (University of Wales MA thesis, 1965), 339.

25 In the case of Elkstone this symmetry was destroyed by the insertion of an upper window to light the west gallery.

26 BFL Clarke, *The Building of the Eighteenth-Century Church* (London, 1963), 100–2; SRO, D922/36.

27 In Colwich parish. Hodson consulted James Trubshaw on the costs of church building before the meeting to found the Diocesan Church Building Society (*Report of the Proceedings at a Meeting . . . for the Purpose of forming a Church Building Society for the Diocese of Lichfield and Coventry* (Birmingham, 1835), 24).

28 Described by 'the Nestor of Ecclesiology', Alexander Beresford Hope, as 'a mock Gothic building without a chancel and with pews extending right up to the altar' and by Benjamin Webb, the Tractarian whom he presented as perpetual curate, as 'a well-meant, but wholly unecclesiastical, structure': HW and I Law, *The Book of the Beresford Hopes* (London, 1925), 184; *Annals of the Diocese of Lichfield* (Newcastle-under-Lyme and London, 1859), 28.

29 Colvin, 70, 643–5; *VCH Staffs.* viii, 23.
30 EA Underhill, *The Story of the Ancient Manor of Sedgley* (Tipton, n.d.), 254–8, 283–5; J Mills, *Annals of the Parish Church, Coseley* (Walsall, 1912), 3–4; Colvin, 359–60.
31 Colvin, 477–8.
32 *Ibid.*, 242–3.
33 *VCH Staffs.* viii, 190.
34 Colvin, 626.
35 *Ibid.*, 188.
36 N Pevsner and A Wedgwood, *The Buildings of England: Warwickshire* (Harmondsworth, 1966), 181.
37 One reason for the method of construction may have been the danger from mining subsidence. This is probably the church referred to in the Midland Mining Commission report of 1843: 'There is an instance in the parish of Sedgley of a church and parsonage-house recently erected composed of wooden frame-work, which will admit of their being screwed up into the perpendicular again whenever they may be thrown out of it'. This report also comments on delays caused to church building in Wednesbury and Dudley by the lack of sites free from the danger of subsidence. See *1st Rep. Com. Midland Mining (S.Staffs)* (London, 1843), pp.iv–v, xiii.
38 Colvin, 687.
39 Colvin, 72. This is the 'Mr Bennett of Tutbury' to whom Hodson in 1837 urged the rebuilding of Chilcote chapel.
40 St. George's, Newcastle-under-Lyme, had 'great appearance of want of strength and substance in the original construction'. Christ Church, Tunstall, was 'very slightly built'.
41 G Hodson, *A Charge . . . Archdeaconry of Stafford, 1839* (Rugeley, 1839), 52.
42 Hodson, *Diocesan Union the Strength and Ornament of the Church*, 17–18.
43 MH Port, *Six Hundred New Churches* (London, 1961), 6, 11.
44 *Ibid.*, 174.
45 *Proceedings at a Meeting . . . for the Purpose of forming a Church Building Society*, 24.
46 This includes a number of chapelries recently given independence. The number of ancient parishes is rather less than this.
47 47 Geo. III, sess. 2, c.114 (local and personal).
48 Underhill, *Ancient Manor of Sedgley*, 296–7, 283–6; JS Roper, *History of Coseley* (Coseley, 1952), pp. ii–iii.
49 *SHC 1915*, 20, 318; White, *Dir. Staffs.* (1834), 612, 552; *VCH Staffs.* viii, 93.
50 See below.
51 *Census of Great Britain, 1851: Religious Worship, England and Wales,* p. ccxlvii. These figures include churches which were outside the archdeacon's jurisdiction in 1830.
52 1831, calculated from Hodson's return (figures based on *Eccles. Revs.* are almost identical); 1851, from *Census of Great Britain, 1851: Religious Worship,* p. ccxcvii; 1881 and 1901, calculated from *Lichfield Diocesan Church Calendar* (1882, 1902).
53 *Diocesan Union the Strength and Ornament of the Church*, 38.
54 Throughout this introduction the use of precise statistics is made difficult by the chapelries and district churches, which can sometimes be counted separately but have sometimes to be included with those for the mother parish.
55 *VCH Staffs.* iii, 71.
56 He notes in his visitation that the one at Norbury seated 60 people for £60.
57 *Proceedings at a Meeting . . . for the Purpose of forming a Church Building Society*, 22.
58 Several churches, such as Woodcote, were described in such terms as 'not in good order – tho' there are no very material instances of neglect observable'.
59 The last three of these at least were fifteenth- or early sixteenth-century: SA Jeavons, 'The Fonts of Staffordshire', *Transactions of Birmingham Archaeological Society*, lxviii, 19–20.
60 LJRO, B/C/5. 1835, 1854.

61 *Ibid.*, 1820, 1824, 1843. The Diocesan Church Building Society recommended that the pulpit should be placed 'so as to intercept the view of the Communion Table as little as possible': *A Summary View of the Object, Plan, and Operations of the Church Building Society, for the Diocese of Lichfield and Coventry with Instructions for carrying its Designs into Effect* (Lichfield, 1835), 26.

62 LJRO, B/C/5, 1825.

63 W Pitt, *A Topographical History of Staffs.* (Newcastle-under-Lyme, 1817), 243.

64 SRO, D1048/6/2. 12 April 1830.

65 Only in a few cases such as Barton-under-Needwood, Hamstall Ridware and Tamworth, does Hodson comment on organists and their payment. In 1830 the parish of Shenstone advertised for an organist at £20 *per annum*; at Seighford, which had a barrel-organ, the grinder in 1840 received 10s. and his blower 5s. (SRO, D1016/3; D731/11).

66 *Charge* (1839), 18.

67 Barlaston, Gayton, Ingestre, Weston-upon-Trent and Weston-under-Lizard (where the sexton let the grass grow too high).

68 The churchwardens of Alstonefield drew seven-ninths of their income from the chapelries in the parish, and had raised large sums for repairs in the previous decade: over £600 between 1824 and 1828 (SRO, D922/36). In his 1839 *Charge* (p.44) Hodson also referred to Marchington and Newborough, which were assessed for the upkeep of their parish church (Hanbury) and also for Christ Church, Needwood. Professor WO Chadwick quotes another North Staffordshire example of a district (Goldenhill) paying church-rates to two tiers within the parochial system (the chapel of Tunstall and the parish church of Wolstanton) in addition to bearing the upkeep of their own chapel: *The Victorian Church* (London, 1966), 85. This dates from 1841.

69 *Diocesan Union the Strength and Ornament of the Church*, 24–5.

70 The information on the social status, professions and trades of churchwardens are taken from White, *Dir. Staffs.* (1834).

71 Law, *Book of the Beresford Hopes*, 193.

72 *Charge* (1839), 17.

73 In addition St. Paul's, Walsall, always had a governor of the school as warden.

74 See *British Museum Catalogue of Printed Books, sub* Price, Humphrey. Ironically Price had been presented to Christ Church by the Crown: LJRO, B/A/3.

75 Butler, *Samuel Butler*, ii, 247–51, 254, 290–1.

76 89 churches had two services; in 28 of them there was only one sermon, and in 9 others a second sermon only in summer.

77 With two exceptions, Alstonefield and Shenstone.

78 There was also a weekly lecture at Tutbury.

79 SRO, D1048/6/2, 1830 *passim*.

80 *Ibid.*, 9 and 30 March 1850.

81 Bloxwich, Holy Trinity, Burton, Checkley, Kinver, Lane End, Leek, St. Giles', Newcastle-under-Lyme, Rocester, St. Mary's, Stafford, Tamworth, Uttoxeter, St. Matthew's, Walsall, All Saints' and Christ Church, West Bromwich, and Worfield. The other four parishes were Aldridge, Blymhill, Enville and Quatt. In addition Communion at Sedgley was intended to be monthly.

82 Compare the figures given in *The State of the Bishopric of Worcester, 1782–1808*, ed. M Ransome (Worcestershire Historical Society, NS vi, 1968), 9; *The Diocese of Exeter in 1821: Bishop Carey's Replies to Queries before Visitation*, ed. M Cook, i (Devon and Cornwall Record Society, NS iii, 1958), pp. xx–xxi; ii (*ibid.*, NS iv, 1960), p. xiv; D McClatchey, *Oxfordshire Clergy, 1777–1869* (Oxford, 1960), 87.

83 Comparison can be made with the Visitations of 1751 and 1772–3 for 89 parishes, in 16 of which there was an increase in frequency of celebration, in 19 a decrease and in 54 there was no change. The changes were usually slight.

84 By 1882 there were two archdeaconries in Staffordshire and Iles's survey covers southern and central Staffordshire: *Report on the Chief Institutions and Year Book of the Diocese of Lichfield, 1882*, 112.

85 *Charge* (1839), 8.

86 SRO, D120/A/PC/311.

87 SRO, D120/A/PV/37.

88 SRO, D120/A/PC/151.

89 *Ibid.*
90 SRO, D120/A/PC/153, 156.
91 SRO, D568/A/PC/2.
92 SRO, D785/16.
93 For the records of these parishes see Original Documents Cited, p. viii and Appendix I.
94 SRO, D233/A/PV/1.
95 LJRO, B/V/5, 1840.
96 Described by HR Hitchcock (*Early Victorian Architecture in Britain* (New Haven, 1954), i, 113) as 'clumsy, fumbling edifices – plaster mouldings, shallow chancels . . . abysmal dullness which more than rivals that of his workhouses'.
97 J Masfen, *Views of the Church of St. Mary at Stafford* (London, 1852), 21–31; *Staffordshire Advertiser,* 21 Dec 1844; *The Ecclesiologist,* i, 64–6; *ibid.,* NS i, 139.
98 GG Scott, *Personal and Professional Recollections* (London, 1879), 96–100, 400, 413–14.
99 The south of the county seems to have resisted ecclesiology, and in 1845 *The Ecclesiologist* (iv, 283), after attacking new churches in Harborne and Handsworth, stated that 'the modern "Gothick" buildings of this neighbourhood make one regret that their architects have wandered beyond their proper province of Anglican paganism. It is a consolation, however, to know that Mr Carpenter is gaining a name here'. Even later (ix, 197) it described St. Mark's, Wolverhampton, as 'one of the poorest designs we have seen for a long time. The style is the First Pointed – as conceived of about the year 1820.'
100 SRO, D874/3/7.
101 SRO, D24/A/PC/483.
102 SRO, D24/A/PC/499–500, 515, 531.
103 James Trubshaw was paid over £30 for the spouting and draining and other structural work, the tiling cost £9 14s. 6d. and the colouring and whitewashing £10 9s. 10d.

VISITATIONS

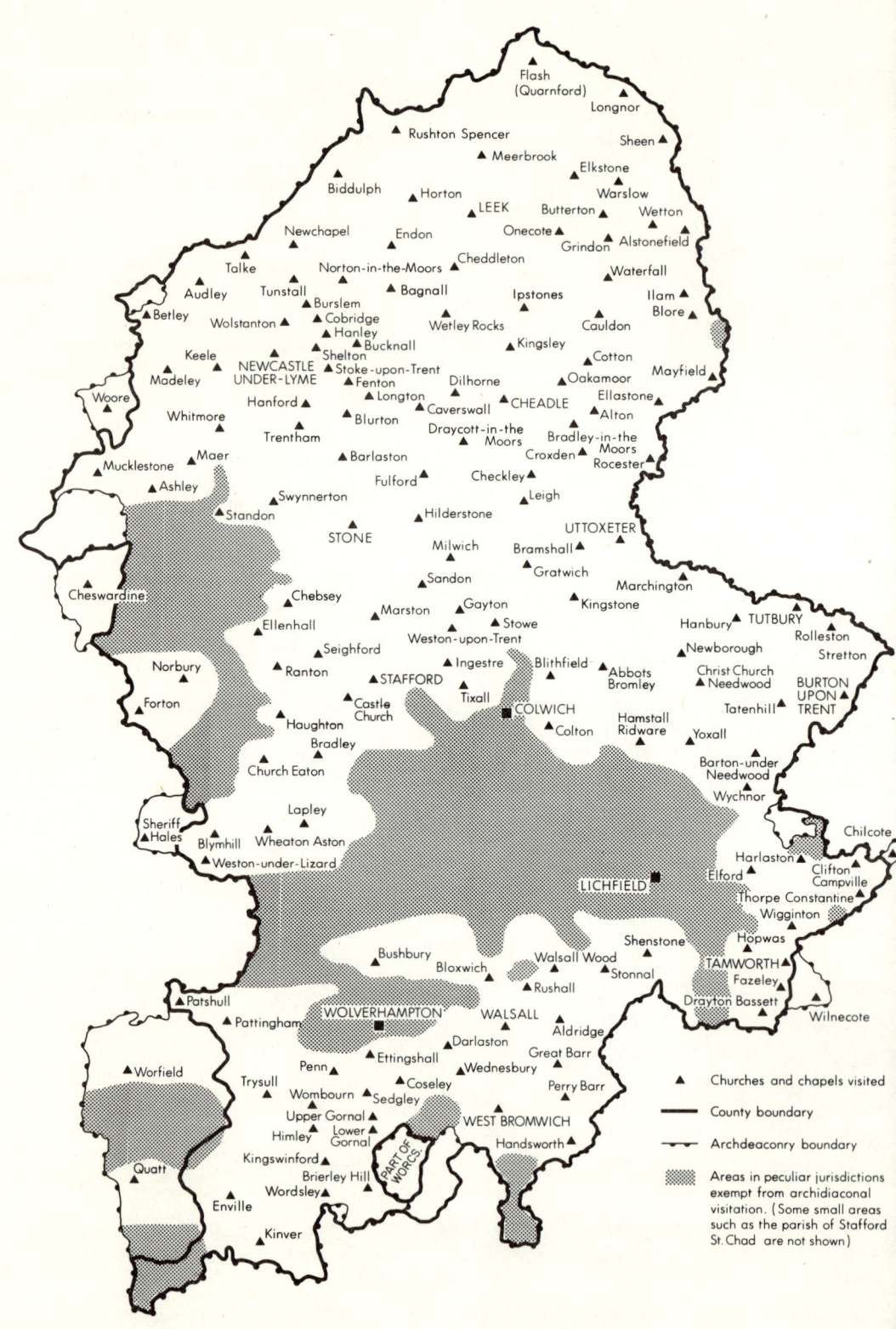

THE ARCHDEACONRY OF STAFFORD IN 1830

ALDRIDGE 17.5.1830 (A/V/1/2,no.24;/3,no.1)

BENEFICE: Aldridge or Aldrich. **Nature:** Rectory. **Ecton:** Kings book £8 1s. 3d. – called a *Vicarage* – Patrons Mr Hoo and Mr Doleman by turns. **Patron:** Sir Edward Scott [Bart.].
CHURCH: Old fashioned Gothic Church – nave and side aisles. **Number it will contain:** 200.[1] **Accommodation for Poor:** None – except in, and under, the singing Gallery. **Roof:** Oak, covered with tile – in good state. **Walls:** Limestone and mortar. **Floor:** Quarries and grave stones[2] – tolerably even. **Windows:** Casements wanted. **Doors:** Pretty good. **Pulpit and Desk:** Old oak – crimson cushions and hangings. **Books:** Good. **Seats:** Oak – in good repair generally, except some of the floors. **Galleries:** Three – one erected in 1770 – in a very inconvenient position, partly extending into the Chancel. **Organ:** A barrel organ, in the corner of the Chancel gallery. **Font:** There is one – but no proper basin for the Water. **Chapels:** None. **Benefaction Tables:** Two – another wanted. **Vestry:** A small one, under the Tower. **Surplices:** Two, in tolerably good state. **Linen:** Provided. **Plate:** Flagon, Chalice, Paten, the Cup want repair. **Chest for Papers:** [None.] **Iron Chest for Register:** In the Vestry. **Register:** Three Vols. – from 1660 – it appears from an entry in the first Vol. that former Registers, from 1558, have been lost. **Porch:** A small one – the wall wants fresh plaistering. **Vaults:** None recently. **Cleanliness:** Attended to. **Damp:** No appearance. **Dimensions:** 29ft. 6in. by 45ft.
CHANCEL: 38ft. 7in. by 15ft. **Table:** Oak – firm. **Ornaments:** [None.] **Repaired by whom:** The Rector – the floor wants laying afresh, both within and without the Communion rails.
STEEPLE: Square tower. **State of:** Good. **Bells:** Five. Good. **Clock:** Good.
CHURCHYARD: **Fence:** Brick wall, belonging to the Parish, except a part of that on the S. side – in good order. **Gates:** Good. **Drains:** None – order'd; and spouting etc. **Graves:** Some too near the walls. **Rubbish:** Some – and earth accumulated against the Church walls. **Cattle:** None.
DIVINE SERVICE: **On Sundays:** Two full services in Summer – Prayers in Afternoon in Winter.[3] **On other Days:** None. **Sacrament:** Monthly. **Communicants:** 28–60 or 70 at the Festivals. **Catechism:** In Lent.
INCUMBENT: **Name and Residence:** Revd H Harding – Rectory. **What Duty he performs:** Whole in general; his Curate at Barr sometimes assists.
PARSONAGE: A new, large, and handsome building – extensive and well fitted up. **State of:** Very good. **Outbuildings:** Stable, Coach House etc. all in good order.
INCOME: **Gross Value:** £1,200.[4] **Tithes:** of 7,000 acres, in Aldridge and Barr. **Glebe:** 60 acres. **Surplice Fees:** About £3. **Easter Dues and small Payments:** None. **Queen Anne's Bounty:** – – – **Terrier:** In the Rector's possession.
SCHOOLS: **Endowed School:** There is one, endowed with upwards of 100 acres of land left 110 years ago – rent about £130 per annum – for boys from 6 to 14 – about 50 attend – there is also a Girls School, supported by Weeley's charity. **Subscription Day School:** A small one, supported by the Rector and his lady. **Sunday School:** 30 boys – 45 girls. **Lancaster School:** None.
DISSENTERS: **Dissenters' School:** ——. **Dissenting Chapels:** ——.
POPULATION: 800.
MISCELLANEOUS: **Monuments:** Some. **Chandeliers, etc.:** None. **Parochial Library:** None.
PARISH CLERK: Thomas Cooke – who is also Schoolmaster. **Appointed by:** The Rector. **Salary:** £21 – besides Surplice Fees.
CHURCHWARDENS: Mr Edward Tongue, Mr John White.
ORDERS MADE: The floor to be laid even, near the Vestry door. Casements made in the Windows. Floors and pannels of Pews repaired. Basin for baptismal font provided. Benefaction Tables completed. Sacramental Cup repaired. Outside walls of Church and Chancel covered afresh with Rough Cast (as now) or Cement. Earth cleared away – drains made and spouting completed.[5]
In consideration of the debt incurred by the Parish by late repairs to the Churchyard fence etc., the completion of the above repairs suffered to occupy three years from present time.
The Church, in general, by no means in a becoming state – a new one very desirable.[6]

Revisited 14.10.1837
Much improved since my former visit. Directed – Pews repaired and oiled. West windows repaired. Floors of pews in N. aisle relaid. Enlargement recommended.

Revisited 23.10.1841
Since my last visit, the Church has been somewhat enlarged, and much improved *internally*; there is reason however to fear that the new roof on South side, has been very insufficiently covered, and that more care has been bestowed on the *ornamental*, than the useful, inside the Church. Directions. (1) The Arch behind the W. Gallery to be opened half way down, and *glazed*, to let in light from West window. (2) The sufficiency of the metal covering of the South Aisle to be ascertained and reported to the *Rural Dean*.

[1] *Eccles. Revs.:* 300. [2] A/V/1/3: 'Quarries and paved stones'. [3] A/V/1/3: '1½ in Winter'. [4] *Eccles. Revs.:* £1,100. [5] A/V/1/3: 'the spowting to be carried all round'. [6] A/V/1/3: 'The Church, in general, is in a very poor condition – by no means suited either to the size of the Parish or to the value of the living – a new one much wanted.'

GREAT BARR 17.5.1830 (A/V/1/2,no.25;/3,no.2)

BENEFICE: Great Barr. **Nature:** Chapel of Ease to Aldridge. **Ecton:** Clear Value £20. **Patron:** The Vicar of Aldridge.
CHURCH: Neat modern-built Chapel, Grecian structure – without side aisles. **Number it will contain:** About 250. **Accommodation for Poor:** About 80 sittings. **Roof:** Oak covered with slates.[1] **Walls:** Brick, faced with cement – good. **Floor:** Flat stones – that of the Chancel tesselated. **Windows:** Very good – those in Chancel, stained glass. **Doors:** Good. **Pulpit and Desk:** Handsome

Oak – velvet cushion. **Books:** The Bible wants a little repair. **Seats:** Very good – oak. **Galleries:** One at the W. end – and partially along the N. and S. sides. **Organ:** There is one. **Font:** There is one. **Chapels:** None. **Benefaction Tables:** None – there are some benefactions not recorded. **Vestry:** A small one, taken off the entrance under the Tower. **Surplices:** Two – one bad; a new one ordered. **Linen:** Table Cloth and Napkin. **Plate:** Flagon, Chalice, 2 Pattens. **Iron Chest for Register:** There is one. **Register:** Two Vols. Oldest 1650 – complete from that time. **Porch:** None. **Vaults:** Two. **Cleanliness:** Attended to. **Damp:** No appearance of it. **Dimensions:** 56ft. 5in. by 26ft.

CHANCEL: [Included in preceding – no separation.] **Table:** Oak – plain and firm. **Ornaments:** Altar Service Book, presented by the present Rector – Velvet Cushions. **Repaired by whom:** The Chapel-wardens, together with the Chapel itself, from the rent of land, which yields £24 per annum – half of which goes to the Clerk.[2]

STEEPLE: Square Tower, with Spire above. **State of:** Good. **Bells:** Six. **Clock:** None.

CHURCHYARD: **Fence:** Brick wall all round – in good order. **Gates:** One – Iron – put up by Sir E Scott. **Drains:** None. **Graves:** None too near the Walls. **Rubbish:** None, except weeds. **Footpaths:** None. **Cattle:** None at present – [sheep occasionally].

DIVINE SERVICE: **On Sundays:** Two full services in Summer – in Winter prayers only Afternoon.[3] **On other Days:** None. **Sacrament:** Four times a year. **Communicants:** 25 [average]–40 at Easter last. **Catechism:** None.

INCUMBENT: **Name and Residence**: Revd H Harding – Aldridge. **What Duty he performs:** [Occasionally changes with his Curate.]

CURATE: **Name and Residence:** Revd GW Luckcock – within a mile from the Chapel. **Licensed:** Not yet. **Salary:** £120 and Surplice Fees. **If serving another church:** None.

PARSONAGE: None.

INCOME: **Gross Value:** [Not ascertained.] **Terrier:** There is one.

SCHOOLS: **Endowed School:** There is one, for education of 5 children, supported by land left by the Scott and Foley families – the present Bart. (Sir Edward Scott) intends to place the Schools on a more complete and effective plan. **Subscription Day School:** None. **Sunday School:** About 50 children. **Lancaster School:** None.

DISSENTERS: **Dissenter's School:** ——. **Dissenting Chapels:** ——.

POPULATION: About 800.

MISCELLANEOUS: **Monuments:** None. **Chandeliers, etc.:** ——. **Parochial Library:** ——.

PARISH CLERK: John Welch. **Appointed by:** The Rector. **Salary:** £12 – from land mentioned Art. 37. Qu? how far is this right?

CHURCHWARDENS: Mr John Brindley – appointed alternately by the Rector and inhabitants.

ORDERS MADE: Bible and Prayer Books to be repaired. Benefactions recorded. New Surplice provided. Spouting – open drains.
Ten Commandments [put up in the Church]. 'Partly done, Articles returned.'

Revisited 14.10.1837
Directions – Prayer Book repaired or new. Window frames repaired and painted. Water tables cleared out. Roof repaired – spouts cleared – drains ditto. Weatherboards restored. Nettles etc removed from Churchyard. Benefaction Tables set up. 'In progress.'

Revisited 23.10.1841
Unless the alterations and enlargement proposed in this Church be effected, the following directions to be observed. (1) Walls to be coloured – ceilings whitewashed. (2) New Prayer Book for reading desk. (3) Wheels of bells repaired and braced, roof of Church examined and repaired. Spouts frequently cleared out. (4) An additional *down pipe* at the SE. of Chancel roof. (5) Trees on N. side lopped, to prevent damage to the Church.

[1] 'tiles' deleted. [2] A/V/1/3: 'The Chapel-wardens, out of the moiety of Rent of land appropriated to the repairs of the whole Chapel – the other half (£12) pays the Clerk.' [3] A/V/1/3: '. . . 1½ in Winter.'

BLOXWICH 17.5.1830 (A/V/1/2,no.28;/3,no.3)

BENEFICE: Bloxwich. **Nature:** Originally Chapel of Ease to Walsall – now a Perpetual Curacy. **Ecton:** £7 clear value. **Patron:** Inhabitants of Great Bloxwich have hitherto been supposed to have the appointment – the Vicar of Walsall disputes the right – The present Minister was appointed by the Bishop, the Benefice having lapsed. **Impropriator:** Col. Walhouse and others.

CHURCH: Plain Modern [brick] building, erected 39 years ago. **Number it will contain:** About 1,000 [– 200 added since, in 1833. (1837).] **Accommodation for Poor:** None, except for the school children and singers and some sittings for the Workhouse poor. **Roof:** Timber covered with slate – not in very good state. **Walls:** Brick – plaistered inside – upright. **Floor:** Quarries – even. **Windows:** Pretty good – casements provided. **Doors:** Good. **Pulpit and Desk:** Good. **Books:** Good. **Seats:** Neat and uniform. **Galleries:** On three sides. **Organ:** None. **Font:** There is. **Chapels:** None. **Benefaction Tables:** Not complete. **Vestry:** A commodious one. **Surplices:** Two – good. **Linen:** Provided. **Plate:** Provided. **Iron Chest for Register:** There is one in the Vestry Closet. **Register:** Two Vols prior to 1813 – oldest date 1733 – previously to which period it is probable that the Registers were kept at Walsall. **Porch:** None. **Vaults:** ——. **Cleanliness:** Pretty well attended to. **Damp:** None, except in the ceiling. **Dimensions:** 65ft. by 40ft.

CHANCEL: **Table:** Oak – good. **Ornaments:** Red Crimson covering – altar services. **Repaired by whom:** The township.

STEEPLE: Square brick Tower. **State of:** Good. **Bells:** One – good. **Clock:** In good repair.

CHURCHYARD: **Fence:** Maintained by the Parish – in good state. **Gates:** Iron – good. **Drains:** Sufficiently provided – spouting wanted on the N. side. **Graves:** Not too near the Walls. **Rubbish:** Weeds etc [– grass not properly kept.] **Footpaths:** None. **Cattle:** None.

DIVINE SERVICE: **On Sundays:** Two full Services on Sundays. **On other Days:** None. **Sacrament:** Monthly. **Communicants:** 15 to 20. **Catechism:** Not in the Church.

INCUMBENT: **Name and Residence:** Revd John Baghe – in the Parsonage house. **What Duty he performs:** The whole.

PARSONAGE: Brick (small) building – 3 sitting rooms – 3 bedrooms, kitchen etc. **State of:** Substantially good. **Outbuildings:** Stable etc. **Gross Value:** About £130. **Tithes:** None. **Glebe:** Six acres – let for £18. **Surplice Fees:** £5. **Easter Dues and small Payments:** Share of an estate at Cannock and £20 per annum from Merchant Taylors School, of which half goes to the National School. **Queen Anne's Bounty:** £90 per annum. **Terrier:** None in the Ministers possession – (at Lichfield there is one as old as 1693 – September 6. GH).

SCHOOLS: **Endowed School:** None. **Subscription Day School:** National School. **Sunday School:** 100 children.

DISSENTERS: **Dissenting Chapels:** Methodist and Roman Catholic.

POPULATION: About 3000, belonging to the Townships.

MISCELLANEOUS: **Parochial Library:** None – assistance in books much wanted.[1]

PARISH CLERK: Thomas Marshall. **Appointed by:** The Minister. **Salary:** Not specified.

CHURCHWARDENS: Mr John James – Edward E Stanley – appointed by Vicar and Parishioners of Walsall.

ORDERS MADE: The roof to be examined and repaired. Benefaction Tables set up. Spouting along the North side of the Chapel. Herbage cleared away [from the Chapel yard].
    Additional accommodation for the School children in the Gallery strongly recommended.

Revisited 12.10.1837
    Spouts to be cleared out. Roof of tower repaired. Roof of Church ditto.

Revisited 20.10.1841
    All in excellent order. (1) Outer doors to be painted. (2) Roof looked over and repaired where needful; especially at the West end and over the North Gallery.

[1] A/V/1/3: 'None — books for use of poor much wanted.'

BRIERLEY HILL 19.5.1830
(A/V/1/2,no.41;/3,no.4)

BENEFICE: Brierley Hill. **Nature:** P Curacy – formerly chapel of ease to K Swinford. **Ecton:** Not mentioned. **Patron:** Rector of Kings Swinford.

CHURCH: Plain modern building enlarged in 1823 by subscription, and aids from the Society. **Number it will contain:** 1,100. **Accommodation for Poor:** 356. 700 additional sittings obtained by the enlargement. **Roof:** Oak – covered with tiles and slates. **Walls:** Brick. **Floor:** Flags. **Windows:** Good. **Doors:** ——. **Pulpit and Desk:** ——. **Books:** The Bible and Clerk's Prayer book need repair. **Seats:** New and uniform. **Galleries:** On three sides. **Font:** There is one. **Chapels:** None. **Vestry:** There is one. **Surplices:** Two, both good. **Linen:** Provided. **Plate:** Two Chalices (plates) and a Paten. **Iron Chest for Register:** At the Minister's house; 1½ mile off. **Register:** [from 1766 (17 July 1838).] **Porch:** None. **Cleanliness:** Attended to. **Damp:** No appearance.

CHANCEL: None distinct from the body. **Table:** [Good.] **Repaired by whom:** [The parish.]

STEEPLE: Square brick Tower. **State of:** Good. **Bells:** Weather boards want repair.

CHURCHYARD: **Fence:** Brick wall – in good repair. **Gates:** Good. **Drains:** ——. **Rubbish and Footpaths:** The herbage not kept properly – a large heap of Ashes near the Gate, *outside* – application to the Surveyors of the Roads recommended, if necessary, for its removal.

DIVINE SERVICE: **On Sundays:** Two full services. **On other days:** None. **Sacrament:** Five times a year. **Communicants:** 45 to 50.

INCUMBENT: Revd C Neave[1] – at Wordsley, in the Parish. **What Duty he performs:** The whole.

CURATE: None.

PARSONAGE: None.

INCOME: [Not ascertained – arises chiefly from pew-rents.][2] **Tithes:** The Income arises partly from Pew-Rents – amount not ascertained.

POPULATION: 14,000 or 15,000[3] – two-thirds of which are near the Chapel.

ORDERS MADE: The interior of the Chapel, and the Fabric generally, being in excellent order, particular enquiries as to many points seemed superfluous. The Chapel yard requires to be kept in better order.

Revisited 17.7.1838
    This Chapel has been much enlarged and greatly improved since my former visit. It now has sittings for 1,516, of which 887 are free.
    Galleries at W. end and on sides. Very little needful in the way of repair; the whole roof being new. The roof of the *Tower,* however (which is old), needs repair – the brick-copings, lead-gutters and flashings, out of order.
    Wheels and gudgeons of bells, window of belfry, repaired. New door at W. entrance, and iron gates.
    Regular footpaths formed from W. and E. corners of Churchyard. New prayer books for Reading and Clerk's desks. 'Not provided 1840.'
    Additional burial ground wanted.

Revisited 19.10.1841
    Directions etc. (1) New books provided. (2) Walls and windows kept clean – windows mended – iron frames of windows painted externally – window sills pointed. (3) Water table for East window. (4) Door at entrance of Tower roof – lead flashings, parapets and tiling of roof repaired. (5) Bells properly furnished. (6) Doors of Church painted outside. (7) Church coloured inside and out – *stone* colour. (8) Delapidated tombs repaired or else walls removed and flag-stone laid on ground.

[1] Also vicar of Kilmersdon (Somerset). [2] *Eccles. Revs.*: gross income £97. [3] *Eccles. Revs.*: 7,800. The figure given above relates to the parish of Kingswinford, including Brierley Hill.

BUSHBURY 18.5.1830 (A/V/1/2,no.48;/3.no.5)

BENEFICE: Bushbury. **Nature:** Vicarage. **Ecton:** Living discharged – £46 Clear yearly value. **Patron:** Ten Trustees.[1] **Impropriator:** The tythes chiefly purchased by the Proprietors of the Lands.

CHURCH: A very old Gothic structure; with some remains of Saxon architecture – the Chancel remarkably handsome internally – The whole [building] however [is] in a [very] dilapidated state, and about to be thoroughly repaired and new modelled inside, on which account particular observations as to the Church itself were unnecessary.[2] **Number it will contain:** 274.[3] **Accommodation for Poor:** At present very insufficient – but in the intended alteration it is proposed to add 250 sittings of which 163 will be for the poor – the remaining 87 are to be disposed of to those who have houses in the Parish but no pews.[4] [This enlargement was effected in the year 1831 or 1832.] **Roof to Chancel:** Not ascertained – in consequence of the state of confusion and disorder preceding the approaching alterations in the Church.[5]

STEEPLE: A Square stone Tower. **State of:** Good. **Bells:** Four – good. **Clock:** There is one.

CHURCHYARD: **Fence:** Wall, partly brick; partly stone. **Drains:** Much wanted. **Graves:** Many much too near the Church walls – the Church itself is almost *buried,* from the accumulation of soil outside.

INCUMBENT: Revd Mr Clare.[6] **If not resident:** At Wolverhampton now (1841) Revd Mr Lister who *resides*. **What Duty he performs:** Two full services (1841).

CURATE: ['Revd W Evans' – in the Parish.] **Licensed:** ['Yes'.]

PARSONAGE: [Modern brick building – I fear not substantially built (1841).][7] **State of:** Tolerably good.

INCOME: **Gross Value:** Not ascertained – the Incumbent himself did not attend.[8]

POPULATION: 1,400.

ORDERS MADE: The whole Parish seems to suffer from the non-residence, or inattention, of the Clergyman. A *Chapel of Ease* is very much wanted – in one of the Townships, Essington, there is a population of 2,000, five miles from the Church. The Churchwarden from that part of the Parish seemed to think that Col Graham, who has property there, would contribute for this purpose – Mr Gough of Perry Hall, has also property in the Parish.[9]

Revisited 12.10.1837
Walls to be coloured. New Prayer Book for Clerk's desk. Windows on N. side repaired – new ties. Pews in S. side repaired. Decayed Panels and wainscoting repaired. Chancel ditto. Timbers and floors of roof repaired. Leadwork of roof repaired. Staircase and weatherboards repaired. Belfry window repaired. Ground cleared outside – and gravel walk made. Chancel spouted. Font repaired.
'nothing done.'

Revisited 20.10.1841
Directions (sent to Mr Briscoe the Churchwarden the following morning.) (1) Wainscoating of Pews on S. side; and of Gallery on ditto to be renewed. (2) Water tables for windows – bars painted. (3) Pews painted (oak), walls coloured (stone), ceilings whitewashed. (4) Roofs of Church and Chancel examined and repaired – especially at E. end of Nave. (5) Roofs of Church and Chancel spouted – open drains all round. (6) Cracked bell re-cast, wheels, ropes, floors of Bell-chamber put into good and sound condition. (7) Battlements, parapets and pinnacles of Tower examined and secured – angles and walls, down to lower string course, *pointed*. (8) Churchyard gates painted – copings of wall repaired; thoroughfare stopped, if possible. N.B. I repeated, in strong terms, my former recommendation of a Chapel of Ease at Essington.

[1] *Eccles. Revs.:* '– Phillips and others.' [2] Faculty granted 6 July 1830 (B/C/2/1829–32, pp.230–35) for the demolition and rebuilding of the south wall and porch and the construction of a new south gallery, and for internal reorganisation. [3] A/V/1/3: '524 (1837)'. *Eccles. Revs.:* 600. [4] A/V/1/3: '163'. [5] A/V/1/3: 'Not ascertained – the Clergyman did not attend and everything appeared to be in confusion; on the prospect of the intended alteration.' [6] Also perpetual curate of Wednesfield: *Eccles. Revs.* [7] *Eccles Revs.:* 'fit'. [8] *Eccles. Revs.* gives the annual gross income as £159 and the Curate's income as £50. [9] A/V/1/3: None – as the Church is on the point of undergoing extensive alterations and repairs, which are much needed. One of the Church Wardens stated that a Chapel of Ease is much wanted in a remote part of the Parish, the Township of Essington, 5 miles from the Church, where there is (he said) a population of 2,000 (but qu? the accuracy of this statement which was afterwards contradicted by the Minister of the Parish.)

CLIFTON CAMPVILLE 24.5.1830 (A/V/1/2,no.17;/3,no.6)

BENEFICE: Clifton Campville – a village about five miles from Tamworth. **Nature:** Rectory. **Ecton:** King's books £30. [(Sir Robert Pye Bart. Patron.)][1] **Patron:** The *present* Patron Revd John Watkins (formerly Rector) as proprietor of the *Clifton Hall* estate to which the living is attached – Ecton, Sir Robert Pye, Bart. Patron. **Impropriator:** None – the Rector has all the Tithes.

CHURCH: A very handsome Gothic building – with Nave, South Aisle (no *North* aisle *remaining*) – but there is a small transept, occupied by the seats belonging to the Hall) – two Chancels – the Rector's separated from the Nave by a handsome Screen. **Number it will contain:** About 400.[2] **Accommodation for Poor:** Not sufficient – the precise number not known. **Roof:** The nave timber covered with tiles – the South Aisle and Chancels [covered with] lead – the *whole* put into complete repair in 1828. **Walls:** Stone – upright. **Floor:** Brick – uneven in several places, owing to *graves* underneath. **Windows:** Good, but *no casements* – ordered four in the Body, two in the Chancels. **Doors:** Old oak – the *South door* wants *lining,* on both sides. **Pulpit and Desk:** Handsome old oak – crimson coverings to Pulpit. **Books:** Good – except some repairs wanted in the *Bible*. **Seats:** Not uniform – many of the floors want repair – floors *brick*. **Galleries:** One, at the W. end; for the singers. **Organ:** None. **Font:** An old stone one at the W. end – in a very dirty state. **Chapels:** None – but there is a side Chancel (or transept see above) on the North side, belonging to the Lord of the Manor. **Benefaction Tables:** None – ordered. **Vestry:** None – one recommended. **Surplices:** Two – one rather bad, never used – its use ordered. **Linen:** Table Cloth and napkin – in bad repair. **Plate:** In a *Chest in the Chancel* are an old, broken, Pewter flagon and two plates – at the Rectory a *silver Cup*. **Iron Chest for Register:** There is one, at the Rectory. **Register:** Several Vols, at the Rectory – oldest 1596 – in indifferent condition – Those belonging to the *Chapels* are kept at the Rectory also. **Porch:** Two – N. and S. – ordered that the light Gates be *kept locked*, and the [inner] doors *open*. **Vaults:** Some, and several [brick] graves, which have done much injury to the floor. **Cleanliness:** *very much neglected* – in every part. **Damp:** A great deal on the walls and floor. **Dimensions:** 58ft. 7in. by 43ft. 2in.

CHANCEL: 53ft. 7in. by 43ft. 2in. **Table:** Square, painted deal – a decent stuff covering. **Ornaments:** None. **Repaired by whom:** The Rector repairs one – the Parish the other – tho' there is some reason to think (from an antient monument in the latter) that it formerly belonged to the Vernon family.

STEEPLE: Stone tower, with a handsome taper Spire above – the latter appears in a very dangerous condition – *both* to be examined. **State of:** very indifferent. **Bells:** Five – in good repair. **Clock:** In good order.

CHURCHYARD: **Fence:** Hedge all round – kept up at the expense of the *whole Parish* – in pretty good order. **Gates:** Want some repairs and painting. **Drains:** None – very much wanted – ordered – and spouts. **Graves:** Too near. **Rubbish:** A great deal – and the soil in heaps against the Church. **Footpaths:** Several – but alleged to be of old standing. **Cattle:** Cows belonging to the late Rector – to keep them from breaking the Windows, rails have been put up, which greatly disfigure the Church.

DIVINE SERVICE: **On Sundays:** Full service morning – prayers afternoon and a second Sermon half the year.[3] **On other Days:** None. **Sacrament:** Four times a year. **Communicants:** 50–70. **Catechism:** Not in the Church.

INCUMBENT: **Name and Residence:** Revd Robert Taylor – resides at *the Hall* – his father-in-law (the *late* Rector) retains the use of the Rectory house, by exchange for his life. **What Duty he performs:** Shares the whole duty of the Parish with his Curate.

CURATE: **Name and Residence:** Revd JB Fisher, – in the Parish ["Cleve"]. **If not resident:** ——. **Licensed:** He is. **Salary:** £100. **If serving another church:** None – except the Chapels.

PARSONAGE: Brick – rough cast; roofed with tile – four sitting rooms and kitchens etc. on the ground floor – five best bedrooms and attics over the whole house.[4] **State of:** Substantially, pretty good – but in a neglected state.[5] **Outbuildings:** Large stable, Coach house etc built by the late Rector, Barn [now] under repair.

INCOME: **Gross Value**: About £1,200.[6] **Tithes and Glebe:** Together £1,000. **Queen Anne's Bounty:** None. **Terrier:** There is one, in the possession of the Rector.

SCHOOLS: **Endowed School:** None. **Subscription Day School:** None – but there is one kept by the *deputy* Clerk – attended by about 60 children. **Sunday School:** 30 boys – 50 girls. **Lancaster School:** None.

DISSENTERS: **Dissenters' School:** ——. **Dissenting Chapels:** Baptist and Methodist *meetings* in *private houses*.

POPULATION: In 1821, 1,030 in *the whole Parish* – viz Clifton 379, Haunton 247, Harlaston 211, Chilcote 192.

MISCELLANEOUS: **Monuments:** Several – particularly to the family of the *Pyes,* a baronetcy (now extinct) to which the Hall estate belonged. **Chandeliers, etc:** None. **Parochial Library:** ——.

PARISH CLERK: Mr Robert Riley – a *farmer,* chosen at the wish of the *Parish* – but the duty done by *Thomas Radford* – much irregularity in the whole affair. **Appointed by:** The Rector. **Salary:** Not fixed – but he is allowed to have the Easter-dues and surplice fees.

CHURCHWARDENS: Mr John Stretton, for *Clifton and Haunton.*

ORDERS MADE: *In the Church:* The floor to be laid even – and *graves* not allowed [within the Church]. The South door repaired – the porch gates kept locked and the doors always open in fine weather. Two additional casements – on each side of the Body of the Church. One additional casement on each side of the Chancel-end.[7] The Bible repaired. Pews repaired where needful – floors of ditto ditto.

I strongly recommend *new pewing* the whole, in a uniform manner, and providing further accommodation in *free sittings* which may easily be done by a better system of pewing.

The Font cleaned and a *basin* provided – benefaction Tables set up – Surplice and Communion Linen repaired or renewed – the old Communion plate fitted for use, or else new substituted. *Cleanliness,* in every part, attended to and *provided* for.[8]

In the Churchyard and outside of the Church:
    The Tower and spire carefully examined and repaired. The earth removed[9] – drains made – rubbish removed – gates repaired and painted – graves not allowed near the Walls – rails on the N. side removed – [a] door [made] to old entrance to School-room on N. side.

The *Parish Clerk* to be properly appointed – and *duties regularly provided for* – a *Vestry* recommended.

Revisited 1.9.1837
    Nothing of importance done since my former visit. I directed – That the Gates of Churchyard be repaired and painted. Drains made round the walls. Down pipes substituted for overshot ditto. Bottom of walls cleared of weeds and fresh pointed. Tower and spire examined by Surveyor and reported. Internal walls cured of damp. Casement in Chancel. Floor at W. end, under Gallery, relaid. Pews newly arranged. New South door – light gate – fresh stuccoed. Windows of Belfry repaired – new leads – bars painted. Weatherboards made good. Door to bell Turrets. South window of Belfry repaired. Porch roof repaired. Thoroughfare of Churchyard stopped,

if possible – old tombstones repaired or removed – hedges trimmed.

'No return from R.D.'

Revisited 3.9.1841
Great improvement has been made – and the Spire repaired, since my last visit. For the purpose of rendering the whole Fabric as complete as possible I *recommended*

That the pews in the area should be removed, and either new and uniform ones erected, or open benches on boarded floors, with backs, kneeling-boards and desks – by which means a sufficient number of sittings would be obtained without the necessity of a Gallery.

I *required:* That the partitions behind the Singers' Gallery be removed, and the West Window restored to view – the bells to be rung *from below.*

That the Gallery be lowered or its position changed, so as not to intercept the Window, if the Gallery cannot be altogether removed.

That the lumber heaped together in the room below the Belfry be removed – separating and reserving for the use of the Church, whatever properly belongs to it. The roofs to be carefully examined – tiling repaired – lead flashings secured – lead water courses laid even – copings over the South side of the Chancel and elsewhere, repaired or secured, roof of old School-room repaired, and old window restored.

(N.B. I *recommend* that this room be converted either into a Vestry, or a room for a Parochial library.) The window-bars and gates leading out of Churchyard *painted.*

I recommend the removal of the over-shot spouts, and the substitution of down-pipes.

[1] A/V/1/3 adds, at left of questionnaire 'Vid: Chilcote, p.7; Harlaston, p.15.' [2] *Eccles Revs.:* 500. [3] A/V/1/3: 'two full services – except in winter'. [4] *Eccles. Revs.:* 'fit'. [5] A/V/1/3: '—— neglected and slovenly condition.' [6] *Eccles. Revs.:* £1,345. [7] A/V/1/3: 'and two at the East end' instead of 'One – chancel end'. [8] 'partly done' written in pencil alongside the section 'In the Church'. [9] A/V/1/3: 'The earth lowered around the walls'.

CHILCOTE 24.5.1830 (A/V/1/2,no.18;/3,no.7)

BENEFICE: Chilcote – a small village in Derbyshire, on the borders of Staffordshire and Leicestershire – 7 miles from Tamworth. **Nature:** Chapelry to Clifton Campville. **Ecton:** Not certified. **Patron:** Rector of Clifton Campville. **Impropriator:** ——.[1]

CHURCH: A small, antient [inelegant] structure, originally perhaps Gothic, but much disfigured by modern alterations – a single body, with a small chancel – in a very ruinous and unsightly condition. **Number it will contain:** About 80, or 100. **Accommodation for Poor:** About half of the whole number of sittings.[2] **Roof:** Oak, covered with tile – said to be now in pretty good state – the ceiling bad. **Walls:** Stone and mud or rubble – very much out of perpendicular, and covered with damp. **Floor:** Brick – very uneven towards the W. end. **Windows:** One good one (of modern shape) on the N. side – one casement; those on the S. very small and bad. **Doors:** One – tolerably good; on the N. side – that on the S. blocked up. **Pulpit and Desk:** No pulpit – reading-desk serves for both purposes – very unsteady. **Books:** Bible wants repairs – Prayer-book rebinding. **Seats:** Oak pews and open benches – floors partly brick; partly boarded – some of the floors need repair. **Galleries:** None. **Organ:** ——. **Font:** There is one. **Chapels:** None. **Benefaction Tables:** None – there are no charities appropriate to the Chapelry. **Vestry:** None. **Surplices:** One, pretty good. **Linen:** Provided. **Plate:** A silver Cup. **Iron Chest for Register** and **Register:** The Registers kept at the Rectory.[3] **Porch:** None at present – there was one formerly on the S. now taken away and the entrance blocked up – ordered it to be re-built. **Vaults:** None. **Cleanliness:** Attended to as well as the state of the fabric will admit. **Damp:** Very much on the walls and floor. **Dimensions:** 34ft. 4in. by 15ft. 6in.

CHANCEL: 17ft. 10in. by 15ft. 6in. **Table:** Old oak frame with moth-eaten cover. **Ornaments:** None – at present there is no access to the Table; the Chancel being filled with pews which bar approach – the Elements have been used to be carried into the Church – ordered that the Pews be removed.[4] **Repaired by whom:** The Parish, hitherto.

STEEPLE: A wooden bell Tower. **State of:** Indifferent. **Bells:** Two – one cracked and without a rope – the other, only half a wheel. **Clock:** None.

CHURCHYARD: **Fence:** A wall all round, kept up by the Parish – some repairs wanting, especially on the South side.[5] **Gates:** One – good. **Drains:** None – ordered, and also spouts. **Graves:** No burials in the Churchyard. **Rubbish:** None – but some trees growing near the walls of the Church on the South side – ordered to be removed. **Footpaths:** None – a gravel walk ordered, from the gate to the Church door. **Cattle:** Sheep sometimes.

DIVINE SERVICE: **On Sundays:** Morning and afternoon alternately with Harlastone. **On other Days:** None. **Sacrament:** Four times a year. **Communicants:** From 15 to 20.

INCUMBENT: **Name and Residence:** Revd R Taylor – as before.[6] **If not Resident:** ——. **What Duty he performs:** ——.

CURATE: **Name and Residence:** (see Clifton). **If not Resident:** ——. **Licensed:** ——. **Salary:** ——. **If serving another Church:** ——.

PARSONAGE: None.[7]

SCHOOLS: **Sunday School:** 20 to 25 children.

PARISH CLERK: Joseph Adams. **Salary:** He receives Easter dues.

CHURCHWARDENS: Mr John Baker, for the Township.

ORDERS MADE: ['In progress']
I strongly urged the necessity of taking down the Chapel and having it re-built, for which I recommended application to the Incorporated Society – Should this however be found impracticable, I directed (1) the state of the walls, roof, etc to be carefully examined, and the whole Fabric put into substantial repair. [A proper access to the Communion Table.] (2) The ceilings to be repaired, and that and the walls whitewashed. (3)

The Bells to be put into complete order. (4) The Churchyard wall to be repaired – a gravel walk made[8] – spouting, open drains etc formed – bushes removed [from the Chapel walls]; the encroachment on the Churchyard by the Clerk's garden, forbidden.

The inhabitants of the Township complain, as usual, of the hardship of having to repair their own Chapel, and *also* to contribute to the repairs of the Mother Church.

Revisited 1.9.1837
A good deal has been done to improve the interior since my former visit. But the fabric still in a wretched state. I strongly urged re-building on the Agent (Mr Bennett of Tutbury) of Mr Robertson the principal proprietor. Mr Bennett replied to my application that he had brought the Subject under Mr Robertson's notice.

Revisited 3.9.1841
Considerable improvements in interior being projected, specific directions deemed unnecessary. See the Agent of Mr Robertson and the builder who is to execute the alterations.
(N.B. The consecration of the Chapel yard strongly *recommended*.)

The Chapel-warden is requested to have the Bible and Prayer Book in the Reading Desk rebound and repaired – and to provide a new Prayer Book for the Clerk.

To restore, if possible, the old baptismal font; if not, to provide a suitable one under the direction of the Rural Dean.

[1] *Eccles. Revs.* gives John Watkins as impropriator (cf. Clifton Campville: see above, p. 4). [2] A/V/1/3: 'about 50'. [3] A/V/1/3: '—— at Clifton'. [4] A/V/1/3: 'None – at present the access to the Table is blocked up by old irregular pews – and the elements have been carried into the Chapel – a discontinuance of this practice and removal of the pews ordered.' [5] A/V/1/3: 'a wall – kept by the Parish – good in general'. [6] A/V/1/3: '(see Clifton)'. [7] *Eccles. Revs.:* 'none'. [8] A/V/1/3: 'a proper pathway made to the entrance of the Chapel.'

DARLASTON 19.4.1830 (A/V/1/2,no.29;/3,no.8)

BENEFICE: Darlaston (Ecton Derlaston). **Nature:** Rectory: **Ecton:** Kings books £3 11s. 5½d. Patron John Crew Offley Esqr. **Patron:** Revd C Simeon and others [as Trustees].[1]

CHURCH: Plain modern building, rebuilt about 25 or 30 years ago – in Grecian style. [Single body.] No Chancel. **Number it will contain:** About 800[2] [now *1500* (1841)]. **Accommodation for Poor:** None except forms in and under the galleries, and seats for the school children. [1841. *558.*] **Roof:** Deal covered with slate – sound. **Walls:** Brick, covered with plaister inside. **Floor:** Quarries and grave-stones. **Windows:** In good order – casements in the gallery. **Doors:** Good. **Pulpit and Desk:** Painted deal – good state – velvet ornaments. **Books:** Good. **Seats:** Ditto – boarded floors. **Galleries:** On the N. W. and S. sides. **Organ:** There is one. **Font:** ——. **Chapels:** None. **Benefaction Tables:** Two, which record all the charities. **Vestry:** There is one. **Surplices:** Three, tolerably good. **Linen, Plate, Chest for Papers, Iron Chest for Register** and **Register:** [Provided – but I] Did not see them owing to the absence of the Rector and illness of the Curate. **Porch:** None. **Vaults:** None made recently. **Cleanliness:** Attended to. **Damp:** No appearance of it. **Dimensions:** 65ft. 2in. by 44ft. 9in.

CHANCEL: [None.] **Table:** Plain painted shelf, on brackets. **Ornaments:** None. **Repaired by whom:** No distinction between Church and Chancel – or rather there is no Chancel – all repaired by the Parish.

STEEPLE: Old square tower, surmounted with steeple. **State of:** Lower part decayed – to be repaired. **Bells:** Eight in good order. **Clock:** There is one – good.

CHURCHYARD: **Fence:** Consists partly of brick wall, partly of houses, the former repaired by the Parish – There is an additional burying ground, given by the Marquis of Stafford. **Gates:** Iron – good. **Drains:** None deemed necessary – spouting ordered. **Graves:** Interments, chiefly in the new burying ground. **Rubbish:** Not much – loose stones lying about. **Footpaths:** None [improper]. **Cattle:** Sheep.

DIVINE SERVICE: **On Sundays:** Two full services. **On other Days:** Wednesday Evening Lecture. **Sacraments:** Eight times a year. **Communicants:** About 70. **Catechism:** Twice a year in the Church – regularly in the School.

INCUMBENT: **Name and Residence:** Revd S Lowe. **If not Resident:** At Walsall. **What Duty he performs:** Preaches on Sunday mornings, when well enough.

CURATE: **Name and Residence:** Revd GW White [in the Parsonage]. **Licensed:** Yes. **Salary:** £100 per annum. **If serving another church:** None.

PARSONAGE: An old building, with two new rooms and staircase at the back – brick with roof partly tile, partly slate – Three Parlours, and small room, and kitchens on ground floor – Four Bedrooms and dark closet above. **State of:** Pretty good, except some part of the roof.[3] **Outbuildings:** Barn, Stable and Gig house – in good repair.

INCOME: ——.[4]

SCHOOLS: **Endowed School:** None. **Subscription Day School:** National school, about 170 boys and 70 girls. **Sunday School:** About 140 children, besides those of the National School. **Lancaster School:** None.

DISSENTERS: **Dissenters' School:** Independents and Methodists. **Dissenting Chapels:** Independents and Methodists – Ranters and Baptist meetings. **POPULATION:** About 6,000.[5]

MISCELLANEOUS: **Parochial Library:** None.

ORDERS MADE: ['Done'.]

The lower part of the Tower to be repaired – (recommend casing it with stone, or Roman cement, to correspond with the Spire). Earth cleared away around the walls – open drains made and spouting all round. The Churchyard to be cleared of loose stones, and other rubbish – and the fence of the additional [burying] ground rendered more [secure and] complete on the sides, where there is no wall.

N.B. There is a great want of more Church room [– especially accommodation for the poor]. The Church will hold little more than one eighth of the population – free seats much needed. The

Church would admit of enlargement. The Bishop to be consulted on the subject.

Revisited 13.10.1837
Since my last visit 210 sittings have been added of which 142 are free; this making the accommodation 1,500 of which 558 free.[6] *Directions.* Weatherboards replaced – spouts and down pipes placed. Windows mended – lead flashings at Tower. Casements in alternate windows.
'Nothing done'.

Revisited 21.10.1841
Directions. (1) A suitable baptismal font – new Prayer Book for *reading desk.* (2) Roof thoroughly repaired – eave spouts – down pipes. (3) Churchyard walls repaired. (4) Stoves for warming the Church at each end. (5) Bells not to be rung without the permission of the *Rector.* (6) Church insured against *fire.*

[1] *Eccles. Revs.:* 'Trustees of J Thornton'. [2] *Eccles. Revs.:* 1,310. [3] *Eccles. Revs.:* 'fit.' [4] *Eccles. Revs.:* £297 Gross Income. [5] *Eccles. Revs.:* 6,667. [6] These figures do not seem to tally with the returns to questions seven and eight in 1830.

DRAYTON BASSETT 25.5.1830
(A/V/1/2,no.23;/3,no.9)

BENEFICE: Drayton Bassett. **Nature:** Rectory. **Ecton:** Kings books £7 8s. 4d. **Patron:** The Lord Chancellor. **Impropriator:** None.
CHURCH: A small modernised building – rebuilt by the Parish about 40 years ago – very plain and inelegant. **Number it will contain:** About 200.[1] **Accommodation for Poor:** Pews below and in the Gallery – sufficient. **Roof:** Oak and deal covered with slate – in very bad state; the whole too flat. **Walls:** Stone – upright. **Floor:** Quarries – even. **Windows:** Pretty good – but the frames want painting – and casements kept open. **Doors:** Good. **Pulpit and Desk:** Good. **Books:** Prayer Book in reading desk wants repairing or renewing. **Seats:** Uniform and good – brick floors. **Galleries:** One at the W. end put up by Subscription, six years ago. **Organ:** There is one. **Font:** None – ordered. **Chapels:** None. **Benefaction Tables:** No benefactions. **Vestry:** None. **Surplices:** One – stolen a few nights before [my visit together with the black cloth put up at the funeral of Sir Robert Peel] – two ordered. **Linen:** Table Cloth and Napkin – good. **Plate:** Silver Cup and Paten. Pewter dish. **Iron Chest for Register:** At the Rectory. **Register:** Three Vols from 1559 – in indifferent preservation. **Porch:** None. **Vaults:** Some. **Cleanliness:** Not properly attended to. **Damp:** Much in the ceiling.
CHANCEL: **Table:** An oak cupboard – crimson cloth stolen a few nights before. **Ornaments:** None. **Repaired by whom:** The Rector.
STEEPLE: Square Tower. **State of:** Good – except the windows. **Bells:** Four – good. **Clock:** Good.
CHURCHYARD: **Fence:** That next the public road kept up by the Parish – partly wall, partly paling of the *Pound*; The other sides, hedges belonging to the adjoining Tenants. **Gates:** Bad. **Drains:** None – nor spouts. **Graves:** Several too near the walls of the Church. **Rubbish:** Much, all round the Church. **Footpaths:** There are several [trespass paths] – long used. **Cattle:** Sheep.
DIVINE SERVICE: **On Sundays:** Two full services. **On other Days:** None. **Sacrament:** Four times a year. **Communicants:** 30.
INCUMBENT: **Name and Residence:** Revd WM Lally. **If not resident:** In Oxford at present. **What Duty he performs:** None.
CURATE: **Name and Residence:** Revd Bedford Kenyon, Rectory House. **Licensed:** He is. **Salary:** £80 – besides the House and Surplice Fees. **If serving another church:** No other.
PARSONAGE: Modern brick building, built by the present Rector, on the site of the old one – capacious and good – four sitting rooms, seven bedrooms – handsome entrance parlour. **State of:** Good.[2] **Outbuildings:** Coach house – Stable and Cow house.
INCOME: **Gross Value:** £240. **Tithes:** £200. **Glebe:** 17 or 18 acres. **Surplice Fees:** Not specified. **Easter Dues and small Payments:** None. **Queen Anne's Bounty:** None. **Terrier:** None.
SCHOOLS: **Endowed School:** None. **Subscription Day School:** None. **Sunday School:** About 60 children **Lancaster School:** None.
DISSENTERS: **Dissenters' School:** ——. **Dissenting Chapels:** ——.
POPULATION: About 500.
MISCELLANEOUS: **Parochial Library:** None.
PARISH CLERK: Joseph Wade. **Appointed by:** The Rector. **Salary:** £5 5s. 0d.
CHURCHWARDENS: Mr Joseph Adams – Rector. Mr Webster – Parish.
ORDERS MADE: ['Done']
The roof to be stripped, and the whole effectually repaired. The window-frames painted. Casements kept open in dry weather. Prayer book repaired or renewed. Font provided. Ten Commandments set up. Church kept properly clean. Holes in the Tower stopped up – window repaired. [(The above repairs reported to me as completed, at my Visitation at Walsall 1831)].

Revisited 31.8.1838.
Much requires attention.
In the Churchyard. Fence repaired – hedge trimmed – herbage kept down; thoroughfare stopped – drains cleared – soil removed. Spouts and down pipes set up. Roof on North side stripped and renewed. Walls pointed – especially on S. side. Tower and Chancel roof repaired.
In the Church. Doors – windows – floors – pews; all need repair. Ceiling whitewashed – walls coloured. Ventilation and cleanliness attended to. Communion rails strengthened – carpet new. Another surplice provided. "Qu? roof on N. side? Chiefly done (RD)"

Revisited 2.9.1841
Books repaired. Doors, window bars and pillars of gallery painted. Roof of Tower repaired and door closed over bells. Soil removed and open drain made. Planks provided for sexton's use in digging graves. Fence on West and South sides in better order. Footpath stopped.

[1] *Eccles. Revs.:* 370. [2] *Eccles. Revs.:* 'fit.'

ELFORD 30.7.1829 (A/V/1/2,no.15;/3,no.10)

BENEFICE: Elford – a small village – six miles from Lichfield, three miles from Tamworth. **Nature:** Rectory. **Ecton:** Kings books £13 6s. 8d. Patron Earl of Suffolk and Berkshire. **Patron:** Mrs Howard. **Impropriator:** None.

CHURCH: One[1] principal aisle – and a side aisle which appears to have been added (*when,* does not appear) – separated from the former by neat Gothic Arches and stone pillars – There is a Chancel at the end of each aisle, one of which belongs to Col. Howard in right of his wife. **Number it will contain:** The whole population that can attend. **Accommodation for Poor:** Benches for children in the Rector's Chancel – and other open seats; sufficient for the Population. **Roof:** The Nave, timber covered with slate – the side Aisle oak, covered with lead. **Walls:** On the North, stone and rubble, in a very unsound state; the South, better (of stone). **Floor:** Brick – except the Chancels and side aisles, which are flagged. **Windows:** In good state – only two casements – another ordered.[2] **Doors:** Two – in good order. **Pulpit and Desk:** Very handsome oak – velvet cushion to Pulpit. **Books:** Prayer Book good – Bible wants repair. **Seats:** Oak, or deal – generally in good condition. **Galleries:** None. **Organ:** None. **Font:** There is one. **Chapels:** None. **Benefaction Tables:** One – which records all the Charities. **Vestry:** None. **Surplices:** One, in bad repair – a new one is being provided. **Linen:** Stated by the Rector to be indifferent – a new supply directed – subject to his opinion. **Plate:** A handsome [silver] Cup and Paten, given by Mrs Howard – besides a smaller one of each, used in *private* administration of Sacrament. **Chest for Papers:** There is one, in the reading desk – used for keeping the Surplice, Cushions etc. **Iron Chest for Register:** In the wall of the passage at the Rectory House. **Register:** Three Vols besides those in use since 1813; in very good state – the oldest reaches as far back as 1558 – within 20 years of the first institution (in 1538/9) of Par. Registers by Cromwell, Vicar-General in the reign of Henry VIII. **Porch:** Stone, repaired with brick – wants repair. **Vaults:** None. **Cleanliness:** Pretty well attended to. **Damp:** No appearance. **Dimensions:** 35ft. 5 in. by 41ft. 3in.

CHANCEL: 32ft. 6in. by 41ft. 3in. **Table:** Oak – neat, with crimson velvet covering. **Ornaments:** Commandments – Lords Prayer and Creed. **Repaired by whom:** The Rector, who has lately, with Col. Howard's assistance battened and plaistered the N. wall.

STEEPLE: Square stone tower – with pinnacles at the Corners, and a Weather-Cock. **State of:** Pretty good. **Bells:** One. **Clock:** None.

CHURCHYARD: **Fence:** Partly stone wall – partly Col. Howard's house, with rails in front – some part of the House seems to be an encroachment on the Churchyard. **Gates:** One *light* Gate – and a swing ditto – pretty good. **Drains:** A surf said to be dug along one part of the wall – but the drainage is insufficient – improvement ordered. **Graves:** Some too near the walls. **Rubbish:** Some – removal ordered. **Footpaths:** No trespass path. **Cattle:** None – except sheep occasionally.

DIVINE SERVICE: **On Sundays:** Prayers and Sermon in the Morning. **On other Days:** None – except on Good Friday and Christmas Day. **Sacrament:** At the Festivals. **Communicants:** From 15 to 30. **Catechism:** Occasionally heard in the Church.

INCUMBENT: **Name and Residence:** Revd John Sneyd – in the Parsonage. **What Duty he performs:** Assists in the Administration of the Sacrament.

CURATE: **Name and Residence:** Revd Cowperthwaite Smith. **If not resident:** Resides at Lichfield. **Licensed:** Yes. **Salary:** 70 Guineas per Annum.[3] **If serving another church:** None.

PARSONAGE: A commodious brick building – roof oak covered with tile – three[4] sitting rooms, one bedroom on ground floor – four best bedrooms, and several over the offices. **State of:** In good substantial repair.[5] **Outbuildings:** Coach house, two Stables, Barn, Cowhouses etc.

INCOME: **Gross Value:** About £300 per annum. **Tithes:** Exchanged in 1766 for Land (which is in the hands of the Rector) – except 60 acres which are titheable. **Glebe:** 260 Acres (viz the exchange land just mentioned.) **Surplice Fees:** Very small – given to the Clerk. **Easter Dues and small Payments:** None demanded. **Queen Anne's Bounty:** None. **Terrier:** There is one, in the hands of the Church Warden.

SCHOOLS: **Endowed School:** There is one – £14 a year for the Master to which Col Howard, the Rector and others give an addition. **Subscription Day School:** None. **Sunday School:** None. **Lancaster School:** ——.

DISSENTERS: **Dissenters' School:** ——. **Dissenting Chapels:** ——.

POPULATION: 400 at last Census.

MISCELLANEOUS: **Monuments:** Several very handsome ones in the Chancels. **Chandeliers etc:** None. **Parochial Library:** ——.

PARISH CLERK: Williscroft. **Appointed by:** The Rector. **Salary:** None – he has a house rent-free – a croft and the Surplice-fees.

CHURCHWARDENS: Only one – Mr William Bourne – appointed by the Rector and Parish jointly.

ORDERS MADE: In the *Church.* An additional casement – new surplice – Bible repaired.

In the *Churchyard.* The Porch repaired. No graves nearer than six feet. The earth, weeds etc removed from the [lower parts of the] Walls – open drain to the depth of the Church floor etc. The wall adjoining the Smaller gate, to be repaired.

I directed also a Surveyor's report of the State of the Walls and Roof to be obtained, and presented to me.

A few weeks after I received a letter from the Churchwarden stating that a *workman* had estimated the necessary expense of *two buttresses* [on the N. side] at £11 – I directed this to be effected; at the same time referring to my former direction respecting the Surveyor's Report –

20.8.1830. I enquired this day of the Churchwarden who assured me that all the above directions had been complied with except the additional casement which had been mentioned to Col. Howard.

Revisited 1.9.1837 and again in the Spring of 1838 North wall in very insecure state. Buttresses, walls etc need pointing and repair. Gates painted. Spouts placed all along N. side of Chancel. Down pipes on S. side. Open drain. Window bars painted. Recommended new pewing lower part of Church.

1838.[6] Report of the Repairs requisite to be done to the Church Tower.

The Parapet, which is in a very decayed and dangerous state, should be taken down and rebuilt with new stone, the weatherings of the buttresses repaired and the joints of the Masonry outside the whole face of the Tower should be raked out and painted with Cement. The probable expense of these repairs I have estimated at £79 0s. 0d.

The Parapet on the south side of the Church nearest the Tower is also much decayed, and requires to be rebuilt with new stone. The expense of which I have estimated at £13 0s. 0d.

The wall of the Church on the north side between the Vestry and the Chancel, described the Red shade on the Plan, should be taken down the whole height and rebuilt to the thickness of the present wall, making the inner part of Brick, with an outer casing of Stone of a proper thickness. The two windows, viz the one a three light and the other a one light, struts full within that length to be new after the design of the present windows. The remaining part of the same wall over the Vestry, and extending towards the Tower to be cased outside with new Stone as plan, in correspondence with the new part. The probable cost of this repair I have estimated at £166 0s. 0d. Lichfield, April 1838. T.P.

Revisited September 1841
Extensive repairs, internal and external, being in progress, I forebore particular directions.

[2] A/V/1/3: begins 'Gothic building, with nave and one side aisle . . .' [2] A/V/1/3: 'In good state – but more casements wanted." [3] *Eccles. Revs.*: £84. [4] Altered from '3' to '4' in A/V/1/3 – no reference to the ground floor bedroom. [5] *Eccles. Revs.*: 'fit.' [6] A loose sheet preserved in A/V/1/3.

ENVILLE 19.5.1830 (A/V/1/2,no.43;/3,no.11)

BENEFICE: Enville (Endfield or Enereld. Ecton).
Nature: Rectory. **Ecton:** K Books £27 2s. 11d.
Patron: The present Rector had the last Presentation, Mrs Jesson will have the next.
CHURCH: A very handsome Saxon building – fine pillars and circular arches separating the Nave from the side Aisles – the Chancel appears to be Gothic. **Number it will contain:** About 600. **Accommodation for Poor:** Sufficient. **Roof:** Oak, covered with tile – newly tiled ten years ago, when the whole Church was put into complete repair.[1] **Walls:** Stone and rubble – cased with brick at the W. end. **Floor:** Flags – very good. **Windows:** Good – but additional casements wanted. **Doors:** Very good. **Pulpit and Desk:** Handsome old oak – very well placed – crimson velvet cushions. **Books:** Bible wants repairs and re-binding. **Seats:** Remarkably handsome – oak – uniform. **Galleries:** One, in the N. aisle. **Organ:** None. **Font:** There is one – a basin wanted for the water. **Chapels:** None – but in the Rector's pew there are the remains of stalls, handsomely carved, formerly belonging to the chantry of Luttley. **Benefaction Tables:** Three – which record all the charities. **Vestry:** A small one, lately built. **Surplices:** Two – good. **Linen:** Good. **Plate:** Very handsome, gilt – given in 1763 by the Earl of Stamford – two flagons, two Cups – two large Dishes – A Paten. **Iron Chest for Register:** At the Rectory. **Register:** Five Vols prior to 1813 – the oldest date 1627 – in which volume there is an entry stating that Parish Registers were first ordered in the 30th year of Henry VIII – by Cromwell, Vicar-General – about 1538. [(see *Elford*).] **Porch:** A small one on the N. side. **Vaults:** Some recently in the Chancel. **Cleanliness:** Very properly attended to. **Damp:** Some on the South wall. **Dimensions:** 60ft. by 51ft.
CHANCEL: 42ft. by 19ft. 10in. **Table:** Handsome oak – no covering – ordered (at the discretion of the Rector). **Ornaments:** The Commandments etc. **Repaired by whom:** The Rector.
STEEPLE: Square Tower – the upper part cased with brick. **State of:** Very good. **Bells:** Six – good. **Clock:** There is one.
CHURCHYARD: **Fence:** Brick, and stone, walls – except some paling on the E. side. **Gates:** Slight repairs wanted. **Drains:** None – ordered. **Graves:** Some too near the Church. **Rubbish:** Very little. **Footpaths:** None[2] except of antient right. **Cattle:** Sheep occasionally.
DIVINE SERVICE: **On Sundays:** Two services – a second Sermon in Summer. **Sacrament:** Monthly. **Communicants:** 30 to 40. **Catechism:** In Lent.
INCUMBENT: **Name and Residence:** Revd Thomas Price, Rectory House. **What Duty he performs:** The whole.
PARSONAGE: A very handsome modern building – rebuilt by the late Rector. **State of:** Very good.[3] **Outbuildings:** Two barns – stable, coach house etc all in good repair.
INCOME: **Gross Value:** £1,000 to £1,100.[4] **Queen Anne's Bounty:** None. **Terrier:** Several copies in the old Registers.
SCHOOLS: **Endowed School:** A small one – £5 a year. **Sunday School:** There is one. **Lancaster School:** None.
DISSENTERS: **Dissenters' School:** ——. **Dissenting Chapels:** ——.
POPULATION: About 750 in 1811 [in 1838 said to be less than 600].
MISCELLANEOUS: **Monuments:** Several – especially to Lord Stamfords family [the Greys].
PARISH CLERK: William Hawkes. **Appointed by:** The Rector. **Salary:** £6 6s. 0d.
CHURCHWARDENS: Mr Samuel Paget for the Rector, Mr Thomas Fownes for the Parish.
ORDERS MADE: ['Done'.]
Two more casements. A basin for the Font. Earth removed from the walls – drains round the Church. Spout at the E. end repaired.
Visited by the Rural Dean in 1837 – by him reported to be out of repair in many respects – to want colouring etc. Stone coping of N. gable of Chancel off. No cushions, cloth or other ornaments for Communion Table, Pulpit etc. Churchyard in bad order.

Revisited by myself 17.7.1838

Found the *Chancel* in *very* bad state, both outside and inside – and many other things shewing marks of neglect.

Ordered: (1) That the roof, copings, buttresses etc of the Chancel be put into a state of thorough repair. (2) Lead-flashings of Tower repaired – gutters cleared out. (3) Gutters of roof cleared out. (4) Copings of gables repaired – spouts kept clean. (5) Pew in North aisle repaired. (6) Church coloured (stone) externally. (7) Gates painted and repaired – thoroughfare stopped. (8) Nettles etc kept down.

Revisited 19.10.1841

Directions etc. (1) Roof of Tower examined and repaired – ridge tiles pointed; gutters cleared; spouts and down pipes examined three or four times a year. (2) East wall of N. aisle, near Vestry, repaired and pointed. (3) Down pipes kept two or three inches from walls. (4) Open drain, or pavement, formed round Church Walls. (5) Roof of Tower repaired; new ladder made, to lead to it from Bell chamber. (6) Water from Tower conveyed to ground by down-pipe, at NW. corner of Tower.

[1] Faculties granted 17.10.1820 (B/C/2/1820–3, pp.73–5) for repewing and erection of north aisle gallery and 14.6.1825 (B/C/2/1823–6, pp.368–70) for a new vestry and the alteration of the positions of the pulpit and reading-desk. [2] A/V/1/3: 'None' altered to 'No trespass paths'. [3] *Eccles. Revs.*: 'fit.' [4] A/V/1/3. pencil addition 'Large, not ascertained – said to be £1,000 per an.'

FAZELEY 25.5.1830 (A/V/1/2, no.22;/3, no.12)

BENEFICE: Fazeley. **Nature:** A perpetual Curacy, in the Parish of Tamworth, endowed by Sir Robert Peel with £2,000 in addition to which Queen Anne's Bounty made a grant to it. **Ecton:** Not mentioned in Ecton. **Patron:** Sir Robert Peel.
CHURCH: A small, modern-built chapel,[1] single body. **Number it will contain:** About 400.[2] **Accommodation for Poor:** About 140. **Roof:** Oak, covered with slate – in good repair. **Walls:** Brick – good. **Floor:** Quarries – even. **Windows:** Good – but some repairs wanting in the frames. **Doors:** Good – but unpainted. **Pulpit and Desk:** Oak – neat and well placed – crimson cushion. **Books:** Clerk's book wants repair. **Seats:** Neat deal pews – uniform but unpainted, brick floors. **Galleries:** On three sides – fronted with oak. **Organ:** There is one. **Font:** None – one ordered. **Chapels:** None. **Benefaction Tables:** None – some charities belonging to the Township are to be recorded. **Vestry:** None – one recommended. **Surplices:** Two – one of them new. **Linen:** Good. **Plate:** Cup and Paten – plated. **Iron Chest for Register:** None. **Register:** Only for baptisms, of which copies are regularly sent to Tamworth – no burials or marriages. **Porch:** None. **Vaults:** One. **Cleanliness:** Attended to. **Damp:** A little; from wet coming in at the Windows. **Dimensions:** 60ft. by 30ft.
CHANCEL: **Table:** Small one – covering. **Repaired by whom:** The township are at the entire charge of repairing the whole Chapel.
STEEPLE: Wooden bell Tower. **State of:** Good. **Bells:** One – in good order. **Clock:** None.
CHURCHYARD: **Fence:** No Chapel yard, excepting a small space between the Street and West entrance.[3] **Gates:** Good. **Drains:** None. **Graves:** No burials. **Rubbish:** None. **Footpaths:** ——. **Cattle:** ——.
DIVINE SERVICE: **On Sundays:** Three full services on Sundays. **On other Days:** None. **Sacrament:** Four times a year (recommended oftener). **Communicants:** 50 to 60. **Catechism:** Occasionally in Lent.
INCUMBENT: **Name and Residence:** Revd Cyprian Thompson; in the Parsonage house close to the Chapel. **What Duty he performs:** Shares the duty with his Curate.
CURATE: **Name and Residence:** Revd Mr [WK] Fletcher, Assistant. **If not resident:** At Tamworth. **Licensed:** He is. **Salary:** None. **If serving another Church:** None.
PARSONAGE: Small brick building – slated roof – two parlours, kitchen, four bedrooms.[4] **State of:** Good. **Outbuildings:** None.
INCOME: **Gross Value:** Not stated – arises partly from Pew Rents, partly from Glebe, partly from Land purchased by Queen Anne's Bounty and Sir Robert Peel's money.[5] **Glebe:** Five or six Acres. An estate of 60 acres at Orton on the Hill. **Easter Dues and small Payments:** None. **Queen Anne's Bounty:** Amount not stated.
SCHOOLS: **Endowed School:** None. **Subscription Day School:** A National School – 140 children. **Sunday School:** 180 children. **Lancaster School:** None.
DISSENTERS: **Dissenting Chapels:** Methodist – with Sunday School.
POPULATION: 1,400, including that of Bonehill.
MISCELLANEOUS: **Parochial Library:** None.
PARISH CLERK: John Roe. **Appointed by:** The Minister. **Salary:** £7 0s. 0d.
CHURCHWARDENS: Mr Mark Cook, for the Minister; Mr John Harding, Inhabitants.
ORDERS MADE: Window frames to be repaired, so as to exclude the wet. A font to be provided. Benefactions recorded publicly. Communion rails repaired. A Drain made, in front of the Chapel, towards the street, so as to carry off the wet from the walls. A Vestry recommended. ['Done']

Revisited 31.8.1838

In good repair – generally. Roof to be examined. 'Done'. Spouts on N. side completed. 'Not'. Pannels (where needful) of pews repaired. 'Not'. Ceiling (where needful) repaired. New Prayer Book for reading desk. 'Not'.

Revisited 2.9.1841

East windows cleaned. Roof examined and torched. Floor leading to gallery and of gallery itself mended. Walls of gallery coloured.

[1] A/V/1/2: '... modern brick building ...' [2] A/V/1/2: pencilled addition '430'. [3] A/V/1/3: '... a brick wall separating the W. end from the Street.' [4] *Eccles. Revs.*: 'fit'. [5] Marg. 'About £240 (July 5, 1831)'. A/V/1/3: 'about £240 – arising partly from pew-rents – Sir Robert Peel endowed it with £2,000, in addition to which Queen Anne's Bounty made a grant.'

GORNAL 30.8.1830 (A/V/1/2,no.39;/3,no.13)

BENEFICE: Gornall Chapel. **Nature:** Beneficed Curacy. **Ecton:** Not mentioned. **Patron:** The Chapel was built by *private Subscription* in 1815, – the present Minister was appointed by the subscribers – who will hereafter have the appointment I was not distinctly informed.[1]

CHURCH: A small plain modern building – single body and roof. **Number it will contain:** 500 or 600, apparently. **Accommodation for Poor:** The N. and S. Galleries. **Roof:** Deal covered with slate – out of repair – ceiling bad. **Walls:** Rough stone – far from sound or strong. **Floor:** Quarries. **Windows:** Bad – no casements. **Doors:** Not good – one blocked up – and Gallery doors bad. **Pulpit and Desk:** Tolerably good and well placed – crimson velvet hangings etc. **Books:** Not in good condition. **Seats:** Neat and uniform, but the timber bad. **Galleries:** On three sides – the woodwork bad, ceilings (underneath) ditto.[2] **Organ:** None. **Font:** None. **Chapels:** ——. **Benefaction Tables:** None. **Vestry:** There is one. **Surplices:** One – bad. **Linen:** Provided. **Plate:** Silver Cup and pewter dish. **Iron Chest for Register:** None. **Porch:** None. **Vaults:** ——. **Cleanliness:** Not properly attended to. **Damp:** No appearance of it.

CHANCEL: **Table:** Firm – blue velvet covering. **Ornaments:** None. **Repaired by whom:** No provision made for the repairs of any part of the Chapel – only £11 per annum allowed from the Parish Church for *all* incidental expenses.

STEEPLE: Square stone Tower. **State of:** Very indifferent – roof bad – windows broken and blocked up with bricks – no floor to the bell chamber. **Bells:** One – out of repair. **Clock:** There is one – much exposed to the weather.[3]

CHURCHYARD: **Fence:** There is no Fence on the South side – on the other three partly a weak stone wall – partly hedge and rails[4] – the wall near the light gates in a ruinous state. **Gates:** Very indifferent. **Drains:** None – nor spouts. **Graves:** None very near the Chapel walls. **Rubbish:** Much. **Footpaths:** Not properly kept – no thoroughfare. **Cattle:** Cows – which ought not to be allowed – at present the want of Fence on the S. side might be pleaded in excuse.

DIVINE SERVICE: **On Sundays:** Two full services. **On other Days:** Wednesday Evening Lecture. **Sacrament:** Five or six times a year. **Communicants:** 10 to 20. **Catechism:** Once a month.

INCUMBENT: **Name and Residence:** Revd T Theodosius – in the Parsonage. **What Duty he performs:** The whole.

PARSONAGE: A newly built brick house – near the Chapel. **State of:** Apparently good.[5]

INCOME: **Gross Value:** Not ascertained (the Minister not being at home) the Income arises from Pew Rents and Glebe.[6] **Glebe:** £9 0s. 0d. per annum. **Queen Anne's Bounty:** £400 given towards the building of the Parsonage house – and something (supposed) in addition [– the Minister being absent I could not learn exactly]. **Terrier:** None.

SCHOOLS: **Endowed School:** None. **Subscription Day School:** A National School – 50 scholars. **Sunday School:** From 150 to 300 children.

DISSENTERS: **Dissenting Chapels:** Independent and Wesleyan.
POPULATION: Of Lower Gornal, about 3,000.
PARISH CLERK: John Fellowes. **Appointed by:** The Minister. **Salary:** £5 0s. 0d. and fees.
CHURCHWARDENS: Mr Eden Guest.
ORDERS MADE: There being no legal provision for defraying the expenses of repairs, I judged it superfluous to leave any orders. The Vicar of the Parish [(Sedgley)] has promised however to use his best efforts for having the Chapel converted into a *District Church,* under the Authority of the Commissioners, by which means the inhabitants of the Chapelry will become liable to repairs – At present a Subscription is being entered into, under the sanction of the Vicar, for doing such repairs at the Chapel as are most urgently wanted.

The securing the outer walls – taking off and repairing the Roof – repairing the Galleries, windows and ceilings – procuring new Books and an Iron Register Chest – putting the roof, walls and windows of the Tower and floor of the Belfry, the Bell, Clock, etc into a state of thorough repair – completing the Fence of the Chapel yard and repairing the wall adjoining the light gate – spouting and draining etc.

Revisited 16.7.1838
The Chapel has been enlarged, and otherwise much improved, since my former visit. It now seats 914 – 520 free.

A few improvements still needful. (1) Eave spouts, and down-pipe to the roofs – down-pipe to the Tower. (2) Roof of Tower repaired – door replaced – weather-board ditto. (3) Doors at the bottom of the Gallery staircases. (4) Copings at W. end of the roof repaired. (5) Roof of Cocklehouse repaired.

The boys school has 80 – the girls 80 – in daily attendance. 140 additional on Sundays.

Revisited 20.10.1841
Directions etc. (1) Plaister round Gallery door repaired – spring placed at top of door frame. (2) Floor of bell chamber repaired and completed – windows mended – weather-board on West side restored. (3) Roof of Tower repaired – door placed at its entrance. (4) Roof of Church examined and repaired. (5) Walls coloured and ceiling white-washed. (6) Outer doors painted – sill of NE. window and crack in wall below, repaired. (7) Iron Register Chest provided, as Law directs.

[1] *Eccles. Revs.:* Earl of Dudley. [2] A/V/1/3: 'On three sides – materials and workmanship bad.' [3] A/V/1/3: '... much injured by exposure to the weather.' [4] A/V/1/3: '... partly a bad hedge.' [5] *Eccles. Revs.:* 'fit.' [6] *Marg.:* 'afterwards I learnt that it is about £137.'

HANDSWORTH 20.4.1830 (A/V/1/2,no,33;/3,no.14)

BENEFICE: Handsworth. **Nature:** Rectory. **Ecton:** King's Books £13 9s. 2d. Patron Mr Birch. **Patron:** Sir Robert Peel (the Right Hon.).
CHURCH: An irregular building – originally Gothic; but the style and symmetry injured by successive alterations and additions. **Number it will contain:**

1,700. Accommodation for Poor: 400. **Roof:** Oak, covered with slate – lead gutters. **Walls:** The old part, stone grouted – the new brick cased with stone – the whole plaistered inside. **Floor:** Flat pavement.[1] **Windows:** Good – casements provided. **Doors:** Good. **Pulpit and Desk:** Handsome – Velvet ornaments. **Books:** Prayer book bad – Bible wants repairs. **Seats:** All oak – new in 1819, boarded floors. **Galleries:** On three sides. **Organ:** There is one. **Font:** There is one. **Chapels:** Lord Dartmouth has a [small] Chancel – and there is a Chapel, opening into the Rectors Chancel erected for the Monument of the late Mr Watt.[2] **Benefaction Tables:** None [since provided, September 1831]. **Vestry:** There is one. **Surplices:** Three – good. **Linen:** Properly provided. **Plate:** Two Flagons (silver), Two Cups Ditto – gilt inside – two plates, one Paten, all very handsome. **Chest for Papers:** In the Vestry. **Iron Chest for Register:** In the Vestry wall. **Register:** Seven Vols, exclusive of those in present use. **Vaults:** Several – no new ones intended. **Porch:** There is one, on the South side. **Cleanliness:** Attended to – except the East Window, and Communion Table. **Damp:** A good deal in different parts of the ceiling and walls.
CHANCEL: **Table:** Oak – crimson velvet covering. **Ornaments:** Commandments – Monuments etc. **Repaired by whom:** The Rector and Lord Dartmouth.
STEEPLE: Square stone Tower. **State of:** Good. **Bells:** Six – in good order. **Clock:** Good.
CHURCHYARD: **Fence:** Brick wall – kept by the Parish – An enlargement of the Churchyard is intended. **Gates:** Good. **Drains:** Surface drains all round. **Graves:** None very near the walls. **Rubbish:** Much ivy growing against the walls. **Footpaths:** None. **Cattle:** Sheep.
DIVINE SERVICE: **On Sundays:** Two full services on Sundays. **On other Days:** None – except Lent etc. **Sacrament:** Eight times a year. **Communicants:** 40 to 70. **Catechism:** During Lent.
INCUMBENT: **Name and Residence:** Revd TL Freer – in the Rectory. **What Duty he performs:** None – from ill health.
CURATE: **Name and Residence:** Revd ND Walton, in the Parish. Revd RL Freer, Assistant Curate, lives with his Father. **Licensed:** He is. **Salary:** 75 Guineas. **If serving another church:** None.
PARSONAGE: A large commodious brick building, much improved by the present Rector. **State of:** Very good.[3] **Outbuildings:** Barn, Coach-house etc – all good.
INCOME: **Gross Value, Tithes, Glebe, Surplice Fees, Easter Dues and small Payments, Queen Anne's Bounty:** Not ascertained, the Rector being too ill to be conversed with. **Terrier:** There is an old one, dated 1600 – not satisfactory to the present Rector.
SCHOOLS: **Endowed School:** None. **Subscription Day School:** A national school – 250 children. **Sunday School:** Between 300 and 400 (including the National School). **Lancaster School:** None.
DISSENTERS: **Dissenters' School:** One. **Dissenting Chapels:** – Independent.
POPULATION: 4,000.
MISCELLANEOUS: **Monuments:** Several – especially a remarkable fine statue to Mr Watt – by Chantry. **Parochial Library:** None.
PARISH CLERK: William Price. **Appointed by:** The Rector. **Salary:** £2 – and perquisites.
CHURCHWARDENS: Mr Haughton for the Rector, C Gallimore for the Parish.
ORDERS MADE: ['Done'.]
A new Prayer Book to be provided. Benefaction Tables put up. Roof [examined and] repaired. Ivy prevented from doing injury to the Walls and roof of the Church.

Revisited 13.10.1837
Found generally in good order – but visit hurried.
Rural dean reported in May 1838 that – The *tower* wants surveying and repairing. Pipes and watercourses examining etc. 'Then order for *Tower.*'

Revisited 21.10.1841
Directions. (1) Water tables to windows; and bars painted. (2) Font lined with lead and used for water. (3) Battlements and parapets of Tower secured and pointed. (4) Pinnacles on S. side of roof restored. (5) Ivy watched and trimmed. (6) Walls on the North side of the Church pointed – especially under *windows.* (7) Outer doors painted.
St. James' Handsworth – built since my last visit – no directions needful further than to watch the *spouts* – lay gravel, or flags, close to the walls all round and have the road leading to the Church kept neat and *fenced.*

[1] A/V/1/3: 'Flat stones'. [2] A/V/1/3: 'and there is a Mausoleum, opening into the Rector's Chancel, containing a monument to the late Mr Watt.' [3] There is no entry for Handsworth in *Eccles. Revs.*

HARLASTON 24.5.1830
(A/V/1/2,no.16;/3,no.15)

BENEFICE: Harlastone; a small village, 2½ miles from Tamworth. **Nature:** Chapelry, belonging to Clifton Campville. **Ecton:** Not mentioned. **Patron:** The Rector of Clifton Campville appoints the Curate to this in common with other parts of his Parish.
CHURCH: A small neat building, originally (as appears from the Chancel) Gothic – modernised – single body – put into new and good condition two years ago by money left for the purpose. **Number it will contain:** About 120 in pews ['200 in all']. **Accommodation for Poor:** 80 – in free sittings and forms. **Roof:** Timber covered with tiles – lately repaired – state good. **Walls:** Brick – upright. **Floor:** Bricks and flat stones – even. **Windows:** Good[1] – casements provided – but not sufficiently opened. **Doors:** New and good. **Pulpit and Desk:** Handsome – Oak – new – Velvet Cushion. **Books:** Bible and Clerks Prayer Book want rebinding. **Seats:** Oak – new and handsome – boarded floors. **Galleries:** None. **Organ:** ——. **Font:** There is one. **Chapels:** None. **Benefaction Tables:** None – there is one Charity belonging to the Parish, of which a public record is to be put up. **Vestry:** None. **Surplices:** One – good. **Linen:** Provided. **Plate:** A silver Cup – the rest Pewter.[2] **Iron Chest for Register:** In the Chancel. **Register:** Only those now in use – the older ones supposed

to be in the possession of the Rector of the Parish. **Porch:** None. **Vaults:** No new ones. **Cleanliness:** Attended to. **Damp:** A little in the Roof, where the Chancel begins – and at the East Window. **Dimensions:** 32ft. by 21ft. 10in.

CHANCEL: 27ft. 4in. by 18ft. 5in. **Table:** Oak Table – no Covering. **Ornaments:** None. **Repaired by whom:** The Rector.

STEEPLE: Wooden bell-tower. **State of:** Good. **Bells:** Three – good. **Clock:** There is – in good order.

CHURCHYARD: **Fence:** On two sides a brick wall kept up by the Parish, on the other two a hedge, part of which belongs to the Rector; both want trimming and otherwise repairing and the ditch adjoining cleared out. **Gates:** One – wants repair. **Drains:** None – ordered, as also Spouts. **Graves:** No burials in the Chapel-yard – Interments at the Parish Church. **Rubbish:** Some remaining from the repairs of the Chapel. **Footpaths:** None. **Cattle:** Large Cattle have been admitted – none to be allowed in future.

DIVINE SERVICE: **On Sundays:** Once – alternately with Chilcote; morning and evening. **On other Days:** None. **Sacrament:** Four times a year. **Communicants:** 14. **Catechism:** No.

INCUMBENT: **Name and Residence:** Revd R Taylor – at the Rectory. **What Duty he performs:** Shares with his Curate.

CURATE: **Name and Residence:** Revd JB Fisher,[3] resides in the Parish. **Licensed:** He is. **Salary:** £100. **If serving another Church:** None, except the other Chapel, and the Mother Church.

PARSONAGE: None.[4]

SCHOOLS: **Endowed School:** None. **Subscription Day School:** None. **Sunday School:** From 16 to 20 children. **Lancaster School:** None.

PARISH CLERK: James Tilly. **Appointed by:** The Rector. **Salary:** £3 18s. 0d.

CHURCHWARDENS: Mr Richard Smith.

ORDERS MADE: ['Partly done'.]
The Bible and Clerk's Prayer book to be rebound. Benefaction Table set up. Wet kept out at the West door and E. window. Spouting and open drains [provided]. Fence trimmed and small gate mended. No large cattle allowed [to feed in the Chapel yard]. Rubbish removed.

Revisited 1.10.1837
Directions. Prayer book new or repaired. Clerk's Prayer book new or repaired. Roof on S. side repaired. Walls repaired, coloured – (inside). Bars of E. window painted – all windows cleaned. Weather boards and slates of bell turrett repaired. Spouts and down pipes – at East end. Walls pointed at bottom. Gates locked.
Mem. *Consecration* of Ch. *yard* recommended. 'R.D. Nothing done.'

Revisited September 1841
The Chapel Yard has been consecrated.
(1) The roof over the porth entry to be examined and repaired. (2) New Prayer Books for Desks. (3) Burials *inside* the Chapel forbidden. (4) Registers better kept. (5) Spouts attended to – wire to windows of bell-chamber.

[1] 'New and' deleted, and omitted in A/V/1/3. [2] A/V/1/3: '—— Pewter flagon etc,'. [3] A/V/1/3 margin: 'now Revd Mr Cleve, September 1831.' [4] *Eccles. Revs.*: 'unfit.'

HIMLEY 21.4.1830 (A/V/1/2,no.38;/3;no.16)

'Not thoroughly visited, owing to the extreme wetness of the day, and the Rector's infirm state of health.' [(Since dead. 1831)].

BENEFICE: Himley.[1] **Nature:** Rectory. **Ecton:** King's Books £3 13s. 4d. **Patron:** Lord Dudley.

CHURCH: Small; neat building. **Number it will contain:** About 300.[2] **Accommodation for Poor:** [Insufficient.] **Roof:** Much out of repair – the wet comes in very much, especially near the W. End. **Walls:** [Upright.] **Floor:** [Quarries.] **Windows:** [Good.] **Doors:** [Ditto.] **Pulpit and Desk:** [Handsome.] **Books:** A new prayer-book much wanted – ordered. **Seats:** [Good.] **Galleries:** [One at W. end.] **Organ:** [There is one.] **Font:** [Too small.] **Chapels:** [None.] **Benefaction Tables:** [There are.] **Vestry:** [None.] **Surplices:** [Good.] **Linen:** [Good.] **Plate:** [Small cup and paten – very indifferent – pewter flagon and paten.] **Iron Chest for Register:** [In the Rectory Room.] **Register:** [From 1661, in good preservation.] **Porch:** [None.] **Vaults:** [——.] **Cleanliness:** [Indifferent.] **Damp:** [No appearance.]

CHANCEL: **Table:** [Sound.] **Ornaments:** [None.] **Repaired by whom:** [The Rector.]

STEEPLE: [Square Tower.] **State of:** [Not good.] **Bells:** [Two – one small.] **Clock:** [None.]

CHURCHYARD: **Fence:** [Good.] **Gates:** [Want painting.] **Graves:** [None too near.] **Rubbish:** [None.] **Footpaths:** [None.] **Cattle:** [None.]

DIVINE SERVICE: **On Sundays:** [Two full services.] **On other Days:** [None.] **Sacrament:** [Eight times hitherto.] **Communicants:** [About 70.]

INCUMBENT: **Name and Residence:** Revd Mr Dudley, in the Rectory.[3] **What Duty he performs:** The principal part.

CURATE: **Name and Residence:** Revd Mr Cartwright, in the Parish.[4]

PARSONAGE: [Very good – brick with stone dressings.] **State of:** [Very good.][5] **Outbuildings:** Chiefly new – rebuilt by Revd R Wrottesley.

INCOME: **Gross Value:** £388 19s. 3d.[6] **Tithes:** £302 0s. 0d. **Glebe:** £81 3s. 9d. **Surplice Fees, Easter Dues and small Payments:** £5 15s. 6d. £388 19s. 3d. **Parish rates:** £18 19s. 3d.

SCHOOLS: **Subscription Day School:** One new building (1838). **Sunday School:** 70 children. **Lancaster School:** None.

DISSENTERS: **Dissenters' School:** ——. **Dissenting Chapels:** ——.

POPULATION: 435.

PARISH CLERK: [Thomas Barron.] **Appointed by:** [The Rector.] **Salary:** [£6 0s. 0d.]

CHURCHWARDENS: Mr Cartwright.

ORDERS MADE: Roof repaired. Spouting, and open drains provided. A new prayer book [procured]. The repairs of the Church neglected under the impression that Lord Dudley will do them.[7]

Revisited 16.7.1838
A plan is in contemplation of enlarging the Church, which is much needed. Should this not be effected (1) Walls coloured and ceiling whitewashed. (2) A more suitable font provided. (3) The Tower (roof and lead gutters) repaired – gutters and roof cleared. (4) The foot which

fastens the Vane refixed. (5) Eave spouts and down pipes to the roofs of the Church. (6) Roof of Church examined and repaired – grass cleared away from NE. end of ditto. (7) Doors and window frames painted. (8) Chancel door repaired and painted. (9) Churchyard gates ditto.

Revisited 19.10.1841
Directions etc. (1) Pews etc cleaned and rubbed with oil. (2) Benefaction tables renewed – Ten Commandments set up – Font provided. (3) Doors of Church, window frames in body and Tower painted – also plinth stones. (4) Roof examined and repaired – ridge tiles pointed. (5) Roof of Tower repaired – gutters cleared out. (6) Soil removed from NE. corner of Chancel.

[1] Most of the returns occur only in /3, where they are for the most part written over pencil entries. These entries apparently relate to the 1838 visitation. [2] A/V/1/3: 'about 200' corrected from 'about 300'. *Eccles. Revs.*: 150. [3] A/V/1/3 adds: '(now Revd R Wrottesley) 1831' and 'Revd Richard Prichard 1838'. [4] A/V/1/3: 'Revd Mr Cartwright' deleted, and 'None 1838' added. [5] *Eccles. Revs.*: 'fit.' [6] *Eccles. Revs.*: £280. [7] A/V/1/3: 'Mem. The Church wants other repairs which appear to have been neglected . . .'

KINVER 19.5.1830 (A/V/1/2,no.42;/3,no.17)

BENEFICE: Kinver or Kinfare. **Nature:** Perpetual Curacy. **Patron:** Trustees – Lord Stamford, Sir G Pigott, Archdeacon Onslow and others. **Impropriator:** John Hodgetts Foley Esq.
CHURCH: An old, handsome Gothic building – Nave; Side Aisles; Chancel – the Arches on the North side seem to have been removed – A handsome pointed arch, at the Chancel entrance. **Number it will contain:** 800 or 900 [967 (1838)]. **Accommodation for Poor:** Sufficient. [256][1] **Roof:** Oak covered with tile – timbers and tiles need repair. **Walls:** Stone and Rubble – good. **Floor:** Flag stones. **Windows:** Good, except of the N. side near the Pulpit, where injured by Ivy – but casements wanting on the South side. **Doors:** Good – a gate wanted at the Porch entrance on the South. **Pulpit and Desk:** Old oak, green velvet hangings – badly placed. **Books:** Bible in bad order. **Seats:** Tolerably uniform. **Galleries:** One on the South side – at the W. end, two not extending the whole way across – the upper one for the Singers, with entrance from the Belfry – also one over the entrance into the Chancel, occupied by the boys of the Free School – very undesirable[2] – qu? as to the *right* [by which the Gallery was erected]. **Organ:** None. **Font:** There is one. **Chapels:** None – but a Chancel, on the N. side; belonging to Mr Foley. **Benefaction Tables:** All the Charities recorded. **Vestry:** None. **Surplices:** A new one wanted. **Linen:** Table Cloth and napkin. **Plate:** Flagon, Chalice, two Plates – all of silver. **Iron Chest for Register:** There is one, kept at a house in the Town [(the Church being remote from the Clergyman's residence)]. **Register:** Five Vols prior to 1813 – oldest date 1560; complete from that time – one of the Vols wants re-binding. **Porch:** There is one on the S. side. **Vaults:** None recently. **Cleanliness:** Attended to. **Damp:** On the North side – owing to Ivy without. **Dimensions:** 57ft. by 45ft.
CHANCEL: 43ft. by 45ft. **Table:** Handsome oak.

Ornaments: None – except some antient monuments. **Repaired by whom:** Mr Foley and others.
STEEPLE: Square stone Tower. **State of:** The top part wants repairing. **Bells:** Six – good. **Clock:** There is one; in good order.
CHURCHYARD: **Fence:** Stone wall, kept up by the Parish – some repairs wanting on the North side. **Gates:** Need repair. **Drains:** None – nor any spouts. **Graves:** Some too near. **Rubbish:** Ivy etc against the North side of the Church. **Footpaths:** None.
DIVINE SERVICE: **On Sundays:** Two full Services. **On other days:** None. **Sacrament:** Monthly and at the Festivals. **Communicants:** 25 to 70. **Catechism:** Not at the Church.
INCUMBENT: **Name and Residence:** Revd H Dudley. **If not resident:** Near Hereford.
CURATE: **Name and Residence:** Revd Thomas Housman. **If not resident:** In the Town. **Licensed:** He is. **Salary:** £80[3] – too small for his duties. **If serving another church:** None.
PARSONAGE: None – the old Parsonage house stated to have been what is now divided into three small tenements, at the lower end of the town, which let for £4 a year each.[4] **State of:** Very indifferent [(of the tenements just mentioned)]. **Outbuildings:** None.
INCOME: **Gross Value:** About £150. **Glebe:** A small field. **Queen Anne's Bounty:** £30 a year. **Terrier:** None known to the Curate.
SCHOOLS: **Endowed school:** [One of] King Edward's [foundation] – open to all the Parish – the Master commonly reported to be not licensed. **Subscription Day School:** None [– one since built and supported by Mr Foley of Prestwood – 60 children. (1838)] **Sunday School:** About 100 children [160 (1838)]. **Lancaster School:** None.
DISSENTERS: **Dissenters' School:** A Sunday School, belonging to **Dissenting Chapels:** A Baptist meeting.
POPULATION: Nearly 2,000.[5]
PARISH CLERK: Samuel Brown. **Appointed by:** The Minister. **Salary:** £8 8s. 0d. per annum.
CHURCHWARDENS: Mr Benjamin Savage and Mr William Griffiths – the *acting* Church Wardens. Appointed alternately by the Minister and Parishioners.
ORDERS MADE: ['Done or doing'.]
Casements [to be made] on the South side of the Church. A new surplice [provided]. Bible repaired. Register rebound. The roof examined and repaired – the [leaden] gutters kept clean. The Tower pointed etc at the top. A Gate placed at the entrance of the Porch. The wall on the N. side of the Churchyard repaired. The Gates repaired and painted. Ivy etc removed from the North side of the Church. Earth cleared away – spouts and drains provided.

I *recommended* the making of a Vestry-room; for which there is a very convenient space afforded, either under the Tower, or near the present Pulpit; where there is an antient doorway,[6] also, a change in the position of the Pulpit etc – which would be much better placed on the side of the Chancel entrance, if the *Gallery* were removed – I directed enquiry to be made into the authority by which it was erected in so objectionable a situation.[7]

15

Revisited 17.7.1838
   Since my former visit this Church has been thoroughly renewed in the interior – new-pewed – Gallery in Chancel entrance removed – and it is now a remarkably handsome and comfortable Church.
   Sittings for 967 of which 256 free. There is still a good deal of damp, at the W. and North sides, owing to the height of the ground outside – which I directed to be lowered as effectually as possible, and an open drain formed – Lead gutters and spouts and pipes to be cleared out. Crest tiles repaired – cross restored at E. end. Additional burial ground.

Revisited 19.10.1841
   Directions etc. (1) Water tables to windows – books repaired. (2) Lead flashings, and battlements of Tower, pointed – gutters cleared. (3) Roof of Church examined and repaired – gutters laid even and frequently cleared – East wall of middle aisle pointed externally. (4) New spout at SE. angle of Church – copings of East gable secured and pointed. (5) South wall carefully examined by Surveyor, and requisite repairs made without delay. (6) Walls of Churchyard repaired and underbuilt – gates painted. (7) Additional burial ground obtained, and if possible, on South side of Church.
   N.B. Strongly recommended erecting a Chapel of Ease at lower part of Town.

[1] In same hand as '967' above. [2] A/V/1/3: 'very improperly placed.' [3] *Eccles. Revs.*: £120. [4] *Eccles. Revs.*: 'unfit.' [5] *Eccles. Revs.*: 856. 1,856 perhaps intended: the 1831 Census states the population as 1,831. [6] A/V/1/3: 'where an antient door-way has been blocked up.' [7] A/V/1/3: '. . . authority by which the *Gallery* in front of the Chancel had been erected in so objectionable a position.'

KINGSWINFORD 19.5.1830
(A/V/1/2,no.40;/3,no.18)

BENEFICE: Kings Swinford. **Nature:** Rectory. Ecton: Kings books £17 3s. 4d. **Patron:** Lord Dudley.
CHURCH: An irregular building altered in 1807 – S. aisle built by Lord Dudley. **Number it will contain:** 900 to 1000.[1] **Accommodation for Poor:** Not more than 60 – more much wanted. **Roof:** Oak covered with tiles and slates in good order. **Walls:** Stone and brick. **Floor:** Flags. **Windows:** Good – two more casements wanted. **Doors:** Good. **Pulpit and Desk:** ——. **Books:** ——. **Seats:** Uniform. **Galleries:** On the W. and North. **Organ:** There is one. **Font:** ——. **Chapels:** None. **Benefaction Tables:** None. **Vestry:** There is one. **Surplices:** Four – good. **Linen:** Table cloth wanted. **Plate:** Two flagons, two cups, two plates – all silver – a large pewter dish. **Iron Chest for Register:** There is one in the Vestry. **Register:** Seven Vols prior to 1813. Oldest date 1603 – perfect except two years from 1692. **Porch:** One at the W. entrance. **Vaults:** None recently. **Cleanliness:** Attended to. **Damp:** Some in the Chancel.
CHANCEL: **Repaired by whom:** The Rector – repair wanting on the N. side – inside and out.[2]
STEEPLE: Square tower, cased with cement. **State of:** Good. **Bells:** Six good. **Clock:** Good.
CHURCHYARD: **Fence:** Wall – kept up by the Parish – in good order. **Gates:** Good. **Drains:** Not sufficient. **Graves:** Some too near the walls. **Rubbish:** Near the Chancel. **Cattle:** Only sheep.
DIVINE SERVICE: **On Sundays:** Two full services. **On other Days:** None. **Sacrament:** Eight times a year. **Communicants:** 45. **Catechism:** In Lent.
INCUMBENT: **Name and Residence:** Revd N Hinds. ['R Foley'.] **If not resident:** Abroad.
CURATE: **Name and Residence:** Revd [Edward] Davies Curate. Revd J Baxter assistant ditto. **If not resident:** Both near the Church. **Licensed:** Both. **Salary:** [Not ascertained.][3] **If serving another church:** [None.]
PARSONAGE: None at present – the former one having been sold, and the money placed in the Accountant General's hands.[4]
INCOME: **Gross Value:** £1,400 or £1,500.[5] **Tithes:** £800. **Glebe:** 380 acres, and an estate at Boningale, £250. **Terrier:** None [known].
SCHOOLS: **Endowed School:** None. **Subscription Day School:** National school 80 boys and 80 girls. **Sunday School:** There is one. **Lancaster School:** None.
DISSENTERS: **Dissenters' School:** ——. **Dissenting Chapels:** ——.
POPULATION: Not ascertained – very large – a new Church building at Wordsley.[6]
MISCELLANEOUS: **Parochial Library:** None.
PARISH CLERK: Thomas Walker. **Appointed by:** The Rector. **Salary:** Ten guineas.
CHURCHWARDENS: Mr Joseph Hughes, Mr John Eades [the latter for Brierly Hill].
ORDERS MADE: Two more casements to be made in the windows in the body of the Church. Benefaction Tables set up. A Linen Table Cloth provided for the Communion. The Chancel wall, on the North side; to be repaired externally – and the part of the Churchyard contiguous to it cleared of Rubbish etc. Open drains all round the Church.
   Application to Lord Dudley, for a Gallery in his aisle, or other accommodation for the poor, *recommended* – At present the free sittings are very insufficient.

Revisited 16.7.1838
   Since my former visit, the new Church at Wordsley has been built and become the Parish Church; and the old Parish Church is now a Benefice without cure of souls, under the name of St. Mary's, Kings Swinford; – a change by no means acceptable to the Parishioners, nor (until districts be attached to each) by any means conducive to the spiritual benefit of the inhabitants.
   The fabric of the Church in good substantial repair – but several minor points much out of order. (1) The Prayer books in the Reading and Clerk's desks should both be renewed – and the Bible repaired. (2) The Pipe which conveys the water from the roof of the Tower, and which from obstructions overflows and does much mischief, must either be removed to the outside of the building, or made to its duty effectually. (3) The roofs of the Church examined and repaired – gutters cleared out. (4) The Thorofare of the Churchyard stopped – and additional burial ground provided.

For the Parish Church at Wordsley see p iii, blank leaves at beginning.[7]

Revisited 19.10.1841
Directions etc. (1) Water tables for windows – plug for Font. (2) Carpet for Communion floor. (3) Walls coloured and ceiling whitewashed. (4) Boarded floors to pews. (5) Weather cock restored – or removed altogether. (6) Parapet wall of Tower repaired. (7) Window on N. side of middle roof restored. (8) Lead gutters of roof cleared – gable at E. end pointed. (9) Chancel spouts cleared. (10) Space laid round Church walls – with gutters. (11) Additional burial ground obtained.

[1] *Eccles. Revs.:* 1,200. [2] A/V/1/3: 'The Rector *ought* to repair it – but the living being sequestered a difficulty has arisen in obtaining the necessary funds.' [3] *Eccles. Revs.:* £200. [4] *Eccles. Revs.:* 'None:' [5] *Eccles. Revs.:* Gross income £1,135. [6] *Eccles. Revs.:* 7,356. [7] See p. 75 below.

PATTINGHAM 18.5.1830
(A/V/1/2,no.46;/3,no.19)

BENEFICE: Pattingham. **Nature:** Vicarage. **Ecton:** Clear yearly value £44 0s. 0d. Mon. de Launda colester Proprietor. **Patron:** Sir George Pigott. **Impropriator:** Ditto.
CHURCH: Handsome old structure, originally Gothic – nave and side aisles – arches on the S. side of nave pointed, on the N. circular; the entrances to the Chancel, and the Chancel itself, modernised – there is a semi-transept on the S. side of the Chancel. **Number it will contain:** 420.[1]
Accommodation for Poor: 40. **Roof:** Oak, covered with lead, in sound repair. **Walls:** Stone, plaistered inside. **Floor:** Quarries, in general even. **Windows:** Good – but casements not properly opened – the Church quite offensive from want of ventilation. **Doors:** Good. **Pulpit and Desk:** Old, but in good condition – velvet ornaments. **Books:** In bad state – new prayer book ordered – and Bible rebound. **Seats:** Old oak pews – pretty uniform – floors in general brick – some of them bad. **Galleries:** A small one at the W. end, built by faculty in 1726. **Organ:** None. **Font:** There is one – but no proper basin. **Chapels:** None. **Benefaction Tables:** Several – all the charities recorded. **Vestry:** There is one. **Surplices:** A new one wanted. **Linen:** Table Cloth and napkin. **Plate:** A pewter flagon and Dish – Silver Cup and Paten. **Iron Chest for Register:** In the Chancel. **Register:** From 1559 to the present time – entire. **Porch:** There are two, N. and S. – light gates to be put up, and doors kept open. **Vaults:** Several, but none very recently – the whole Church floor seems to be undermined[2] with graves. **Cleanliness:** Not properly attended to. **Damp:** Not much, except in the Chancel. **Dimensions:** 6ft. 8in. by 54ft. 8in.
CHANCEL: 35ft. 10in. by 17ft. 9in. **Table:** Oak – firm. **Ornaments:** Old figured covering to the Table. **Repaired by whom:** The Patron – Casements much wanted – much damp upon the walls, and below the window.
STEEPLE: Handsome Square Tower. **State of:** Good. **Bells:** Six – good. **Clock:** There is one.
CHURCHYARD: **Fence:** Stone wall – good repair. **Gates:** Good. **Drains:** None. **Graves:** Too near the walls. **Rubbish:** Weeds. **Footpaths:** One – claimed as antient.[3] **Cattle:** A horse – forbidden.
DIVINE SERVICE: **On Sundays:** Morning Prayers and Sermon at half past ten – Afternoon prayers at three. **On other Days:** None. **Sacrament:** Six times a year and festivals. **Communicants:** 20 at Easter last. **Catechism:** Every Monday morning.
INCUMBENT: **Name and Residence:** Revd R Thursfield, Vicarage.[4] **What Duty he performs:** The whole.
PARSONAGE: A large brick building, of which the present Vicar occupies only a small part at one end – (owing to embarrassed circumstances). **State of:** Very much [neglected and] dilapidated.[5] **Outbuildings:** Stable and barn.
INCOME: **Gross Value:** About £300 per annum[6] [(stated nearly 400 July 1838)]. **Tithes:** £240. **Glebe:** One acre. **Terrier:** There is one.
SCHOOLS: **Endowed School:** A small one. **Subscription Day School:** A national school intended. **Sunday School:** Not at present – there was one. **Lancaster School:** None.
DISSENTERS: **Dissenters' School:** ——. **Dissenting Chapels:** ——.
POPULATION: 1,000 to 1,100 (in 1838 said to be *700*).[7]
MISCELLANEOUS: **Monuments:** There are some. **Parochial Library:** None.
PARISH CLERK: Thomas Devey. **Appointed by:** The Vicar.
CHURCHWARDENS: Mr Christopher Callum, and Thomas Pawton [(Mr James Offley, Great Moor, Pattingham. Warden 1838)].
ORDERS MADE: 'See Articles of Enquiry'.
The Prayer Book and Bible repaired or renewed. A new surplice provided – and basin for the Font. Casements to be kept properly open in fine weather. Casements to be provided in the *Chancel*. The floors and pannels of some of the Pews repaired. The floors in the Gallery, and plaister on the wall repaired. Ladder, and rubbish of various kinds removed from the N. aisle. The doors on the N. and S. side to be protected by light gates, and kept open in fine weather. The South Porch repaired. The earth cleared away [from the walls] – open drains formed – spouts fixed. No graves [allowed] near the walls – Horse not allowed in the Churchyard. The Fence on the North side, adjoining the Vicarage, repaired. The Plate to be kept in a more secure place. The Chancel floor relaid – windows new-leaded – old mats removed etc. The erection of a *Vestry* recommended. The Church wardens [directed] to enquire respecting certain lands left for the repairs of the Church.

Revisited 18.7.1838
Greatly improved since my former visit. Chancel windows to be repaired – spouts ditto – new casements. Pews oiled – old mats taken out. New prayer book – leaves of Bible pressed. Pannels and floor of Vicarage Pew repaired and painted. Gallery repaired – Clock weight enclosed. Spouts and pipes on N. side. Overshot spout removed – down pipe instead, as E. end. Wall at bottom underbuilt.

Revisited 18.10.1841
Directions etc. (1) Communion Table planed, cleaned, and rubbed with oil. (2) Mat, or carpet,

laid on Communion floor. (3) Water tables made for windows. (4) Floors of pews boarded, especially on North side of Church. (5) Wheel of *Clock Bell* repaired and strengthened. (6) Vestry enclosed at North entrance, without obstructing access to seats in North Aisle. (7) Walls of Tower *pointed,* under *string moulding;* and stones at N. and S. angles pointed and secured with cramping-irons – Conductor taken down. (8) Water conveyed from roof of Tower at NW. side, by iron spout to ground – instead of being projected upon roofs of Church. (9) Lead flashings under upper windows on S. side pointed afresh. (10) Chancel spouted, and pavement formed all round walls of Church and Chancel, with gutter to carry off the wet. (11) Register kept in Iron Chest, and regularly filled up.

[1] *Eccles. Revs.:* 700. [2] A/V/1/3: 'the chancel almost undermined ——'. [3] A/V/1/3: 'one, deemed an antient right'. [4] Also perpetual curate of Patshull. [5] *Eccles. Revs.:* 'fit'. [6] *Eccles. Revs.:* £199. [7] *Eccles. Revs.:* 840.

PATSHULL 18.5.1830 (A/V/1/2,no.47;/3,no.20)

BENEFICE: Patshull (Patteshall, Ecton). **Nature:** Perpetual Curacy. **Ecton:** College of Wolverhampton Proprietor. £7 14s. 0d. Clear Value. **Patron:** Sir G Pigott. **Impropriator:** ——.
CHURCH: A modern stone building (about 90 years old) of Grecian Architecture, resembling a private Chapel, which indeed it has nearly become from the depopulation of the Parish. **Number it will contain:** About 80.[1] **Accommodation for Poor:** None required. **Roof:** Wants repair. **Walls:** Suffering much from Ivy, and apparently from a *settling* of the building – especially near the Windows. **Windows:** Open casements wanted. **Doors:** Wants painting. **Pulpit and Desk:** Good. **Books:** ——. **Seats:** Very neat and commodious. **Galleries:** None. **Organ:** ——. **Font:** There is. **Chapels:** None. **Benefaction Tables:** ——. **Vestry:** ——. **Register:** Kept at Pattingham – four Vols from 1559 to those in present use – in good preservation. **Damp:** Very much. **Dimensions:** 67ft. by 22ft.
CHANCEL: **Repaired by whom:** Sir G Pigott – who however seems to take very little care of the building. Roof and walls much injured by Ivy.
STEEPLE: Small Cupola. **State of:** Injured, like every other part of the Church, by Ivy.
CHURCHYARD: **Fence:** The whole Churchyard is overgrown (especially on the N. side) by Trees.[2] **Graves:** None near the Church. **Cattle:** None.
DIVINE SERVICE: **On Sundays:** Single duty – at 12 o'clock. **Sacrament:** Six times a year – alternately with Pattingham.
INCUMBENT: **Name and Residence:** Revd R Thursfield.[3] **If not resident:** At Pattingham. **What Duty he performs:** The whole.
CURATE: **Name and Residence:** None.
PARSONAGE: None.[4]
POPULATION: Small – much lessened of late years, owing to the enlargement of the Park.[5]
MISCELLANEOUS: **Monuments:** A large one to Sir Jacob Astley – two to the family of the Pigotts – who succeeded to the Astleys, by purchase.
ORDERS MADE: As the Church is little more than a family Chapel attached to the Hall (having been removed to its present situation about 90 years ago when the Hall was built; at or since which period, a great part of the former houses have been taken down, to form the Park) it seemed scarcely necessary to give particular directions *for the Church warden* (whom, indeed, I did not see) – I requested the Clergyman, however, to point out to Sir G or the Church Warden, the serious injury which the Building is sustaining from Ivy, both in the body and the Chancel – and to recommend *casements* for Ventilation in the Chancel.

It appears that the Parish Church formerly stood about half a mile off its present situation – but was removed (when the Hall was built about 90 years ago) for the convenience of the Proprietor.

Revisited 18.7.1838
This Church still in a shamefully neglected state – much injury has been done by ivy, tho' now partially removed.

Directed that Ivy removed from SW. window, under the Tower. The Cracks in the walls filled up – walls coloured, ceilings white-washed. Pannels of pews repaired. Prayer book repaired or new. Weeds removed from roof – copings secured. Bars of windows painted externally.

Revisited 18.10.1841
Directions etc. (1) New Prayer Books for Reading and Clerk's Desks. (2) Lead work of roof examined and repaired; water from roof carried off by down pipes and spouts on each side of Church. (3) Cracks in walls neatly filled up, and ivy prevented from injuring walls etc. (4) Ornaments of Tower restored. (5) Pavement formed all round the walls. (6) Copings of roof, at East end, pointed.

[1] *Eccles. Revs.:* 150. [2] A/V/1/3: 'Wall and Ledge – but it can scarcely be called a Churchyard – The whole is overgrown by trees.' [3] Also vicar of Pattingham. [4] *Eccles. Revs.:* 'None'; £80 gross income. [5] *Eccles. Revs.:* 132.

PENN 21.4.1830 (A/V/1/2,no.35;/3,no.21)

BENEFICE: Penn. **Nature:** Vicarage. **Ecton:** Living discharged – clear yearly value £43. **Patron:** The Bishop of the Diocese. **Impropriator:** The Lay Vicars in Lichfield Cathedral – Mrs Marsh and Mr Piershouse are the Lessees [under them].
CHURCH: Antiently Gothic – but much disfigured by modern alterations – a nave and one side Aisle – the Chancel separated from the body by a wide irregular Arch. **Number it will contain:** 300.[1] **Accommodation for Poor:** 50. **Roof:** Oak covered with Tile – needs some repair. **Walls:** The old part stone – the new brick. **Floor:** Bricks and grave-stones; very uneven on the North side. **Windows:** Only two casements – another ordered. **Doors:** Pretty good. **Pulpit and Desk:** Handsome old oak – velvet hangings. **Books:** Good and very handsome. **Seats:** Pews very irregular – most of them boarded floors. **Galleries:** One, at the W. end. **Organ:** None. **Font:** There is one. **Chapels:** None – but the North Aisle retains the name of the 'Lady's Chancel'. **Benefaction Tables:** Imperfect. **Vestry:** There is one, large and commodious, under the Tower. **Surplices:** Three – good. **Linen:** Table

Cloth and Napkin. **Plate:** Silver flagon, Chalice: two Plates. **Iron Chest for Register:** In the Vestry. **Register:** Three Vols prior to 1813 – oldest date 1570 – complete and in good preservation. **Porch:** There is one. **Vaults:** None recently. **Cleanliness:** Attended to. **Damp:** Very much on the North side. **Dimensions:** 34ft. 10in. by 39ft.

CHANCEL: 36ft. 2in. by 17ft. 4in. **Table:** Oak – velvet Covering. **Ornaments:** None. **Repaired by whom:** The lessees of the Impropriators – the Chancel is in a very bad state from damp – the floor wants repair – the Books at the Table bad.[2]

STEEPLE: Square brick Tower. **State of:** Good. **Bells:** Five – The weather boards want mending – and the Gudgeons of the Bells. **Clock:** None.

CHURCHYARD: **Fence:** Brick wall – much out of repair in some places – repairs belong to the Parish. **Gates:** Iron – good. **Drains:** None – much wanted. **Grves:** Many too near the walls. **Rubbish:** A good deal. **Footpaths:** None – the Church is injured exceedingly by the *entrances to Vaults* on the North side; which have produced great accumulations of earth against the Walls.[5] **Cattle:** Sheep occasionally.

DIVINE SERVICE: **On Sundays:** Two services – a second sermon half the year.[4] **On other Days:** Occasionally. **Sacrament:** Four times a year. **Communicants:** 40. **Catechism:** In the Sunday School.

INCUMBENT: **Name and Residence:** Revd GA Thursby.[5] **If not resident:** Resides in London. **What Duty he performs:** None – except on occasional visits.

CURATE: **Name and Residence:** Revd H Thursby – Vicarage. **Licensed:** He is. **Salary:** £75 and the House. **If serving another church:** None.

PARSONAGE: Old brick building, with modern enlargements. **State of:** Good.[6] **Outbuildings:** Stable etc in good order.

INCOME: **Gross Value:** About £300.[7] **Queen Anne's Bounty:** There is a grant, which has been laid out in land – the amount not ascertained. **Terrier:** None, so far as the Curate knows.

SCHOOLS: **Endowed School:** A free school, endowed by a former Vicar. **Subscription Day School:** None. **Sunday School:** About 80 [children]. **Lancaster School:** None.

DISSENTERS: **Dissenters' School:** ——. **Dissenting Chapels:** ——.

POPULATION: 700[8] (between 8 and 9. July 1838).

MISCELLANEOUS: **Monuments:** Some. **Parochial Library:** None.

PARISH CLERK: Edward Davies. **Appointed by:** The Vicar. **Salary:** £2 – and fees.

CHURCHWARDENS: Mr Deakin and Mr Perry.

ORDERS MADE: ['Done'.]
The soil to be cleared away all round the Church walls (as far as the arches of the Vaults will permit), and open drains of sufficient depth and width made and carefully preserved. The roof carefully examined and repaired. The floor of the N. aisle taken up and laid afresh. An additional casement made. Benefaction tables completed. The door, walls, windows, floor, of the Chancel repaired – and a new Altar service provided. Bells put into good order – weather boards mended – and door placed to the aperture above.

Walls of the Churchyard, on the N. propped. Rubbish removed from the Churchyard. [Articles returned. Benefaction Table *not* put up.]

Revisited 19.7.1838
Still much damp, owing to the height of ground outside and want of ventilation. Additional casements on South side; iron gates at W. entrance – a fresh arrangement of sittings – alteration of pews, with view of obtaining increase of accommodation – extending the gallery to North wall – for use of the poor – *strongly recommended*. The floors of several pews repaired, in centre and North aisle. Locks removed from pews. Benefaction tables set up in Church. Walls of Vestry coloured – ceiling washed. New prayer book for Clerk. Battlements of Tower refixed – bell-wheels repaired. Spouts and pipes put up. East window repaired. Walls cemented at bottom. Outer doors painted. Floor of Chancel re-laid – walls coloured – ceiling washed.

Revisited 21.10.1841
Directions etc. (1) Cover of Communion table and tables of Commandments etc renewed. (2) Pews repaired and rubbed with oil – decayed floors and panels repaired. (3) More free sittings obtained. (4) Whole of roofs carefully examined and repaired – crest tiles restored and pointed – gutters re-laid with lead – ceilings inside coloured – roof at W. end flashed with lead – copings at E. gable re-laid and pointed – open drains kept clear – walks cleaned – spouts of chancel cleared. (5) Weather boards of bell chamber repaired – new staves to ladder of the Tower.

[1] *Eccles. Revs.:* 450. [2] A/V/1/3: 'The floor sunk – Altar services much injured'. [3] A/V/1/3: 'None, trespass'. [4] A/V/1/3: 'In summer, two Sermons'. [5] *Eccles. Revs.:* Also rector of Abington (Northants). [6] *Eccles. Revs.:* 'fit'. [7] *Eccles. Revs.:* £226. [8] *Eccles. Revs.:* 863.

QUATT 19.5.1830 (A/V/1/2,no.44;/3,no.22)

BENEFICE: Quatt. **Nature:** Rectory. **Ecton:** Kings books £14 5s. 0d. – Prior de Malvern Magna 20s. **Patron:** Woolrich Whitmore Esqr.

CHURCH: An old Gothic structure – spoilt by modern alterations, about 60 years ago. **Number it will contain:** 200.[1] **Accommodation for Poor:** 60.[1] **Roof:** Oak covered with lead. **Walls:** Stone – cased with brick. **Floor:** Brick and flat Tombstones – uneven in many places. **Windows:** Good – two casements. **Doors:** Want repair – and gates outside. **Pulpit and Desk:** Very handsome old carved oak – some repair wanted – and new hangings. **Books:** Bible out of repair. **Seats:** Very irregular and inconvenient – new pewing much wanted. **Galleries:** One, at the W. end. **Organ:** There is. **Font:** A very old one. **Chapels:** None – the N. chancel belongs to the Patron. **Benefaction Tables:** None – ordered. **Vestry:** None – one recommended. **Surplices:** Two – one indifferent. **Linen:** Table Cloth and Napkin – good. **Plate:** Silver Flagon and Cup – two plates ditto. **Iron Chest for Register:** At the Rectory. **Register:** Four Vols, prior to 1813 – oldest 1672, in good preservation – reported that the previous registers were destroyed by a former Rector. **Porch:** None. **Vaults:** None recently. **Cleanliness:**

Not properly attended to. **Damp:** Much on the walls. **Dimensions:** 45ft. 11in. by 32ft. 8in.
CHANCEL: 28ft. 6in. by 29ft. **Table:** Old oak, wants cleaning; and the Prayer book rebound. **Ornaments:** None. **Repaired by whom:** The Rector and Patron, each his own – both in a very indifferent state – walls, floors, doors, windows.
STEEPLE: Square stone Tower, cased with brick. **State of:** Good. **Bells:** Six – good. **Clock:** There is one – in bad order.
CHURCHYARD: **Fence:** Part belongs to the Parish – part to the occupiers of adjoining land – repairs wanted. **Gates:** A new one wanted at the principal entrance. **Drains:** None – much wanted – spouts also. **Graves:** Too near the Walls. **Rubbish:** Trees etc growing upon the Buttresses. **Footpaths:** One [(trespass)] leading to some gardens, which ought to be forbidden. **Cattle:** Cows – not to be allowed.
DIVINE SERVICE: **On Sundays:** Morning and afternoon – second Sermon in the Summer months. **Sacrament:** Eight times a year – and the Festivals. **Communicants:** 35 to 50.
INCUMBENT: **Name and Residence:** Revd Edmund Carr – Rectory.[2] **What Duty he performs:** The whole.
PARSONAGE: A commodious dwelling – three sitting rooms, nine bedrooms etc. **State of:** Good.[3] **Outbuildings:** Stable – Coach-house, Barn etc – good repair.
INCOME: **Gross Value:** £450. **Glebe:** None. **Queen Anne's Bounty:** None. **Terrier:** There is one.
SCHOOLS: **Endowed School:** None. **Subscription Day School:** A small one. **Lancaster School:** None.
DISSENTERS: **Dissenters' School:** ——. **Dissenting Chapels:** A meeting of *Ranters*.
POPULATION: 330.
MISCELLANEOUS: **Monuments:** Some [belonging] to the Woolryche family. **Parochial Library:** None.
PARISH CLERK: John Hay. **Appointed by:** The Rector.
CHURCHWARDENS: Mr John Goodwin, for the Parish.
ORDERS MADE: ['Principally done'.]
The floor to be laid even, and the injury done to the Font by the sinking of the floor repaired. The doors mended – and [light] gates placed outside. The Pulpit, with its coverings, repaired. Bible and Communion Prayer book repaired. Benefaction Tables set up. Both Chancels thoroughly repaired – and walls coloured.[4] The Fence in the Churchyard repaired – and [the trespass] footpath stopped. Earth removed – drains made – spouting provided. Buttresses cleared of trees and otherwise repaired. A new Gate put up.
A Vestry, New pewing the Church, *strongly urged*. ['Articles returned. Qu? *Terrier* wanted'.]

Revisited 18.7.1838
Sittings 303, of which 141 free.
Greatly improved since my former visit – both internally and externally – new-pewed and thorofare stopped. No orders necessary – except to have the new pewing painted – old oak oiled or varnished – ventilation better attended to – iron gates at W. entrance – drain on S. side kept clear.

Churchyard gates painted. Roof of tower repaired, gutters, spouts etc cleared out.

Revisited 18.10.1841
Directions etc. (1) Water tables to windows. (2) Prayer Book in Clergyman's desk repaired. (3) Tiling of roof examined and repaired – gutters cleared. (4) Same in roof of *Tower* – copings pointed. (5) Broken cross at E. end of Chancel restored. (6) Down-spout placed at NW. end of Church. (7) Principal beam of Bell chamber examined and repaired. (8) Weather boards repaired and secured. (9) Wooden frame put up on ground floor, beneath *Clock weight,* to prevent danger in case of its falling. (10) Chancel spouts cleared out, door oiled on outside, buttresses cleaned and pointed. (11) Open drain, or pavement with gutter, laid down round walls of Church and chancel. (12) Fence on N. and E. sides of Churchyard repaired and kept in order – grass kept short by sheep etc. (13) A new gate at NW. entrance, to be kept locked. (14) Thoroughfare stopped and trespass paths forbidden.

[1] A/V/1/3 adds: 'now 303, 141 July 1838'. [2] *Eccles. Revs.:* Also rector of Woolstaston (Salop). [3] *Eccles. Revs.:* 'fit'. [4] A/V/1/3: 'and the walls whitewashed or otherwise cleaned.'

RUSHALL 17.5.1830 (A/V/1/2,no.26;/3,no.23)

BENEFICE: Rushall. **Nature:** Formerly a Chapel of Ease to Walsall – now a Vicarage. **Ecton:** Clear yearly value £30 0s. 0d. Abb. Halesowen Propr. William Leigh Esqr. Patron. **Patron:** Revd Edward Mellish (present Dean of Hereford) as having married into the Leigh family, to whom it belongs.[1] **Impropriator:** The Tithes belong partly to the Patron, partly to other families.
CHURCH: An irregular building – rebuilt two years ago – the old walls [remain] – single body – with a semi-transept on the NW. and SE. sides [(not in one line)]. **Number it will contain:** About 250. **Accommodation for Poor:** About 100. **Roof:** Oak covered with tiles. **Walls:** Stone – covered with plaister [inside]. **Floor:** Flat Stones. **Windows:** Very good. **Doors:** Good. **Pulpit and Desk:** Good and well placed – velvet Cushion. **Books:** Clerk's Prayer Book wants repair. **Seats:** Good. **Galleries:** [One for the] Singers. **Organ:** None. **Font:** There is one. **Chapels:** None – the SE. Transept belongs to the Lord of Manor. **Benefaction Tables:** None – one benefaction ['£2 12s. 0d.']; to be recorded. **Vestry:** A small one. **Surplices:** Two, good. **Linen:** Provided. **Plate:** Three Plate Dishes – two Silver Cups – Pewter Flagon and Plate. **Iron Chest for Register:** At the Curate's house. **Register:** At the Curate's house – three Vols prior to 1813 – oldest date 1686 – not very regularly kept formerly. **Porch:** A small one. **Vaults:** None recently. **Cleanliness:** Pretty well attended to. **Damp:** No appearance. **Dimensions:** 57ft. 6in. by 19ft. 6in.
CHANCEL: **Table:** Painted wood – cloth Covering. **Ornaments:** Crimson coverings to Table – Altar Services. **Repaired by whom:** The Parish, by agreement with Mr Mellish.
STEEPLE: Old Tower – Stone and Rubble. **State of:**

Pretty good. **Bells:** Five – good. **Clock:** None.
CHURCHYARD: **Fence:** Wall all around – kept up by the Parish. **Gates:** Pretty good. **Drains:** None. **Graves:** Some too near the Walls. **Rubbish:** None. **Footpaths:** A right of footpath thro' the Churchyard. **Cattle:** None.
DIVINE SERVICE: **On Sundays:** Full Service Morning, all the year round – second Sermon afternoon half the year. **On other Days:** None. **Sacrament:** Six times a year. **Communicants:** 20 to 30. **Catechism:** In the Summer.
INCUMBENT: **Name and Residence:** Revd J Whalley – Vicarage. **What Duty he performs:** Shares it with his Curate.
CURATE: **Name and Residence:** Revd W Cowley – in the Parish. **Licensed:** Yes. **Salary:** £50.[2]
PARSONAGE: A small brick building, erected in 1816 – two parlours, four bedrooms and dressing room – kitchens etc. **State of:** Good.[3] **Outbuildings:** Stable, Coach-house etc – good order.
INCOME: **Gross Value:** About £300. **Tithes:** £140. **Glebe:** 70 Acres. **Surplice Fees:** 50s. **Easter Dues and small Payments:** Not demanded. **Queen Anne's Bounty:** £60. **Terrier:** In the Vicar's possession.
SCHOOLS: **Endowed School:** None. **Subscription Day School:** There is a school, supported chiefly by the Vicar. **Sunday School:** 70 children. **Lancaster School:** None.
DISSENTERS: **Dissenters' School:** ——. **Dissenting Chapels:** ——.
POPULATION: 670.
MISCELLANEOUS: **Parochial Library:** None.
PARISH CLERK: Thomas Dean. **Appointed by:** The Vicar. **Salary:** £8 8s. 0d.
CHURCHWARDENS: Mr John Brown – Joseph Hulme.
ORDERS MADE: ['Done – Articles returned. Qu? Benefaction recorded.']
 Clerk's Prayer book rebound. Register Ditto. Spouting and Drains provided.

Revisited 14.10.1837
 Window frames to be painted. Ground lowered outside, and gravel walk formed. Thoroughfare of Churchyard stopped. Chancel spouted. Tower repaired.

Revisited 23.10.1841
 This Church in admirable order – very much improved since my last visits – a neat gravel walk has been made round the Church and the Churchyard closed.
 I had only to require (1) A new Prayer Book for the Reading desk. (2) The East Window sill flashed with lead outside – and the bars of the windows painted.

[1] Eccles. Revs.: 'W Mellish and B Gurdan, trustees.' [2] Eccles. Revs.: £94. [3] Eccles. Revs.: 'fit'.

SEDGLEY   21.4.1830   (A/V/1/2,no.34;/3,no.24)

BENEFICE: Sedgley. **Nature:** Vicarage – endowed with the Small Tythes of the whole Parish and the great Tythes of a part. **Ecton:** Kings books £5 12s. 8½d. – Pri: Dudley Propr. **Patron:** The Earl of Dudley.
CHURCH: New Gothic structure, plain and substantial, tho' somewhat heavy – nave and side aisles – no Chancel – Galleries.[1] **Number it will contain:** 1,400. **Accommodation for Poor:** 500. **Roof:** Deal, covered partly with slates, partly with lead. **Walls:** Brick faced with stone. **Floor:** Flags. **Windows:** Lead[2] frames, Stone mullions – Casements insufficient. **Doors:** New and good. **Pulpit and Desk:** New and good – Crimson moreen hangings. **Books:** Very handsome. **Seats:** Painted oak colour – board floors. **Galleries:** On three sides. **Organ:** There is. **Font:** At the W. end. **Chapels:** None. **Benefaction Tables:** Not yet put up. **Vestry:** A small one, under the Tower. **Surplices:** Four – good. **Linen:** Table Cloth and Napkin. **Plate:** Silver Cup and Paten. **Iron Chest for Register:** At the Vicarage. **Register:** In good preservation. **Porch:** At the West entrance. **Vaults:** [None.] **Cleanliness:** Attended to. **Damp:** Stone on the S. side near the Tower. **Dimensions:** 71ft. 6in. by 35ft. 6in.
CHANCEL: There is no space distinct from the body of the Church. **Table:** Oak – velvet covering. **Ornaments:** None at present – the Commandments intended.
STEEPLE: Tower, with a spire above. **State of:** Good. **Bells:** Eight – good. **Clock:** Good.
CHURCHYARD: **Fence:** Not yet completed – stone wall, with iron palisades. **Gates:** Iron. **Drains:** Not wanted – the space all round the Church being clear and open. **Graves:** None near. **Rubbish:** None – except arising from the unfinished state of the Churchyard. **Footpaths:** —— **Cattle:** None – There is a new burying ground, in front of the Vicarage, in which the interments take place.
DIVINE SERVICE: **On Sundays:** Morning and Afternoon – Prayers and Sermon. **On other Days:** None – except Good Friday, Ascension Day etc. **Sacrament:** Eight times a year – intended to be monthly. **Communicants:** 50 to 100. **Catechism:** Not in the Church.
INCUMBENT: **Name and Residence:** Revd C Girdlestone – in the Vicarage. **What Duty he performs:** Half the duty.
CURATE: **Name and Residence:** Revd GW Woodhouse – in the Parish. **Licensed:** Not yet. **Salary:** £100. **If serving another church:** Not any.
PARSONAGE: Brick building, covered with Cement – much improved and enlarged by the present Lord Dudley, who has laid out £1,000 upon it – three sitting rooms – seven bedrooms, kitchens etc. **State of:** Good.[3] **Outbuildings:** Coach house – Stable, Cow house, dairy etc.
INCOME: **Gross Value:** £550.[4] **Tithes:** £450. **Glebe:** Seven Acres granted, but not yet made over. **Surplice Fees:** £50. **Easter Dues and small Payments:** £50. **Queen Anne's Bounty:** None. **Terrier:** Several Copies in the hands of the Vicar's Agent – also a Deed of Endowment in the Court of Lichfield.
SCHOOLS: **Endowed School:** There is one, in the hands of the Presbyterians – enquiry to be made into the grounds of their tenure. **Subscription Day School:** A national School – 200 in all – an infant School about to be opened. **Sunday School:** About 200 children in addition to the preceding. **Lancaster School:** None.
DISSENTERS: **Dissenters' School:** Several on

Sundays. **Dissenting Chapels:** Several – and a Roman Catholic seminary.
POPULATION: 20,000 – (a new chapel at Coseley – Chapel at Gornall).[5]
MISCELLANEOUS: **Monuments:** Not any. **Chandeliers, etc:** ——. **Parochial Library:** None.
PARISH CLERK: John Newton. **Appointed by:** The Vicar. **Salary:** £5 0s. 0d. and perquisites.
CHURCHWARDENS: Mr JT Ferriday and Mr Josiah Tay.
ORDERS MADE: None necessary – (the Church being new and the Churchyard enclosure etc in progress) except one or two additional Casements for further Ventilation – It is intended to place Iron Gates[6] at the W. entrance, so as to admit of the Inner door being kept open.
['Done'.]

Revisited 16.7.1838
Orders.
Cleanliness better attended to – especially in Galleries – Walls coloured – ceilings washed. Two or more casements in W. window. Dilapidated tomb-stones in Churchyard restored or removed. The population of this Parish stated now (July 1838) to be 21,700 – of which: 8,000 attached to Parish Church (including Upper Gornall); 8,000 attached to Coseley; 3,124 attached to Lower Gornall. The remainder, it is supposed, to Ettingshall, which however provides, chiefly, for the two adjoining parishes of Wolverhampton and Bilston.

It is intended, speedily to build a new Church at Upper Gornall, to hold 900 – An additional Church much wanted near Coseley.

The Parish Church has sittings for 1,300; Coseley 2,000; Ettinghall 928; Lower Gornall 914; Upper Gornall (when built will have) 900: 6,042. There is an Infant School with 74 children, a boys National ditto with 80 ditto, a girls ditto ditto with 70 ditto in average daily attendance near the Parish Church besides which there are Sunday Schools in other parts of the Parish Church district, with *150* – and Infant Schools with *80* – children in attendance.

Revisited 19.10.1841
Directions etc. (1) Walls of Galleries coloured – ceilings white washed. (2) Ridge-flashings of roof secured. (3) Iron fence of Churchyard, down pipes and other iron work painted. (4) Ladders provided for roofs, and kept near the Church. (5) Porch – roof examined and repaired. (6) Proper rope for large bell.

[1] Faculty dated 2.5.1826 (B/C/3/1823–26). The architect was Thomas Lee. [2] A/V/1/3 adds marginal note 'Qu? Cast Iron?'. [3] *Eccles. Revs.*: 'fit'. [4] *Eccles. Revs.*: Gross income £626. [5] A/V/1/3: '20,000, in the whole Parish – partly taken off by Gornall and Coseley Chapels.' *Eccles. Revs.* gives the population as 8,643. [6] A/V/1/3: 'a light iron casement'.

COSELEY 16.7.1838
(A/V/1/3,no.25;[not in A/V/1/2])

BENEFICE: Coseley Chapel (Sedgley). **Nature:** District Church. **Patron:** The Vicar of Sedgley. **Impropriator:** Lord Ward.[1]
CHURCH: Handsome stone Church; in Gothic style, center and side aisles, pointed arches. **Number it will contain:** 2,000. **Accommodation for Poor:** 900. **Roof:** Timber covered with slate. **Walls:** Stone. **Floor:** Quarries. **Windows:** Good. **Doors:** Good – but want painting. **Pulpit and Desk:** Very handsome. **Books:** Good, except binding of Bible. **Seats:** Good – painted oak colour. **Galleries:** West and two sides. **Organ:** There is none. **Font:** Good. **Chapels:** None. **Benefaction Tables:** None. **Vestry:** Two. **Surplices:** Not seen. **Iron Chest for Register:** None provided. **Porch:** None. **Vaults:** ——. **Cleanliness:** Pretty well. **Damp:** No appearance, except above the Galleries.
STEEPLE: Handsome tower. **State of:** Good.
INCUMBENT: **Name and Residence:** Revd C M Provand, in the District.
CURATE: **Name and Residence:** Revd – Grey. **If not resident:** In the district.
PARSONAGE: None.[2]
ORDERS MADE: Lead Gutters above the Galleries examined and repaired. Walls coloured – ceilings white washed – doors painted. Windows mended – Clock weight inclosed. Spouts from the Tower cleared out – door leading on to the roof of ditto replaced. Iron Register Chest provided.

Revisited 19.10.1841
Directions etc. (1) Bible re-bound – ten commandments set up. (2) Inclosure for Clock weight, in case of falling. (3) Spring to prevent Gallery door from slamming. (4) Lead flashings at base of Tower and along parapet walls, laid close to walls. (5) East window guarded by water table. (6) Slates under ridge at E. end of roof replaced. (7) Door on roof of Tower replaced. (8) Lead gutter of chancel roof cleared out.

[1] *Eccles. Revs.*: 'Earl of Dudley.' [2] *Eccles. Revs.*: 'none'.

SHENSTONE 21.7.1829
(A/V/1/2,no.13;/3,no.26)

BENEFICE: Shenstone, a village three miles from Lichfield on the Birmingham road. **Nature:** Vicarage. **Ecton:** Living discharged – clearly yearly value £30 – Decano et Cap. Lich. 10s. Abb. Oseney in Co. Oxon.Propr. Sam Hill Esqr. Patron. **Patron:** Sir Robert Peel. **Impropriator:** Mr Leigh of Aston (late Mr Tenant) as purchaser of the Great tithes from Sir R Peel.
CHURCH: Of a very mixed kind, both in architecture and materials, partly Gothic, partly Grecian, part stone, part brick. Nave, transept, one side aisle – Chancel of very modern date. **Number it will contain:** It is said upwards of 500 in pews. Nearly 700 in all. **Accommodation for Poor:** 160 in the Chancel, Galleries etc. **Roof:** Oak, covered with brown tiles, side aisles covered with lead, not any part in very sound repair apparently. **Walls:** Principally stone – part brick. **Floor:** Quarries. **Windows:** In a good state [casements sufficient]. **Doors:** Very good. **Pulpit and Desk:** Oak, in good repair, velvet covering and cushion to pulpit. **Books:** Not in good repair – repairs ordered. **Seats:** Oak – floors some board, some brick or quarry – some of the pannels need repairing. **Galleries:** Three, including one

recently built, chiefly for poor. **Organ:** There is one – in good repair. **Font:** In the side aisle. **Chapels:** None. **Benefaction Tables:** Five – which record all the benefactions, except one (advised the Churchwardens to have *that* recorded.) **Vestry:** Very comfortable. **Surplices:** Two – one very old – new one ordered. **Linen:** A large table cloth and smaller ditto in good state. **Plate:** Flagon, Cup, Paten, Plate: all silver, neat. **Chest for Papers:** There is an old one; but no papers of any importance appear to be kept in it. **Iron Chest for Register:** There is one – kept at the Vicarage. **Register:** Eight Vols (including those at present in use) earliest date 1579 – nearly complete and in good preservation. **Porch:** One on the S. side – part brick, part stone. **Vaults:** Several – one lately in the side aisle. **Cleanliness:** Attended to. **Damp:** Great appearance of it, in the Walls all round, and the ceiling of the side aisle. **Dimensions:** 56ft. 3in. by 37ft. 12in. [*sic*] (including side aisles) Transept 65ft. 6in.

CHANCEL: 30ft. by 17ft. 6in. **Table:** Oak – good, covered with handsome red moreen. **Ornaments:** None. **Repaired by whom:** Sir Robert Peel.

STEEPLE: Square stone tower, with pinnacles at the corners. **State of:** Appears in good repair. **Bells:** Six in good order [– weather boards wanted]. **Clock:** There is one.

CHURCHYARD: **Fence:** Stone or brick wall all round – kept up by the Parish. Next the Vicarage garden, there is a palisade (within the wall) enclosing a small shrubbery, which appears to have been an encroachment. **Gates:** Three large; and three small adjoining for foot passengers. **Drains:** None – except a surf, said to run along a very small part of the south side – no provision for carrying off the water from the walls [– ordered]. **Graves:** Several close to the walls – the Churchyard much too full. (Additional ground wanted.) **Rubbish:** None – except what has been occasioned by late repairs. **Footpaths:** Three gravel walks; and one footpath across the Churchyard said to have been used immemorially for passengers. A dispute has late arisen[1] about the right of the Vicar and Mr Grove to make use of a Church way, leading from the East side of the Church to the Hall; as also of the Parishioners to bring their corpses up it – As the opposition made by a late Purchaser of the property has recently been withdrawn, advised the Vicar etc to continue to use the Way as formerly – and if fresh obstructions should take place, to bring their action against the Restrictor. **Cattle:** Sheep only.

DIVINE SERVICE: **On Sundays:** Full service morning, Prayers afternoon – occasionally a lecture in the Afternoon in Summer. **On other Days:** Friday Prayers – not attended. **Sacrament:** Four times a year. **Communicants:** 40 or 50. **Catechism:** The Sunday school children, occasionally examined in Church.

INCUMBENT: **Name and Residence:** Revd James Hargreaves – in the Vicarage. **What Duty he performs:** The whole – with his son's occasional assistance.

PARSONAGE: Commodious brick building – rough cast, and white washed – roof blue tiles. Three sitting – five bedrooms. The whole in good repair, and very comfortable state. **State of:** Very good.[2] **Outbuildings:** Stable, Coach house, Granary, Dairy, Barn.

INCOME: **Gross Value** and **Tithes:** £400[3] per annum including Vicarial tithes and Easter dues. **Glebe:** 4¾ acres, including the Churchyard, garden, site of house etc. **Surplice Fees:** About £5 a year. **Queen Anne's Bounty:** 35 acres purchased by Money from the Bounty Board. **Terrier:** There is one in the Vicar's possession, specifying the nature and value of the Vicarial tithes, Easter dues, Surplice fees, Extent of Glebe etc.

SCHOOLS: **Endowed School:** None. **Subscription Day School:** None in Shenstone itself (there has been one in Stonnal chapelry, about to be resumed). **Sunday School:** 35 girls 15 boys. **Lancaster School:** None.

DISSENTERS: **Dissenters' School:** One occasionally used as a place of worship. **Dissenting Chapels:** [*bracketed with Dissenters' School.*]

POPULATION: 1,700 last Census (including the Chapelry).

MISCELLANEOUS: **Monuments:** There are some in the Chancel. **Parochial Library:** None.

PARISH CLERK: Thomas Adlam Tonks. **Appointed by:** The Parish. **Salary:** Five Pounds, besides Fees etc.

CHURCHWARDENS: Edward White appointed by the Vicar, Samuel Adcock appointed by the Parish.

ORDERS MADE: ['Done. Articles returned']
The Churchwardens desired to obtain a Surveyor's report of the state of the roof, to be submitted to me – the lead over the side aisle to be repaired.

In the Church.
The Bible and Prayer books in reading and Clerk's desk, to be forthwith repaired. The state of the floors beneath the Pews, in the South Chancel to be examined and rectified. The Pews, where needful repaired; and the walls and ceiling white washed. An additional Benefaction table provided. A new Surplice provided.

In the Churchyard.
The Earth to be removed, all round the Church, to at least the depth of the Church floor – and *if possible* a drain all round, to convey the wet from the walls and foundation of the Church. If this cannot be done on account of the graves, the most effectual method, practicable, to be adopted.

September 1831. Visited the Church again – and found all the material repairs completed, as far as circumstances would allow – viz the Roofs put into sound repair – the sough[4] carried all round, and an open space round the walls paved with bricks – spouts put up where wanted – weatherboards to the belfry etc.

Revisited 31.8.1837 – several matters require attention.
1. In the *Churchyard*
The grass, weeds, etc to be cleared away round the walls (especially of the chancel) and the drain kept open. Nettles and other weeds removed from different parts of the Churchyard – especially near the fence on the E. and S. sides – and the herbage kept shorter. The trespass

path from the SW. corner to the NE. to be stopped. The tomb-stones on the E. repaired.

2. In the *exterior* of the fabric

The windows of the East Chancel to be mended. The lower part of the window in the NE. chancel, which has been blocked up, to be re-opened, in order to give more light in the Church. The brick work, at the base of the Tower on the N. side, immediately above the Vestry, repaired. Some of the higher branches of the Trees which obscure the Clock from the Parishioners to be lopped off.

3. *Inside the Church*

Additional ventilation to be procured, by opening one or two more casements, and by providing light gates for N. and S. doors, to be kept open in fine weather. Two casements opened in the *Chancel,* and the leads of the windows repaired. The panels and floors of the pews repaired, where needful – especially those in the N. and S. Chancels, *below,* and those in the Gallery over the N. Chancel, several of the floors of which are in a state of near decay. The Clerk's Prayer Book repaired or renewed. *Recommended,* that the oak pews in the body of the Church be *varnished,* and the hinges painted – 'Qu: *floors* etc.'

Revisited 2.9.1841

Directions to Churchwardens – Pews in N. and S. Chancels to be repaired when needful. Lead gutters, copings, ridge-tiles etc. Down-pipes instead of overshot spouts.

(N.B.) I recommended the removal of the Pulpit and Reading Desk, so as not to intercept the Chancel. Churchyard kept neat – Fences repaired.

[1] A/V/1/3: '. . . respecting the right of Church way thro' a field adjoining the Churchyard – the way however is still used, the Proprietor not urging his opposition, tho' refusing to put up proper gates etc.' [2] *Eccles. Revs.:* 'fit'. [3] *Eccles. Revs.:* £512. [4] Altered from 'surf'.

STONNALL 21.7.1829 (A/V/1/2,no.14;/3,no.27)

BENEFICE: Stonnal Chapel – in Shenstone parish – about three miles from the church. **Nature:** Perpetual Curacy. **Patron:** Vicar of Shenstone.
CHURCH: Plain, neat building, with pointed arches – area undivided – no Chancel. **Number it will contain:** 400 including 96 free sittings in the body of the Church and gallery. **Roof:** Oak covered with slate. **Walls:** Brick. **Floor:** Quarries – a pipe for warm air runs along the floor. **Windows:** In good order. **Doors:** Oak – front door needs repainting. **Pulpit and Desk:** Oak – very neat, and neatly covered and cushioned. **Books:** Almost new. **Seats:** Deal unpainted – (painting ordered). **Galleries:** One for singers, and school children. **Organ:** A small one. **Font:** There is one. **Chapels:** None. **Vestry:** There is one. **Surplices:** One. **Linen:** Provided. **Plate:** Similar to those in the Parish church – but plated. **Chest for Papers:** None. **Iron Chest for Register:** None – one ordered. **Register:** There is one. **Porch:** None. **Vaults:** ——. **Cleanliness:** Duly attended to. **Damp:** No appearance of it, except a little on the ceiling. **Dimensions:** 50ft. by 30ft.
CHANCEL: There is no Chancel. **Table:** Neat and neatly covered. **Ornaments:** The ten commandments and belief; and an account of the appropriation of sittings, their number etc.
STEEPLE: Square brick tower. **State of:** Good. **Bells:** One. **Clock:** None.
CHURCHYARD: **Fence:** Brick wall, next the road, the rest a quick hedge – the whole in good state. **Gates:** Two – good. **Drains:** One, on the N. side – ordered that a drain or surf, be made all round. **Graves:** None near the walls. **Rubbish:** None. **Footpaths:** One, and one carriage road. **Cattle:** None.
DIVINE SERVICE: **On Sundays:** Morning and Afternoon, alternately. **On other Days:** Ash Wednesday. **Sacrament:** Four times a year. **Communicants:** 30. **Catechism:** Taught in the Vestry.
INCUMBENT: **Name and Residence:** Revd James Hargreaves Jnr. **If not resident:** Lives with his Father [in the Vicarage] – 2½ miles off. **What Duty he performs:** All.
PARSONAGE: None.[1]
INCOME: **Gross Value:** About £107. **Surplice Fees:** Very small – sum not specified. **Easter Dues and small Payments:** None. **Queen Anne's Bounty:** £2,020 granted, to be laid out in land. **Terrier:** None.
SCHOOLS: **Endowed School:** None. **Subscription Day School:** There has been one, given up for want of support; but about to be renewed. **Sunday School:** 50 or 60 children. **Lancaster School:** None.
POPULATION: 700 last Census.
MISCELLANEOUS: **Monuments:** None.
PARISH CLERK: George Holmes. **Appointed by:** The Vicar of Shenstone. **Salary:** £12 per annum.
CHURCHWARDENS: George Wright, and R Caddick.
ORDERS MADE: ['Done except painting. Articles returned'.]

The pews to be painted. The doors repainted. Iron Chest for Register, provided.

The Chapel being entirely new, no further orders needful within the building.

Proper draining, *externally,* directed, as a means of *preserving* the Chapel, in good repair.

(N.B.) A difficulty in doing repairs at the Chapel, from there being no *legal* provision for Church rates for the Chapelry.

Reported by Rural dean in 1838 to be all good. 'Qu? Pews painted? Ch. rates?'

Revisited 2.10.1841

Roof and flashings of Tower to be repaired.

[1] *Eccles. Revs.:* 'none'.

TAMWORTH 25.5.1830 (A/V/1/2,no.20;/3,no.28)

BENEFICE: Tamworth. **Nature:** A Vicarage. **Ecton:** Olim Collegium – certif. val. £16 – (supposed by Mr Blick to refer to the two annual payments of £8 each, allowed [by the Crown] from the time of Henry VIII, for the maintenance of two Curates – in addition to [the payment of] £20 per annum to the 'King's Vicar'. **Patron:** CE Repington Esqr as Lay-Dean of the Collegiate Church of Tamworth. **Impropriator:** Mr

Repington has part of the Tythes – the six Prebendaries of the Church a part.

CHURCH: A large handsome Gothic building; with Center and side Aisles – pointed arches; The Chancel seems of more antient date – some of the arches Saxon order. **Number it will contain:** Not ascertained[1] – should suppose from 1,200 to 1,500. **Accommodation for Poor:** Considerable,[2] but insufficient. **Roof:** Remarkably handsome open oak ceilings – timbers oak covered with lead; the ceiling of the North gallery needs some repair. **Walls:** Stone – upright and good, internally – much injured externally. **Floor:** Flat Stones. **Windows:** Good – and well provided with casements – except in the S. Chancel. **Doors:** Good. **Pulpit and Desk:** Very handsome and well placed – velvet Cushion and hangings. **Books:** Very good. **Seats:** New in 1809 – boarded floors – uniform. **Galleries:** On three sides. **Organ:** There is one – organist paid partly by the Parish, partly by Subscription. **Font:** There is, in one of the Chancels – not kept properly – a basin ordered. **Chapels:** There are two Chancels, besides the Rector's – one of which belongs to the Parish – the other formerly belonged in part to the Comberford Prebend – but now the whole is kept up by the Parish. **Benefaction Tables:** Not complete. **Vestry:** A very large and Commodious one. **Surplices:** Three – good. **Linen:** Table Cloth and two napkins – good. **Plate:** Two silver flagons – two ditto Patens and Chalices – two Pewter Plates. **Iron Chest for Register:** Kept at a lodging occasionally used by the Vicar; near the Church. **Register:** Five Vols, from *1538* to those in present use. **Porch:** None. **Vaults:** No recent ones. **Cleanliness:** Not sufficiently attended to. **Damp:** A little on the N. side.

CHANCEL: **Table:** Handsome Oak stand with Marble Slab – blue cloth Covering. **Ornaments:** Several [old and] handsome monuments. **Repaired by whom:** The Prebendaries of the Collegiate Church.

STEEPLE: A square Tower, with four pinnacles. **State of:** By no means good – the stone much injured – large crack all the way down [one side] – windows defaced by bricks. **Bells:** Six – all good. **Clock:** Good.

CHURCHYARD: **Fence:** Walls and houses – some of the latter with windows overlooking the Churchyard, supposed to be encroachments – the walls kept up chiefly by the Parish. **Gates:** Good. **Drains:** None. **Graves:** Several much too near. **Rubbish:** A good deal on the N. side – and the herbage in a very overgrown state. **Footpaths:** A public road thro' the Churchyard. **Cattle:** None.

DIVINE SERVICE: **On Sundays:** Three full services. **On other Days:** Wednesday Prayers – Thursday Evening Prayers and Lecture. **Sacrament:** Monthly. **Communicants:** 80 to 100. **Catechism:** Not in the Church.

INCUMBENT: **Name and Residence:** Revd F Blick – lives about ¾ mile from the Church – but sleeps one night in each week near the Parish Church. **What Duty he performs:** Shares the whole with his Curate.

CURATE: **Name and Residence:** Revd James Pearson – Tamworth. **Licensed:** He is. **Salary:** £100. **If serving another church:** None.

PARSONAGE: The present Parsonage house is a new brick building purchased a few years ago with money arising from the sale of the former one – the present yearly Tenant is Mr Brown, a Surgeon. **State of:** Very good.[3] **Outbuildings:** Coach house, Stable etc in the yard.

INCOME: cir. £150 per annum – as follows:

	£	s.	d.
from debenture paid by the Crown from the Exchequer in lieu of all Tithes, herbage, Easter dues etc annually	26	7	3
Surplice Fees	20	17	6
a bequest of Mr C Budd, three small closes let (on average) for	21	0	0
Queen Anne's Bounty: Land formerly purchased by	40	0	0
Imperial grants lately assigned, upon an average, annually	40	14	6
	148	19	3

SCHOOLS: **Endowed School:** A grammar School, [the Mastership] in the Gift of the Corporation – supported by Land. **Subscription Day School:** A national and Infant School. **Sunday School:** About 400 children. **Lancaster School:** None.

DISSENTERS: **Dissenters' School:** Sunday Schools attached to all the **Dissenting Chapels**, which are numerous.

POPULATION: 3,500 in the Town – about the same number in the Townships[4] – a new Chapel is much wanted. Note: there are remains of an old Chapel at Amington in the Parish.

MISCELLANEOUS: **Monuments:** Several. **Chandeliers, etc:** There are Lamps and Chandeliers.

PARISH CLERK: Thomas Jones. **Appointed by:** The Vicar. **Salary:** £20 a year.

CHURCHWARDENS: Mr Thomas Marshall, for the Vicar, Mr Richard Barrett, for the Parish.

ORDERS MADE: ['Articles returned but directions not executed'.]
Benefaction Tables to be completed. Communion Plate repaired, and a suitable box provided for keeping it in. More attention paid to *cleaning* and *ventilating* the Church – an additional casement in the S. Chancel. The Tower to be examined and watched with great care, with a view of guarding against further mischief.[5] Bricks to be removed from the apertures. The earth cleared away, and open drains made, all round – the whole of the N. side of the Church put into complete repair [externally], as soon as funds can be raised. The herbage to be kept in better order. Enquiry to be made as to the right of door-way out of one of the Cottages; near the Street into the Churchyard – and if it be a recent encroachment, the door to be blocked up.

Revisited 31.8.1837
Directions to Churchwardens. The exterior walls, buttresses and tower to be put into thorough repair as soon as practicable. Herbage etc – cleared away from walls. Windows thoroughly repaired. Walls (inside) coloured. Down-pipes put up.

May 1838. The Rural Dean reported that an estimate had been obtained of the expense needful for putting the Fabric into thorough repair – £1,200.

Revisited 2.10.1841
No directions till Surveyor's report received.

[1] marginal: 'July 5, 1831. Stated by Mr Blick to be 2,100'. *Eccles. Revs.:* 2,500. [2] marginal: 'about 100, for *adults*, and some 100 for children'. [3] *Eccles. Revs.:* 'fit'. [4] marginal: 'Stated in a letter from Mr Blick to the Bishop, January 1831, to be about 5,400, exclusive of the Townships – in all 7,184 in 1821, but much increased since that time'. [5] A/V/1/3: '. . . guarding against any increase of insecurity'.

THORPE CONSTANTINE 24.5.1830
(A/V/1/2,no.19;/3,no.29)

BENEFICE: Thorpe Constantine. **Nature:** Rectory. **Ecton:** King's books £5 5s. 5d. **Patron:** William Phillips Inge Esqr. **Impropriator:** None.
CHURCH: A small, modernized building; rebuilt in 1778 on a much smaller scale than formerly. **Number it will contain:** About 80. **Accommodation for Poor:** None needed – there being no day labourers – the whole of the working population live in service [and sit in their employers pews]. **Roof:** Oak and deal – covered with slate – the whole new about four years ago. **Walls:** Stone – sound and upright. **Floor:** Flat stones – even. **Windows:** Good – properly supplied with Casements. **Doors:** Very good. **Pulpit and Desk:** Handsome, painted oak [colour] – velvet cushions and hangings. **Books:** New – very good.[1] **Seats:** All new and in excellent order. **Galleries:** None. **Organ:** ——. **Font:** Near the West entrance. **Chapels:** None. **Benefaction Tables:** None – there is a benefaction arising from land at Northampton. **Vestry:** None. **Surplices:** Two – good. **Linen:** Very good. **Plate:** Two Silver Patens, Ditto Flagon and Chalice. **Iron Chest for Register:** At the Rectory. **Register:** Two Vols prior to 1813 – oldest date 1538 – all in good order and entire. **Porch:** None. **Vaults:** One belonging to the Inge family. **Cleanliness:** Thoroughly attended to. **Damp:** No appearance of it. **Dimensions:** 47ft. by 20ft.
CHANCEL: None, separate from the rest of the Church. **Table:** Painted deal; crimson cover. **Ornaments:** Handsome altar services – No table of Ten Commandments – ordered. **Repaired by whom:** The Rector, or rather the Patron – who in fact repairs the whole [Church].
STEEPLE: Square Tower, surmounted by a Spire. **State of:** Very good – except one of the small windows. **Bells:** One – in good order – but no weather-boards. **Clock:** None.
CHURCHYARD: **Fence, Gates, Drains, Graves, Rubbish, Footpaths, Cattle:** The whole in excellent order – open drains formed last Autumn; no cattle allowed.
DIVINE SERVICE: **On Sundays:** Full service; morning and afternoon alternately. **On other Days:** None. **Sacrament:** Four times a year. **Communicants:** About 15.
INCUMBENT: **Name and Residence:** Revd G Inge – with his father, at the family Mansion,[2] close by the Church. **What Duty he performs:** The whole, usually.
CURATE: **Name and Residence:** None.
PARSONAGE: A small, ill-built house, close to the Churchyard – walls partly brick, partly mud – very damp – One parlour, kitchen and back kitchen; three bedrooms, three attics – Roof good. **State of:** As good as the nature of the building will admit of.[3] **Outbuildings:** Stable and Cowhouse; brick and mud buildings, in tolerable order.
INCOME: **Gross Value:** Valued in 1815 at about £360 exclusive of the House. **Tithes:** Of the whole Parish. **Glebe:** About 100 acres; *now* lying contiguous to the Rectory – by exchange recently made with the Patron. **Surplice Fees:** Very small. **Easter Dues and small Payments:** None. **Queen Anne's Bounty:** None. **Terrier:** There is an old one – the Rector is taking measures for having one made better adapted to the present state of the Parish [and the benefice].
SCHOOLS: **Endowed School:** None. **Subscription Day School:** None. **Sunday School:** None needed – from the smallness of the Parish. **Lancaster School:** None.
DISSENTERS: **Dissenters' School:** ——. **Dissenting Chapels:** ——.
POPULATION: From 50 to 60.
PARISH CLERK: John Ball – his son William officiates for him. **Appointed by:** The Rector. **Salary:** £2 2s. 0d. a year.
CHURCHWARDENS: Mr William Dennett – appointed by the Rector and Parish jointly.
ORDERS MADE: (1) The benefaction arising from land at Northampton to be recorded in the Church. (2) The Commandments set up in the Church. (3) The Mullions in the East Window of the Spire restored – and weather-boards put up. ['Articles returned'.]

Revisited 3.10.1841
No orders requisite – Everything in the best order.

[1] A/V/1/3: 'new and handsome'. [2] A/V/1/3: '. . . at the Hall . . .' [3] *Eccles Revs.:* 'fit'.

TRYSULL 21.4.1830 (A/V/1/2,no.37;/3,no.30)

BENEFICE: Trysull or Triezull or Treosle. **Nature:** Vicarage united with Wombourn. **Ecton:** See Wombourn. **Patron:** Same as Wombourn. **Impropriator:** None – the proprietors [of the land] have bought the tithes – Vicar's tithes exchanged for land.
CHURCH: An old Gothic building – pointed arches – nave, and two side aisles – spoilt by modern alterations. **Number it will contain:** 270. **Accommodation for Poor:** 40. **Roof:** Oak, covered with tiles – out of repair. **Walls:** Solid stone – upright.[1] **Floor:** Quarries and bricks – uneven especially in the N. aisle. **Windows:** Good – but no casements. **Doors:** N. door – bad. **Pulpit and Desk:** Old oak – firm and well placed. **Books:** Clerk's prayer book bad. **Seats:** Very irregular – new pewing much wanted. **Galleries:** One for the singers. **Organ:** None. **Font:** There is. **Chapels:** A private chancel. **Benefaction Tables:** Five – some benefactions have been lost. **Vestry:** There is,

under the Tower. **Surplices:** Two – a new one wanted. **Linen:** Table cloth and napkin. **Plate:** Flagon, cup – three silver plates – paten. **Iron Chest for Register:** None – one ordered. **Register:** Five vols prior to 1813 – oldest date 1560 – in good preservation. **Porch:** One on S. side – with oaken gates. **Vaults:** None recently. **Cleanliness:** Not Attended to. **Damp:** Some. **Dimensions:** 30ft. 2in. by 41ft.
CHANCEL: 28ft. 3in. by 23ft. **Table:** Old – not very firm. **Ornaments:** None. **Repaired by whom:** Different owners of land tithe free or Sir John Wrottesley.[2] The floor within the rails, table, rails, chancel floor, want repair. Two casements wanted.
STEEPLE: Old square tower. **State of:** Good. **Bells:** Five – one cracked. **Clock:** Pretty good.
CHURCHYARD: **Fence:** Wall all round – good – kept by Parish. **Gates:** Pretty good. **Drains:** None – much wanted. **Graves:** Too near the walls. **Rubbish:** Much both inside and out. **Cattle:** A Donkey.
DIVINE SERVICE: **On Sundays:** Two full services. **On other Days:** None. **Sacrament:** Six times a year. **Communicants:** 18. **Catechism:** None.[3]
INCUMBENT: **Name and Residence:** Same as Wombourn. **What Duty he performs:** None.
CURATE: **Name and Residence:** Revd JC Pigott, in the Parish. **Licensed:** He is. **If serving another church:** Alternates with Wombourn.
PARSONAGE: [None.]
INCOME: **Gross Value:** Not exceeding £300. **Tithes:** Land in lieu of tithes. **Easter Dues and small Payments:** Collected. **Queen Anne's Bounty:** None.
SCHOOLS: **Endowed School:** There is one, endowed with land – open to the whole parish. **Subscription Day School:** None. **Sunday School:** 40 or 45. **Lancaster School:** None.
DISSENTERS: **Dissenters' School:** ——. **Dissenting Chapels:** ——.
POPULATION: From 450 to 500.
MISCELLANEOUS: **Monuments:** There are [some]. **Chandeliers, etc:** None. **Parochial Library:** None.
PARISH CLERK: John Griffin. **Appointed by:** The Vicar. **Salary:** £3 and Christmas offerings.
CHURCHWARDENS: William Robotham, by the Parish.
ORDERS MADE: I   In the *Church*
['Done'.]
The floor to be taken up and laid even where needful – especially in the *N. Aisle*. Casements made in the Windows – The North door lined inside. A new Prayer book provided for the Clerk. The Plaister near the Gallery window repaired. Cleanliness properly attended to and enforced.

II   In the *Vestry*
A Register Chest provided, according to Act of Parliament. A new surplice provided.

III   In the *Chancel*
The door, floor, rails, table repaired. A casement on each side made.

IV   In the *Fabric*
The roof and NE. wall carefully examined and repaired.

V   In the *Churchyard*
Earth cleared away, and open drains made, all round. I strongly *recommended* the *new pewing* of the Church.

Revisited 18.7.1838
Improved since my last visit, but still much required.
The Communion Table and rails refixed – pews etc oiled. E. window repaired – windows, generally, new leaded and tied – and kept clean. Bell recast – weather-boards made good. Crest tiles of roofs and windows repaired – roofs ditto. Roof of Tower repaired – slates and lead work. Lead gutters, between roofs, cleared – roofs spouted. Casement in Vestry. Cleanliness, generally, in Church. Gates of Churchyard repaired and painted. Thoro'fare stopped – Churchyard enlarged – nettles destroyed. Space under eaves stopped with bricks or wood.

Revisited 21.10.1841
In hope of speedy improvement in whole of interior, directions concerning inside of Church postponed except to work up again the old oak pews – restore the screen etc – and provide *free* sittings. (1) Roof of *Tower* repaired without delay – gutters cleared and flashings restored. (2) Cracked bell re-cast – weatherboards made good – bell chamber cleaned. (3) Practice of having *fire* in Belfry, and ringers allowed to sit and drink there stopped immediately. (4) Gutters between roofs cleared out – roof repaired – open drain outside church cleared – trespass path stopped. (5) New gates at principal entrance, when the Church is done.

[1] A/V/1/3: 'Solid stone – good in general'. [2] A/V/1/3: 'Different owners of tithe-free land – Sir J Wrottesley a part'. [3] A/V/1/3: 'Not in Church'.

WALSALL 19.4.1830 (A/V/1/2,no.27;/3,no.31)

BENEFICE: **Walsall** [(St. Matthew's – Parish Church)]. **Nature:** Vicarage. **Ecton:** King's books £10 19s. 7d. Abb. Halesowen 7s. 8d. Abb. Halesowen Propr. **Patron:** Lord Bradford. **Impropriator:** Lord B and Col Walhouse.
CHURCH: A modern Pseudo-Gothic structure, with Nave and side aisles – the Chancel antient. The modern part, built about seven years ago, on a very faulty plan, by Mr Goodwin. **Number it will contain:** About 2,000 (stated in 1841 to be 2,500). **Accommodation for Poor:** (900 included in the 2,000). **Roof:** Timber covered with slate – part of the side aisles with thin sheets of copper – not in a good state. **Walls:** Brick faced with stone, and lined with cement [– upright]. **Floor:** Plaister – tolerably level. **Windows:** [Cast] Iron frames, with stone mullions – good order – Casements in all the gallery windows. **Doors:** Good. **Pulpit and Desk:** Oak – good condition. Velvet cushion to Pulpit. **Books:** Good order – except trifling repairs wanted in Bible. **Seats:** Oak – boarded floors – in good state. **Galleries:** All round the body of the Church. **Organ:** There is one. **Font:** A very handsome ancient one, at the entrance into the Chancel. **Chapels:** None. **Benefaction Tables:** There are some – said to be incomplete – not publicly exhibited. **Vestry:** Large and

commodious. **Surplices:** Four – two of them in tolerable order – one new one wanted. **Linen:** Two table cloths – one pretty good – a napkin ditto. **Plate:** Silver flagon – two Chalices – two Patens – one dish. **Chest for Papers:** At the Workhouse. **Iron Chest for Register:** A small one – a larger ordered. **Register:** Seven Vols in good preservation, and nearly entire – some interpolations, made by the last clerk – oldest date 1570. **Porch:** One – in good state. **Vaults:** None made recently. **Cleanliness:** Attended to – but ceiling wants white-washing. **Damp:** Some on the walls and ceiling, from the imperfect state of the roof. **Dimensions:** 89ft. by 62ft.

CHANCEL: 47ft. 10in. by 19ft. 1in. **Table:** White marble slab, on iron frame. **Ornaments:** None. **Repaired by whom:** The Impropriator; but the windows, roof, and ancient stalls are much out of repair.

STEEPLE: Tower, surmounted with a spire – the former cased with cement. **State of:** Good. **Bells:** Eight good; but not sufficiently protected from weather.[1] **Clock:** An old one – out of repair.

CHURCHYARD: **Fence:** Some doubt as to the extent of the Churchyard[2] – there is a brick wall, or houses, or palisade, all round – and within a public walk – the burying ground much trespassed upon. The doubt seems to be whether the Churchyard extends to the wall, or only to the road. **Gates:** Iron – good. **Drains:** Insufficient, much attention wanted in this respect. **Graves:** None lately made [too] near the walls. **Rubbish:** A good deal, and sad nuisances [all] around the walls. **Footpaths:** Several – the children, and worst characters of the town, make it a place of common resort. **Cattle:** None.

DIVINE SERVICES: **On Sundays:** Two full services. **On other Days:** Prayers Wednesday, Friday and Saints days. **Sacrament:** Monthly, and at the Festivals. **Communicants:** 160 at Easter, from 50 to 60 other times. **Catechism:** Occasionally in the Church.

INCUMBENT: **Name and Residence:** Revd John Baron – Vicarage. **What Duty he performs:** Takes part with his Curate.

CURATE: **Name and Residence:** Revd S Lowe – (Revd W Bagnall, Assistant curate). In the Town.[3] **If not resident:** In the Town. **Licensed:** Yes. **Salary:** £70.[4] **If serving another church:** None.

PARSONAGE: Brick building, faced with Plaister – new tiles – consists of three sitting rooms and kitchen on ground floor – eight rooms of different sizes above. **State of:** Good – the present Vicar has laid out a good deal of money in repairs etc.[5] **Outbuildings:** Stable – Coach-house – Cart shed.

INCOME: **Gross Value:** £400 per annum. **Tithes:** Worth about £180. **Glebe:** £150. **Surplice Fees:** £80 to £100. **Easter Dues and small Payments:** £20. **Queen Anne's Bounty:** None. **Terrier:** A copy in the possession of the Vicar.

SCHOOLS: **Endowed School:** A free grammar school, endowed by Queen Mary in the first year of her reign – funds large. There are two schools – one classics; and the other for inferior education.[6] **Subscription Day School:** A national school. **Sunday School:** Two – not very well attended – about 170 all. **Lancaster School:** None.

DISSENTERS: **Dissenters' School:** Independents, Methodists – on Sundays. **Dissenting Chapels:** Four including a new Catholic Chapel.

POPULATION: 13,000[7] in the Parish – about 8,000 in the Town.

MISCELLANEOUS: **Monuments:** Several. **Chandeliers, etc:** None. **Parochial Library:** ——.

PARISH CLERK: John Sheldon. **Appointed by:** The Vicar. **Salary:** Only £3 from the Parish.

CHURCHWARDENS: Mr Thomas Franklin for the Vicar, Joseph Cotterill for the Parish.

ORDERS MADE: A complete table of benefactions to be made out, and fixed publicly in the Church. A new surplice provided, and new Table cloth for Communion Table. An Iron Chest, capable of holding all the Registers. Chancel roof, windows, stalls to be repaired. Bells protected by weatherboards. Churchyard fenced and protected from encroachment, Churchyard cleared of nuisances. *Drains* to carry off the wet from the Church walls.

State of fabric, examined by Architect and reported. *Recommend* increase of Clerk's salary.

Revisited 13.10.1837
The support of the Galleries being in progress, and other improvements in contemplation, I found particular directions unnecessary.

Revisited 21.10.1841
'Churchyard fence – qu?'

Great improvement since my last visit. The Galleries have been effectively propped – no longer apprehension of danger in the Fabric. The Churchyard has been surrounded with a substantial iron palisade; and there is a general appearance of neatness and order about the Church, affording a satisfactory contrast to former times.

I had only to *suggest* (1) The prudence of insuring the Church against *fire.* (2) The importance of having the water courses and pipes kept clear. And to *enjoin* (3) The procuring of additional *burial ground.*

[1] A/V/1/3: 'Eight – good – weather-boards defective'. [2] A/V/1/3: 'viz whether it extends to the *wall*; or only to the *walk*'. [3] A/V/1/3: 'Revd S Lowe (since; Revd W Bagnall (1831))'. [4] *Eccles. Revs.:* £30. [5] *Eccles. Revs.:* 'fit'. [6] A/V/1/3: '. . . one classical, the other commercial'. [7] *Eccles. Revs.:* 15,066, including Walsall Foreign and Bloxwich.

ST. PAUL'S, WALSALL 19.4.1830
(A/V/1/2,no.27;/3,no.32 (with Walsall))

A/V/1/2
St. Paul's Chapel, Walsall – visited the same day – but the particulars omitted (by mistake) in this place.

The Chapel being new, no particular observations were called for, except as to the new-colouring of the Chapel, and repair of Prayer-book.

A/V/1/3
BENEFICE: St. Paul's, Walsall. **Nature:** Chapelry, built (by special Act of Parliament) by the Governors of the Free Grammar School. **Patron:** The Governors – the Chapel however is annexed by Act of Parliament to the Mastership of the School.

CHURCH: Small, neat building – modern Grecian style – middle and two side aisles. **Number it will contain:** About 700 (in 1841 said to be *600*).[1] **Accommodation for Poor:** 60. **Roof:** Timber covered with slate – good. **Walls:** Want colouring or white-washing. **Floor, Windows, Doors, Pulpit and Desk:** All good. **Books:** Prayer Book wants repairing. **Seats:** Good. **Galleries:** ——.
DIVINE SERVICE: **On Sundays:** Two full services. **On other Days:** Wednesday Evening Lecture (voluntary on the part of the Minister). **Sacrament:** Once in five weeks. **Communicants:** About 40.
INCUMBENT: **Name and Residence:** Revd T Rogers. Now (1841) Revd WG Barker. **What Duty he performs:** The whole.
PARSONAGE: The Minister has the house provided for the Master of the School.
INCOME: **Gross Value:** £50 – paid by the Governors.
PARISH CLERK: William Hayward. **Appointed by:** The Governors.
CHURCHWARDENS: Always one of the Governors of the School.
ORDERS MADE: ['Done'.]
The Chapel being new, no directions were found necessary, except for having the Prayer book repaired, and the walls and ceiling fresh white-washed and coloured.

Revisited 13.10.1837
New books for *reading desk*. Gratings to cover the pipes from the roof.
'Qu? Dry rot on N. side?'

Revisited 21.10.1841
Directions (1) Outer doors painted – loose board for notices. (2) Churchyard fence completed. (3) Decayed wainscoating of pews repaired – precaution against dry-rot. (4) A lead gutter to carry off the wet from the pipe on the East side of the Tower to the lead gutter of the roof. (5) The roof, *adjoining the Tower*, flashed with lead. (6) Walls coloured, ceilings white-washed, as soon as convenient. (7) New carpet for Pulpit Staircase.
St. Peter's, Walsall – see blank page at the beginning of the book – p. 1.[2]

[1] Eccles. Revs.: 800. [2] See p. 75 below.

WEDNESBURY 19.4.1830
(A/V/1/2,no.30;/3,no.33)

BENEFICE: Wednesbury. **Nature:** Vicarage. **Ecton:** Clear yearly value £40 – Abb. Halesowen 40s. Abb. Halesowen propr. **Patron:** Lord Chancellor. **Impropriator:** Sir Edward Scott and Hon. – Foley.[1]
CHURCH: A remarkably handsome modern structure in the Gothic style – lately erected – Nave, side aisles, Transept, Chancel. **Number it will contain:** 1,299. **Accommodation for Poor:** 674 (113 childrens' seats). **Roof:** Fir and Oak – covered with slates – Transept and Chancel with lead. **Walls:** Rubble Stone – the Transept solid stone. **Floor:** Flag stones. **Windows:** Cast Iron frames – stone mullions – casements to each. **Doors:** Very good. **Pulpit and Desk:** The pulpit [old and] remarkably handsome oak (date 1611). **Books:** Good – except the Bible in some places. **Seats:** Painted oak colour – all handsome and uniform. **Galleries:** On three sides. **Organ:** An old one – about to be exchanged [(since done) 1831]. **Font:** At the W. end. **Chapels:** None. **Benefaction Tables:** Several – all the Charities recorded. **Vestry:** There is one. **Surplices:** Two – one of them indifferent. **Linen:** Table Cloth and Napkin – good. **Plate:** Pewter flagon – silver Chalice; Paten and Dish. **Iron Chest for Register:** There is one. **Register:** 18 Vols – oldest date 1561 – entire with exception of 50 years. **Porch:** Two – in good state. **Vaults:** No recent ones. **Cleanliness:** Attended to. **Damp:** Very little. **Dimensions:** 69ft. by 60ft.
CHANCEL: 25ft by 24ft. **Table:** Marble slab – on iron frame. **Ornaments:** Ten Commandments, Creed, Lords Prayer. **Repaired by whom:** The Impropriators – [it has been] rebuilt, however, by the Parish.
STEEPLE: Tower – surmounted by Steeple. **State of:** Good. **Bells:** Eight – all in good order. **Clock:** There is [one].
CHURCHYARD: **Fence:** Brick wall, on all sides – well kept up. **Gates:** Good. **Drains:** Sufficiently provided. **Graves:** None near the Church. **Rubbish:** None. **Footpaths:** ——. **Cattle:** Sheep.
DIVINE SERVICE: **On Sundays:** Two full services. **On other Days:** None. **Sacrament:** Eight times a year. **Communicants:** 45. **Catechism:** Not in the Church.
INCUMBENT: **Name and Residence:** Revd I Clarkson – Vicarage. **What Duty he performs:** The whole.
CURATE: **Name and Residence:** – Hunt.[2]
PARSONAGE: A small house in Cottage style – not good, nor in very good repair. An exchange meditated.[3] **Outbuildings:** Stable – Gig-house – good order,.
INCOME: **Gross Value:** About £300[4] the proper value – the present Vicar receives about £200. **Tithes:** £140. **Glebe:** Garden to the Vicarage. **Surplice Fees:** £10. **Easter Dues and small Payments:** None. **Terrier:** In the possession of the Vicar.
SCHOOLS: **Endowed School:** None. **Subscription Day School:** None at present – a national School about to be opened. **Sunday School:** 280 [children]. **Lancaster School:** One of 70 boys.
DISSENTERS: **Dissenters' School:** Methodist and Independent. **Dissenting Chapels:** Three.
POPULATION: 6,471 last Census.[5]
MISCELLANEOUS: **Monuments:** Some very antient ones. **Chandeliers, etc:** There are. **Parochial Library:** None.
PARISH CLERK: GW Court. **Appointed by:** The Vicar. **Salary:** £3 10s. 0d. and perquisites.
CHURCHWARDENS: Mr John Addison – John Parkes.
ORDERS MADE: None necessary – everything in the Church and Churchyard in a remarkable good and satisfactory state – The Church is one of the handsomest newly erected Churches that I have seen.
['Articles returned'.]

Revisited 13.10.1837
(1) A new Prayer Book. (2) Water tables of Windows cleaned out. (3) Copings of the N. roof replaced – lead flashings repaired of all the roofs. (4) The door of the bell-chamber repaired. (5) Drains for down-pipes; ground lowered – grass

removed. (6) Sill of window of S. Transept repaired. (7) Iron Gates at N. and S. Porches. (8) Walls coloured as soon as convenient. 'Not done'.

Revisited 21.10.1841
All in good order – Directions (1) Pinnacles and battlements at SE. of Church and Chancel secured. (2) Pipes of roof over middle aisle cleared at the mouths. (3) Down-pipe from the roof of Tower cleared at the mouth.

[1] Thomas Edward Foley. [2] This is a late insertion in A/V/1/3. William Hunt was licensed as curate, 23.1.1831 (B/A/11a/E (1830–4) p.56). [3] *Eccles. Revs.:* 'unfit'. [4] *Eccles. Revs.:* gross income £350. [5] *Eccles. Revs.:* 8,437.

WEST BROMWICH 20.4.1830
(A/V/1/2, no.31;/3, no.34)

BENEFICE: West Bromwich. **Nature:** Perpetual Curacy. **Ecton:** Clear value £22 – Pri: Tickford Propr. **Patron:** Lord Dartmouth. **Impropriator:** Ditto.
CHURCH: An irregular building, originally Gothic but much disfigured by modern alterations; one or two remaining pointed arches indicate the ancient style of structure. **Number it will contain:** About 600.[1] **Accommodation for Poor:** 250, exclusive of children. **Roof:** Timber covered with slate. **Walls:** Stone, rough-cast; upright. **Floor:** Flat stones. **Windows:** Pretty good – casements [provided]. **Doors:** Good. **Pulpit and Desk:** Oak – good state – crimson moreen hangings. **Books:** Prayer book needs repair. **Seats:** Pews, oak and deal unpainted – good condition. **Galleries:** On the W. – and part of the N. and S. sides. **Organ:** There is one. **Font:** ——. **Chapels:** None – Lord Dartmouth has a private chancel, on the S. side. **Benefaction Tables:** Two small ones – other charities not recorded. **Vestry:** There is one. **Surplices:** Three – Good. **Linen:** Table Cloth and napkin – good. **Plate:** Plated flagon, two silver Cups and plates – two pewter dishes. **Iron Chest for Register:** In the wall of the Vestry. **Register:** Eleven Vols prior to 1813 – oldest date 1608; they appear not to have been regularly preserved. **Porch:** There is one – of brick. **Vaults:** Several. **Cleanliness:** Not properly attended to. **Damp:** No appearance. **Dimensions:** 64ft. 6in. by 28ft. 4in.
CHANCEL: 24ft. 5in. by 28ft. 4in. **Table:** Oak, covered with crimson cloth. **Ornaments:** None – no table of commandments etc. **Repaired by whom:** Lord Dartmouth.
STEEPLE: Square Tower – steeple above. **State of:** Good. **Bells:** Six – two of them cracked. ['Qu? Articles say *one*.] **Clock:** There is one – in good order.
CHURCHYARD: **Fence:** Stone wall – kept by the Parish. **Gates:** Good. **Drains:** None – ordered. **Graves:** Not many too near the walls – but many of them left in a very unsightly state, from not being covered with turf – stones etc lying about. **Rubbish:** [Stones etc.] **Footpaths:** None. **Cattle:** Sheep.
DIVINE SERVICE: **On Sundays:** Two full services. **On other Days:** None. **Sacrament:** Monthly. **Communicants:** 65. **Catechism:** In Lent.
INCUMBENT: **Name and Residence:** Revd C Townsend – resides half the year. **What Duty he performs:** Half, when resident.
CURATE: **Name and Residence:** Revd PG Harper – in the Parish. **Licensed:** He is. **Salary:** £100. **If serving another church:** None.
PARSONAGE: A large brick house, belonging to Lord Dartmouth, who has assigned it for the residence of the Minister, and engages to provide another, satisfactory to the Bishop, should he resume possession of the present one. **State of:** Good.[2] **Outbuildings:** Coach-house, Stables etc. spacious and good.
INCOME: **Gross Value:** £580. **Tithes:** None. **Glebe:** None – but Lord D has assigned some acres of land ['about 20 acres'] together with the house, for the use of the Minister. **Surplice Fees:** From £80 to £90. **Easter Dues and small Payments:** £100 paid yearly from Stanley's Trust to support a Lectureship. **Queen Anne's Bounty:** £98, in money.
SCHOOLS: **Endowed School:** None. **Subscription Day School:** National and Infant Schools. **Sunday School:** There is [one]. **Lancaster School:** None.
DISSENTERS: **Dissenters' School:** Several. **Dissenting Chapels:** Five.
POPULATION: 15,000 – rapidly increased and increasing.
MISCELLANEOUS: **Monuments:** There are. **Parochial Library:** None.
PARISH CLERK: William Barton. **Appointed by:** The Minister. **Salary:** £2 2s. 0d. – and £7 7s. 0d. for cleaning the Church which he greatly neglects.
CHURCHWARDENS: Mr Hood and Mr Haynes.
ORDERS MADE: ['Done except the *Bible*. Articles returned.']
Prayer book to be repaired. Ten Commandments put up. Benefaction tables completed. Bells repaired. Earth cleared away round the Church – and open drains made. Spouting completed. Rubbish removed from the Churchyard, and more attention paid to neatness and cleanliness both in the Church and yard.

Revisited 13.10.1837
Directions. (1) Water-tables to the windows. (2) Walls coloured; *doors painted*. (3) Battlements of Tower secured – lock on roof door. (4) Eave-spouts cleared out, and made effectual. (5) Open drain on N. side of Church cleared out – and gravel walk formed round the Church. (6) Windows mended – font removed. 'Not done, for want of funds.'

Revisited 21.10.1841
(1) Roof examined and repaired. (2) New pewing, with *better arrangement* for room; strongly *recommend*.
N.B. After my visit I wrote to Revd James Spry the Incumbent urging him to consider the propriety of *re-building* the Church, on a larger scale, and in a more central position.
I heard from him in reply, that Lord Dartmouth was not favorable to the proposition.

[1] *Eccles. Revs.:* 1,072. [2] *Eccles. Revs.:* 'none'.

CHRIST CHURCH, WEST BROMWICH
20.4.1830 (A/V/1/2, no. 32;/3, no. 35)

BENEFICE: Christ Church, West Bromwich. **Nature:** Chapel of Ease to the Parish Church – but intended to be [made] a district church. **Patron:** Trustees – of whom Lord Dartmouth is one.
CHURCH: A new structure, in the florid Gothic style – nave and side aisles – Galleries – no division for Chancel.[1] **Number it will contain:** 1,230.[2] **Accommodation for Poor:** 800. **Roof:** Lets in the wet in some places. **Walls, Floor, Windows, Doors, Pulpit and Desk, Books, Seats, Galleries, Organ, Font, Chapels:** All new, handsome and in good order. **Vestry:** There is one. **Surplices:** One – another ordered. **Plate:** Provided. **Register:** None wanted at present.
DIVINE SERVICE: **On Sundays:** Two full services, Morning and Evening. **Sacrament:** Monthly and at the Festivals. **Communicants:** 50 at Easter.
INCUMBENT: **Name and Residence:** Revd W Gordon – in a house of Lord Dartmouths, in the Parish.[3] **What Duty he performs:** The whole.
INCOME: **Gross Value:** About £300[4] – of which £100 from Stanleys Trust, £200 from Pew Rents.
PARISH CLERK: Joseph Perkins. **Appointed by:** The Minister. **Salary:** £15.
CHURCHWARDENS: *Churchwardens* deleted, and replaced by *Sidesmen*: Mr Izon and Mr Dawes.
ORDERS MADE: ['Done']
New Surplice to be provided. Roof examined and repaired. Weather-boards put up.
N.B. The Chapel being quite new, particular entries as to many parts unnecessary.

Revisited 13.10.1837
Better Water-tables to windows. Walls etc coloured.

Revisited 21.10.1841
All in 'capital' order, *internally*; but there is much reason to suspect the stability of the *pinnacles* of the Tower, and indeed of the Tower itself.
(1) The attention of the Churchwardens was specifically directed to this point – and also the pointing, externally, of the window sills, and walls under the windows. (2) The roof to be examined and repaired where needful.
Two new Churches have been built; and one of them consecrated, since my last Visitation.
(1) *Trinity* Church – with accommodation for 932.
(2) *Hill Top* Church: nearly finished – and to be opened, under licence from the Bishop, in a few weeks – accommodation 1,000.

[1] A/V/1/3: 'No distinct Chancel'. [2] *Eccles. Revs.:* 1,420. [3] *Eccles. Revs.:* 'None'. [4] *Eccles. Revs.:* gross income £330.

WYCHNOR 27.7.1829 (A/V/1/2,no.10;/3,no.36)

BENEFICE: Wichnor; a small hamlet, about seven miles from Lichfield and five or six miles from Burton. **Nature:** Perpetual Curacy – formerly Chapelry to Tatenhill. **Ecton:** £16 13s. 4d. clear yearly value. **Patron:** Theophilus Levett Esqr. **Impropriator:** There are no tithes – a modus is paid to the Dean of Lichfield, as Rector of Tatenhill.
CHURCH: Nave, one side aisle and chancel, originally of Gothic architecture, but injured by modern alterations. **Number it will contain:** About 80 in pews. **Accommodation for Poor:** From 30 to 50 on forms and benches. **Roof:** Oak timber, covered with Tiles – in good repair. **Walls:** Stone covered with Plaister [inside]. **Floor:** Brick – very good and even. **Windows:** In good order: four with casements – kept properly open. **Doors:** One: in a sound state. **Pulpit and Desk:** Oak: very neat – handsome velvet Cushion for Pulpit, and red cloth coverings for desk. **Books:** Handsome; and in good preservation. **Seats:** Oak: with boarded floors – in very good condition generally. **Galleries:** None. **Organ:** None. **Font:** Handsome old stone font. **Chapels:** None. **Benefaction Tables:** None – no benefactions belonging to the Parish: it is in fact a chapel of ease to Tatenhill. **Vestry:** None. **Surplices:** One in indifferent condition – the present Curate uses his own, but considering the circumstances of the Cure, I did not think it necessary to order a new one. **Linen:** Table Cloth and Napkin – in good state. **Plate:** Silver Cup and Plate – no flagon. **Chest for Papers:** There is a chest in the Chancel. **Iron Chest for Register:** There is one – in the Chancel. **Register:** Two vols: besides those now in use, the earliest date 1731. **Porch:** None. **Vaults:** None recently made. **Cleanliness:** Not fully attended to – directions given. **Damp:** Some appearance of it; but stated to have been much diminished of late.
Dimensions: 37ft. 9in. long; 29ft. 11in. broad.
CHANCEL: 19ft. 5in. long; 16ft. 2in. broad. **Table:** Oak: good. Covered with a neat green cloth. **Ornaments:** None. **Repaired by whom:** Theophilus Levett Esqr. [The Patron.]
STEEPLE: Square [stone] tower: the upper part brick. **State of:** Not very good – repairs ordered. **Bells:** One. **Clock:** None.
CHURCHYARD: **Fence:** A quick hedge, in very good state – kept up by one of the principal farmers, who has the herbage in compensation. **Gates:** Two – not very good – repairs ordered. **Drains:** There is a surf along the South side of the Church and part of the North – ordered to be continued. **Graves:** None – the few interments have all been in the Church. **Rubbish:** Some – ordered to be removed – as also nettles and earth near the wall – and Tree too near the Church. **Footpaths:** Two – one gravel walk. **Cattle:** Sheep occasionally.
DIVINE SERVICE: **On Sundays:** Prayers and sermon in the morning. **On other Days:** None. **Sacrament:** Four times a year. **Communicants:** From 25 to 30. **Catechism:** Taught at the Sunday School.
INCUMBENT: **Name and Residence:** Revd Thomas Levett. **If not resident:** Resides at Packington. **What Duty he performs:** None.
CURATE: **Name and Residence:** Revd John Hinckley. **If not resident:** Resides at Lichfield. **Licensed:** Yes. **Salary:** £86 (£40 of which is a voluntary addition of the present Incumbent). **If serving another church:** Not at present [(now *Alrewas* 1831)].
PARSONAGE: There is none.[1]
INCOME: **Gross Value:** £46 arising from land in Kings Bromley parish. **Tithes:** None. **Glebe:** None –

except that mentioned in Gross Value. **Surplice Fees:** Very little surplice duty. **Easter Dues and small Payments:** None. **Queen Anne's Bounty:** ——. **Terrier:** None.

SCHOOLS: **Endowed School:** None. **Subscription Day School:** None. **Sunday School:** 15 boys – 10 girls. **Lancaster School:** None.

POPULATION: About 100.

MISCELLANEOUS: **Monuments:** None.

PARISH CLERK: William Holland. **Appointed by:** The Incumbent. **Salary:** Four Guineas.

CHURCHWARDENS: Charles Hall and – Hixon.[2] The duty done by one. (The four principal farmers take it in succession.)

ORDERS MADE: ['nearly done except the Tower'.]
In the Church.
    The walls to be white-washed. Pews to be repaired, where needful. Communion rails, ditto.
In the Churchyard.
    The drain carried all round the Church. Earth and weeds to be removed from the walls. A Tree cut down, which injures the [Church] wall. The Gates repaired, or renewed. The Steeple fresh pointed, and otherwise repaired.
['Articles returned – qu? *Tower*'.]

Revisited 5.9.1837
    Found the exterior of the Church much neglected – the Spouts out of order and causing much dampness to the walls – herbage, etc collecting round the base of the walls – walls wanting repair etc. I wrote to the Rural Dean requesting him to see that these matters were attended to – and especially that a *down*-pipe, of metal, be substituted for the old decayed wooden spout at the E. end of the South aisle – ivy etc cleared away from the walls on the North side – also that the *Tower* be pointed and battlements repaired. Owing to the lateness of the Evening, and the heavy rain, I could not fully ascertain the state of the *interior* of the Church – but directed the attention of the Rural Dean to it. 'Qu? done. Damp? Spouts etc.'

[1] *Eccles. Revs.:* 'none'. [2] Edward Hickson.

WIGGINTON 15.9.1829
(A/V/1/2,no.150;/3,no.37) ['omitted after no.20']

BENEFICE: Wigginton. **Nature:** Chapelry under Tamworth – Perpetual Curacy.[1] **Ecton:** Value not certified. **Patron:** The Vicar of Tamworth.

CHURCH: A plain rectangular [brick] building, in one compartment – without side aisles or Chancel. **Number it will contain:** About 120 adults.[2] **Accommodation for Poor:** About 45 including children. **Roof:** Timber covered with tiles – ceiling and tiles both in bad state. **Walls:** Brick – firm and upright. **Floor:** Brick and quarries – much appearance of damp. **Windows:** Pretty good. **Doors:** One – wants painting and repair. **Pulpit and Desk:** Deal – some repairs wanted. **Books:** Out of repair. **Seats:** Pannels good – floors brick and very damp. **Galleries:** One at W. end – capable of holding 25 or 30 children. **Organ:** None. **Font:** There is one. **Chapels:** None. **Benefaction Tables:** None – wanted. **Vestry:** One – not in good order. **Linen:** Table Cloth and napkins – pretty good. **Plate:** Cup and salver plated – not good. **Chest for Papers:** None. **Iron Chest for Register:** None. **Register:** None kept – all burials and christenings are registered at Tamworth – improperly. **Porch:** None. **Vaults:** None since 1820. **Cleanliness:** Not properly attended to. **Damp:** Much on the floor – rain beats in at the windows. **Dimensions:** 37ft. 6in. by 16ft. 9in.

CHANCEL: No chancel. **Table:** Plain oak – uncovered. **Ornaments:** None. **Repaired by whom:** Much difficulty on this subject – the Chapel was built about 50 years ago by subscription – and has since been repaired out of the surplus of money then collected; that fund being now exhausted, the inhabitants refuse to raise money by rate for repairs.

STEEPLE: Small bell-tower. **State of:** Very poor. **Bells:** One – pretty good. **Clock:** None.

CHURCHYARD: **Fence:** Partly brick wall – partly quick hedge; the latter not properly kept. **Gates:** One – entrance insufficient. **Drains:** None. **Graves:** None near the walls. **Rubbish:** ——. **Footpaths:** ——. **Cattle:** A cow kept by the Clerk, by permission of the Minister.

DIVINE SERVICE: **On Sundays:** Morning and afternoon – alternately with Wilnecote. **On other Days:** Good Friday and Christmas day. **Sacrament:** Four times a year. **Communicants:** 12 or 15. **Catechism:** During Lent in Chapel – in the School at other times.

INCUMBENT: **Name and Residence:** Revd Robert Lloyd, Tamworth.[3] **If not resident:** [At Tamworth.] **What Duty he performs:** None.

CURATE: **Name and Residence:** Revd Philip Palmer – Tamworth (now G Harrison 1830). **If not resident:** [At Tamworth.] **Licensed:** He is. **Salary:** 60 Guineas per annum – and board and lodging – equal to £90.[4] **If serving another church:** Wilnecote Chapel.

PARSONAGE: None.[5]

INCOME: **Gross Value:** About £95 – arising from same sources, nearly, as that of Wilnecote (see p.21).

SCHOOLS: **Endowed School:** One at Hopwas, within the Chapelry. **Subscription Day School:** None. **Sunday School:** About 50 boys and girls. **Lancaster School:** None.

DISSENTERS: **Dissenters' School:** ——. **Dissenting Chapels:** A small Gothic Chapel at Hopwas.

POPULATION: 335.

MISCELLANEOUS: **Monuments:** One, to Mrs Blakesley. **Chandeliers, etc:** None. **Parochial Library:** ——.

PARISH CLERK: Joseph Vaughton. **Appointed by:** The Vicar of Tamworth. **Salary:** No stated salary – paid by voluntary subscription.

CHURCHWARDENS: Mr Matthew Ingle.

ORDERS MADE: The books to be renewed – Register book and chest to be provided. Measures taken for removing the damp. Other more important repairs not ordered, as it is intended to take immediate measures for enlarging the Chapel.

1830. Plans, Estimates etc for enlarging the Chapel were laid before me – with a view to application for aid from the Incorporated Society.

1831. The Chapel, enlarged and repaired, was re-opened for service in the Spring of this year.

Revisited 1.9.1837
Enlarged since my former visit and generally in good order – Napkin wanted at Communion Table. Rails of ditto to be re-fixed. Prayer Book new – Bible repaired – Clerk's Prayer Book new. New Surplice. Herbage cleared from walls. Spouts and down-pipes. East end of Church pointed externally. Walk cleared of weeds. Hedges trimmed. Entrance gates and rails painted. 'Partially done.'

Revisited 3.9.1841
New Prayer books for Reading Desk and Clerk's Desk. An iron stay for Communion rails. The Commandments, Creed, and Lord's Prayer set up on each side of the East window. Grass cleared away round walls, and space of about three feet laid with gravel, tiles or bricks, to keep the lower part of the Walls dry. Stays of eave-spouts, down-pipes, and gates of Churchyard painted.

[1] A/V/1/3: 'Perpetual Curacy – originally Chapel of ease to Tamworth'. [2] A/V/1/3 adds, 'Since this time, it has been enlarged by the addition of a new aisle.' *Eccles. Revs.:* 270. [3] Also perpetual curate of Wilnecote. [4] *Eccles. Revs.:* £45. (The figure given above is presumably the total income of Palmer as curate of Wigginton and Wilnecote.) [5] *Eccles. Revs.:* 'None'.

WILNECOTE 15.9.1829
(A/V/1/2,no.21;/3,no.38)
At head of A/V/1/2 'for *Wigginton* Chapel see p.150'.

BENEFICE: Wilnecote Chapel. **Nature:** Perpetual Curacy [Chapelry in Tamworth Parish]. **Ecton:** Not mentioned. **Patron:** The Vicar of Tamworth. **Impropriator:** None.
CHURCH: A neat, modern, oblong building – without chancel or side aisles, enlarged (and nearly rebuilt) in 1821. **Number it will contain:** About 650. **Accommodation for Poor:** 482. **Roof:** Timber covered with tiles. **Walls:** Brick, faced on the S. and W. sides with stone; upright and solid. **Floor:** Quarries. **Windows:** Good. **Doors:** Good. **Pulpit and Desk:** Ditto; but very strangely[1] placed, within the Communion rail – the passage from one to the other, being actually *over* the Table. **Books:** The Prayer book, in reading desk, wants rebinding. **Seats:** The Pews, deal – boarded floors – the free sittings below, open benches. **Galleries:** Three. **Organ:** None. **Font:** None. **Chapels:** None. **Benefaction Tables:** None. **Vestry:** There is one: but much affected by damp, owing to want of proper drainage outside; and to water cask being placed against the wall – orders given accordingly. **Surplices:** One – in good state. **Linen:** Pretty good – Table cloth and napkin. **Plate:** Cup and Pallett[2] – silver. **Chest for Papers:** There is one, in the Vestry. **Iron Chest for Register:** None. **Register:** None – baptisms registered at Tamworth – no burials performed here. **Porch:** None. **Vaults:** None. **Cleanliness:** Attended to. **Damp:** Very little, except from rain beating in at the windows. **Dimensions:** 67ft. 4in. by 32ft.
CHANCEL: **Table:** Oak. **Ornaments:** None. **Repaired by whom:** Out of the Poor rates.
STEEPLE: Square – stone [tower]. **State of:** Good. **Bells:** One – good. **Clock:** None.
CHURCHYARD: **Fence:** None at present – there has been a talk of enclosing the Chapel, on the S. and W. sides – on the N. is a garden belonging to Mr Lloyd. The enclosure strongly urged. (This has since been done. 1831.)
DIVINE SERVICE: **On Sundays:** Alternate Morning and Afternoon duty with Wigginton. **On other Days:** Good Friday and Christmas day. **Sacrament:** Four times a year. **Communicants:** About 35. **Catechism:** At the School.
INCUMBENT: **Name and Residence:** Revd R Lloyd – Tamworth.[3] **If not resident:** Not. **What Duty he performs:** None.
CURATE: **Name and Residence:** Revd G Harrison – Tamworth.[4] **Licensed:** He is. **Salary:** 60 Guineas a year, with board and lodging – in all £90. **If serving another church:** None other – except Wigginton Chapel.
PARSONAGE: None.[5]
INCOME: **Gross Value:** About £95 – as follows –

	£
Moiety of rent of Estate purchased by Bounty money – at £56 rent	28
Ditto of remainder of Bounty money and of Parliamentary grant – £98	49
Annual payment from the Estate of Lord Weymouth	10
Other payments, fees etc cir.	8
	95

SCHOOLS: **Endowed School:** None. **Subscription Day School:** None. **Sunday School:** 40 boys – 50 girls. **Lancaster School:** None.
DISSENTERS: **Dissenters' School:** None. **Dissenting Chapels:** None.
POPULATION: About 700.
MISCELLANEOUS: **Monuments:** None. **Chandeliers, etc:** None. **Parochial Library:** None.
PARISH CLERK: Joseph Hodgkinson. **Appointed by:** Vicar of Tamworth. **Salary:** None, except voluntary subscriptions.
CHURCHWARDENS: Mr Paul.
ORDERS MADE: The causes of dampness in the Vestry to be removed. The windows to be secured against [the beating in of] rain. A baptismal font, register, and register chest, to be provided.
  Recommended. To alter the position of the Reading desk, and Pulpit. To paint all the woodwork [(pews, pulpit etc)] which has never been painted. To enclose the Chapel on the S. and W. sides. The East end cannot well be enclosed, with encroaching on the Public street – the N. side is protected by a garden. The Chapel was rebuilt in 1821, when 250 additional free sittings were procured; partly by private subscription; partly by aid from the Society for enlarging etc.

Revisited 31.8.1837
Directions. Two additional casements in lower parts of windows on each side. Ventilation to be attended to. Window bars painted. 'Not done'. Lock on Iron Gates. Grass cleared from walls.

Revisited 2.9.1841
Dry rot – pews to be repaired. Bars of windows painted. Baptismal Font provided.
Mem: District and Parish much wanted.

[1] A/V/1/3: 'awkwardly'. [2] A/V/1/3: 'Paten'. [3] Also perpetual curate of Wigginton. [4] 'Philip Palmer' deleted. [5] *Eccles. Revs.:* 'None'.

WOMBOURN 21.4.1830
(A/V/1/2, no.36;/3, no.39)

BENEFICE: Wombourn. **Nature:** Vicarage. **Ecton:** Living discharged – clear yearly value £49 – prior: Dudley olim propr. **Patron:** Trustees – JH Foley Esqr, Sir Thomas Wynnington and others. **Impropriator:** Sir John Wrottesley.
CHURCH: Old Gothic structure with modern additions – nave and north aisle – chancel, with circular arch. **Number it will contain:** 425. **Accommodation for Poor:** About 50. **Roof:** Oak covered with tile. **Walls:** Stone – upright. **Floor:** Flags. **Windows:** Pretty good – two casements. **Doors:** Repairs and painting wanted. **Pulpit and Desk:** Mahogany. Handsome coverings. **Books:** Very handsome, but want [slight] repair – given by Sir Samuel Hellier. **Seats:** New pewed in 1825. **Galleries:** On the W. and North. **Organ:** There is one. **Font:** ——. **Chapels:** None. **Benefaction Tables:** None – ordered. **Vestry:** A small one – damp. **Surplices:** One – a new one wanted. **Linen:** [Provided.] **Plate:** Remarkably handsome – silver gilt flagon, chalice, dish, paten, and cup for baptisms, given by Sir S Hellier. **Chest for Papers:** There is one. **Iron Chest for Register:** There is [one]. **Register:** Seven vols prior to 1813 – oldest date 1570, entire from that time. **Porch:** None. **Vaults:** Several. **Cleanliness:** Attended to. **Damp:** Much on the N. side and chancel. **Dimensions:** 42ft. 4in. by 33ft.
CHANCEL: 26ft. by 14ft. 6in. **Table:** Old oak table. **Ornaments:** None. **Repaired by whom:** Sir John Wrottesley – much out of repair, in roof, walls, mullions of windows, steps at the door – the children sit within the communion rails.
STEEPLE: Square stone tower – spire above – top of tower wants repair. **State of:** That of Spire good. **Bells:** Six – in good order. **Clock:** Out of repair.
CHURCHYARD: **Fence:** On the S. a wall, kept up by the Parish, on the East, vicarage garden hedge – N. and W., hedges belonging to tenants of adjoining lands. The two latter need repair, and the ditch on the W. keeping in order.[1] **Gates:** Good. **Drains:** None – ordered. **Graves:** Several – near the walls. **Rubbish:** Some. **Footpaths:** Two [trespass paths] – one to be stopped if possible. **Cattle:** A poney.
DIVINE SERVICE: **On Sundays:** Two full services. **On other Days:** None. **Sacrament:** Four times a year. **Communicants:** 30 to 40. **Catechism:** Occasionally.
INCUMBENT: **Name and Residence:** Revd TP Foley, Old Swinford.[2] **What Duty he performs:** None.
CURATE: **Name and Residence:** Revd James Bevan, Vicarage. **Licensed:** He is. **Salary:** £60 – Fees and [the] house.[3] **If serving another church:** Alternate with Trysull.
PARSONAGE: An old building – half brick – half timber. **State of:** Tolerably good.[4] **Outbuildings:** Barn – Stable etc and some smaller tenements in village – all out of repair.
INCOME: **Gross Value:** Upwards of £500.[5] **Tithes:** An allotment of land, in lieu of tithes in one of the hamlets. **Glebe:** 37 acres. **Surplice Fees:** About £6. **Easter Dues and small Payments:**[6] Collected. **Queen Anne's Bounty:** None. **Terrier:** There is [one].
SCHOOLS: **Endowed School:** None **Subscription Day School:** A charity school. **Sunday School:** 63 girls – 57 boys. **Lancaster School:** None.
DISSENTERS: **Dissenters' School:** One at Swindon. **Dissenting Chapels:** A Wesleyan chapel.
POPULATION: About 1,600.
MISCELLANEOUS: **Monuments:** There are some. **Parochial Library:** None – the curate lends books.
PARISH CLERK: George Frior. **Appointed by:** The Vicar. **Salary:** £8 for Clerk's duty, and other services.
CHURCHWARDENS: Mr John Perry. Mr John Hill.
ORDERS MADE: ['Done except the Chancel'.]
The doors to be repaired and painted. Bible and Prayer-book repaired. Benefactions recorded. New surplice provided.
The Chancel put into complete repair. Sittings provided for the children, so as to prevent the necessity of their sitting within the Rails. The upper part of the Tower repaired. The Hedge on the N. and W. sides of the Churchyard and the ditch adjoining kept in better order. The footpath, along the [side nearest the] Vicarage garden, stopped up if possible. The earth cleared away, open drains made etc.
There is great want of further accommodation – and plans have been formed for the enlargement of the Church; which it is hoped will be carried into effect, if the concurrence of the [Lay-] Impropriator can be obtained.
I found the out-buildings belonging to the Vicarage, and some small tenements attached to it, much out of repair – and wrote to the Vicar on the subject, who promised to put them into repair without delay – [(this has since, I understand, been done)].

Revisited 18.7.1838
This Church still suffers greatly from damp.
I directed the Churchwarden to consult an experienced workman as to the most effectual and practicable means of lowering the soil at the N. and E. ends of the Church – and to have it lowered on the South side – to provide additional casements on the North and South sides of the Church, and place iron gates at the South door. The beams above N. gallery examined. The *Tower* to be examined by a competent builder and *reported* to me – the roof carefully examined and repaired – eave-spouts and down-pipes placed – crest tiles repaired – gutters cleared out. Battlements of Tower repaired – gutters cleared out; weatherboards replaced. Outer doors painted – walls pointed with cement – at Chancel end. A Chapel of Ease much wanted at Swindon. The Vicar is about to re-build the Parsonage house on a better site.

Revisited 21.10.1841
Directions etc. (1) Mat or carpet for Communion

floor. (2) Font provided and suitably placed. (3) Buttresses pointed – herbage cleared from N. side of Church. (4) Window at W. end of N. aisle repaired or enlarged so as to light the gallery. (5) Battlements secured and gutters kept clear, till Tower is repaired. (6) Gravel walk or flagged space laid round Church – when improvements in Church and Churchyard are completed.

[1] A/V/1/3: '. . . which want trimming and ditches clearing out'. [2] Also vicar of Trysull and rector of Old Swinford. [3] *Eccles. Revs.*: £128. [4] *Eccles. Revs.*: 'fit'. [5] *Eccles. Revs.*: £643, including income of the vicarage of Trysull. [6] A/V/1/3 encloses 'and small payments' in brackets.

WORFIELD 18.5.1830 (A/V/1/2,no.45;/3,no.40)

BENEFICE: Worfield. **Nature:** Vicarage. **Ecton:** Living discharged – clear yearly value £35 0s. 0d. **Patron:** The Davenport family.[1] **Impropriator:** Ditto.[1] (Ecton says Dec. et Cap. Lich. Impropriators.)
CHURCH: A very handsome Gothic structure, with Nave, side aisles and Chancel – but suffering much from want of timely repairs. **Number it will contain:** 1,000. **Accommodation for Poor:** Very insufficient – galleries have been talked of. **Roof:** Oak, covered with tiles – in good state. **Walls:** Stone – that on the S. side appears to be in a very insecure state. **Floor:** Quarries – uneven. **Windows:** An additional casement wanted. **Doors:** Good. **Pulpit and Desk:** Good – but not well situated. **Books:** The Bible wants repair. **Seats:** Irregular – [much room lost –] a different arrangement highly desirable. **Galleries:** One or two small ones. **Organ:** There is [one]. **Font:** ———. **Chapels:** [None.] **Benefaction Tables:** All the Charities recorded. **Vestry:** A small one. **Surplices:** Two – a new one wanted. **Linen:** Good. **Plate:** A plated Flagon – two silver Cups and [a] Paten. **Iron Chest for Register:** There is one. **Register:** From 1562 to present time; one of the Vols needs re-binding. **Porch:** On the S. side – iron gates about to be put up. **Damp:** Very much – owing to the accumulation of soil outside. **Dimensions:** 78ft. by 66ft.
CHANCEL: 53ft. by 20ft. **Table:** Plain [and firm]. **Ornaments:** None. **Repaired by whom:** The Impropriator[2] – in good repair; but an additional casement required.
STEEPLE: Square stone tower, with [handsome] spire above. **State of:** Much weakened, apparently, by a *settling* at the base. **Bells:** Six – good. **Clock:** There is one.
CHURCHYARD: **Fence:** Kept up partly by the Rector, partly by the Parish – in good repair. **Gates:** Good. **Drains:** None. **Graves:** Many too near the walls. **Rubbish:** Some – and much ivy growing upon the Church. **Footpaths:** None [improperly]. **Cattle:** A Poney.
DIVINE SERVICE: **On Sundays:** Full morning service – prayers on the afternoon. **On other Days:** [None.] **Sacrament:** Monthly and at the Festivals. **Communicants:** 60 to 90. **Catechism:** Not in the Church.
INCUMBENT: **Name and Residence:** Revd ES Davenport, in the Rectory.[3] **What Duty he performs:** The whole, when his health permits.
CURATE: **Name and Residence:** None at present.
PARSONAGE: A small old building, adjoining the Rectory – in good repair; but insufficient for the present Vicar's family, who lives in the Rectory, but occupies also a part of the Vicarage. **State of:** Good.[4] **Outbuildings:** A Barn – dilapidated.
INCOME: **Gross Value:** £200. **Glebe:** 19 acres – [value] £25. **Terrier:** There is one.
SCHOOLS: **Endowed School:** There is one, for boys, supported by land. **Subscription Day School:** The Vicar's lady has a [small] weekly school. **Sunday School:** 100 children. **Lancaster School:** None.
DISSENTERS: **Dissenters' School:** ———. **Dissenting Chapels:** ——— a small meeting in a private room.
POPULATION: 1,400.[5] [Said (in 1838) to be 1,800.]
MISCELLANEOUS: **Monuments:** To the Bromley family. **Parochial Library:** None.
PARISH CLERK: Thomas Rogers. **Appointed by:** The Vicar. **Salary:** £5 5s. 0d.
CHURCHWARDENS: Mr John Meredith, Mr Powel.
ORDERS MADE: ['Chiefly done. Articles returned.'] The floor to be laid even, where necessary. The Bible re-bound. One Vol of the Registers re-bound. Casements (additional) provided. A new surplice provided. The state of the Tower to be carefully examined by an experienced Architect, and the necessary steps taken for its security – the same, as to the *South wall*. The earth to be dug out and cleared away, all round, to the level, at least, of the Church floor, and open drains made – spouting to be provided. The Buttresses to be repaired – and Ivy either removed, or prevented from injuring the walls and roof – the Window on the N. side, now blocked up, to be restored. No graves to be allowed within six feet of the Walls. Removal of pulpit.[6] Erection of galleries. Different arrangement of Pews and open seats for better accommodation of the Poor – strongly recommended.

Revisited 18.7.1838

This very handsome Church has been re-pewed and in many other respects very greatly improved, both in its interior and exterior condition; since my former visit – it is now one of the handsomest and neatest Churches in the Archdeaconry. Accommodation now for 851 – of which 185 free.

The lead gutters of roof to be cleared and repaired. Thorofare of Churchyard stopped if possible.

I urged the Vicar to take down and re-build his Vicarage, which is in a most ruinous condition; he himself living (now) at Davenport House – I recommended also a second Sermon.

Revisited 18.10.1841

Directions etc. (1) Door placed at top of staircase leading to Tower – and lower window of spire, near entrance of Tower, guarded by weatherboards. (2) Water from Tower conveyed to ground by *Iron down-pipe*, at NW. side. (3) Weather-boards of bell chamber placed on *inside* of window jambs. (4) New bell ropes provided. (5) Gravel walk made from North entrance of Churchyard to Church door. (6) Churchyard secured from trespass, by keeping principal gate locked. (7) Children kept from playing in Churchyard – idle persons, misbehaving in

Churchyard during Service time, admonished or punished.

[1] *Eccles. Revs.:* WY Davenport. [2] A/V/1/2: 'Patron' deleted. [3] Also rector of Lydham (Salop). [4] *Eccles. Revs.:* 'unfit'. [5] *Eccles. Revs.:* 1,591. [6] A/V/1/3: 'A change in the position of the Pulpit'.

PERRY BARR 13.10.1837 (A/V/1/3,no.41)
Not in A/V/1/2.

BENEFICE: Perry Barr. **Nature:** Proprietary Chapel – built in 1833 or 4. **Patron:** John Gough Esqr. **Impropriator:** ——.
CHURCH: Neat Gothic building. **Number it will contain:** 266. 216 in pews (50 in Gallery). [Now (1841) 340.]
INCUMBENT: **Name and Residence:** Revd H Wyatt.
ORDERS MADE: Visited in 1837 – and again in 1841. All in the best order – accommodation (1841) increased to 340.
No directions needful – (O si sic omnia!)

FORTON[1] 9.6.1830 (A/V/1/2,no.64;/3,no.42)

BENEFICE: Forton. **Nature:** Rectory. **Ecton:** Kings Books £20 19s. 2d. Mr Baldwyn Patron. **Patron:** Sir Thomas Bowey. **Impropriator:** None – but the Aqualate property (consisting of 800 acres) is tithe-free, as well as some other parts of the Parish – nor is there any hay-tithe – the Parish contains 3,600 acres in the whole.
CHURCH: Originally Gothic, but much spoilt by modern alterations – the nave re-built in 1713 – separated from the north aisle by modern circular arches – no South aisle. **Number it will contain:** Upwards of 300. **Accommodation for Poor:** Sufficient. **Roof:** Timber covered with tile – lately examined and repaired; the ceiling in the N. aisle wants whitewashing – and NW. end also. **Walls:** Stone, upright. **Floor:** Brick and flat stones, generally even, except in N. aisle. **Windows:** Two more casements wanted. **Doors:** Want painting outside. **Pulpit and Desk:** Good and well placed – crimson velvet cushion. **Books:** Bible defective in some parts, Clerk's prayer book out of repair. **Seats:** Oak – uniform – brick floors – some of them out of repair. **Galleries:** None. **Organ:** ——. **Font:** Near the W. end – a basin wanted. **Chapels:** None. **Benefaction Tables:** None – ordered. **Vestry:** There is one – but no place for surplice etc. **Surplices:** Two – good. **Linen:** Provided. **Plate:** Flagon – Cup, two patens. **Iron Chest for Register:** At the Rectory. **Register:** From 1558 to present time, complete, and in good preservation. **Porch:** None. **Vaults:** None recently. **Cleanliness:** Attended to, except the Windows. **Damp:** Much on the N. wall.
CHANCEL: **Table:** Oak – firm; but wants cleaning. **Ornaments:** None. **Repaired by whom:** The Rector – the window wants repair.
STEEPLE: A square stone tower, with modern coping. **State of:** Good. **Bells:** Five – good, but no weatherboards – some of the windows stopped up with bricks. **Clock:** None.
CHURCHYARD: **Fence:** Kept by the Parish – wants repair on the N. and W. **Gates:** One wants repair.

Drains: None – nor spouts. **Graves:** Too near [the walls]. **Rubbish:** Trees, Ivy etc on and near the Walls. **Footpaths:** Properly kept. **Cattle:** Sheep.
DIVINE SERVICE: **On Sundays:** Full service morning – prayers afternoon. **Sacrament:** Five times a year. **Communicants:** 20. **Catechism:** In Lent.
INCUMBENT: **Name and Residence:** Revd TS Bright, the Rectory.[2] **What Duty he performs:** The whole.
PARSONAGE: Brick house, partly re-built by the present Rector; three good sitting rooms and kitchen[3] on ground floor, six Bedrooms and Attics above. **State of:** Very good.[4] **Outbuildings:** Barn – two Stables – Coach-house, built by present Rector.
INCOME: **Gross Value:** ——.[5] **Tithes:** ——. **Glebe:** 44 acres. **Easter Dues and small Payments:** Collected.
SCHOOLS: **Endowed School:** A small one. **Subscription Day School:** None. **Sunday School:** None.
POPULATION: Upwards of 700.[6]
PARISH CLERK: John Beetenson. **Appointed by:** The Rector. **Salary:** £4 4s. 0d.
CHURCHWARDENS: Peter Whitmore, the other lately dead.
ORDERS MADE: ['In progress'.]
The walls and ceiling of the N. aisle to be whitewashed or coloured. The floor of the N. aisle laid even where needful. Two additional casements made, and all the casements kept open in dry weather. Bible, and Clerk's Prayer book repaired. Some of the Pew-floors repaired. A Basin for the Font. Benefaction Tables set up. Vestry properly fitted up. Windows kept clean – dampness remedied if possible. Commandments set up – Chancel windows repaired. Weather-boards put in the Tower – bricks removed from some of the windows – and others mended. Fence of Churchyard repaired where needful, and one of the Gates. Earth removed – open drains formed – spouts and pipes put up. Ivy and other trees removed from the walls – no graves allowed within six feet of walls.

Revisited 10.10.1837
Directions to the Churchwardens. (1) The roof of the Tower repaired – roof of Church examined and repaired – lead gutters cleared out. (2) Windows repaired and fresh *tied*. (3) Pews etc *oiled*. (4) Vestry walls coloured – window bars painted. (5) Benefaction table set up. (6) Decayed straw mats removed. (7) Churchyard gates painted. 'Qu? *done* ? or in progress. R.D. doubtful.'

Revisited 22.11.1841
New roof in progress – outward appearance to be improved.

[1] A note explains that this and the following three parishes were omitted from their proper place (after Ellenhall) and inserted in front of the entry for Ashley, the first parish in alphabetical order on the Stafford call. [2] Also prebendary in St David's cathedral. [3] A/V/1/3: 'offices'. [4] *Eccles. Revs.:* 'fit'. [5] *Eccles. Revs.:* £524. [6] *Eccles. Revs.:* 904.

HANFORD 17.6.1830 (A/V/1/2,no.85;/3,no.43)

BENEFICE: Hanford. **Nature:** Chapel of Ease to Trentham – intended to be a distinct Parish – already endowed with two acres of land by Marquis of Stafford – so as to be a Perpetual Curacy. **Ecton:** Not mentioned. **Patron:** The Marquis of Stafford.
CHURCH: A small; neat building – single body – some *imitation* of Gothic Architecture in windows etc built in 1827, cost £1,300. **Number it will contain:** 470. **Accommodation for Poor:** 350. **Roof:** Deal covered with tiles – lead gutters. **Walls:** Brick. **Floor:** Quarries – those of Pews and Benches [have] boarded floors. **Windows:** Good. **Doors:** ——. **Pulpit and Desk:** ——. **Books:** Good – but injured by damp. **Seats:** ——. **Galleries:** One at the W. end. **Organ:** None. **Font:** There is one. **Chapels:** None. **Benefaction Tables:** None. **Vestry:** None – one intended. **Surplices:** One – good. **Linen:** Good. **Plate:** Silver Cup and Paten. **Iron Chest for Register:** None. **Register:** Only those in present use, for baptisms and burials [– no marriages]. **Porch:** None. **Vaults:** One under the Communion Table. **Cleanliness:** Attended to. **Damp:** Much on the walls – not yet dry.[1]
CHANCEL: **Table:** Painted deal. **Ornaments:** Handsome covering to Table – commandments etc on neat wooden tablets. **Repaired by whom:** The Hamlet.
STEEPLE: Brick tower – with stone pinnacles. **State of:** Good. **Bells:** One – good. **Clock:** None.
CHURCHYARD: **Fence:** Incomplete, as yet. **Gates:** Putting up. **Drains:** None. **Graves:** None [too] near the Chapel. **Rubbish:** ——. **Footpaths:** ——. **Cattle:** ——.
DIVINE SERVICE: **On Sundays:** Morning and Evening – full service. **On other Days:** On Saints Days, and before the Sacrament. **Sacrament:** Six times a year. **Communicants:** 40. **Catechism:** In the School.
INCUMBENT: **Name and Residence:** Revd J Hutchinson. **If not resident:** At Blurton, in the Parish. **What Duty he performs:** Shares with his Curate.
CURATE: **Name and Residence:** Revd Jeremiah Bowen – in a house, near the Chapel, allowed by Marquis of Stafford. **Licensed:** He is. **Salary:** £60 – and the use of the house and land etc.[2] **If serving another church:** Assists at Blurton and Trentham.
PARSONAGE: None.[3]
INCOME: **Gross Value:** About 80.[4]
SCHOOLS: **Subscription Day School:** National School at Trentham. **Sunday School:** There is. **Lancaster School:** None.
DISSENTERS: **Dissenters' School:** ——. **Dissenting Chapels:** ——.
POPULATION: 600.
PARISH CLERK: Thomas Napper. **Appointed by:** The Minister. **Salary:** 52s. [per annum].
CHURCHWARDENS: Mr William Asbury.
ORDERS MADE: ['Done'.]
Casements to be regularly open in fine weather. Spouts and Pipes put up. Register Chest to be provided.

Revisited 25.9.1837
The outer doors to be painted – 'deferred'. The roofs and water-courses carefully examined, so as to ascertain and remove the causes of dampness in the walls and ceiling inside – 'examined but not done'.
The windows painted – and iron bars etc painted – 'deferred'. Iron Register Chest provided – 'not done'. 'Qu?'

Revisited 17.9.1841
The outer doors to be painted. Situation of Pulpit and Reading Desk changed. Pannels and floor of Pew in NE. corner, repaired. Water tables of windows enlarged.
[1] A/V/1/3: 'Much on the walls, which have never yet become thoroughly dry.' [2] *Eccles. Revs.:* £80. [3] *Eccles. Revs.:* 'None'. [4] *Eccles. Revs.:* £140.

HAUGHTON 15.10.1829 (A/V/1/2,no.73;/3,no.44)

BENEFICE: Haughton. **Nature:** Rectory. **Ecton:** Kings Books £9 11s. 3d. Eccl. de Gnosall 2s. 10d. – Mr Young and others Patrons. **Patron:** James Royds Esqr Mount Failings, Lancashire [by purchase]. **Impropriator:** None.
CHURCH: The body and Chancel a modern brick building, with circular windows on the S. side; those on the other seem to have formed part of the antient Church. **Number it will contain:** About 200 in pews.[1] **Accommodation for Poor:** One or two pews, and forms up the Middle aisle for the children. The present Rector is building a transept at his own expense. **Roof:** Oak covered with tiles – good repair. **Walls:** Brick – sound and good. **Floor:** Brick – in some places out of repair.[2] **Windows:** Good – three casements. **Doors:** Good. **Pulpit and Desk:** Handsome oak – well situated. **Books:** Not in good condition. **Seats:** In a very indifferent state, both pannels and floors. **Galleries:** One for the singers – entrance thro' the Belfry. **Organ:** None. **Font:** There is one. **Chapels:** None. **Benefaction Tables:** One – a benefaction not recorded said to have been lost; enquiry directed. **Vestry:** A small one – very incommodious – brick floor, uneven. **Surplices:** One – another wanted. **Linen:** Provided. **Plate:** Cup and Paten, given by the present Rector. **Chest for Papers:** There is one – but no papers in it. **Iron Chest for Register:** At the Rectory. **Register:** Three Vols, prior to 1813; oldest date 1711, regularly kept since that date; the former Registers supposed to be lost. **Porch:** None. **Vaults:** None. **Cleanliness:** Not sufficiently attended to. **Damp:** None observable. **Dimensions:** 45ft. by 21ft.
CHANCEL: 18ft. by 18ft. **Table:** Oak frame, marble slab. **Ornaments:** None. **Repaired by whom:** The Rector – who intends to lay a new floor, both within and without the rails, at his own expense.
STEEPLE: Square stone tower with minarets[3] – two of them broken off. **State of:** Very good. **Bells:** Five – good. **Clock:** There is one, out of repair.
CHURCHYARD: **Fence:** On the South side; next the street, a good brick wall recently built by the Parish – on the West, a hedge claimed by Mr Haughton of Birmingham,[4] but in a very bad state – on the E. rectory garden – on the N. no fence but that of a Cottage garden.[5] **Gates:** Pretty good. **Drains:** All round – made by the present

Rector, and a gravel walk, on a level with the floor of the Church. **Graves:** None near the walls. **Rubbish:** None. **Footpaths:** There are two, or three, which if possible should be stopped up – one leading from a School (built by the late Incumbent close to the Church) to a Privy in the Churchyard for the use of the Scholars – the state of the Churchyard generally is slovenly and unbecoming. **Cattle:** Sheep.

DIVINE SERVICE: **On Sundays:** Two full services – the second Sermon commenced by the present Rector. **On other Days:** On the Friday before the Sacrament. **Sacrament:** Six times a year. **Communicants:** 78 the last time. **Catechism:** During Lent [in the Church] – at other times in the School.

INCUMBENT: **Name and Residence:** Revd Charles S Royds – in the Parsonage. **What Duty he performs:** Half.

CURATE: **Name and Residence:** Revd George Norman – Stafford. **Licensed:** Not yet. **Salary:** £75 per annum.[6] **If serving another church:** None.

PARSONAGE: A good substantial brick building, roofed with slate – built by the late Rector. Three sitting rooms, butler's pantry etc[7] on the ground floor; two stories above with four bedrooms on each. **State of:** Very good.[8] **Outbuildings:** Small Coach-house, and two stables; not in good repair.

INCOME: **Gross Value:** About £420. **Tithes:** £300. **Glebe:** 78 acres. **Surplice Fees:** Very small. **Easter Dues and small Payments:** No Easter dues collected. **Queen Anne's Bounty:** None. **Terrier:** There is a Copy, in the Register Chest.

SCHOOLS: **Endowed School:** None. **Subscription Day School:** A small [day] school, on the National Plan, and a Dame's School. **Sunday School:** 68 children. **Lancaster School:** None.

DISSENTERS: **Dissenters' School:** ——. **Dissenting Chapels:** ——.

POPULATION: About 500.

MISCELLANEOUS: **Monuments:** One or two; one supposed to be that of the Founder. **Chandeliers, etc:** None. **Parochial Library:** ——.

PARISH CLERK: (Not learnt.)

CHURCHWARDENS: Mr Allen and Mr Hart.

ORDERS MADE: ['Nearly finished'.]
A new Bible to be provided, and the Clerk's Prayer-book rebound. A second surplice [provided]. Pannels of Pews strengthened and otherwise repaired; also the floors, and the floors of the Aisle in some places: (*boarded* floors to the Pews *recommended*). The Vestry-floor to be new laid, with boards, and a new fire place provided. The clock repaired; and also the Staircase leading to the Gallery, the Gallery Pews, and the Belfry-floor. The fence of the Churchyard to be kept in proper order by the parties respectively concerned – the true *boundary* on the N. side to be ascertained and *fixed* – the thoroughfare, if possible, to be diverted. Enquiry to be made concerning the Benefaction said to be lost. More attention paid to cleanliness and ventilation in the Church.

Revisited 8.9.1837
I Inside
(1) Casement made in window of South transept. (2) Iron bars of windows painted. (3) Windows kept clean. (4) Pews both of Nave and Gallery refixed and repaired. Doors and sides varnished and *hinges painted*. 'Chiefly done'.

N.B. I strongly recommend that the *brick* floors of the Pews be taken up and boarded floors put instead. The present floors are neither sufficiently comfortable nor decent. 'Complied with'.

II Outside
(1) Weather boards of tower replaced. (2) Sufficient fence placed along the N. boundary of the Churchyard. (A brick wall is the cheapest and most durable.) (3) Spouts and down pipes placed on both sides of the Church, and soil and herbage cleared away, and a clear space of three feet laid all round the walls. (4) Thoroughfare stopped by means of a footpath along W. and N. sides of Churchyard, or *outside* the *fence*. 'Not done. Drains laid.'

P.S. I strongly recommend an application to the Ordinary for a better arrangement of Pews (or sittings) so as to enable whole families to sit together — and provide for those at present unprovided — if the Rector and Churchwardens can fix upon such an arrangement, the Ordinary will *confirm* it.

[Orders of 1841[9]]
(1) Should the Rector not speedily execute his intention of putting in new windows, it is desirable to have *water tables* made for the present ones, and the bars painted. (2) The covering of the Communion Table should be renewed. (3) The roof of the Tower repaired; the lead flashings put in order; the gutters cleared out and the battlements secured. (4) The belfry *ceiled*, so as to keep out the cold from the Gallery. (5) The bells properly fitted for ringing. (6) An open space, of three or four feet round the walls of the Church, to be laid with flags, tiles, or gravel, so as to prevent the growth of grass, and other herbage close to the walls. (7) The gutters in the roof, formed by the *Transepts*, to be flashed with lead, as a preventive against the admission of wet – the pipes to be removed a few inches from the walls.

I must again repeat my earnest recommendation to have the thoroughfare of the Churchyard stopped, and a proper fence provided on the West and North sides. It is shamefully unprotected and trespassed upon at present.

[1] *Eccles. Revs.:* 300. [2] A/V/1/3: 'Brick – in some places uneven.' [3] A/V/1/3: 'pinnacles'. [4] A/V/1/3: '. . . on the W. a hedge belonging to the owner of the adjacent property . . .' [5] A/V/1/3: '. . . on the N. – no definite boundary, only cottages.' [6] *Eccles. Revs.:* £50. [7] A/V/1/3: 'three sitting rooms, offices, etc . . .' [8] *Eccles. Revs.:* 'fit'. [9] Loose sheet preserved in A/V/1/3.

INGESTRE 7.6.1830 (A/V/1/2,no.52;/3,no.45)

BENEFICE: Ingestre. **Nature:** Rectory. **Ecton:** Kings books £10 17s. 6d. 'Walter Chetwynd Esqr offered upon the altar the Tythes of Hopton as an addition to the Rectory.' **Patron:** Lord Talbot. **Impropriator:** None.

CHURCH: A Grecian building, erected by Walter Chetwynd, in 1676 – about 200 yards from the site of the antient Parish Church. **Number it will contain:** Upwards of 200.[1] **Accommodation for**

Poor: Sufficient. **Roof:** Oak, covered with lead – good repair. **Walls:** Solid stone – good repair. **Floor:** Flags. **Windows:** Good – eight casements, not sufficiently kept open. **Doors:** Oak – good. **Pulpit and Desk:** Handsome oak, well placed – velvet cushions. **Books:** Slight repairs wanted. **Seats:** Very neat, old oak, uniform, boarded floors. **Galleries:** None. **Organ:** There is one. **Font:** A handsome one, of white marble – a basin wanted. **Chapels:** None. **Benefaction Tables:** No benefactions, tho' some private charities at the option of present members of the family. **Vestry:** None. **Surplices:** Two – kept at the house; good. **Linen:** Provided, from the House. **Plate:** Two Dishes, a Paten and Cup; gilt; and a smaller Cup of silver. **Iron Chest for Register:** In the Chancel. **Register:** Not seen, owing to the Rectors absence from home. **Porch:** None, except at the W. entrance under the Tower. **Vaults:** None except that belonging to the Talbot family. **Cleanliness:** Attended to, except in the Belfry and Organ loft. **Damp:** Some occasioned by ivy on the North side. **Dimensions:** 65ft. by 42ft.
CHANCEL: (Included in the former.) **Table:** Handsome carved oak – crimson velvet ornaments. **Ornaments:** No commandments etc. **Repaired by whom:** The Patron for the Rector – all in very good state – handsome marble floor.
STEEPLE: Square stone Tower. **State of:** Very good. **Bells:** Six – good.
CHURCHYARD: **Fence:** Stone wall, kept up by Lord Talbot. **Gates:** One – of iron; handsome. **Drains:** None – nor spouts – both ordered. **Graves:** Not very near the walls. **Rubbish:** Ivy, weeds etc in abundance. **Footpaths:** None. **Cattle:** None – the grass is mown.
DIVINE SERVICE: **On Sundays:** Full morning service – afternoon prayers. **On other Days:** None. **Sacrament:** Four times a year. **Communicants:** Vary from 30 to 80. **Catechism:** In Lent.
INCUMBENT: **Name and Residence:** Hon. and Revd Arthur Talbot – in the Rectory.[2] **What Duty he performs:** The whole usually – occasional assistance from
CURATE: **Name and Residence:** Revd Mr Oldershaw, Curate of the adjoining Parish of Weston.
PARSONAGE: Not seen, owing to the Rectors absence.[3]
SCHOOLS: **Endowed School:** None – but the present Earl built a school in the adjoining Township of Salt, free for 40 children – others are allowed to attend, on payment to the Master. **Sunday School:** Those belonging to the free school attend. **Lancaster School:** None.
DISSENTERS: **Dissenters' School:** ——. **Dissenting Chapels:** ——.
POPULATION: About 200 – including the family at the House.
MISCELLANEOUS: **Monuments:** Several to the Talbot family.
PARISH CLERK: Thomas Hill. **Appointed by:** The Rector. **Salary:** Not known.
CHURCHWARDENS: Jeremiah Genders Junr. Eli Knight.
ORDERS MADE: ['Done.']
The casements to be kept regularly open, in dry weather. A basin provided for the Font. Spouts to be put up, and an open drain all round the Church. Ivy to be removed from the Walls; and the herbage in the Churchyard kept under; nettles etc cleared away.

Revisited 9.9.1837
Everything here in excellent order, except the *Ivy*, which is still doing some mischief.

[1] *Eccles. Revs.:* 140. [2] Also rector of Church Eaton. [3] Gross income given as £569 in *Eccles. Revs.* and the parsonage described as 'fit'.

ASHLEY 4.10.1830 (A/V/1/2,no.143;/3,no.46)

BENEFICE: Ashley. **Nature:** Rectory. **Ecton:** Kings Books £10 2s. 8½d. Patron. Lord Chetwynd two turns, Mr Meynell one turn. **Patron:** Hugh Meynell Esqr of Hoar Cross two turns – Thomas Kinnersly Esqr of Clough Hall one turn. **Impropriator:** None.
CHURCH: An antient building – Gothic style – nave and side aisles – pointed arches. **Number it will contain:** About 218 exclusive of the Gallery.[1] **Accommodation for Poor:** Not sufficient. **Roof:** Not very good. **Walls:** Stone – upright. **Floor:** Quarries – even, except near the S. door. **Windows:** Not in good condition – casements insufficient. **Doors:** Pretty good. **Pulpit and Desk:** Slight repair wanted in reading desk door. **Books:** New and handsome. **Seats:** Uniform – some repairs wanted – and *cleaning*. **Galleries:** One for the singers. **Organ:** None. **Font:** An antient one, projecting from the back part of one of the pillars near the W. end – with a Canopy above. **Chapels:** None – but an old mausoleum to the Gerard family, and a new one, now building, by Mr Kynnersley. **Benefaction Tables:** One – recording several benefactions in money which have been laid out in land, and the rents given to the poor on St Thomas day. **Vestry:** None – one recommended. **Surplices:** One – not properly kept. **Linen:** Much stained. **Plate:** Small silver Cup and paten. **Chest for Papers:** Provided. **Iron Chest for Register:** At the Rectory. **Register:** From 1551 in good preservation. **Porch:** One on the S. side – no outer gate. **Vaults:** None lately. **Cleanliness:** Not properly attended to. **Damp:** On the wall above the Pulpit.
CHANCEL: **Table:** A shelf projecting from the E. wall and supported by an iron frame – no cover. **Ornaments:** Commandments and figures of Moses and Aaron, cherubs' heads etc painted on wood – in very bad taste. **Repaired by whom:** The Rector – repairs much wanted and a general attention to neatness.
STEEPLE: Square stone tower, with battlements and pinnacles. **State of:** Not good. **Bells:** Three, good – but no weatherboards – a rope wanted to the small bell. **Clock:** There is one.
CHURCHYARD: **Fence:** Sunk fence all round, except on the N. side. **Gates:** Want painting. **Drains:** None – much earth accumulated against the walls. **Graves:** Many too near the walls – more room wanted. **Rubbish:** Much, owing [partly] to building of [the Kinnerslys] Mausoleum – weeds also and other deformities.[2] **Footpaths:** Not properly kept. **Cattle:** None.
DIVINE SERVICE: **On Sundays:** Two full services in

Summer – 1½ in winter.³ **On other Days:** None.
Sacrament: Three or four times a year.
Communicants: About 40 – increased of late.
Catechism: In Lent.
INCUMBENT: **Name and Residence:** Revd James Troughton Junr.⁴ **If not resident:** At Coventry. **What Duty he performs:** None.
CURATE: **Name and Residence:** Revd William Thickins. **If not resident:** In the Rectory. **Licensed:** He is. **Salary:** £120 and the house. **If serving another church:** None.
PARSONAGE: An old building, thatched roof, two sitting rooms, six bedrooms – offices. **State of:** Roof not very good.⁵ **Outbuildings:** Barn, Stable etc – the latter new – the barn intended to be re-built.
INCOME: **Gross Value:** £4 or 500 [per annum]. **Tithes:** Modus in lieu of Hay. **Glebe:** 30 acres.
SCHOOLS: **Endowed School:** None. **Subscription Day School:** A small number of children are taught free. **Sunday School:** 60 or 70 children. **Lancaster School:** None.
DISSENTERS: **Dissenters' School:** ——. **Dissenting Chapels:** Calvinist – Methodist – Roman Catholic.
POPULATION: 700 or 800.
MISCELLANEOUS: **Monuments:** To the late Thomas Kinnersly Esqr of Clough Hall – tablet to William Lord Viscount Chetwynd who died in 1770 – and a very large monument to the family of the Lord Gerard, Baron of Gerards Bromley, title now extinct.
PARISH CLERK: John Lightfoot. **Appointed by:** The Rector. **Salary:** None fixed.
CHURCHWARDENS: Mr John Dicken by the Rector. Mr Richard Steele by the Parish.
ORDERS MADE: ['In progress'.]
The roof to be made weather-proof over the Pulpit – the walls whitewashed – the floor laid even near the South door. An additional casement to be made on each side; and at the E. and W. ends [of the Church]. The lead work of windows repaired – iron bars painted – frames mended etc. New hinges on the door of the reading-desk – the pannels of the Pews fixed. A suitable basin provided for the Font, and cover for the Table.
A vestry *recommended*.
A new Surplice provided – the Surplices and Table linen better kept. A light gate put up at the Porch-entrance. The bricks removed from the East windows (of both Chancels) – the iron bars painted – the floor laid even and Communion rails fixed. The Battlements of Meynells Chancel secured – those of the Tower and Body of Church ditto. The tower pointed – weather-boards put up – bricks removed from the windows – rope attached to small bell. The Gates painted and locked – earth removed from near the walls – [down] pipes affixed to convey wet from roof to *ground*. The Buttresses on the N. side pointed and otherwise repaired. Weeds etc removed. No graves within 10 feet.

Revisited 9.10.1837
Much improved – except the roofs of the *Chancels* – which are out of repair. *Walls* pointed in some places – pinnacles on SW. secured. Roof of porch repaired – and lock on door. Floors of a few pews on N. side repaired. 'Not done.' One of the weatherboards refixed. 'Not done.' An Iron Register Chest provided. 'Not done.' 'Mem. Par. Clerk.⁶ Roof and gutters done.'

Revisited 13.10.1841
Directions etc. (1) Bible and Prayer book in reading desk, and *Clerk's* Prayer Book, to be repaired and re-bound. (2) Pews well cleaned, and rubbed with boiled linseed oil. (3) Roof of Tower thoroughly repaired – battlements and parapet secured – gutters cleared out and *kept* clear – lead flashings re-placed, door placed at entrance of roof, and a proper ladder inside. (4) Roof of Church examined and repaired, especially on North side. (5) Battlements, copings, parapets of *Chancel*, examined and secured; gutters kept clear, lead flashings etc replaced. (6) Walk laid all round Church and Chancels. (7) Wet from Roof brought to ground by *down pipes* – no tombstones within six feet of walls of Church. (8) Communion plate and Registers kept at Parsonage – free from damp. (9) Window on West side of 'Meynell's Chancel' re-opened and restored.

[1] *Eccles. Revs.:* 300. [2] A/V/1/3: '. . . the whole Churchyard ill-kept.' [3] A/V/1/3: '. . . prayers only afternoon in winter.' [4] Also perpetual curate of Wyken (Coventry) and of the donative of Binley (Warwicks). [5] *Eccles. Revs.:* 'fit'. [6] This probably refers to the parish clerk's having no fixed salary.

AUDLEY 5.10.1830 (A/V/1/2,no.135;/3,no.47)

BENEFICE: Audley. **Nature:** Vicarage. **Ecton:** Capella de Bettley 15s. Abb. Hilton Propr. Clear value £42 0s. 0d. **Patron:** G Tollett Esqr. **Impropriator:** ——.
CHURCH: A remarkably handsome antient building – Gothic architecture; nave, side-aisles and Chancel – pointed Arches – ceiling now flat¹ – the South side altered 50 years ago. **Number it will contain:** 7 or 800.² **Accommodation for Poor:** Pews, and benches for children – sufficient. **Roof:** Oak covered with slate and tile – the side aisles with lead – in good repair. **Walls:** Solid stone – upright. **Floor:** Quarries – and grave-stones. **Windows:** Not very good – more casements wanted. **Doors:** Pretty good – the South door wants repair and painting. **Pulpit and Desk:** Good and well placed – moreen cushion to pulpit. **Books:** Good, except the Clerk's Prayer Book. **Seats:** Very handsome – put up 38 years ago. **Galleries:** One at the W. end, belonging to Sir Thomas Boughey, but *rented* by the Parish – not in good state. **Organ:** There is one. **Font:** An antient one. **Chapels:** None. **Benefaction Tables:** Several – all the benefactions preserved. **Vestry:** One in progress. **Surplices:** Two – good. **Linen:** Provided – good. **Plate:** Two handsome silver Cups and Patens. **Iron Chest for Register:** At the Vicarage. **Register:** From *1538* to the present time – in good preservation. **Porch:** None. **Vaults:** None lately. **Cleanliness:** Attended to. **Damp:** On the floor and lower parts of the walls.
CHANCEL: **Table:** Pretty good – a new Cloth Covering. **Ornaments:** Monuments to E Vernon Esqr and others – niches in the walls. **Repaired by**

whom: Mr Tollett – (the Impropriator) not in good state either inside or out.
STEEPLE: An old square stone Tower. **State of:** Not very good. **Bells:** Six – good. **Clock:** There is one.
CHURCHYARD: Fence: Bad on the South side – the Churchyard is about to be enlarged on that side. **Gates:** Good. **Drains:** None – nor spouts. **Graves:** Many too near the walls. **Rubbish:** None, except from present building of Vestry etc. **Footpaths:** Well attended to. **Cattle:** None.
DIVINE SERVICE: On Sundays: Two full services. **On other Days:** None. **Sacrament:** Five times a year. **Communicants:** 30 to 40. **Catechism:** Not lately.
INCUMBENT: Name and Residence: Revd W Hickin – Vicarage. **What Duty he performs:** None – from age and infirmity.
CURATE: Name and Residence: Revd Thomas Garratt (who is to be the next incumbent).[3] **If not resident:** In the Parish. **Licensed:** He is. **If serving another church:** None.
PARSONAGE: An old building – lath and plaister walls – thatched roof: four rooms below, the same number above. **State of:** Good.[4] **Outbuildings:** Two barns – coach-house, etc good.
INCOME: Gross Value: Not ascertained.[5] **Glebe:** 40 acres. **Easter Dues and small payments:**[6] Collected. **Terrier:** There is one – dated 1786.
SCHOOLS: Endowed School: [There is one – income] £150 a year – free to all the Parish. **Subscription Day School:** None at present – a national school intended; Sir T Boughey has given land for the purpose. **Sunday School:** A small one. **Lancaster School:** None.
DISSENTERS: Dissenters' School: Methodist. **Dissenting Chapels:** Methodist.
POPULATION: Of the *whole* Parish 3,000 – of Audley itself 2,000.
MISCELLANEOUS: Monuments: Several antient ones.
PARISH CLERK: Thomas Wareham. **Appointed by:** The Vicar. **Salary:** £5 0s. 0d. per annum.
CHURCHWARDENS: Mr Daniel Eardley for the Vicar. Mr William Wilson for the Parish.
ORDERS MADE: ['In progress'.]
The lead work of the windows to be repaired; iron bars painted; two more casements on each side, and one at the W. end. The South door to be repaired and painted. The walls [whitewashed or] neatly coloured and ceiling whitewashed. A new Prayer book for the Clerk – the Gallery put in repair. The roof of the *Tower* mended – walls pointed – bricks removed from the windows, bush from the wall – the water carried off by a *pipe* [or down spout] to *the ground*. The roofs of *the Church* to be spouted – and pipes put up. The earth lowered all round – and an open drain (or surf) made. The walls pointed and under built.
In the *Chancel*
The old windows to be restored and the mullions repaired – the walls coloured and ceiling whitewashed. The Buttresses repaired – walls pointed etc ground lowered. The removal of *the screen* (a *modern* one, which greatly disfigures the entrance into the Chancel) *recommended*.
[October 1830.] (I wrote to Mr Tollett, from Eccleshall, begging his attention to the above particulars – and also to [others respecting] Talk Chapel) [(vid p.33. Vol.2)].

Revisited 19.9.1837
Found the state of the Church and Chancel still *very* unsatisfactory – especially the *Chancel* – Directions given to the Churchwardens – (those relating to the Chancel to be communicated to Mr Tollett or his agent).

I   *Chancel*
Roof to be examined and repaired before winter – (down-pipes *recommended* instead of overshot spouts) – ground lowered and open drain, or gravel walk, formed all round the walls – buttresses and walls pointed – mullions of windows repaired and parts blocked up restored. *Walls (inside)* re-plaistered and repaired – windows mended and new-leaded; bars painted; water-tables or lead-flashings made. *Brick floors* re-laid; (*boarded floors recommended*) and rotten mats taken away. *Walls (when dry)* coloured (grey), and ceilings whitewashed.

II   *Church – inside*
Walls coloured; ceilings washed; brick-floors re-laid (or *boarded*). Two *casements* on each side; windows and doors opened in fine weather. Iron bars of windows painted – gallery benches repaired.

Church – outside
Roof examined and repaired; buttresses and walls pointed – gutters cleared out and raised where needful. Ground lowered, and walk, or open drain, formed, as directed for the Chancel.

Revisited 16.9.1841
Directions to Churchwardens –

I   In the *Chancel*
Window bars painted. Water-tables formed on window sills to carry off the wet *outside*. Window frames painted externally. Pews repaired, and well rubbed with boiled linseed oil.
Recommended – that the pews be provided with *boarded* floors instead of *brick*.

2   In the body of the Church, *internally*
Old Font restored, and sponge provided to take up the water after baptisms. Window bars painted, where needful.

3   *Externally*
Roof of Tower examined and repaired. Pinnacles pointed with mortar or cement. Ridge tiles flashed – lead gutters laid even. Door leading on Roof mended. *Walls of Tower* pointed throughout, with Barrow lime. Walls and buttresses of Church pointed, where needful, and decayed stones made good. Roofs of Church looked over, tiling repaired in places. *Chancel* buttresses need much repair – South and East windows re-opened and restored.

[1] A/V/1/3: 'Ceiling underdrawn.' [2] *Eccles. Revs.:* 950. [3] *Eccles. Revs.:* £75 curate's stipend. [4] Eccles. Revs.: 'fit'. [5] *Eccles. Revs.:* £177. [6] 'And small Payments' enclosed in brackets.

BARLASTON 14.6.1830
(A/V/1/3, p.48; A/V/1/2, p.75)

BENEFICE: Barlaston. **Nature:** Perpetual Curacy. **Ecton:** Pri: Trentham Propr. £9 clear value. **Patron:** The Marquis of Stafford. **Impropriator:** The Marquis of Stafford.

CHURCH: A small neat edifice – rebuilt in 1762; single body, pointed Arches and Windows etc. The tower *old*. **Number it will contain:** About 190[1] (including the private and singing Gallery). **Accommodation for Poor:** Only one pew, and benches for the children *within Communion rails*; very insufficient for the Population. Five in all. **Roof:** Oak covered with tile – wants examining.[2] **Walls:** Brick – good. **Floor:** Quarries; even. **Windows:** Good – well provided with casements. **Doors:** Good. **Pulpit and Desk:** Good – the cushion of cloth – wants new covering. **Books:** Prayer book bad. **Seats:** Neat and uniform; in good repair. **Galleries:** One (a private Pew), and one for the singers. **Organ:** None. **Font:** Provided. **Chapels:** None. **Benefaction Tables:** Two. **Vestry:** None. **Surplices:** Two – good. **Linen:** Table Cloth and napkin. **Plate:** Two Pewter flagons (not used) and plate-silver Cup. **Iron Chest for Register:** In the Singers Gallery. **Register:** Three Vols prior to 1813 – in good preservation. **Porch:** None. **Vaults:** None recently. **Cleanliness:** Pretty well [attended to]. **Damp:** Much on the floor. **Dimensions:** 45ft. by 20ft.

CHANCEL: Old (original) square Tower. **State of:** Good. **Bells:** Three – good. **Clock:** Good.

CHURCHYARD: **Fence:** Partially removed, adjoining the pleasure grounds of Ralph Adderley Esqr, who has placed *stones* to mark the boundary. **Gates:** One – not very suitable, but substantial. **Drains:** There is one – but not kept in order. **Graves:** Not too near. **Rubbish:** None. **Footpaths:** ——. **Cattle:** None – the grass mowed and given away.

DIVINE SERVICE: **On Sundays:** Full service morning – prayers afternoon. **On other Days:** None. **Sacrament:** Four times a year. **Communicants:** 20.

INCUMBENT: **Name and Residence:** Revd Benjamin Adams, in the Parish. **What Duty he performs:** The whole.

PARSONAGE: A small, poor cottage, altogether unfit for the Clergyman's residence; occupied by a Labourer. **State of:** Indifferent.[3] **Gross Value:** £150 or £160. **Tithes:** Of Hay. **Glebe:** 70 acres. **Easter Dues and small payments:** Collected. **Queen Anne's Bounty:** The Glebe (or part of it) supposed to have been purchased by means of a Grant.

SCHOOLS: **Endowed School:** £500, 3 Per Cents left by Mr Thomas Mills, 80 years ago, for instruction of 20 children. **Subscription Day School:** None. **Sunday School:** 40 or 50 children. **Lancaster School:** None.

DISSENTERS: **Dissenters' School:** ——. **Dissenting Chapels:** ——.

POPULATION: 500.

PARISH CLERK: George Benbow. **Appointed by:** The Minister. **Salary:** £10.

CHURCHWARDENS: Mr. John Aston.

ORDERS MADE: The roof to be examined and put in repair. A new Prayer-book provided. The Pewter flagons, for the Communion; repaired, and kept in use until better provided. The drain in the Churchyard cleared out. Casements to be kept open. The accommodation is very insufficient for the wants of the Parish – a North aisle might easily be added. I strongly recommended the Churchwarden and Mr Adderley to take immediate measures for having this effected. 12.4.1830 Mr Aston, the Churchwarden, called upon me, together with Mr Hamilton, the Architect, to state that the Parish had determined to add a North aisle to the Church, upon a plan of Mr Hamiltons – [by means of which] 81 additional pew sittings, 41 free ditto are to be obtained.[4] 14.2.1831. The proposed alteration not being satisfactory to the Society, a new arrangement has been made, by which 183 additional sittings will be obtained – viz 90 in Pews, 93 in Free sittings.

Revisited 25.9.1837
Directions to Churchwardens.
The Churchyard to be mapped and boundaries accurately marked, and map placed in the Parish Chest (signed by Mr Adderley, the Minister and Churchwardens). 'In progress – R.D.'
The vault on the S. side to be filled up with clay, so as to prevent the deposit of wet in it, which causes damp to the floor of the Church – an open drain or gravel walk to be formed round the walls. 'Done – R.D.'
The water courses of the tower and roofs cleared out and relaid (where needful) to carry off the wet; the spouts and pipes made to carry off the wet without overflowing – lead-flashings at the junction of the roof and tower – branches of trees near the tower lopped off. 'Done – R.D.' A new Prayer Book for Clerk's desk – altar-service book – West window repaired. 'Leading still defective – R.D.'

Revisited 17.9.1841
Directions to Churchwardens.
New Prayer Book provided. New Bell ropes. Roof of Church and Chancel examined – tiling and eaves mended – lead flashings secured – copings flashed. Lead flashings of Tower replaced and pointed; weatherboards placed at window of Clock Chamber – holes in window seat filled up.
N.B. Expenses of settling disputes between incumbent and Mr A cannot be charged upon Church rates.

[1] *Eccles. Revs.*: 373. [2] A/V/1/3: '. . . not in good state.' [3] *Eccles. Revs.*: 'Unfit.' [4] Faculty granted 10.9.1830 (B/C/2/1829–32, p.259) for the construction of a new north aisle and vestry. The Architect was GE Hamilton of Stone.

BETLEY 5.10.1831 (A/V/1/3, p.49; A/V/1/2, p.136)

BENEFICE: Betley. **Nature:** Perpetual Curacy. **Ecton:** Pri: Ronton Prop. – not certified. **Patron:** Mr Tollett – (Ecton. Mr Crew). **Impropriator:** Mr Tollett – (Ecton. Mr Crew).

CHURCH: An antient building (except the side aisles, which are modern) – centre and side aisles and Chancel. **Number it will contain:** About 300.[1] **Accommodation for Poor:** A pew at the W. end, and benches for children, not sufficient. **Roof:** Timber covered with tile. **Walls:** The old part stone – the side walls brick and timber. **Floor:** Quarries, pretty even. **Windows:** Good – casements sufficient. **Doors:** Not good. **Pulpit and Desk:** Good – handsome velvet cushion and hangings. **Books:** Not in good condition. **Seats:** Pretty good and uniform. **Galleries:** One at the W. end, and part of the N. and S. sides. **Organ:** None. **Font:** A small modern one, in the Chancel. **Chapels:** None. **Benefaction Table:** Several – all the benefactions preserved. **Vestry:** A small one, formed out of the Tower. **Surplices:** Two. **Linen:** Provided. **Plate:** Handsome silver flagon; cup and paten. **Iron Chest for Register:** Provided in the Chancel. **Register:** From *1538* to *1623* – in good preservation. **Porch:** None. **Vaults:** ——. **Cleanliness:** Attended to. **Damp:** No appearance.

CHANCEL: **Table:** Good – crimson velvet covering. **Ornaments:** An ancient screen at the entrance. **Repaired by whom:** Mr Tollett.

STEEPLE: Square stone tower – modern. **State of:** Appears good. **Bells:** Five – good; but weatherboards bad. **Clock:** One – much out of repair.

CHURCHYARD: **Fence:** Wants repair on the South side, where there are rails. **Gates:** Good. **Drains:** None – nor spouts – ground wants lowering. **Graves:** Some too near [the walls]. **Rubbish:** None. **Footpaths:** Properly attended to. **Cattle:** None.

DIVINE SERVICE: **On Sundays:** Two full services. **On other Days:** None – except in Passion week etc. **Sacrament:** Six times a year. **Communicants:** 40 to 50. **Catechism:** In Lent.

INCUMBENT: **Name and Residence:** Revd HV Turton – Parsonage. **What duty he performs:** The whole.

PARSONAGE: A new brick building – erected by the present Incumbent – commodious and well built. **State of:** Good.[2]

INCOME: **Gross Value:** About £150 – out to be £200. **Tithes:** Small tithes £35. **Glebe:** 60 acres – purchased by bounty money. **Easter Dues and small payments:** £6 a year paid from the Impropriation. **Queen Anne's Bounty:** See *Glebe*. **Terrier:** There is one, in the possession of the Minister.

SCHOOLS: **Endowed Schools:** There is one for instruction of 10 boys in English – endowment in land. **Subscription Day School:** A national school incorporated with the above – 70 boys and 60 girls. **Sunday School:** 70 or 80 in each school.

DISSENTERS: **Dissenters' School:** One. **Dissenting Chapels:** Methodist – one.

POPULATION: 935.

MISCELLANEOUS: **Monuments:** To the Egertons and Tolletts.

PARISH CLERK: – Cockbayne. **Appointed by:** The Clergyman. **Salary:** £15 – and £30 as schoolmaster.

CHURCHWARDENS: – Brayford for the Clergyman – Brassington for the Parish.

ORDERS MADE: ['Nearly finished'.]
A new door to be made on the South side [of the Church]. New Prayer Book for the Reading desk – Clerk's Prayer Book rebound – the *N.T.* of the Clergyman's Bible to be new. The Registers bound. The windows of the Chancel repaired – iron bars painted. The Chancel and side aisles spouted. The earth lowered outside the walls – no graves within 10 feet. The roof of the Tower, and weatherboards repaired. The rails on the South side of the Churchyard repaired.

Revisited September 1837
The state of the Fabric so insecure, and accommodation so insufficient that I strongly recommended *rebuilding* the body of the Church. Tower to be repaired – weatherboards ditto. Bible and Prayer Book to be new. Churchyard fence improved etc but *this* to be deferred till Church re-built, together with several other repairs and improvements needful in different parts of the Church. 'Re-building determined'.
In the following Spring I had the satisfaction of receiving information from Mr Turton, the Vicar, that it was determined to *re-build* the Church – which was confirmed also in the Report of the Rural Dean.[3]

Revisited 18.9.1841
I recommend that a sufficient number of Free sittings be reserved in front of the pulpit, for old and infirm people. If the Church be heated, care must be taken not to bring the flues near the oak pillars, or any woodwork.

[1] *Eccles. Revs.:* 500. [2] *Eccles. Revs.:* 'fit'. [3] Faculty granted 22.6.1841 (B/C/2/1841–6,pp.38–42) for the enlargement of the church on the N. and S. sides and for a new W. gallery. The architects were Scott and Moffatt.

BLYMHILL 10.6.1830
(A/V/1/3,p.50;A/V/1/2,p.67)

BENEFICE: Blymhill. **Nature:** Rectory. **Ecton:** Kings Books £13 1s. 7½d. **Patron:** Lord Bradford (Ecton. Lord Bradford *two turns.* Mr Manning *one*). **Impropriator:** None.

CHURCH: Neat Gothic building – windows modernized – nave and chancel – no side aisles. **Number it will contain:** About 300. **Accommodation for Poor:** 150 including children, some of whom sit on *flap* – benches, between the pews. **Roof:** Good. **Walls:** Stone – good state. **Floor:** Quarries – even. **Windows:** Good – two more casements wanted. **Doors:** Good. **Pulpit and Desk:** Well placed – handsome green velvet cushions. **Books:** Out of repair – new Bible and Prayer Book wanted. **Seats:** Oak pews uniform; some of the floors want repair. **Galleries:** One, at the W. end. **Organ:** There is. **Font:** ——. **Chapels:** None. **Benefaction Tables:** Three – all the charities recorded. **Vestry:** There is one. **Surplices:** Two – good. **Linen:** No napkin. **Plate:** Pewter flagon (not used) silver Cup and two Patens. **Iron Chest for Register:** In the Vestry wall. **Register:** Six Vols prior to 1813 – tolerably good [state] – some deficiencies from 1644 to 1662. **Porch:** None – except the entrances at the W. end. **Vaults:** None. **Cleanliness:** Not properly attended to. **Damp:** Much on the walls and floor – especially at the E. end. **Dimensions:** 45ft. 3in. by 30ft. 9in.

CHANCEL: 20ft. by 16ft. 7in. **Table:** Oak – wants cleaning. **Ornaments:** Table of Commandments etc – handsome wrought cloth covering to Table – and some monuments. **Repaired by whom:** The Rector.

STEEPLE: Square stone tower. **State of:** Good – but some of the windows stopped up with bricks.

43

Bells: Four – one cracked and wheel bad; all want looking over – the floor wants repair – and door above closing. **Clock:** There is one.
CHURCHYARD: **Fence:** A hedge – kept up by the Parish and Rector. **Gates:** Good. **Drains:** None, nor spouts. **Graves:** Many too near [the walls]. **Rubbish:** The Churchyard is sadly overrun by herbage[1] – and the Church walls surrounded with grass, Ivy etc. **Footpaths:** Properly kept; there is a thoroughfare, about to be stopped, if possible. **Cattle:** Sheep sometimes.
DIVINE SERVICE: **On Sundays:** Two full duties. **Sacrament:** Monthly. **Communicants:** Vary from 30 to 90. **Catechism:** In the School.
INCUMBENT: **Name and Residence:** Hon and Revd Henry Bridgman, in the Rectory. **What Duty he performs:** The whole at present [a Curate since (1831)].
CURATE: **Name and Residence:** None at present.
PARSONAGE: A handsome, spacious house, chiefly built by the present Rector, at considerable expense. **State of:** Good.[2] **Outbuildings:** Stable, Coach-house etc re-built by present Rector.
INCOME: **Gross Value:** (Not ascertained.)[3] **Glebe:** 60 acres. **Terrier:** There are several copies in the hands of the farmers – but the Rector deems them incorrect.
SCHOOLS: **Endowed School:** There is a small endowment, of £3 5s. 0d. per annum. **Subscription Day School:** A national school, built by the present rector – with which the children maintained by the endowment above-mentioned are incorporated. **Sunday School:** 60 or 70 children. **Lancaster School:** None.
POPULATION: 700.[4]
MISCELLANEOUS: **Monuments:** Several. **Parochial Library:** None.
PARISH CLERK: Benjamin Jones. **Appointed by:** The Rector. **Salary:** £5.
CHURCHWARDENS: Mr Wright and Mr Madden.
ORDERS MADE: ['Nearly done'.]
A new Bible and Prayer book to be provided for the Reading Desk. Two more casements made in the Windows; and all the casements kept open. The Pew-floors repaired where needful. A napkin provided [for the Communion]. Cleaning of the Church better attended to. Dampness remedied, if possible. Communion Table cleaned. Bricks removed from the windows of the Tower, and the stones of the Tower pointed. The cracked bell re-cast, and all the frames, wheels etc put into complete order – the floor of the Belfry mended, and trap-door closed. The earth, herbage etc cleared away round the walls – open drain made – herbage of Churchyard kept down – Ivy removed etc.[5] Spouts put up. No graves allowed near the Church walls.

Revisited 13.10.1837
Church and Churchyard generally in excellent order – much improved since my former visit. Lead gutters to be attended to – and flashings. Tiles in places, need repair. Roof of Tower needs repair.

Revisited 15.10.1841
Directions etc. (1) Gutters of Tower cleared, and parapets secured. (2) Bell Chamber cleaned – gudgeons of wheels oiled and *covered* – broken bell re-cast. (3) Walk round Church kept free from weeds – thoroughfare of Churchyard stopped.

[1] A/V/1/3: '... overgrown by nettles etc.' [2] *Eccles. Revs.:* 'Fit.' [3] *Eccles. Revs.:* £630. [4] *Eccles. Revs.:* 566. [5] A/V/1/3: 'Ivy removed, where injurious'.

BLURTON 14.6.1830
(A/V/1/3,p.51;A/V/1/2,p.76)

BENEFICE: Blurton. **Nature:** Perpetual Curacy (under Trentham) – intended to form a separate Parish. **Ecton:** £32 2s. 6d. clear value. **Patron:** Marquis of Stafford, and others, as Trustees. **Impropriator:** Supposed, Mr Heathcote of Longton.
CHURCH: A small irregular building, enlarged in 1822 by the Marquis of Stafford. **Number it will contain:** 400. **Accommodation for Poor:** Sufficient. **Roof:** Wants fresh tiling. **Walls:** Good. **Floor:** Bricks – (the floor of the new part, beneath the Benches, board). **Windows:** Good – ivy creeping in at the W. end. **Doors:** ——. **Pulpit and Desk:** ——. **Books:** ——. **Seats:** ——. **Galleries:** On two sides. **Organ:** None. **Font:** Provided. **Chapels:** None. **Benefaction Tables:** ——. **Vestry:** A small one. **Surplices:** One – bad. **Linen:** Provided. **Plate:** Cup – plate – paten. **Iron Chest for Register:** In the Vestry. **Register:** Not seen (the Curate being from home). **Porch:** None. **Vaults:** ——. **Cleanliness:** Attended to. **Damp:** Much on the walls.
CHANCEL: **Table:** Oak. **Repaired by whom:** Mr Heathcote of Longton – the roof wants repair.
STEEPLE: A small, very shabby, bell-tower. **State of:** Bad. **Bells:** One. **Clock:** None.
CHURCHYARD: **Fence:** Brick wall, good. **Gates:** Good. **Drains:** Want clearing out – and spouts to the roof. **Graves:** Not too near. **Rubbish:** None. **Footpaths:** ——. **Cattle:** None.
DIVINE SERVICE: **On Sundays:** Two full services. **Sacrament:** Four times a year – and occasionally at other times. **Communicants:** 40.
INCUMBENT: **Name and Residence:** Revd John Blunt.[1] **If not resident:** At Lilleshall in Shropshire.
CURATE: **Name and Residence:** Revd John Hutchinson, Parsonage. **Licensed:** He is. **Salary:** £55 and the house.[2] **If serving another church:** He is Curate of *the Parish,* and shares the duty of the Mother Church, and Hanford Chapel, with the Ministers of both.
PARSONAGE: A commodious house, in Cottage style – four rooms on ground floor, six bedrooms. **State of:** Good.[3] **Outbuildings:** A stable.
INCOME:[4]
SCHOOLS: **Endowed School:** None. **Subscription Day School:** An Evening school. **Sunday School:** 130 children. **Lancaster School:** None.
DISSENTERS: **Dissenters' School:** ——. **Dissenting Chapels:** ——.
POPULATION: 840.
CHURCHWARDENS: Mr John Swift acts as *Chapel-warden* to Blurton and Churchwarden to Trentham.
ORDERS MADE: 'Old Church Warden did not appear.' The Roofs, of Church and Chancel, to be repaired. A new Surplice provided. Spouts and

pipes put up. Drain cleared out. Ivy removed from the W. end of the Church. The casements to be kept open.

Revisited 25.9.1837
Directions. A new Prayer Book for reading desk and altar services for Table. Chancel pews and windows to be repaired. Recommended that Chancel be spouted, and down-pipes put up – open drain of flags or gravel. 'Not done.' Walls of Church and Chancel painted all round and lead flashing at junction of Tower with Church. 'In preparation.' Ivy checked. 'Not done.' 'Communion Cloth wanted.' 'Altar services.' 'Ivy.'

Revisited 17.9.1841
Directions to Churchwardens. (1) New Prayer Book for Reading Desk, Bible repaired. (2) Pews rubbed with linseed oil. (3) Window frames pointed externally, timbers and casements painted. (4) Gallery and staircase walls re-coloured. (5) West door repaired. (6) Spout on North side of Chancel repaired and painted. (7) Roof of Chancel examined and repaired – walls pointed at bottom.

[1] Also vicar of Lilleshall (Salop). [2] *Eccles. Revs.*: £80. [3] *Eccles. Revs.*: 'Fit.' [4] *Eccles. Revs.*: £189.

BRADLEY 30.7.1830
(A/V/1/3,p.52;A/V/1/2,p.72)

BENEFICE: Bradley or Bradeley (juxta Stafford. Ecton). **Nature:** Perpetual Curacy. **Ecton:** Coll. St. Tho. in Staff. Propr. £16 10s. 0d. Clear value. **Patron:** Lord Stafford – by purchase from the Anson family. **Impropriator:** Lord Anson has part of the Tithes – Dr Bright part.
CHURCH: An old Gothic Church with some remains of very handsome architecture – tall pillars and pointed Arches separating the nave from *the N. aisle* – no South aisle – the building much disfigured by modern alterations. **Number it will contain:** About 400.[1] **Accommodation for Poor:** Sufficient. **Roof:** Oak, covered with slate – formerly with lead, which was sold a few years ago; and a flat modern ceiling substituted for the former handsome open woodwork. **Walls:** Stone – pretty good. **Floor:** Bricks and flagstones;[2] very uneven. **Windows:** Indifferent – no casements. **Doors:** Not in good state. **Pulpit and Desk:** Want cleaning and repairs. **Books:** Out of repair.[3] **Seats:** Very bad and irregular – new pewing very much wanted. **Galleries:** One at the W. end. **Organ:** None. **Font:** There is an antient one, near the W. Door; not properly kept. **Chapels:** None. **Benefaction Tables:** Sufficient. **Vestry:** A small one at the E. end of the N. chancel, in bad condition. **Surplices:** Two – one of them new. **Linen:** Provided. **Plate:** Handsome silver Cup, Patin and Salver. **Iron Chest for Register:** Provided – at the Parsonage. **Register:** From *1538* to present time; the oldest Vol. mutilated. **Porch:** There is one – no gate – roof out of repair. **Vaults:** Many – but none very recent. **Cleanliness:** Much neglected. **Damp:** Much on the walls both of the Church and Chancel. **Table:** Oak – the top loose, the whole out of condition.
Ornaments: None. **Repaired by whom:** Lord Stafford.
STEEPLE: Square stone Tower. **State of:** The roof much out of repair. **Bells:** Five – in pretty good state. **Clock:** There is one.
CHURCHYARD: **Fence:** Partly a stone wall – partly posts and rails; formerly the whole was repaired in *doles*; most of the parishioners however have agreed to keep up the whole at the general expense. **Gates:** Much out of repair. **Drains:** None – nor spouts. **Graves:** Many too near the walls of the Church. **Rubbish:** Much; both in the Church and Churchyard. **Footpaths:** Many trespass paths, and a gate from a private house; which seems wholly unauthorised; the proper Church ways ill kept. **Cattle:** The Curate's horse.
DIVINE SERVICE: **On Sundays:** Full service morning – prayers afternoon. **On other Days:** None. **Sacrament:** Five times a year. **Communicants:** From 30 to 40. **Catechism:** In the School.
INCUMBENT: **Name and Residence:** Revd EC Wright.[4] **If not resident:** In Northamptonshire.
CURATE: **Name and Residence:** Revd Thomas Browne – in the School house near the Church. **Licensed:** He is. **Salary:**[5] **If serving another Church:** The neighbouring parish of Copnall (or Dunston).
PARSONAGE: Two small cottages, adjoining – now occupied by labourers – near the Church – thatched roofs.[6] **State of:** Indifferent. **Outbuildings:** A small shed.
INCOME: **Gross Value:** About £90 per annum. **Glebe:** Purchased by Queen Anne's Bounty (quantity not stated). **Easter Dues and small Payments:** £15 per annum from the great Tythes. **Terrier:** The Churchwarden has a Copy.
SCHOOLS: **Endowed Schools:** There is an old one, free to all the Parish – in two departments, one for boys the other for girls – endowment in land. **Subscription Day:** None. **Sunday School:** None at present. **Lancaster School:** None.
DISSENTERS: **Dissenting Chapels:** None – a Wesleyan meeting in private house.
POPULATION: Upwards of 500.[7]
PARISH CLERK: Thomas Johnson. **Appointed by:** The Clergyman. **Salary:** £6 per annum.
CHURCHWARDENS: Mr Sampson Byrd for the Minister, Mr John Ward for the Parish.
ORDERS MADE: ['In progress'.]
The floor to be taken up, and laid afresh, *hollow* – the earth beneath being first secured from further depression (I *recommended the raising* of the floor considerably higher, so as to be more nearly on a level with the Churchyard outside). Four casements to be made in the Nave of the Church – two in the Chancel – one in the Gallery. The doors, Pulpit steps, Reading desk, pannels and floors of Pews, to be put into complete repair – (*new pewing recommended*).

The roof of the Porch repaired and a light gate placed at the entrance. The books to be repaired and re-bound – the Font cleaned and a new Cover provided – the Table repaired and cleaned – the Vestry ceiling repaired and walls white-washed. The floor of the Chancel re-laid, the walls whitewashed, the windows repaired – the external walls pointed. Coals not to be kept in the Pew near the Vestry. The roof of the Tower repaired – lead gutters of Church roof cleaned out. The roofs to be spouted, proper drain[s] made round the walls – fence of Churchyard made good and sufficient where defective – trespass footpaths and private entrance stopped – Church ways properly kept – No graves allowed within ten feet of walls outside, nor any new ones inside the Church.

Revisited 11.10.1837
Great improvements have been made since my former visit. The Church has been new-pewed at an expense of £540. Directions to Church-wardens. Bible to be re-backed or otherwise renewed. Casement on S. side of Nave – ditto in Chancel. Basin for baptismal font. Windows on north side of Church fresh tied. Walls of Church and Vestry coloured – ceilings whitewashed. Roof of Tower repaired – lead gutters cleared out – weatherboards repaired. Broken bell re-cast – gudgeons oiled. Ground lowered on N. side – spouts and down-pipes. Chancel roof at gable, mended – roof spouted. Fence on E. side of Churchyard repaired. Rails of decayed monuments repaired. Down-pipes to roof. 'Not attended to'.

Revisited 5.10.1841
Directions etc. (1) Flags of Communion Floor laid afresh – mat, or decent carpet provided. (2) Window bars painted – Font cleaned and restored to use. (3) Door placed at entrance upon roof of Tower – tiling repaired – lead gutters and flashings attended to. (4) Broken spout on S. side of Church repaired – gutters kept clear, and mouths of down-pipes guarded by caps of lead or wire. (5) Walls and buttresses of Chancel pointed, ridge tiles pointed and gutters cleared – weatherboard of E. gable repaired and painted. (6) Chancel roof *spouted* at eaves on both sides – wet brought to ground by down-pipes. (7) Grass etc cleared away from walls – open space laid all round.

[1] *Eccles. Revs.*: 'Sufficient'. [2] A/V/1/3: 'flat stones'. [3] A/V/1/3: 'in bad condition'. [4] Also rector of Pisford (Northants). [5] *Eccles. Revs.*: £65. [6] *Eccles. Revs.*: 'unfit'. [7] *Eccles. Revs.*: 731.

CASTLE CHURCH 30.7.1830
(A/V/1/3,p.53;A/V/1/2,p.74)

BENEFICE: Castle Church. **Nature:** Perpetual Curacy. **Ecton:** £9 6s. 8d. clear value. **Patron:** The Lord Chancellor. **Impropriator:** None – the land tithe-free.[1]

CHURCH: A plain, modern building – rebuilt about 30 years ago, except the Tower – single body – no Chancel. **Number it will contain:** 150 in pews and about 20 in the Gallery.[2] **Accommodation for Poor:** All the sittings are in fact free, as not being claimed, except the Minister's pew. **Roof:** Timber covered with tiles – not in good state. **Walls:** Stone – cased with brick on the South side. **Floor:** Brick; and some gravestones – sunk in some places. **Windows:** Pretty good – casements provided but not sufficiently used. **Doors:** Good. **Pulpit and Desk:** The pulpit not well fixed – velvet cushion. **Books:** Out of repair. **Seats:** Good – but not sufficient in number. **Galleries:** One at the W. end, which might easily be enlarged. **Organ:** None. **Font:** None. **Benefaction Tables:** Two – which record all the Charities. **Vestry:** A small one. **Surplices:** One. **Linen:** Provided. **Plate:** A Chalice and Patin. **Iron Chest for Register:** At the Clergyman's house. **Register:** From 1567. **Porch:** None. **Vaults:** Several brick graves – the floor much injured by them. **Cleanliness:** Not well attended to. **Damp:** On the walls – which are much discoloured.

CHANCEL: **Table:** Oak – firm; but uncovered. **Ornaments:** None. **Repaired by whom:** The Parish – but not in good repair; some of the windows have been blocked up – the walls very dirty.

STEEPLE: Old Square stone tower. **State of:** Not good – battlements want securing; the walls painting etc. **Bells:** Three – but only one of them in a state fit for use. **Clock:** None.

CHURCHYARD: **Fence:** Hedge all round – belonging to Lord Stafford, who claims the churchyard. **Gates:** Pretty good. **Drains:** Not sufficiently provided. **Graves:** Many too near, especially on the South side. **Rubbish:** A good deal behind the Tower – and the whole Churchyard in a slovenly state. **Footpaths:** There is one across the Churchyard, which may easily be carried thro' the adjoining field – the Churchwarden (who is Lord Stafford's Agent) promised to effect this alteration. **Cattle:** Sheep.

DIVINE SERVICE: **On Sundays:** Only in the afternoons – except on Sacrament days. **On other Days:** None. **Sacrament:** Four or five times a year. **Communicants:** From 20 to 30. **Catechism:** Not in the Church.

INCUMBENT: **Name and Residence:** Revd Robert Anlezark – in the Parish.[3] **What Duty he performs:** The whole.

PARSONAGE: None.[4]

INCOME: **Gross Value:** About £120. **Glebe:** About 34 acres. **Easter Dues and small Payments:** £5 5s. 0d. paid by the Crown; and a portion of an estate at Cannock. **Queen Anne's Bounty:** £500 – of which the interest is received. **Terrier:** None.

SCHOOLS: **Endowed School:** None – but the land on which the National School room is built belongs to the parish. **Subscription Day School:** A national school. **Sunday School:** About 35 girls – 32 boys. **Lancaster School:** None.

DISSENTERS: **Dissenters' School:** A Roman Catholic School, close to Stafford. **Dissenting Chapels:** A private Wesleyan Meeting.

POPULATION: Upwards of 1,400.[5]

PARISH CLERK: William Wynne. **Appointed by:** The Minister. **Salary:** £6 and Easter dues.

CHURCHWARDENS: Mr P Seckerson – by the Minister.

ORDERS MADE: 'In progress'.
The roof to be examined and repaired – the walls, inside, whitewashed or neatly coloured – cleanliness, in general better attended to, and the casements properly opened.

The pannels of the Pulpit re-fixed, and the books in the Reading Desk repaired. A Font to be provided; and a [proper] covering for the Table. No earth-graves to be allowed within the Church.

The Gallery (recommended) to be enlarged and a separate entrance made into the Belfry.

The roof of the Tower to be repaired – the

cracked bells re-cast, the weatherboards and timbers made good – bricks removed from the windows – the battlements'secured – stones pointed – bush removed from the N. side etc.

The windows of the Chancel restored which have been blocked up. The earth to be removed round the walls of the Church, and an open drain formed – the spouts re-fixed and repaired – the East end of the Church secured and repaired – rubbish removed from the Churchyard, and the footpath (if practicable) stopped.

Revisited 8.9.1837
I Inside
(1) Window on N. side of Chancel, which has been blocked up, to be reopened. (2) A suitable *basin* provided for the baptismal font. (3) Books in reading desk repaired. (4) Pews varnished and floors repaired. (5) Windows cleaned and repaired and bars painted – especially in Belfry.

II Outside
(1) Doors varnished or painted oak. (2) Bricks removed from window of W. side of the Tower – and window restored. (3) Lower part of Tower fresh pointed. (4) Buttresses on N. side of Church repaired. (5) Privy on NE. side of Churchyard taken away. (6) Hedges trimmed, grass and weeds cleared away round the walls of the Church. Lock put upon Lich Gates.

[1841 Orders[6]]
The Churchwardens are requested – (1) To have the Baptismal Font lined, with lead, so as to admit of pouring water into it when used for baptisms. (2) To have the Communion Table cleaned, and well rubbed with boiled linseed oil. (3) To have the floors of the Clerk's seat and some others which are decayed, or sunk, repaired, and also the rail on the North side of the Gallery. (4) To have the roof of the Tower re-tiled, the gutters kept clear of weeds etc; and the small window in the chamber above the belfry, which is now bricked up, opened and protected by weatherboards. (5) To have the roof of the Church examined and repaired where needful; and the spouts attended to. (6) To have the open drain on the North side of the Church kept clear – the Churchyard fence kept in due order – and the gates painted.

N.B. No *heavy cattle* to be allowed in the Churchyard.

[1] *Eccles. Revs.:* Lord Stafford and others. [2] *Eccles. Revs.:* 250. [3] Also vicar of S. Chad, Stafford. [4] *Eccles. Revs.:* 'None'. [5] Corrected in pencil in A/V/1/2 to 'about 1363 – in 1821, 1118'. [6] Loose sheet preserved in A/V/1/3.

CHEBSEY 2.10.1830
(A/V/1/3,p.54;A/V/1/2,p.145)

BENEFICE: Chebsey (*Ecton Chebley* al. Shebley). **Nature:** Vicarage. **Ecton:** King's books £5 7s. 6d. **Patron:** Dean and Chapter of Lichfield, and the Bishop, alternately. **Impropriator:** Swinfin Jarvis Esqr – Darlaston near Stone.[1]

CHURCH: A neat, but irregular, building; the South aisle seems to have been added to the original structure – Circular pillars, pointed arches; windows of Nave square, of Chancel pointed.
Number it will contain: Upwards of 200.[2] **Accommodation for Poor:** Benches in the Chancel and [forms] for children. **Roof:** Oak covered with tiles – lately put into good repair. **Walls:** Stone – apparently out of the perpendicular on the S. side – to be examined. **Floor:** Handford quarries – recently laid afresh. **Windows:** Good – casements about to be made. **Doors:** Good. **Pulpit and Desk:** New and handsome – well placed – handsome crimson velvet cushions. **Books:** Bible wants repair. **Seats:** Newly varnished and neat – pretty uniform, floors good. **Galleries:** A small one at the West End, for singers. **Organ:** None. **Font:** Near the W. end – a suitable basin wanted. **Chapels:** None. **Benefaction:** None. **Vestry:** None. **Surplices:** One good – another wanted. **Linen:** Provided. **Plate:** Silver Cup and Patin. **Chest for Papers:** There is one. **Iron Chest for Register:** Within the Communion rails. **Register:** None exhibited older than 1754 – the old Vols said to be at Gnosall, in the possession of the Curate who lives there. **Porch:** There is one – but no gate to it. **Vaults:** None made later than 1818. **Cleanliness:** Attended to. **Damp:** No appearance.

CHANCEL: **Table:** Wants a covering. **Ornaments:** None. **Repaired by whom:** Mr Jarvis – the mullions of the windows want repairing – a casement also wanted, and the iron bars painting.

STEEPLE: Square stone Tower. **State of:** Good. **Bells:** Four – good. **Clock:** Good.

CHURCHYARD: **Fence:** Brick walls, and hedge; the latter not well kept. **Gates:** Good. **Drains:** None – nor spouts. **Graves:** Not too near. **Rubbish:** None. **Footpaths:** Several – and some private entrances and roads which ought not to be allowed.[3] **Cattle:** Cows – [forbidden].

DIVINE SERVICE: **On Sundays:** Two full services. **On other Days:** None. **Sacrament:** Four or five times a year. **Communicants:** From 12 to 20. **Catechism:** Not in the Church.

INCUMBENT: **Name and Residence:** Revd H White – Lichfield.[4] **If not resident:** [Lichfield.] **What duty he performs:** None.

CURATE: **Name and Residence:** Revd Fearon Jenkinson. **If not resident:** At Gnosall. **Licensed:** He is. **Salary:** 60 guineas. **If serving another Church:** Gnosall.

PARSONAGE: A straggling brick building, occupied as a farm house – thatched roof, principally. **State of:** Much out of repair.[5] **Outbuildings:** Much out of repair.

INCOME: **Gross Value:** From £250 to £300. **Glebe:** 80 acres. **Easter dues and small payments:**[6] Collected. **Terrier:** None known of.

SCHOOLS: **Endowed School:** None. **Subscription Day School:** None. **Sunday School:** About 20 children. **Lancaster School:** None.

POPULATION: About 200.[7]

PARISH CLERK: William Picken. **Appointed by:** The Vicar. **Salary:** £2 7s. 6d. from rent of land, and perquisites.

CHURCHWARDENS: Mr Richard Aspley for the Vicar. Mr Marsh for the Parish.

ORDERS MADE: ['In progress'.]
The state of the South wall to be examined – the Church and Chancel to be spouted – iron bars of windows, and iron work of bells, painted.

The Bible to be repaired – a Benefaction Table set up, and a basin provided for the Font. A second Surplice to be provided and covering for the Communion Table – *all* the Registers to be kept in the Register Chest.

A Light gate to be put up at the Porch entrance.

A casement to be made in the Chancel window, and the mullions repaired. The weather-boards to be put in repair – the gutters of the Tower cleared out. A drain formed all round the Church. The hedges trimmed and kept in order – the private entrances into the Churchyard stopped,[8] and, if possible, the footpaths also. ['Qu? *Cow* in Churchyard. Paths stopped?']

Revisited 10.10.1837
Directions etc. (1) The *table* to be *repaired* or renewed. (2) A light gate at the entrance of the Porch and the roof of the porch repaired. (3) The *walls pointed,* at the bottom; and open spaces under the roofs filled up. (4) Eave spouts and down-pipes – *recommended.* 'Qu? *roofs* done? spouts?'.

Revisited 12.10.1841
Directions etc. (1) Water tables made inside windows – and iron bars painted – windows kept neat and clean. (2) Singing Gallery swept out weekly and kept neat.

N.B. I strongly recommend the removal of the Gallery – which is not *needful* in point of accommodation.

(3) Roof of Tower repaired, gutters kept clear, lead flashings kept in their places, and a door placed at top of staircase. As the weather-cock seems useless, the Pole had better be taken down, as the action of the winds injures the Tower. (4) Gravel walk or open drain laid with flags, bricks or tiles, to be formed all round the Church and Chancel, close to the walls, to keep them free from soil, grass etc. A Vestry ought to be provided – place for it, and plan, left to the judgment of the Rural Dean, with the Vicar and Churchwardens.

[1] *Eccles. Revs.:* 'Dean and Chapter of Lichfield'. [2] *Eccles. Revs.:* 'Sufficient'. [3] A/V/1/3: 'Several which ought not to be – private entrances and roads from adjoining cottages'. [4] Also sacrist of Lichfield cathedral, vicar of Dilhorne and perpetual curate of Pipe Ridware and S. Chad, Lichfield. [6] '*and small Payments*' enclosed in brackets. [5] *Eccles. Revs.:* 'Fit'. [7] *Eccles. Revs.:* 377. [8] A/V/1/3: 'The private entrance into the Churchyard, from the Clerk's premises, stopped'.

CHESWARDINE 8.10.1830
(A/V/1/3,p.55;A/V/1/2,p.147)

BENEFICE: Cheswardine. **Nature:** Vicarage. **Ecton:** Clear value £40 – Abb. Hagmond Propr. **Patron:** William Harding Esqr of Liverpool. **Impropriator:** Revd Mr Otter, Chetwynd ['Bishop of Chichester'].
CHURCH: An old building, Gothic structure – middle and side aisles – on S. side pointed arches; on N. circular – Chancel arch circular – ceiling of N. Chancel, handsome carved wood-work. **Number it will contain:** 420. **Accommodation for Poor:** 24 persons – [very] insufficient. **Roof:** Timber covered with tile – not very good. **Walls:** Stone [– good]. **Floor:** Flags and quarries; even. **Windows:** Pretty good – more casements wanted. **Doors:** Good. **Pulpit and Desk:** Neat and well placed – crimson velvet Cushion – faded. **Books:** Not good – a new Bible has been ordered. **Seats:** Good – new 20 years ago. **Galleries:** On W. and part of N. side. **Organ:** None. **Font:** A small modern one. **Chapels:** None. **Benefaction Tables:** Sufficient. **Vestry:** Under the Tower. **Surplices:** Good. **Linen:** Provided. **Plate:** Handsome silver flagon – two Cups and a Patin. **Iron Chest for Registers:** Provided. **Register:** From 1559 – in pretty good order. **Porch:** None. **Vaults:** None, except in the Chancel. **Cleanliness:** Attended to. **Damp:** No appearance except on the roof.
CHANCEL: **Table:** Good – handsome cover. **Ornaments:** None – except some rude paintings of Moses and Aaron etc. The commandments are put up. **Repaired by whom:** The Impropriator – roof wants examining. ['A second Chancel formerly belonging to Lord Shrewsbury – now to the Parish'.]
STEEPLE: Square stone Tower. **State of:** Roof wants repair – and pipes. **Bells:** Four – one broken – another cracked, weatherboards bad. **Clock:** Good.
CHURCHYARD: **Fence:** Bad, on the East side. **Gates:** Good. **Drains:** None. **Graves:** Not too near. **Rubbish:** None. **Footpaths:** Well kept. **Cattle:** Sheep.
DIVINE SERVICE: **On Sundays:** Two full services. **On other days:** None. **Sacrament:** Every two months. **Communicants:** 60. **Catechism:** In Lent.
INCUMBENT: **Name and Residence:** Revd JH Bromby.[1] **If not resident:** Near Hull. **What duty he performs:** None.
CURATE: **Name and Residence:** Revd C Miller. **If not resident:** In the Vicarage. **Licensed:** He is. **Salary:** £120 and the house. **If serving another Church:** [None.]
PARSONAGE: Brick house, covered with tile – the front built by the late Vicar – not [very] substantial. **State of:** Good.[2] **Outbuildings:** Tithe barn; stable etc – not very good.
INCOME: **Gross Value:** £250. **Glebe:** 30 acres. **Easter Dues and small Payments:**[3] Collected. **Queen Anne's Bounty:** None. **Terrier:** A copy from 1755.
SCHOOLS: **Endowed School:** £4 a year paid for educating four poor children from Tithes in the parish of High Ercall. **Subscription Day School:** None. **Sunday School:** 100 children. **Lancaster School:** None.
DISSENTERS: **Dissenting Chapels:** A meeting four miles from the Church.
POPULATION: 940 in 1821.[4]
PARISH CLERK: Charles Shaw. **Appointed by:** The Vicar. **Salary:** Paid by Easter dues.
CHURCHWARDENS: John Icke – Vicar. Thomas Bedston – Parish.
ORDERS MADE: ['In progress'.]
The roof of the Body of the Church, and of the Tower to be examined and repaired. Eave spouts, and down-pipes from the Tower [put up]. A casement to be made on the S. side of the Nave – and one on N. of Chancel. The Clerk's Prayer Book to be repaired. The Bells re-cast and weatherboards mended.

The Fence on the East end of Churchyard repaired – the ground kept clear on the N. side. The iron work around the Church[5] to be painted. More free seats and enlargement of Galleries recommended.

In the Chancel
The walls to be painted all round – buttresses ditto. The roof examined and repaired. Spouts and pipes put up. ['Qu? *Bells – Fences*'.]

N.B. The Churchwardens in their Articles of Enquiry (returned at my Visitation in 1831) state that there are *lands* left for the purpose of Church repairs – Qu?

Revisited 11.10.1837
(1) *Chancel* roof spouted; windows repaired and strengthened. (2) Bells re-cast – weatherboards repaired. (3) Roof of Tower repaired – gutters cleared out; pinnacles secured. 'Not done'. (4) Windows mended – iron-frames painted. (5) *Tower walls,* and *buttresses,* repaired and painted. (6) Spouts and gutters cleared out – drains kept clear. (7) Churchyard kept neat – nettles removed etc. (8) Ground, outside the Churchyard wall etc on N. side lowered. 'Qu?'

Revisited 22.11.1841
Directions etc. Battlements of Tower fresh cemented – roof of Chancel repaired and spouted – windows flashed – gallery pews oiled.

[1] *Eccles. Revs.*: Also vicar of Holy Trinity, Kingston-upon-Hull. [2] *Eccles. Revs.*: 'Fit'. [3] 'And small Payments' enclosed in brackets. [4] *Eccles. Revs.*: 1,065. [5] A/V/1/3: 'Iron bars of windows etc painted'.

CHURCH EATON 10.6.1830
(A/V/1/3,p.56;A/V/1/2,p.71)

BENEFICE: Church Eaton (Ecton. Ch. *Eyton*). **Nature:** Rectory. **Ecton:** King's Books £14 19s. 9½d. **Pens.** Abbatissae Polesworth £13 6s. 8d. **Patron:** Lord Talbot. **Impropriator:** None.
CHURCH: A large irregular building – (no South aisle) nave and *North* aisle, separated by pointed arches – the Chancel thrown open by a wide circular arch – the East window modern painted glass. **Number it will contain:** 250 in pews.[1] **Accommodation for Poor:** The sittings in the Gallery and one or two pews below – not sufficient. **Roof:** Oak covered with tiles – out of repair. **Walls:** Solid stone chiefly — not upright. **Floor:** Bricks – even but very damp. **Windows:** No casements – (ordered). **Doors:** Pretty good, but want painting – the porch gate wanting. **Pulpit and Desk:** Good – but awkwardly placed in the Chancel; before the Altar – a large wood pillar supporting a sounding board. **Books:** Clerk's prayer book wants re-binding. **Seats:** Uniform and good – oak – boarded floors. **Galleries:** One at the W. end – might easily be enlarged. **Organ:** None. **Font:** There is one – not kept clean – a basin wanted. **Chapels:** None. **Benefaction Tables:** Four – all the charities recorded, but some lost. **Vestry:** A small one – no closet for surplices etc. **Surplices:** Two – one bad. **Linen:** Provided. **Plate:** A Pewter flagon and Dish – silver Cup. **Iron Chest for Register:** At the Rectory. **Register:** Two Vols. from *1538* to 1813 – pretty complete. **Porch:** One at the South side – the gate wanting. **Vaults:** No recent ones. **Cleanliness:** Pretty well attended to. **Damp:** Much in the North aisle, and on the floors.
CHANCEL: **Table:** Oak – good – purple Cloth covering. **Ornaments:** None. **Repaired by whom:** The Rector – the children are allowed to sit within the Communion Rails.
STEEPLE: Square stone Tower, surmounted by an ornamented spire. **State of:** Good – but weatherboards wanting. **Bells:** Five – good. **Clock:** There is one.
CHURCHYARD: **Fence:** Sunk fence – stone wall and the end of an old Barn – the latter in bad state – and a privy adjoining, with entrance from the Churchyard, for use of the Scholars. **Drains:** A surf – not sufficient for keeping off damp – no spouts. **Graves:** Some too near. **Rubbish:** Not much. **Footpaths:** The boys from the free school go thro' the Churchyard. **Cattle:** The Curate's horse.
DIVINE SERVICE: **On Sundays:** Full service morning – prayers afternoon. **Sacrament:** Five times a year. **Communicants:** 70 to 80.
INCUMBENT: **Name and Residence:** Hon and Revd A Talbot.[2] **If not resident:** At Ingestre.
CURATE: **Name and Residence:** Revd William Bird, in the Rectory House. **Licensed:** He is. **Salary:** £100 and surplice fees – with house, orchard and garden. **If serving another Church:** None.
PARSONAGE: A brick building – *nine bays* – tiled roof – three storeys – comfortable parlours and entrance hall below. **State of:** Not very good – the new Rector means to repair.[3] **Outbuildings:** Barn, stables, Coach-house – all good. **Glebe:** 60 acres.[4] **Surplice Fees:** £3. **Terrier:** There are two copies.
SCHOOLS: **Endowed School:** A free grammar school, endowed with land from the Chetwynd family and others – £120 a year – free to all the boys in the Parish – from 20 to 50 attend. **Subscription Day School:** None. **Sunday School:** 30 boys – 40 or 50 girls. **Lancaster School:** None.
DISSENTERS: **Dissenters' School:** ——. **Dissenting Chapels:** ——.
POPULATION: 830.
PARISH CLERK: Robert Stevens. **Appointed by:** The Rector.
CHURCHWARDENS: Mr Crockett (Rector) and Mr Cotterill (Parish).
ORDERS MADE: ['Nearly complete'.]
The roofs to be stripped, and put into complete repair. Two casements to be made on each side of the Church. The doors to be painted outside, and the Porch gate restored. The Pulpit Cushion to have a new covering – and the Clerk's prayer book re-bound. A closet to be put up [for the Surplices etc] in the Vestry. Children not to [be allowed to] sit within the Communion rails. Weatherboards to be put up in the Spire. Spouting to be carried all round – [down] pipes affixed – and an open space laid all round the walls with tiles or bricks.[5] Additional sittings to be obtained in the Gallery for the children. The bricks removed from the outside of the Windows on the North side of the Chancel. Measures to be taken, if practicable, for preventing the trespass of the school boys upon the Churchyard – by

making an entrance into the School from *the road,* and removing the Privy[6] to another place, out of the Churchyard. Alteration of the position of the Pulpit and reading desk *recommended.*

Revisited 11.10.1837

Orders. Chancel door to be repaired or new. Proper basin for Baptismal font. Spouts and down-pipes. Windows cleaned and bars painted. Roof examined and repaired – ceiling repaired. Pulpit removed to S. side of Chancel. Oak pews etc rubbed with oil. Pannels of doors of pews examined and repaired. Gallery extended in front. Thoro'fare of Churchyard stopped. Better allotment of *Pews*. 'Apparently nothing done'.

Revisited 15.10.1841

Directions etc. (1) Water tables for windows – window bars cleaned and painted. (2) Prayer Book and Bible in Reading Desk repaired – Communion table and rails rubbed with boiled linseed oil. (3) Pews, Pulpit and Reading Desk cleaned and oiled – book boards repaired. Font kept clean and in use – North door repaired and oiled or painted – Wainscoting on S. side repaired. (4) Gutters of Tower cleared – parapet pointed – weatherboard replaced. (5) Dumb bell made to speak and replaced – wheels of bells repaired. (6) Eave spouts to roofs on both sides – down-pipes placed so as not to touch the wall. (7) Walls and buttresses on North side cleared and pointed. (8) Open drain or gravel walk formed all round the Church. (9) Tree near Church on South side removed. Blind provided for window behind pulpit.

Advisable to have the School removed from the Churchyard.

[1] *Eccles. Revs.:* 400. [2] Also Vicar of Ingestre. [3] *Eccles. Revs.:* 'Fit.' [4] *Eccles. Revs.:* Gross Income £1,078. [5] A/V/1/3: 'and an open drain made' instead of 'and an open . . . bricks'. [6] A/V/1/3: 'the *Nuisance*'.

COLTON 14.10.1829
(A/V/1/3,p.57;A/V/1/2,p.50)

BENEFICE: Colton. **Nature:** Rectory. **Ecton:** Kings books £5. **Patron:** A member of the Landor family. **Impropriator:** Mr Green of Lichfield has a moiety of the Tithes.

CHURCH: Formerly a Gothic building, divided into two aisles (as the Chancel still is) by pillars, and pointed arches. In 1799 the body of the Church being ruinous was taken down and rebuilt, in a plain, modern style – circular windows – [single body] – S. side brick wall, N. the old stone wall, partly cased with brick. **Number it will contain:** 300 besides children in the Chancel. **Accommodation for Poor:** 15 sittings, besides benches for children. **Roof:** Oak – covered with slates – in good repair. **Walls:** In good substantial repair. **Floor:** Brick – even, but very damp. **Windows:** In good repair – but open casements wanted. **Doors:** The S. door, leading into the Porch, should be cased.[1] **Pulpit and Desk:** Unpainted deal – wood suffering from the damp. **Books:** Pretty good; but suffering from damp. Clerk's Prayer Book wants re-binding. **Seats:** Those in the body pretty uniform, but the floors much out of repair. **Galleries:** One for the singers, at the W. end – erected by two individuals at their own expense.

Organ: None. **Font:** An old-fashioned one.[2] **Chapel:** None. **Benefaction Tables:** Two – which record all the Charities. **Vestry:** None. **Surplices:** One – [much] injured by damp. **Linen:** Table cloth and napkin – good. **Plate:** Silver Chalice, Cup, two Patens and a dish – very good; but kept improperly at the Clerk's. **Chest for Papers:** There is one. **Iron Chest for Register:** At the Rectory. **Register:** Stated (in the absence of the Rector) to consist of *one* vol. (earliest date 1682) besides those in present use. **Porch:** One on the S. side lately repaired. **Vaults:** None of recent date. **Cleanliness:** Attended to. **Damp:** Very much – owing to the low situation of the Church [– and the proximity of the brook]. **Dimensions:** About 93ft. long and 33ft. broad.

CHANCEL: Included in Dimensions above. **Table:** An old oak table, covered with a moth-eaten cloth. **Ornaments:** None. **Repaired by whom:** The S. Chancel by Mr Green: the N. by the Rector – but both Chancels are much out of repair and apparently very insecure.

STEEPLE: Square stone tower, belonging to the original Church. **State of:** Pretty good. **Bells:** Two – good. **Clock:** None.

CHURCHYARD: **Fence:** On three sides, hedge belonging to the Rector – the fourth wall side a wall kept up by the Parish – the Churchyard extremely wet, and much too small – might be enlarged on the S. side. **Gates:** Pretty good. **Drains:** None[3] – ordered – at three feet deep, the graves full of water. **Graves:** Several too near the walls. **Rubbish:** Several heaps. **Footpaths:** One from the new Parsonage to the stables etc belonging to the *old* Parsonage house.

DIVINE SERVICE: **On Sundays:** Morning – Prayers and sermon – Prayers afternoon. **On other days:** None. **Sacrament:** Six times a year. **Communicants:** From 12 to 15 or 20. **Catechism:** In Lent.

INCUMBENT: **Name and Residence:** Revd Charles Landor – in the Rectory. **What duty he performs:** The whole.

CURATE: **Name and Residence:** None.

PARSONAGE: (Not visited, the Rector's mother having just died) but stated to have been built by the present Rector in place of the former house, which was situated, very low and damp, on the W. side of the Churchyard.[4]

SCHOOLS: **Endowed School:** [Two –] One endowed with two houses and a small portion of land, another with 20 acres of land at Uttoxeter – the former seems to be used as a kind of preparatory school to the latter, which is taught by the Clerk. Lord Anson, Rector of Colton, Rector of Blithfield, three of the Trustees. **Subscription Day School:** No other. **Sunday School:** The children of the above schools – about 20. **Lancaster School:** None.

POPULATION: Upwards of 600.[5]

MISCELLANEOUS: **Monuments:** Several to the family of Mr Taylor, the former Rector. **Chandeliers, etc:** None.

PARISH CLERK: William Simpson. **Appointed by:** The Rector. **Salary:** The rent of land, left for his maintenance.

CHURCHWARDENS: Mr Thomas Hodgkinson, and Joseph Walkedon.

ORDERS MADE: 'Partly done'.

Additional casements to open – the [inner] door leading to the S. porch, cased on the inside (recommend putting a door with rails,[6] in the place of the outer door of the Porch, so as to admit of free ventilation by leaving the inner door open – the same on the N. side).

The floors of the Pews repaired. Pulpit and Desk painted, also the Pews. Clerks Prayer Book, re-bound – a second surplice provided. Communion plate, kept in a place of safety. A surface drain, made all round the Church; and spouts to the roof, weeds etc removed; and effectual measures adopted for draining off the wet from the Churchyard.[7] The Chancels to be carefully examined and repaired, inside and out.

Revisited 28.3.1838

Much improved since my former visit – *less* damp – cleanliness *better* attended to – pulpit and desk painted – new Gallery erected at the West end, and benches below for the poor.

More attention however still required to ventilation. I *again* urged having lattice gates put up at the North and South entrances, and also at the *Chancel* ditto. Pannels, doors and floors of *pews* repaired – old oak pews to be rubbed with linseed oil; and hinges painted. New covering for Communion table and suitable basin for baptismal font. Roof, pinnacles and battlements of *Tower* to be thoroughly repaired and secured.

Rector's Chancel in a very insecure state – especially the roof – too bad to admit of *substantial* repair – ridging tiles, buttresses and windows to be replaced and repaired – some slight repairs also in the Lay Rector's chancel.

[1] A/V/1/3: '... wants lining'. [2] A/V/1/3: 'An antient one'. [3] A/V/1/3: 'None – not easy to drain sufficiently...' [4] *Eccles. Revs.*: £461 gross revenue, glebe house 'fit'. [5] *Eccles. Revs.*: 765. [6] A/V/1/3: 'a light – gate'. [7] A/V/1/3: Instead of 'A surface ... Churchyard'; 'The most effectual measures which the situation of the Churchyard (which is *extremely low,* and close to the water) admits of it to be taken for draining off the wet from the Church and Churchyard.'

HILDERSTONE 28.9.1837 (A/V/1/3,p.58;(Not in A/V/1/2))

BENEFICE: Hilderstone. **Nature:** Chapel of Ease to Stone built under 1 and 2nd William 4 – for the *Manor of Hilderstone.* **Patron:** Ralph Bourne Esqr (deceased) who endowed it with £45 per annum.

CHURCH: A very elegant Gothic structure – with centre and side aisles – beautiful stained glass in E. window. **Number it will contain:** 540.[1] **Accommodation for Poor:** One third. **Roof:** Timber covered with slate – lead gutters and stone battlements. **Walls:** Stone. **Iron Chest for Register:** Not provided – the Parish Wardens having hitherto refused to grant any money. **Register:** Not provided.

ORDERS MADE: Ventilation to be attended to – *recommended* the introduction of some kind of warm air apparatus, to preserve the building from damp, of which there is at present some appearance.

The Chapel being new, no other directions appeared needful.

Revisited 27.9.1841

New Prayer Book for the Clerk. Wider trough for Water-tables. The copings of roof pointed all round – as also the mouldings and heads of the windows – the spouts kept clear. The oval stones at each end of the roof secured – flashings on S. side of Tower. Flagging all round the walls of Church.

[1] *Eccles. Revs.*: 420. This source gives the population as 800, the gross income as £70, and states that there was no glebe house.

ELLENHALL 8.10.1830
(A/V/1/3,p.59;A/V/1/2,p.146)

BENEFICE: Ellenhall. **Nature:** Perpetual Curacy – formerly attached to Ranton Abbey. **Ecton:** Clear value £4 13s. 4d. **Patron:** Lord Anson – formerly Sir Jonathan Cope, and Earl Aboyne. **Impropriator:** Ditto.

CHURCH: A small building, rebuilt in 1752 – single body, flat ceiling – Chancel arch very ugly. **Number it will contain:** 150 to 200.[1] **Accommodation for Poor:** The seats in the Gallery, and forms in the Chancel.[2] **Roof:** Oak covered with tile – good. **Walls:** Brick – firm. **Floor:** Quarries. **Windows:** Pretty good – but no casements provided. **Doors:** Good. **Pulpit and Desk:** Good – velvet Cushion, enmbroidered hangings. **Books:** Bible and Clerk's prayer book want repair. **Seats:** Good – but some of the floors and mats in bad order. **Galleries:** At the W. end. **Organ:** None. **Font:** A small one – modern. **Chapels:** None. **Benefaction Tables:** No benefactions. **Vestry:** None. **Surplices:** Two – good. **Linen:** Provided. **Plate:** Silver Cup and old patin – two pewter plates. **Iron Chest for Register:** Provided. **Register:** One old Vol. from *1539* bound up with more recent ones. **Porch:** None, except at the W. entrance – light gate wanted. **Vaults:** None. **Cleanliness:** Attended to. **Damp:** No appearance.

CHANCEL: **Table:** Wants repair – the rails ditto. **Ornaments:** None. **Repaired by whom:** Lord Anson – repairs much wanted.

STEEPLE: Square brick tower. **State of:** Windows bad. **Bells:** One. **Clock:** None.

CHURCHYARD: **Fence:** Wants repair on the East and South sides. **Gates:** Not in good condition. **Drains:** None, nor spouts. **Graves:** Not many too near. **Rubbish:** Weeds etc. **Footpaths:** There is a thoroughfare both for carts and foot passengers.[3] **Cattle:** Sheep.

DIVINE SERVICE: **On Sundays:** Morning and Afternoon alternately. **On other days:** None. **Sacrament:** Four times a year. **Communicants:** 12. **Catechism:** Not in the Church.

INCUMBENT: **Name and Residence:** Revd W Hickin. **If not resident:** At Audmore, three or four miles off. **What duty he performs:** The whole.

PARSONAGE: None.[4]

INCOME: **Gross Value:** £89 0s. 8d. [arising from] rent of land – and a rent charge (from the Tithes) of £5 0s. 8d. (the latter is perhaps included in the £89 0s. 8d.). **Glebe:** 69 acres. **Queen Anne's Bounty:** Supposed that the glebe was purchased by means of money from the Bounty. **Terrier:** There is one – from a Copy in 1765.

SCHOOLS: **Endowed School:** None. **Subscription Day**

School: None. **Sunday School:** 51 children. **Lancaster School:** None.
DISSENTERS: **Dissenters' School:** None. **Dissenting Chapels:** None.
POPULATION: 250.
MISCELLANEOUS: **Monuments:** None.
PARISH CLERK: Thomas Bagnall. **Salary:** £2 2s. 0d.
CHURCHWARDENS: Mr W Whittingham.
ORDERS MADE: ['Art. and suggestions not retd.']
Two casements to be made on the South side; one on the North – the [iron] bars of the windows painted. Light Gate to be put up at the W. entrance. The Bible and Clerk's Prayer Book to be repaired and re-bound. The floors and mats of the Pews (where needful) repaired and renewed. The windows of the Tower repaired – the roofs spouted – earth lowered round the walls. The fence made good (especially on the *East* side) – the Gates repaired and painted.

In the Chancel
The Table *and rails* to be repaired – door and window ditto – roof and wall examined and repaired – the walls pointed outside – the ground lowered – buttresses repaired – spouts and pipes put up.[5] A casement made in the East window.

Revisited 11.10.1837
(1) Floors of pews, repaired, where needful. 'Not done'. (2) A cover for the *Communion table.* (3) Floor of the Belfry repaired. (4) A lock on iron gate at West entrance.[6] (5) Fence of Churchyard made good and trimmed etc. (6) *Roof, door,* and *windows* of the Chancel repaired – and walls and ceiling whitewashed. 'Not entirely done'.

Revisited 22.11.1841
(1) Lead to be repaired at top of Tower – belfry floor repaired. (2) Fresh stays to Communion rails. (3) Soil removed – iron gate painted – Chancel spouted. (4) Church door, roof and floor, in a disgraceful state.

[1] *Eccles. Revs.:* 'Sufficient'. [2] 'Sufficient for the population' bracketed against 7 and 8. [3] A/V/1/3: '... carts and horses'. [4] *Eccles. Revs.:* 'None'. [5] A/V/1/3 has 'done' in pencil, referring to the Chancel works generally, the repair of the roof and walls or to the pointing of the wall. [6] 'Not done', in pencil, relating either to 3 or 4.

KEELE 7.10.1830 (A/V/1/3, p.60; A/V/1/2, p.138)

BENEFICE: Keele. **Nature:** Perpetual Curacy – formerly attached to Woolstanton. **Ecton:** Knights Templars Propr. Clear Value £24. **Patron:** Ralph Sneyd Esqr – (Ecton Mr Chetwynd). **Impropriator:** Ditto.
CHURCH: The body of the Church [re-]built 48 years ago, in modern style, single roof, by no means ecclesiastical – the Tower old. **Number it will contain:** About 400. **Accommodation for Poor:** Insufficient. **Roof:** Oak covered with slate. **Walls:** Stone – upright. **Floor:** Flags. **Windows:** Good – well provided with casements. **Doors:** Good. **Pulpit and Desk:** Not commodiously arranged – to be altered. **Books:** The Prayer book not good. **Seats:** Good and uniform. **Galleries:** One at the W. end. **Organ:** None. **Font:** There is one. **Chapels:** None. **Benefaction Tables:** None at present – an old one to be replaced. **Vestry:** None – one recommended. **Surplices:** Two – one of them bad. **Linen:** Provided. **Plate:** Silver flagon; Chalice and small Patin – a larger patin wanted. **Chest for Papers:** ——. **Iron Chest for Register:** There is one. **Register:** From 1540 – in good preservation. **Porch:** None. **Vaults:** None, except a family one belonging to the Sneyds. **Cleanliness:** Attended to. **Damp:** No appearance.
CHANCEL: **Table:** Not in good state. **Ornaments:** None – except monuments; no Commandments. **Repaired by whom:** Mr Sneyd.
STEEPLE: Square stone (Tower). **State of:** Wants pointing and weatherboards. **Bells:** Six – good. **Clock:** In good order.
CHURCHYARD: **Fence:** Wants repair – on South and East sides. **Gates:** Want painting and repairs. **Drains:** There is a surf – no pipes from the roof. **Graves:** None too near. **Rubbish:** None. **Footpath:** Well kept. **Cattle:** None.
DIVINE SERVICE: **On Sundays:** Two full services. **On other Days:** None. **Sacrament:** Six times a year. **Communicants:** From 60 to 70. **Catechism:** In Lent, at the Church – in the School at other times.
INCUMBENT: **Name and Residence:** Revd G Styche – near the Church. **If not resident:** ——. **What duty he performs:** The whole.
PARSONAGE: None – the present Incumbent lives in a house belonging to the Patron, but it is not appropriated as a Parsonage.[1] **State of:** Good.
INCOME: **Gross Value:** About £170 – paid by the Patron in one entire sum [in lieu of all dues etc]. **Tithes:** Vicarial Tythes paid. **Glebe:** Upwards of 20 acres – let for four guineas. **Easter Dues and small payments:** Collected.[2] **Terrier:** None.
SCHOOLS: **Endowed School:** The interest of £100 (5 per cent) was left by one of the Sneyds for the instruction of 12 girls – augmented by the present Mr Sneyd for education of 30. **Subscription Day School:** None else. **Sunday School:** About 130 children. **Lancaster School:** ——.
DISSENTERS: **Dissenters' School:** Sunday. **Dissenting Chapels:** Methodist.
POPULATION: 1,100 last Census.
PARISH CLERK: Joseph Cooper officiating as such at present. **Appointed by:** The Clergyman. **Salary:** £5.
CHURCHWARDENS: Mr Stubbs and Mr Booth.
ORDERS MADE: 'In progress'.
The Pulpit and reading-desk to be rendered more commodious. The approach to the Gallery altered – and a Vestry made.[3] A new Prayer Book for the Clerk – Benefaction Table set up – Commandments ditto.
  The Communion Table and rails to be repaired. The Tower pointed – weatherboards completed. [Down] pipes put up to carry off the wet from the roofs. A clear open space to be kept all round the Church. The fence to be put into complete repair all round.

Revisited 21.9.1837
Directions to Churchwardens. 'Done or to be done'. (1) A new prayer book for Clerk's desk. Ten Commandments. A Vestry recommended and a new access to the Gallery. (2) Battlements of roof of Church to be secured – roof itself examined and repaired – lead flashings secured and weatherboards repaired. Stone steps leading to Belfry repaired. Overshot spouts removed and

down-pipes substituted. Grass etc removed on North side – Water tub removed. Herbage kept under, and neatness in Churchyard generally. Old tombstones and rails repaired or removed. Gates and wall at West corner repaired – trespass paths stopped. Bricks and rubbish removed. 'April 1838. Reported by Rural Dean as done or in progress.'

Revisited 7.9.1841
    Directions to Churchwardens. Pews rubbed with boiled linseed oil. Steps of staircase landing to bell-chamber, repaired or renewed. Battlements and parapet of roof secured – slates and flashings at West end, secured.
    Roof of Tower examined and repaired – battlements fresh pointed – vane secured – mouths of spouts cleaned out. *Recommended* – making new approach to gallery, near North door.

[1] *Eccles. Revs.:* 'None.' [2] 'And small Payments' enclosed in brackets. [3] A/V/1/3: 'A Vestry *recommended* connected with the preceding alteration'.

LAPLEY 10.6.1830 (A/V/1/3,p.61;A/V/1/2,p.70)

BENEFICE: Lapley. **Nature:** Vicarage. **Ecton:** Clear yearly value £31 10s. 0d. College Tonge Propr. **Patron:** Mr Swinfen of Swinfen (Ecton, Sir Theophilus Biddulph). **Impropriator:** Ditto.
CHURCH: The remains of a [very] fine old Gothic Church, formerly belonging to the Priory of Lapley – but [now] much dilapidated and disfigured – the Transept destroyed – the interior sadly spoilt. **Number it will contain:** About 350.[1] **Accommodation for Poor:** Very insufficient. **Roof:** Now tolerably good – but the ceiling tumbled down last year. **Walls:** Stone – not upright. **Floor:** Quarries – even, but very damp. **Windows:** Only two casements – more [much] wanted, on the S. side. **Doors:** Want painting outside. **Pulpit and Desk:** Oak – pretty good – crimson moreen cushion. **Books:** In very bad condition. **Seats:** Oak – tolerably good. **Galleries:** One at the W. end, for singers and children – about 30 children may sit there. **Organ:** None. **Font:** None, at present; there is a large stone font [antient] lying in the Churchyard said to have been used by the former Vicar for feeding his calves. **Chapels:** None. **Benefaction Tables:** Several. **Vestry:** None. **Surplices:** Two – one very bad. **Iron Chest for Register:** None. **Register:** Four Vols from *1538* to 1813 – pretty complete – one vol. wants binding. **Porch:** None. **Vaults:** There are several *graves* in the Chancel. **Cleanliness:** Much neglected. **Damp:** A great deal. **Dimensions:** 78ft. 5in. by 26ft.
CHANCEL: 36ft. 5in. by 16ft. 3in. **Table:** Plain painted wood. **Ornaments:** None – the Ten Commandments are in the body of the Church. **Repaired by whom:** The Impropriator – the floor is much undermined by graves.
STEEPLE: A very large handsome square stone Tower. **State of:** Apparently very insecure at the Top. **Bells:** Five – one cracked – the small one wants a handle. **Clock:** There is one.
CHURCHYARD: **Fence:** A stone wall; much overgrown by trees etc – and a hedge which separates it from a garden at the E. end of the Church. The garden has evident marks of having been an encroachment. **Gates:** Pretty good. **Drains:** None, nor any spouts. **Graves:** Several, close to the walls of the Church. **Rubbish:** There is much [accumulation of] soil and herbage and bushes etc of all kinds close to, and upon, the walls – in fact the Church is almost *buried* – much Ivy on the walls – in one place, the buttress has been cut away to make room for a tomb-stone. **Cattle:** A poney.
DIVINE SERVICE: **On Sundays:** Morning service only. **On other days:** None. **Sacrament:** Three times a year. **Communicants:** Under 30.
INCUMBENT: **Name and Residence:** Revd Michael Ward, in the Vicarage house. **What duty he performs:** The whole.
CURATE: **Name and Residence:** None.
PARSONAGE: A small brick building – two sitting rooms, kitchen etc on ground floor – drawing room, and bedrooms above. **State of:** Now under repair.[2] **Outbuildings:** A Barn and stable.
INCOME: **Gross Value:** Under £130 per annum. **Glebe:** 23 acres. **Queen Anne's Bounty:** None – application for it recommended. **Terrier:** There is one.
SCHOOLS: None – except the one at Wheaton Aston, before mentioned. **Subscription Day School:** None. **Sunday School:** 33 children. **Lancaster School:** None.
DISSENTERS: **Dissenters' School:** At Wheaton Aston [in the Parish]. **Dissenting Chapels:** Ditto, and some Catholics (no Chapel).
POPULATION: About 120 in *Lapley itself*; the principal [part of the] population is at Wheaton Aston.[3]
PARISH CLERK: Benjamin Blakemore. **Appointed by:** The Vicar. **Salary:** £5 0s. 0d.
CHURCHWARDENS: Mr Grundy for Lapley. [Mr Smith for Wheaton Aston].
ORDERS MADE: 'Nothing done'.
    Two additional casements – new Bible and Prayer book for Reading desk – Clerk's Prayer book repaired – a new surplice – the Font properly fixed – the doors painted outside – an iron Register Chest provided. A new entrance to the Belfry, to prevent the Ringers from passing thro' the Church and Chancel. The tower examined and secured – the cracked bell re-cast, and the small one repaired [and made fit for use]. Enquiry to be made respecting the origin of the encroachment upon the Churchyard [at the East end] with a view to its removal. The earth, herbage etc to be cleared away to the level of the floor inside *at least,* and a large open space laid all round with tiles or bricks – [Eave] spouts and pipes put up – Ivy and other trees removed – no graves allowed near the walls.

Wheaton Aston, Chapel of Ease – parish of Lapley.

Lapley revisited 12.10.1837
    Still in a very neglected state – many of the former orders renewed – especially, as relates to the roof of the Tower – weatherboards – bells – clearing away of ivy, open ground round the walls.
    The thoro'fare and trespass paths to be stopped.

Ceiling under belfry repaired – walls coloured etc. Chancel walls, windows and roof to be repaired. 'Nothing done'.

The Chapel being much dilapidated and in a very unseemly condition, I recommended application to the Incorporated Society for aid towards the enlargement, or re-building of it – in a more suitable situation. Whether this be adopted or no, I ordered (1) New books for the Reading and Clerk's desks. (2) A new surplice. (3) Repairs to the Pulpit, reading and Clerk's desks. (4) Communion rails (at present there are *none*). (5) Repairs to the Pews, and Gallery seats. (6) Repairs to Bell-tower.

I received at the ensuing Visitation at Stafford a respectful letter from the inhabitants, urging their inability to *rebuild*; but promising the repairs which I had ordered (Letter annexed).

Revisited 15.10.1841
(1) Water tables for windows, and bars painted. (2) Ladders leading to roof of Tower repaired – lead gutters of Tower cleared out – flashings re-laid, and battlements secured. (3) Bells re-cast, wheels etc repaired. (4) Chancel stove repaired. (5) Walls and buttresses pointed – grass cleared from walls, gravel walk laid. (6) *Recommended* – to raise the belfry-floor – to restore to the Church that part of the antient Churchyard now occupied as a garden – to restore the antient *sedilia* and *piscina* on S. side of Chancel, near Communion rails.

[1] *Eccles. Revs.:* 200 in Lapley parish church, 160 in Wheaton Aston chapel. [2] *Eccles. Revs.:* 'Fit'. [3] *Eccles. Revs.:* 200 at Lapley, 800 at Wheaton Aston.

MADELEY 5.10.1830
(A/V/1/3,p.62;A/V/1/2,p.137)

BENEFICE: Madeley. **Nature:** Vicarage. **Ecton:** Clear value £11 10s. 0d. Pri. Stone Propr. **Patron:** Lord Crewe's representatives. **Impropriator:** Hon. Mrs Cunliffe Offley – daughter of the late Lord Crewe.
CHURCH: A remarkably handsome Gothic structure – middle and side aisles, transept and Chancel – pointed arches – some of the windows antient. **Number it will contain:** About 500.[1] **Accommodation for Poor:** Sufficient. **Roof:** Oak covered with lead – the side aisles [have] open carved ceilings – the centre underdrawn. **Walls:** Solid stone [– good]. **Floor:** Quarries and tombstones; even. **Windows:** Not sufficiently provided with casements. **Doors:** Very good. **Pulpit and Desk:** Old carved oak, painted – faded velvet cushion. **Books:** Bible wants repair. **Seats:** Very good and neat. **Galleries:** At the W. end, for singers. **Organ:** There is one. **Font:** An old one, near the S. door. **Chapels:** The N. and S. transepts belong to Earl Wilton. **Benefaction Tables:** A large one in the Chancel, and two in the body of the Church – the former records the munificent donations of Sir John Offley, Knight. **Vestry:** A very handsome one – formerly a private Chapel. **Surplices:** Two – good. **Linen:** Provided. **Plate:** Silver flagon, cup and patin. **Iron Chest for Register:** In the Vestry. **Register:** From 1678 only – well kept from that time – the earlier Vols said to have been destroyed. **Porch:** There is one on the S. side – in good state. **Vaults** Two within the last 12 years – no new ones intended. **Cleanliness:** Well attended to. **Damp:** Some on the walls.
CHANCEL: **Table:** Firm and good – crimson velvet covering. **Ornaments:** The Commandments etc. **Repaired by whom:** Lord Crewe's heir – the window on the South side wants repair.
STEEPLE: A square stone tower, with pinnacles at the corners. **State of:** Good. **Bells:** Six – in good order. **Clock:** There is one – good.
CHURCHYARD: **Fence:** Sunk fence and rails – well kept. **Gates:** Good – one old and superfluous – to be stopped. **Drains:** Not sufficient – ground too high on N. side. **Graves:** Many too near the walls. **Rubbish:** Not any. **Footpaths:** Want cleaning – some trespass footpaths – to be stopped. **Cattle:** None.
DIVINE SERVICE: **On Sundays:** Two full services. **On other Days:** None. **Sacrament:** Seven times a year. **Communicants:** About 30. **Catechism:** In the school.
INCUMBENT: **Name and Residence:** Revd John Stevenson Catlow[2] – Vicarage. **What duty he performs:** The whole.
PARSONAGE: A good, commodious brick house – pleasantly situated below the Church – three sitting rooms etc. **State of:** Very good.[3] **Outbuildings:** New.
INCOME: **Gross Value:** Not ascertained.[4] **Tithes:** The late Lord Crewe gave part of the Corn Tythe. **Terrier:** There is one at the Vicarage.
SCHOOLS: **Endowed School:** There are two – one for boys, the other for girls – about 50 in each; endowed with land by Sir J Offley – £60 a year – taught on the National system. **Subscription Day School:** None besides the preceding. **Sunday School:** The same as the weekly schools [Art 72]. **Lancaster School:** None.
DISSENTERS: **Dissenters' School:** None. **Dissenting Chapels:** None – a small Methodist meeting.
POPULATION: About 1,000.[5]
MISCELLANEOUS: **Monuments:** To the Crewe family.
PARISH CLERK: Thomas Sneyd. **Appointed by:** The Parishioners. **Salary:** £5 per annum.
CHURCHWARDENS: Mr John Sutton Wilkinson. Mr B Roberts.
ORDERS MADE: 'In progress'.
The ground to be lowered, especially on the N. side of the Church – drain of sufficient depth formed – Chancel and Transept roofs spouted – paths kept clear from weeds. The Bible repaired – a casement made on each side of the nave. The windows of the Chancel and belfry repaired – the buttresses also repaired. [(Qu? as to the *inconvenient height* of some of *the Pews*).

Revisited 25.10.1837
The state of this Church greatly improved since my former visit. Some repairs and alterations still needed.

I: *Inside* the Church
Windows on South of Chancel repaired – new ones wanted. East window bars painted. Ditto of Vestry. Prayer Book repaired – Bible ditto – and leaves pressed. Lumber removed from S. Chancel. Water tables to windows. Pannels of

Pews in S. aisle repaired. Baptismal basin provided.

II. Outside

Walls underbuilt and repaired – and pointed, where needful. Battlements of tower repaired – lead flashings renewed. Steps to tower refixed. Lead roof over North side examined and repaired – flashings and mortar ditto – water courses cleared out. Roof over N. transept stripped and renewed.

Ridging tiles of N. transept repaired – water courses cleared. Ridging tiles of South transept repaired – water courses cleared and ceiling repaired inside.

Battlements repaired and secured. 'Done or in progress. R.D.'

Revisited 18.9.1841

Directions to Churchwardens. Cover of Communion table and pulpit dyed afresh – and preserved during the week from exposure to Sun. Reading Desk covered – to preserve the books from injury. Wainscoting of pews on S. side repaired. Baptismal Font restored, and Christening Pew separated. Wheels of bells repaired, head of window arch in bell-chamber restored, and joints in window-sill filled up. Stone roof over little door leading into Tower repaired and door kept closed. Parapets and battlements pointed – iron cramps etc painted – and lead flashings secured. Roof of Chancel, used as a Vestry, examined and repaired.

Recommended. Floors of pews to be boarded. Churchyard enlarged – on N. side of burial ground – if Mrs Cunliffe Offley will give piece of ground.

[1] *Eccles. Revs.:* 650. [2] A/V/1/3: pencil deletion of Catlow and replacement by 'Daltry'. Catlow also rector of Coppenhall (Cheshire). [3] *Eccles. Revs.:* 'Fit'. [4] *Eccles. Revs.:* Gross income £314. [5] *Eccles. Revs.:* 1,160.

MAER 7.10.1830 (A/V/1/3, p.63; A/V/1/2, p.140)

BENEFICE: Maer – olim Meare. **Nature:** Perpetual Curacy – endowed with Corn Tithe by Lady Bowyer, a former Patroness. **Ecton:** Coll. Sti. Thom. Staff. Propr. Clear [yearly] value £20 6s. 8d. **Patron:** Josiah Wedgwood Esqr. **Impropriator:** The Patron has the small tithes.
CHURCH: An antient, low, building – rebuilt (as appears from a date upon the Tower) in 1610; pillars and pointed arches on N. side of nave – no South aisle. **Number it will contain:** 200. **Accommodation for Poor:** The Gallery sittings, and some below. **Roof:** Timber covered with tile – new in 1805. **Walls:** Stone. **Floor:** Bricks and flags; the latter very uneven. **Windows:** Tolerably good – casements sufficient. **Doors:** Good. **Pulpit and Desk:** Pretty good. **Books:** New prayer book wanted. **Seats:** Oak – good. **Galleries:** One at the W. end. **Organ:** None. **Font:** Of stone at the W. end, attached to the wall. **Chapels:** None. **Benefaction Tables:** None – wanted. **Vestry:** A small one at the W. end. **Surplices:** One. **Linen:** Provided. **Plate:** Pewter flagon and patin – silver Cup. **Iron Chest for Register:** Provided. **Register:** From 1558 – want rebinding. **Porch:** There is one – a lock wanted on the door. **Vaults:** None lately. **Cleanliness:** Attended to. **Damp:** Not much appearance.
CHANCEL: **Table:** Firm – blue cloth covering. **Ornaments:** Commandments. **Repaired by whom:** The Incumbent, as having the great tithes.
STEEPLE: A square stone tower. **State of:** Good externally – but no weatherboards. **Bells:** One – [the] wheel broken – floor of belfry bad etc. **Clock:** None.
CHURCHYARD: **Fence:** Not very good. **Gates:** Good. **Drains:** None. **Graves:** Many too near the walls. **Rubbish:** Weeds etc. **Footpaths:** Trespass paths. **Cattle:** Poney, occasionally.
DIVINE SERVICE: **On Sundays:** At present only one service on account of the infirm health of the Incumbent – formerly two. **On other days:** None. **Sacrament:** Four times a year. **Communicants:** 25 or 30. **Catechism:** Not lately.
INCUMBENT: **Name and Residence:** Revd J Allen Wedgwood – Parsonage. **What duty he performs:** The whole.
CURATE: **Name and Residence:** None at present – his brother did assist him.
PARSONAGE: An old stone building – tiled roof – small and not very commodious. **State of:** Not very good.[1] **Outbuildings:** Stable, barn etc.
INCOME: **Gross Value:** £150 to £180. **Terrier:** There is one, dated 1773.
SCHOOLS: **Endowed School:** None. **Subscription Day School:** None. **Sunday School:** From 50 to 60 children. **Lancaster School:** None.
DISSENTERS: **Dissenters' School:** ——. **Dissenting Chapels:** —— a licensed meeting house.
POPULATION: About 400.[2]
MISCELLANEOUS: **Monuments:** One to Sir John and Lady Bowyer – 1604.
PARISH CLERK: Richard Slaney. **Appointed by:** The Parish. **Salary:** £4 4s. 0d. a year – and £1 1s. 0d. for cleaning.
CHURCHWARDENS: Moses Harding – for the Minister, Williams Hitchins – for the Parish.
ORDERS MADE: ['Nearly done'.]
The floor in the North aisle to be laid even and hollow – the floors of the pews also to be laid afresh. Benefaction table set up – new Prayer Book for reading desk. A lock on the Porch door; the bell-wheel mended; weatherboards put up – floor of belfry repaired and also the door. The drain round the Church cleaned out – the roofs spouted. The fence put into good repair – weeds removed, and the thoroughfare, if possible, stopped. The road leading up to the Church made more easy of ascent.

Revisited 9.10.1837

In a very damp and neglected state.
Directions.

I. Outside

Drains kept clear – walls and buttresses pointed – eave-spouts and drain-pipes. Roof examined – repaired – cleared of moss etc. Branches of trees overhanging the Church to be lopped off – (other trees removed). Buttresses – tower walls etc pointed and cracks filled up. Windows kept in proper repair.

II. Inside

Floor of Communion rail relaid – chimney in corner removed – Stone steps leading to Chancel re-laid. Pews etc oiled. Walls and ceiling whitewashed. Lath and plaistering under Gallery repaired. Roof of Tower examined and repaired. Porch whitewashed – lock put on door. Footpath from SE. corner of Churchyard stopped. Additional burial ground provided. 'All done. R.D.'

Revisited 13.10.1841
Directions etc. (1) Baptismal Font cleaned and restored to use – mat, or decent Carpet, provided for Communion floor. (2) Floors of pews *boarded*. (3) New wheel for one of the bells. (4) Roof examined and repaired – spouts repaired and painted.

[1] *Eccles. Revs.:* 'Fit'. [2] *Eccles. Revs.:* 505.

MARSTON 2.10.1830
(A/V/1/3,p.64;A/V/1/2,p.59)

BENEFICE: Marston. **Nature:** Chapel of ease to St. Mary Stafford. **Ecton:** Clear yearly value £15 6s. 8d. **Patron:** The Rector of Stafford. **Impropriator:** The Corporation of Stafford (hitherto).
CHURCH: A small; very plain building – the body antient – the south side new 30 years ago – the Chancel and West Porch added 10 years ago. **Number it will contain:** About 150. **Accommodation for Poor:** Five pews. **Roof:** Not in good condition, apparently. **Walls:** Stone – want whitewashing [inside]. **Floor:** Quarries – pretty good. **Windows:** Pretty good – but dirty; casements not opened daily. **Doors:** ——. **Pulpit and Desk:** Not good – unpainted deal. **Books:** Prayer book in reading desk wants rebinding. **Seats:** Pretty good – floors damp – pannels want painting. **Galleries:** None. **Organ:** ——. **Font:** An old one, in the Chancel. **Chapels:** None. **Benefaction Tables:** One. **Vestry:** None. **Surplices:** One. **Linen:** Provided. **Plate:** Pewter Cup and two plates. **Iron Chest for Register:** In the Chancel. **Register:** From 1569 to 1718 – from that time till 1768 not kept regularly. **Porch:** At the W. end – a light gate wanted. **Vaults:** None lately. **Cleanliness:** Not properly attended to – no one paid for cleaning. **Damp:** Much on the floor.
CHANCEL: **Table:** Deal – uncovered. **Ornaments:** None. **Repaired by whom:** The repairs said to belong to the Corporation [of Stafford] as receivers of the Great Tithes – in consequence however of the late disputes and law-suit they have refused to repair – (the whole in a very bad state).
STEEPLE: A small bell-tower. **State of:** Pretty good. **Bells:** One. **Clock:** None.
CHURCHYARD: **Fence:** Quick hedge – not properly kept. **Gates:** Indifferent. **Drains:** None – nor spouts. **Graves:** None too near. **Rubbish:** None. **Footpaths:** Not properly attended to. **Cattle:** Sheep.
DIVINE SERVICE: **On Sundays:** Prayers and Sermon *once a fortnight* only, in the Afternoon – used to be *every Sunday*. **On other Days:** None. **Sacrament:** Only *twice a year*. **Communicants:** From 10 to 20. **Catechism:** Occasionally.
INCUMBENT: **Name and Residence:** Revd Joseph Ellerton – Baswich, six miles off. **If not resident:** Not. **What duty he performs:** The whole.
PARSONAGE: None.[1]
INCOME: **Gross Value:** Supposed about £50 per annum – a copy of Terrier in the Register states the payments as follows: £8 per annum paid by the Corporation (out of the Tythes). £6 13s. 4d. from WR Cartwright Esq. £14 0s. 0d. from estate in Standon Parish, purchased by Queen Anne's Bounty in 1792. £4 0s. 0d. interest of 200 granted by Queen Anne's Bounty. Total £32 13s. 4d. **Terrier:** In the Register.
SCHOOLS: **Endowed School:** None. **Subscription Day School:** None. **Sunday School:** None – the Clerk promised to commence one. **Lancaster School:** ——.
DISSENTERS: **Dissenters' School:** ——. **Dissenting Chapels:** ——.
POPULATION: In 1811, 200.
PARISH CLERK: William Goodwin. **Appointed by:** The Minister and Parishioners jointly. **Salary:** £2 2s. 0d.
CHAPELWARDEN: John Ponder.
ORDERS MADE: The timbers of the roof to be examined and necessary repairs to be done – the ceiling also repaired near the trap-door leading to Belfry. The ceiling and walls to be whitewashed – the windows kept clean and regularly opened – the iron bars painted. Light gate put up at the Porch entrance. The Prayer Book in reading-desk re-bound; pulpit and communion rail made secure – covering provided for the Communion Table. The roof, walls and windows of the Chancel put into thorough repair. The roof spouted all round – pipes put up – drain formed. The hedge kept neatly trimmed and in good repair – the Church ways properly kept.

Revisited 8.10.1837
Much required both inside and outside.
I. Inside
(1) Walls coloured – ceiling whitewashed, ? repaired. (2) Windows repaired, cleaned, bars painted. (3) Casement in Church – ditto in Chancel. (4) Pipe of stove carried thro' wall or ceiling, not window. (5) Pews thoroughly repaired – hinges painted. (6) Bible and Prayer Book in Desk repaired or new. (7) Rails of Communion painted – Cover for Table.

II. Outside
(1) Roof repaired – especially Chancel. (2) Eave spouts on both sides – down pipes. (3) Churchyard – grass cleared out – open drain. (4) Bell Turret painted stone colour. (5) Walk to Door of Church properly laid. (6) Hedge trimmed all round. (7) Gates painted.
   'Nothing done. Tower.'

[1] *Eccles. Revs.:* 'None'.

MILWICH 5.7.1830 (A/V/1/3,p.65;A/V/1/2,p.57)

BENEFICE: Milwich. **Nature:** Vicarage. **Ecton:** Clear yearly value £31 10s. 0d. Pri. Sti. Wolfhadi in Stone Impr. – Mrs Dyve Patron. **Patron:** Mr Dive[1] of London. **Impropriator:** The Patron [has] two-thirds of the Corn Tithes – the Vicar one third.
CHURCH: A plain building, re-erected (except the Tower which is old) in 1792–5 – single body – a

small chancel, separated from the Nave by a low ugly arch. **Number it will contain:** About 200 in all. **Accommodation for Poor:** 20 on benches – and forms for children within the Communion rails. **Roof:** Deal covered with slates – a large crack runs across the ceiling towards the lower end – and one or two considerable ones near the E. end. **Walls:** Brick – surbase stone – appear good. **Floor:** Flags – even. **Windows:** More casements wanted. **Doors:** Good – but a light gate wanted at the W. end. **Pulpit and Desk:** Well placed – crimson cushion – wants covering. **Books:** Good. **Seats:** Oak pannels – boarded floors – neat and uniform – doors want easing. **Galleries:** One for singers at the W. end. **Organ:** None. **Font:** There is one – awkwardly placed under the Tower, outside the entrance into the body of the Church – fastened to the wall. **Chapels:** None. **Benefaction Tables:** Two – sufficient. **Vestry:** There is one – used only by the Parish – much out of repair. **Surplices:** One – a new one wanted. **Linen:** Table Cloth and napkin. **Plate:** Silver Cup – Two Patines – Pewter dish. **Chest for Papers:** There is one. **Iron Chest for Register:** There is one in the Parish Chest – not used at present for the Registers – Ordered to be used for that purpose, and kept at the Vicarage. **Register:** Not inspected. **Porch:** None. **Vaults:** None recently. **Cleanliness:** Pretty well attended to. **Damp:** Some on the floor, and Chancel roof. **Dimensions:** 50ft. 1in. by 27ft. 1in.

CHANCEL: Very small. **Table:** Oak – to be cleaned. **Ornaments:** None. **Repaired by whom:** The Impropriator – roof wants repair.

STEEPLE: An old stone square Tower – wants pointing and underbuilding. **State of:** Not good. **Bells:** Three – in good state – weatherboards out of repair. **Clock:** None.

CHURCHYARD: **Fence:** Hedge – partly kept by the Vicar, partly by the Parish – in good state. **Gates:** Good. **Drains:** None – nor spouts. **Graves:** None too near the walls. **Rubbish:** None observable. **Footpaths:** Not in good order. **Cattle:** A small poney, belonging to the Curate.

DIVINE SERVICE: **On Sundays:** Alternate morning and evening service. **On other Days:** None. **Sacrament:** Four times a year. **Communicants:** 8 or 10.

INCUMBENT: **Name and Residence:** Revd John Owen. **If not resident:** Denbigh.

CURATE: **Name and Residence:** Revd John Sell, in the Vicarage. **Licensed:** He is. **Salary:** £60 and surplice fees. **If serving another Church:** Fradswell – within two miles.

PARSONAGE: An old, small and very incommodious house – two rooms and kitchen etc below – three or four very inconvenient bedrooms above.[2] **State of:** Indifferent. **Outbuildings:** Stables etc.

INCOME: **Gross Value:** About £120. **Glebe:** One acre, **Surplice Fees:** £4. **Easter Dues and small Payments:**[3] Collected. **Queen Anne's Bounty:** None. **Terrier:** There is a Copy.

SCHOOLS: **Endowed School:** £5 left by Lady Buller (or her ancestors) for instructing ten children in English.[4] **Subscription Day School:** None. **Sunday School:** 30 children. **Lancaster School:** None.

DISSENTERS: **Dissenting Chapels:** A Methodist meeting.

POPULATION: About 600.

PARISH CLERK: James Smith. **Appointed by:** The Vicar. **Salary:** None fixed.

CHURCHWARDENS: John Cotton – only one at present – the Curate has neglected to appoint one.

ORDERS MADE: ['In progress'.]
The state of the beams and timbers of the roof to be carefully examined, with a view of ascertaining the cause of the *cracks* in the ceiling – necessary repairs to be done forthwith. Two more casements to be made in the body of the Church, and one in the Chancel – the lead-work of the windows repaired, and the Iron frames painted. The Pulpit Cushion to be covered afresh. The doors of the Pews eased, so as to open and shut without noise. The Vestry to be put into proper repair – a casement made in the window. A new Surplice provided – the Iron Chest removed to the Vicarage and the Registers kept in it. The Communion Table to be cleaned. The Tower to be under-built, and pointed and otherwise secured at the top. The weather-boards renewed, and door above the Belfry *closed*. Spouts and pipes affixed – an open drain all round.[5] The Church ways kept in better order – encroachments [on the Churchyard] prevented, and no thoroughfare allowed, but such as can be claimed by long established custom.

Revisited 9.9.1837
We found this Church in a very gratifying state of repair and neatness. Much has been done for its improvement since my former visit. The only directions I had to give to the Churchwardens were – (1) To have the oak pannels of the Pulpit, Reading desk and pews, varnished. (2) The chancel roof secured by lead flashings from admitting the wet, and down spouts at N. angle continued to the ground so as to convey the rain from the roof into a *drain*; and thus prevent the dampness caused on that side of the Chancel. (3) The S. side spouts painted, and brought down as in No. 2. (4) New Lich Gates at NE. entrance of Churchyard.

I strongly *recommended* the extension of the West gallery, so as to give free sittings for 50 or 60 persons, promising them aid from the Diocesan Church Building Society. '*All* done'.

Visited 10.10.1841[6]
Directions to the Churchwardens. (1) New linen to be provided for the Communion Table, and a new Prayer-book for the Reading desk. (2) The lead basin to be disused in the Baptismal Font, and the water poured into *the Font itself*.
(I *recommend* – as more in character with the rest of the Chancel, and neater – that *smaller* tables; with the Commandments etc, should be put up, instead of the present large ones. I do not, however, think it necessary to *enjoin* it.) (3) *Water-tables* to be made for the windows, so that the wet may be carried *outside,* instead of streaming down the walls. (4) A table of the 'Bourne benefactions' to be set up. (5) The pinnacles at the four corners of the Tower to be either taken down or else restored in more becoming state; the battlements and parapets fixed

securely; the lead flashings laid close to the walls. (6) The roof of the Church carefully examined and repaired; and the buttresses, at the SE. and NE. angles of the Tower, pointed and secured from dilapidation. (7) The West front of the Tower, and the buttresses, to be well pointed with good mortar or cement. (8) The Spouts to be repaired, where needful, and painted – the iron stays also to be painted. (9) The thoroughfare of the Churchyard to be stopped, if it can be done with the concurrence and good-will of the parishioners generally.

[1] A/V/1/3: 'G Dyve Esqr.' [2] *Eccles. Revs.:* 'Fit'. [3] A/V/1/3: 'and small Payments' deleted. [4] A/V/1/3: '. . . in reading'. [5] A/V/1/3: 'Spouts and pipes all round – a drain formed'. [6] Loose sheet inserted in A/V/1/3.

MUCKLESTONE 4.10.1830
(A/V/1/3, p.66; A/V/1/2, p.141)

BENEFICE: Muckleston (alias Muggleston, or Munxton). **Nature:** Rectory. **Ecton:** Kings Books £20 3s. 9d. **Patron:** Patronage now in the hands of Trustees – appointed by the late Lord Crewe. **Impropriator:** None.
CHURCH: An antient Church modernised in 1789 – single body, flat ceiling. **Number it will contain:** About 400.[1] **Accommodation for Poor:** The gallery, and benches below for children. **Roof:** Oak, covered with slate. **Walls:** Stone – upright. **Floor:** Flags. **Windows:** Good – casements sufficiently provided. **Doors:** Good. **Pulpit and Desk:** Very handsome and well placed – velvet cushion. **Books:** Good in general. **Seats:** Very neat and uniform. **Galleries:** One at the W. end. **Organ:** There is. **Font:** ——. **Chapels:** None. **Benefaction Tables:** Three – one out of repair. **Vestry:** There is one – not used. **Surplices:** Two – good. **Linen:** Napkin indifferent. **Plate:** Handsome silver flagon, cup and patin. **Iron Chest for Register:** Provided. **Register:** From 1556 – three old vols not in good repair. **Porch:** None. **Vaults:** Only two – belonging to Sir J Chetwood and the Crewe family. **Cleanliness:** Attended to. **Damp:** No appearance.
CHANCEL: **Table:** Firm – cover wanted. **Ornaments:** Commandments – texts of Psalms. **Repaired by whom:** The Rector – Sir J Chetwood in part.
STEEPLE: Square stone tower. **State of:** Good externally – weatherboards imperfect – floor bad. **Bells:** Five – one cracked – frame wants repair. **Clock:** There is one – the dial wants painting.
CHURCHYARD: **Fence:** Stone walls, and sunk fence – good. **Gates:** Good. **Drains:** A surf – spouts are being prepared. **Graves:** Not too near. **Rubbish:** None. **Footpaths:** One or two trespass paths – and one unnecessary road, recommended to be stopped up, to gain more room for burials. **Cattle:** None.
DIVINE SERVICE: **On Sundays:** Two full duties. **On other Days:** None. **Sacrament:** Quarterly. **Communicants:** 50 to 60. **Catechism:** In Lent.
INCUMBENT: **Name and Residence:** Revd Offley Crewe – Rectory. **What duty he performs:** None.
CURATE: **Name and Residence:** Revd William Thornes – close to the Church. **Licensed:** He is. **Salary:** £100. **If serving another Church:** None.

PARSONAGE: A commodious house, much enlarged and improved by the present Rector – walls brick, rough-cast, roof tiled – nine bedrooms, three sitting rooms.[2] **State of:** Good – lately put into complete repair. **Outbuildings:** Extensive – newly repaired.
INCOME: **Gross Value:** Not ascertained.[3] **Tithes:** Corn – modus for hay partially. **Glebe:** 24 acres. **Easter dues and small payments:**[4] Collected. **Terrier:** Not seen.
SCHOOLS: **Endowed School:** None. **Subscription Day School:** A national school, supported at present by subscriptions, intended to be endowed. **Sunday School:** About 60 children. **Lancaster School:** None.
DISSENTERS: **Dissenters' School:** One. **Dissenting Chapels:** One.
POPULATION: Of Munxton itself, 800–1,000 at Woore.[5]
PARISH CLERK: William Skelhorne. **Appointed by:** The Rector. **Salary:** £2 12s. 0d. and 5s. for cleaning.
CHURCHWARDENS: Richard Stanway, by the Rector and Parish jointly.
ORDERS MADE: ['Nearly finished'.]
A new covering for the Communion Table – and napkin for the Sacrament. The Bible and Benefaction Table repaired. The tower pointed at the top – Ivy removed or checked. The frame of the Bells secured – the floor mended.
The cracked bell recast (a) – the weatherboards made good. Spouts to be carried *all round* the roof – and pipes affixed.[6] The footpath leading from the NW. corner of the Churchyard to be stopped (b).
(a) Suspended till a more favourable opportunity, in compliance with a request of the Parishioners communicated in a letter to me from the Churchwarden December 14th 1830.
(b) Revoked, on the application of the Parishioners who wish to substitute the ground under the *centre path,* leading to the S. door (which is flagged) for interments.[7]

Revisited 9.10.1837
Directions. (1) Oak work of pews, pulpit etc *oiled.* (2) Doors, and iron work of windows, *painted.* (3) A *new door* to the *Chancel.* (4) Lead flashing of roof of tower replaced – pinnacles secured – water courses cleared out – weatherboards repaired. (5) Broken bell recast or replaced, and wheels etc repaired *within two years.* (6) Walls and buttresses of Tower; and walls of Church and Chancel to be pointed along the bottom. (7) Each side of Church and Chancel spouted, and down-pipes on both sides of the Church – spout on N. side cleared out, and made to carry off the wet.

Revisited 12.10.1841
Directions. (1) Water tables to windows – pews rubbed with boiled linseed oil – doors and windows set open in dry weather. (2) Floor in front of Pulpit, taken up and laid even – Prayer Book repaired. (3) Vestry ceiling repaired and chimney completed. (4) Gutters and lead flashings of *Tower,* properly attended to. (5) Soil lowered round Church walls, and open drain or gravel walk formed all round. (6) East end of Church *spouted* – roof at SW. end repaired –

chimney removed and slates secured. (7) Old Registers carefully covered.

[1] *Eccles. Revs.:* 560. [2] *Eccles. Revs.:* 'Fit'. [3] *Eccles. Revs.:* Gross income £900. [4] A/V/1/3: 'and small Payments' enclosed in brackets. [5] *Eccles. Revs.:* 2,045. [6] A/V/1/3: 'down pipes put up'. [7] A/V/1/3: '*revoked*, on the same ground' (i.e. the churchwardens' letter).

NORBURY 9.6.1830
(A/V/1/3,p.67;A/V/1/2,p.62)

BENEFICE: Norbury. **Nature:** Rectory. **Ecton:** Kings Books £10 2s. 6d. Mr Baldwyn Patron. **Patron:** Lord Anson. **Impropriator:** None – the Rector has all the Tithes.
CHURCH: A very neat plain building, with pointed Arches; a very handsome one at the Chancel entrance. **Number it will contain:** 310.[1] **Accommodation for Poor:** Sufficient. **Roof:** Oak, covered with tile – in very good repair. **Walls:** Solid stone. **Floor:** Flags. **Windows:** Very good – but no casements. **Doors:** Ditto. **Pulpit and Desk:** Very handsome oak, well placed; a black velvet cushion. **Books:** Very handsome – Baskett Bible 1716. **Seats:** Very uniform and neat; boarded floors. **Galleries:** A small one at the W. end recently erected, at an expense of £60 – holds 60 people. **Organ:** None. **Font:** Near the Vestry door. **Chapels:** None. **Benefaction Tables:** None at present, having been taken down for the repairs of the Church [– intended]. **Vestry:** A new one, very neat; but a closet wanted. **Surplices:** Two – good. **Linen:** Table Cloth and napkin. **Plate:** Pewter flagon – silver Cup and patin. **Iron Chest for Register:** At the Rectory. **Register:** One Vol. in excellent preservation from *1538* (the first year of Registers) – marriage register from 1754 – and those in present use. **Porch:** None. **Vaults:** ——. **Cleanliness:** Pretty well attended to; an arrangement to be made for its being better observed. **Damp:** No appearance. **Dimensions:** 53ft by 25ft.
CHANCEL: 41ft. by 21ft. **Table:** Plain oak. **Ornaments:** None. **Repaired by whom:** The Rector – all in excellent order and neatness; the present Rector has bestowed much pains both on the Church and Chancel.
STEEPLE: A square brick tower; about 100 years old. **State of:** Good. **Bells:** Four, and a small one; the latter wants a *handle*; weatherboards incomplete. **Clock:** None.
CHURCHYARD: **Fence:** A wall; kept up by the Parish; an enlargement of the Churchyard is now taking place. **Gates:** New ones about to be put up. **Drains:** None – no spouts. **Graves:** Not too near. **Rubbish:** None. **Footpaths:** ——. **Cattle:** Sheep, intended.
DIVINE SERVICE: **On Sundays:** Full service morning – prayers [only] at six (in the evening) *in the Summer.* **On other days:** None. **Sacrament:** Six times a year. **Communicants:** 30.
INCUMBENT: **Name and Residence:** Revd WH Cynric Lloyd – in the Rectory.[2] **What duty he performs:** The whole [since that time, his brother has been ordained as his Assistant (1831)].
PARSONAGE: A handsome brick building – large and commodious; great additions made to it by the present Rector – there is a small house and garden attached to it; occupied by the Clerk.[3] **State of:** Very good. **Outbuildings:** Very complete and spacious – good repair.
INCOME: **Gross Value:** ——.[4] **Tithes:** Of whole parish – except Hay, for which a modus. **Glebe:** 58 acres. **Terrier:** There is one – date 1758.
SCHOOLS: **Endowed School:** None. **Subscription Day School:** None. **Sunday School:** 30 children. **Lancaster School:** None.
DISSENTERS: **Dissenters' School:** ——. **Dissenting Chapels:** ——.
POPULATION: 306.[5]
MISCELLANEOUS: **Monuments:** To the Skrymshires, formerly Lords of the Manor. **Parochial Library:** None.
PARISH CLERK: John Rutter. **Appointed by:** The Rector. **Salary:** £4 0s. 0d. per annum (£2 2s. 0d. to be added for cleaning the Church).
CHURCHWARDENS: Mr W Derington for Norbury Liberty; Joseph Brooke for Weston Jones Liberty.
ORDERS MADE: ['In progress'.]
Casements to be made. Commandments to be put up. Small bell repaired – weatherboards completed; the door above the Bells closed. A partition to be put up between the Belfry and Gallery door. Drains and spouts provided.

Revisited 11.10.1837
Directions to the Churchwardens. (1) *Walls* of Church, Chancel, and Vestry to be coloured (grey) and *ceilings whitewashed.* (2) Windows repaired – lead ties new – water tables. (3) Oak pews etc oiled. (4) Roof of Tower re-tiled; roof of Church, near Tower, cemented or flashed with lead. (5) Eave-spouts and down pipes. (6) *Gravel* on *walks*. '*In progress*'.

Revisited 22.11.1841
In excellent order – turf to be removed wider from the Church.

[1] *Eccles. Revs.:* 250. [2] Also vicar of Ranton. [3] *Eccles. Revs.:* 'Fit'. [4] *Eccles. Revs.:* Gross income £533. [5] *Eccles. Revs.:* 447.

NEWCASTLE-UNDER-LYME (PARISH CHURCH) 16.6.1830(A/V/1/3,p.68;A/V/1/2,p.83)

BENEFICE: Newcastle (Parish Church). **Nature:** Rectory [(formerly a part of Stoke Parish)]. **Ecton:** Chapelry to Stoke – £25 9s. 6d. Clear value. **Patron:** Revd C Simeon. **Impropriator:** None.
CHURCH: A modern building, in Grecian style – [built in] 1721 – a single body and roof – spacious East end – but no separate Chancel. **Number it will contain:** 830. **Accommodation for Poor:** 2 or 300. **Roof:** Oak, covered with lead – in good repair. **Walls:** Stone – in good repair. **Floor:** Bricks of a dark colour – even. **Windows:** Good – but casements not sufficiently opened[1] – additional ones wanted. **Doors:** Good – but want painting. **Pulpit and Desk:** Good and well placed – crimson ornaments. **Books:** Prayer books out of repair. **Seats:** Uniform and in good condition. **Galleries:** On three sides. **Organ:** There is one. **Font:** There is – but not a suitable basin. **Chapels:** None. **Benefaction Tables:** Sufficient. **Vestry:** There is one. **Surplices:** Three – all good. **Linen:** Provided. **Plate:** A Flagon – two Cups – two Patins – silver – handsome. **Iron**

Chest for Registers: At the Rectory. **Register:** Several Vols – in good preservation. **Porch:** None. **Vaults:** None recently. **Cleanliness:** Attended to. **Damp:** Appearance of it: on the floor.
CHANCEL: **Table:** Mahogany – good [order]. **Ornaments:** Covering to Table – Commandments etc. **Repaired by whom:** The Rector.
STEEPLE: Old stone Tower. **State of:** The stones much dilapidated externally – especially towards the bottom. **Bells:** Eight – good. **Clock:** There is.
CHURCHYARD: **Fence:** Out of repair – and incomplete in several places – brick wall, maintained partly by the Parish, partly by adjoining proprietors. **Gates:** One wanting at the W. end. **Drains:** None – nor spouts. **Graves:** Several close to the walls. **Rubbish:** Not much. **Footpaths:** There is a public thoroughfare, which occasions much disturbance at Funerals etc. **Cattle:** None.
DIVINE SERVICE: **On Sundays:** Two full services – Morning and Evening. **On other Days:** Wednesday Evening service. **Sacrament:** Monthly. **Communicants:** From 60 to 100.
INCUMBENT: **Name and Residence:** Revd Clement Leigh – Rectory. **What duty he performs:** Shares with his Curate.
CURATE: **Name and Residence:** Revd John Porter (in the Town). **Salary:** ——.[2] **If serving another Church:** None.
PARSONAGE: A good house; substantially built, and commodious – three sitting rooms, kitchens etc on ground floor – several bedrooms above. **State of:** Very good.[3] **Outbuildings:** Stable, Coachhouse etc built by present Rector.
INCOME: **Gross Value:** £400.[4]
SCHOOLS: **Endowed School:** There is one – an English School – income £170 – to be put on a better footing for the poor generally. There is also a Grammar School. **Subscription Day School:** National School – upwards of 300 children. **Sunday School:** There is. **Lancaster School:** None.
DISSENTERS: **Dissenters' School:** ——. **Dissenting Chapels:** There are several.
POPULATION: 8,000.
PARISH CLERK: Andrew Shufflebotham. **Appointed by:** The Rector. **Salary:** £10 – he is also Sexton.
CHURCHWARDENS: Mr Baylie and Mr Hancock.
ORDERS MADE: ['See Articles.']
(1) Additional casements to be made in the Gallery windows and those of the staircases leading to them – and care taken that they be *opened*. (2) The doors to be painted outside. (3) Prayerbooks repaired or renewed. (4) Tower underbuilt, or cased with stone, bricks, or cement. (*Reference to Surveyor.*) (5) *Churchyard* Fence repaired and completed – the thoroughfare (if possible) stopped. (6) Spouts and Pipes to be put up. (7) No graves within six feet of walls.

Revisited 20.9.1837
Happily the thoroughfare of the Churchyard has at length been stopped – much however is still needful to put the Church into a proper state.
Directions to the Churchwardens. (1) *Inside.* The *walls* to be coloured, and ceilings whitewashed – pews varnished and repaired – windows cleaned and painted. (2) *Outside.* Buttresses of Tower under-built and otherwise repaired; (*recommended* that the Tower be cased with brick or cement). Lead gutters of roof cleared out and raised. Private doors into Churchyard and walks leading from them taken away.
Recommended – That the titles on which many of the Parishioners claim the right of altering, letting and even *selling pews*, be carefully examined and a practice so injurious put a stop to.

Revisited 16.9.1841
Directions to Churchwardens – Buttresses of Tower restored, and the whole cased. Flat stones and bricks on North side of Church taken up and laid even – weeds cleared away, and the whole kept neat and clean. Drain formed to carry off the water from the roofs thro' the pipes – instead of overflowing the walks. Groins, window dressings, plinths etc repaired – pipes oiled and painted – walls on SW. side of Church raised, to prevent trespass on the Churchyard.

[1] A/V/1/3: '. . . but casements insufficient and not duly opened'. [2] *Eccles. Revs.:* Curate's income £100. [3] *Eccles. Revs.:* 'Fit'. [4] *Eccles. Revs.:* gross income £352.

ST. GEORGE, NEWCASTLE-UNDER-LYME
17.6.1830 (A/V/1/3,p.69;A/V/1/2,p.84)

BENEFICE: St. George's Chapel, Newcastle. **Nature:** At present, Chapel of Ease to the Parish Church – [intended] to become a *district* Church. **Ecton:** Not mentioned. **Patron:** The Rector of the Parish.[1]
CHURCH: A new Gothic building – nave and small Chancel in one body and under one roof [– no side aisles]. **Number it will contain:** 1,517. **Accommodation for Poor:** 800 sittings and upwards. **Walls:** 'Damp at present.' **Floor:** [Refers to 9–19]. All new and in good condition. **Pulpit and Desk:** 'Situation lately altered – not improved, tho' said to be easier to the Speaker.' **Plate:** 'None as yet.' **Iron Chest for Register:** 'None'. **Damp:** A good deal on the Walls – not yet dry.
CHURCHYARD: **Fence:** Not yet in complete order.
INCUMBENT: **Name and Residence:** 'Revd G Crakebill'.[2]
INCOME: ——.[3]
ORDERS MADE: Communion Plate to be provided. A Register Chest to be provided. Windows and (as far as possible) *doors* to be kept open. The walks kept clean. The Fence on the W. side of the Chapel yard properly secured.

Revisited 20.9.1837
Great appearance of want of strength and substance in the original construction of this Church. The *lead gutters* and *flashings* of *the roof* to be examined and kept in a proper state – *additional* down-pipes seem requisite, (one at least on each side) to carry off the wet. The *windows* to be strengthened with iron bars and lead ties. Weatherboards to be put up in the belfry – and the doors and window in the chamber *above* it closed. Water tables to be provided *inside*. The *walls* coloured – prayer book and reading desk new or repaired. The window above the West door to be put into a suitable state of repair.

Revisited 16.9.1841

Directions to Churchwardens. (1) Water-tables for windows – and new bell-ropes. (2) Parapets and battlements of Tower secured, and door leading to top of Tower kept shut. (3) The water which falls on the *roof* from the Tower, to be conveyed by a pipe to the ground. (4) East window strengthened. (5) Obstruction to digging of graves, from trees in Churchyard, guarded against.

[1] *Eccles. Revs.*: 'C Simeon'. [2] deleted in A/V/1/3 and replaced by 'Revd John Wright'. [3] *Eccles. Revs.*: Gross income £108, no glebe house.

RANTON 9.6.1830 (A/V/1/3,p.70;A/V/1/2,p.63)

BENEFICE: Ranton or Ronton. **Nature:** Vicarage. **Ecton:** Curacy – formerly an Abbey, Sir John Cope Patron. £6 16s. 8d. Clear value. **Patron:** Lord Anson. **Impropriator:** Mr Eld, except of a small part which he has sold to Lord Anson (on his Lordship's farms).

CHURCH: A small neat Gothic building – nave and Chancel – neat pointed Arch at the entrance into the Chancel and at the East end. **Number it will contain:** About 180, including benches for children – some within the Communion rails. **Accommodation for Poor:** 50 (included in the former) – more wanted. **Roof:** In good repair. **Walls:** Stone – good. **Floor:** Bricks – even. **Windows:** No casements. **Doors:** Good. **Pulpit and Desk:** Good – but no kneeling board in the Pulpit – a green cloth cushion; much moth-eaten. **Books:** Want re-binding. **Seats:** Oak – neat and uniform; new pewed, by brief, 25 years ago but not firm[1] – board floor, except of free seats. **Galleries:** None. **Organ:** ——. **Font:** Under the Arch leading into the Chancel – very dirty – no basin. **Chapels:** None. **Benefaction Tables:** One, recording a benefaction left in 1815 which cannot be obtained – there is another, not recorded. **Vestry:** A small one, [very] damp and brick floor – no furniture. **Surplices:** One – good but not properly kept. **Linen:** Table Cloth and napkin. **Plate:** Silver Cup and Patin – Pewter flagon. **Iron Chest for Registers:** In the Vestry – had better be kept at the house adjoining the Churchyard, on account of the dampness of the Vestry. **Register:** Two vols prior to 1813 – in good preservation; oldest date 1655. **Porch:** One on the S. side of the Church in good repair – a lock to be put upon the gate at its entrance and the inner door kept open. **Vaults:** None. **Cleanliness:** Not properly attended to.[2] **Damp:** Much on the floors and lower part of walls. **Dimensions:** 34ft. by 21ft. 5in.

CHANCEL: 21ft. 7in. by 14ft. **Table:** Very old and infirm; not at all becoming; no covering. **Ornaments:** None – the rails very bad, floor damp. **Repaired by whom:** The Lay Rector – but in very bad repair; the floor very damp and windows let in rain – walls very dirty.

STEEPLE: A small bell tower. **State of:** Pretty good – one or two tiles off. **Bells:** Two – good. **Clock:** None.

CHURCHYARD: **Fence:** Hedge – kept up partly by the Lay Rector, partly by occupiers of land[3] and, consequently, much neglected. **Gates:** Very bad. **Drains:** None – nor any spouts. **Graves:** Some too near the walls. **Rubbish:** Much – the whole Churchyard in very bad order.[4] **Footpaths:** Not properly attended to. **Cattle:** Cows and horses, belonging to the Impropriator's tenant – not to be allowed – it does not appear on what ground the Impropriator claims the Churchyard.

DIVINE SERVICE: **On Sundays:** Only in the afternoon; except on Sacrament Sundays. **On other days:** None. **Sacrament:** Three times a year. **Communicants:** Six. **Catechism:** Not in the Church.

INCUMBENT: **Name and Residence:** Revd WHC Lloyd.[5] **If not resident:** Resides at Norbury, about four miles off. **What duty he performs:** The whole.

CURATE: **Name and Residence:** None.

PARSONAGE: None.[6]

INCOME: **Gross Value:** About £90 per annum. **Tithes:** None – received by the Vicar – the Impropriator pays £5 6s. 8d. annually as a composition (it is supposed) for Tithes – enquiry should be made into this. **Queen Anne's Bounty:** Laid out in the purchase of land, from which the whole income of the living arises, with the exception of the £5 6s. 8d. mentioned above. **Terrier:** Two old ones.

SCHOOLS: **Endowed School:** None. **Subscription Day School:** None. **Sunday School:** 30 children, some of whom sit within the Communion rails. **Lancaster School:** None.

DISSENTERS: **Dissenters' School:** ——. **Dissenting Chapels:** ——.

POPULATION: 335 in 1821 – that of the Abbey 11 in addition.

MISCELLANEOUS: **Parochial Library:** None.

PARISH CLERK: Joseph Evans. **Appointed by:** The Vicar. **Salary:** £2 12s. 0d. and four shillings for washing the Surplice.

CHURCHWARDENS: Mr William Hall – who fills the office from year to year – and has given in no accounts for several years.

ORDERS MADE: Casements be made in the windows, on each side.

The Bible and Prayer books repaired. The Pulpit cushion new covered ; and a kneeling board or hassock provided for the Pulpit. The pannels and floors of the Pews repaired. The baptismal font cleaned, and a proper basin provided. The Benefaction tables completed. The Vestry boarded – and a Table, Chair and Closet provided. A new Communion Table provided, and the rails repaired. Cleanliness better attended to, and damp remedied. Children not to be allowed to sit within the Communion rails. Ten commandments to be put up. The Bell tower repaired – and a lock put on the Porch-gate. The mode of keeping up the fence altered – and a the whole put into proper repair. The earth removed and drains made etc, spouts put up etc. The gates repaired – paths improved; and Churchyard kept clear of weeds, briers and other rubbish.

Revisited 8.9.1837
I. Inside the Church
(1) Pannels and floors of pews, both in Church and Chancel, carefully looked over and repaired where needful. (2) Walls of Church, Chancel,

and Vestry, neatly colored and ceilings white-washed. (3) Floor of chancel re-laid, new communion rails put up and a new window at East end.

II. *Outside*
(1) Walls of chancel pointed. (2) Roofs of Church and Chancel repaired. (3) The soil and herbage cleared away round walls of Church and Chancel, and eave spouts and down pipes affixed to roofs of both. (4) New gates at N. West end entrance of Churchyard – fence repaired adjoining the Gates. ['Done or in progress – Qu? Chancel floor.']

[1841 Orders[7]]. Visited October 12th
So much has been done for the improvement of this neat little Church and its precincts that I have nothing to desire further than that all things may be kept in their present excellent state.
It would be well to have the *Bible re-bound*.

[1] A/V/1/3: '... but not in a substantial manner'. [2] A/V/1/3: 'Neglected'. [3] A/V/1/3: '... Lay Rector – partly in doles by the Parishioners ...'. [4] A/V/1/3: '... in a neglected state'. [5] Also rector of Norbury. [6] *Eccles. Revs.:* 'None'. [7] Loose sheet preserved in A/V/1/3.

SANDON 14.6.1830
(A/V/1/3,p.71;A/V/1/2,p.56.)

BENEFICE: Sandon. **Nature:** Vicarage – (in Ecton called a Rectory). **Ecton:** Living discharged – Clear yearly value £47 10s. 0d. **Patron:** Lord Harrowby – (Ecton. Lord Archibald Hamilton). **Impropriator:** Lord H. has a part of the great Tithes – the Vicar the remainder.
CHURCH: A very neat, regularly-built, structure; nave and 2 side aisles – pointed Arches; the Arch which separates the Chancel from the body of the Church modernised. **Number it will contain:** 400 including children. **Accommodation for Poor:** About 200 – sufficient for the wants of *the Parish*. **Roof:** Timber covered with tiles – in good repair, but in danger of injury from Ivy. **Walls:** Stone – upright. **Floor:** Quarries and grave stones – some of the latter have sunk. **Windows:** Good – but not sufficiently supplied with casements. **Doors:** Good. **Pulpit and Desk:** Well placed and good – crimson cloth cushion etc. **Books:** Want repairing. **Seats:** Uniform – floors partly brick, partly board – some repairs wanted in the floors. **Galleries:** One over the Chancel entrance, belonging to Ld. H. – another at the SW. end of the Church. **Organ:** None. **Font:** Near the W. end. **Chapels:** None. **Benefaction Tables:** None. **Vestry:** None – might easily be provided. **Surplices:** Two, in good order. **Linen:** Table Cloth and napkin. **Plate:** Small plated flagon – silver Cup; no paten. **Chest for Papers:** There is. **Iron Chest for Register:** At the Vicarage. **Register:** From *1635* to present time – in good repair. **Porch:** There is one, in good order. **Vaults:** None recently – several formerly, much to the injury of the floor etc. **Cleanliness:** Not sufficiently attended to. **Damp:** Much on the lower parts of the walls. **Dimensions:** 38ft. 11in. by 52ft. 3in.
CHANCEL: 38ft. 2in. by 14ft. 7in. **Table:** Oak – firm – wants cleaning. **Ornaments:** Crimson cloth covering to the Table. **Repaired by whom:** The Patron – in good order, excepting damp at the East end – and on the ceiling.
STEEPLE: Square stone tower, covered with Ivy. **State of:** Injured by Ivy – the pinnacles want securing. **Bells:** Three and a small one – the iron parts want painting – and some repairs. **Clock:** None.
CHURCHYARD: **Fence:** Kept up partly by the Vicar, partly by the Parish – the latter wants raising to keep out sheep etc. **Gates:** Good. **Drains:** There are – but not kept sufficiently clear – no spouts. **Graves:** Not many too near the walls. **Rubbish:** Weeds and Ivy in great abundance – but no heaps of rubbish. **Footpaths:** Well kept. **Cattle:** None.
DIVINE SERVICE: **On Sundays:** Two full services. **On other Days:** None, regularly. **Sacrament:** Four times a year. **Communicants:** 30.
INCUMBENT: **Name and Residence:** Revd WE Coldwell, Stafford.[1] **What duty he performs:** Occasionally comes over and takes a part.
CURATE: **Name and Residence:** Revd EB Seckerson, in the Vicarage. **If not resident:** ——. **Licensed:** He is. **Salary:** 120 Guineas – together with the House, Garden, Churchyard and Paddock adjoining. **If serving another church:** None.[2]
PARSONAGE: A small house, in Cottage form – thatched roof – two parlours, kitchens etc below – six bedrooms. **State of:** Good, excepting the Thatch. **Outbuildings:** Stable – Cowhouses – Barn, in good repair.
INCOME: **Gross Value:** £350. **Tithes:** Vicarial, and one-third of the Corn tithe. **Glebe:** Seven acres. **Easter Dues and small Payments:** None. **Queen Anne's Bounty:** ——. **Terrier:** There is one – 1824.
SCHOOLS: **Endowed School:** None. **Subscription Day School:** A national school – 120 children; supported partly by Lord Harrowby. **Sunday School:** The same children as in the week. **Lancaster School:** None.
DISSENTERS: **Dissenting Chapels:** One Methodist.
POPULATION: About 500.
PARISH CLERK: John Dix. **Appointed by:** The Vicar.
CHURCHWARDENS: Brian Ellsmore, the Vicar; Hugh Davidson, the Parish.
ORDERS MADE: ['In progress'.]
The Bible and Prayer-book repaired – two more casements in the body of the Church, the *iron* frames of the windows painted – the floor repaired, in the Cross aisle, at the upper end of the Church – and also the floors of some of the Pews, Benefaction Tables, and the Commandments to be set up in the Church.
The Communion Table cleaned, the Cover taken off during the week, and the regular cleaning of the Church more duly attended to.
(A *Vestry recommended*.) A Paten for the Sacrament-bread.
The pinnacles of the Tower secured; and Ivy removed from the *roofs* of the Church and Chancel, the inside of the Tower, and elsewhere where injurious.
The Bells repaired where needful, and cleaned – the iron work painted.
The open drains round the Church kept properly cleared.

The fence on the E. end of the Churchyard raised.

The trees on the N. side cut down where they interfere with digging the graves.

Revisited 9.9.1837
Much reparation needed both externally and internally, especially the former. Roofs, gables, copings, lead gutters and flashings; the roof, battlements and pinnacles of the Tower, the spouts on NW. side of Church – are sustaining much injury and causing much dampness and discoloration of walls and ceilings; with decay of floors and pannels and wainscoting of pews adjoining the walls – *within* the Church. As Mr Thomas Trubshaw is now altering and adding to the Church I suggested to the Vicar and Churchwardens the propriety of desiring him to make a careful survey of the whole Fabric, and a report of the necessary repairs, with an estimate of the expense required for thoroughly repairing the whole. The floors of some of the pews near the South door, must be taken up and re-laid, and when these alterations are ended, the walls must be neatly coloured and the ceilings whitewashed. 'Under thorough repair.'

[1] Also rector of St. Mary's, Stafford. [2] *Eccles. Revs.*: 'None'.

SEIGHFORD 8.6.1830
(A/V/1/3,p.72;A/V/1/2,p.61)

BENEFICE: Seighford (Ecton, Sightford). **Nature:** Vicarage. **Ecton:** Clear yearly value £41 2s. 8d. – Pri: Ronton Impr. **Patron:** The Lord Chancellor. **Impropriator:** Francis Eld Esqr except of a small portion of the great Tithes which belong to the Vicar.
CHURCH: An old Saxon structure, as appears from the massy pillars and circular arches which separate the body of the Church from the North Aisle – there is however no corresponding South Aisle; the S. side seems to have been taken down and re-built in modern style. **Number it will contain:** About 450.[1] **Accommodation for Poor:** Only a small gallery, and two or three pews below. **Roof:** Oak covered with tile; in good repair; the leaden gutters want cleaning. **Walls:** The North, stone – the South brick, erected in 1752, – all good. **Floor:** Quarries, bricks and flat stones – very uneven towards the NE. end. **Windows:** Good – but only one casement; others ordered. **Doors:** One, at the W. end – good. **Pulpit and Desk:** Old oak, painted; well placed – old crimson hangings – new crimson cushion. **Books:** Repairs wanted. **Seats:** Oak, uniform; brick floors, except in the Chancel. **Galleries:** One for singers at the W. end; and one in the N. aisle. **Organ:** None. **Font:** There is one – but no basin. **Chapels:** None – the North chancel has an old monument to the Bower family. **Benefaction Tables:** Two; one of the charities, arising from land at Bushbury, has not been received (tho' applied for) for 27 years. **Vestry:** A small one, taken off from the N. aisle. **Surplices:** Two, one very bad, a new one to be provided [– ordered]; and both kept at the Vicarage. **Linen:** Provided. **Plate:** Two Pewter Flagons and plates; and a small silver Cup; not sufficient for convenience; the Flagons out of use and repair. **Chest for Papers:** In the entrance to the Church – where the Flagons are kept. **Iron Chest for Register:** At the Vicarage. **Register:** Three Vols prior to 1813 – oldest 1560; complete. **Porch:** The entrance at the W. end, under the Tower; ceiling wants repair. **Vaults:** Only in the Chancel – belonging to the Eld family. **Cleanliness:** Not sufficiently attended to, [especially] in the Windows and Gallery. **Damp:** In the Chancels. **Dimensions:** 41ft. 6in. by 37ft. 4in.
CHANCEL: 39ft. by 37ft. 4in., the breadth of both chancels together as well as of the Church. **Table:** Old oak; wants repair and cleaning. **Ornaments:** Crimson velvet covering to the Table. **Repaired by whom:** The Lay Rector; – the roof, walls and floor want repair, and protection from damp – the windows cleaning and making weathertight; the Iron frames painting etc.
STEEPLE: Square brick tower, [re-]built in 1752. **State of:** Good, except the battlements at the Top. **Bells:** Five – one of them wants the wheel and rope mended; the floor of the Belfry repaired – door above the Bells closed and weatherboards completed; walls of belfry whitewashed. **Clock:** There is; in good repair.
CHURCHYARD: **Fence:** Kept up by different parishioners [in doles]; partly hedge – partly rails; much out of repair and order. **Gates:** One of them needs to be repaired, or renewed. **Drains:** None, nor spouts; both ordered. **Graves:** Not many too near. **Rubbish:** Ivy on the N. and E. – and rubbish near the School, which is kept under the Tower. **Footpaths:** None trespass. **Cattle:** Sheep occasionally.
DIVINE SERVICE: **On Sundays:** Full service morning – prayers afternoon. **On other Days:** None regularly. **Sacrament:** Three or four times a year, and the festivals. **Communicants:** From 30 to 40 at the festivals. **Catechism:** Taught in the School.
INCUMBENT: **Name and Residence:** Revd T Watkin Richards.[2] **If not resident:** Resides on his other living at Puttenham, Surrey, at present Chaplain to the British Embassy at Vienna.
CURATE: **Name and Residence:** Revd EJ Rathbone, in the Vicarage. **Licensed:** He is. **Salary:** The whole endowment of the living; deducting the necessary repairs of the Parsonage house. **If serving another church:** None.
PARSONAGE: A brick building, partly rebuilt by Mr Whitby, the former Vicar; three parlours and kitchen on the ground floor – five bedrooms and dressing room above.[3] **State of:** Good, in general. **Outbuildings:** Barn, Coach-house, two stables.
INCOME: **Gross Value:** £110 per annum. **Tithes:** Small [tithes] of the whole Parish, and [the] large of a small portion. **Glebe:** 45 acres, **Surplice Fees:** £5 a year. **Easter Dues and small Payments:** Easter dues, collected. **Terrier:** The Curate has a Copy of one dated 1726.
SCHOOLS: **Endowed School:** A small one (taught under the Church) £3 a year, chargeable on land; for *four* children; others attend and pay. **Subscription Day School:** None. **Sunday School:** 35 children, (including the day school).
DISSENTERS: **Dissenters' School:** One at Bridgford.

Dissenting Chapels: A Methodist meeting.
POPULATION: About 900.
MISCELLANEOUS: **Monuments:** To the Eld family – and one to the Bowers. **Parochial Library:** None.
PARISH CLERK: William Hodgetts. **Appointed by:** The Vicar. **Salary:** £6 0s. 0d. (£2 5s. 0d. specified by the Terrier).
CHURCHWARDENS: Richard Woolams – Hubbart.
ORDERS MADE: ['Finished'.]
   Cleanliness to be better attended to, especially in the Galleries, Windows, Belfry. Two more casements in the Church – and two ditto in the Chancels. Gutters of the Roof cleared, and the lead repaired, where sunk. Floor in the North Chancel laid even. Prayer Book and Bible repaired. Basin provided for the Font. A new surplice; surplices better taken care of. The Flagons repaired and kept in use. The tower repaired at the Top; wheel and rope of one of the Bells repaired – belfry floor repaired – walls whitewashed; weatherboards completed, door closed. The walls and windows of the Chancel repaired and cleaned. The Fence and Gates in the Churchyard repaired; and the present method of keeping up the Fence (in doles) altered. Earth cleared away – open drains – spouts put up; Ivy and rubbish removed. Ventilation properly attended to. The benefaction from Bushbury re-claimed.

Revisited 8.9.1837
   'Church *and* Chancel.'

   I. *Inside the Church*
   (1) The walls of the Church to be neatly coloured. (2) The cracks of the ceiling filled up; ceiling repaired and whitewashed. (3) The floor of the north chancel to be taken up, and re-laid, even, with tiles and bricks. (4) A new Prayer book for the Clergyman's desk, and new surplice, to be provided.

   II. *Outside*
   (1) Eave spouts to be placed along the roof on both sides of the Church, and *down spouts* of metal to carry off the water into a drain of sufficient depth and fall. (2) The buttresses to be *repaired* and *pointed*. (3) Walls to be pointed along the lower parts. (4) Fences all round the churchyard to be repaired where needful – hedges trimmed and gates painted. (5) Church paths weeded and trespass paths stopped. (6) Roofs, especially at North side of the Church examined and repaired, and lead flashings placed at the junctions of Roof and Tower. Weatherboards secured in the Belfry. (7) The *privy* on North side of the Churchyard taken away and fence made up 'In progress and promised to be completed. Qu? *Chancel*'.
   Mem: I strongly urged the Clergyman to take measures for getting a School room erected in the Parish, so as to avoid keeping the School in the precincts of the Church.

Chancel of Seighford Church
Revisited September 8th.
   The *Chancel* requires much reparation both *externally* and *internally*.

Externally
Buttresses repaired and strengthened. Eave spouts and down pipes put up. Soil and herbage cleared away properly round the walls, and an open drain formed with bricks or tiles. Roof repaired and lead flashings placed at the junction with the body of the Church.

Internally
Windows repaired and iron bars painted. Walls coloured to match those of the Church, and ceiling whitewashed. Top of Communion table made fast.

[1841 Orders[4]]
   (1) A mat, or *Carpet,* or oil cloth to be provided for the Communion floor. (2) New books for the Clergyman's and Clerk's desks. (3) Water tables to the windows. (4) The old pews rubbed with boiled linseed oil. (5) The roof of the Tower re-tiled, and the weather-cock taken down. (6) The roofs to be spouted at the eaves, and the wet conveyed to the ground by down-pipes. (7) A gravel walk, or pavement of flags, tiles or bricks, to be formed close to the walls, all round, to keep the walls dry.
   N.B. I strongly *recommend* that the Galleries *on the North side* of the Church be taken down, and the West Gallery brought further forward, so as to seat the School children – *also,* that the footpaths through the Churchyard be stopped, and the *nuisance* on the North side of it, removed.

[1] *Eccles. Revs.:* 560. [2] Also rector of Puttenham (Surrey): *Eccles. Revs.* [3] *Eccles. Revs.:* 'Fit'. [4] Loose sheet inserted in A/V/1/3.

STAFFORD 8.6.1830
(A/V/1/3,p.73;A/V/1/2,p.60)

BENEFICE: Stafford. **Nature:** Rectory – endowed with a portion of four Prebends formerly belonging, together with a Deanery and two other Prebends, to the Collegiate Church of Stafford, restored by Queen Elizabeth in 1572. **Ecton:** Olim a College – not in charge or certified. **Patron:** The Lord Chancellor. **Impropriator:** None.
CHURCH: A very handsome antient Gothic Church, resembling a Cathedral in its structure; Nave, side Aisles, Transept and Chancel with two side Chancels – plain pointed Arches. **Number it will contain:** 1,200 conveniently – 1,400 may be accommodated. **Accommodation for Poor:** 278 – besides about 250 in the Chancel, for children. **Roof:** Oak, covered with lead, except the South Chancel, which is tiled. **Walls:** Solid stone, upright; the outward facing much decayed by weather. **Floor:** Brick, and grave stones – very uneven in several places.[1] **Windows:** Good, and well provided with casements. **Doors:** That at the SW. side wants a weatherboard; and all of them *painting.* **Pulpit and Desk:** Not very well placed – but neat; handsome crimson velvet ornaments.[2]
Books: Prayer book wants repairing or renewing.
Seats: Not very uniform, or well arranged – more accommodation (which is much needed) might be obtained by a better arrangement of the Pews.
Galleries: On two sides and at the W. end.

Organ: There is one. **Font:** In the North transept – a very antient one; a *basin* wanted. **Chapels:** None – part of the N. transept is railed off as burying place for the Clifford family. **Benefaction Tables:** Several – all the charities recorded, except a recent one, which will be added. **Vestry:** There is a small one. **Surplices:** Three – good. **Linen:** Table Cloth and two napkins good. **Plate:** Two Silver flagons, two Patins, one Chalice; two [large] Dishes – very handsome – another Cup wanted. **Chest for Papers:** In the Vestry. **Iron Chest for Registers:** Two – in the Vestry. **Register:** Nine Vols, prior to 1813 – oldest date 1559 – all in good preservation, and appear perfect, except a few years between 1650 and 1660. **Porch:** At each end of the Transept, a small one. **Vaults:** Many, both in the Church and Chancel – frequently opened. **Cleanliness:** Not sufficiently attended to. **Damp:** No appearance of it. **Dimensions:** 72ft. 6in. by 60ft. Transept 95ft. by about 25ft.

CHANCEL: 65ft. 6in. by 71ft. **Table:** An old, and very plain, oak table – wants cleaning and ornaments. **Ornaments:** Commandments etc. Two handsome Altar Services given by the present Rector. **Repaired by whom:** Out of funds left for the purpose (in common with the repairs of the Church) *as far as they will go* – other portions of the money arising from the Prebends have been allotted to the repairs.

STEEPLE: An octangular base; formerly surmounted by a spire, which was blown down, and a cornice put to the Tower in 1777. **State of:** Not very good – especially at the *lower part,* which formed the *base* of the antient spire. **Bells:** Eight besides the small one – good. **Clock:** There is one, and also chimes – but no *dial* plate.

CHURCHYARD: **Fence:** Brick wall, and houses; the former chiefly repaired by the Churchwardens[3] – the Churchyard is an open thoroughfare. **Gates:** Good. **Drains:** None – nor pipes, (in general) to convey the water from the roof. **Graves:** Several close to the walls. **Rubbish:** Very much – and earth, weeds etc accumulated against the walls. **Footpaths:** Several – one a *trespass path*. **Cattle:** None.

DIVINE SERVICE: **On Sundays:** Three full services. **On other Days:** Wednesday and Friday Prayers – Wednesday Evening Lecture.[4] **Sacrament:** Monthly and at the Festivals. **Communicants:** 150 to 200. **Catechism:** During Lent.

INCUMBENT: **Name and Residence:** Revd WE Coldwell, Rectory.[5] **What duty he performs:** Shares the whole with his Curate.

CURATE: **Name and Residence:** Revd R Temple, near the Church. **Licensed:** He is. **Salary:** £100. **If serving another Church:** None.

PARSONAGE: A commodious house in the Town, provided, about 130 years ago, by the Corporation in exchange for the old Rectory which stood in the Churchyard – four stories high – entrance hall, parlour, kitchens [etc] on ground floor, two sitting rooms, seven bedrooms above.[6] **State of:** Good throughout. **Outbuildings:** None – but there is a garden.

INCOME: **Gross Value:** [Will be about] £400, when the present dispute is finally adjusted.[7] **Surplice Fees:** About £50. **Terrier:** None – except an antient grant of Queen Elizabeth.

SCHOOLS: **Endowed School:** There is a school of King Edward's endowment – £450 per annum – open to all the Town. **Subscription Day School:** National Schools. 240 children. **Sunday School:** 220 children. **Lancaster School:** None.

DISSENTERS: **Dissenters' School:** Three Sunday Schools. **Dissenting Chapels:** Methodists and Independents.

POPULATION: Of the whole Parish about 7,000, of which 6,000 in the Town – there is a Perpetual Curacy of Marston, appended to the Rectory – and three other Townships, without chapels.

MISCELLANEOUS: **Monuments:** Several. **Parochial Library:** None.

PARISH CLERK: John Tinnesley.

CHURCHWARDENS: Mr Fowke and Mr ['Shaw'].

ORDERS MADE: The doors to be painted externally, and a new weatherboard to that at the lower end of the Church on the South side. The Prayer book in the Reading desk to be repaired, or a new one provided. A proper basin for the Baptismal Font to be provided. The Communion Table cleaned and varnished or otherwise beautified. The buttresses, battlements, base of the Tower to be carefully examined, and the stones secured by mortar or iron-cramps, as the case may require. The walls to be repaired where the surface has been injured by the weather – and underbuilt where the plinth has been dilapidated by soil and damp.

The earth cleared away all round the Church, and an open drain, three feet wide, formed – spouting to be completed and pipes to convey the wet from the roofs and walls. No graves to be allowed within six feet of the Church walls. The grass to be kept mown, and all weeds and rubbish to be cleared away. The trespass footpath to be stopped up.

Revisited 8.9.1837
1. St. Mary's Stafford.

Memorandum
The state of this Church and its precincts is all so dilapidated that instead of giving directions to the Churchwardens as to minute points requiring attention, I thought it better to direct them to have the entire fabric thoroughly examined by an experienced and skilful Architect, and to send me his report together with an estimate of the expense necessary for putting the roofs, walls, buttresses, parapets, Tower, floors, ceilings etc into a state of complete and substantial repair. This report and estimate being obtained I shall advise the Churchwardens to apply to the Court of Chancery for a sum of money sufficient (if the funds at its disposal will allow) for the above purposes; and at the same time to endeavour to raise, by an appeal to the public, a sufficient sum to enable them to enclose the Church and Churchyard, and thus protect the sacred precincts from the disgraceful profanation to which they are now exposed. Should the above application prove unsuccessful I must call upon them, at all events, to have –

(1) The buttress at the *SE.* aisle of the Church effectually repaired. (2) The other buttresses pointed and repaired where needful. (3) The lead

roofing of the N. Chancel completed. (4) The ridging of S. Chancel roof repaired and secured. (5) Lead gutters cleaned out. (6) Windows mended. (7) Churchyard cleaned from nettles and other accumulations.

'Nothing done – urge Subscription.'[8]

[1] A/V/1/3: '... much sunk in several places.' [2] A/V/1/3: '... in good condition.' [3] A/V/1/3: '... by the parish.' [4] A/V/1/3: '... Wednesday Evenings – Service.' [5] Also vicar of Sandon. [6] *Eccles. Revs.:* 'Fit'. [7] A/V/1/3; '... law-suit is settled.' *Eccles. Revs.:* gives the gross income as £221. [8] Faculty granted 25.8.1841 (B/C/2/1841-6, pp.51-63) for restoration, including repewing, removal of galleries and erection of a West gallery. The architects were Scott and Moffatt.

STANDON 4.10.1830
(A/V/1/3,p.74;A/V/1/2,p.144)

BENEFICE: Standon. **Nature:** Rectory. **Ecton:** King's Books £6 18s. 4d. **Patron:** Revd Mr Walker (the present Rector) formerly W Vyse Esqr. **Impropriator:** None.
CHURCH: An old irregular building – apparently Gothic – centre and two side aisles – pillars and pointed Arches of unequal height on the two sides – a low circular arch leading into the Chancel. **Number it will contain:** About 250. **Accommodation for Poor:** Sufficient. **Roof:** Timber covered with tiles, and lead gutters – to be examined – flat ceiling. **Walls:** Stone – not very upright. **Floor:** Brick – even but damp. **Windows:** Good – well provided with casements. **Doors:** Want lining inside, and new weatherboards. **Pulpit and Desk:** Pretty good and well placed. **Books:** Much out of repair. **Seats:** Some out of repair, especially in the S. aisle – floors bad. **Galleries:** One at the W. end for singers and others. **Organ:** None. **Font:** An old one near the South door – the cover wants repair. **Chapels:** None. **Benefaction Tables:** One. **Vestry:** There is one – casements wanted, and walls whitewashed. **Surplices:** One, bad – another ordered. **Linen:** Provided. **Plate:** An old, very small, Cup and patin, of silver – pewter flagon and basin. **Chest for Papers:** There is one. **Iron Chest for Registers:** At the Rectory. **Register:** From 1558 – entire and in good preservation. **Porch:** There is one, in good repair. **Vaults:** None recently. **Cleanliness:** Attended to, except in the Pews. **Damp:** On the floor and lower parts of Walls.
CHANCEL: **Table:** Oak, firm but dirty – rails also want cleaning. **Ornaments:** Commandments – old Monument and flat tombstones. **Repaired by whom:** The Rector.
STEEPLE: Square stone tower. **State of:** Wants pointing. **Bells:** Three – gudgeons want repair – the weatherboards ditto. **Clock:** Good.
CHURCHYARD: **Fence:** Stone wall, and sunk fence – good state. **Gates:** Pretty good. **Drains:** None – nor spouts and pipes. **Graves:** Not many [too] near the walls. **Rubbish:** None. **Footpaths:** A thoroughfare – to be stopped if possible. **Cattle:** None.
DIVINE SERVICE: **On Sundays:** Full service morning – prayers afternoon. **On other days:** None. **Sacrament:** Four times a year – formerly eight times. **Communicants:** About 14. **Catechism:** Not now.
INCUMBENT: **Name and Residence:** Revd Thomas Walker – Rectory. **What duty he performs:** None – from ill health.
CURATE: **Name and Residence:** Revd Alfred Hadfield – in the Parish. **Licensed:** He is. **Salary:** £60 per annum. **If serving another church:** None.
PARSONAGE: A substantial brick building, tiled roof – three sitting rooms below, kitchens etc, seven bedrooms above. **State of:** Good. **Outbuildings:** Coach-house – Stable etc all good.
INCOME: **Gross Value:** £500 or £600 [a year]. **Tithes:** All – except a modus for Hay in one of the Townships. **Glebe:** 90 acres. **Terrier:** Two copies in the Parish Book.
SCHOOLS: **Endowed School:** None. **Subscription Day School:** None. **Sunday School:** Taught in the Vestry – about 50; a school-room about to be built. **Lancaster School:** None.
DISSENTERS: **Dissenters' School:** ——. **Dissenting Chapels:** A small Independent Meeting.
POPULATION: 420.
PARISH CLERK: Shadrach Ashley. **Appointed by:** The Rector. **Salary:** 50s. a year.
CHURCHWARDENS: John Swinnerton – Rector. John Grimshaw – Parish.
ORDERS MADE: The roof to be examined and repaired – lead gutters cleaned out and repaired. Eave spouts to be placed along the roofs – and down-pipes to convey the wet from the tower and roofs to the ground. The earth removed to a sufficient depth round the walls, and a drain formed to carry off the damp. The inner South door to be lined inside, and a new weatherboard made. The Books repaired or renewed. The Pews in the North Chancel to be put into repair – the floors laid with bricks or boards, hollow. A new Surplice provided – a rail, put up in the Gallery at the North end, for security. A casement put in the Vestry window – the walls whitewashed – Cover of Font repaired. The Communion Table, and rails, oiled and cleaned. The floor of the Chancel relaid, within and without the rails. The Chancel spouted, and earth lowered, as [directed for] the body of the Church. The Tower pointed – new Gudgeons and bells; weatherboards – trap-door to roof – ladder leading to Belfry mended, or a new one. The thoroughfare through the Churchyard stopped, *if possible*.

Revisited 9.10.1837
In a very good state. (1) Roof, at juncture with tower, cemented or flashed with lead. (2) Walls pointed where needful. (3) Thoroughfare of Churchyard stopped, if possible. (It being dark, I did not see the Tower etc.) 'Qu? *floors* of pews and quarries *see* Mr Grimshaw'.

Revisited 13.10.1841
Directions etc. (1) Bible in Reading Desk rebound – Prayer Book repaired. (2) Mat, or carpet, for Communion Floor – Communion Table and rails. Cleaned and rubbed with boiled linseed oil – old oak pewing oiled in same manner. (3) Floors of pews *boarded*. Floors of side aisles, at NW. and SE. ends, repaired and re-laid.

(N.B. Recommended that *North Aisle* be fitted up with open seats with a boarded platform, for use of poor.)

(4) Roofs of Tower and Church examined and repaired, also West wall of Tower. (5) Walls of buttresses repaired and pointed – especially at lower parts.

SHERIFF HALES 9.6.1830
(A/V/1/3,p.75;A/V/1/2,p.66)

BENEFICE: Sheriffhales (Ecton. *Shref* – hales). **Nature:** Vicarage. **Ecton:** King's Books £11 1s. 8d. Pri. Shene in Surr. Impr. **Patron:** Lord Gower. **Impropriator:** Ditto.
CHURCH: A large Gothic building – modernised in several respects; but a remarkably handsome open wood roof[1] remaining. **Number it will contain:** About 600.[2] **Accommodation for Poor:** In the Gallery – not sufficient for the population. **Roof:** Oak covered with tile. **Walls:** Solid stone. **Floor:** Flags – very good. **Windows:** Very good – casements sufficient. **Doors:** ——. **Pulpit and Desk:** Handsome and well situated; purple velvet cushion. **Books:** Bible and Prayer-book want re-binding. **Seats:** Uniform and very good – oak. **Galleries:** One at the W. end, for singers and children – a casement wanted in it. **Organ:** None. **Font:** There is one – but no proper basin. **Chapels:** None. **Benefaction Table:** Two – all the charities recorded. **Vestry:** A small one, very dark, **Surplices:** Two – good. **Linen:** Lately stolen out of the Church. **Plate:** Silver Cup and Paten. **Iron Chest for Register:** At the Vicarage. **Register:** Four Vols prior to 1813 – in good pre-servation. **Porch:** None. **Vaults:** None recently. **Cleanliness:** Attended to. **Damp:** Much on the walls – especially at the W. end.
CHANCEL: **Table:** Neat oak table. **Ornaments:** None. **Repaired by whom:** Lord Gower – in good repair.
STEEPLE: Square stone Tower. **State of:** Pointing wanted – bushes growing upon it. **Bells:** Five and a small one – good. **Clock:** There is one.
CHURCHYARD: **Fence:** Kept up by the Parish – in good order. **Gates:** Some repairs wanted. **Drains:** There is a surf – but still much damp upon the walls – spouts provided – but some alteration wanted in the placing of the pipes. **Graves:** Too near. **Rubbish:** Not any observable. **Footpaths:** Pretty well kept. **Cattle:** A donkey.
DIVINE SERVICE: **On Sundays:** *One* full service – in the morning three Sundays in the month, after-noon the fourth alternated with Woodcote chapel. **Sacrament:** At the festivals. **Communicants:** Uncertain.
INCUMBENT: **Name and Residence:** Revd WH Molineux. ['Since *dead* – John Hinckley new Incumbent.'] **If not resident:** Near Tong.
CURATE: **Name and Residence:** Revd Mr Dean – in the Vicarage. **Licensed:** Yes. **If serving another church:** Woodcote Chapel [– in the Parish].
PARSONAGE: Brick building – two sitting rooms; and kitchens on the ground floor – four bedrooms. **State of:** Good, in general.[3] **Outbuildings:** Stable etc.
INCOME: **Gross Value:** £500.[4] **Tithes:** About £300 from Woodcote. **Terrier:** There is one.
SCHOOLS: **Endowed School:** None. **Subscription Day School:** A National school. **Sunday School:** None.
DISSENTERS: **Dissenting Chapels:** A Methodist meeting.
POPULATION: 920.
PARISH CLERK: Thomas Teke. **Appointed by:** The Vicar or his Curate. **Salary:** £6 10s. 0d.
CHURCHWARDENS: Mr Robert Pearse, Mr Thomas Whittle.
ORDERS MADE: ['Done – see Mr Dean's letter.'] The Bible and Prayer-book to be re-bound. A basin provided for the Font. A casement made in the Gallery window. Roof examined and repaired at the W. end. The Tower pointed – and pipes better connected with the spouts. A clear open space preserved all round the walls. Gates repaired and painted.

Revisited 12.10.1837 – all in good order. Baptismal basin wanted. Roof and ridging tiles repaired. Ditto of Tower repaired. Lead gutters cleaned out. Thoroughfare stopped. 'Nothing done.'

Revisited 15.10.1841
Could not judge of state of interior, owing to an Organ being erected – recommended to *spout* the N. side of Chancel – and bring the wet by down-pipes from between the two roofs – to lay a gravel walk all round the Church.

[1] A/V/1/3: '. . . handsome open carved ceiling remain-ing.' [2] *Eccles. Revs.*: 300. [3] *Eccles. Revs.*: 'Unfit'. [4] *Eccles. Revs.*: Gross income £675.

WOODCOTE 9.6.1830
(A/V/1/3 with Sheriffhales;A/V/1/2,p.65)

BENEFICE: Woodcote or Woodcoat Chapel.[1] **Nature:** Chapel of ease to Sheriff hales – but in point of situation and size has every character of a private domestic chapel attached to Woodcote Hall. Mr Cotes – the Chapelry has its own warden, and maintains its own poor. **Ecton:** Not certified. **Patron:** The Vicar of Sheriffhales appoints the Curate.
CHURCH: A small building, Gothic architecture;[2] single body – no chancel. **Number it will contain:** About 50. **Accommodation for Poor:** None in particular. **Books:** Bible wants repair.
CHURCHYARD: **Drains:** None. **Rubbish:** Much ivy upon the E. end of the Chapel.
DIVINE SERVICE: **On Sundays:** In the Morning once in the month – at other times in the afternoon.
CURATE: **Name and Residence:** Revd Mr Dean – Sheriff-hales; upwards of 80 – not adequate to the proper performance of the duty.[3]
ORDERS MADE: [Other particulars not noted – there being no one to give information. The Chapel is not kept in good order – tho' there are no very material instances of neglect observable.]
The Bible to be repaired – spouts put up – an open drain all round. Ivy removed – weather-board put up.

[1] 'Particular enquiries not made – partly from want of time, partly from the absence of the Curate, Warden etc. No one to give correct information'. [2] A/V/1/3: 'Gothic windows'. [3] *Eccles. Revs.* states that the population was 195.

STONE 14.6.1830 (A/V/1/3,p.76;A/V/1/2,p.58)

BENEFICE: Stone. **Nature:** Perpetual Curacy. **Ecton:** £4 13s. 0d. clear value – Pri. Stone Propr. **Patron:** The Lord Chancellor. **Impropriator:** Mr Swinfin Jervis of Swinfen, as Lessee.[1]
CHURCH: A neat modern structure – erected about 60 years ago – single body. **Number it will contain:** About 1,400 in pews. **Accommodation for Poor:** 150 – more needed. **Roof:** Oak, covered with lead – in good repair generally. **Walls:** Stone – good and upright. **Floor:** Flags. **Windows:** Good, and well provided with casements; but the casements not properly kept open. **Doors:** Good. **Pulpit and Desk:** Handsome – oak, well situated; crimson velvet cushion and hangings. **Books:** Not in good repair – new ones ordered. **Seats:** Neat and uniform. **Galleries:** On three sides. **Organ:** There is one. **Font:** Handsome marble – near the W. door – basin wanted. **Chapels:** None. **Benefaction Tables:** Two – sufficient. **Vestry:** A small one, not convenient.[2] **Surplices:** Three – good. **Linen:** Provided – but not good. **Plate:** Silver flagon – two silver Cups and Dishes – one paten. **Iron Chest for Register:** In the Vestry. **Register:** Several Vols from 1568 – in good preservation. **Porch:** None. **Vaults:** None recently. **Cleanliness:** Well attended to. **Damp:** No appearance.
CHANCEL: *No Chancel* (properly speaking). **Table:** Handsome mahogany table. **Ornaments:** Velvet Covering to Table. **Repaired by whom:** The Parish.
STEEPLE: Square stone Tower. **State of:** Good. **Bells:** Six – in good order. **Clock:** Good.
CHURCHYARD: **Fence:** Brick wall, good – kept up by Parish. **Gates:** Good – iron. **Drains:** Under ground – sufficient. **Graves:** Not near the Church – which is surrounded by a good, broad gravel walk. **Footpaths:** Properly kept in general. **Cattle:** None.
DIVINE SERVICES: **On Sundays:** Two full services. **On other Days:** Prayers on Wednesday and Friday. **Sacrament:** Eight times a year. **Communicants:** 50 to 60. **Catechism:** Not in the Church.
INCUMBENT: **Name and Residence:** Revd JT Hinds, Parsonage.[3] **What Duty he performs:** The whole [since this period he has removed to London – and the duty is done by a Curate – Revd Mr Sneyd].[4]
CURATE: **Name and Residence:** None.
PARSONAGE: A brick house – [neat and] commodious – much improved by the present Incumbent, who has laid out a great deal of money upon it. **State of:** Good.[5] **Outbuildings:** Stable, coach-house etc.
INCOME: **Gross Value:** £200. **Glebe:** Eight or ten acres. **Queen Anne's Bounty:** £110 a year – arising (I presume) from this source – but I could not learn – the Incumbent being absent. **Terrier:** None exhibited.
SCHOOLS: **Endowed School:** There is one – of which the Master is appointed by Trinity College, Cambridge – the present Master[6] however receives the Stipend and lives at *Tixall*; the subject under enquiry. **Subscription Day School:** None. **Sunday School:** About 300 children. **Lancaster School:** None.

POPULATION: 4,000.
PARISH CLERK: Samuel Hughes. **Appointed by:** The Incumbent. **Salary:** £12 12s. 0d.
CHURCHWARDENS: Mr Vaughan and Mr Joule.
ORDERS MADE: ['Done'.]
A new Bible and Prayer book. New Table Cloth for the Communion Table. A basin for the Font.

Revisited 25.9.1837
Directions to Churchwardens. (1) The thoroughfare of the Churchyard stopped (in concurrence with Lord Granville's agent) and a new road provided for the public in its stead – 'not done'. (2) Nettles etc removed; herbage kept down – decayed tomb-stones repaired or removed – 'in part'. (3) Lead gutters of roof repaired and kept clear; chimney re-built and properly coped – 'not done. R.D.'. (4) Walls of the Church and Gallery stair-case coloured, ceilings whitewashed – windows of Staircase repaired and made secure against admission of wet – 'not done'. (5) New Prayer Book for Clerk's desk – that in Reading desk repaired – 'not done'.
Recommended. A curtain for the whole length of the East window – 'not done'. 'Stove recommended'. 'Christ Church, Stone, consecrated 1830, 830 sittings – 300 free.'

Revisited 18.9.1841
Outer doors painted – and down-pipes from roof. Loose board provided for notices on Church doors.

[1] No impropriator named in *Eccles. Revs.* [2] A/V/1/3; '. . . very inconvenient'. [3] *Eccles. Revs.:* Also rector of Pulham (Dorset). [4] The curate's stipend was given in *Eccles. Revs.* as £100. [5] *Eccles. Revs.:* 'Fit'. [6] A/V/1/3: '. . . the present Master does no duty, living at Tixall'.

SWYNNERTON 17.6.1830 (A/V/1/3,p.77;A/V/1/2,p.87)

BENEFICE: Swinnerton. **Nature:** Rectory. **Ecton:** King's Books £10 2s. 6d. Prior de Stone 40s. Mr Fitzherbert Patron. **Patron:** The Rector. **Impropriator:** None – the Rector has all the Tithes.
CHURCH: An old Gothic structure; nave and side aisles – pointed Arches; the North aisle appears to be modern, not corresponding to the rest of the building. **Number it will contain:** About 450 or 500.[1] **Accommodation for Poor:** Sufficient. **Roof:** Oak covered with tiles – in good repair. **Walls:** Stone; the South wall far from upright; and much dilapidated externally. **Floor:** Quarries – tolerably good. **Windows:** Good – two more casements wanted. **Doors:** Good. **Pulpit and Desk:** The latter wants repair. **Books:** Prayer book bad. **Seats:** Very irregular; the woodwork very unsound, patched etc. **Galleries:** None. **Organ:** ——. **Font:** There is one. **Chapels:** Mr Fitzherbert claims the South Chancel – the grounds of his claim do not appear. **Benefaction Tables:** Several – sufficient. **Vestry:** None, except the South Chancel, which the Rector claims the right of using for this purpose. **Surplices:** Two – both bad. **Linen:** Furnished by the Rector.[2] **Plate:** Silver Cup, Dish and Paten – handsome. **Iron Chest for Register:** At the Rectory. **Register:** Oldest date 1558 – many

chasms; especially from 1628 to 1736 – in good preservation. **Porch:** There is one in the N. – but no gate to it. **Vaults:** One lately made under the Chancel floor – not under the body of the Church. **Cleanliness:** Not attended to. **Damp:** Very much – especially in the Chancel.

CHANCEL: **Table:** Oak – no covering. **Ornaments:** None. **Repaired by whom:** The Rector – the floor very bad and uneven.

STEEPLE: Old Square stone tower, with modern cornice. **State of:** Wants pointing. **Bells:** Five – good, except the ropes. **Clock:** Good.

CHURCHYARD: **Fence:** In a very bad and improper state – down in many places – belongs to the Parish. **Gates:** Some taken away – others out of repair. **Drains:** None – nor spouts. **Graves:** None very near the walls. **Rubbish:** A large heap of ashes near the S. chancel – nettles etc in abundance. **Footpaths:** The larger ones not properly kept – and several trespass paths in all directions. **Cattle:** Sheep occasionally.

DIVINE SERVICE: **On Sundays:** Full service morning – prayers afternoon. **On other Days:** None. **Sacrament:** Four times a year. **Communicants:** 26 to 40. **Catechism:** In the School.

INCUMBENT: **Name and Residence:** Revd Christopher Dodsley – in the Rectory. **What duty he performs:** The whole.

CURATE: **Name and Residence:** None.

PARSONAGE: A large brick building, apparently not very substantial – much neglected (as everything about the Church seems to have been) by the late Curate – commodious and well furnished with offices etc. **State of:** Now good – still undergoing improvements. **Outbuildings:** Barns, stables etc extensive.

INCOME: **Gross Value:** Not ascertained. **Terrier:** Several copies.

SCHOOLS: **Endowed School:** None – but a Roman Catholic schoolmaster (formerly the Parish Clerk) is allowed to teach a weekly school in the S. Chancel, – under the sanction of Mr Fitzherbert. **Subscription Day School:** None. **Sunday School:** About 40 children.

DISSENTERS: **Dissenting Chapels:** A private Catholic Chapel at the Hall.

POPULATION: Under 600.

MISCELLANEOUS: **Monuments:** Some antient ones.

PARISH CLERK: Mesech Ashley. **Appointed by:** The Rector. **Salary:** £10 per annum.

CHURCHWARDENS: Mr James Warner, Mr Richard Ford.

ORDERS MADE: ['In progress'.]
Two more casements in the body of the Church – casements *open* in dry weather. Reading Desk repaired – Prayer-book ditto. Pannels and floors of the pews repaired – (*new pewing*, urged). New surplices provided – and covering for the Communion Table. [Light] Gate put up at the entrance of the Porch – with a lock upon it. Cleanliness more duly attended to – the floor of the chancel laid even. The South wall to be rendered secure, or else re-built. The walls all round, and buttresses, carefully pointed, underbuilt, filled up, etc. The tower pointed. An open drain formed all round – earth cleared away – spouts and pipes etc put up. The fence all round thoroughly repaired – new gates put up and others repaired. Trespass-Footpaths, if possible, prevented – and the proper ones better kept. The South Chancel put into complete repair, inside and out. Rubbish removed, nettles etc kept down. A stop to be put to the profanation of the South Chancel by teaching a weekly school in it.

Revisited 25.9.1837
Much improvement in the *exterior* of the building since my former visit; the interior still in a very unsatisfactory state.

Directions. (1) In the *Churchyard* – the thoroughfare to be stopped – gates locked; paths kept neat; grass etc cleared away round the walls of the Chancel. 'Vestry repaired.' 'Attended to.'[3] (2) *Inside the Church*. The walls of the Church and Chancel to be coloured, ceilings, whitewashed – ceiling of Rector's chancel repaired – South Chancel repaired, cleaned and coloured at the *Parish expense,* and the Chancel kept free from improper uses – (weekly school).

The floors and pannels of the pews repaired – brick floors re-laid where needful, and decayed straw mats taken out – 'done or under consideration'. (I strongly recommended *boarded* floors and *new pewing*) 'under consideration'. Railing and covering of baptismal font repaired and cleaned – 'not done'. Windows repaired where needful, and iron pipes of stove kept from discolouring the walls – 'done'.

Revisited 18.9.1841
Directions to Churchwardens. Re-pewing of Church on uniform plan, strongly recommended – with boarded floors – making use of old materials – one side done at a time, to diminish expense. Oak pewing, whether remaining as at present, or used for uniform re-pewing, to be well rubbed with boiled linseed oil. Communion table and rails oiled in like manner – as also the screen – and new stone steps placed before the rails. Two casements made in S. Chancel – and walls neatly coloured. Wheels of bells braced afresh – and iron work painted. Lead flashings of Tower, roof etc – repaired and secured. Guard for Clock weight, in belfry beneath the Tower, to prevent injury in case of its falling. Roofs carefully examined and thoroughly repaired, especially that of S. Chancel – lead flashings restored – copings pointed – lead gutters kept clear. Weatherboards at E. end of Nave repaired and painted. Walls pointed externally, at the base – thoroughfare of Churchyard stopped.

[1] There is no return for this parish in *Eccles. Revs.* [2] A/V/1/3: 'None provided by the Parish – the Rector supplies it.' [3] 'Attended to' refers to the whole of the directions.

TIXALL 5.10.1829 (A/V/1/3,p.78;A/V/1/2,p.51)

BENEFICE: Tixall. **Nature:** Rectory. **Ecton:** Living discharged – Clear yearly value £46 10s. 0d. **Patron:** Sir [Thomas Aston] Clifford Constable, Bart. (Ecton Lord Aston). **Impropriator:** [I] could not ascertain – arrangement [relative to tithes] said to exist between the Patron and Rector.

CHURCH: Plain building, with circular windows – single body, separated from chancel, by circular arch. **Number it will contain:** About 100.

Accommodation for Poor: None specified, but there is room for any who attend. **Roof:** Timber covered with tiles. **Walls:** That on the S. side wants inspection. **Floor:** Brick–even. **Windows:** Good– open casements. **Doors:** Double doors, at the W. entrance. **Pulpit and Desk:** Oak: good. **Books:** The Prayer book, in reading desk, needs repair. **Seats:** In good order. **Galleries:** None. **Organ:** ——. **Font:** There is one. **Chapels:** None. **Benefaction Table:** None. **Vestry:** None. **Linen:** Table cloth and Napkin. **Plate:** Two Cups and a Paten – not well kept. **Chest for Papers:** There is one. **Iron Chest for Register:** At the Rectory. **Register:** Only two vols besides those now in use: the oldest date 1707– it is said that the older vols were destroyed by a former Rector– Revd Thomas Holbroke, early in the 18th century – see Topographical Account of Tixall, by Sir T Clifford and Mr Arthur Clifford, p.75. **Porch:** None. **Vaults:** None. **Cleanliness:** Attended to. **Damp:** Very little at the bottom of the walls. **Dimensions:** 36ft. 5in. by 16ft. 8in.
CHANCEL: 14ft. 2in. [by 16ft. 8in.] The Church being much dilapidated, was partially taken down, and re-built on a *smaller* extent, about 50 years ago. **Table:** Plain oak. **Ornaments:** None. **Repaired by whom:** The Rector.
STEEPLE: Low square tower, surmounted Lead Cupola and Vane. **State of:** Good externally. **Bells:** Two– one out of order– wood work said to need repair. **Clock:** None.
CHURCHYARD: **Fence:** On the E. and S. walls of the Rectory garden; and road leading to the Rectory. W. and N. a low wall, or bank belonging to the Parish. The garden wall, in an insecure state. **Gates:** Good. **Drains:** None– directed. **Graves:** A few too near the wall. **Rubbish:** A little. **Footpaths:** None. **Cattle:** The Curate's horse.
DIVINE SERVICE: **On Sundays:** Morning Prayers and Sermon– Afternoon Prayers. **On other Days:** None. **Sacrament:** Four times a year. **Communicants:** About 10. **Catechism:** Not in the Church.
INCUMBENT: **Name and Residence:** Revd Thomas Walker, Standon, Eccleshall. **If not resident:** Not. **What duty he performs:** None.
CURATE: **Name and Residence:** Revd Joseph Smith, in the Rectory. **Licensed:** Yes. **Salary:** £80 and the house. **If serving another Church:** None.
PARSONAGE: An old brick, rough cast, building, with two parlours and kitchen– four bedrooms, garret and lumber rooms. Beer-house. A new one stated to have been promised by Sir C Constable to the present Rector. **State of:** Very much out of repair – especially the roof and ceilings.[1] **Outbuildings:** Granary, Stables, Coach-house, Cart sheds– some of theme exceedingly out of repair.
INCOME: **Gross Value:** About £200. **Glebe:** 40 acres. **Surplice Fees:** £1 per annum. **Easter Dues and small Payments:** None. **Queen Anne's Bounty:** The Patronage being in a Catholic family, it is difficult to ascertain the nature of the arrangement, subsisting between the Patron and present Rector. The latter is said to receive a fixed sum in lieu of Tithes, Glebe etc. **Terrier:** None, that the Curate knows of.
SCHOOLS: **Endowed School:** None. **Subscription Day School:** None. **Sunday School:** None– the children being all Catholics. **Lancaster School:** None.
DISSENTERS: **Dissenters' School:** A Catholic Sunday school– about 20. **Dissenting Chapels:** Catholic Chapel at Sir Clifford's [house].
POPULATION: About 100.
MISCELLANEOUS: **Monuments:** None. **Chandeliers, etc:** None. **Parochial Library:** None.
PARISH CLERK: Walter Malpass. **Appointed by:** The Rector. **Salary:** £4 a year and burial fees.
CHURCHWARDENS: Mr John Cliffe.
ORDERS MADE: ['Done'.]
The state of the South Wall, and of the Roof to be examined and necessary repairs performed. An open drain made all round to carry off the wet. Ivy etc to be removed from the walls and plinth. The Rectory garden wall secured. The Communion Plate repaired, and better preserved. The Clergyman's Prayer book repaired. Windows in Church and Belfry mended. State of Bells, and wood work, connected with them examined and [where needful] repaired. 'Nothing done.'

The principal repairs, however, are wanted in the Rectory House and Offices, concerning which the Rector to be written to.

[1841 Orders[2]]: Visited October 12th Directions to the Churchwardens. (1) The state of the Fabric to be examined by a competent Surveyor, with reference, more especially, to the cracks in the North and South walls of the Chancel; and his opinion reported to the Archdeacon. (2) The outer door at the West end of the Church to be well oiled with boiled linseed oil, and a new weatherboard put to the bottom of it: the inner door to be painted. (3) The Communion Table, and oak pewing, to be well rubbed with boiled linseed oil. (4) The coping stones, at each end of the roof, to be well pointed. (5) The open drain round the Church to be kept clear from weeds and other herbage. (6) The Churchyard gate to be repaired and painted.

N.B. It would on many accounts be extremely desirable to take down the body of the Church, and re-build it. Should this be done, the above directions will, of course, be superseded. I have written to Mr Marsland on this subject.

[1] *Eccles. Revs.:* 'Fit'. [2] Loose sheet in A/V/1/3.

TRENTHAM 17.6.1830
(A/V/1/3,p.79;A/V/1/2,p.86)

BENEFICE: Trentham. **Nature:** Perpetual Curacy. **Ecton:** Formerly a Priory– £14 clear value. **Patron:** The Marquess of Stafford. **Impropriator:** Ditto.
CHURCH: An old, irregular building– originally Gothic; but the Tower taken down some years ago; and a modern W. end substituted in its place; also a South aisle, belonging to the Marquess. **Number it will contain:** Sufficient for the wants of the Parish,[1] Hanford Chapel supplying much additional accommodation. **Roof:** Oak, covered with tiles– not in good repair. **Walls:** Stone; that on the North side much out of the perpendicular– in a very insecure state. **Floor:** Quarries– and flags in the S. aisle, some of the latter want levelling.

Windows: Good– casements want opening and frames painting. **Doors:** Good, but want painting outside; the window above the S. door wants mending. **Pulpit and Desk:** Good– old oak; handsome ornaments of crimson velvet much ornamented; formerly the trappings of a Mameluke saddle, given by Lord Gower. **Books:** Good. **Seats:** Very irregular, and much out of repair– both in the floor and pannels. **Galleries:** Two– one of them the Marquis' pew. **Organ:** None. **Font:** There is one. **Chapels:** None. **Benefaction Tables:** Several. **Vestry:** None– parish meetings [said to be] held at the Inn. **Surplices:** Three– good. **Linen:** Provided from the Hall. **Plate:** Silver Flagon, Chalice, two patens. **Iron Chest for Registers:** At the Clergyman's house. **Register:** Several Vols prior to 1813– oldest date 1558– in good preservation. **Porch:** There is one, on the N. side; [much] out of repair in front. **Vaults:** Some in the S. aisle; flags above want laying even. **Cleanliness:** Much neglected. **Damp:** Very much, especially on the N. and E.
CHANCEL: **Table:** Old oak– wants cleaning. **Ornaments:** Purple Cloth Covering. **Repaired by whom:** The Marquess.
STEEPLE: **None**– the old tower taken away. **Bells:** Said to have been sold to Woolstanton. **Clock:** None.
CHURCHYARD: **Fence:** Brick wall; on three sides– Lord Stafford's yard on the S. **Gates:** Good. **Drains:** None– much wanted; and no spouts. **Graves:** The interments, now, in the burying ground behind the Mausoleum.
DIVINE SERVICE: **On Sundays:** Two full services– formerly prayers only in the afternoon. **On other days:** None. **Sacrament:** Six times a year. **Communicants:** 55 (average). **Catechism:** Occasionally [in the Church].
INCUMBENT: **Name and Residence:** Revd Mr Butt,[2] parsonage house. **What Duty he performs:** Shares the whole with his Curate.
CURATE: **Name and Residence:** Revd John Hutchinson. **If not resident:** [At Blurton.] **Licensed:** He is. **Salary:** £80 a year. **If serving another Church:** None, except part of the duty of Hanford Chapel, and Blurton, in the Parish.
PARSONAGE: A new, handsome house, built by the Marquess, and enlarged by the present Incumbent. **State of:** Very good.[3] **Outbuildings:** Coach-house, barn, stables etc– all new.
INCOME: **Gross Value:** A little upwards of £100. **Tithes:** The Marquess pays £50 a year to the living. The Marquess pays £27 7s. as domestic Chaplain. **Easter dues and small Payments:** £7 12s. **Queen Anne's Bounty:** Interest on £400. **Terrier:** There is.
SCHOOLS: **Endowed School:** There is £400, the interest on which payable to a Master for teaching the children of the Parish– £20 per annum paid– now incorporated with the National School. **Subscription Day School:** Naional School, as above. **Sunday School:** [One] in each division of the Parish– Trentham, Hanford, Blurton.
DISSENTERS: **Dissenters' School:** None. **Dissenting Chapels:** ——.
POPULATION: In 1821, 2,203 – now supposed to be 2,314 viz. Trentham proper 869, Blurton 844, Hanford 601.
MISCELLANEOUS: **Monuments:** Some old ones. **Chandeliers, etc:** None. **Parochial Library:** ——.
CHURCHWARDENS: ['Mr RW Kirkby. Mr Jonathan Davenport for Blurton. Mr Wardle, Sidesman for Blurton. D Glover, Sidesman for Trentham and Church Warden.']
ORDERS MADE: ['In progress.']
The whole Church in a very neglected, and in many parts dilapidated and dangerous state– it is highly expedient to *re-build the whole,* perhaps in a different site.
But if this be not done– (1) The *north wall* must be either taken down and re-built, or else firmly buttressed. (2) The walls, externally, all round must be carefully pointed, and where necessary, underbuilt. (3) The earth must be removed, all round, to the depth *at least* of the floor inside– an open drain formed, and spouts and pipes put up. (4) The roof must be put in thorough repair. (5) The doors painted, outside, and the Porch entrance repaired. (6) The pews put in complete repair, both floors and pannels– (indeed the whole should be *new-pewed,* in a uniform manner)– the floor of the S. aisle laid even. (7) Ivy and other shrubs removed from the W. end– and the Coal-place taken away from the E. end of the S. aisle. (8) Cleanliness properly attended to in the Church – *generally*; the Communion table cleaned and beautified; and damp [at the Table] remedied. (9) *Vestry* strongly *recommended*; at present the Parish Meetings are held at the *Inn*.

Revisited 26.9.1837
Suggestions. (1) That the pews in the N. aisle be taken up and re-placed with the same materials, of a uniform plan, and with *boarded floors*; all the pews in the body of the Church to be varnished or oiled. (2) The walls coloured – ceilings white-washed– plaister at W. end repaired– door leading to Hall painted. (3) A Vestry recommended, at the NE. end of Church. (4) The roof of the South aisle to be repaired or renewed– the water courses and spouts cleared out; copings at E. end fresh pointed.

Revisited 17.9.1841
Unless the Church be restored or rebuilt, the directions given to Churchwardens can only be repeated – i.e. as to the Reparation and cleaning of interior of Church. Substitution of boarded floors for brick to the pews. Examination and repair of roofs, water courses, spouts, battlements, parapets etc. Repair and painting of windows. Removal of herbage round the walls. Formation of broad walk. Vestry recommended– at NE. end of Church.

[1] *Eccles. Revs.:* 350. [2] Also vicar of Kinnersley (Salop): *Eccles. Revs.* [3] *Eccles. Revs.:* 'Fit.'

WESTON UNDER LIZARD 10.6.1830
(A/V/1/3, p.80; A/V/1/2, p.68)

BENEFICE: Weston under Lizard. **Nature:** Rectory. **Ecton:** Living discharged. Clear yearly value £41 10s. 0d. **Patron:** Lord Bradford. **Impropriator:** None.
CHURCH: A very neat plain building– rebuilt in 1700 and subsequently altered– the East window retains the original Gothic form[1]– a nave and Chancel. **Number it will contain:** About 160 exclusive of

the Gallery.[2] **Accommodation for Poor:** Sufficient. **Roof:** In Good state. **Walls:** Stone– good. **Floor:** Flags. **Windows:** Good– but two more casements wanted. **Doors:** Good. **Pulpit and Desk:** Very handsome, and well situated. **Books:** A good deal out of repair. **Seats:** Oak– very neat, boarded floors. **Galleries:** One, at the W. end. **Organ:** There is one. **Font:** ——. **Chapels:** None. **Benefaction Tables:** None. **Vestry:** There is one. **Surplices:** Two– one not good. **Linen:** Provided. **Plate:** Two Flagons, one Cup, two Dishes, all silver, no Patin. **Iron Chest for Register:** In the Vestry. **Register:** Only two vols before 1813– oldest 1701; preserved as appears only since the re-building of the Church. **Porch:** At the W. end. **Vaults:** One in the Chancel, belonging to the Family. **Cleanliness:** Attended to. **Damp:** In the Chancel, much. **Dimensions:** 42ft.6in. by 22ft.2in. CHANCEL: 22ft. 8in. **Table:** A marble stand– wood deal top. **Ornaments:** Purple Cloth covering– Marble tablets with commandments etc inscribed. **Repaired by whom:** The Rector.

STEEPLE: A handsome square stone tower. **State of:** Pretty good– except the weatherboards. **Bells:** Three– good. **Clock:** There is one.

CHURCHYARD: **Fence:** Brick wall, and part of Lord Bradford's house. **Gates:** Good. **Drains:** None, nor spouts. **Graves:** None near the walls. **Rubbish:** Much Ivy upon the Church – and trees growing inconveniently near the entrance into the Churchyard. **Cattle:** None– the grass is kept for mowing by the Sexton, and is much too high.

DIVINE SERVICE: **On Sundays:** Full service morning– prayers afternoon. **On other Days:** None. **Sacrament:** Four times a year. **Communicants:** 30 or 40. **Catechism:** In the School.

INCUMBENT: **Name and Residence:** Hon and Revd George Bridgman. **If not resident:** Wigan, in Lancashire.

CURATE: **Name and Residence:** Revd Oswald Feilden, in the Rectory House. **Licensed:** He is– but has not received his Licence. **Salary:** £80 and the House. **If serving another church:** None.

PARSONAGE: A very good handsome house; the front built by the present Rector. **State of:** Good in general.[3]

INCOME: **Gross Value:** About £500.

SCHOOLS: **Endowed School:** None. **Subscription Day School:** A small one supported by Lord Bradfords family. **Sunday School:** 40 children. **Lancaster School:** None.

DISSENTERS: **Dissenters' School:** ——. **Dissenting Chapels:** ——.

POPULATION: Nearly 500.[4]

MISCELLANEOUS: **Monuments:** Several in the Chancel belonging to the Ancestors of the Bridgemans. **Parochial Library:** None.

PARISH CLERK: John Warrender, the acting Clerk. **Salary:** £5 0s. 0d.

CHURCHWARDENS: Mr John Jellicoe for the Rector. Mr Richards for the Parish.

ORDERS MADE: ['Nearly done.']
Two more casements to be made in the windows and the casements always open in dry weather, and also the doors. Prayer book and Bible repaired; the parts in the Bible which are torn out, supplied. Parish Benefactions recorded. Weatherboards in the Tower completed, and roof [of Tower] repaired. Ivy removed from the walls and roof– and trees near the entrance into the Churchyard cut down [so far as necessary to prevent inconvenience to the Parishioners coming to Church]. The grass kept down, by mowing or sheep. An open space, free from earth, herbage etc kept all round the Church walls.

Revisited 12.10.1837
New surplice to be provided. Pews rubbed with oil. Overshot spouts removed. Gutters cleared out. North roof repaired. 'Not done.'

Revisited 15.10.1841
Directions etc. (1) Roof of Tower re-tiled– new bell-ropes provided. (2) Correct copy of Terrier deposited in Parish Chest. (3) Require the late Churchwardens to deliver in their accounts without delay.

[1] A/V/1/3: '. . . the early Gothic form'. [2] *Eccles. Revs.:* 300. [3] *Eccles. Revs.:* 'Fit.' [4] *Eccles. Revs.:* 257.

WESTON UPON TRENT 12.10.1829
(A/V/1/3,p.81;A/V/1/2,p.54)

BENEFICE: Weston upon Trent. **Nature:** Vicarage. **Ecton:** Coll. Sti Tho. Staff. Propr. £8 4s. 10d. clear value. **Patron:** Revd Mr Inge of Rugeley, and Mr Lane of Kings Bromley, have the alternate presentation. **Impropriator:** William Moore Esqr of Wychdon Lodge, in the adjoining Parish of Stowe. There are about 12 acres of Glebe, belonging to the Rectory– great and small tythes.

CHURCH: A very neat stone building; in the Gothic style, a middle and two side aisles, the latter separated from the former by plain pointed arches – the Chancel arch of the same description. **Number it will contain:** About 300. **Accommodation for Poor:** 100 (included in the above). **Roof:** Oak: covered with tiles– in good repair. **Walls:** Upright, and in good repair. **Floor:** Quarries, brick or flat stones– even. **Windows:** In good repair, a second casement wanted, on N. side. **Doors:** Good. **Pulpit and Desk:** Very neat, oak, with plain ornaments. **Books:** The Bible wants re-binding. **Seats:** Very neat; and in good order. **Galleries:** One for the singers, under the Tower. **Organ:** None. **Font:** There is one. **Chapels:** None. **Benefaction Tables:** One, recording the only Charity stated to belong to the Parish – a bequest in 1782 of the interest of £10, annually to the poor. **Vestry:** None. **Surplices:** Two– good, kept in the Chancel. **Linen:** Table cloth and napkin. **Plate:** Cup, Plate, very handsome silver– given by Mr Moore. **Chest for Papers:** There is one. **Iron Chest for Register:** In the Chancel. **Register:** Three vols [prior to 1813], besides those now in use, oldest date 1585– seem complete, and in pretty good preservation. **Porch:** There is one – in good repair. **Vaults:** None. **Cleanliness:** Attended to. **Damp:** A little on the walls, and Chancel floor. **Dimensions:** 50ft. 8in. by 33ft. 8in. CHANCEL: 28ft. by 24ft. **Table:** Very handsome, plain oak Table – modern. **Ornaments:** None – except stained glass windows. The whole Chancel is very handsome – re-built five years ago, by Mr Moore – with centre and two side chancels – gothic. **Repaired by whom:** Mr Moore.

STEEPLE: Square stone tower, surmounted by a neat Spire. **State of:** Very much dilapidated, and insecure, injured by Ivy. **Bells:** Two – there used to be a third which has been lost. **Clock:** None.
CHURCHYARD: **Fence:** On two sides a brook – on the E. and S. a sunk fence supported by a stone wall – the whole kept in repair by Mr Moore. **Gates:** Good. **Drains:** None at present – ordered all round. **Graves:** Some too near the walls. **Rubbish:** None. **Footpaths:** None. **Cattle:** None – the Curate mows the grass.
DIVINE SERVICE: **On Sundays:** Alternate, Morning and Afternoon. **On other Days:** None. **Sacrament:** Four times a year. **Communicants:** About 20. **Catechism:** Not.
INCUMBENT: **Name and Residence:** Revd C Inge – in Leicestershire. **If not resident:** Not. **What duty he performs:** ——.
CURATE: **Name and Residence:** Revd Henry Oldershaw – in the Vicarage. **Licensed:** He is. **Salary:** £35. **If serving another Church:** Not at present.[1]
PARSONAGE: A small, low building, in the cottage style, a parlour, kitchen, back-kitchen, two bedrooms. **State of:** Good – the present curate has done a good deal to it.[2] **Outbuildings:** Stable – adjoining the house.
INCOME: **Gross Value:** About £90 (including the Bounty). **Tithes:** Value not known. **Surplice Fees:** £2 or 3. **Easter Dues and small Payments:** £10.[3] **Queen Anne's Bounty:** Not received on account of the non-residence of the Vicar. The amount not known by the Curate. **Terrier:** There is, at the end of an old Volume of the Register, specifying the Buildings, Glebe etc belonging both to the Rector and Vicar – dated 1701.
SCHOOLS: **Endowed School:** None. **Subscription Day School:** None. **Sunday School:** None – the Curate urged to form one. **Lancaster School:** ——.
DISSENTERS: **Dissenters' School:** ——. **Dissenting Chapels:** ——.
POPULATION: 514, at the last Census.
MISCELLANEOUS: **Monuments:** None. **Chandeliers, etc:** ——. **Parochial Library:** ——.
PARISH CLERK: Thomas Lister. **Appointed by:** The Vicar. **Salary:** £2 10s. per annum, formerly there was a small piece of land, out of which he was paid – now lost.
CHURCHWARDENS: Only one – Mr Joseph Horobin.
ORDERS MADE: ['Done.']
That the state of the Tower and steeple be [examined and] reported [on] by an Architect, and put in thorough repair. [1830/1. The steeple has been taken down and re-built in consequence.] The earth removed; and a drain made all round the Church. The Bible to be rebound, and a new casement made, on the South side of the Church.

Revisited 9.9.1837
I. *Inside*
(1) The plastering of the wall on the South side to be repaired and the walls of the body of the Church neatly coloured and ceilings whitewashed. (2) More attention paid to *ventilating* the Church, by setting open doors and windows in fine weather.

II. *Outside*
(1) Roof of Porch to be repaired and walls whitewashed. (2) Porch Gates painted and a lock put on so as to admit of opening the door of the Church in fine weather. (3) Eave spouts put up on both sides of the Church and *down-pipes* to carry the wet into a *drain*. (4) Soil and weeds cleared away round the walls both of Church and Chancel. (5) The down spout at the North angle of the Church kept from touching the wall, and extended to the ground so as to convey the water into a drain. (6) The base of the Tower to be pointed. (7) The walks kept free from weeds, and the herbage and weeds generally in the Churchyard, kept down. 'Everything done. R.D. May 1838.'

[1841 Orders[4]]
Visited 10.10.1841
The Churchwardens are requested – (1) To have *water tables* formed for the windows, and the iron bars and frames of the casements painted. (2) To have the roof *spouted,* and down-pipes placed to bring the water to the ground. (3) To keep the open drains clear from weeds and other herbage. (4) To have the walls *well pointed* on the outside, *at the lower parts* especially; as also, the walls and *buttresses* of *the Tower*. (5) To prevent the admission of Cows, and other heavy cattle, into the Churchyard.

[1] A/V/1/3: 'Not regularly.' **[2]** *Eccles. Revs.:* 'Unfit.' **[3]** A/V/1/3 has 'and small Payments' enclosed in brackets. **[4]** Loose sheet preserved in A/V/1/3.

WHITMORE 7.10.1830
(A/V/1/3, p.82; A/V/1/2, p.139)

BENEFICE: Whitmore. **Nature:** Rectory – formerly a Chapelry under Stoke. **Ecton:** Chapelry to Stoke – of no value. **Patron:** – Mainwaring Esqr. **Impropriator:** None.
CHURCH: A small old building – single body and roof, flat ceiling – windows square. **Number it will contain:** About 100, exclusive of the Gallery.[1] **Accommodation for Poor:** Seats in the Gallery – and benches beneath. **Roof:** Oak covered with tile. **Walls:** Stone – not solid. **Floor:** Quarries. **Windows:** Pretty good – casements provided. **Doors:** Good. **Pulpit and Desk:** Good – purple cloth cushion and hangings. **Books:** Good – except the Clerk's Prayer Book. **Seats:** Neat and uniform – boarded floors. **Galleries:** One for singers and boys at W. end – repairs wanted. **Organ:** None. **Font:** There is one. **Chapels:** None. **Benefaction Tables:** One – not complete. **Vestry:** None – recommended. **Surplices:** Two – one not very good. **Linen:** Provided – handsome. **Plate:** Ditto. **Iron Chest for Register:** Provided. **Register:** From 1558. **Porch:** None. **Vaults:** None – except the family vault of the Mainwarings. **Cleanliness:** Attended to. **Damp:** No appearance except on the floor of the Chancel.
CHANCEL: **Table:** The top wants re-fixing. **Ornaments:** Monuments etc. **Repaired by whom:** The Patron – windows want repair.
STEEPLE: Small square [bell] tower – stuccoed. **State of:** Good. **Bells:** Three – one cracked – wheels out of order. **Clock:** None.

CHURCHYARD: **Fence:** Good – kept on two sides by the Parish – on two by Mr Mainwaring. **Gates:** Good. **Drains:** None – earth much accumulated. **Graves:** Several too near the walls. **Rubbish:** Much rubbish and weeds. **Footpaths:** Not properly kept. **Cattle:** None.
DIVINE SERVICE: **On Sundays:** Two full services. **On other Days:** None. **Sacrament:** Four times a year. **Communicants:** 20. **Catechism:** Not at Church.
INCUMBENT: **Name and Residence:** Revd John Isaac Brazier. **If not resident:** Abroad. **What duty he performs:** None.
CURATE: **Name and Residence:** Revd T Hardinge. **If not resident:** At Holly Bank – three miles from the Parish. **Licensed:** He is. **Salary:** £90 and [surplice] fees. **If serving another church:** None.
PARSONAGE: An unfinished brick building – much too large for the living – occupied at present by a Farmer, and the rooms used for Cow-house, Barn, etc.[2] **Outbuildings:** None, at present but piggeries.
INCOME: **Gross Value:** Said to be worth £500 in good times – does not exceed £300 at present – [the living] is sequestered.[3] **Glebe:** 30 acres. **Terrier:** Not known.
SCHOOLS: **Endowed School:** None. **Subscription Day School:** A girls school, supported by Miss Mainwaring. **Sunday School:** 22 girls and a few boys. **Lancaster School:** None.
DISSENTERS: **Dissenters' School:** ——. **Dissenting Chapels:** ——.
POPULATION: 300.
MISCELLANEOUS: **Monuments:** To the Mainwaring family. **Parochial Library:** None.
PARISH CLERK: James Bates. **Appointed by:** The Rector. **Salary:** £2 2s. 0d. and 5s. for cleaning.
CHURCHWARDENS: Mr James Furnival for the Rector. Mr Benjamin Packhorn for the Parish.
ORDERS MADE: ['Done.']
The roof to be spouted all round and pipes put up – the casings repaired. The walls pointed – the Ivy kept from doing injury to the windows and roof. The lead work of the windows repaired – benches and floor of the Gallery repaired – the Benefaction Table completed. The Communion Table repaired and oiled.[4] The cracked bell re-cast* – wheels repaired – new trap-door.
*Suspended, at the request of the Parishioners, conveyed in a letter from Mr Hardinge, December 1830.
The earth cleared away round the walls – and a drain made. No graves near the walls – the Churchyard kept neat and free from weeds.

Revisited 26.9.1837
Directions. (1) New Surplice – baptismal basin repaired and used 'not' – Bible repaired and re-bound – 'not properly' – Clerk's desk – 'partially' – and seat in reading desk re-fixed. (2) Pannels and floors of pews in N. aisle repaired – and also in the Chancel – Communion floor dried and cleaned – 'done'. (3) Ground lowered – drain formed, so as to carry off wet. (4) Roof of bell-turret repaired – 'done' – wheels of bells ditto – cracked bell re-cast – 'not done' (5) Roof of Church repaired – ivy checked – old tombstones removed – lich-gates repaired, and locked. 'Done or promised.' 'Done in part – but imperfectly. Mr Stone not licensed.'

Revisited 18.9.1841
Directions to Churchwardens. Water tables made for windows, and East window repaired. Floors of pews on S. side of Chancel repaired. Reading and clerk's desks covered, to preserve the books. Beam over Gallery repaired and secured – plaister of ceilings whitewashed. Cracked bell re-cast, and wheels of Bells repaired and braced. Roof examined and repaired – copings pointed or flashed – ridge tiles made good. Lintel and side posts of S. Door repaired and renewed, and means adopted for keeping out the cold. Additional sittings, if required, to be provided at W. end of Church. Suitable sittings for Sunday school children. Loose board for notices at outer door of Church. Walls pointed externally, at the base.

[1] *Eccles. Revs.*: 250. [2] *Eccles. Revs.*: 'Unfit.' [3] *Eccles. Revs.*: Gross income £470. [4] A/V/1/3: '. . . repaired and cleaned.'

WOORE 4.10.1830 (A/V/1/3,p.83;A/V/1/2,p.142)

BENEFICE: Woore. **Nature:** Perpetual Curacy [in the Parish of Munxton]. **Ecton:** Chapelry to Muggleston – £18 clear value. **Patron:** The Mackworth family.[1] **Impropriator:** Supposed, the Rector of Munxton.[2]
CHURCH: A new Chapel in progress – expected to be ready for consecration next Summer – plain brick building, covered with cement – plaister inside – single roof. **Number it will contain:** 590 – being an addition of 285 to the former chapel. **Accommodation for Poor:** 226. **Walls:** Brick. **Windows:** Well provided with casements. **Galleries:** One at the W. end.
STEEPLE: A small bell tower.
INCUMBENT: **Name and Residence:** Revd John Hawksworth, lately appointed – service performed at present in the National School room.[3]
SCHOOLS: **Subscription Day School:** National School.
POPULATION: 1,000.[4]
CHURCHWARDENS: Mr Wilkinson.
ORDERS MADE: [None necessary – a new Chapel being in progress.]

Revisited 9.10.1837
Directions. Roof examined and made weather-tight. Spouts and pipes cleared out. Ditto and doors *painted*. Chapel yard *drained* effectually – 'done'. Stove, or warm air apparatus, *recommended* – 'done'. 'Turf to be cut away. New books. Iron Chest. R.D.'

Revisited 13.10.1841
Directions etc. (1) Provide new books for Reading and Clerk's Desks. (2) Procure an Iron Register Chest, *as Act of Parliament requires*. (3) Form a drain along *outside* of Gravel walks, to carry off the wet. Everything in admirable order.

[1] *Eccles. Revs.:* 'Disputed'. [2] No impropriator named in *Eccles. Revs.* [3] *Eccles. Revs.* states that the benefice income was £50, and the glebe house unfit. [4] *Eccles. Revs.:* 890.

WALSALL WOOD (A/V/1/3,p.a,i)

Walsall Wood – consecrated in August 1837.
> Neat plain building – brick, with small tower – 450 sittings – chiefly free.

23.8.1841
> I was grieved to find, on revisiting this Church, that external damp has already made sad ravages in this neat little Church and that the *ceiling* is already coming down at the West end of the body of the Church.
> I directed. (1) The roof to be thoroughly repaired and ceiling restored. (2) Water tables to the windows. (3) Spouts cleared out – herbage removed from walls – gravel or tiles etc laid round the walls. (4) The walls externally, stuccoed or otherwise secured against damp.

HOPWAS (A/V/1/3,p.a,i)

Hopwas Chapel – Tamworth. Population 300. Small chapel with sittings for 140. Endowed with £1,000 – a small house and garden about to be purchased.

Visited 3.9.1841
> A baptismal font wanted.

ST. PETER, WALSALL (A/V/1/3,p.1[11])

St. Peter's, Walsall – consecrated in 1841 – accommodation for 1,140.

ETTINGSHALL (A/V/1/3,p.ii)

Ettingshall – Chapel of Ease to Sedgley – timber frame Church – visited 16.7.1838. No district yet attached.
> Sittings for 928 of which 904 free; the whole of the lower area (except four pews) and all the Gallery sittings, being free. It is doubtful whether the plan on which the Church is built will answer; the walls being only four inches thick admit much damp, especially on the South side. I recommended covering that side with slates. The roof, windows, furniture of the Church are very good. There is a small parsonage, and three schools connected with the Church – all built in the same manner as the Church – the schools in excellent order. The Infant School has 131 children in attendance. The boys National school 112 children. The girls National school 114.
> I recommended that the South and West walls of the Church should be protected with slates, and the internal walls coloured.

Revisited 19.10.1841
> Directions etc. (1) South side of Church protected against wet and cold. (2) Window sills painted on outside – water tables inside. (3) Spouts cleared out.

WORDSLEY (A/V/1/3,p.iii)

Wordsley – new Parish Church of Kingswinford – visited 17.7.1838.
> A remarkably handsome new Church, stone, with handsome Tower, pointed arches etc. Sittings for 1,200 of which 800 free – furnished in a very handsome manner. All in good order as might be expected, except that injury has been done to the ceilings above the N. and S. galleries, owing to the lead pipes not carrying off the wet effectually from the roofs – the Churchwardens directed to have this defect remedied. Too much room taken up in the Churchyard by vaults.

Revisited 9.10.1841
> Directions not needful – except to fence the Churchyard, on South side – and paint the iron palisades and gates.

ST. PAUL'S, WOLVERHAMPTON (A/V/1/3,p.iv)

St. Paul's, Wolverhampton – visited 19.7.1838 New Church, built under 1 and 2 William IV. Sittings for 1,460 – of which 620 free. Insured for £2,000. In general in good order – excepting the windows which have been done very badly – wet comes in; and the plaister much injured. Lead gutters to be carefully cleared and kept clear. Air-holes to pews, underneath. A National School – boys 220 – 60 additional Sundays, girls 150 – 50 additional Sundays. Sacrament 16 times per annum – 170 Communicants.
> I recommended a rate on pews for incidental expenses.

Revisited 18.10.1841
> Directions etc. (1) Lead gutters formed at each end of roof of Church, to convey the water from upper water-courses to lower. (2) Overflow of water from cistern prevented. (3) Position of Reading desk and Pulpit altered, to afford more space for Communicants and persons attending Baptisms, yet not so as to render the prayers inaudible in back seats of North Gallery.

UPPER GORNAL (A/V/1/3,p.v)

Upper Gornall – parish of Sedgley.

Visited 20.10.1841
> Directions etc. (1) Lower casements made to open more easily – vent to carry off the wet from the water-tables.
> N.B. Strongly *recommended* to enlarge the Churchyard on N. and S. sides – and to provide for burials there, without loss of fees to the Mother Church.

CHRIST CHURCH, STONE (A/V/1/3,p.vi)

Christ Church, Stone.[1]

[1] The heading is entered, but there is no description of the Church.

ALSTONEFIELD 19.7.1830 (A/V/1/4,p.1;A/V/1/2,p.113)

BENEFICE: Alstonfield. **Nature:** Vicarage. **Ecton:** Mon. Combermere Propr. Sir H Harpur Bart. Patron – Clear yearly value £40 10s. 0d. **Patron:** Sir George Crewe. **Impropriator:** Ditto.
CHURCH: A remarkably handsome, spacious building – in the early Gothic style; Nave and side Aisles – Chancel Arch circular, the others

pointed. **Number it will contain:** About 400. **Accommodation for Poor:** Sufficient. **Roof:** Oak, covered with lead – the open wood ceiling has been underdrawn (fresh plaistered) by the present Vicar. **Walls:** Stone, upright. **Floor:** Flags – even. **Windows:** Very good – double row on each side; casements not sufficient. **Doors:** Good. **Pulpit and Desk:** Old carved oak, painted blue!!; crimson velvet Cushion. **Books:** Bible wants re-binding. **Seats:** Very neat – oak pannels, boarded floors. **Galleries:** A small one for the Organ at the W. end. **Organ:** There is one. **Font.** There is – not a proper basin. **Chapels:** None. **Benefaction Tables:** Two – not complete, several benefactions have been lost. **Vestry:** There is one. **Surplices:** A new one wanted. **Linen:** Provided. **Plate:** A flagon, Cup, Paten and dish. **Iron Chest for Register:** There is one. **Register:** From *1538* – complete and in good preservation. **Porch:** One on the South side – not in good repair. **Vaults:** Only one. **Cleanliness:** Attended to. **Damp:** Much on the walls.

CHANCEL: **Table:** In good condition. **Ornaments:** None. **Repaired by whom:** The Patron.

STEEPLE: Handsome square stone tower, with battlements and pinnacles. **State of:** Pinnacles out of the perpendicular. **Bells:** Three – iron work wants painting; and floor of belfry repairing. **Clock:** Pretty good.

CHURCHYARD: **Fence:** Stone wall – condition indifferent. **Gates:** Good. **Drains:** None – much wanted. **Graves:** Many too near the walls. **Rubbish:** A good deal at present, owing to recent repairs. **Footpaths:** Several trespass paths. **Cattle:** A horse, belonging to the Vicar.

DIVINE SERVICE: **On Sundays:** Two full services. **On other Days:** Wednesday Evening Lecture. **Sacrament:** Four times a year. **Communicants:** 20 to 25. **Catechism:** Not in the Church.

INCUMBENT: **Name and Residence:** Revd John Simpson, in the Vicarage. **What Duty he performs:** The whole.

PARSONAGE: A substantial stone building, just finished; built partly by direction of Sir G Crewe, partly by grant of £600 from the Bounty Board. **State of:** Good.[1] **Outbuildings:** Good.

INCOME: **Gross Value:** £120. **Tithes:** All the small Tythes, and a Modus for Hay. **Glebe:** Four acres, including the Garden and site of the House. **Easter Dues and Payments:**[2] Collected. **Queen Anne's Bounty:** Grant towards the building of the Parsonage. **Terrier:** The Vicar has a Copy.

SCHOOLS: **Endowed School:** Upwards of £20, partly in land, partly in money, 35 boys and girls taught. **Subscription Day School:** No other. **Sunday School:** About 100 children. **Lancaster School:** None.

DISSENTERS: **Dissenters' School:** ——. **Dissenting Chapels:** Wesleyans.

POPULATION: (Of *Alstonfield proper)* 6 or 700 – of the whole Parish 6,000 – 13 miles in extent – four Chapelries.

PARISH CLERK: Not ascertained. **Appointed by:** Not ascertained. **Salary:** Not ascertained.

CHURCHWARDENS: Not ascertained.

ORDERS MADE: Two additional casements in the *upper* row of windows. The Bible re-bound, Benefaction Tables corrected and completed. A new surplice provided – the floor of the Belfry repaired – iron work of bells painted.
The fence repaired – earth cleared away round the Church, and an open drain formed. The lead gutters cleared out all round the roof. No graves to be allowed within ten feet of Church walls. No large cattle to feed in the Churchyard.

Revisited 14.9.1837
The inside in excellent order, except the top of the walls which are injured by wet coming in at the ceiling.
Directions. (1) Water-courses of roofs cleared out, and kept clear. (2) Coping of NW. roof pointed. (3) Walls all round pointed at bottom. (4) Weatherboards of tower made good, and pinnacles secured. (5) Thoroughfare of Churchyard stopped. (6) Down-pipes instead of overshot spouts.

Revisited 10.9.1841
(1) Pew-doors looked over and eased; and pannels repaired. (2) Beresford pew repaired – Prayer Book ditto. (3) Copings of walls and gable of roof pointed. (4) Walls of Church pointed at bottom. (5) Old font placed in convenient situation, or else broken up.

[1] *Eccles. Revs.:* 'Fit.' [2] A/V/1/3: 'and small Payments' enclosed in brackets.

BIDDULPH 23.7.1830
(A/V/1/4,p.2;A/V/1/2,p.128)

BENEFICE: Biddulph. **Nature:** Vicarage. **Ecton:** Pri. Hilton Propr. – Sir Thomas Gresley Bart. Patron. Clear value £30 0s. 0d. **Patron:** John Bateman Esqr. **Impropriator:** Ditto.

CHURCH: An antient Gothic structure (said to be 400 years old); middle and side aisles, open carved ceilings; a handsome screen before the Chancel. **Number it will contain:** About 400. **Accommodation for Poor:** Very insufficient. **Roof:** Oak covered with tile – side aisles covered with flag-slates – the whole roof much out of repair. **Walls:** Stone – much out of perpendicular. **Floor:** Flags – very uneven. **Windows:** Very bad – no casements. **Doors:** Old and bad. **Pulpit and Desk:** Inconveniently situated – and not good.[1] **Books:** In very bad condition. **Seats:** Very bad and irregular – floors very bad. **Galleries:** None. **Organ:** ——. **Font:** An old one. **Chapels:** None. **Benefaction Tables:** Four – not sufficient; many benefactions lost. **Vestry:** A very bad one. **Surplices:** Two – one good. **Linen:** Provided. **Plate:** Gilt Silver Cup (1690), another of silver, and silver patin. **Chest for Papers:** There is one. **Iron Chest for Register:** In the Church – in very damp situation. **Register:** From 1558, pretty entire, but in bad preservation. **Porch:** There is one – out of repair. **Vaults:** None very lately. **Cleanliness:** Attended to. **Damp:** Much on floor and walls.

CHANCEL: **Table:** Old oak – top wants refixing. **Ornaments:** None. **Repaired by whom:** The Impropriator.

STEEPLE: A square stone Tower. **State of:** Very bad. **Bells:** Six – two of them cracked. **Clock:** The remains of one.

CHURCHYARD: **Fence:** Kept by the parish – pretty good. **Gates:** Want locks, to keep out trespassers. **Drains:** None. **Graves:** Too near the walls. **Footpaths:** [Trespass –] to be stopped, as unnecessary.
DIVINE SERVICE: **On Sundays:** Prayers in Morning – prayers and sermon in Afternoon. **On other Days:** None. **Sacrament:** Four times a year. **Communicants:** 30. **Catechism:** Occasionally.
INCUMBENT: **Name and Residence:** Revd James Sewell – in the Parish [since dead (1831) Revd Mr Holt now the Vicar].
INCUMBENT: **What Duty he performs:** The whole. **PARSONAGE:** None.[2]
INCOME:[3] **Tithes:** Vicarial. **Glebe:** 36 acres. **Queen Anne's Bounty:** Interest of £1,000 from Parliamentary grant and Bounty Board.
SCHOOLS: **Endowed School:** A small one for 12 children. **Subscription Day School:** None. **Sunday School:** About 90 children.
DISSENTERS: **Dissenters' School:** Methodist. **Dissenting Chapels:** Ditto.
POPULATION: 2,000.
MISCELLANEOUS: **Monuments:** Some antient ones to the Bowyer family.
PARISH CLERK: James Partington. **Appointed by:** The Vicar. **Salary:** £10 – including payment for cleaning etc.

Finding the Church altogether in a very dilapidated and apparently insecure condition, I directed the Churchwardens to call in an experienced Architect; and lay before me his report of its state.

The general opinion in the Parish seems decidedly to be that the Church must be rebuilt.

Revisited 15.9.1837

The Church re-built since my former visit – in same style of Architecture as old Church – very beautiful – to hold 658 – of which 211 free.[4]

I strongly urged the provision of a Chapel of Ease; in one of the remote and populous hamlets of this extensive Parish.

Directions to the Churchwardens. (1) An additional casement to be made on each side of the Church, and one in the Vestry – casements regularly open – and doors – an iron gate to be placed at the W. entrance. (2) The water-courses of the tower and roof kept clear. (3) Down-pipes to be placed instead of overshot spouts.

Revisited 13.9.1841

Great want of *attention*. (1) Casements made to open easily and kept open in fine weather. (2) Bars of windows painted – windows cleaned. (3) More attention to ventilation and cleanliness. (4) Open gates for West entrance to be provided. (5) Down-pipes from Tower – Roof of ditto repaired – cracked bells re-cast, wheels repaired. (6) Crosses at E. and W. ends of Church secured – ridge tiles pointed – copings ditto – tiling mended. (7) Dry rot in floor.

[1] A/V/1/3: 'Bad – and ill-placed.' [2] *Eccles. Revs.*: 'Unfit.' [3] *Eccles. Revs.*: £122. [4] A faculty was issued 13.11.1832 (B/C/2/1832–6,p.89) for the extension of the church southwards and eastwards, the construction of N. and SE. galleries and a new baptistry, and for repewing the church, to the plans of Thomas Trubshaw of Great Haywood. Another was issued 6.10.1836 (B/C/2/1836–41, p.29) permitting deviations from the 1832 faculty plan, and permitting the commissioners for the re-pewing to allot pews in the old parts of the church as well as the new.

BAGNALL 24.7.1830
(A/V/1/4,p.3;A/V/1/2,p.132)

BENEFICE: Bagnall. **Nature:** United Rectory with Bucknall (vid. p.78).[1] **Ecton:** Chapelry to Stoke £3 clear value. **Patron:** Revd E Powys.
CHURCH: A very small old building, in so bad a state that it must be re-built. [Re-built since my first visit.] **Number it will contain:** [About 160.] **Accommodation for Poor:** [120.] Roof, Walls, Floor, Windows, Doors, Pulpit and Desk, Books, Seats, Gallieres: [All new and good.] **Books:** [Good.] **Galleries:** [At West end.]
INCUMBENT: **Name and Residence:** [Revd E Powys, Cheddleton.] **What Duty he performs:** [One duty.]
PARSONAGE: [None.][2]
ORDERS MADE: 12.9.1837
Spouts and down-pipes to be placed to each roof. The walls and window frames pointed where needful. The walks and herbage of Churchyard kept in order. The weatherboards enlarged to keep out the wet.

Revisited 15.9.1841
(1) Water-tables to windows. (2) Quarries of floor laid afresh. (3) Door from belfry to roof kept open – to ventilate the roof. (4) Tiling of roof repaired. (5) Eave-spouts and down-pipes. (6) Basement stones at E. end pointed. (7) Ground lowered – open drain – herbage kept away.

[1] A/V/1/4: 'vid. p.4.' [2] *Eccles. Revs.* states the population to be 170.

BUCKNALL 15.6.1830 (A/V/1/4,p.4; A/V/1/2,p.78)

BENEFICE: Bucknall. **Nature:** Rectory united with Bagnall (formerly Chapelry to Stoke). **Ecton:** £10 clear value. **Patron:** Revd E Powys, near Cheddleton.
CHURCH: A small, ill-built church – nave and Chancel – built (as appears) [or *re-built*] in 1718. **Number it will contain:** About 200.[1] **Accommodation for Poor:** All the pews open. **Roof:** Not in good repair – tiles bad. **Walls:** Stone – pretty good. **Floor:** Bricks and flags – very uneven and bad. **Windows:** No casements. **Doors:** Want repair. **Pulpit and Desk:** Pretty good. **Books:** Ditto. **Seats:** Some of them want repair. **Galleries:** One at the W. end for children. **Organ:** None. **Font:** There is one – not used. **Chapels:** None. **Benefaction Tables:** One – not complete. **Vestry:** None. **Surplices:** One. **Plate:** Pewter Dish and Flagon. **Iron Chest for Register:** In the Chancel. **Register:** Not seen – the minister being absent. **Porch:** None. **Vaults:** ——. **Cleanliness:** Pretty well attended to. **Damp:** Not much.
CHANCEL: **Table:** Old and shabby – no covering. **Ornaments:** None. **Repaired by whom:** The Parish.
STEEPLE: Square stone tower. **State of:** Good. **Bells:** One – good. **Clock:** None.

CHURCHYARD: **Fence:** Belongs principally to the Parish – in a very bad state. **Gates:** Very indifferent – under repair. **Drains:** None – nor spouts. **Graves:** Too near [the walls]. **Rubbish:** A good deal. **Cattle:** A poney.
DIVINE SERVICE: **On Sundays:** One – alternately morning and afternoon. **On other Days:** None. **Sacrament:** Four times a year. **Communicants:** 15.
INCUMBENT: **Name and Residence:** Revd E Powys.[2] **If not resident:** Leigh House, near Cheddleton.
CURATE: **Name and Residence:** Revd J Smith. **If not resident:** Resides at Fosbrook, 6 miles off. **Licensed:** He is. **Salary:** ——.[3]
PARSONAGE: None.[4]
INCOME: **Gross Value:** £300 a year. **Glebe:** 50 or 60 acres.
SCHOOLS: **Endowed School:** £5 chargeable on land for 12 children. **Subscription Day School:** None. **Sunday School:** 40 or 50.
POPULATION: Upwards of 300.
PARISH CLERK: Samuel Allen. **Salary:** 50s. a year.
CHURCHWARDEN: Mr George Twigg.
ORDERS MADE: Two casements, at least, to be made in the windows. The floor to be laid even. A proper baptismal basin provided. The benefaction table completed. The Communion Table cleaned and covered. The roof stripped and re-tiled. Earth cleared away round the Walls of the Church – open drains made – spouts and pipes fixed. The fence put in order, all round. Rubbish removed – no graves allowed within six feet. The brick chimney removed from the East end of the Church.

Revisited 18.9.1837
I found this Church in so dilapidated and comfortless a state that, learning from the Clergyman that he had thoughts of enlarging it by an extension of the Chancel, I strongly urged him and the Churchwardens to have the entire fabric taken down and a new one built in its stead, promising to obtain for him all the assistance from Societies I could. They seemed much inclined to adopt my suggestion and I left it with them for consideration; superseding all directions as to minute points in the state of the Church and Churchyard etc which would otherwise have required attention.
If the plan is adopted, there must be a new fence to the Churchyard, and the School removed from within it, or else fenced off.

Revisited 15.9.1841
The Church still in the same disgraceful state – no directions, except (as before) to re-build with enlargement – to enlarge and fence the Churchyard – remove the School. Churchyard protected from trespass. Roof of Tower thoroughly repaired.

[1] *Eccles. Revs.:* 'Sufficient.' [2] Also perpetual curate of Cheddleton. [3] *Eccles. Revs.:* £80. [4] *Eccles. Revs.:* 'None.'

BURSLEM 15.6.1830 (A/V/1/4,p.5;A/V/1/2,p.81)

BENEFICE: Burslem. **Nature:** Rectory. **Ecton:** Chapelry to Stoke £22 9s. 6d. clear value. **Patron:** William Adams Esqr. of Cowbridge. **Impropriator:** None.
CHURCH: The nave re-built in 1788 – the old Tower remains – single body and roof. **Number it will contain:** 800 exclusive of children. **Accommodation for Poor:** None – except forms for children. **Roof:** Oak, covered with slate – lead gutters – good repair. **Walls:** Brick – upright. **Floor:** Flags. **Windows:** Good – casements sufficient. **Doors:** Good. **Pulpit and Desk:** Handsome – well placed – velvet Cushion to Pulpit. **Books:** Good. **Seats:** ——. **Galleries:** All round the body of the Church. **Organ:** There is. **Font:** There is no proper basin. **Chapels:** None. **Benefaction Tables:** Two. **Vestry:** There is – not well fitted up.[1] **Surplices:** Three – good, but not clean. **Linen:** Table Cloth – two napkins. **Plate:** Flagon, Cup, Paten – handsome. **Iron Chest for Register:** In the Vestry. **Register:** Several Vols – the old ones imperfect. **Porch:** None. **Vaults:** ——. **Cleanliness:** Attended to. **Damp:** From wet coming in at the Windows.
CHANCEL: **Table:** Oak – handsomely carved. **Repaired by whom:** The Parish.
STEEPLE: Old stone Tower. **State of:** Wants pointing. **Bells:** Six – good. **Clock:** None.
CHURCHYARD: **Fence:** Good. **Gates:** ——. **Drains:** None – nor spouts. **Graves:** Too near the walls – more room wanted to bury in. **Footpaths:** A thoroughfare – to be stopped, if possible. **Cattle:** None.
DIVINE SERVICE: **On Sundays:** Two full services. **On other Days:** Tuesday Evening. **Sacrament:** Nine times a year. **Communicants:** 80.
INCUMBENT: **Name and Residence:** Revd E Whieldon, near Cheadle.[2]
CURATE: **Name and Residence:** Revd J Bateman, in the Parsonage House. [Now Revd – Cooper (1831).] **Licensed:** He is. **Salary:** Not ascertained.[3] **If serving another church:** None other.
PARSONAGE: A new house – brick covered with cement – not very substantial – seven rooms on ground floor. **State of:** Good at present – but roof seems not very good.[4]
INCOME: **Gross Value:** '4 or 500.' **Terrier:** At the Parish office.[5]
SCHOOLS: **Endowed School:** £30 [per annum] from a farm – to support an English School for 20 boys and 10 girls. **Subscription Day School:** National School, about 120 children. **Sunday School:** 260 children.
DISSENTERS: **Dissenting Chapels:** Several.
POPULATION: 11 or 12,000 – a new Chapel lately built (consecrated 19.1.1831) to hold 2,080[6] – 600 free sittings.
PARISH CLERK: Bagnal Wood Beach. **Appointed by:** The Rector. **Salary:** £5 5s. 0d. and surplice fees.
CHURCHWARDENS: John Haywood for the Rector. Thomas Brindley for the Parish.
ORDERS MADE: Spouts and pipes to be put up – and drain all round to carry off the wet. The nuisance occasioned by the Chimney on the South side adjoining the Churchyard to be *abated*. The

Tower to be pointed. No graves within six feet of the Walls. The thoroughfare thro' the Churchyard to be stopped, *if possible*. The windows secured against the admission of rain. A closet to be put in the Vestry for the Surplices etc. The communion plate better secured.[7] 'Not complied with. 1831.'

Revisited 20.9.1837
Directions to the Churchwardens. The roofs to be carefully examined; and the necessary means taken to secure the carrying off the wet. The roof of the *tower* examined and repaired – watercourses cleared out. Staircase leading to belfry repaired. The ceiling (within the Church) whitewashed. Spouts and down-pipes *recommended*.

Revisited 16.9.1841
Directions to Churchwardens. (1) Two additional casements made on each side of the Church. (2) Eave-spouts and down-pipes on both sides of Church. (3) Roof of Tower repaired, and door at top of Staircase kept closed.

[1] A/V/1/3: 'Not well furnished.' [2] Also perpetual curate of Bradley-le-Moors. [3] *Eccles. Revs.*: £158. [4] *Eccles. Revs.*: 'Fit.' [5] A/V/1/3: 'At the Parish Vestry room.' [6] A/V/1/3: 'January 19. 2,200.' [7] A/V/1/3: 'The communion plate to be kept in a place of greater security than the Vestry.'

ST. PAUL, BURSLEM
(A/V/1/4,p.6; not in A/V/1/2)

'Not finished when I visited Burslem in 1830.'

BENEFICE: St. Paul's, Burslem. **Nature:** Chapel of Ease at present.
CHURCH: **Number it will contain:** 2,200. **Accommodation for Poor:** 600.
INCUMBENT: **Name and Residence:** Revd Thomas Nunns.[1]
ORDERS MADE: 20.9.1837
Further precautions to be used for carrying off the wet from the roofs of the Church and Tower. The woodwork etc painted, and walls coloured.

Revisited 16.9.1841
Directions to Churchwardens. (1) Floor taken up and laid even, where it has sunk. (2) Water-tables completed, to carry the wet outside the windows. (3) Conductor placed for spout at East end of North Aisle.
N.B. To confer with the Bishop respecting contraction of lower part of St. Paul's Church.

[1] Deleted and replaced by 'R Mayor' in pencil and 'J Noble' in ink. *Eccles. Revs.* states the population to be 5,000, gross income £123, and that there was no glebe house.

BUTTERTON 21.7.1830
(A/V/1/4,p.7;A/V/1/2,p.119)

BENEFICE: Butterton. **Nature:** Perpetual Curacy – endowed with hay-tithe, £400 Bounty money and £1,400 from Parliamentary grant. **Ecton:** Chapelry to Mathfield. £17 clear value. **Patron:** The Vicar of [Mathfield or] Mayfield. **Impropriator:** Duke of Devonshire.
CHURCH: An old building, partly re-built in 1781 – single body, open oak ceiling – Chancel arch circular. **Number it will contain:** About 150.[1] **Accommodation for Poor:** Very small. **Roof:** Oak covered with lead – good. **Walls:** Freestone, upright – want whitewashing. **Floor:** Flags – uneven. **Windows:** Not good – no casements. **Doors:** Want painting. **Pulpit and Desk:** Want re-fixing and otherwise repairing. **Books:** Not good. **Seats:** Many of them out of repair. **Galleries:** A small one, under the belfry. **Organ:** None. **Font:** There is one – near the W. end. **Chapels:** None. **Benefaction Tables:** Two – another wanted, to record the free school benefaction. **Vestry:** None. **Surplices:** One – not good. **Linen:** Provided. **Plate:** Plated flagon, Cup, patin and plate. **Iron Chest for Register:** None. **Register:** From 1676 – irregularly kept. **Porch:** None. **Vaults:** Several in the Chancel. **Cleanliness:** Not attended to. **Damp:** Much on the walls and Chancel floor.
CHANCEL: **Table:** Not firm – nor properly cleaned. **Ornaments:** None. **Repaired by whom:** The Parish.
STEEPLE: Square stone tower. **State of:** Not good. **Bells:** Two, good – wheels out of order. **Clock:** None.
CHURCHYARD: **Fence:** Stone wall, and hedges – partly kept by the Parish, partly by tenants of adjoining lands. **Gates:** Want painting. **Graves:** Some too near. **Footpaths:** Church way wanted.[2] **Cattle:** A Cow, belonging to the Clerk [– not to be allowed].
DIVINE SERVICE: **On Sundays:** One service; alternately Morning and Afternoon. **On other Days:** None. **Sacrament:** Four times a year. **Communicants:** About 12. **Catechism:** Occasionally.
INCUMBENT: **Name and Residence:** Revd W Richardson, Butterton Moor.[3] **What Duty he performs:** The whole.
PARSONAGE: None.[4]
INCOME: **Gross Value:** Supposed about £100. **Tithes:** One-fourth of the Parish pays Hay Tithe to the Minister, the other three-fourths pay a modus of 13s. 4d. to the Vicar of Mayfield – and 6s. 8d. for the Churchyard. **Easter Dues and small Payments:** Collected.[5] £10 per annum from Mrs Stubbs' will. [(See Art. 72.)] **Queen Anne's Bounty:** £1,500, 3 per Cents from Parliamentary grant. £8 per annum (i.e. 2 per Cent of £400) [from Queen Anne's Bounty]. **Terrier:** The Minister has one.
SCHOOLS: **Endowed School:** Mrs Ruth Stubbs left land in Grindon Parish for support of a school – present Rent £16 per annum. **Subscription Day School:** None. **Sunday School:** None at present.
POPULATION: About 500.[6]
PARISH CLERK: Moses Smith. **Appointed by:** The Minister. **Salary:** £2 10s. 0d. and 3s. 6d. for cleaning.
CHURCHWARDENS: Mr Thomas Salt.
ORDERS MADE: The floor to be laid even in Church and Chancel – and no more graves allowed inside the Church [– 'done']. The Pews repaired by the respective claimants – walls whitewashed [– 'done']. Three Casements to be made in the lower windows – one in the Gallery. The Pulpit and Reading Desk made firm – Bible and Clerk's Prayer Book repaired [– 'done']. Iron Register

Chest provided [– 'done'] – Free School benefaction recorded. The Communion Table fixed and oiled – new Chancel door. The tower examined and repaired – wheel of bell ditto. The fence put into good repair – gates painted. A proper Church-way made – earth lowered round the Church.

Revisited 14.9.1837
Much improved since my former visit. (1) Windows to be looked over and repaired – sills fresh pointed outside. (2) Ceiling above the Chancel window repaired. (3) Doorway of Chancel enlarged, to admit of taking coffins out at funerals – and a new door put up. (4) Pews repaired, where needful, in Church and Chancel; and a stay to the Pulpit. (5) Free School benefaction recorded. (6) Copings of roof fresh pointed, and water-courses cleared. (7) Thoro'fare of Churchyard stopped – gates locked – gravel walks to be formed to the door of the Church.

Revisited 11.9.1841
(1) Chancel ceiling repaired – Harrison's pew repaired or removed – decayed matting taken away. (2) New Surplice – Bible repaired. (3) Gallery floor and walls ditto. (4) Door Lintels inside Tower renewed. (5) Lower part of Chancel walls repaired and pointed. (6) Down-pipe at E. end. (7) Trespass path of Churchyard stopped. (8) Enquiry as to appointment of new Trustees and proper School-Master. Sunday School much needed.

[1] *Eccles. Revs.:* 300. [2] A/V/1/3: '*Church-way* not properly kept.' [3] Also perpetual curate of Onecote. [4] *Eccles. Revs.:* 'None.' [5] Inserted after 'Easter Dues'. [6] *Eccles. Revs.:* 346.

CAVERSWALL 15.7.1830
(A/V/1/4, p.8¦; A/V/1/2, p.98)

BENEFICE: Caverswall (Ecton. Careswall). **Nature:** Vicarage. **Ecton:** Living discharged. Clear value £40 0s. 0d. Pri. Sti. Thomae Staff: Impr. **Patron:** Thomas H Parker Esqr. (Ecton: G Parker Esqr. 1715). **Impropriator:** Ditto.
CHURCH: An antient Saxon structure – nave, side aisles and Chancel – massy pillars and circular arches; pointed windows. **Number it will contain:** About 280 – including the Gallery.[1] **Accommodation for Poor:** Only two pews; very insufficient. **Roof:** Oak; covered, the nave with tile, N. aisle with slate, S. aisle with lead – the latter is at present being new-roofed. **Walls:** Solid stone, good. **Floor:** Flags. **Windows:** Good – one additional casement on the S. side wanted. **Doors:** Old oak – repairs wanted. **Pulpit and Desk:** Not in very good condition. **Books:** Good. Seats: Very irregular, and insufficient for the population. **Galleries:** A small one at the W. end, for children. **Organ:** None. **Font:** An antient one of stone, lined with lead. **Chapels:** None. **Benefaction Tables:** Provided. **Vestry:** The belfry is used for this purpose – should be separated. **Surplices:** Good. **Linen:** Provided. **Plate:** Flagon, Chalice, Patin, Two Dishes – Silver gilt. **Iron Chest for Register:** There is one. **Register:** From 1559 to present time – the old Vols want re-binding. **Porch:** On the S. side; to be repaired;
and light gates put up. **Vaults:** Some. **Cleanliness:** Attended to. **Damp:** Not much. **Dimensions:** 57ft. 5in. by 37ft. 7in.
CHANCEL: 27ft. 6in. by 17ft. 7in. **Table:** Firm – wants cleaning and a new cover. **Ornaments:** None – except monuments. **Repaired by whom:** The Lay Impropriator.
STEEPLE: An old square Tower. **State of:** Not good. **Bells:** Three – one of them cracked. **Clock:** Good.
CHURCHYARD: **Fence:** Stone wall, kept up principally by the Parish – on the South side the boundary seems uncertain; a barn forms the present boundary – which is not in good repair. **Gates:** Want painting. **Drains:** None. **Graves:** Many too near. **Rubbish:** Much – partly owing to present repairs of Church. **Footpaths:** There is one, a thoroughfare, along the N. side, which seems very unnecessary, as the road is close by. **Cattle:** None at present.
DIVINE SERVICE: **On Sundays:** Full service morning – prayers afternoon. **On other Days:** None regularly (except Good Friday, Christmas Day etc). **Sacrament:** Seven times a year. **Communicants:** 35.
INCUMBENT: **Name and Residence:** Revd Alexander Goode, Vicarage. **What Duty he performs:** The whole.
PARSONAGE: A new house (free-stone) built – partly by private subscription, partly by money from the Bounty board – cost £1,073. **State of:** ['Good'.][2]
INCOME: **Gross Value:** About £200.[3] **Glebe:** 24 acres – rent about £40. **Queen Anne's Bounty:** A grant obtained towards building the Parsonage. [(62.)] **Terrier:** There is one.
SCHOOLS: **Endowed School:** None. **Subscription Day School:** A national school, established in 1824. **Sunday School:** About 100 children.
DISSENTERS: **Dissenters' School:** A Roman Catholic school – 50 children. **Dissenting Chapels:** One, Methodist.
POPULATION: Upwards of 1,200.
MISCELLANEOUS: **Monuments:** Several in the Chancel – to the Parker family.
PARISH CLERK: Joseph Woolley. **Appointed by:** The Vicar. **Salary:** £10 and £1 for cleaning.
CHURCHWARDENS: Mr Whalley for the Vicar. Mr Shaw for the Parish.
ORDERS MADE: An additional casement to be made on the South side. The Iron bars of the windows etc painted. The doors repaired – Porch ditto and iron (or wood) light gates placed at the N. and S. entrances. The Church to be new-pewed – the Gallery removed, or rebuilt.[4] Font repaired and cleaned, a basin provided; the Vestry enclosed, the window [of ditto] repaired, and a separate entrance, if possible, made to the Belfry. The Communion Table to be cleaned, and a new Cover provided; the Chancel window repaired. The old Registers to be re-bound. The Tower repaired at the Top and pointed all over; weatherboards provided; the cracked bell re-cast; the Clock weight secured and protected – and the Clock-face re-painted, or renewed.

Revisited 27.9.1837
> Much improved – Churchyard closed – buildings on S. side repaired. Directions to the Churchwardens.
>
> I   Outside
> (1) Porch roof repaired, and ground lowered on each side – the iron gates removed to the entrance of *the Porch,* and painted; gates at N. entrance likewise painted. (2) Ivy removed from roof of tower, roof repaired and wheel of bell; battlements and pinnacles secured; clock-face painted, and down-pipe instead of overshot spout. (3) Roof on N. side repaired – spouts cleared out; battlements on S. side re-pointed. (4) Chancel roof spouted, and window new leaded – iron rails of Gilbert's burial ground *painted.*
>
> II   *Inside the Church*
> (5) *Walls* coloured; *ceilings* whitewashed – pipes of stove made not to discolour the walls. (6) *Pews rubbed with oil* and hinges painted – back of pulpit painted – and screen re-painted under direction of Vicar. ['Nothing done. Chancel promised'.]

Revisited 27.9.1841
> Directions to Churchwardens.
>
> I.   In the Church
> Oak pews rubbed with linseed oil. Decayed floors and skirting of pews on S. side repaired. Wheels of bells repaired, and cracked bell re-cast. Joints of parapets pointed. Porch kept in sound repair, or (if the Patron approves) taken down. Wall at SW. corner of Church, under-built – eave spout on that side taken down, and wet from roof brought to ground by ground-pipes. Open drains carried all round the Church.
>
> II.   In the Chancel
> Water tables made for windows. Old pews rubbed with oil, and repaired. East gable pointed, or flashed. Spouts placed so as to carry the wet from the roof, and painted.

[1] *Eccles. Revs.:* 348. [2] *Eccles. Revs.:* 'Fit'. [3] *Eccles. Revs.:* gross income £233. [4] 'Repaired and enlarged' deleted and replaced by 'rebuilt'.

CAULDON 20.7.1830
(A/V/1/4, p.9; A/V/1/2, p.114)

BENEFICE: Cauldon. **Nature:** Perpetual Curacy. **Ecton:** Chapelry to Mathfield – £8 19s. 8d. Clear value. **Patron:** Mrs Wilmot (of Derbyshire). **Impropriator:** Ditto.
CHURCH: A small Church, the body rebuilt in 1784 – the Chancel old, separated by a circular arch. **Number it will contain:** About 170. **Accommodation for Poor:** 46. **Roof:** Timber covered with lead – several cracks all along the ceiling seem to indicate want of strength in the Timbers. **Walls:** Brick, faced with grit-stone [upright]. **Floor:** Flags – uneven in some places. **Windows:** Good – no casements. **Doors:** Good. **Pulpit and Desk:** Good – handsomely ornamented. **Books:** Slight repairs wanted. **Seats:** Somewhat out of repair. **Galleries:** One at the W. end, not in good repair. **Organ:** None. **Font:** Provided. **Chapels:** None. **Benefaction Tables:** None. **Vestry:** None. **Surplices:** Two – one new. **Linen:** Good. **Plate:** Small silver Cup and two small patins. **Iron Chest for Register:** In the Church. **Register:** Oldest appears to be 1675 – but they have been very irregularly kept. **Porch:** None. **Vaults:** Only one recently. **Cleanliness:** Attended to. **Damp:** Some appearance on the walls.
CHANCEL: **Table:** Firm – wants cleaning. **Ornaments:** None. **Repaired by whom:** Mrs Wilmot – several repairs needed.
STEEPLE: Square stone tower. **State of:** Good. **Bells:** Three – new and good. **Clock:** None.
CHURCHYARD: **Fence:** Stone wall, good. **Gates:** Good. **Drains:** None – nor pipes to carry wet from roof. **Graves:** Some too near. **Rubbish:** None. **Footpaths:** Some which should be stopped. **Cattle:** None.
DIVINE SERVICE: **On Sundays:** One full service – afternoon. **On other Days:** None. **Sacrament:** Three times a year. **Communicants:** About 20. **Catechism:** At Easter.
INCUMBENT: **Name and Residence:** Revd Richard Ward.[1] **If not resident:** At Kingsley – 3½ miles off. **What Duty he performs:** The whole.
PARSONAGE: None.[2]
INCOME: **Gross Value:** Not ascertained.[3] **Tithes:** Have been purchased for the Minister (as I understand) by four several grants of £200 each from Queen Anne's Bounty. **Terrier:** There is one.
SCHOOLS: **Endowed School:** None. **Subscription Day School:** About 60 children. **Sunday School:** 150 – including children from neighbouring parishes. **Lancaster School:** None.
DISSENTERS: **Dissenters' School:** ——. **Dissenting Chapels:** None.
POPULATION: About 300.
PARISH CLERK: William Woolley. **Appointed by:** The Minister. **Salary:** 52s. a year.
CHURCHWARDENS: Mr John Rushton.
ORDERS MADE: The roof to be carefully examined, and also the Timbers and ceiling etc. The lead gutters to be regularly cleaned out. The floor to be repaired where needful – and pannels of pews repaired. Two additional casements to be made in the body of the Church, and one in the Gallery. The Bible to be rebound, and Prayer Book repaired. The Table and Communion-rails to be cleaned with oil. The wood-work of Pews etc to be painted, and walls whitewashed. The Chancel roof to be examined and repaired – the floor laid even, the walls and ceiling whitewashed – door repaired or renewed – casements made. Pipes to be put up to carry the rain from the roof – an open drain made. Footpaths to be stopped.

Revisited 16.9.1837
> Lead-gutters to be cleaned out – ground cleared away around the walls – thoroughfare of Churchyard stopped. Walls and ceilings of Church coloured and whitewashed. Books repaired. 'Qu? Thoroughfare'.

Revisited 14.9.1841
> (1) Water tables to windows – bars painted. (2) Communion Table and rails oiled. (3) Battlements of roof repaired and pointed. (4) Copings of Chancel laid afresh – Chancel floor re-laid with quarries – and pews repaired. (5) Open drain all round.

[1] Also perpetual curate of Waterfall and of the donative of Calton. [2] *Eccles. Revs.:* 'None'. [3] *Eccles. Revs.:* £57.

CHEDDLETON 24.7.1830
(A/V/1/4,p.10;A/V/1/2,p.131)

BENEFICE: Cheddleton (Ecton. Ched*u*lton). **Nature:** Perpetual Curacy [stated to have been] formerly a Chapelry under Alstonfield [but] qu? Leek, more probably. **Ecton:** Olim Chapelry *to Leeke*. Abb.[1] Dulacres Propr. £7 15s. 10d. Clear value. **Patron:** The Powys family.[2] **Impropriator:** The principal part of the land is Tythe free – formerly it was under the Abbey de la Crux.

CHURCH: An old Gothic church[3] – the architecture altered at different times; centre and side aisles; pointed arches, antient windows. **Number it will contain:** 397. **Accommodation for Poor:** 30. **Roof:** Oak covered with tile; not very good. **Walls:** Stone, upright. **Floor:** Flags – much sunk, owing to interments underneath. **Windows:** Good – more casements wanted. **Doors:** Good. **Pulpit and Desk:** Good and well placed. **Books:** Pretty good. **Seats:** Some of them very irregular – too high. **Galleries:** At the W. end. **Organ:** There is one. **Font:** A very old one. **Chapels:** None. **Benefaction Tables:** Several. **Vestry:** Under the Belfry. **Surplices:** Three – good. **Linen:** Provided. **Plate:** Three very handsome silver Cups – ditto patin and plate. **Iron Chest for Register:** At the Clergyman's house. **Register:** Oldest about 1680 – in good preservation. [I did not see them – the house being distant.] **Porch:** There is one – a light gate wanted. **Vaults:** Several. **Cleanliness:** Attended to. **Damp:** On the floor.

CHANCEL: **Table:** A Mahogany Table – no covering. **Ornaments:** None. **Repaired by whom:** The Parish.

STEEPLE: Stone square tower. **State of:** Some repairs wanted on the roof. **Bells:** Three – good in general. **Clock:** Good.

CHURCHYARD: **Fence:** Good. **Gates:** ——. **Drains:** None. **Graves:** Too near. **Rubbish:** Not much. **Footpaths:** Trespass paths several. **Cattle:** A horse.

DIVINE SERVICE: **On Sundays:** Alternately Morning and Afternoon. **On other Days:** None. **Sacrament:** Five times a year. **Communicants:** 30 to 40. **Catechism:** Occasionally.

INCUMBENT: **Name and Residence:** Revd E Powys [(or Powis)] – 1¼ miles off. **If not resident:** [1¼ miles from the Church.] **What Duty he performs:** The whole.

PARSONAGE: None.[4]

INCOME: **Gross Value:** About £200.[5] **Queen Anne's Bounty:** £1,400, 3 per Cents. **Terrier:** The Clergyman has one.

SCHOOLS: **Endowed School:** Two endowments, together £13 per annum – 40 children taught free. **Sunday School:** 40 children.

DISSENTERS: **Dissenting Chapels:** Lady Huntingdon's, and Methodist, at Wetley Rocks.

POPULATION: About 1,700 (a chapel about to be built at Wetley Rocks).

PARISH CLERK: Thomas Dawson. **Appointed by:** The Minister. **Salary:** 30s. – too little.

CHURCHWARDENS: Joshua Braddock. John Hughes.

ORDERS MADE: The roof to be examined and repaired. The floor taken up and laid afresh – both in Church and Chancel. Two new casements in the body of the Church – and one in the Gallery and Vestry. The window on the N. side enlarged; and that at the E. end renewed. The [free] Pews in the North aisle to be re-modelled, on a uniform plan. The large Pew in the Chancel lowered [– 'done']. The floors of the pews laid with boards, hollow [– 'done']. Light gates put up at the Porch entrance and Chancel door [– 'done']. A covering provided for the Communion Table [– 'will be done']. The roof of the Tower, and wheels of the bells, repaired. Spouts put up on the North side and Chancel roof. The earth cleared away,[6] and an open drain formed. Footpaths stopped, if possible; and no graves within ten feet of walls. The new pews, and Iron bars of windows etc painted.

Revisited 18.9.1837
Directions to the Churchwardens. (1) The pews to be thoroughly repaired, especially those in the North aisle, and Chancel. (2) A covering to be provided for the Communion Table, and new Pulpit Cushion. (3) Bell-wheels repaired – roof of tower ditto – water-courses kept clear – eavespouts and down-pipes on north roof of Church and both roofs of Chancel – down-pipes instead of overshot spouts of tower and S. side of Church. (4) Roofs carefully examined and repaired; soil and herbage cleared away, walls pointed. (5) Proper gravel walk formed from the East gate to the door of the Church.

N.B. The Church has been much improved since my former visit; and most of my directions carried into effect. 'Qu – Spouts? Registers filled up?'

Revisited 14.9.1841
(1) Roof examined – tiling repaired – ridge tiles and copings pointed. (2) W. end of roof repointed or flashed. (3) Weights of clocks to hang more safely – case provided. (4) Wheels of bells repaired – flashings of Tower Roof secured – gutters levelled. (5) Chancel roof examined and repaired. (6) Eave-spouts and down-pipes. (7) Open space – (two feet wide) soil removed. (8) Recommended – new pewing on N. side.

[1] A/V/1/4 adds marginal 'qu? *de la Crux*?' [2] A/V/1/4: 'The present Incumbent's family.' [3] A/V/1/4: 'originally Gothic'. [4] *Eccles. Revs.:* 'None'. [5] *Eccles. Revs.:* gross income £170. [6] A/V/1/3: 'lowered'.

COTTON 16.7.1830
(A/V/1/4,p.11;A/V/1/2,p.102)

BENEFICE: Cotton Chapel. **Nature:** A donative, in the Parish of Alveton, three miles from the Parish Church. **Ecton:** Not mentioned. **Patron:** Revd Thomas Gilbert – the son of the Gentleman[1] who built and endowed it. **Impropriator:** No tithes belonging to the Chapel.

CHURCH: A small, [modern,] inelegant building, coved roof, two arched recesses on the N. and S. sides [of the body of the Chapel]. **Number it will contain:** About 160. **Accommodation for Poor:** All the sittings free, except three in the Chancel. **Roof:** Timber covered with slate –

lead gutters and ridgings. **Walls:** Brick. **Floor:** Flags. **Windows:** Good – but dirty, and casements out of order. **Doors:** Good – light gates recommended instead of the outer door. **Pulpit and Desk:** Firm and well placed – old cloth Cushion – moth-eaten. **Books:** Very bad. **Seats:** Good – all open benches with backs, except three pews near the E. end. **Galleries:** None – except a small one for organ and singers. **Organ:** A barrel organ. **Font:** There is one – but no proper basin. **Chapels:** None. **Benefaction Tables:** None required. **Vestry:** A very small one. **Surplices:** One. **Linen:** Provided. **Plate:** Handsome silver Cup and Cover, and Patin. **Iron Chest for Register:** None. **Register:** No registers have been kept hitherto; baptisms only performed and very occasionally burials. **Porch:** None. **Vaults:** One or two. **Cleanliness:** Not properly attended to; no provision made for cleaning. **Damp:** On the walls and ceiling. **Dimensions:** 51ft. by 21ft.

CHANCEL: Included in above. **Table:** Good – green cloth covering and cushions moth-eaten and dirty. **Repaired by whom:** All the repairs of the Chapel lie upon the family of the founder, Mr Gilbert.

STEEPLE: A wooden bell tower, over the centre of the Chapel, surmounted with a vane – sheeted with lead at the bottom. **State of:** The rain comes in.[2] **Bells:** One. **Footpaths:** None.

CHURCHYARD: **Fence:** Wall and hedge, in good order. **Gates:** Good. **Drains:** None – much wet on the N. side. **Graves:** None. **Rubbish:** ——. **Footpaths:** ——. **Cattle:** ——.

DIVINE SERVICE: **On Sundays:** Full service morning and afternoon, alternately. **On other Days:** None. **Sacrament:** Two or three times a year. **Communicants:** 14 last time. **Catechism:** None.

INCUMBENT: **Name and Residence:** Revd T Gilbert. **If not resident:** Abroad.

CURATE: **Name and Residence:** The duty done pro tempore by Revd E Whieldon. **If not resident:** At Wood-houses near Cheadle.

PARSONAGE: None.[3]

INCOME: **Gross Value:** £50 or 60, arising partly from endowment, partly from Queen Anne's Bounty.

INCOME: **Queen Anne's Bounty:** Amount not stated. **Terrier:** None, except the Consecration Deed.

SCHOOLS: **Endowed School:** None. **Subscription Day School:** None. **Sunday School:** None. **Lancaster School:** None.

DISSENTERS: **Dissenters' School:** None. **Dissenting Chapels:** None.

POPULATION: 600.[4]

PARISH CLERK: John Mellor. **Appointed by:** The Minister (supposed). **Salary:** £3 12s. 0d. paid hitherto by the Township.

CHURCHWARDENS: Mr John Prince.

ORDERS MADE: The casements of the windows to be put in order, and regularly opened. The iron bars painted – roof examined and repaired, where the wet comes in – and the ceiling whitewashed. New Bible and Prayer Book for reading-desk; Clerk's Prayer Book repaired. New Surplice – and basin for the Font. The Communion rails made firm – table and coverings cleaned; and the screen of the circular window above, either removed or renewed. A Trap door made to the Belfry – Registers and an Iron Chest provided. The earth removed round the Chapel walls; and effectual means used for drawing off the wet from the North side of the Chapel.

Revisited 28.9.1837
Directions to the Churchwarden. (1) To have the oak pews, Pulpit etc. Communion rails and table *rubbed with linseed oil* – the deal benches etc painted oak colour, and the doors, and screen at the E. end. (2) Iron bars of windows painted – skirting board along the floor where it is sunk. (3) Lead gutters of roof cleared out – eave-spouts and down-pipes. (4) Trees removed from E. end – copings of roof at W. end secured. (5) Registers and Register Chest provided. *'Nothing done'*.

Revisited 28.9.1841
There being no Churchwarden, and there being reason to doubt whether the Chapel, as a Donative, be not exempt from Episcopal jurisdiction, I merely recommend that the Fabric be preserved from injury by draining the Chapel-yard – by altering the structure of the roof, or taking precautions to keep out the wet – by putting up eave-spouts and down-pipes, and by securing the window frames against the weather, by pointing externally and internally.

N.B. As baptisms are solemnized in this Chapel, there ought to be separate Register books and an Iron Register Chest in which to keep them. 52 G. 3.c.146.

[1] A/V/1/4: '. . . of Revd Mr G, the builder and endower'. [2] A/V/1/4: 'Not very good.' [3] *Eccles. Revs.:* 'None'. [4] *Eccles. Revs.:* 470.

DILHORNE 15.7.1830
(A/V/1/4,p.12;A/V/1/2,p.97)

BENEFICE: Dilhorne (alias Dilherne). **Nature:** Vicarage. **Ecton:** Clear value £49 0s. 0d. **Patron:** Dean and Chapter of Lichfield. **Impropriator:** Henry Potts Esqr of Chester, as Lessee under the D. and C.

CHURCH: An old structure, in Gothic style – nave and two side aisles – pointed Arches – flat ceiling. **Number it will contain:** About 500. **Accommodation for Poor:** 30 and benches for children. **Roof:** Deal covered with slate, side aisles [with] lead. **Walls:** Stone; upright, but want whitewashing or colouring.[1] **Floor:** Quarries and grave-stones; sunk in some places. **Windows:** Good. **Doors:** ——. **Pulpit and Desk:** Firm and well-placed as to the *Pulpit* – pannels want cleaning – the reading desk too far back. **Books:** Not good. **Seats:** Neat and uniform; hinges of doors want painting. **Galleries:** A small one at the W. end, in ruinous condition. **Organ:** None. **Font:** An antient one – basin wanted. **Chapels:** None. **Benefaction Tables:** One – a benefaction lost. **Vestry:** None – recommended. **Surplices:** Two. **Linen:** Provided. **Plate:** Silver Cup and Patin. **Chest for Papers:** There is [one]. **Iron Chest for Register:** In the Chancel. **Register:** Five vols prior to 1813 – the old ones to be re-bound. **Porch:** None. **Vaults:** Several – not to be allowed in future. **Cleanliness:** Want of it on the walls. **Damp:** Much on the walls and floor of Chancel. **Dimensions:** 46ft. 4in. by 47ft. 4in.

CHANCEL: 27ft. 4in. by 14ft. 9in. **Table:** In proper

state. **Ornaments:** None. **Repaired by whom:** The Lessee of the Dean and Chapter – the roof wants repair – walls colouring – another casement.

STEEPLE: Octagonal stone tower. **State of:** Roof wants repair – lower windows glazed. **Bells:** Five – good. **Clock:** There is one.

CHURCHYARD: **Fence:** Hedge, and sunk fence – the wall of the latter next the road, wants repairing. **Gates:** Out of repair. **Drains:** Not sufficient. **Graves:** Some too near. **Rubbish:** Some. **Footpaths:** A thoroughfare in two directions – the Church-ways well kept. **Cattle:** A horse.

DIVINE SERVICE: **On Sundays:** Full service in Mornings – prayers Afternoon. **On other Days:** None. **Sacrament:** Five times a year. **Communicants:** 30 or 40. **Catechism:** In Lent.

INCUMBENT: **Name and Residence:** Revd H White.[2] **If not resident:** Lichfield. **What Duty he performs:** None.

CURATE: **Name and Residence:** Revd Thomas Macdougal, Vicarage. **Licensed:** He is. **Salary:** £75 – fees £5 – and the house. **If serving another church:** None.

PARSONAGE: An old fashioned brick building – tiled roof; rough-cast in front. **State of:** Not very good.[3] **Outbuildings:** Barn and two stables – good repair.

INCOME: **Gross Value:** About £200. **Tithes:** A composition for Tithes and Easter dues. **Terrier:** There is a Copy.

SCHOOLS: **Endowed School:** There is one – a grammar school – free to [all] the Parishioners – supported by land which lets for £300 per annum – there is also an English school – £28 per annum. **Subscription Day School:** None. **Sunday School:** About 30 children – supported by Lady Buller. **Lancaster School:** None.

DISSENTERS: **Dissenters' School:** ——. **Dissenting Chapels:** Three.

POPULATION: 1,500.

MISCELLANEOUS: **Monuments:** Several in the Chancel. **Parochial Library:** None.

PARISH CLERK: Jonathan Whalley. **Appointed by:** The Vicar. **Salary:** None.

CHURCHWARDENS: Mr Whitehurst, Mr Bradbury.

ORDERS MADE: The Gallery to be taken down and re-built; (recommended that it be reserved for the *School children,* and one or two pews below, now free, be given in exchange for the pews in the present Gallery). The floor laid even, where needful – light gates to be set up at the N. and S. entrances. The hinges of the pews, bars of windows, straps of Bells etc painted. The pannels of the Pulpit and Pews to be cleaned – reading desk *advanced.* The walls coloured or white-washed – the ceiling whitewashed. A new Prayer Book for reading desk – Bible re-bound. Clerk's Prayer Book repaired. A basin for the Baptismal Font – Iron Register Chest removed to the Vicarage – old Registers re-bound – A Vestry *recommended.* The Chancel floor [to be] re-laid, door repaired and painted – ceiling made good – casement made on S. side; walls and ceiling whitewashed. The roof of the Tower repaired; walls pointed – weatherboards completed – lower windows glazed – a close door placed at the entrance from the Church into the Belfry. Earth removed from walls of the Church – open drain formed; the thoroughfare stopped, if possible – wall next the street repaired, and no large cattle allowed to feed in the Churchyard.

I visited the Church again on 2.12.1834 – and finding that the Gallery had not yet been repaired, nor the books renewed, nor the earth properly removed from the walls, I wrote a strong letter to the Churchwardens on the subject – The Gallery is *under orders*; but the execution has been delayed.

Revisited 27.9.1837

Since the last memorandum, a good deal has been done; a new gallery has been erected; the roofs and ceilings repaired etc. Still much is wanted, especially *outside* the Church – An addition to the burial ground is much wanted, and a plan has been suggested for the enlargement of the present Churchyard on the SW. and W. sides; by means of which also the public road through the Churchyard may be stopped.

Directions to the Churchwardens. (1) The earth to be cleared away all round the Church and Chancel (especially the latter) and a gravel walk, or open drain formed – walls pointed – down-pipe restored at the SE. angle – roof of Tower repaired – weatherboards put up; *battlements of Tower secured.* (2) Walls of the Church and Chancel coloured – ceilings whitewashed; pews rubbed with linseed oil; floor within Communion rails repaired – Chancel window and pews, and floors of pews, repaired. 'Done or in progress.'

Recommended
A new covering for the Table; and ditto for Pulpit and reading desk. A *salary for the Clerk* – £5 per annum.

Revisited 27.9.1841

Directions to Churchwardens. (1) Baptismal basin provided for Font. (2) New floor for Communion table – either boarded or bricks laid on Cinders – rails new or repaired. (3) Old pews in Chancel (if not claimed on sufficient authority) taken down, and open benches placed for School children. The temporary Vestry removed, and placed under the Tower. (4) Walls of Chancel pointed all round, especially at lower parts, and kept clear of grass etc – spouts painted. (5) Wet conveyed from roof of Tower by down-pipe, instead of overshot pipe – injuring walls, battlements, roofs etc. (6) Lead pipes at NW. end of Church repaired. (7) No heavy cattle allowed in Churchyard. (8) Churchyard enlarged and fenced, and no thoroughfare or trespass paths hereafter allowed.

[1] A/V/1/4: '. . . but want cleaning.' [2] See under Chebsey, above p. 47. [3] *Eccles. Revs.:* 'Fit'.

ELKSTONE 21.9.1830
(A/V/1/4,p.13;A/V/1/2,p.120)

BENEFICE: Upper Elkstone. **Nature:** Chapelry under Alstonfield – Perpetual Curacy. **Ecton:** 6s. 8d. clear value. **Patron:** The Vicar of Alstonfield. **Impropriator:** Sir G Crewe.

CHURCH: A very small plain building, rebuilt in 1788 – single body. **Number it will contain:** 180.

Accommodation for Poor: Sufficient. **Roof:** Red deal, covered with tile – good repair. **Walls:** Stone – good. **Floor:** Flags. **Windows:** Good. **Doors:** Good. **Pulpit and Desk:** ——. **Books:** Not good. **Seats:** Floors bad. **Galleries:** One at W. end for singers; and some private pews. **Organ:** None. **Font:** There is one. **Chapels:** None. **Benefaction Tables:** No benefactions. **Vestry:** None. **Surplices:** One – new. **Linen:** Provided. **Plate:** The same as at Warslow. **Iron Chest for Register:** None. **Register:** At Warslow. **Porch:** None. **Vaults:** None lately. **Cleanliness:** Attended to. **Damp:** No appearance, except a little on W. wall. **Dimensions:** About 20ft. by 15ft.
CHANCEL: No Chancel. **Table:** Painted deal. **Ornaments:** None. **Repaired by whom:** The Parish.
STEEPLE: A bell tower. **State of:** Not very good. **Bells:** One. **Clock:** None.
CHURCHYARD: **Fence:** Stone wall on three sides – a dingle and sloping bank planted with trees on the fourth. **Gates:** Good. **Drains:** Not wanted. **Graves:** Some too near. **Rubbish:** None. **Cattle:** Sheep and calves.
DIVINE SERVICE: **On Sundays:** Alternately [morning and afternoon] with Warslow. **On other Days:** None. **Sacrament:** Four times a year. **Communicants:** 12.
INCUMBENT: **Name and Residence:** Revd R Burton Pidcock.[1] **If not resident:** At Warslow 2½ miles off. **What Duty he performs:** The whole.
PARSONAGE: None.[2]
INCOME: **Gross Value:** ——.[3] **Tithes:** About 50 acres of land, purchased by Bounty money. **Terrier:** At Alstonfield.
SCHOOLS: **Endowed School:** None. **Subscription Day School:** None. **Sunday School:** None at present.
POPULATION: About 300.
PARISH CLERK: John Milward. **Appointed by:** The Vicar of Alstonfield. **Salary:** £2 12s. 0d. per annum.
CHURCHWARDENS: Mr Thomas Bestwick, appointed by the Vicar of Alstonfield.
ORDERS MADE: The Prayer Book and Bible to be repaired – new Prayer Book for the Clerk. The Coverings of the Pulpit and Communion Table to be restored. Floors of the Pews to be flagged or boarded. The bell-tower repaired – no graves near the walls. The earth cleared away from the Chapel walls – and stairs leading to the Belfry (at W. end) pointed,[4] so as to exclude the wet from the Wall. ['Everything done [——] – floors boarded – new prayer book [——] repaired.']

Revisited 14.9.1837
Much improved – nothing further necessary at present except (1) Eave-spouts and down-pipes on *N. side*. (2) Open drain all round. (3) Register Chest – in which Warslow may join. 'Not done. Qu. Register Chest.'

Revisited 11.9.1841
(1) Bible re-bound – new Prayer Book for Clerk. (2) Covers of Table and Pulpit died afresh. (3) Iron bars and casements of windows painted – outer door ditto. (4) New rail etc to Gallery steps. (5) Wall under East window repaired – grass removed from bottom of walls. (6) Churchyard gate re-hung and painted.

[1] Also perpetual curate of Warslow. [2] *Eccles. Revs.:* 'None.' [3] *Eccles. Revs.:* Gross income £74. [4] A/V/1/4: 'repaired'.

ENDON 23.7.1830 (A/V/1/4,p.14;A/V/1/2,p.130)

BENEFICE: Endon. **Nature:** Perpetual Curacy – Chapelry under Leek. **Ecton:** 'Of *no value*'. **Patron:** Lord Macclesfield. **Impropriator:** No tythes.
CHURCH: A neat small building, erected 120 years ago – single body. **Number it will contain:** About 200. **Accommodation for Poor:** All the Gallery sittings. **Roof:** Oak covered with lead. **Walls:** Freestone – good. **Floor:** Bricks – even. **Windows:** Good – but casements wanted. **Doors:** Good. **Pulpit and Desk:** Neat – velvet cushion. **Books:** Good. **Seats:** Very neat and uniform; boarded floors. **Galleries:** Two. **Organ:** None. **Font:** Provided. **Chapels:** None. **Benefaction Tables:** Three. **Vestry:** There is one. **Surplices:** One – another ordered. **Linen:** Provided. **Plate:** Silver Cup and Patin – plated flagon and dish. **iron Chest for Register:** There is one. **Register:** From 1731. **Porch:** None. **Vaults:** ——. **Cleanliness:** Attended to. **Damp:** Not much.
CHANCEL: **Table:** Neat. **Ornaments:** None. **Repaired by whom:** The Townships.
STEEPLE: **Description:** Square stone Tower. **State of:** Good. **Bells:** One. **Clock:** None.
CHURCHYARD: **Fence:** Kept up by the Townships – part of the Chapel yard has been turned into a garden – very improperly. **Gates:** Good. **Drains:** None – earth too high. **Cattle:** None.
DIVINE SERVICE: **On Sundays:** Two full services. **On other Days:** None. **Sacrament:** Five times a year. **Communicants:** 20. **Catechism:** Not in the Chapel.
INCUMBENT: **Name and Residence:** Revd John Salt. **What Duty he performs:** The whole.
PARSONAGE: None.[1]
INCOME: **Gross Value:** About £100 per annum. **Glebe:** An estate at Rushton Spenser. **Queen Anne's Bounty:** Amount not stated. **Terrier:** There is one.
SCHOOLS: **Endowed School:** £7 or 8 per annum charged on land. **Subscription Day School:** None. **Sunday School:** 40 or 50 children. **Lancaster School:** None.
DISSENTERS: **Dissenters' School:** None. **Dissenting Chapels:** None.
POPULATION: 350.[2]
PARISH CLERK: John Mountford. **Appointed by:** The Minister. **Salary:** £5.
CHURCHWARDENS: William Hand.
ORDERS MADE: Two casements to be made on the S. side; one on the N. Another surplice to be provided. The earth lowered outside the Chapel – especially at the W. end.

Revisited 18.9.1837
Directions to the Churchwardens. (1) To have the mats removed from the Pews, and those which at present have no *floors, boarded* at the common expense; the boarded floors of some of the others, repaired. (2) The floor near the Communion rails repaired – the rails, table, pulpit, desk, pews, varnished or oiled; the pulpit door fixed; and a new floor laid, with boards or quarries, within the Communion rails. (3) A new

prayer book for the Reading Desk; the present one transferred to the Clerk's desk. (4) The ladder to the belfry mended; gudgeons of wheel oiled and covered; down-pipes substituted for overshot spouts. (5) The staircase leading to the gallery *pointed* at its juncture with the wall of the Church – the ground lowered and bush removed near the Vestry; the grass etc cleared away round the walls of the Church – the trespass paths stopped, and gates kept locked. 'Apparently nothing done.'

Revisited 13.9.1841
(1) Bible re-bound – Desk altered – Stand for Clergyman. (2) Communion Table oiled – new Cover to ditto. (3) Brick floors removed, or laid afresh – decayed mats removed. (4) Water tables to windows – bars and frames of ditto painted. (5) Vestry ceiling repaired – battlements of roof secured. (6) Open drain – Churchyard gates painted.

[1] *Eccles. Revs.:* 'None.' [2] *Eccles. Revs.:* 605.

GRINDON 20.7.1830
(A/V/1/4,p.15;A/V/1/2,p.116)

BENEFICE: Grindon or Grendon. **Nature:** Rectory. **Ecton:** King's Books £15 14s. 2d. Abb. Burton 14s. – Duke of Montague Patron. **Patron:** Mrs Bradshaw, as the present representative of the Clowes family. **Impropriator:** None.
CHURCH: An antient Gothic building – low pointed Arches – very handsome open carved ceiling – the side aisles modernized. **Number it will contain:** About 200[1] – exclusive of the Gallery. **Accommodation for Poor:** About 50 – including benches for children. **Roof:** Oak covered with lead – in good repair. **Walls:** Free stone – good. **Floor:** Flags – uneven. **Windows:** No casements – iron bars want painting. **Doors:** Old – but in tolerable repair. **Pulpit and Desk:** Antient oak – motheaten cushion. **Books:** Good. **Seats:** Oak – some out of repair, floors bad. **Galleries:** The space under the Tower fitted up for singers. **Organ:** None. **Font:** A very antient stone font. **Chapels:** None. **Benefaction Tables:** Several – recording amongst others an endowment of the Charity school by Mr Hall. **Vestry:** None. **Surplices:** Only one. **Linen:** Provided. **Plate:** A silver Cup – pewter flagon and plate. **Chest for Papers:** There is. **Iron Chest for Registers:** None. **Register:** Not seen. **Porch:** There is one – not in repair. **Vaults:** None lately. **Cleanliness:** Attended to. **Damp:** Some at the bottoms of the walls.
CHANCEL: **Table:** Oak – wants cleaning – the rails to be new.[2] **Ornaments:** None. **Repaired by whom:** The Rector.
STEEPLE: A square stone Tower, with pinnacles. **State of:** Out of repair at the top. **Bells:** Three – sound – but the wheels want repair etc. **Clock:** None.
CHURCHYARD: **Fence:** Pretty good. **Gates:** Want painting. **Drains:** None. **Graves:** Some too near. **Rubbish:** Some. **Footpaths:** To be stopped if possible. **Cattle:** None.
DIVINE SERVICE: **On Sundays:** Morning and afternoon alternately. **On other Days:** None.
Sacrament: Four times a year. **Communicants:** About 10. **Catechism:** Occasionally.
INCUMBENT: **Name and Residence:** Revd John Clowes – qu? the ground of his non-residence. Fellow of Collegiate Church of Manchester. **If not resident:** At Manchester.
CURATE: **Name and Residence:** Revd W Carlisle. **If not resident:** Belmont, Ipstones [four miles off]. **Licensed:** He is. **Salary:** £90 a year. **If serving another church:** Ipstones.
PARSONAGE: A stone building, occupied as a farm house. **State of:** Very much out of repair, and [apparently] insecure.[3]
INCOME: **Gross Value:** About 400.[4] (Stated to me £300 and £600 [by different persons].) **Terrier:** None exhibited.
SCHOOLS: **Endowed School:** £25 per annum arising from land – for instruction of 18 children. The school adjoins the Chancel, at the East end – and appears formerly to have been part of it. **Subscription Day School:** None. **Sunday School:** 35 children. **Lancaster School:** None.
DISSENTERS: **Dissenters' School:** None. **Dissenting Chapels:** None.
POPULATION: Under 300.[5]
CHURCHWARDENS: Thomas Derbyshire; James Burnett.
ORDERS MADE: The floor to be laid even – two casements on each side of the Church. Iron work of windows, bells, doors etc to be painted. A new Cushion for the Pulpit – and basin for the Font. The pannels and floors of the Pews repaired – the Porch made secure and light gates placed at the Entrance. The Communion Table cleaned and covered – new rails. The floor of the Chancel re-laid – walls pointed externally. The Clerk's seat and Rector's pew put in proper repair. The Tower made secure at the top – the bell wheels mended, floor of Belfry, and that underneath (on the ground floor) repaired – the rails in front of the Gallery fixed. The Gates painted – earth removed from the Church walls – the walls, all round, cleared of weeds and pointed. No graves to be dug near the walls.

Revisited 13.9.1837
Much improved since my former visit. (1) Porch roof to be repaired – down-pipe instead of the overshot spouts which empty the water upon it from the roof. (2) Windows, both of Church and Chancel, repaired and bars painted. (3) Floors of pews, in places, repaired. (4) New Prayer Book – Bible repaired. (5) Water-course of roofs cleared out and laid even. (6) The Lich-gates repaired and painted – thoroughfare stopped up if possible – Rector's fence improved. (7) The School, *if possible,* removed from the east end of the Church. (8) No large cattle in the Churchyard. 'Qu? Churchyard.'

Revisited 10.9.1841
Inside
(1) Oak pews, pulpit, Reading desk, *open ceiling* etc oiled. (2) Floors of pews repaired – flags of aisle re-laid. (3) Outer door repaired and oiled. (4) Casement on S. side.

Outside
(1) Pinnacles and battlements of Tower secured – joints pointed – window jambs and heads

pointed. (2) Walls of Church pointed all round. (3) Wall under upper windows on N. side, repaired. (4) Lead work of roof repaired and secured. (5) Roof, generally, repaired. (6) Walls and roof of Porch repaired.

Mem. New Gate about to be put up; and thoroughfare stopped. Chancel about to be repaired by Rector – conformity to original style.

[1] *Eccles. Revs.:* 300. [2] A/V/1/4: '. . . the rails bad'. **&3***
[3] *Eccles. Revs.:* 'Fit'. [4] *Eccles. Revs.:* Gross income £341. [5] *Eccles. Revs.:* 422.

HANLEY 15.6.1830 (A/V/1/4,p.16;A/V/1/2,p.79)

BENEFICE: Hanley. **Nature:** Perpetual Curacy – under Stoke but intended to be a Parish Church and a Rectory. **Ecton:** Not mentioned. **Patron:** At present the patronage is in the hands of Trustees – but is to be given up to the Bishop. **Impropriator:**[1]
CHURCH: A modern building – erected in 1737 – rebuilt in 1790 – a single body – no chancel. **Number it will contain:** 1,000 in pews. **Accommodation for Poor:** 80 in pews – 200 in benches. **Roof:** Oak covered with tile – large crack in the ceiling – but the roof stated to be good. **Walls:** Brick – solid. **Floor:** Quarries [– even]. **Windows:** Well provided with casements. **Doors:** Good. **Pulpit and Desk:** Oak, well placed – crimson velvet cushions. **Books:** Not good. **Seats:** Very good. **Galleries:** On three sides – beside two (above that on the W.) for children. **organ:** There is one. **Font:** ——. **Chapels:** None. **Benefaction Tables:** None. **Vestry:** A very good one. **Surplices:** Two – good. **Linen:** Table Cloth and napkin – good. **Plate:** Silver flagon, Cup and Patin. **Iron Chest for Register:** At the Parsonage. **Register:** Six Vols [prior to 1813] – oldest 1754 (the Chapel built in 1737) in excellent preservation, and beautifully kept. **Porch:** None. **Vaults:** ——. **Cleanliness:** Attended to. **Damp:** No appearance.
CHANCEL: **Table:** Handsome mahogany. **Ornaments:** Crimson velvet covering – Commandments. **Repaired by whom:** The pew-owners.
STEEPLE: Square brick tower. **State of:** Good. **Bells:** Eight – good. **Clock:** Good.
CHURCHYARD: **Fence:** Brick wall and iron palisades – good repair. **Gates:** Iron. **Graves:** Too near the walls. **Rubbish:** None. **Cattle:** None.
DIVINE SERVICE: **On Sundays:** Two full services. **On other Days:** Every Tuesday Evening. **Sacrament:** Seven times a year. **Communicants:** 60 to 80. **Catechism:** At the School.
INCUMBENT: **Name and Residence:** Revd RE Aitkens – Parsonage. **What Duty he performs:** The whole.
PARSONAGE: A good brick building – purchased 17 years ago with money raised by subscription – improved by the present Minister – three parlours, several bedrooms etc. **State of:** Good.[2]
Outbuildings: Stable, Coach-house etc good.
INCOME: ——.[3]
SCHOOLS: **Endowed School:** None. **Subscription Day School:** National schools. **Sunday School:** There is.
DISSENTERS: **Dissenting Chapels:** 11 – capable of holding 7,300.

POPULATION: Of Hanley and Shelton 14,000 or 15,000.
PARISH CLERK: Abraham Dutton. **Salary:** £10 (or 15) and fees which are large.
CHURCHWARDENS: Mr Yates.
ORDERS MADE: A new Bible and Prayer-book for the Reading desk. Benefaction Tables set up. Spouts and pipes affixed. Graves not to be allowed within six feet of the Chapel walls.

Revisited 20.9.1837
Directions to the Churchwardens. (1) Weather-boards of tower to be re-placed – water-courses cleared out – roof new-leaded; battlements secured. (2) A casement opened in each Gallery staircase. (3) The crack in the wall, under the Tower, examined and repaired. (4) Spouts and down-pipes. (5) Thoroughfare of Churchyard stopped – and additional burial ground provided.

Revisited 16.9.1841
(1) Cracks in the walls of Church on S. and SW. to be filled up. (2) Window frames painted – stone plinth mended, on S. side. (3) No graves near the walls – down spouts – brick wall mended.

I again advised iron palisades as a protection to the Churchyard.

[1] *Eccles. Revs.:* 'Rector of Stoke-upon-Trent'. [2] *Eccles. Revs.:* 'Fit'. [3] *Eccles. Revs.:* Gross income £220.

HORTON 23.7.1830 (A/V/1/4,p.17;A/V/1/2,p.129)

BENEFICE: Horton. **Nature:** Perpetual Curacy, formerly under Leek. **Ecton:** £20 clear value. **Patron:** The Antrobus family. **Impropriator:** No tythes.
CHURCH: Appears to have been a regular Gothic structure – at present however there are pillars and arches on the North side of the middle aisle, only – the ceiling underdrawn. **Number it will contain:** About 300. **Accommodation for Poor:** Sufficient. **Roof:** Oak covered with flag slate. **Walls:** Stone – upright. **Floor:** Flags, even. **Windows:** Not in good repair – casements wanted. **Doors:** Pretty good. **Pulpit and Desk:** —— crimson velvet cushion. **Books:** The Bible wants rebinding. **Seats:** Several of them want repair. **Galleries:** At the W. end, and along part of the N. side. **Organ:** None. **Font:** There is. **Chapels:** None. **Benefaction Tables:** Sufficient. **Vestry:** None. **Surplices:** Provided. **Line:** Provided. **Plate:** Silver Cup and Patin – plated flagon. **Iron Chest for Register:** At the Parsonage. **Register:** From 1653 – in good preservation. **Porch:** There is one. **Vaults:** Some – not very lately. **Cleanliness:** Attended to.
CHANCEL: **Table:** Painted deal – firm. **Ornaments:** Tablets to the Wedgwood family. **Repaired by whom:** The Patron.
STEEPLE: Square stone tower. **State of:** Good – except the weatherboards. **Bells:** Four – in good state. **Clock:** None.
CHURCHYARD: **Fence:** Kept by the Parish and tenants of adjoining lands. **Gates:** Good. **Drains:** None –

earth wants removing. **Graves:** Too near. **Rubbish:** Weeds etc. **Footpaths:** Some trespass-paths; no proper Church-way.
DIVINE SERVICE: **On Sundays:** Prayers in Morning – Prayers and Sermon Afternoon. **On other Days:** None. **Sacrament:** Four times a year. **Communicants:** 15 or 16. **Catechism:** In Lent.
INCUMBENT: **Name and Residence:** Revd Thomas Bowness – Parsonage [since dead (1831)]. **What duty he performs:** Part.
CURATE: **Name and Residence:** Revd James Bostock. **Licensed:** He is. **Salary:** £50.
PARSONAGE: A good substantial brick house – four rooms on ground floor – five bedrooms – five attics. **State of:** Good.[1] **Outbuildings:** Stable, barn, cowhouse – tolerable repair.
INCOME:[2] **Glebe:** 61 acres – 17 in exchange for tythes – 44 purchased by money from the Bounty. **Easter Dues and small Payments:** A rent-charge of £20 per annum on Horton Hall Estate – and some payments for Sermons. **Terrier:** There is one.
SCHOOLS: **Endowed School:** None. **Subscription Day School:** There is a school *house*, built by subscription. **Sunday School:** 30 children.
DISSENTERS: **Dissenters' School:** A small Sunday School. **Dissenting Chapels:** A small Chapel.
POPULATION: 1,000.
MISCELLANEOUS: **Monuments:** Tablets to some of the Wedgwood family.
PARISH CLERK: William Pointon. **Appointed by:** The Minister. **Salary:** £4 0s. 0d. [per annum].
CHURCHWARDENS: William Lawton, Francis Cotterill.
ORDERS MADE: The Bible to be re-bound; the pannels and floors of the Pews repaired; especially at the E. end of the N. aisle, and in the Chancel; also the back of the West Gallery. Two casements to be made in the Chancel – and the floor repaired. The lead-work of windows repaired; iron bars painted, hinges of doors etc. ditto. Wooden weather-boards put up – the bush growing on the side of the Tower removed.
The Chancel to be spouted etc and pipes affixed. Open drain all round, laid with flags. The footpaths stopped – Church way formed – no graves within ten feet.[3] The doors and casements to be regularly opened in fine weather. A person appointed to keep the Church clean.

Revisited 15.9.1837
Directions. (1) New Bible for reading desk. (2) Floors of pews and open benches in North aisle, taken up and relaid. (3) Water-courses of roofs and tower kept clear; belfry cleaned. (4) Eave-spouts and down-pipes; walls pointed; overshot spouts removed. (5) Thoroughfare of Church-yard stopped; lich-gates painted. (6) *Chancel windows* and *pews* repaired – casement on each side.
New-pewing of the Church strongly urged – Minister and Churchwardens promised to take immediate measures for this being done. Additional burial ground to be provided the first opportunity. 'Qu? new pewing? – Thorofare?'

Revisited 14.9.1841
(1) Chancel roof examined and repaired. (2) Walls and windows pointed. (3) Bars of ditto painted – lead ties renewed. (4) Two casements in Chancel. (5) Service book for Table – old pews oiled – rights to pews ascertained – high-backs lowered; or new arrangement and distribution of sittings effected. (6) Battlements and Tower pointed; lead flashings re-placed and secured. (7) Iron work of bells painted – stays secured. (8) Trespass paths stopped – thoro'fare forbidden.
I recommended a new *arrangement* and pewing of interior.
(9) Roof of Chancel restored.

[1] *Eccles. Revs.:* 'Fit'. [2] *Eccles. Revs.:* Gross income £105. [3] A/V/1/4: '... six feet'.

ILAM 20.7.1830 (A/V/1/4, p. 18; A/V/1/2, p. 111)

BENEFICE: Ilam. **Nature:** Vicarage; endowed with the great tythes – [qu? *Rectory*?]. **Ecton:** King's Books £6 13s. 4d. Abb. Burton 13s. 4d. Abb. Burton Propr. – G Port Esqr. Patron. **Patron:** Mr Watts Russell, by purchase from the Port family in whose hands it has been for many generations. **Impropriator:** None – the Vicar has the Great Tythes.
CHURCH: A neat small building – originally Gothic but rebuilt in modern style, with square windows – single body, neat Chancel. **Number it will contain:** About 150. **Accommodation for Poor:** Sufficient. **Roof:** Oak and deal covered with lead. **Walls:** Limestone – upright, but very damp. **Floor:** Flags – even. **Windows:** Very neat – some modern stained glass – more casements wanted, and another window on the N. side. **Doors:** Good. **Pulpit and Desk:** Handsome old oak – well placed; crimson velvet hangings and cushion. **Books:** In bad condition. **Seats:** Neat and uniform – oak pannels; some injured by damp. **Galleries:** None – benches are placed for children under the Tower. **Organ:** A barrel organ. **Font:** A very antient one at the W. end – no basin. **Chapels:** None – but there is a Chancel, or aisle, on the South side which appears to have been added in 1618 – there is also a Mausoleum belonging to the Russell family. **Benefaction Tables:** None. **Vestry:** None – a small compartment is boarded off from the S. Chancel. **Surplices:** Two – good. **Linen:** Not in good condition. **Plate:** Silver-gilt cup and patin – silver salver. **Iron Chest for Register:** At the Vicarage. **Register:** From 1656 to present time – entire and in pretty good preservation. **Porch:** There is one – out of repair – much injured by Ivy. **Vaults:** None recently. **Cleanliness:** Not sufficiently provided for. **Damp:** On the Chancel floor. **Dimensions:** 43ft. by 18ft.
CHANCEL: 23ft. by 17ft. 5in. **Table:** Firm and good – wants cleaning. **Ornaments:** Handsome crimson velvet covering to the Table and Cushions – Silver Candlesticks – ornamented wainscot. **Repaired by whom:** Hitherto by the Patron.
STEEPLE: A square stone tower. **State of:** Not easy to judge, owing to the vast accumulation of Ivy which completely hides it. **Bells:** Two – one cracked. **Clock:** Good.
CHURCHYARD: **Fence:** Removed, towards Mr Watts Russell's [house and] pleasure grounds – it seems necessary that *some* fence should be replaced.[1] **Gates:** Good. **Drains:** None – nor spouts: earth

[much] accumulated against the walls. **Graves:** Not too near. **Rubbish:** None – but the grass and weeds want keeping under. **Footpaths:** Properly kept. **Cattle:** None.

DIVINE SERVICE: **On Sundays:** Once. **On other Days:** None. **Sacrament:** Four times a year. **Communicants:** 30 to 40. **Catechism:** Not in the Church.

INCUMBENT: **Name and Residence:** Revd Bernard Port, Vicarage house.[2] **What duty he performs:** The whole.

CURATE: **Name and Residence:** None.

PARSONAGE: A new, handsome and commodious house; built of stone – roof slate. **State of:** Very good.[3] **Outbuildings:** Barn, Stables, Coach-house etc.

INCOME: **Gross Value:** Not ascertained.[4] **Tithes:** Not valuable, as there is very little corn grown [in the Parish – land chiefly pasture]. **Glebe:** A small quantity round the house.

SCHOOLS: **Endowed School:** £4 0s. 0d. per annum for instruction of eight boys – now merged in a larger school supported by Mr Watts Russell, who receives the £4. **Sunday School:** A small one. **Lancaster School:** None.

DISSENTERS: **Dissenters' School:** None. **Dissenting Chapels:** None.

POPULATION: 250.

MISCELLANEOUS: **Monuments:** Several [old ones] to the Ports – and a very handsome [new] one by Chantrey to Mrs Watts Russell's father.

PARISH CLERK: Robert Fern. **Appointed by:** The Vicar. **Salary:** 52s. a year.

CHURCHWARDENS: Thomas Oakden.

ORDERS MADE: An additional window to be made on the N. side of the Church and a casement on the South side. A new Bible and Prayer Book to be provided for the Reading desk – Clerk's Prayer-book also to be repaired or renewed. A suitable Basin for the Font. The roof and walls of the Porch to be repaired. The growth of Ivy to be checked on the Tower and walls – and not suffered to be injurious to the roofs and windows. The cracked bell re-cast; both bells cleaned and iron-work painted; the weather-boards restored – rubbish cleared away etc. A sufficient fence to be placed all round the Churchyard. Spouts all round the roofs and pipes – earth cleared away and open drain made. An allowance to be made for cleaning the Church.

Revisited 13.9.1837
(1) The order for the new window on the North side of the Church renewed. (2) The Clerk's Prayer Book to be repaired, and a suitable basin provided for the font. (3) Lead-gutters and pipes at the bottoms of the windows. (4) The pannels and floors of the pews, where needful, repaired. (5) The Chancel roof repaired and the water-courses cleared. (6) The tower repaired – weather-board on the East side – the Ivy trimmed and prevented from getting on the roof of the tower and in the windows. (7) The entrance into the Belfry to be closed (for warmth) and a door placed there – the children's seats to be removed before the door or into the Chancel. (8) The ground lowered round the Church – an open drain laid with flags or bricks – Eave spouts and down-pipe on North side – Down-pipe on S. side and the spout rectified. (9) Ivy checked and hindered from injuring the fabric, roofs, and windows.

Recommended. That a stove be put in the Church. That an allowance be made to the Clerk for cleaning the Church. That a wire-fence or fine hedge of withies be placed along the boundary of the Churchyard. 'Qu? attended to?'

Revisited 10.9.1841
(1) Floors and pannels of pews to be looked over and repaired. (2) Wainscot of ditto repaired – doors, pannels and wainscoting rubbed with oil. (3) Water-tables to windows. (4) Bible and Clerk's Prayer Book repaired – skirting of Pulpit staircase on E. side repaired. (5) Coping stones of roof at E. end laid afresh. (6) Chancel roofs stripped and re-tiled. (7) Ivy removed from inside of Tower windows. (8) Holes in Tower walls filled up. (9) Weather-boards in Tower windows. (10) Dilapidated monument on S. side of Church repaired or laid flat.

[1] A/V/1/4: '. . . it seemed right to direct that some fence or boundary to the Churchyard should be put up.' [2] *Eccles. Revs.:* also rector of Honiley (Warks.). [3] *Eccles. Revs.:* 'Fit'. [4] *Eccles. Revs.:* Gross income £380.

IPSTONES 20.7.1830
(A/V/1/4, p.19; A/V/1/2, p.117)

BENEFICE: Ipstones. **Nature:** Perpetual Curacy. **Ecton:** Abb. Dulacres Propr. Bishop of Lichfield Patr. £13 6s. 8d. clear value. **Patron:** The freeholders. **Impropriator:** The freeholders have the land tythe free.

CHURCH: A small edifice, rebuilt in 1790, single body, pointed windows – no chancel. **Number it will contain:** 220[1] [– much too small]. **Accommodation for Poor:** Not sufficient.[2] **Roof:** Oak, covered with blue slate. **Walls:** Stone – upright. **Floor:** Flags. **Windows:** Good – two casements. **Doors:** ——. **Pulpit and Desk:** —— crimson cushion and hangings. **Books:** Bible to be new.[3] **Seats:** Good – but insufficient for the population. **Galleries:** One at the W. end. **Organ:** None. **Font:** There is one. **Chapels:** None. **Benefaction Tables:** Two – some benefactions lost. **Vestry:** One lately made, under the Tower. **Surplices:** Two – good. **Linen:** Provided. **Plate:** No patin. **Iron Chest for Register:** None. **Register:** From 1571 – in bad preservation and very irregularly kept. **Porch:** None. **Vaults:** None recently. **Cleanliness:** Attended to. **Damp:** Some on the East wall.

CHANCEL: **Table:** Good – but no covering. **Ornaments:** None. **Repaired by whom:** The Parish.

STEEPLE: Neat square stone tower. **State of:** Roof wants repair. **Bells:** One – good. **Clock:** Out of repair.

CHURCHYARD: **Fence:** Stone wall – good; additional burial ground sadly wanted – the Minister and Churchwardens have promised to procure some [– this has since been done, and the additional ground consecrated. 1831.]. **Gates:** Good. **Graves:** Too near – from want of room. **Rubbish:**

None. **Footpaths:** A thoroughfare – which will be stopped when the Churchyard is enlarged. **Cattle:** None.

DIVINE SERVICE: **On Sundays:** Morning and afternoon alternately with Grindon; in summer an evening service once a fortnight. **On other Days:** None. **Sacrament:** Four times a year. **Communicants:** 30.

INCUMBENT: **Name and Residence:** Revd W Carlisle, Belmont in the Parish.[4] **What duty he performs:** The whole.

PARSONAGE: None.[5]

INCOME: **Gross Value:** About £150 – chiefly from Bounty Board. **Terrier:** In the Register there is a Copy.

SCHOOLS: **Endowed School:** 22 children taught free – from an endowment of 20 or 25 acres of land – present salary [of Master] £15 per annum.

POPULATION: Upwards of 1,500.[6]

PARISH CLERK: George Clowes. **Salary:** £2 0s. 0d.

CHURCHWARDENS: Mr Thomas Johnson. Samuel Tatten.

ORDERS MADE: A new Bible to be procured for the Reading Desk. Pictures to be removed from the walls. A Patin to be provided for the Communion Table, and a Cover for the Table. An Iron Register Chest ditto. The roof of the Tower, and floor of Belfry to be repaired – the Clock also. Additional burying ground to be obtained as soon as possible and the thoroughfare of the Churchyard stopped. An open drain formed round the Church.

Revisited 16.9.1837

Directions. (1) New Prayer Book for Clergyman – *his* repaired and put into Clerk's desk. (2) New Altar Services. (3) Lead-flashing to the windows – and pipe – water courses of roofs cleared out – roof of tower stripped and new covered – door closed at top – weather-boards repaired – belfry floor and window mended. (4) Pews of W. Gallery, adjoining the end wall, repaired. (5) Fences, kept by Mr Beech and Malkin, made suitable. (6) Thoroughfare of Churchyard stopped. (7) A Stove, or warm air flues, *strongly recommended.*
  'Done or in progress.'

Revisited 14.9.1841

(1) Pew-floors on N. side repaired. (2) Roof examined – battlements, spouts, and gutters examined. (3) Down-pipe – open drain – soil removed.

[1] *Eccles. Revs.:* 420. [2] A/V/1/4: 'Very insufficient.' [3] A/V/1/4: 'Bible bad.' [4] Also rector of Sutton-cum-Duckmanton and perpetual curate of Earl Sterndale (both Derbys): *Eccles. Revs.* [5] *Eccles. Revs.:* 'None.' [6] *Eccles. Revs.:* 1,384.

KINGSLEY 16.7.1830
(A/V/1/4,p.20;A/V/1/2,p.101)

BENEFICE: Kingsley. **Nature:** Rectory. **Ecton:** King's Books £16 15s. 0d. Abb. Burton 14s. Countess of Oxford Patr. **Patron:** James Beech Esqr of the Shaw. **Impropriator:** None.

CHURCH: A neat, open building, re-built 10 years ago,[1] nearly on the old foundations – single body – pointed arches[2] – small chancel. **Number it will contain:** 306 in pews. **Accommodation for Poor:** 192 including the Gallery. **Roof:** Red deal covered with slate; ridge lead. **Walls:** Stone, solid and upright. **Floor:** Quarries, even. **Windows:** Good – and well provided with Casements. **Doors:** Good. **Pulpit and Desk:** Very neat and well placed – crimson velvet cushion. **Books:** Not in good repair. **Seats:** Very neat and uniform; oak pannels, boarded floors. **Galleries:** At the W. end. **Organ:** None. **Font:** There is. **Chapels:** None. **Benefaction Tables:** Three. **Vestry:** Under the Tower. **Surplices:** One – a new one wanted. **Linen:** Provided. **Plate:** Silver Flagon, Cup and Patin. **Iron Chest for Register:** None – ordered. **Register:** From 1682 – in good preservation. **Porch:** None. **Vaults:** None. **Cleanliness:** Attended to. **Damp:** No appearance. **Dimensions:** 69ft. 9in. by 35ft.

CHANCEL: 34ft. 10in. by 15ft. **Table:** Oak – good and firm. **Ornaments:** None. **Repaired by whom:** The Rector.

STEEPLE: An old square Tower. **State of:** Pretty good – secured at the top by cramping Irons. **Bells:** Five – good. **Clock:** Good.

CHURCHYARD: **Fence:** Stone wall, kept by the Parish. **Gates:** Not good. **Drains:** None – nor spouts. **Graves:** Not too near. **Rubbish:** None. **Footpaths:** Several [trespass] – to be stopped. **Cattle:** A horse – forbidden.

DIVINE SERVICE: **On Sundays:** Two full services. **On other Days:** None. **Sacrament:** Four times a year. **Communicants:** About 30. **Catechism:** On Sunday Evenings.

INCUMBENT: **Name and Residence:** Revd John Wood, nr Alfreton, Derbyshire.[3] **What Duty he performs:** None.

CURATE: **Name and Residence:** Revd Richard Ward, Rectory. **Licensed:** He is. **Salary:** £75 and Fees – and apartments in the Rectory house. **If serving another church:** Cauldon in the Afternoon.

PARSONAGE: A new, substantial brick house, erected eight years ago. **State of:** Good.[4] **Outbuildings:** Barn and stables – pretty good.

INCOME: **Gross Value:** Not ascertained.[5] **Glebe:** 89 acres, let for £84 0s. 0d.

SCHOOLS: **Endowed School:** There is one – endowed with £60 per annum in land and money in the Funds. **Subscription Day School:** No other. **Sunday School:** 140 children.

DISSENTERS: **Dissenters' School:** None. **Dissenting Chapels:** Methodist Chapel.

POPULATION: 1,500.

MISCELLANEOUS: **Parochial Library:** There is one, belonging to Mr Beech.

PARISH CLERK: Philip Hall. **Appointed by:** The Rector. **Salary:** 16s. 4d.

CHURCHWARDENS: Mr John Thorley, for the Rector. George Locker, for the Parish.

ORDERS MADE: The roof to be examined and repaired; the windows secured against rain. New Prayer books for Reading and Clerk's Desks – and Bible rebound. A new Surplice [– 'done']; and Iron Chest for Register. Iron work of the Church, Bells etc[6] painted. The Tower pointed and roof repaired. New gates to the Churchyard – footpaths stopped [if possible] and no large cattle allowed. The walls kept free from accumulation of herbage etc and spouts [and pipes] placed all round the roof. No graves allowed within ten feet of walls.

Revisited 27.9.1837
Directions to Churchwardens. New Prayer Book for Clerk's Desk – new Bible for Reading Desk – and new Altar Services. Iron Chest for Register. Water table at East window – frames of windows painted. Suitable linen for table – communion plate repaired etc. Roof, ridging tiles, slates, weather-boards of *tower* repaired. Battlements secured. Down-pipes and spouts to roofs. Thoro'fare of Churchyard stopped, if possible. Earth cleared away from walls. Lich gates repaired and painted. Church ventilated during the week.
'All done or doing. R.D.'

Revisited 28.9.1841
Directions to Churchwardens. (1) Church doors painted, or rubbed with boiled linseed oil inside. (2) Roof of Tower stripped and re-tiled – water courses kept clear – lead flashings replaced and secured – battlements and parapets pointed. (3) Walls and buttresses of Tower well pointed, and pipes placed on NW. side of Tower – to conduct the wet from the roof into a drain instead of overshot spout – pipe kept two or three inches off the wall. (4) Lead pipes at SE. corner of body of Church repaired. (5) I strongly urge the stopping of the thoroughfare of the Churchyard – either by voluntary consent of inhabitants, or by application to Church Commissioners, who are empowered by 59 G. 3. c 134. sec. 39. to stop any Churchyard footway, with consent of two Justices of Peace.
N.B. I have written to Mr Trubshaw respecting the money said to be due to him.

[1] Faculty dated 2 March 1820 (B/C/2/1816–20 p.705). The architect was James Trubshaw of Great Haywood. [2] 'Arches' altered to 'windows' in A/V/1/4. [3] *Eccles. Revs.*: also vicar of Pentrich with Ripley (Derbys). [4] *Eccles. Revs.*: 'Fit'. [5] *Eccles. Revs.*: Gross income £259. [6] A/V/1/4: 'Iron work of windows, bells etc painted.'

LANE END 15.6.1830
(A/V/1/4,p.21;A/V/1/2,p.77)

BENEFICE: Lane End. **Nature:** Perpetual Curacy – intended to become a Vicarage [on a vacancy in Stoke upon Trent]. **Ecton:** Not mentioned. **Patron:** Trustees. **Impropriator:** The Rector of Stoke (in which parish it is) has the Tithes – Mr Tomlinson is his Lessee.
CHURCH: A large, plain, modern building, single body and roof – built 70 years ago, but re-built in different parts since that time, in consequence of injury done by the Mines – enlarged, at the E., two years ago. **Number it will contain:** 1,500, exclusive of forms for the children. **Accommodation for Poor:** 486 – besides forms for the children. **Roof:** Oak and deal – lately repaired, and now in good state. **Walls:** Brick – very substantial. **Floor:** Flags – even. **Windows:** Good – well provided with casements. **Doors:** Very good. **Pulpit and Desk:** Very good – purple cloth hangings [etc] – very handsome. **Books:** New and handsome. **Seats:** Very uniform and neat. **Galleries:** On three sides. **Organ:** There is.
Font: ——. **Chapels:** None. **Benefaction Tables:** One. **Vestry:** There is. **Surplices:** Two – not very good. **Linen:** Table Cloth and napkin; good. **Plate:** Pewter flagon and Dish – Silver Cup and Patin. **Iron Chest for Register:** At the Parsonage. **Porch:** None. **Vaults:** None. **Cleanliness:** Attended to. **Damp:** Some on the walls, and roof at E. end.
CHANCEL: **Table:** Handsome – mahogany. **Ornaments:** Purple Cloth covering and hangings – Commandments about to be set up, as soon as the Walls are [sufficiently] dry. **Repaired by whom:** The Township.
STEEPLE: Square Tower [– brick]. **State of:** Good. **Bells:** Eight – good. **Clock:** Good.
CHURCHYARD: **Fence:** A brick wall, kept up by the *Pew-owners*. **Gates:** Good. **Drains:** Provided. **Graves:** None [too] near the Chapel. **Rubbish:** Some; thrown over by inhabitants of premises adjoining. **Footpaths:** None; the thoroughfare has been done away with – good gravel walks all round, and across the Chapel yard. **Cattle:** None.
DIVINE SERVICE: **On Sundays:** Two full services. **On other Days:** None. **Sacrament:** Monthly and at the Festivals. **Communicants:** 100.
INCUMBENT: **Name and Residence:** Revd Isaac Temple – Parsonage. [Joseph Kingsmill. September 1837.] **What Duty he performs:** The whole.
PARSONAGE: A brick building, commodious for a small family – built about 20 years ago. **State of:** Good.[1]
INCOME: **Gross Value:** About £150 a year. **Glebe:** 18 acres. (£72.) **Surplice Fees:** £26. **Queen Anne's Bounty:** £54. **Terrier:** None.
SCHOOLS: **Endowed School:** There is one, endowed with [rents of certain] houses in 1760 for instruction *in English* of *30* children; or more if the Trustees think fit – income £70 at present – part of the Rent (£40) applied to the *National* School. **Subscription Day School:** National, and Infant Schools – the former, 142 boys, 114 girls. **Sunday School:** 800 children.
DISSENTERS: **Dissenters' School:** Several. **Dissenting Chapels:** Several.
POPULATION: Of Lane End and Longton 9,000 – a new Chapel about to be built at Longton.
PARISH CLERK: —— Shaw. **Appointed by:** The Minister. **Salary:** Arises from fees.
CHURCHWARDENS: Mr Meakin and Mr Simpkin.
ORDERS MADE: The Commandments to be set up at E. end. Gallery doors, and the inner door at the W. end to be painted. The walls coloured, and ceiling whitewashed. Casements made in Gallery staircases. Lead Gutters repaired. Rubbish forbidden in Chapel-yard. Space near E. end kept clear of Grass etc. New Surplices provided.

Revisited 21.9.1837
Walls to be coloured – ceiling whitewashed – walls and ceilings of Gallery staircases repaired and washed. Windows cleaned – and water tables provided. Gallery floors, and staircases, repaired where needful. Roof of tower, and lead-flashings of NE. transept roof – repaired. *Cracks in S. wall* examined and filled up. Churchyard fence repaired.

Revisited 17.9.1841
   Directions to Churchwardens. (1) Wall adjoining SW. Gallery door repaired, and *spring* attached. (2) Water-tables made for Gallery windows – flashings in roof of Tower pointed – Conductors placed on roof of Church, to carry off the wet from roof of Tower. (3) Wheels of bells repaired and *braced* – weather-boards of bell-chamber restored. (4) Mouths of down-pipes *capped*.

[1] *Eccles. Revs.:* 'Fit'.

LEEK 22.7.1830 (A/V/1/4,p.22;A/V/1/2,p.125)

BENEFICE: Leek. **Nature:** Vicarage. **Ecton:** Clear value £42 16s. 8d. Mon. Dulacres Propr. **Patron:** Lord Macclesfield. **Impropriator:** None – the land tithe-free; having formerly belonged to the Monastery of Leek.
CHURCH: A spacious, handsome Church, in mixed style; centre and side aisles; pointed Arch to Chancel. **Number it will contain:** 1,000, exclusive of benches – insufficient. **Accommodation for Poor:** About 200 sittings. **Roof:** Oak covered with lead. **Walls:** Freestone – good. **Floor:** Flags – even. **Windows:** Very good – and well provided with casements. **Doors:** Good. **Pulpit and Desk:** Very handsome. **Books:** Good. **Seats:** Very good in general. **Galleries:** Partially on the W., N. and S. sides. **Organ:** There is one. **Font:** ——. **Chapels:** None: but there is an antient Pew claimed by the occupiers of different estates formerly belonging to the Abbey. **Vestry:** A very commodious one – ventilation wanted. **Surplices:** Well provided. **Linen:** Provided. **Plate:** Handsome silver Flagon – two Cups, two Patins. **Iron Chest for Register:** In the Vestry and at the Vicarage. **Register:** From 1634 – not perfect. **Porch:** None. **Vaults:** None recently. **Cleanliness:** Attended to. **Damp:** A little on the walls, N. and W.
CHANCEL: **Table:** Good. **Ornaments:** None. **Repaired by whom:** Lord Macclesfield – the roof wants spouting.
STEEPLE: Square stone tower. **State of:** Good. **Bells:** Six – good. **Clock:** In good repair.
CHURCHYARD: **Fence:** Kept by the Parish – stone walls and iron palisades [– very good]. **Gates:** Good. **Drains:** Not sufficient. **Graves:** Too near the walls. **Rubbish:** None. **Footpaths:** There is a thoroughfare, which it is said cannot be stopped. **Cattle:** None.
DIVINE SERVICE: **On Sundays:** Two full services, morning and afternoon. **On other Days:** Weekly prayers, Wednesday and Friday. **Sacrament:** Monthly. **Communicants:** 30 or 40. **Catechism:** At the School.
INCUMBENT: **Name and Residence:** Revd TH Heathcote, Vicarage. **What Duty he performs:** Shares the whole.
CURATE: **Name and Residence:** Revd James Turner, in Leek. **Licensed:** He is. **Salary:** £50. **If serving another church:** Meerbrook Chapel.
PARSONAGE: A good, well-built modern house. **State of:** Good.[1] **Outbuildings:** A stable and coach-house.
INCOME: **Gross Value:** About £200. **Tithes:** None. **Glebe:** 66 acres. **Easter Dues and small Payments:**[2] Collected. **Queen Anne's Bounty:** Amount not specified. **Terrier:** Several Copies.
SCHOOLS: **Endowed School:** £9 14s. 0d. per annum, from money left for endowment of free school.[3] **Subscription Day School:** None. **Sunday School:** 200 children.
DISSENTERS: **Dissenters' School:** Methodist Sunday School. **Dissenting Chapels:** Methodist and Roman Catholic.
POPULATION: 6,000[4] of *Leek* [and Lowe], exclusive of [the other] Townships.
PARISH CLERK: Francis Hilyard. **Appointed by:** The Vicar. **Salary:** £10 and fees.
CHURCHWARDENS: Mr Jessimond* – appointed by the Vicar and Parishioners.
 *It has been usual, for many years, to appoint *one* Churchwarden for the Townships of Leek and Lowe, and three others for the Chapelries (of which there are three, each containing more than one Township) in the extensive Parish. Of late differences have arisen between the Mother Church and some of the Chapelries, especially that of Rushton, respecting the liability of the latter to pay Church-rates to the Parish Church; in consequence of which there is at present only *one* Churchwarden for the whole Parish.
   A casement to be made in the Chancel, and one in the Vestry. The Chancel to be spouted. The ground lowered on the N. side of the Church. No graves allowed within ten feet.

Revisited 16.9.1837
   Directions. (1) Windows repaired and guarded from admission of wet. (2) Crack in W. Gallery examined and repaired. (3) More attention to keeping Church *clean*. (4) Walls to be coloured, as soon as alterations completed. (5) Spouting of Chancel completed – water-courses of roofs cleared out and leading repaired. (6) Ground lowered – open drain formed. (7) Old Baptismal font removed into the inside of the Church. (8) Thoro'fare of Churchyard stopped.

Revisited 14.9.1841[5]
   (1) Water-tables to windows. (2) Additional casement in N. and S. galleries, and on N. side (below) of Church. (3) Roof examined where sunk – lead flashings and gutters levelled. (4) Pinnacles on S. side secured – battlements ditto. (5) Door to roof repaired – wheels of treble and tenor bells repaired. (6) Buttresses pointed.

[1] *Eccles. Revs.:* 'Fit'. [2] 'And small payments' enclosed in brackets. [3] A/V/1/4: '£9 14s. 0d. per annum arising from land'. [4] 7,310 in *Eccles. Revs.*, which treats the other townships separately. [5] Faculty granted 3.1.1839 (B/C/2/1836–41,p.291) for the enlargement of the N., S. and W. galleries, new porches, and alterations to the pewing and the positions of pulpit and reading-desk.

LONGNOR 22.7.1830 (A/V/1/4,p.23;A/V/1/2,p.123)

BENEFICE: Longnor. **Nature:** Perpetual Curacy, under Alstonfield. **Ecton:** £3 clear value. **Patron:** The Vicar of Alstonfield. **Impropriator:** Sir G Crewe.
CHURCH: A neat modern Chapel; re-built 48 years ago, and heightened 19 years ago. **Number it will contan:** 468.[1] **Accommodation for Poor:** None appropriated.[2] **Roof:** Deal covered with slate – good. **Walls:** Stone – good. **Floor:** Flags – even.

Windows: Good – but no casements. **Door:** Wants repairing and painting. **Pulpit and Desk:** Firm and well-placed; faded velvet cushion. **Books:** Bad. **Seats:** Painted deal – many of them without proper floors. **Galleries:** One at the W. end, and singing Gallery [on the S.] over the door. **Organ:** None. **Font:** An old one in the Churchyard – to be replaced. **Chapels:** None. **Benefaction Tables:** One. **Vestry:** None – but one intended. **Surplices:** One – another wanted. **Linen:** Provided. **Plate:** Silver Cup and patin – plated flagon and dish. **Iron Chest for Register:** None. **Register:** One or two old Vols, from the early part of the last Century – sadly neglected till within the last few years. **Porch:** None. **Vaults:** ——. **Cleanliness:** Attended to. **Damp:** A good deal at the East end and on the floor. **Dimensions:** 55ft. 6in. by 36ft. 4in.
CHANCEL: No separate Chancel. **Table:** A very shabby one – no covering. **Repaired by whom:** The township.
STEEPLE: Square stone tower – roof covered with lead. **State of:** Good – except the floors of the Belfry and Chambers underneath. **Bells:** Good. **Clock:** There is one.
CHURCHYARD: **Fence:** Stone wall, and houses – at the East end of the Chapel is a Garden, which ought to be laid to the Chapel yard – additional burying ground being much wanted. **Gates:** Want repair and painting. **Drains:** None – ground wants lowering – especially at E. end. **Graves:** Many too near. **Rubbish:** Heaps of stones on N. side. **Footpaths:** Several – which greatly disfigure and injure the Chapel yard – to be stopped. **Cattle:** None.
DIVINE SERVICE: **On Sundays:** Only one at present – alternately Morning and Afternoon. **On other days:** None at present. **Sacrament:** Four times a year. **Communicants:** About 20. **Catechism:** Once a year.
INCUMBENT: **Name and Residence:** Revd W Buckwell (just appointed) in the Parish, quarter of a mile from the Town. **What Duty he performs:** The whole.
PARSONAGE: None at present. It is hoped that Sir G Crewe will promote the building of one, as he has already done at the other Chapelries upon his [extensive] Estate.[3]
INCOME: **Gross Value:** Not ascertained.[4] **Queen Anne's Bounty:** Amount not stated. **Terrier:** None in the Clergyman's possession.
SCHOOLS: **Endowed School:** There is a small sum of money left for the instruction of two or three children. **Subscription Day School:** None. **Sunday School:** None – at present. **Lancaster School:** None.
DISSENTERS: **Dissenters' School:** Sunday School – about 50 children. **Dissenting Chapels:** Methodist.
POPULATION: of *the whole Chapelry* 2,600 – but there is another Chapel at the Flash.
PARISH CLERK: George Harrison. **Appointed by:** The Vicar of Alstonfield. **Salary:** £3 per annum and fees etc.
CHURCHWARDENS: Mr John Plant, Junr.
ORDERS MADE: Three large casements to be made on each side; above and below. The door repaired and painted – pulpit cushion new or fresh-dyed. The floors of the Pews laid hollow with flags or boards. A Vestry to be made under the Tower, as soon as practicable. A new Surplice provided and an Iron Chest for the Registers. The floors of the Bell chamber and Belfry repaired – and the steps leading to them. The ground to be lowered on the NW. and East sides of the Chapel, and the Garden at the East end obtained (if possible) for the enlargement of the Chapel yard. The gates to be repaired and painted – no graves near the Walls – Rubbish cleared away – footpaths stopped.

Revisited 14.9.1837
Very much improved – the Churchyard now free from trespasses – handsome gates put up etc.
Directions. (1) New Prayer Book for Clerk's desk – Clergyman's ditto or repaired. (2) Floors and pannels of pews repaired where needful – also woodwork and plaister of S. window, West end of the Church. (3) Floors of Singers Gallery, and Belfry repaired. (4) Pinnacles of Tower secured – water-courses cleared. (5) New Gallery staircase, *within* the Church. (6) Soil cleared away – open drain with flags. (7) Old font restored to the inside of the Church.
'Qu? directions attended to'.

Revisited 11.9.1841
(1) New Prayer Books. (2) Water tables for windows' sills – plaister repaired. (3) New window seats on S. side. (4) Plaister on E. wall repaired: chink under E. window filled up. (5) Two large casements on each side of the Church. (6) Old Font removed into Church or clean new one. (7) Gallery staircase altered – spouts painted. (8) Window on N. Side of Tower taken out and weatherboards put in, to admit air. (9) Light gate at S. door, for ventilation.

[1] *Eccles. Revs.:* 600. [2] A/V/1/4: 'None in particular'. [3] *Eccles. Revs.:* 'None'. [4] *Eccles. Revs.:* £102.

MEERBROOK 23.7.1830
(A/V/1/4,p.24;A/V/1/2,p.126)

BENEFICE: Meerbrook. (Ecton. Marbrook.) **Nature:** Perpetual Curacy, under Leek. Ecton: £11 12s. 0d. clear value. **Patron:** The Vicar of Leek. **Impropriator:** The land tythe free.
CHURCH: A small old building – open roof; single body, separate Chancel – the original Chapel founded by Sir Ralph Bagnal in the time of Queen Elizabeth. **Number it will contain:** About 200.[1] **Accommodation for Poor:** Sufficient. **Roof:** Timber covered with flagslates – lately put in repair. **Walls:** Stone; not quite upright; to be examined. **Floor:** Flags; even. **Windows:** Not provided with casements. **Doors:** Good. **Pulpit and Desk:** Very neat and good – faded velvet cushion. **Books:** Good. **Seats:** —— many of them new. **Galleries:** An old one at the W. end. **Organ:** None. **Font:** There is one. **Chapels:** None. **Benefaction Tables:** Two – recording benefactions both to the Minister and the poor. **Vestry:** None. **Surplices:** One – good. **Linen:** Provided. **Plate:** A plated Cup and pewter patin. **Iron Chest for Register:** There is one. **Register:** From 1767. **Porch:** None. **Vaults:** Not recently. **Cleanliness:** Pretty well attended to. **Damp:** Some at the lower parts of the walls.

CHANCEL: **Table:** Neat and firm – no covering. **Ornaments:** None. **Repaired by whom:** The townships.
STEEPLE: A small square bell Tower. **State of:** Not very good. **Bells:** One – the frame work wants repairing. **Clock:** None.
CHURCHYARD: **Fence:** Quick hedge – good in general. **Gates:** Want repairs. **Drains:** None – nor spouts. **Graves:** Not too near. **Rubbish:** None, except behind the Tower. **Footpaths:** More than necessary – some to be stopped. **Cattle:** A Cow.
DIVINE SERVICE: **On Sundays:** Once – usually afternoon. **On other Days:** None. **Sacrament:** Four times a year. **Communicants:** From 10 to 20. **Catechism:** Occasionally.
INCUMBENT: **Name and Residence:** Revd James Turner. **If not resident:** At Leek, 3½ miles distant. **What Duty he performs:** The principal part – but he is assisted occasionally by his brother who lives on the spot.
PARSONAGE: A good substantial building, re-built within these few years. **State of:** Good.[2] **Outbuildings:** A stable, in ruinous condition.
INCOME: **Gross Value:** About £90 – arising from land, partly given by Sir Ralph Bagnal, partly purchased by Queen Anne's Bounty.
SCHOOLS: **Endowed School:** 28 children taught free, from a rent-charge on land – salary of the Master £12 0s. 0d., and a house to live in. **Subscription Day School:** None. **Sunday School:** A small one. **Lancaster School:** None.
DISSENTERS: **Dissenters' School:** None. **Dissenting Chapels:** None.
POPULATION: 800.
PARISH CLERK: James Maberley. **Salary:** £2 0s. 0d.
CHURCHWARDENS: Mr Carter.
ORDERS MADE: Two casements to be made in the Chapel – iron bars painted. The [new] benches painted – oak colour [– 'done']. A covering provided for the Communion Table [– 'done']. The roof of the Bell-tower repaired – the stones pointed – walls inside, underneath [the gallery] whitewashed. The Chapel yard to be drained – on the North side. The earth cleared away round the walls. [Footpaths stopped.]

Revisited 15.9.1837
Directions. (1) New surplice, and basin for font. (2) Walls of Chapel coloured – ceiling, and wall of belfry, whitewashed. 'Qu?' (3) Casement on South side – arching behind the Gallery filled up, and a door made, for warmth. 'Qu?' (4) Bell-wheel fixed, roof at W. gable pointed – eave-spouts and down-pipes. (5) Earth cleared away – open drains. 'Qu?' (6) Thoro'fare of Churchyard stopped. 'Qu?'
Admonition to the Parish Clerk on account of Drunkenness. Further tried at next Visitation.

Revisited 13.9.1841
(1) Bible re-bound. (2) Water table to E. window – iron window bars and frames painted. (3) Quarries of floors scraped and laid down on dry materials. (4) Roof examined – ridge-tiles pointed. (5) Doors and windows set open in fine weather. (6) Tower pointed at the Top.

[1] *Eccles. Revs.:* 300. [2] *Eccles. Revs.:* 'Fit'.

NEWCHAPEL 6.10.1830
(A/V/1/4,p.25;A/V/1/2,p.149)[1]

BENEFICE: Newchapel. **Nature:** Perpetual Curacy, under Wolstanton. **Patron:** The appointment said to be jointly in the *Lawton* and *Sneyd families*. **Impropriator:** Col. Sneyd.
CHURCH: A modern building (single body) erected 60 years ago – the former Chapel said to have been built in the 13th Century. **Number it will contain:** From 5 to 600. **Accommodation for Poor:** Sufficient. **Roof:** Oak covered with tiles – very good. **Walls:** Solid brick – upright. **Floor:** Brick – even. **Windows:** Good – but casements insufficient. **Doors:** Slight repairs wanted. **Pulpit and Desk:** Good – handsome velvet cushion. **Books:** Not in good order. **Seats:** Very neat and uniform – oak. **Galleries:** One, at the W. end. **Organ:** None. **Font:** An old one – out of repair. **Chapels:** None. **Benefaction Tables:** There are. **Vestry:** There is one – wall wants repair. **Surplices:** Two. **Linen:** Provided. **Plate:** A silver gilt flagon – Chalice and patin. **Iron Chest for Register:** None. **Register:** Not seen – the Minister (who did not attend) keeps them at his own house [some distance off]. **Porch:** None. **Vaults:** Several. **Cleanliness:** Attended to. **Damp:** On the floor.
CHANCEL: **Table:** Good. **Ornaments:** None, except the Commandments. **Repaired by whom:** The different townships for whose use the Chapel was built.
STEEPLE: A small bell-house. **State of:** Good. **Bells:** One – good. **Clock:** None.
CHURCHYARD: **Fence:** Good. **Gates:** ——. **Drains:** Provided. **Graves:** None very near. **Footpaths:** A thoroughfare. **Cattle:** None.
DIVINE SERVICE: **On Sundays:** Two services. ['Qu? Articles of Enquiry say *Alternate*'.] **On other Days:** None. **Sacrament:** Four times a year. **Communicants:** From 12 to 15 or 20. **Catechism:** Not lately.
INCUMBENT: **Name and Residence:** Revd J Lawton [since dead September 1831]. **If not resident:** At Lawton, in Cheshire. **What Duty he performs:** Occasionally assists.
CURATE: **Name and Residence:** Revd Mr Carter [– now the incumbent]. **Licensed:** He is.
PARSONAGE: None.[2]
INCOME: **Gross Value:** Said to be under £100. **Glebe:** 50 or 60 acres. **Queen Anne's Bounty:** Not ascertained.
SCHOOLS: **Endowed School:** £63 per annum said to have been left by Dr Hulme of Cheshire for educating 18 poor children. **Subscription Day School:** No other. **Sunday School:** None.
DISSENTERS: **Dissenters' School:** Several – by the Methodists. **Dissenting Chapels:** Several – ditto.
POPULATION: 2 or 3,000, in the eight hamlets[3] [– a new Chapel is being built in one of them – at Tunstal Moss].
PARISH CLERK: William Pope. **Appointed by:** The Minister. **Salary:** £5 0s. 0d. and fees.
CHURCHWARDENS: Mr George Goodwin for the Minister. Mr James Goodwin for the Parishioners.
ORDERS MADE: An additional casement to be made on each side of the Chapel. The Books repaired – font restored – Register Chest provided, and the

Registers kept in it. The Vestry wall and window repaired – the windows at W. end of Chapel ditto. No new interments to be made inside the Chapel. The thoroughfare of the Chapel yard, to be stopped if possible.

Revisited 19.9.1837
In a very damp and comfortless state. Ordered – (1) That the ground be lowered, and grass etc removed, and open drain formed all round the walls. (2) That the wall surrounding the Churchyard be repaired where needful, and the thoroughfare of the Church stopped. (3) That the walls (inside) be coloured, and ceilings whitewashed. (4) That the Bible in the Reading desk be repaired. (5) *Recommended* – (i) That the Church be warmed in winter. (ii) That the brick floors of the pews be taken up and boarded floors substituted.

Revisited 16.9.1841
Much improved since my last visit. Directions to Churchwardens. (1) New Bible for Reading Desk. Prayer book repaired. (2) Baptismal Font, of Stone, provided. (3) Iron bars of windows painted. (4) Roofs of Chapel and Bell-chamber carefully looked over and repaired where needful. (5) Weather-boards at West end of Church fresh painted.

[1] 'Omitted after Wolstanton p.80.' [2] *Eccles. Revs.:* 'None.' [3] *Eccles. Revs.:* 500 in Newchapel chapelry only.

NORTON IN THE MOORS 24.7.1830
(A/V/1/4,p.26;A/V/1/2,p.133)

BENEFICE: Norton [in the Moors]. **Nature:** Rectory – formerly a part of Stoke Parish – separated by Act of Parliament in 1826. **Ecton:** Chapelry to Stoke, £20 clear value. **Patron:** The family of the present Rector. **Impropriator:** None.
CHURCH: A modern structure – built 90 years ago – centre and side aisles – circular arches – small Chancel. **Number it will contain:** 309 [– too small]. **Accommodation for Poor:** Under 20 [– very insufficient]. **Roof:** Oak, covered with flagslates – pretty good. **Walls:** Brick. **Windows:** Good – well provided with casements. **Doors:** Good. **Pulpit and Desk:** Handsome. **Books:** Clerk's Prayer Book bad. **Seats:** Very neat and uniform. **Galleries:** At the E. and W. ends; the former for singers: another wanted and intended. **Organ:** None. **Font:** There is one. **Chapels:** None. **Benefaction Tables:** Sufficient. **Vestry:** None. **Surplices:** Two – good. **Linen:** Provided. **Plate:** Silver flagon. Chalice and patin. **Iron Chest for Registe:** There is one. **Register:** From 1575 to present time – in pretty good state. **Porch:** None. **Vaults:** ——. **Cleanliness:** Attended to. **Damp:** Some appearance at E. and W. ends.
CHANCEL: **Table:** Firm and good – purple cloth covering. **Ornaments:** None. **Repaired by whom:** The Rector.
STEEPLE: A square brick tower. **State of:** Wants pointing. **Bells:** Six – good and well furnished – newly done. **Clock:** There is one, with a face inside the Church.
CHURCHYARD: **Fence:** Hedge – well kept; additional burying ground wanted. **Gates:** Good. **Drains:** Provided. **Graves:** Not many too near. **Rubbish:** None. **Footpaths:** Properly regulated. **Cattle:** None.
DIVINE SERVICE: **On Sundays:** Prayers Morning – prayers and sermon afternoon. **On other Days:** None (except Christmas day etc.). **Sacrament:** Four times a year. **Communicants:** 30. **Catechism:** After morning prayers in the Chancel; and annually before the Congregation.
INCUMBENT: **Name and Residence:** Revd G Burgess Wildig, in the Rectory. **What Duty he performs:** The whole.
PARSONAGE: A very handsome, well-built, new house. Commodious and well situated. **State of:** Good – all new.[1]
INCOME: **Gross Value:** About £510.[2] **Tithes** and Easter dues compounded for about £480. **Surplice Fees:** £20. **Terrier:** None older than 1720 or 1730.
SCHOOLS: **Endowed School:** A small one for four children. **Subscription Day School:** A girls' school, under the direction of the Rector's lady – 70 [children] at present. **Sunday School:** 160 boys – 80 girls.
DISSENTERS: **Dissenters' School:** Two Sunday Schools. **Dissenting Chapels:** Two Methodist – one Calvinist.
POPULATION: 3,000. [2,400 in 1831.]
PARISH CLERK: Joseph Steele. **Appointed by:** The Rector. **Salary:** £5.
CHURCHWARDENS: Hugh Henshall Williams Esqr, Mr Richard Dean.
ORDERS MADE: Larger casements – walls and tower pointed – open space round the walls laid with flags [or bricks]. A Vestry and additional gallery recommended.

Revisited 18.9.1837
Much dampness. Directed the Churchwardens to have the roofs examined and repaired, gutters cleared out etc. New staircase to Gallery, *within* the Church. The Church, however, is so lamentably inadequate to the wants of the Parish that I strongly urged the Rector to take measures for having it enlarged, and one or more Chapels of ease erected.

Revisited 13.9.1841
Church very damp and unsightly – brick floors of pews should be removed – Church rebuilt and enlarged – or Chapels of Ease erected – Churchyard enlarged. (1) Tiling of roof repaired – ridge tiles repointed. (2) Roof of Tower examined – proper weather-boards. (3) Door above the bell-chamber closed. (4) Spouts examined and kept clear.
N.B. Only one sermon on Sunday.

[1] *Eccles. Revs.:* 'Fit.' [2] *Eccles. Revs.:* Gross income £457.

ONECOTE 21.7.1830
(A/V/1/4,p.27;A/V/1/2,p.118)

BENEFICE: Oncote. **Nature:** Perpetual Curacy – a Chapelry under Leek. **Ecton:** Not mentioned. **Patron:** The Vicar of Leek. **Impropriator:** The land tythe free.
CHURCH: A small, very plain[1] building, erected by subscription in 1753 – single body, small circular windows. **Number it will contain:** About 150,[2] exclusive of gallery. **Accommodation for Poor:**

Sufficient. **Roof:** Oak covered with tile – the ceiling bad. **Walls:** Stone – upright. **Floor:** Flags, even. **Windows:** No casements. **Doors:** Want repair and painting. **Pulpit and Desk:** In very indifferent condition. **Books:** Bad. **Seats:** Good – but the floors very bad. **Galleries:** A small one, on the N. side. **Organ:** None. **Font:** There is one. **Chapels:** None. **Benefaction Tables:** None. **Vestry:** None. **Surplices:** One – good. **Linen:** Provided. **Plate:** Plated Cup and patin. **Iron Chest for Register:** Provided. **Register:** From 1765. **Porch:** None. **Vaults:** ——. **Cleanliness:** Attended to. **Damp:** Much on the walls. **Dimensions:** 39ft. 4in. by 22ft. 4in.

CHANCEL: **Table:** Oak frame – limestone slab. **Ornaments:** None. **Repaired by whom:** The Townships of Oncote and Bradnop.

STEEPLE: A wood bell-tower. **State of:** Much out of repair. **Bells:** One. **Clock:** None.

CHURCHYARD: **Fence:** Stone wall – good. **Gates:** Want painting. **Drains:** None. **Graves:** Some too near. **Rubbish:** None.

DIVINE SERVICE: **On Sundays:** Morning and Afternoon alternately. **On other Days:** None. **Sacrament:** Four times a year. **Communicants:** 8 or 10. **Catechism:** Before confirmations.

INCUMBENT: **Name and Residence:** Revd William Richardson.[3] **If not resident:** On Butterton Moor, a mile from the Church. **What duty he performs:** The whole.

PARSONAGE: None.[4]

INCOME: **Gross Value:** £80 or 90 per annum. **Queen Anne's Bounty:** Supplies nearly the whole Income. **Terrier:** None.

SCHOOLS: **Endowed School:** None. **Subscription Day School:** ——. **Sunday School:** ——. **Lancaster School:** ——.

DISSENTERS: **Dissenters' School, Dissenting Chapels:** A Sunday School attached to the Methodist Chapel.

POPULATION: 4 or 500.

CHURCHWARDENS: William Barker.

ORDERS MADE: The ceiling to be put into complete repair, and the whole whitewashed – the walls ditto. The bell-tower, bell frame etc thoroughly repaired, inside and out. The pews repaired – floor near the Gallery staircase paved. The door repaired and painted – pulpit and reading desk repaired. A new Bible procured – Prayer book and service book re-bound. The bars of the windows, hinges of doors etc painted. An open space round the Chapel walls laid with flags.

Revisited 16.9.1837

This Chapel is being enlarged and much improved. No directions necessary but to have the *North* wall strengthened by buttresses — and, if needful, the *South* also. 'Qu? finished.'

Revisited 14.9.1841

(1) Pulpit, desk, and pews – oiled. (2) Clerk's Prayer Book re-bound. (3) Window bars painted, inside and out. (4) Copings of roof at E. end pointed. (5) Walls pointed – spouts and down-pipes. (6) Open drain. (7) Old Font re-placed in Church. (8) Cracks on S. side of Church filled up and ridge tiles of Chancel re-pointed.

[1] A/V/1/4: '. . . very ordinary'. [2] *Eccles. Revs.:* 300.
[3] Also perpetual curate of Butterton. [4] *Eccles. Revs.:* 'None.'

QUARNFORD 22.7.1830
(A/V/1/4,p.28;A/V/1/2,p.120)

BENEFICE: Quarnford (or Flash). **Nature:** Chapelry, *under Longnor* – and also under Alstonfield. **Ecton:** Not mentioned. **Patron:** Sir G Crewe. **Impropriator:** Ditto.

CHURCH: A small building, erected by subscription in 1744 – plain, single body – much disfigured [and blocked up] by Galleries etc. **Number it will contain:** 315. **Accommodation for Poor:** None appropriated.[1] **Roof:** Oak and deal – covered with flag-slates. **Walls:** Stone – pretty good. **Floor:** Flags. **Windows:** No casements. **Doors:** Pretty good. **Pulpit and Desk:** Good – crimson velvet cushion. **Books:** Much injured by damp. **Seats:** Much injured; both pannels and floors. **Galleries:** One at the W. end, and another at the E. and part of S. **Organ:** None. **Font:** A small one. **Chapels:** None. **Benefaction Tables:** Not complete. **Vestry:** A small enclosure on the N. side of the Communion Table. **Linen:** Provided. **Plate:** Silver Cup – plated flagon and dish. **Iron Chest for Register:** There is one. **Register:** From 1744 – the early ones mutilated. **Porch:** None. **Vaults:** Only one, which will not be reopened. **Cleanliness:** Tolerably well attended to. **Damp:** Much on the floors and walls.

CHANCEL: **Table:** A very common one – no covering. **Ornaments:** None. **Repaired by whom:** The *Pew owners;* the Inhabitants pay rates to Longnor and Alstonfield, but none to the repairs of their own Chapel.

STEEPLE: A small stone tower. **State of:** Tolerably good. **Bells:** One. **Clock:** None.

CHURCHYARD: **Fence:** Stone wall – good. **Drains:** None – the earth on N. side much too high. **Graves:** Not many near the Walls. **Rubbish:** Grass not properly kept. **Footpaths:** Some – to be stopped. **Cattle:** None.

DIVINE SERVICE: **On Sundays:** The usual service alternately Morning and Afternoon. **On other Days:** None. **Sacrament:** Four times a year. **Communicants:** 20. **Catechism:** Not at present.

INCUMBENT: **Name and Residence:** Revd James Roberts – a short distance from the Chapel. **What Duty he performs:** The whole.

PARSONAGE: There is no house that can be *claimed* as a Parsonage – but Sir G Crewe built one in 1822 for the present Minister which he will probably continue to allot to the Clergyman's use.[2] **State of:** Suffers much from damp. **Outbuildings:** Small Cowhouse and stable.

INCOME: **Gross Value:** About £80 per annum – viz. £10 from Pew owners, £30 from rent of land purchased by Queen Anne's Bounty, £5 rent-charge on land given by Sir H Crewe,[3] and interest of £1,000 [Parliamentary grant, (I suppose)]. £90 4s. 6d., including Surplice Fees. Mr Roberts told me. September 1831. **Queen Anne's Bounty:** £400 invested in land.

SCHOOLS: **Endowed School:** None. **Subscription Day School:** None. **Sunday School:** None exclusively belonging to the Chapel – the Methodists and Church-inhabitants have a Sunday School in common.

DISSENTERS: **Dissenting Chapels:** One.

POPULATION: 730 of the Chapelry.

PARISH CLERK: Isaac Brunt. **Appointed by:** The Minister. **Salary:** No fixed Salary.
CHURCHWARDENS: Mr Thomas Slack.
ORDERS MADE: Two casements to be made on each side of the Chapel. Light gates to be placed at the doors. The Books re-bound – covering provided for the Communion Table. The pannels and floors of the Pews repaired – floors laid hollow. The Earth lowered on the N. and E. sides; and an open drain formed. The Chapel to be spouted all round – and pipes affixed. Footpaths stopped.

I was not able to reach this Chapel in my Parochial Visitation 1837 owing to the roads and the distance. From the Report of the Rural Dean the following Spring I learnt that repairs are needed in the interior of the Church – especially the W. Gallery walls want pointing – and staircase which leads to the Belfry is much out of order. Thoroughfare of the Churchyard *not* yet discontinued. *Roof* reported in unsafe state in 1839.

Revisited September 1841
The fabric in tolerable repair – but the floor and indeed the whole building seemed very damp. I desired that the walls might be pointed – the floor laid afresh on dry materials – the windows painted – the spouts made water-tight.

With the heavy burdens, however, to which the Chapelry is subject from having to pay rates to Alstonfield and Longnor, as well as to support their own Chapel, I really could not enjoin much upon them – they would, I believe, gladly rebuild the Chapel, if they might be freed from their other obligations.

[1] A/V/1/4: 'None in particular.' [2] *Eccles. Revs.:* 'None.' [3] A/V/1/4: 'Sir G Crewe.'

RUSHTON SPENCER 23.7.1830
(A/V/1/4, p.29; A/V/1/2, p.127)

BENEFICE: Rushton Spencer. **Nature:** Perpetual Curacy – under Leek. **Ecton:** Chapelry to Leeke – £13 10s. 0d. Clear value. **Patron:** The Vicar of Leek. **Impropriator:** The land tythe-free.
CHURCH: A very old low building – divided into two aisles by pillars and arches – a low lean-to on the N. side. **Number it will contain:** About 230, exclusive of Gallery. **Accommodation for Poor:** The benches in the Gallery. **Roof:** Oak, covered with flag-slates – in very bad state. **Walls:** Stone – not good. **Floor:** Flags – uneven; the floors of the pews generally mud earth. **Windows:** Pretty good – but no casements. **Doors:** Out of repair. **Pulpit and Desk:** Pretty good – handsome embroidered velvet cushion and hangings – faded. **Books:** Bible bad. **Seats:** Very old, irregular and out of repair. **Galleries:** One at the W. end. **Organ:** None. **Font:** An old one – not properly kept clean. **Chapels:** None – but Mr Trafford claims the North Chancel, and has a family vault there. **Benefaction Tables:** None – wanted. **Vestry:** None – one might be fitted up under the Belfry. **Surplices:** One – good. **Linen:** Provided. **Plate:** Handsome silver cup and patin – given in 1706 and 1727. **Chest for Papers:** There is one. **Iron Chest for Register:** [Provided.] **Register:** From 1700 to the present time – in good preservation.
Porch: There is one – much out of repair. **Vaults:** None very lately – the floor sunk from former ones. **Cleanliness:** Pretty well attended to. **Damp:** Not much, except on the floor. **Dimensions:** 57ft. by 27ft.
CHANCEL: Included above. **Table:** Firm – but no communion-rails – the Elements administered at the Seats. **Ornaments:** None. **Repaired by whom:** The Townships comprising the Chapelry.
STEEPLE: An old bell tower. **State of:** In very bad repair. **Bells:** One – [not good state –] wants attention. **Clock:** None.
CHURCHYARD: **Fence:** Hedge all round – well kept. **Gates:** Want repair and painting. **Drains:** None. **Graves:** Several too near [the walls]. **Footpaths:** One thro' the Chapel yard, leading to other parts of the Township. **Cattle:** A horse occasionally.
DIVINE SERVICE: **On Sundays:** Morning and Afternoon alternately. **On other Days:** None. **Sacrament:** Four times a year. **Communicants:** 15 or 20. **Catechism:** Every Spring.
INCUMBENT: **Name and Residence:** Revd G Mounsey.[1] **If not resident:** At Fairfield near Buxton. **What Duty he performs:** Occasionally comes over.
CURATE: **Name and Residence:** Revd Daniel Turner. **If not resident:** At Meerbrook, 4 miles off. **Licensed:** He is. **Salary:** £30 – and the rent of six acres of land; formerly left for the encouragement of a *resident Minister*. **If serving another church:** None.
PARSONAGE: None.[2]
INCOME: **Gross Value:** From £70 to 80 – from rent of land left to the Chapel, and Bounty Money.
SCHOOLS: **Endowed School:** None free.[3] **Subscription Day School:** None **Sunday School:** None.
DISSENTERS: **Dissenters' School:** Methodist Sunday School. **Dissenting Chapels:** ——.
POPULATION: About 1,000.[4]
PARISH CLERK: John Armitt. **Appointed by:** The Minister. **Salary:** £5 and fees.
CHURCHWARDENS: William Gould [*acts as* such, but has had no regular appointment comformable to the antient ways of the Parish – see Leek p.22].
ORDERS MADE: The roof of the Chapel to be stripped and covered afresh. The roof of the Chancel ditto – and the East wall buttressed. The bell tower put into complete repair; bell apparatus ditto. The ground lowered round the walls – footpath stopped, if possible. The doors of the Chapel and both Chancels repaired. Light gates put up at the Porch entrance. Casements made in the windows – iron bars painted. A new Bible, or else the present one rebound. The floor laid afresh – Communion space properly separated by rails.

I strongly recommended, however, that the present ruinous building, very inconveniently situated on a steep hill some distance from the inhabitants, should be taken down, and a new Chapel erected, in the plain below, as has been much wished by some of the more respectable parishioners.

Revisited 15.9.1837
Directions. (1) Windows cleaned – roof examined and repaired – roof of N. Chancel repaired –

watercourses cleared out – battlements secured – ceiling below repaired. (2) Bell-wheel repaired; ground lowered round the walls.

Revisited 11.9.1841
(1) New Covers for Pulpit and Table. (2) East end of Church pointed and watched – buttresses if needful. (3) Roof of Trafford's Chancel repaired – copings pointed – wooden weather boards at E. end of body of Church repaired and painted.
(4) Roof of bell-turret repaired and painted.
(5) Ditto of Church and Porch repaired. (6) Mr Yardley to surrender the old Parish Chest.
Additional burial ground much wanted – Church should be re-built in the plain.

[1] Also curate of donative of Fairfield and perpetual curate of Forest Chapel (both Derbys): *Eccles. Revs.* [2] *Eccles. Revs.*: 'None.' [3] A/V/1/4: 'None.' [4] *Eccles. Revs.*: 360.

SHEEN 21.7.1830 (A/V/1/4,p.30;A/V/1/2,p.122)

BENEFICE: Sheen. **Nature:** Perpetual Curacy. **Ecton:** Mo. Burton Propr. £4 13s. 0d. Clear value. **Patron:** The late Sir Hugh Bateman's representatives.[1] **Impropriator:** None – the Tithes have been bought up except on three farms.
CHURCH: A new building, just erected; no regular style of Architecture. **Number it will contain:** About 300. **Accommodation for Poor:** Sufficient. **Roof:** Oak, covered with Welsh slate. **Walls:** Stone. **Floor:** Flags. **Windows:** Good – another casement wanted on N. side. **Doors:** Good. **Pulpit and Desk:** New. **Books:** Want repairing or renewing. **Seats:** New and good – boarded floors. **Galleries:** One at W. end. **Organ:** None. **Font:** There is a handsome old one, now in the Churchyard. **Chapels:** None. **Benefaction Tables:** Not complete. **Vestry:** One about to be made. **Surplices:** Good. **Linen:** Provided. **Plate:** Silver Cup and patin – pewter flagon. **Iron Chest for Register:** None. **Register:** From 1595 – in bad preservation. **Vaults:** None to be allowed in the new Church. **Cleanliness:** Attended to. **Damp:** None.
CHANCEL: **Table:** Firm. **Ornaments:** None. **Repaired by whom:** The Parish.
STEEPLE: Square stone tower – with four ugly pinnacles. **State of:** Doubtful – there is a large crack, occasioned by a settling in the wall. **Bells:** Three – good. **Clock:** None.
CHURCHYARD: **Fence:** Good stone wall. **Gates:** Good. **Drains:** Surf. **Graves, Rubbish, Footpaths, Cattle:** From the state of the building, and rubbish [not yet removed] – not possible to judge of these particulars.
DIVINE SERVICE: **On Sundays:** Only once – in the Afternoons. **On other Days:** None. **Sacrament:** Four times a year. **Communicants:** Six. **Catechism:** None.
INCUMBENT: **Name and Residence:** Revd Matthew Beetham, in the Parsonage house. **What Duty he performs:** The whole.
PARSONAGE: A small house, rebuilt and enlarged by the present Incumbent. **State of:** Good.[2] **Outbuildings:** ——.
INCOME: **Gross Value:** Said not to exceed £100 per annum.[3] **Glebe:** 50 acres.

SCHOOLS: **Endowed School:** 16 children taught free – £4 arising from land – £8 from money subscribed. **Subscription Day School:** None. **Sunday School:** 20 or 30 children. **Lancaster School:** None.
DISSENTERS: **Dissenters' School:** ——. **Dissenting Chapels:** ——.
POPULATION: About 500.[4]
PARISH CLERK: James Slack. **Appointed by:** The Clergyman. **Salary:** 52s.
CHURCHWARDENS: Mr Thomas Gilman.
ORDERS MADE: A Register Chest to be provided and new Books for the Reading desk. (Further orders not required, the Church being wholly new. I was, however, much concerned to see so much appearance of neglect in the [spiritual] state of the Parish – during upwards of a year, whilst the Church has been rebuilding there has been no duty – there ought to be *two* services on the Sunday.)

Revisited 14.9.1837
Directions. (1) New Books. (2) Air holes under the floors of the pews. (3) Walls coloured – ceilings whitewashed. (4) Benefaction Table. (5) A new ladder to lead upon the Roof of the Tower. (6) Watercourses of roofs frequently cleared out. (7) Earth lowered – open drain with flags, or gravel. 'Qu? directions.'

Revisited 11.9.1841
(1) New Prayer Books, immediately. (2) Floors of Pews in N. aisle, and of Vestry, repaired. (3) Communion Table cleaned, and cover provided. (4) Windows pointed externally. (5) Back-seat but one in Gallery repaired. (6) Window arches on N. side pointed at the heads. (7) Key stone of Vestry window secured. (8) Bricks at W. end of Tower, and SW. of Body, above the door, carefully pointed and watched. (9) Soil removed from bottoms of walls – open drain. (10) Stones of wall on N. side, near the spout, secured. (11) Churchyard gates repaired and painted. (12) Iron frames of windows painted – and outer door of Church. (13) Copings at E. end of Roof pointed.

[1] *Eccles. Revs.*: 'Trustees of the late Sir H Bateman, and J Gould'. [2] *Eccles. Revs.*: 'Fit.' [3] *Eccles. Revs.*: Gross income £71. [4] *Eccles. Revs.*: 371.

STOKE UPON TRENT 16.6.1830 (A/V/1/4,p.31;A/V/1/2,p.82)

BENEFICE: Stoke upon Trent. **Nature:** Rectory. **Ecton:** King's Books £41 0s. 10d. **Patron:** John Tomlinson Esqr. **Impropriator:** Ditto as Lessee under the Rector (the Dean of Lichfield).
CHURCH: A handsome Gothic structure, just erected – and not yet consecrated – (consecrated 6.10.1830).[1] **Number it will contain:** 1,531. **Accommodation for Poor:** 500. **Roof:** Deal – covered with slate. **Walls:** Stone. **Floor:** Flags. **Windows:** Good. **Doors:** ——. **Pulpit and Desk:** Too low; the latter to be raised. **Books:** None yet provided for the new Church – those of the old Church exceeding bad. **Seats:** New and handsome. **Galleries:** On three sides. **Organ:** One just being put up. **Font:** One at the old Church – to be removed, I suppose, to the new one. **Chapels:** None. **Benefaction Tables:** At the old Church.

Vestry: There is one. **Surplices:** At the old Church – new ones wanted. **Linen:** Provided. **Plate:** Two flagons, two chalices, two Patens; silver, gilt inside. **Iron Chest for Register:** At the Rectory. **Register:** Several Vols – oldest date 1631; in good order. **Porch:** None. **Vaults, Cleanliness, Damp, Dimensions:** The Church being new, several of these points not enquired into.

CHANCEL: **Dimensions, Table, Ornaments:** The Church being new, several of these points not enquired into.

STEEPLE: Square stone tower. **State of:** New. **Bells:** Six in the old Church – two additional ones talked of. **Clock:** At the old Church.

CHURCHYARD: **Fence:** Not yet completed – much altercation has arisen about it between the Patron and the Parish; I received an assurance however that my injunction should be attended to [– (since finished (1831)) and the Church consecrated]. **Gates, Drains, Graves, Rubbish, Footpaths, Cattle:** [Not yet completed.]

DIVINE SERVICE: **On Sundays:** Two full services. **On other Days:** None, except during Lent etc. **Sacrament:** Eight times a year. **Communicants:** Vary from 50 to 100.

INCUMBENT: **Name and Residence:** The Dean of Lichfield [resigned the living 30.9.1831]. **If not resident:** At Lichfield. **What Duty he performs:** None.

CURATE: **Name and Residence:** Revd Benjamin Vale, Rectory. **Licensed:** He is. **Salary:** ——.[2]

PARSONAGE: Now very good, large and commodious; the Patron has recently enlarged and improved the old Rectory house, at much expense. **State of:** Very good – chiefly new.[3] **Outbuildings:** Very extensive; in good repair.

INCOME: **Gross Value:** Not stated – I believe [considerably] upwards of £1,000.[4] **Terrier:** Several copies.

SCHOOLS: **Endowed School:** More than one in the Parish. **Subscription Day School:** A National School, to which the present Rector (Dean of Lichfield) has lately granted an endowment – 150 children at present [attend]. **Sunday School:** 150 in addition to the National School.

DISSENTERS: **Dissenting Chapels:** Several – and Sunday Schools attached to each.

POPULATION of *Stoke proper:* 9,000 – of whole Parish 34,000.

CHURCHWARDENS: Mr Herbert Minton and Mr James Greaves.

ORDERS MADE: New Bible and Prayer book – the reading Desk to be raised higher. New Surplices to be provided. Benefaction Tables to be removed from the old Church. Additional casements to be made in the Chancel and Gallery staircase windows. The new Churchyard enclosed by a solid and sufficient Fence.

In consequence of a report which reached me, in the progress of my Parochial Visitations (1837) that the roof of this handsome Church was in a dangerous state, I examined it myself (September 20) and directed Mr Trubshaw (the builder) to do so, very carefully – He assures me (September 29) that all is perfectly secure.

I have nothing to direct; except that the wheels of the bells be repaired where needful.

Revisited 17.9.1841

Directions to Churchwardens. (1) To consult Mr Trubshaw about securing the Church from danger arising from hot air flues and to have the Church *insured.* (2) To provide *water-tables* for windows, service books for Communion Tables, and new bell-ropes. (3) Iron bars of windows painted, walls re-coloured, water-courses of roofs over NW. and SW. entrances, cleared, pinnacles examined and strengthened, water from roof of Tower conducted by a pipe into lead gutters of roof – lead flashings of roof of Tower secured and parapets pointed, where needful. (4) Door placed at top of Staircase leading to Tower; – wheels, frames, and brasses of bells repaired and strengthened – and iron work oiled and painted. (5) External roof of Church repaired where needful.

[1] The note enclosed in brackets added later. Faculty dated 1.10.1828 (B/C/2/1826–9, p.531). [2] *Eccles. Revs.:* Curate's stipend £195. [3] *Eccles. Revs.:* 'Fit.' [4] *Eccles. Revs.:* Gross income £3,000.

TALKE 5.10.1830 (A/V/1/4, p.33; A/V/1/2, p.134)

BENEFICE: Talk o' th' Hill. **Nature:** Perpetual Curacy. **Ecton:** Chapelry to Audley – Clear value £5 14s. 0d. **Patron:** The Vicar of Audley. **Impropriator:** G Tollett Esqr.

CHURCH: A small brick building – erected about 60 years ago; single body, very plain. **Number it will contain:** About 180.[1] [Stated to be *150* in an application for enlargement – May 1832.] **Accommodation for Poor:** [30.] **Roof:** Timber covered with tile – apparently not in good repair. **Walls:** Brick – want pointing externally. **Floor:** Bricks – damp. **Windows:** Not in good repair. **Doors:** Good – the outer door wants painting. **Pulpit and Desk:** Good – old oak – velvet crimson cushion to pulpit. **Books:** Want repair. **Seats:** Neat and uniform. **Galleries:** Two small ones at the W. end. **Organ:** None. **Chapels:** None. **Benefaction Tables:** None. **Vestry:** There is one. **Surplices:** One, new. **Linen:** Provided. **Plate:** Silver Cup and Patin – pewter flagon. **Iron Chest for Register:** None. **Register:** None kept at Talk – registers sent to Audley. **Porch:** None. **Vaults:** ——. **Cleanliness:** Pretty well. **Damp:** On the floor.

CHANCEL: No Chancel distinct from the rest of the Chapel. **Table:** Neat mahogany – green cloth cover. **Ornaments:** None – Commandments up.

STEEPLE: Small bell tower, covered with lead. **State of:** Not good – weather-boards bad. **Bells:** One – good. **Clock:** Out of repair.

CHURCHYARD: **Fence:** Not properly kept up [– there is scarcely any Chapel yard – but on the S. side is a garden, which I should judge to have been originally intended for such]. **Gates:** One – bad. **Drains:** None – nor spouts. **Graves:** No burials at present. **Rubbish:** None. **Footpaths:** The Chapel yard appears to have been encroached upon – on the S. side is a garden, almost close to the Chapel walls – on the N. a very small space walled off from the road. **Cattle:** None.

DIVINE SERVICE: **On Sundays:** Once – alternately Morning and Afternoon. **On other Days:** None. **Sacrament:** Four times a year. **Communicants:**

Uncertain. **Catechism:** Not in the Chapel.
INCUMBENT: **Name and Residence:** Revd Robert Hill [since dead, and Revd Mr Garratt, the Curate of Audley, appointed, 1831]. **If not resident:** At the Hough – ten miles off. **What Duty he performs:** None.
CURATE: **Name and Residence:** Revd JD Hill, grandson to the Incumbent, just ordained to the Chapel. **If not resident:** At present with his grandfather – till a lodging can be procured. **Licensed:** He is. **Salary:** ——.[2] **If serving another church:** None.
PARSONAGE: None.[3]
INCOME: **Gross Value, Tithes, Glebe, Surplice Fees, Easter Dues and small Payments, Queen Anne's Bounty:** These particulars not ascertained – neither the Incumbent nor Curate appearing.[4]
SCHOOLS: **Endowed School:** Land given by Mr Tollett for education of 14 boys and girls – yearly value £14. **Subscription Day School:** None. **Sunday School:** None. **Lancaster School:** ——.
DISSENTERS: **Dissenters' School:** Methodist – weekly and Sunday. **Dissenting Chapels:** Methodist.
POPULATION: 3 or 400.[5] [In an application made to the Society for enlargement etc – May 1832 – this is stated at *1,300*.]
MISCELLANEOUS: **Monuments:** None.
PARISH CLERK: James Foster. **Appointed by:** The Minister. **Salary:** None fixed.
CHURCHWARDENS: Samuel Johnson, appointed at Audley.
ORDERS MADE: The roof to be examined and repaired – spouts and pipes affixed. The wall of the Chapel yard to be repaired – the Gate ditto – shrubs removed from the North side – and the proper boundary of the yard to be carefully ascertained and restored if necessary. The walls of the Chapel to be pointed all round – the windows repaired – casements made – the outer door and bars of windows painted – the bell-house put in proper repair – weather-boards put up. The Clock repaired and the dial painted afresh. The Bible (O.T.) to be re-bound; a new Copy of the N.T. provided; the Prayer-books repaired – Iron Register Chest, and Register books provided.

It seems very desirable that a *burial* ground should be attached to the Chapel, which is full three miles distant from the Mother Church – along very bad roads – I wrote on the subject to Mr Tollett, [as also respecting Audley,] but have received no answer. September 1831.[6]

The Chapel has been enlarged so as to contain about 300 and much improved since my former visit – still there is much that needs attention. (1) The old gate, on the North side, to be renewed. (2) The weeds etc, within the wall on the N. side, taken away. (3) A casement to be opened in the window of the ante-room leading to the gallery, or on the staircase – the plaister of the window-cills repaired. (4) The Gallery pews to be painted, oak colour. (5) The walls to be coloured and the ceiling whitewashed. (6) The Prayer Book belonging to the Reading desk repaired and replaced; that in the Reading desk restored to the Clerk's desk. (7) The windows repaired – lead gutters and pipes. (8) An additional casement on the South side. (9) The roof on the South side repaired, and spouting carried all along the roof – and a down-pipe put up. (10) The drain, on the South side, cleared out. (11) A burial ground *strongly recommended*.

Revisited 16.9.1841

Directions to Churchwardens. (1) Water-tables provided for windows – bars painted – windows set open in fine weather. (2) New Prayer-book for Reading-desk. (3) Baptismal Font, of *stone*. (4) Walls in room leading to gallery, to be fresh plastered and coloured – window frame painted, and casement made to open. (5) Pews in Gallery well rubbed with boiled linseed oil. (6) Parapet walls of tower to be well pointed, and lead gutters cleared. (7) Roof of Chapel examined and repaired – especially the *old* part towards East end. (8) Eave-spouts and down-pipes on *both* sides of the Chapel. (9) Fence wall repaired and coping stones replaced.

[1] *Eccles. Revs.:* 300. [2] *Eccles. Revs.:* £50. [3] *Eccles. Revs.:* 'None.' [4] *Eccles. Revs.:* Gross income £122. [5] *Eccles. Revs.:* 1,196. [6] '. . . but . . . 1831' added later.

WARSLOW 21.7.1830
(A/V/1/4, p.34; A/V/1/2, p.121)

BENEFICE: Warslow. **Nature:** Perpetual Curacy – under Alstonfield. **Ecton:** £1 10s. 0d. Clear value. **Patron:** Vicar of Alstonfield. **Impropriator:** Sir G Crewe.
CHURCH: A small building, erected in 1820 (the old one in 1631) single body – flat ceiling – no Chancel. **Number it will contain:** 314. **Accommodation for Poor:** Sufficient. **Roof:** Deal covered with slate, lead gutters. **Walls:** Stone – good. **Floor:** Flags – even. **Windows:** Good – but not sufficiently provided with casements. **Doors:** Good. **Pulpit and Desk:** Very neat – faded crimson velvet Cushion. **Books:** Very good. **Seats:** Ditto. **Galleries:** One at the W. end. **Organ:** None. **Font:** A small one. **Chapels:** None. **Benefaction Tables:** None. **Vestry:** A small one. **Surplices:** One. **Linen:** Provided – napkin not good. **Plate:** Silver Cup and Patin – plated flagon. **Iron Chest for Register:** None. **Register:** From 1785 – not regularly kept. **Porch:** None. **Vaults:** None. **Cleanliness:** Attended to. **Damp:** Some on the walls.
CHANCEL: **Table:** Good – velvet covering. **Ornaments:** None. **Repaired by whom:** The Parish.
STEEPLE: Square Tower. **State of:** Good. **Bells:** One. **Clock:** None.
CHURCHYARD: **Fence:** Good. **Gates:** Want painting. **Drains:** None. **Graves:** Too near. **Rubbish:** None. **Footpaths:** Several across the yard – not necessary. **Cattle:** No large ones.
DIVINE SERVICE: **On Sundays:** Alternately with Elkstone. **On other Days:** None. **Sacrament:** Four times a year. **Communicants:** About 20. **Catechism:** In the School.
INCUMBENT: **Name and Residence:** Revd RB Pidcock, Parsonage.[1] **What Duty he performs:** The whole.
PARSONAGE: A substantial house, of stone, not yet finished; roof red-deal covered with slate.[2] **State of:** Good.

INCOME:[3] **Glebe:** About 50 acres [of land] purchased by Bounty money. **Queen Anne's Bounty:** Interest of £250 in addition to the above. **Terrier:** At Alstonfield.
SCHOOLS: **Endowed School:** There is one, endowed with land (present income £27 per annum) for instruction of 25 children. **Subscription Day School:** No other. **Sunday School:** There is one.
POPULATION: About 500.[4]
PARISH CLERK: John Milward. **Appointed by:** Vicar of Alstonfield. **Salary:** 52s. per annum.
CHURCHWARDENS: Mr John Barker – by the Vicar of Alstonfield.
ORDERS MADE: Additional casements to be made on each side. Iron Chest to be provided for the Registers. The lead gutter of the roof raised, so as to carry off the wet. The earth removed from the Chapel walls, and an open drain made. Gates painted – footpaths stopped – no graves near the walls.

Revisited 14.9.1837
Very much improved – the thoroughfare of the Churchyard stopped – new entrance and handsome gates – new Clock etc.
  Directions. (1) A large casement on each side of the Church. (2) An iron Register Chest, conjointly with Elkstone. (3) The stove guarded by sheet iron. (4) Spouts along the N. side of the roof, and down-pipe. (5) No large cattle. 'Qu? Register Chest? Spouts.'

Revisited 11.9.1841
(1) Floors of pews repaired – ditto of reading-desk. (2) Coverings of Communion Table and Pulpit died afresh. (3) Bible rebound, new Prayer Book for Desk. (4) Water tables to windows. (5) Clock-weight secured – frame provided. (6) New bell-ropes. (7) Large casement on each side of Church. (8) Spout at NE. angle brought to ground. (9) Drain kept open. (10) Ridge of roof pointed, or flashed.

[1] Also perpetual curacy of Elkstone. [2] *Eccles. Revs.:* 'Fit.' [3] *Eccles. Revs.:* Gross income £105. [4] *Eccles. Revs.:* 620.

WATERFALL 20.7.1830
(A/V/1/4,p.35;A/V/1/2,p.115)

BENEFICE: Waterfall. **Nature:** Perpetual Curacy. **Ecton:** Chapelry to Rocettur. £7 clear value.
Patron: Mrs Wilmot. **Impropriator:** Mr Townsend.
CHURCH: A small building, the body modern. **Number it will contain:** 150. **Accommodation for Poor:** Sufficient. **Roof:** Oak, covered with lead. **Walls:** Lime and gritstone. **Floor:** Flags – much injured by graves; to be re-laid. **Windows:** Good – but unprovided with casements. **Doors:** Good. **Pulpit and Desk:** Good – pulpit cushion bad. **Books:** Prayer book wants repair. **Seats:** The pannels etc good – floors bad. **Galleries:** One at the W. end. **Organ:** None. **Font:** There is. **Chapels:** None. **Benefaction Tables:** None – the endowment of the School to be recorded. **Vestry:** None. **Surplices:** One – much injured by damp. **Linen:** Provided. **Plate:** Small silver Cup – pewter flagon – patin. **Iron Chest for Register:** There is one. **Register:** In bad preservation – oldest date about 1600. **Vaults:** Several, or rather *graves* – not to be allowed henceforth. **Cleanliness:** Attended to. **Damp:** No appearance.
CHANCEL: **Table:** Wants cleaning – purple Cloth covering. **Ornaments:** None. **Repaired by whom:** The Impropriator.
STEEPLE: Square stone Tower. **State of:** Good – lead roof. **Bells:** Three, good. **Clock:** None.
CHURCHYARD: **Fence:** Not well kept. **Gates:** Want painting. **Drains:** None – the earth accumulated. **Graves:** Many too near the walls. **Footpaths:** Trespass – no proper Church-way. **Cattle:** Sheep.
DIVINE SERVICE: **On Sundays:** Morning and Afternoon alternately. **On other Days:** None. **Sacrament:** Four times a year. **Communicants:** 20. **Catechism:** Once a year.
INCUMBENT: **Name and Residence:** Revd Elias Saunders.[1] **If not resident:** At Calton, two miles off. **What Duty he performs:** The whole.
PARSONAGE: None.[2]
INCOME: **Gross Value:** Not ascertained.[3] **Glebe:** Purchased by Queen Anne's Bounty. **Queen Anne's Bounty:** See *Glebe*. **Terrier:** The Minister has one.
SCHOOLS: **Endowed School:** Five acres of land were allotted by the Parishioners, 87 years ago, for the education of eight children. **Subscription Day School:** None. **Sunday School:** None – the children attend the School at Cauldon.
DISSENTERS: **Dissenters' School:** A Sunday School. **Dissenting Chapels:** Methodist.
POPULATION: 500.
PARISH CLERK: Thomas Wardle. **Appointed by:** The Minister. **Salary:** £2 0s. 0d. and Easter dues.
CHURCHWARDENS: Mr Isaac Smith – appointed by the Parish.
ORDERS MADE: The floor to be re-laid, where necessary – the floors of the Pews to be laid afresh with bricks or boards; and no more graves allowed within the Church. Casements on each side of the Church – and one in the Gallery. The Prayer book repaired – a new Cushion for the Pulpit. The School endowment to be recorded in the Church. The iron bars of the windows, bells etc to be painted. The Communion Table and rails, and Pulpit oiled – the Surplice better kept. The Chancel to be spouted – and walls pointed outside. An open drain formed – footpaths stopped – gates painted – a proper Churchway made. No graves within ten feet – no large cattle.

Revisited 13.9.1837
Much improved, as regards the interior of *the Church*. The Chancel still in a damp and slovenly state – ordered (1) That the parish chest be removed from within the Communion rails, and the Table placed close to the wall. (2) That the ground round the Chancel be lowered – down-pipes put up – spout on NE., and wall, repaired. (3) No large cattle in Churchyard – Church walk made of proper width – trespass paths stopped, fence mended and thoroughfare stopped, if possible – Lich gates repaired and painted. (4) Down-pipe on SW. side of Church, near the door, repaired – also belfry floor – window bars painted. 'Qu? directions.'

Revisited 11.9.1841
(1) Oak pews in Church and Chancel rubbed with

oil: Communion Table ditto. (2) New steps and kneeling mats to rails of Communion. (3) Prayer Book re-bound. (4) Wheels of bells repaired – iron work painted. (5) Copings of roof pointed – stones from gutters. (6) Chancel roof under coping stones repaired. (7) NE. corner of Chancel wall (adjoining Church), repaired at bottom. (8) Base of Tower pointed – and Staircase to Gallery. (9) Thoroughfare of Churchyard stopped.

[1] Also perpetual curate of Cauldon and of the donative of Calton. [2] *Eccles. Revs.:* 'None.' [3] *Eccles. Revs.:* Gross income £65.

WETTON 19.7.1830
(A/V/1/4,p.36;A/V/1/2,p.112)

BENEFICE: Wetton. **Nature:** Perpetual Curacy. **Ecton:** Chapelry to Tutbury. Clear value £7 13s. 4d. **Patron:** Montague Burgoyne Esqr. **Impropriator:** ——.[1]
CHURCH: A small modern building; rebuilt eight or ten years ago; single body. **Number it will contain:** About 150 – exclusive of benches for children. **Accommodation for Poor:** None appropriated.[2] **Roof:** Deal, covered with slate [– good]. **Walls:** Limestone and gritstone – upright. **Floor:** Flags – even. **Windows:** Good – more casements wanted. **Doors:** Good. **Pulpit and Desk:** Well placed – old moth eaten Cushion. **Books:** Clerk's Prayer Book out of repair [– bad]. **Seats:** Neat and uniform. **Galleries:** None – one might easily be put up opposite the door. **Organ:** None. **Font:** Not a proper one. **Chapels:** None. **Benefaction Tables:** Not complete. **Vestry:** A small one – in a Pew. **Surplices:** One – pretty good. **Linen:** Provided. **Plate:** Pewter flagon and dish. **Iron Chest for Register:** At the Clerk's. **Register:** From 1660 to present time. **Porch:** A small one. **Vaults:** None since the re-building of the Church. **Cleanliness:** Attended to. **Damp:** Much on the walls.
CHANCEL: **Table:** An oak table – firm and good; no covering. **Ornaments:** None. **Repaired by whom:** The Parish.
STEEPLE: A square stone Tower. **State of:** Good. **Bells:** Three – good. **Clock:** There is one.
CHURCHYARD: **Fence:** Wall of loose stones – kept up by the Parish. The Churchyard itself is claimed by a Mr Cantrell who says he bought it, and keeps his cattle in it. **Gates:** Good. **Drains:** None – no spouts or pipes. **Graves:** Some too near. **Rubbish:** Some – and a sink runs into the Churchyard from the neighbouring Cottages. **Footpaths:** Several, very improperly. **Cattle:** A horse.
DIVINE SERVICE: **On Sundays:** Alternately Morning and Afternoon. **On other Days:** None. **Sacrament:** Three times a year. **Communicants:** 12 or 14. **Catechism:** Two or three times a year.
INCUMBENT: **Name and Residence:** Revd WM Ward. **If not resident:** At Beresford Hall, two miles off. **What Duty he performs:** The whole. **If serving another church:** Hartington.
PARSONAGE: None.[3]
INCOME: **Gross Value, Tithes, Glebe, Surplice Fees, Easter Dues and small Payments, Queen Anne's Bounty:** Not ascertained;[4] the Clergyman did not appear. **Terrier:** None.

SCHOOLS: **Endowed School:** None. **Subscription Day School:** ——. **Sunday School:** 30 children. **Lancaster School:** None.
DISSENTERS: **Dissenters' School:** ——. **Dissenting Chapels:** Methodist.
POPULATION: 4 or 500.
PARISH CLERK: John Robinson. **Appointed by:** The Minister. **Salary:** 52s. and 5s. for cleaning.
CHURCHWARDENS: Richard Fallows for the Minister. George Beardmore for the Parish.
ORDERS MADE: Two more casements to be made – the iron bars of the windows, straps of Bells etc to be painted. New Cushion for the Pulpit – Clerk's Prayer Book repaired or renewed. The Font altered – Benefactions fully recorded. Spouts[, pipes] to be put up – and an open drain formed. Rubbish removed – trespass footpaths stopped – nuisances prohibited. A Gallery, on the North side, *recommended*.

Revisited 13.9.1837
Much improved. Directions. (1) New Prayerbooks for Reading and Clerk's Desks – and new Office book. (2) Lead gutters and pipe for the windows. (3) Walls, when dry, to be coloured, *grey* stone colour. (4) Porch roof repaired. (5) West side of Tower pointed – down-pipes. (6) Copings of roof at E. end pointed. (7) Gudgeons of bells protected, and new beds for them. (8) Thoroughfare of Churchyard stopped – locks on gates. (9) No heavy cattle in Churchyard.

Revisited 10.9.1841
(1) New Prayer Book for Desk – Bible re-bound.[5] (2) Communion Table and rails rubbed with oil.[5] (3) Ivy planted upon N. side of Church by way of experiment. (4) Gutters of roof of Tower laid even – flashings secured – walls pointed – downpipe set up. (5) Wheels of bells repaired – iron cramps etc painted; also iron bars of windows, and Churchyard gates.

[1] *Eccles. Revs.:* 'Duke of Devonshire'. [2] A/V/1/4: 'None in particular.' [3] *Eccles. Revs.:* 'None.' [4] *Eccles. Revs.:* Gross income £90. [5] These directions are marked with a tick.

WOLSTANTON 15.6.1830
(A/V/1/4,p.37;A/V/1/2,p.80)

BENEFICE: Wolstanton. **Nature:** Vicarage. **Ecton:** Ecton calls it a Rectory – but says in a note 'The Bishop of Lichfield is Impropriator of the Rectory – the Parish is only a Curacy, with the Chapel called New Chapel certified at £9 15s. 0d. clear value. Value of the *Rectory* in the Kings Books £32 3s. 9d.' **Patron:** The Sneyds of Keele – to whose family the Rectory was granted by Queen Elizabeth in 1567, on condition of endowing a Vicarage. **Impropriator:** Col. Sneyd.
CHURCH: An old stone building, with a handsome spire – but the stone much dilapidated externally – remains of a handsome Church – wood roofs[1] and pointed Arches. **Number it will contain:** About 600.[2] **Accommodation for Poor:** Sufficient. **Roof:** Out of repair – ceilings ditto. **Walls:** Stone – not upright. **Floor:** Quarries and flags. **Windows:** No casements. **Doors:** Not sufficiently close – much wind comes in. **Pulpit and Desk:** Good – velvet cushions. **Books:** Not

good. **Seats:** Out of repair. **Galleries:** A small one at the W. end. **Organ:** None. **Font:** There is one. **Benefaction Tables:** There are. **Vestry:** A very good one. **Surplices:** Two – good. **Linen:** Provided. **Plate:** Two flagons – two Cups – a Paten, plated. **Iron Chest for Register:** In the Vicarage. **Register:** Several Volumes – from 1628 – in bad preservation – mutilated in some parts. **Porch:** There is one – out of repair – outer gate wanted. **Vaults:** None recently. **Cleanliness:** Pretty well attended to. **Damp:** Much in all parts of the Church.

CHANCEL: **Table:** Oak – covered with purple Cloth. **Repaired by whom:** The Impropriator – much injury done by damp.

STEEPLE: Square Tower, with spire above. **State of:** Good. **Bells:** Six – good. **Clock:** Good.

CHURCHYARD: **Fence:** A good brick wall. **Drains:** Wanted. **Graves:** Many close to the walls.

DIVINE SERVICE: **On Sundays:** Prayers in the morning – full service afternoon. **On other Days:** None. **Sacrament:** Four times a year. **Communicants:** Under 30.

INCUMBENT: **Name and Residence:** Revd R Bagot, Vicarage (holds the living for Mr Sneyd). **What duty he performs:** The whole.

PARSONAGE: An old, straggling, inconvenient building – '3 bays of building'. **State of:** In very bad repair.[3] **Outbuildings:** Ample – but much dilapidated.

INCOME: **Gross Value:** About £300 per annum. **Glebe:** 30 acres. **Terrier:** There is an old one.

SCHOOLS: **Endowed School:** £5 yearly. **Subscription Day School:** None. **Sunday School:** 60 to 100 children. **Lancaster School:** None.

DISSENTERS: **Dissenters' School:** ——. **Dissenting Chapels:** ——.

POPULATION: 10,000 [a Chapel at Newchapel].

PARISH CLERK: **John Hassall.**

CHURCHWARDENS: William Cartledge, Abraham Wood.

ORDERS MADE: The doors to be repaired – and an inner door to be put up at the W. end of the Church. The roof and ceilings to be examined and repaired. Two casements to be made on each side of the Nave – and one in the Chancel. The Porch to be repaired and a light gate placed at its entrance. The Bible to be repaired, and a new Prayer book provided. The Pews to be repaired where needful. The earth to be cleared away round the walls – an open drain made – spouts and pipes put up. Graves forbidden within six feet. The nuisance to be removed from the Corner of the Churchyard. The Vicarage house, outbuildings etc to be put into substantial repair. See p. 149 for Newchapel.

Revisited 19.9.1837

The Church still in a very damp, uncomfortable and dilapidated state. Ordered (1) That the walls of the Church and Chancel be coloured (grey) in the Spring, and the ceilings whitewashed. (2) That a new mat, or carpet, be provided for the Communion floor, and the Table cleaned; the cover of the Table kept in a box or chest during the week or covered – the kneeling cushions kept clean. (3) The windows of the Chancel repaired and bars painted; the ivy prevented from coming in at the windows. (4) The floors of the Church laid level, where sunk; and the windows, all round, cleaned and repaired. (5) The belfry whitewashed – the weatherboards replaced; the water-courses and battlements of Tower put in order. (6) Externally – The roofs carefully looked over – lead flashings repaired – gutters cleared out and laid even – roof and spouts of chancel repaired and put in order – The overshot spouts taken away and down-pipes substituted. (7) The buttresses repaired and underbuilt – ivy removed from Chancel – ground lowered, all round, below the level of the floor inside. (8) The wall round the Churchyard, to be repaired at the NE. corner, and raised at the NW. so as to conceal the nuisance in the adjoining yard. (9) The gate to be kept locked – the Vestry ruin removed – the tombstones repaired, or else the rails and stones removed. (10) Doors and windows kept open in fine weather.

Revisited 16.9.1841

Directions to Churchwardens. (1) *Inside the Church.* West window repaired at bottom. Casement made at each end of South Aisle. Windows and doors kept open in fine weather. (2) *Outside.* Parapets and battlements of roof examined and secured, on both sides of Church. Buttresses repaired and pointed, all round the Church.

N.B. To be informed by what authority the building on the NE. side of the Church was originally erected, and is now used for the business of the Vestry Clerk. To be removed if no sufficient authority. To write to Mr Sneyd respecting *Chancel.*

[1] A/V/1/4: '. . . wood ceilings.' [2] *Eccles. Revs.:* 500. [3] *Eccles. Revs.:* 'Fit.'

WETLEY ROCKS 18.9.1837
(A/V/1/4,p.38; not in A/V/1/2)

BENEFICE: Wetley Rocks. **Nature:** Chapel of Ease to Cheddleton – with district annexed – built 1833/4. **Patron:** Mrs Sneyd of Ashcombe, Leek.[1]

CHURCH: A neat stone building, in Gothic style – centre and side aisles – small chancel. **Number it will contain:** About 564. **Accommodaion for Poor:** 364. **Roof:** Timber covered with slate. **Walls:** Stone. **Floor:** Brick. **Windows:** Good. **Doors:** ——. **Pulpit and Desk:** ——. **Books:** —— **Seats:** ——. **Galleries:** West end. **Organ:** None. **Chapels:** None. **Benefaction Tables:** ——. **Vestry:** There is one. **Linen:** Provided. **Porch:** None. **Vaults:** ——. **Cleanliness:** Attended to. **Damp:** Very little.

CHANCEL: **Table:** Suitable. **Repaired by whom:** Mrs Sneyd.

STEEPLE: Tower. **State of:** Good. **Bells:** One. **Clock:** None.

CHURCHYARD: **Fence:** Good. **Gates:** ——. **Drains:** ——. **Graves:** ——. **Rubbish:** ——. **Footpaths:** ——. **Cattle:** ——.

DIVINE SERVICE: **On Sundays:** Two services. **On other Days:** None.

INCUMBENT: **Name and Residence:** Revd Henry Sneyd.

PARSONAGE: None at present.

ORDERS MADE: The Communion rails to be properly fixed. The weatherboard of the Tower to be made larger, and sufficient means provided for carrying off the wet. The ridging tiles examined. Eave-spouts and down-pipes put up.

Revisited 15.9.1841
(1) Window water tables deeper – bars painted. (2) Plaister and timber at SW. end (over gallery) repaired. (3) Battlements and Tower pointed – lead on roof levelled. (4) Copings at E. gable flashed – eave-spouts and down-pipes. (5) Walls kept clear from herbage.

[1] Near Leek, but in the parish of Cheddleton.

TUNSTALL 19.9.1837
(A/V/1/4,p.39; not in A/V/1/2)

BENEFICE: Tunstall. **Nature:** District Church in parish of Wolstanton. **Patron:** Vicar (or Patron) of Wolstanton.
CHURCH: New Church, in Gothic style – very slightly built – centre and side aisles – pointed arches – small chancel. **Number it will contain:** 1,008. **Roof:** Timber covered with slate. **Walls:** Good. **Floor:** ——. **Windows:** —— not securely made. **Doors:** Good. **Pulpit and Desk:** ——. **Books:** —— ——. **Seats:** ——. **Galleries:** On three sides. **Organ:** There is one. **Font:** ——. **Chapels:** None. **Benefaction Tables:** ——. **Vestry:** There is one.
STEEPLE: Tower, surmounted by spire. **State of:** Good.
CHURCHYARD: **Fence:** Brick wall. **Gates:** Iron – good. **Drains:** Not sufficient. **Footpaths:** None. **Cattle:** None.
INCUMBENT: **Name and Residence:** Revd Th Campbell.[1]
CURATE: **Salary:** ——.[2]
PARSONAGE: None.
ORDERS MADE: The window frames and bars to be painted and strengthened with additional bars. The quarries at the East end repaired. The pews etc painted. Casements, in *lower* parts of the windows, in alternate windows. The lead gutters cleaned out – an additional down-pipe placed for each roof. The Churchyard drained.

Revisited 16.9.1841
Directions to Churchwardens. (1) Four additional Casements made in lower parts of windows – two on each side of Church. (2) New Prayer-book for Clergyman's desk. (3) Iron bars of windows painted. (4) Pinnacles secured. (5) Overflow of spouts and pipes guarded against – mouths of pipes guarded from obstruction, and the whole frequently examined and cleaned.

[1] 'G Harvey, Horton' deleted. [2] The stipend of the curate of Wolstanton with Tunstall is given as £60 in *Eccles. Revs.*

SHELTON 20.9.1837
(A/V/1/4,p.40; not in A/V/1/2)

BENEFICE: Shelton.
ORDERS MADE: Pinnacles of the tower to be secured. The water-courses and flashings of the roof to be examined and kept in good order – so as to carry off the wet – *suggested* additional down-pipes, (or larger ones) to prevent overflow of water. Windows repaired and strengthened – water-table provided. The outer doors varnished – pews and Galleries painted – walls coloured (as soon as *funds can be obtained*).

Revisited 16.9.1841
(1) The outer doors and down-pipes to be painted – windows mended. (2) The SW. and NW. pinnacles of Tower secured, or else taken down – the broken off pinnacles re-placed. (3) The joints of battlements pointed. (4) Window bars painted – walls, internally, coloured.
I recommend that the church should be insured against *fire* – and enjoined strict precautions against fire; especially near the Pulpit.

LONGTON 21.9.1837
(A/V/1/4,p.41; not in A/V/1/2)

BENEFICE: Longton.
ORDERS MADE: Wood, and iron work to be *painted*. Walls coloured etc as soon as possible.

Revisited 17.9.1841
Directions to Churchwardens. (1) Water-tables made for windows. (2) Wainscoting on South side repaired, and dry-rot prevented. (3) Walls of Church coloured, and ceiling whitewashed. (4) Pinnacles pointed at joints, and lead flashings secured. (5) Warm air apparatus repaired.

COBRIDGE (A/V/1/4,p.42; not in A/V/1/2)

BENEFICE: Cobridge, consecrated 16.4.1841. **Patron:** Rector of Burslem.
CHURCH: Neat brick building – centre and two side Aisles – small Chancel – pointed arches and neat windows – Tower. **Number it will contain:** 566. **Accommodation for Poor:** '364 (included in above).' **Roof:** Timber covered with slate.

ABBOTS BROMLEY 6.7.1830
(A/V/1/4,p.43;A/V/1/2,p.89)

BENEFICE: Abbots Bromley. **Nature:** Vicarage. **Ecton:** Living discharged – Clear value £30. Abb. Burton Propr. **Patron:** Marquis of Anglesey. **Impropriator:** Lord Bagot, by purchase from Lord Anglesey of the principal part of the Tythes.[1]
CHURCH: A handsome spacious Gothic structure – nave and two side aisles – pointed Arches, except that leading into the Chancel which, as well as the Tower, were rebuilt in modern style about 1700. **Number it will contain:** 648 in pews.[2] **Accommodation for Poor:** 100 – obtained by grant from the Society in 1826. **Roof:** Deal covered principally with lead – one aisle and Chancel with tiles – the ceiling open [carved] wood work. **Walls:** Stone – good. **Floor:** Quarries – even. **Windows:** Pretty good – four more casements wanted. **Doors:** Good – those on N. and S. new. **Pulpit and Desk:** Neat, but ill-placed – handsome velvet cushions. **Books:** Out of repair. **Seats:** New five years ago – uniform, painted deal. **Galleries:** Organ gallery. **Organ:** There is one – just put up. **Font:** [There is one.] **Chapels:** None. **Benefaction Tables:** Two – sufficient. **Vestry:** None – one recommended. **Surplices:** Two – one very bad. **Linen:** Provided. **Plate:** Flagon, Chalice; two Patins and Plate for offerings. **Iron Chest for Register:** At the Vicarage.

Register: From 1558 to present time, perfect and in excellent preservation. **Porch:** None. **Vaults:** Several – no new ones to be allowed. **Cleanliness:** Not properly attended to. **Damp:** Not much appearance. **Dimensions:** 58ft. 6in. by 62ft.
CHANCEL: 40ft. by 22ft. **Table:** Firm and good – wants cleaning. **Ornaments:** None. **Repaired by whom:** The Marquis of Anglesey.
STEEPLE: A square stone Tower, built in 1700. **State of:** Good. **Bells:** Five – good. **Clock:** There is one.
CHURCHYARD: **Fence:** Partly brick walls – partly rails and posts; kept [up] by the Parish. **Gates:** The principal ones iron – new. **Drains:** There are – but not in good order. **Graves:** Too near the walls. **Rubbish:** Weeds and nettles in abundance. **Footpaths:** A thoroughfare through the Churchyard; which is to be stopped if possible. **Cattle:** The Curate's horse.
DIVINE SERVICE: **On Sundays:** Full service morning and evening on Sundays. **On other Days:** None (except on Good Friday etc). **Sacrament:** Eight times a year. **Communicants:** From 20 to 50.
INCUMBENT: **Name and Residence:** Revd HF Cary. **If not resident:** At the British Museum [London].
CURATE: **Name and Residence:** Revd John Neale, Vicarage. **Licensed:** He is. **Salary:** £75 and the house. **If serving another church:** Gayton [since discontinued 1831].
PARSONAGE: A brick building, consisting of three sitting rooms, kitchen and pantry on ground floor – five bedrooms. **State of:** Good substantial repair.[3] **Outbuildings:** Stable and Gig-house – good repair.
INCOME: **Gross Value:** £210 per annum. **Tithes:** £60 or 70. **Glebe:** 38 acres. **Easter Dues and small Payments:**[4] Collected. **Queen Anne's Bounty:** None. **Terrier:** The Clerk has one.
SCHOOLS: **Endowed School:** A Free Grammar School, endowed with £20 per annum (charged on land near Cheadle) and a house – left by a Mr Clark. **Subscription Day School:** None. **Sunday School:** There are two – 70 in each. **Lancaster School:** None.
DISSENTERS: **Dissenters' School:** ——. **Dissenting Chapels:** Independent.
POPULATION: In 1821, 1,535.
PARISH CLERK: William Eason. **Appointed by:** The Vicar. **Salary:** £6 0s. 0d.
CHURCHWARDENS: Mr John Williams for the Parish. Mr John Woodrooffe for the Vicar.
ORDERS MADE: Four additional casements to be made in the body of the Church and one in the Chancel. The Bible and Prayer Books to be repaired, and a new Surplice provided. Cleanliness more duly attended to, and neatness in the Churchyard. The drains cleared out and kept open. The thoroughfare of the Churchyard to be stopped, if practicable. A Vestry *recommended*.

Revisited 11.9.1837
Directions to the Churchwardens. (1) The roofs of the Chancel and Tower to be repaired. (2) Overshot spouts removed and down-pipes substituted. (3) Metal spouts and pipes *painted*. (4) Windows, all round, repaired and bars painted. (5) Chancel ceilings repaired and whitewashed. (6) Wainscot of pews on S. side repaired. (7) Bible and Prayer Book repaired or renewed – new Surplice. (8) Nettles etc removed from walls – a brick drain or gravel walk formed all round. (9) Walks kept clear. (10) East wall of Churchyard repaired and the trespass of Churchyard prevented by building a wall on the NW. side of the Churchyard.
Recommended – change of position of Pulpit. 'Nothing done (R.D.). Surplice.'

Revisited 8.9.1841
(1) New Prayer Books for Clergyman and Clerk – Bible rebound. (2) Bars of windows painted.
Outside. (3) The plinth stones to be carefully pointed with cement. (4) The open drain kept clear of weeds. (5) The North Chancel roofs examined and repaired – weatherboards pointed – tiles repaired – gutters laid level – copings pointed. (6) The NE. corner of the Chancel, at the lower part, to be secured – copings of W. roof ditto.
Churchyard. (7) Fence on South side to be raised, and the stile taken away, and trespass paths stopped – gate placed at the SW. corner. (8) The window sill on the W. of the Tower repaired; weatherboards to circular window of ditto.

[1] 'Marquis of Anglesey' in *Eccles. Revs.* [2] *Eccles. Revs.:* 800. [3] *Eccles. Revs.:* 'Fit.' [4] A/V/1/4: 'and small Payments' enclosed in brackets.

ALTON 16.7.1830 (A/V/1/4,p.44;A/V/1/2,p.104)

BENEFICE: Alveton (or Alton). Ecton Alneton. **Nature:** Vicarage. **Ecton:** Mon. Croxden Impr. Clear value £41 0s. 0d. **Patron:** The Earl of Shrewsbury. **Impropriator:** Mr Bill of Farley and Mr Saunders of Burton.[1]
CHURCH: An antient Saxon building, as appears from the circular pillars and arches on the North side of the Nave, and circular arch leading to the Chancel. **Number it will contain:** 344[2] – as stated in the application for Aid to the Incorporated Society. **Accommodation for Poor:** 65[3] – as stated in the application for Aid to the Incorporated Society. **Roof:** Oak covered with lead. **Walls:** Stone – that on the North side lately re-built. **Floor:** Flags – very uneven and bad; much undermined by graves. **Windows:** Those on the N. side new – on the S. bad and broken – *no casements*. **Doors:** One – old and very bad. **Pulpit and Desk:** Old and infirm – stone steps leading to them. **Books:** New – in the Reading Desk. **Seats:** Most of them very bad and irregular – a few new ones built without authority, or any regard to uniformity of appearance or general convenience. **Galleries:** One at the W. end. **Organ:** None. **Font:** There is one – no basin. **Chapels:** None. **Benefaction Tables:** There are. **Vestry:** A new one – very damp. **Surplices:** Two – one new. **Linen:** Provided. **Plate:** Silver Cup and Patin; pewter flagon and dish. **Iron Chest for Register:** In the Vestry. **Register:** None earlier than *1681*, and not regularly kept from that time. **Porch:** An old one, on the S. side, much out of repair – no light gates. **Vaults:** Several – or rather *earthgraves*, under the whole floor. **Cleanliness:** Much neglected. **Damp:** Much in every part. **Dimensions:** 56ft. by 39ft. 3in.

CHANCEL: 23ft. 7in. by 20ft. 10in. **Table:** Oak – wants cleaning. **Ornaments:** None. **Repaired by whom:** The Impropriators – much however is wanting to put it into proper state. The roof and ceiling out of repair – pews bad – floor damp – one window blocked up.
STEEPLE: Square stone tower. **State of:** Not very good – a large crack down one side – pointing wanted. **Bells:** Six – good; the belfry wants whitewashing and weatherboards put up.[4] **Clock:** There is one, much out of repair.
CHURCHYARD: **Fence:** Stone wall – good – kept up by the Parish; an addition has lately been made to the Churchyard, which is now being enclosed, very handsomely. **Gates:** Good – those at the principal entrance [new –] iron. **Drains:** None – earth much accumulated against the walls. **Graves:** Many too near the walls. **Rubbish:** None. **Footpaths:** The proper Paths well kept; no trespass paths. **Cattle:** A horse hitherto.
DIVINE SERVICE: **On Sundays:** Two full services. **On other Days:** None. **Sacrament:** Four times a year. **Communicants:** 15 to 20. **Catechism:** Not at present.
INCUMBENT: **Name and Residence:** Revd John Pike Jones.[5] **If not resident:** In Devonshire.
CURATE: **Name and Residence:** Revd John Cotterill, in lodgings in the Parish. **Licensed:** Licence not yet received from the Bishop. **If serving another church:** No other.
PARSONAGE: A small house; unfit in its present state for the residence of the Clergyman, and now occupied by a labourer – in the service of Lord Shrewsbury. **State of:** Not very good.[6] **Outbuildings:** A small stable.
INCOME: **Gross Value:** About £150. **Easter Dues and small Payments:**[7] Collected. **Queen Anne's Bounty:** Not ascertained. **Terrier:** In the Register there is a Copy.
SCHOOLS: **Endowed School:** There is one, for instruction of 12 boys – arising from land, £12 per annum. **Subscription Day School:** A Girls' school just established. **Sunday School:** 70 or 80. **Lancaster School:** None.
DISSENTERS: **Dissenters' School:** A Roman Catholic School, supported by Lord Shrewsbury – about 40 attend – Calvinist Sunday School. **Dissenting Chapels:** Calvinists and Primitive Methodists.
POPULATION: Of the whole Parish 2,000 [last census] – 1,500 within two miles of the Church – 2,356 (1830).
PARISH CLERK: Godfrey Wilson – incapable of duty – his son officiates. **Appointed by:** The Vicar.
CHURCHWARDENS: Mr Charles Smith – Sidesmen appointed for Farley and Cotton.
ORDERS MADE: The roof to be carefully examined and put in thorough repair – the floor taken up, raised and laid even. Two casements to be made on each side of the Nave – one each side of the Chancel. The windows mended – new door on the South side; and light gates at the Porch entrance – the Porch repaired. The Pulpit and reading desk repaired and proper steps made (*recommended* that the whole be new). A Basin for the Font – cleanliness attended to – no more graves inside [the Church]. The S. aisle to be *new-pewed*, on a regular plan, and so as to afford more room for the poor.

In the Chancel. The roof and ceiling to be put in thorough repair – the floor cleared from damp – the pews repaired or renewed – the window on the North side restored – the Table and rails cleaned with oil. The Tower to be examined and secured – weatherboards put up – the lower window of the Tower glazed – the belfry whitewashed and clock repaired. The earth removed to a proper depth outside the walls – and an open drain formed – no graves allowed within ten feet. No large cattle allowed to feed in the Churchyard.

Since my visit, and in consequence of my suggestions, the Church has been thoroughly repaired and the South aisle enlarged, new floored and new pewed – Pulpit and reading desk new – several additional sittings for the poor, both below and in the Gallery obtained.

For these important improvements a grant was obtained from the Society – the remaining expenses defrayed partly by Subscribers, partly by money borrowed on the credit of the Church rates (1831).[8]

Revisited 28.9.1837
Directions. Additional burial ground consecrated. Open drain kept clear. Gallery roof ditto – roof protected by lead flashings at E. and W. ends. Skylight ditto. Belfry staircase repaired – door placed at the going out on *the tower*. East window repaired – water table formed – casement on each side of Chancel. Kneeling board for Clerk's desk. Down-pipe at SW. angle repaired – all pipes painted. Thoroughfare of Churchyard stopped – children kept out – nettles and rubbish cleared away and tomb-stones removed from East wall. South door varnished.

Revisited 28.9.1841
Directions to Churchwardens. (1) Tower to be carefully examined by an experienced Surveyor, and his opinion taken respecting the cause of the violent disjunction of the battlements at the SW. angles of the Tower – which must be replaced and secured according to his recommendations. I wish his opinion also to be taken as to the prudence of leaving the NW. side of the Tower unsupported by a buttress. If he deems it needful, the buttress must be restored – if otherwise the surface of the wall must be cased where the buttress formerly stood. (2) Lead flashings on roof of Tower replaced and secured. (3) Roof of Church examined and repaired where needful. (4) Chancel walls pointed externally at base – ground lowered, and open drains formed on S. side. (5) Drain formed to carry off the wet from S. side of Church – also from N. and S. sides of Tower. (6) Churchyard wall on N. side raised – or road lowered, to prevent the Churchyard from being made a playground – and otherwise trespassed upon. Gravel walks cleansed, and kept free from weeds. Nettles eradicated, or kept down. No heavy cattle suffered to graze in Churchyard. (7) Additional burial ground obtained immediately, and consecrated. (8) Thoroughfare of Churchyard stopped, and trespass paths forbidden. (9) Broken windows of Church and Chancel mended.

[1] *Eccles. Revs.:* 'Earl of Shrewsbury and others'. [2] 'About 500' deleted. *Eccles. Revs.:* 1,000. [3] 'About 100' deleted. [4] A/V/1/4: 'repaired'. [5] Also rector of Butterleigh (Devon): *Eccles. Revs.* [6] *Eccles. Revs.:* 'Unfit.' [7] 'And small Payments' enclosed in brackets. [8] Faculty granted 19.10.1830 (B/C/2/1829–32.p.290) for the repewing and internal replanning of the church, rebuilding the S. aisle and extending the W. gallery.

BARTON UNDER NEEDWOOD 14.7.1829
(A/V/1/4,p.45;A/V/1/2,p.9)

BENEFICE: Barton under Needwood – eight miles from Lichfield – formerly chapel of ease to Tatenhill – but recently made a perpetual Curacy. **Nature:** Perpetual Curacy. **Ecton:** £25 clear value. **Patron:** Dean of Lichfield. **Impropriator.**[1]
CHURCH: A handsome Gothic stone building, with a middle and two side aisles. **Number it will contain:** 900 including. **Accommodation for Poor:** 250 in addition to sittings for children. **Roof:** Timber covered with lead. **Walls:** Stone, in a very good sound state. **Floor:** Along the *aisles*, brick, the pews have *boarded* floors. **Windows:** Whole and in good repair, except that of the belfry. **Doors:** In good order. **Pulpit and Desk:** Oak: in good repair, velvet covering to reading desk, and cushion to the Pulpit. **Books:** In very good state. **Seats:** Of oak: in good repair, excepting one or two of the floors. **Galleries:** One over the west entrance, for the organ and singers, and one over each side aisle. **Organ:** There is one given by Mr Wyatt: organist paid by the Parish. **Font:** Of stone. **Chapels:** None. **Benefaction Tables:** There are three; but there are other bequests not recorded publicly in the church. **Vestry:** There is one – small, but convenient, and in good repair. **Surplices:** Three – in good repair. **Linen:** One table cloth – one napkin – both good. **Plate:** Only a small silver Cup and Paten – the Flagon and salver of Pewter – very shabby. **Chest for Papers:** There is one of Oak in the Vestry – proposed to remove it to the select vestry room, at the Workhouse. **Iron Chest for Register:** There is one. **Register:** Six vols: commencing from 1571, all, at present, kept in the Clerk's house, except those now in use. **Porch:** None. **Vaults:** None recently made. **Cleanliness:** Attended to. **Damp:** Very little appearance of it. **Dimensions:** 62ft. 6in. long, 39ft. 3in. wide.
CHANCEL: 43ft. long, 16ft. wide. **Table:** Of oak – good in itself; but without any other covering than an old green cloth, in poor condition. **Ornaments:** None: except some good painted glass[2] in the East window. **Repaired by whom:** The township of Barton – since the separation of the Church from the Mother church of Tatenhill – it is at present in good repair and order.
STEEPLE: Square stone tower. **State of:** Apparently very good. **Bells:** Six: one a little cracked. **Clock:** There is one – in good order.
CHURCHYARD: **Fence:** On the north side a brick wall, on the east side, palisades, repaired by the Township. On the south and west, posts and rails, repaired in *doles*, except a garden wall for some part on the West side. No part in very good repair. **Gates:** Five in number, besides light gates for funerals etc. **Drains:** None, the water conveyed from the roof by projecting spouts – no provision for receiving or carrying off the water. **Graves:** Several quite close to the walls. **Rubbish:** None. **Footpaths:** Five good ones – besides which a *trespass* path has been made, across some of the graves. **Cattle:** Sheep only – the herbage belongs to the Incumbent, who lets the Clerk have the use of it.
DIVINE SERVICE: **On Sundays:** Two full services – Morning and Afternoon. **On other Days:** None, except on Good Friday and Christmas day. Prayers on Saints' days, and on Wednesday and Friday in Lent. **Sacrament:** Seven times yearly. **Communicants:** Average 70. **Catechism:** Taught at the Sunday school.
INCUMBENT: **Name and Residence:** Revd James Gisborne, resides in the Parsonage house. **If not resident:** ——. **What Duty he performs:** All the duty ordinarily.
CURATE: **Name and Residence:** None.
PARSONAGE: Built in 1816, on land appropriated by Queen Anne's Bounty; small and comfortable – two parlours, small study, four bedrooms. **State of:** In perfect repair.[3] **Outbuildings:** None, except common household offices.
INCOME: **Gross Value:** £135 per annum (including the augmentation mentioned under article 70). **Tithes:** None. **Surplice Fees:** £2 10s. 0d. per annum. **Easter Dues and small Payments:** None. **Queen Anne's Bounty:** £53 per annum. **Terrier:** There is one, upon a brass plate in the Chancel wall recording the annual payment, which used to be made to the Curate, whilst it was a chapel of ease to Tatenhill and also the surplice fees.
SCHOOLS: **Endowed School:** A free school for boys, endowed by the Drapers' company, London – attended by about 75 boys – recently placed on the footing of a National school. **Subscription Day School:** A girls' school containing from 60 to 70. **Sunday School:** 75 boys – 65 or 70 girls. **Lancaster School:** None.
DISSENTERS: **Dissenters' School:** None. **Dissenting Chapels:** Two: Baptist and Methodist – erected within the last two years – about 50 together attend.
POPULATION: 1,500.[4]
MISCELLANEOUS: **Monuments:** Two: in the Chancel. **Chandeliers, etc:** Church lighted with lamps, suspended from the roof. **Parochial Library:** There is one – kept in the Vestry.
PARISH CLERK: John Scarratt. **Appointed by:** The Incumbent. **Salary:** Five Pounds.
CHURCHWARDENS: Stephen Hawkesworth and Francis Shaw, one appointed by the Minister, other by parishioners.
ORDERS MADE: In the Chancel. A new covering for the Table – the rails repaired – the Sunday School boys to be removed from within the rails. Vestry. A large iron chest, capable of holding *all* the Registers. Belfry. The present entrance into the Organ gallery, blocked up, and a new one made, *from below;* without going through the belfry. Nave. The floors of some of the pews to be repaired. Churchyard. The *trespass path,* prohibited – earth removed from the walls – some method of carrying off the water, to be provided. No more graves to be allowed nearer the walls than six feet. The palisade fence, and the wall in some places put in repair.

[The latter order however accompanied with

a strong recommendation to the Churchwardens, to endeavour to prevail upon the Parish (or Township) to take upon themselves the repair of *the whole,* west side) and build a wall on the East, South, and west sides.

An enquiry also into the right of private entrance into the Churchyard, through a door in the garden wall, recommended to the Churchwardens.]

The procuring of a silver Flagon and Salver, in lieu of the Pewter one, *recommended,* but not *ordered.*

Revisited 1.9.1837

The state of the Church and its precincts much improved since my last visit. The dilapidated wooden fence on the E., N. and NW. sides of the Churchyard has been removed, and a brick wall built in its stead – The Church itself neat and clean.

The only directions needful were – (1) That the water from the roofs should be more effectually carried away from the foot of the walls; for which purpose I strongly *recommended* the substitution of *down-pipes* for the *over-shot* spouts now in use. (2) That the gate on the N. side of the Churchyard – now used for the admission of carriages at weddings and occasionally on Sundays – but not needful for any legitimate purposes – should be closed – or rather, *taken away* and the wall built up. (3) That the Bible in the Reading Desk be repaired. (I omitted to enquire whether my former order as to the Iron Register Chest had been complied with; and did not think it necessary to repeat the order as to the Gallery entrances.)

Revisited 7.9.1841

(1) Roofs inspected – lead work, gutters and flashings repaired. (2) Battlements, copings, and pinnacles secured. (3) Clerestory windows repaired – also skylights. (4) Mouths of down-pipes protected by coverings. (5) Churchyard gates locked – thoroughfare stopped.

[1] *Eccles. Revs.:* 'Dean of Lichfield'. [2] A/V/1/4: '... some handsome old stained glass . . .' [3] *Eccles. Revs.:* 'Fit.' [4] *Eccles. Revs.:* 1,344.

BLITHFIELD 13.7.1830
(A/V/1/4,p.46;A/V/1/2,p.88)

BENEFICE: Blithfield. **Nature:** Rectory. **Ecton:** Kings Books £10 19s. 2d. **Patron:** Lord Bagot.
CHURCH: A very handsome, regular, Gothic building – nave, side aisles and Chancel – pointed Arches – open carved ceiling. **Number it will contain:** 150 to 200.[1] **Accommodation for Poor:** About 50 – sufficient for population. **Roof:** In good repair. **Walls:** Stone – upright. **Floor:** Quarries – even and dry. **Windows:** Good – but more casements wanted. **Doors:** Good. **Pulpit and Desk:** Handsome and well placed. **Books:** Good, except the Clerk's Prayer Book. **Seats:** In good condition – pews and open seats. **Galleries:** One at the W. end. **Organ:** There is one. **Font:** Qu? **Chapels:** None. **Benefaction Tables:** Three. **Vestry:** A small one is now being built. **Surplices:** Two. **Linen:** Table Cloth and Napkin. **Plate:** Flagon, two Cups, Patin – a basin for offerings. **Chest for Papers:** Two. **Iron Chest for Register:** Kept at the Parsonage. **Register:** From 1538 to 1650, and from 1658 to 1812 – and thence to present time. **Porch:** None, except at the W. entrance – which is guarded by a light iron gate. **Vaults:** None recently. **Cleanliness:** Attended to. **Damp:** No appearance.
CHANCEL: **Table:** Handsome. **Ornaments:** Old painted glass – and several monuments to the Bagot family. **Repaired by whom:** Lord Bagot – everything very neat and in excellent order.
STEEPLE: Square stone tower – with a cornice apparently modern. **State of:** Good, except in some parts near the base, which have been injured by ivy. **Bells:** Three – good.
CHURCHYARD: **Fence:** Stone wall and paling – good. **Gates:** Good. **Drains:** None near the walls – but a gravel walk all round. **Graves, Rubbish, Footpaths, Cattle:** Everything properly attended to.
DIVINE SERVICE: **On Sundays:** Two services. **On other Days:** None regularly. **Sacrament:** Six times [in the year] at least. **Communicants:** Vary from 40 to 111. **Catechism:** During Lent.
INCUMBENT: **Name and Residence:** Hon. and Rt. Revd Lord Bishop of Oxford. **What Duty he performs:** Shares with his Curate, when in residence.
CURATE: **Name and Residence:** John James Cory, Blithfield. ['Hon. Francis Paget.'] **Licensed:** Not. **Salary:** Liberal – but not specified.[2] **If serving another church:** None.
PARSONAGE: A new handsome spacious house.[3] **State of:** In complete repair. **Outbuildings:** Ditto.
INCOME: **Gross Value, Tithes, Glebe, Surplice Fees, Easter Dues and small Payments, Queen Anne's Bounty, Terrier:** Not ascertained – neither the Incumbent nor his Curate being at home when I visited the Church.[4]
SCHOOLS: **Endowed School:** None. **Subscription Day School:** None – but Lord Bagot supports two schools, one for boys, the other for girls, the latter of whom are also clothed. **Sunday School:** One for both sexes. **Lancaster School:** None.
DISSENTERS: **Dissenters' School:** None. **Dissenting Chapels:** None.
POPULATION: 475 at the last census.
MISCELLANEOUS: **Monument:** Several to the Bagot family, and some others. **Parochial Library:** There is one; containing 44 Vols.
PARISH CLERK: Thomas Cooke. **Appointed by:** The Rector. **Salary:** £5 per annum.
CHURCHWARDENS: Mr John Kent and Lewis Burgess.
ORDERS MADE: Additional casements in the Church. The walls of the Church to be under-built and otherwise repaired where necessary – especially at the East end and North side. The paling (for sheep) at the NE. side of the Church to be removed.

Revisited 28.3.1838

Everything in excellent order, both externally and internally. Attention directed to some of the copings and one of the pinnacles on the North side of the Church – and to the necessity of keeping the water-courses of the roofs free from obstruction.

[1] *Eccles. Revs.:* 'Sufficient'. [2] *Eccles. Revs.:* £150. [3] *Eccles. Revs.:* 'Fit'. [4] *Eccles. Revs.:* Gross income £468.

BLORE 19.7.1830 (A/V/1/4,p.47;A/V/1/2,p.110)

BENEFICE: Blore (Ecton. Blore Roy). **Nature:** Rectory. **Ecton:** Clear value £47 0s. 0d. Abb. Burton 13s. 4d. **Patron:** Mr Shore of Sheffield. (Ecton. Duke of Newcastle.)
CHURCH: An antient Gothic structure – said to be 800 years old – two aisles separated by pointed Arches and pillars; Chancel with pointed Arch. **Number it will contain:** About 200. **Accommodation for Poor:** Sufficient. **Roof:** Oak, covered with lead – wants repair. **Walls:** Stone – upright; – but very dirty. **Floor:** Brick – even. **Windows:** Pretty good – additional casements wanted, and some repairs. **Doors:** Good. **Pulpit and Desk:** Very good – handsome crimson velvet cushion and hangings. **Books:** Good – slight repairs wanted. **Seats:** [Good.] **Galleries:** A small one at the W. end. **Organ:** None. **Font:** A very handsome old one – cover and basin wanted. **Chapels:** None – but at the end of the N. aisle is an enclosure containing a remarkably handsome monument to William Bassett, stated (in the inscription) to have obtained his estate from William the Conqueror. **Benefaction Tables:** None. **Vestry:** None. **Surplices:** One – very dirty. **Linen:** Provided – but not well kept. **Plate:** A plated Cup, and old pewter flagon. **Chest for Papers:** An old one – wants repair. **Iron Chest for Register:** None. **Register:** Kept by the Rector, at Ashbourn; not seen. **Porch:** There is one – out of repair. **Vaults:** None lately. **Cleanliness:** Not sufficiently attended to. **Damp:** Much on the walls. **Dimensions:** 36ft. 2in. by 31ft. 3in.
CHANCEL: 29ft. 9in. by 13ft. 11in. **Table:** Oak – wants repair and cleaning. **Ornaments:** Some remains of old painted glass, and tabernacle work against the walls. **Repaired by whom:** The Rector – the ceiling, wainscot and windows need repair.
STEEPLE: Square stone tower. **State of:** Pointing wanted and battlements secured. **Bells:** Three. **Clock:** None.
CHURCHYARD: **Fence:** Wall of loose stones – pretty good. **Gates:** Good. **Drains:** None – earth much accumulated. **Graves:** Some too near. **Rubbish:** Weeds etc. **Footpaths:** Thoroughfare. **Cattle:** A horse.
DIVINE SERVICE: **On Sundays:** Once – in the afternoon, except first Sunday in the month. **On other Days:** None (except Good Friday etc). **Sacrament:** Three times a year. **Communicants:** Seven or eight. **Catechism:** Before the Confirmation.
INCUMBENT: **Name and Residence:** Revd W Bayliffe. **If not resident:** At Ashborn. **What Duty he performs:** The whole.
PARSONAGE: There is one – but not fit for the Clergyman's residence.[1]
INCOME: **Gross Value:** From £120 to 150 per annum. **Easter Dues and small Payments:**[2] Collected. **Terrier:** There is one.
SCHOOLS: **Endowed School:** None. **Subscription Day School:** None. **Sunday School:** None – the children attend the schools at Mayfield and Ilam.[3]
DISSENTERS: **Dissenting Chapels:** A Methodist meeting.
POPULATION: Under 600.[4]

PARISH CLERK: John Waterfall. **Appointed by:** The Rector. **Salary:** None fixed.
CHURCHWARDENS: Mr Sutton.
ORDERS MADE: The roof to be examined and repaired – the lead gutters cleaned out; the Tower pointed; battlements repaired – iron cramps of Tower, and iron-work of the Bells etc painted – Belfry door put up and floor repaired, Bell-chamber cleared of rubbish, and walls of belfry whitewashed – Ivy and other shrubs to be removed from the walls – the walls and buttresses pointed and otherwise repaired. The earth cleared away all round the walls, and an open drain formed – pipes put up to convey the wet from the roof. Two casements made in the body of the Church, the lead-work of the windows repaired and iron bars painted. The Books put in good repair – a Cover and basin provided for the Font – the Parish Chest repaired and the Flagon now in it made fit for use. The floor and window of the North Chancel repaired – the Communion Table repaired and cleaned – Wainscot and screen of the Rector's Chancel repaired – and the roof and windows put into proper state. The Surplice and Communion Linen kept clean, and cleanliness better attended to, generally, throughout the Church.

Revisited 13.9.1837
The Church and its precincts still in a sad state of dilapidation and disorder: scarcely anything done to it since my former visit.
Directed – (1) That the roofs be thoroughly examined by an experienced Architect, and repaired according to his report. The lead covering, if incapable of repair, to be taken off, and slate substituted in its stead. (2) The walls, buttresses, tower etc to be examined, repaired, pointed and otherwise repaired – likewise the bells and belfry floor. (3) The windows repaired and the iron bars painted. (4) The floors of both Chancels relaid – the stalls and pews of the Rector's Chancel repaired; the windows mended etc. (5) Eave-spouts, down-pipes, drain, open drain all round. (6) Roof of Porch repaired. (7) Trespass paths stopped, and a gravel walk formed leading to the Church door.
Two years allowed for the above repairs. 'Nothing done.'

Revisited 20.9.1841
Found the Church undergoing thorough repair.

[1] *Eccles. Revs.:* 'Unfit.' [2] 'And small payments' enclosed in brackets. [3] This comment relates to questions 73 and 74. [4] *Eccles. Revs.:* 299.

BRADLEY IN THE MOORS 16.7.1830 (A/V/1/4,p.48;A/V/1/2,p.105)

BENEFICE: Bradley in the Moors. **Nature:** Perpetual Curacy. **Ecton:** Note. Bradley is an Impropriation in Sir Nathanael Curzon – only a Curacy remains, which is certified to be of the yearly value of £3 6s. 8d. **Patron:** Lord Shrewsbury. **Impropriator:** Ditto.
CHURCH: A small neat building; rebuilt in 1750, single body, small chancel, circular arches. **Number it will contain:** 150. **Accommodation for Poor:** Sufficient. **Roof:** Timber covered with tile

– in good repair. **Walls:** Stone – good. **Floor:** Bricks – even. **Windows:** Good – but casements insufficient. **Doors:** Good. **Pulpit and Desk:** Very neat – velvet hangings and cushion. **Books:** Good. **Seats:** ——. **Galleries:** None. **Organ:** ——. **Font:** There is one. **Chapels:** None. **Benefaction Tables:** None – a small one wanted. **Vestry:** None. **Surplices:** One, good. **Linen:** Provided. **Plate:** Silver Cup, (flagon, Basin for Alms) – Pewter. **Iron Chest for Register:** In the wall of the Church. **Register:** From 1708 to present time. **Porch:** None. **Vaults:** Some – not to be allowed henceforth. **Cleanliness:** Attended to. **Damp:** No appearance.

CHANCEL: **Table:** Very good – but wants cleaning; as do the rails. **Ornaments:** None. **Repaired by whom:** Lord Shrewsbury.

STEEPLE: **Square stone Tower. State of:** Good. **Bells:** Two. **Clock:** None.

CHURCHYARD: **Fence:** Partly by the Parish, partly tenants of the adjoining land; the hedges want trimming. **Gates:** Good. **Drains:** None. **Graves:** Some too near. **Rubbish:** None. **Footpaths:** No improper ones. **Cattle:** Cows – not to be continued.

DIVINE SERVICE: **On Sundays:** Alternately Morning and Afternoon. **On other Days:** None. **Sacrament:** Five times a year. **Communicants:** 12. **Catechism:** In the School.

INCUMBENT: **Name and Residence:** Revd E Whieldon. **If not resident:** 3½ miles from the Church. **What Duty he performs:** The whole.

PARSONAGE: None.

INCOME: Tithes: £3 6s. 8d. paid in lieu of Tithes. **Queen Anne's Bounty:** £53. **Terrier:** None.

SCHOOLS: **Endowed School:** None. **Subscription Day School:** None. **Sunday School:** 38 children. **Lancaster School:** None.

DISSENTERS: **Dissenters' School:** ——. **Dissenting Chapels:** ——.

POPULATION: About 70.

PARISH CLERK: G Hervey. **Appointed by:** The Minister. **Salary:** £2 0s. 0d. and fees.

CHURCHWARDENS: Mr John Smith.

ORDERS MADE: The bars of the windows to be painted. Benefaction recorded. The hedges in the Churchyard trimmed and ditches cleared out. Spouts, pipes and open drain – no graves too near [the walls]. No large cattle to feed in the Churchyard.

Revisited 28.9.1837
Footpath to be stopped and locks put on gates [– 'done']. Roof of tower examined [– 'will be']. Vestry *recommended*.

28.9.1841
Not visited – but Prayer Book for Clerk ordered to be provided.

BRAMSHALL 14.7.1830
(A/V/1/4,p.49;A/V/1/2,p.93)

BENEFICE: Bromshall [or Bromshelf] ('olim Bromshelfe, alias Bromshif'). **Nature:** Rectory. **Ecton:** Living discharged. Clear value £39 0s. 0d. **Patron:** Lord Willoughby de Broke. **Impropriator:** None.

CHURCH: An old inelegant building – single body – pointed Arches. **Number it will contain:** 150 exclusive of Gallery.[1] **Accommodation for Poor:** Sufficient. **Roof:** Oak – covered with shingles – out of repair. **Walls:** Solid stone – much out of perpendicular and dangerous at the SE. side. **Floor:** Quarries and flags – sunk in one part. **Windows:** No casements – iron bars want painting. **Doors:** Tolerably good – lining wanted. **Pulpit and Desk:** Good – velvet Cushion to Pulpit. **Books:** New Prayer Book wanted for Clerk. **Seats:** Not in good repair. **Galleries:** A small one for singers. **Organ:** None. **Font:** There is [one]. **Chapels:** None. **Benefaction Tables:** Provided. **Vestry:** A new one. **Surplices:** Two. **Linen:** Provided. **Plate:** Chalice and Patin – Britannia metal. **Iron Chest for Register:** Not a suitable one. **Register:** Only from 1770. **Porch:** There is one – an iron or other light gate wanted. **Vaults:** Only one of recent date. **Cleanliness:** Not sufficiently attended to. **Damp:** No appearance. **Dimensions:** 42ft. by 22ft. 6in.

CHANCEL: 25ft. 6in. **Table:** Oak – wants cleaning. **Ornaments:** None. **Repaired by whom:** The Rector – it is in a very dangerous state – held together only by iron cramps which gird the outer walls.

STEEPLE: Bell tower. **State of:** Bad repair. **Bells:** Three – wheels want looking over.[2] **Clock:** None.

CHURCHYARD: **Fence:** Posts and rails all round; kept up by the Parish; not in good state. **Gates:** Bad. **Drains:** None – nor spouts. **Graves:** Several too near the walls. **Rubbish:** Some heaps of bricks. **Footpaths:** There are some which ought to be stopped; the proper Church ways are not properly kept. **Cattle:** Cows – to be forbidden.

DIVINE SERVICE: **On Sundays:** Morning and afternoon alternately. **On other Days:** None. **Sacrament:** Four times a year. **Communicants:** From 20 to 30. **Catechism:** At the Sunday School.

INCUMBENT: **Name and Residence:** Revd John Sneyd. **If not resident:** At Elford, his other living. **What duty he performs:** None.

CURATE: **Name and Residence:** Revd Brian Sneyd Broughton, in the Parsonage house. **Licensed:** Licence not yet received – but papers sent in. **Salary:** £50 and surplice fees. **If serving another church:** Stowe, at present.

PARSONAGE: A small neat building – erected in 1809 – two parlours etc. **State of:** Good.[3] **Outbuildings:** Barn, stable etc.

INCOME: **Gross Value:** About £150[4] per annum (as far as I could collect). **Tithes:** £64 10s. 0d. **Glebe:** £76. **Easter Dues and small Payments:**[5] £2 3s. 4d. **Terrier:** The Church warden has a Copy – dated 1809.

SCHOOLS: **Endowed School:** None. **Subscription Day School:** None. **Sunday School:** 50 children. **Lancaster School:** None.

DISSENTERS: **Dissenters' School:** ——. **Dissenting Chapels:** ——.

POPULATION: In 1821, 189.

PARISH CLERK: Joseph Foster. **Appointed by:** The Rector. **Salary:** 15s. by the Parish; he collects 12s. besides.

CHURCHWARDENS: Mr Thomas Warner.

ORDERS MADE: The state of the South wall and Chancel to be examined by an Architect and reported. The roof examined and repaired – the Bell tower do and coping stones at the W. end of the roof. Spouts, pipes and an open drain. The Churchyard fence repaired – gates ditto – ways widened – rubbish removed – cows not allowed – no graves within ten feet. The floors of the Pews to be repaired, and that of the middle Aisle [lain even], where sunk. Four casements to be made, and the iron bars of the windows painted. The doors to be lined inside. A new Prayer Book provided for the Clerk – and a proper iron Register Chest.

Revisited 11.9.1837

A new and substantial Church has been built since my former visit – capable of containing, I should think, from 100 to 150 persons.[6] I found however much appearance of *damp*, arising apparently from want of Ventilation. I directed a Casement to be opened in the Vestry window – and attention to be paid to having the windows regularly set open in fine weather. A *new Bible* to be provided for the Reading desk. The thoroughfare of the Churchyard to be stopped. The Surplice to be kept at the Clerk's house, till the Vestry is free from damp. 'Qu? attended to?'

Revisited September 1841

The book-desk repaired – roof examined. Churchyard kept neat and clean from nettles and herbage cleared away from the walls – thoroughfare stopped, if possible.

[1] *Eccles. Revs.:* 'Sufficient'. [2] A/V/1/4: '. . . want repair'. [3] *Eccles. Revs.:* 'Fit.' [4] *Eccles. Revs.:* Gross income £100. [5] 'And small Payments' enclosed in brackets. [6] Faculty granted 1.7.1835 (B/C/2/1832–6, p.502). The architect was WM Crowther.

BURTON UPON TRENT 1.10.1829
(A/V/1/4,p.50;A/V/1/2,p.1)

BENEFICE: Old Church, Burton [on Trent]. **Nature:** Perpetual Curacy. **Ecton:** Not certified – olim an Abbey – living discharged. **Patron:** Marquis of Anglesey. **Impropriator:** Ditto.
CHURCH: Modern Grecian building – middle and side aisles; and small Chancel (which latter is little more than the space formed by the circular form of the Church at the East end). **Number it will contain:** 1,800.[1] **Accommodation for Poor:** 30 on benches in the middle aisle, and children along the walls in the gallery. **Roof:** Oak covered with lead. **Walls:** Stone – upright and in good repair. **Floor:** Flags – even and in good state; but in some places, damp. **Windows:** Good – six casements to open – two additional ones wanted in the Chancel. **Doors:** Good – double ones at the bottom of the aisles; besides outer ones. **Pulpit and Desk:** Handsome oak, with velvet coverings and cushions. **Books:** In very good repair. **Seats:** Oak, in good condition – boarded floors. **Galleries:** On both sides, and all the West end. **Organ:** There is one. **Font:** ——. **Chapels:** None. **Benefaction Tables:** Only two – though there are several benefactions. **Vestry:** A small [very inconvenient] one near the South door – a large one upstairs. **Surplices:** Two – good. **Linen:** Table cloth and napkin – good. **Plate:** Two flagons, two cups, two dishes and a patin – all silver. **Chest for Papers:** There is one. **Iron Chest for Register:** There is one. **Register:** Nine volumes [– prior to 1813 –] besides those now in use; oldest date 1539 – generally in good condition. **Porch:** None. **Vaults:** None of recent date. **Cleanliness:** Attended to. **Damp:** Very little. **Dimensions:** 81ft. 3in. by 57ft. 8in.
CHANCEL: Only the circular end of the Church. **Table:** Neat oak: with handsome velvet coverings. **Ornaments:** King's arms over the Table – no Commandments. **Repaired by whom:** Marquis of Anglesey – casements wanted in the windows.
STEEPLE: Square stone Tower, with crosses and pinnacles. **State of:** Good. **Bells:** Eight in good order. **Clock:** There is one.
CHURCHYARD: **Fence:** On the West side, houses – North, a wall bounding a field of Lord Anglesey's. East, the river – South, abbey garden wall. **Gates:** Iron – good. **Drains:** A surf which conveys the wet, by spouts, from the Church. **Graves:** None near the walls. **Rubbish:** None. **Footpaths:** None; but of late years horses and gigs have been brought into the churchyard – a manifest encroachment [– to be prohibited]. **Cattle:** Sheep – and donkeys occasionally.
DIVINE SERVICE: **On Sundays:** Two full services – Morning and Afternoon. **On other Days:** Wednesday and Friday Prayers – Lecture on Thursdays – Prayers on Saints' days. **Sacrament:** Eight times a year. **Communicants:** About 70. **Catechism:** In the Schools.
INCUMBENT: **Name and Residence:** Revd Hugh Jones – in Burton. **What Duty he performs:** The whole, now.
CURATE: **Name and Residence:** None.
PARSONAGE: None.[2]
INCOME: **Gross Value:** A little upwards of £200 including the Lecture, Surplice Fees etc. **Tithes:** None. **Glebe:** None. **Surplice Fees:** Not stated. **Easter Dues and small Payments:** About £50 – Lord Anglesey [pays] £50. **Queen Anne's Bounty:** Interest of £1,400 – 3 per Cents. **Terrier:** In the Churchwardens' books.
SCHOOLS: **Endowed School:** A Free Grammar School supported by lands. **Subscription Day School:** None. **Sunday School:** 90 boys, 80 girls.
DISSENTERS: **Dissenters' School:** There is [one]. **Dissenting Chapels:** Several in the Town.
POPULATION: 4,000, belonging to this district of the Town.
MISCELLANEOUS: **Monuments:** Several. **Chandeliers, etc:** There are. **Parochial Library:** There is one – not much used.
PARISH CLERK: William Shelton. **Appointed by:** The Incumbent. **Salary:** No fixed sum. Surplice Fees, and a few small payments.
CHURCHWARDENS: Mr Robert Thornewill and Mr William Worthington, both chosen by the Parish.
ORDERS MADE: Gallery staircase, repaired in one or two places. Casements opened in the Chancel. Encroachments on Churchyard prohibited, unless a legal right can be established to the contrary.

Revisited 25.8.1837

The Church generally in a very good state – two large casements have been put in the Chancel window.

The only direction needful respected the

Churchyard, in which the herbage is allowed to grow much too high – the Churchwardens farm it of the Marquis of Anglesey, and let it out as suits their convenience – I desired that it might be kept regularly mowed and kept neat.

Revisited 7.9.1841
(1) Water tables to South windows – windows cleaned and mended. (2) More attention to cleanliness – especially in windows. (3) North roof examined – gutter to carry off wet. (4) Churchyard guarded against encroachment and trespass from Schoolboys and foot-paths.

[1] *Eccles. Revs.:* 1,080. [2] *Eccles. Revs.:* 'None.'

BURTON ON TRENT, HOLY TRINITY
1.10.1829 (A/V/1/4,p.51;A/V/1/2,p.2)

BENEFICE: Trinity Chapel, Burton [on Trent]. **Nature:** Perpetual Curacy. **Patron:** Lord Anglesey. **Impropriator.**[1]
CHURCH: New Gothic building, ornamented style – centre and side aisles – pillars and [pointed] arches – Chancel formed by the shape of the East end of the Church. **Number it will contain:** 8 or 900. **Accommodation for Poor:** 650. **Roof:** Timber covered with slate – good. **Walls:** Brick – cased inside and out with cement – stone arches. **Floor:** Board. **Windows:** In good repair, six open casements. **Doors:** Good. **Pulpit and Desk:** Handsome. **Books:** New. **Seats:** Good. **Galleries:** On three sides. **Organ:** There is one. **Font:** ——. **Chapels:** None. **Benefaction Tables:** None. **Vestry:** A very good one. **Surplices:** Two. **Linen:** Table cloth and Napkin – good. **Plate:** Flagon, Cup, two dishes – silver. **Chest for Papers:** None needed. **Iron Chest for Register:** There is one. **Register:** Those now in use. The chapel has been built only five years. **Porch:** None. **Vaults:** ——. **Cleanliness:** Attended to. **Damp:** No appearance of any. **Dimensions:** 81ft. by 45ft.
CHANCEL: **Table:** Plain deal – green cloth covering. **Ornaments:** None at present. The Commandments etc are directed[2] to be painted on the pannels over the Table. **Repaired by whom:** The Parish.
STEEPLE: **Square Tower. State of:** Good. **Bells:** One. **Clock:** There is one.
CHURCHYARD: **Fence:** Good brick wall on two sides, hedge on the South, iron rails on the West. **Gates:** Iron Railing. **Drains:** A surf goes round. **Graves:** None near the wall. **Rubbish:** None. **Footpaths:** None. **Cattle:** Sheep.
DIVINE SERVICE: **On Sundays:** Morning and Evening – full services. **On other Days:** On Festivals – Passion week etc. **Sacrament:** Once a month. **Communicants:** 60. **Catechism:** At School.
INCUMBENT: **Name and Residence:** Revd P French – At the Abbey. **What Duty he performs:** The whole.
CURATE: **Name and Residence:** None.
PARSONAGE: None.[3]
INCOME: **Gross Value:** About £200.[4] **Easter Dues and small Payments:** £15 from a benefactor. **Queen Anne's Bounty:** [Interest of] £2,000 in 3 per Cents. **Terrier:** None.
SCHOOLS: **Endowed School:** Free Grammar School – open to the whole Town. [The same mentioned under the Old Church (p.50).] **Subscription Day School:** National school containing 120. **Sunday School:** 250 children. **Lancaster School:** None.
DISSENTERS: **Dissenters' School:** Methodist schools. **Dissenting Chapels:** Many.
POPULATION: 2,200, of *this* district of the Parish.[5]
MISCELLANEOUS: **Monuments:** None. **Chandeliers, etc:** Lamps. **Parochial Library:** None.
PARISH CLERK: John Shelly. **Appointed by:** The Minister, who also appoints the Sexton. **Salary:** £6 14s. 0d. per annum.
CHURCHWARDENS: John Tibberton and Joseph Hopkins.
ORDERS MADE: Commandments to be placed above the Table. Font placed near the Communion rail [for public convenience]. The chapel being new, no repairs wanted.

Revisited 25.8.1837
No directions needful, except to have more attention paid to *ventilation*, and keeping the gutters of the roofs clear.

Revisited 7.9.1841
(1) Bible repaired – walls and windows kept clean – walls coloured and ceiling whitewashed. (2) Churchyard wall, adjoining the street, secured.

[1] *Eccles. Revs.:* 'Marquis of Anglesey'. [2] A/V/1/4: '... intended to put the Ten Commandments over the Table'. [3] *Eccles. Revs.:* 'None'. [4] *Eccles. Revs.:* Gross income £261. [5] *Eccles. Revs.:* 2,580.

CHEADLE 15.7.1830
(A/V/1/4,p.52;A/V/1/2,p.96)

BENEFICE: Cheadle (Ecton. Chedull). **Nature:** Rectory. **Ecton:** King's Books £12 9s. 2d. Abb. Croxden 7s. 8d. **Patron:** Trinity College, Cambridge. **Impropriator:** None.
CHURCH: A handsome Gothic building – nave, side-aisles and Chancel – pointed Arches – open ceiling. **Number it will contain:** About 400.[1] **Accommodation for Poor:** Only *5* free sittings (one pew). **Roof:** Oak covered with lead. **Walls:** Stone, upright. **Floor:** Quarries – even but damp. **Windows:** Good – but casements not sufficient. **Doors:** Good. **Pulpit and Desk:** Handsome and well-placed; crimson velvet hangings and cushion. **Books:** The Bible wants repair or binding. **Seats:** Neat and uniform – oak pannels; but much of the wainscoting against the South wall out of repair. **Galleries:** Organ gallery at W. end – and on the N., and part of the South, sides. **Organ:** There is one. **Font:** A small one – inconveniently placed. **Chapels:** None. **Benefaction Tables:** In the Chancel – all the charities recorded. **Vestry:** None – a small closet enclosed in the Belfry – very unsuitable.[2] **Surplices:** Three – good. **Linen:** Provided. **Plate:** Silver Cup, flagon and patin. **Chest for Papers:** There is one. **Iron Chest for Register:** At the Rectory. **Register:** From 1568 to present time; in tolerable preservation. **Porch:** There is one on the South side – no light gate. **Vaults:** None recently. **Cleanliness:** Not properly attended to; especially in Organ Gallery. **Damp:** Much on the walls and floor.
CHANCEL: **Table:** Firm – old faded Velvet Cover. **Ornaments:** Some old painted glass. **Repaired by whom:** The Rector – slight repairs wanted in the

floor and pews – a crack in the SE. corner – the bottom of the walls injured by damp – especially on N. side.

STEEPLE: A square stone Tower. **State of:** Good. **Bells:** Six – good. **Clock:** A new one.

CHURCHYARD: **Fence:** Iron rails and high wall next the street – the rest chiefly brick wall, kept up principally by the Parish. **Gates:** Good. **Drains:** None. **Graves:** Many too near. **Rubbish:** Some. **Footpaths:** Many trespass paths – the Churchyard is made a complete thoroughfare. **Cattle:** None.

DIVINE SERVICE: **On Sundays:** Full service morning – prayers afternoon. **On other Days:** Prayers, on Wednesdays, Fridays and Saints' days. **Sacrament:** Seven times a year. **Communicants:** 50. **Catechism:** In Lent.

INCUMBENT: **Name and Residence:** Revd Delabere Pritchett, Rectory.[3] **What Duty he performs:** The whole.

PARSONAGE: A good substantial brick house – tiled roof – built in 1758 – three rooms on ground floor, eight above. **State of:** Good.[4] **Outbuildings:** Tithe barn, stable and Coach-house – in good repair.

INCOME: **Gross Value:** Estimated at £800 or £1,000 – present value £500. **Tithes:** Corn-modus for Hay over 1,500 acres. **Glebe:** £44 per annum. **Easter Dues and small Payments:**[5] Not collected now. **Terrier:** There is a Copy dated 1762.

SCHOOLS: **Endowed School:** One for education of 12 boys in English. **Subscription Day School:** An Infant School – 90 children. **Sunday School:** About 170 children. **Lancaster School:** None.

DISSENTERS: **Dissenters' School:** Roman Catholic. **Dissenting Chapels:** Four.

POPULATION: Of whole Parish 4,000 – of the Town 3,000.

MISCELLANEOUS: **Monuments:** Several in the Chancel – none remarkable. **Parochial Library:** None.

PARISH CLERK: Thomas Chawner. **Appointed by:** The Rector. **Salary:** £1 8s. 0d. per annum.

CHURCHWARDENS: George Askew for the Rector. John Malkin for the Parish.

ORDERS MADE: Light iron gates to be placed at the Porch entrance. Two additional casements on each side [the Church]. Pews and their floors on South side repaired. Cleanliness attended to – especially in Organ Gallery. Covering of Table to be renewed. The Belfry walls, ceiling etc repaired and whitewashed. The earth to be cleared away on the North side of the Church – and an open drain formed – Pipes to carry the wet from the spouts. The thoroughfare of the Churchyard to be stopped if possible, and at all events unnecessary footpaths prevented. A suitable Vestry *recommended.*

The attention of the Rector was strongly called to the urgent importance of *enlarging* the Church (if possible) and building a Chapel of Ease (or School) at Oakamoor, a populous hamlet three miles from the Mother Church. [This latter suggestion is now being acted upon – a Chapel is in progress at Oakamoor – 1831.]

Revisited 27.9.1837

The old Church has been taken down and a new one is in progress – expected to be completed before the close of next year.[6] No directions needful.

Revisited 28.9.1841

Directions to Churchwardens. (1) Walls of Church, inside, neatly stone-coloured, and ceilings whitewashed. (2) Water-tables provided for all the windows – to carry the wet outside. (3) Boards protecting lead water-courses of roof, painted or tarred, to preserve them from decay. (4) Roof of Vestry sloped, and lead covering relaid, to carry off the wet at NW. angle. (5) No damp soil or herbage allowed to accumulate around walls – which should be surrounded, at the base, by broad flags or tiles etc.

[1] *Eccles. Revs.:* 920. [2] A/V/1/4: 'None – a small partition off the Belfry used for this purpose.' [3] *Eccles. Revs.:* also prebendary of St. David's Cathedral. [4] *Eccles. Revs.:* 'Fit.' [5] 'And small Payments' enclosed in brackets. [6] Faculty for the new church granted 13.7.1837 (B/C/2/1836–41, p.124). The architect was JP Pritchett of York.

CHECKLEY 14.7.1830
(A/V/1/4,p.53;A/V/1/2,p.95)

BENEFICE: Checkley. **Nature:** Rectory. **Ecton:** King's Books £20 2s. 6d. Mon. de Stone 20s. Eccl. de Uttoxeter 4s. Mr Langley Patron. **Patron:** Thomas Hutchinson Esqr by purchase from the family of the present Rector.[1] **Impropriator:** None.

CHURCH: A neat Gothic structure – nave and side aisles, separated by two rows of handsome pillars and pointed Arches – Chancel arch, sharp pointed – open wood ceiling in Church and Chancel. **Number it will contain:** About 600 in all.[2] **Accommodation for Poor:** 65.[3] **Roof:** Oak covered with lead – out of repair on North side. **Walls:** Stone – upright. **Floor:** Quarries and flags – uneven in many places, especially in S. aisle. **Windows:** Not sufficiently provided with casements. **Doors:** The North door wants lining inside. **Pulpit and Desk:** Oak – not well placed; too high for pews in S. Aisle – doors of Pulpit and Reading desk out of repair. **Books:** Clerk's prayer book bad. **Seats:** Very irregular – and many of them much out of repair – much room might be gained by a new disposition of the Pews. **Galleries:** On three sides. **Organ:** There is one. **Font:** An old one, at the W. end. **Benefaction Tables:** Two. **Vestry:** A small and very incommodious one; near the S. door. **Surplices:** Two – good. **Linen:** Provided. **Plate:** A plated flagon (which cannot be used)[4] and small Cup and Patin. **Chest for Papers:** There is one – containing a valuable old Bible. **Iron Chest for Register:** At the Rectory. **Register:** From 1625 to present time – in bad condition. **Porch:** There is one on the South side. **Vaults:** None recently. **Cleanliness:** Attended to. **Damp:** Not much, except at the foot of the walls. **Dimensions:** 48ft. 9in. by 48ft. 10in.

CHANCEL: 48ft. 10in. by 20ft. 9in.[5] **Table:** Neat and good – handsome velvet covering. **Ornaments:** Remains of handsome stained glass; and some antient stalls, which have been suffered to fall very much into decay. **Repaired by whom:** The Rector – who has lately put on a new roof – and put the windows into repair. There are pews

very awkwardly placed, and the floor much out of repair.
- **STEEPLE**: Square stone Tower. **State of:** Good. **Bells:** Six – good. **Clock:** There is one.
- **CHURCHYARD: Fence:** Stone wall (forming a *sunk* fence) – partly kept up by the Rector, partly by the Parish – wants pointing, and the ground outside lowering in some parts. **Gates:** Pretty good. **Drains:** None. **Graves:** Many much too near. **Rubbish:** The whole Churchyard is in a very disorderly state – much encroached upon by footpaths, and a school house and dwelling inhabited by the Clerk. **Footpaths:** A thoroughfare, which may easily be stopped. **Cattle:** Cows kept by the Clerk – to be forbidden.
- **DIVINE SERVICE: On Sundays:** Two services – *two sermons* every *alternate* Sunday. **On other Days:** None. **Sacrament:** Monthly and at the festivals. **Communicants:** 17 or 18. **Catechism:** In Lent.
- **INCUMBENT: Name and Residence:** Revd Samuel Langley – Rectory. **What Duty he performs:** All the weekly duty and part on Sundays.
- **CURATE: Name and Residence:** Revd William Higton, at Tean, in the Parish. **Licensed:** He is. **Salary.**[6] **If serving another church;** Croxden.
- **PARSONAGE:** An old brick whitewashed house – tiled roof; stands low, near the River – the interior resembles a Farmhouse. **State of:** In miserable condition.[7] **Outbuildings:** Very extensive, but in ruinous state.
- **INCOME: Gross Value:** Considerable – at least £700, if rightly managed.[8] **Glebe:** 140 acres. **Easter Dues and small Payments:**[9] Collected. **Terrier:** A copy dated 1701.
- **SCHOOLS: Endowed School:** There was formerly an endowment of £3 10s. 0d. per annum, now lost. **Subscription Day School:** None. **Sunday School:** 45 children. **Lancaster School:** At Tean; and an Infant School, supported by Mr Phillips, who is a Socinian.
- **DISSENTERS: Dissenters' School:** ——. **Dissenting Chapels:** Four.
- **POPULATION:** 2,200.
- **PARISH CLERK:** William Hall. **Appointed by:** The Rector. **Salary:** £2 0s. 0d. as Clerk – and Easter offerings.
- **CHURCHWARDENS:** Jacob Milner, Enoch Harris.
- **ORDERS MADE:** The roof and ceiling of the North Gallery to be repaired – the North door lined inside – two more casements to be made on each side of the Church – and one [on each side] in the Chancel. The doors of the Pulpit and Reading desk eased – new Prayer Book for Clerk. The lower part of the Church to be new-pewed, and a basin provided for the Font. Cleanliness and ventilation properly attended to. The *pews* removed from the Chancel – the stalls and door repaired – floor laid even, and bars of windows outside repaired. The Churchyard fence pointed, and the ground lowered where needful. The thoroughfare of the Churchyard stopped, if possible, and the encroachments caused by the occupation of the School-house; dung-heaps etc put a stop to. An open drain to be made all round the Church – and the wet properly carried from the roofs to the ground. Cows not to feed in the Churchyard – no graves to be dug within ten feet of the walls. The new-pewing etc to be completed *within two years.*

Revisited 11.9.1837
The new-pewing, roofing etc of the Church has been done, and the whole state of the *body* of the Church as satisfactory as formerly it was disgraceful.[10]

Still the *Chancel* remains in disorder, owing to the impracticable temper of the Rector, in consequence of which, also, the floor, at the foot of the Pulpit stairs, remains incomplete.

Ordered – (1) That the flooring be completed. (2) Communion rails varnished. (3) Bars of windows painted. (4) Stalls in the Chancel repaired. (5) Roof examined and repaired where needful. (6) Wheels of the bells and floor of belfry repaired – weatherboards put up. (7) Pannels and seats of some of the pews in the N. gallery repaired. (8) The *spouts* and *down-pipes*, on both sides of the Church made to carry off the wet, without injuring the walls. (9) A casement made in the Vestry window. (10) The wall, at the NW. corner of the Churchyard raised, and the trespass on Churchyard stopped. 'Qu. pinnacles of the tower. Thoroughfare. Spouts etc.'

Revisited 9.9.1841
The Church and Chancel in excellent order. (1) Water tables to windows – Bible rebound. (2) Base of walls – buttresses – copings of roof, pointed with good cement. (3) Lead flashings of roof secured. (4) Weatherboards in small window of clock-chamber. (5) Removal of over-shot spouts recommended to the Rector.

[1] *Eccles. Revs.*: 'Appears to be in dispute'. [2] *Eccles. Revs.*: 1,000. [3] A/V/1/4: '47 – very insufficient'. [4] A/V/1/4: 'Unfit for use'. [5] Altered in A/V/1/4 to '19ft. 6in.' [6] *Eccles. Revs.*: £50. [7] *Eccles. Revs.*: 'Fit'. [8] *Eccles. Revs.*: Gross income £580. [9] 'And small Payments' enclosed in brackets. [10] Faculty for repewing granted 2.8.1832 (B/C/2/1832–6, p.23).

CHRIST CHURCH, NEEDWOOD 6.7.1830
(A/V/1/4,p.54;A/V/1/2,p.49)

Owing to the peculiar circumstances and character of the Minister of this Chapel who had been liberated from prison a few days before my visit, I could not satisfactorily make the usual enquiries. This was the less important, as the Chapel is of very recent date; the most important defects strike the eye at once, and were pointed out in a letter to the Churchwardens.

- **BENEFICE:** Christ Church, Needwood. **Nature:** Perpetual Curacy. **Ecton:** Not mentioned. **Patron:** Trustees – of whom Revd T Gisborne of Yoxall Lodge, the principal.
- **CHURCH:** A modern building, in imitation of Gothic – pointed windows – open roof, the span of which is too wide for safety – and is pressing the walls out of the perpendicular. **Number it will contain:**[1] ——. **Walls:** Brick. **Floor:** Flags. **Windows:** Good. **Doors:** ——. **Pulpit and Desk:** ——. **Books:** ——. **Seats:** ——. **Galleries:** None.
- **CHURCHYARD: Fence:** In a very neglected state – overgrown with weeds and bushes – no gate at the entrance.
- **INCUMBENT: Name and Residence:** Revd Humphrey Price, in the Parsonage. **What duty he performs:** The whole, at present.
- **CURATE: If serving another church:** No other.

PARSONAGE: A plain brick building. **State of:** Seems to have suffered from want of occupation during the last year.²

INCOME: **Gross Value.**³

CHURCHWARDENS: **Mr Fearn and J Rigby Esqr.**

ORDERS MADE: The walls to be secured against further injury. The causes of damp, in the interior, to be ascertained and removed. The roofs to be spouted, and drain round the walls cleared out. The Ivy to be removed from the windows – and the Churchyard cleared of thistles etc. Gate to be put up at the W. entrance.

24.10.1832
Visited the Church a second time and likewise the Parsonage. Nothing appears to have been done to the former in pursuance of my former directions, with the exception of putting up gates at the entrance of the Churchyard. I have accordingly directed fresh attention to the state of the fabric – especially the roofs of the Tower and body of the Church, which need repair – also to the Churchyard wall.

The Parsonage is in a sadly neglected condition, and will, I fear, suffer materially from the strange conduct of the present Incumbent, who seems determined to let everything run to waste. I pointed out, in a letter to the Churchwardens, what ought to be done, and requested their attention to the subject. I doubt however whether it may not be necessary to enforce the repairs on the Incumbent by a sequestration.

26.8.1837
Things still in the same forlorn condition – on account of the almost impossible difficulty of making and collecting a rate.

The Churchwarden thinks however that he can raise money, by *voluntary contributions* in the neighbourhood, towards the repairs of the Church.

I desired therefore that Mr Trubshaw might be called in to survey and report to me the state of the Church, Mr Price pledging himself to defray the expense of the survey; to the extent of £5.

31.7.1838
Mr Trubshaw having neglected to survey the Church, Arthur Hinckley Esqr. (Churchwarden for the present year) called in Mr Smith of Repton, on whose recommendation I directed as follows:

(1) The side walls to be secured by iron rods across the body of the Church. (2) The floor, joists, wainscoting etc on the S. side of the Church to be renewed and repaired. (3) The walls coloured, ceiling whitewashed. (4) A sough, or open drain, formed all round. (5) The Vestry walls underbuilt and otherwise repaired. (6) The roof of the Tower to be new slated – to which I added (7) Spouts and down-pipes to the roofs – the roof examined – Chancel lead-flashings. (8) The Church to be re-coloured externally. (9) New gates to Churchyard – wall repaired.

Revisited 6.9.1841
Chancel – window cleaned – communion table and space within rails kept clear – covering for Table – kneeling boards fresh covered.

Church – more attention to cleanliness – especially to windows. Covering to reading desk – to protect the books.

Outside – Eave-spouts and down-pipes. Open space round walls. Weatherboard in circular opening of Tower. Churchyard kept neat and clear. (The Church has been repaired – new-roofed – and much improved – since my last visit.)

The *Parsonage House* much out of repair.

[1] *Eccles. Revs.:* Accommodation for 280. [2] *Eccles. Revs.:* 'Fit'. [3] *Eccles. Revs.:* Gross income £150.

CROXDEN 17.7.1830
(A/V/1/4,p.55;A/V/1/2,p.108)

BENEFICE: Croxden. **Nature:** Perpetual Curacy – formerly attached to Rocester. **Ecton:** Formerly an Abbey – £12 clear value. **Patron:** Lord Macclesfield. **Impropriator:** No Tythes – having been, probably, Abbey Land – there is a remarkably fine ruin of an antient abbey still remaining.

CHURCH: A small irregular building – single body – no chancel. **Number it will contain:** 113 in pews – total 153. **Accommodation for Poor:** 50, including children. **Roof:** Oak covered with tiles. **Walls:** Stone – grouted; not firm. **Floor:** Brick – even. **Windows:** Not very good – none on the N. side, nor casements except one at E. end. **Doors:** Good. **Pulpit and Desk:** Good – handsome covering of crimson *cotton* velvet – 3s. 4d. per yard. **Books:** In bad state. **Seats:** Good. **Galleries:** None. **Organ:** ——. **Font:** An antient one – very handsome. **Chapels:** None. **Benefaction Tables:** Not complete. **Vestry:** None – recommended. **Surplices:** One – another wanted. **Linen:** A table Cloth wanted. **Plate:** Cup and small Patin – Cup wants repair. **Iron Chest for Register:** In the wall of the Church. **Register:** From 1680 to present time. **Porch:** None. **Vaults:** None lately. **Cleanliness:** Attended to. **Damp:** Much on the E. and S. walls. **Dimensions:** 51ft. 6in. by 18ft. 6in.

CHANCEL: **Table:** A handsome mahogany Coffer – in which the Velvet hangings [of the Pulpit] etc are kept. **Ornaments:** None. **Repaired by whom:** The Parish.

STEEPLE: A small bell tower. **State of:** Pretty good. **Bells:** Good. **Clock:** None.

CHURCHYARD: **Fence:** In good order. **Gates:** Want repair and painting. **Drains:** None – nor spouts. **Graves:** Some too near. **Footpaths:** Churchways want putting in order. **Cattle:** A horse has been accustomed to feed there.

DIVINE SERVICE: **On Sundays:** Single duty – alternately Morning and Afternoon. **On other Days:** None. **Sacrament:** Four times a year. **Communicants:** Eight or ten. **Catechism:** In Lent.

INCUMBENT: **Name and Residence:** Revd W Higton; Tean, four miles off. **What duty he performs:** The whole.

PARSONAGE: None.¹

INCOME: **Gross Value:** Not stated.² **Easter Dues and small Payments:** Annual Payment of £15 [paid (I presume) out of the Abbey lands]. **Queen Anne's Bounty:** £1,400 10s. 0d. – part laid out in land, part at interest. **Terrier:** There is one.

SCHOOLS: **Endowed School:** None. **Subscription Day School:** None. **Sunday School:** 39 children. **Lancaster School:** None.

DISSENTERS: **Dissenters' School:** None. **Dissenting Chapels:** None.

POPULATION: 250.

PARISH CLERK: Thomas Middleton. **Appointed by:** The Minister. **Salary:** £1 10s. 0d. to be increased.

CHURCHWARDENS: Mr Thomas Harvey.

ORDERS MADE: A window to be made on the N. side of the Church [– 'not needed']. The Prayer book and Service book repaired. Benefaction Table completed. Table Cloth for the Communion – larger Patin – Cup repaired. The Gates repaired and painted – Church way properly kept. Spouts, pipes and an open drain [– 'done']. Ivy cleared from the roof – no large cattle. A Vestry recommended.

Revisited 12.9.1837
Much improved since my former visit – still a good deal of damp arising from want of spouts etc on the North side; and want of pointing etc. Directed – (1) That a lead gutter and pipe be made at the East window so as to carry the wet outside. (2) That the decayed mats be taken out of the Pews. (3) That the ceiling under the bell-turret be repaired, and the turret itself made weather-tight by lead-flashings. (4) That the walls and buttresses, all round, be carefully repaired and pointed – holes filled up etc. (5) That the spouts and down-pipes on N. side – and drain cleared of nettles etc as on the S. side. (6) That part of the Churchyard wall at the East end against the Church, removed, to prevent damp to the Church. 'Qu?'

Revisited 9.9.1841
The whole greatly improved. The books to be repaired – pulpit cushions and hangings re-dyed. Drain on N. side cleaned out – and kept clear. Roofs examined.

[1] *Eccles. Revs.:* 'None.' [2] *Eccles. Revs.:* Gross income £92.

DRAYCOTT 15.7.1830
(A/V/1/4,p.56;A/V/1/2,p.100)

BENEFICE: Draycott. **Nature:** Rectory. **Ecton:** King's Books £9 6s. 8d. Eccl. de Checkley 3s. 4d. Abb. Combermere 3s. 4d. – Patr. Lord Langdale. **Patron:** The Stourton family (Roman Catholic) – present, Dowager Lady Stourton. **Impropriator:** None.

CHURCH: A spacious building, formerly Gothic; re-built 100 years ago, without any regard to antient style of structure, arches and windows circular. **Number it will contain:** About 250. **Accommodation for Poor:** Sufficient. **Roof:** Oak, covered with lead – good repair. **Walls:** Stone – upright. **Floor:** Flags. **Windows:** More casements wanted. **Doors:** Not very good. **Pulpit and Desk:** Good, well placed – purple Cloth coverings. **Books:** Good. **Seats:** ——. **Galleries:** A small one for the singers. **Organ:** None. **Font:** At the W. end. **Chapels:** A private *Chancel*, belonging to the Stourtons. **Benefaction Tables:** Two. **Vestry:** None. **Surplices:** Good. **Linen:** Provided. **Plate:** Silver Cup, Patin and Dish. **Iron Chest for Register:** At the Rectory. **Register:** None older than 1670 – and thence imperfect. **Porch:** None. **Vaults:** None recently. **Cleanliness:** Attended to. **Damp:** Much in the Chancels. **Dimensions:** 40ft. 2in. by 43ft. 8in.

CHANCEL: 29ft. 2in. by 16ft. **Table:** Oak, wants repair. **Ornaments:** None – except an antient monument to the Draycott family. **Repaired by whom:** The Rector, who is now putting it into complete repair.

STEEPLE: An old Square Tower. **State of:** Wants pointing. **Bells:** Five, good – much rubbish on the belfry floor. **Clock:** Good.

CHURCHYARD: **Fence:** Stone wall, and hedge – good. **Gate:** Want painting. **Drains:** None. **Graves:** Some too near. **Rubbish:** None. **Footpaths:** There is a thoroughfare which is to be stopped; the Church ways well kept. **Cattle:** None.

DIVINE SERVICE: **On Sundays:** Two services – one Sermon. **On other Days:** None. **Sacrament:** At the Festivals and Michaelmas. **Communicants:** 25. **Catechism:** In Lent.

INCUMBENT: **Name and Residence:** Revd R Porter, the Rectory. **What Duty he performs:** The whole.

PARSONAGE: A commodious house – two parlours and kitchen etc on ground floor – seven rooms above – very pleasantly situated; excellent garden. **State of:** In good repair; but not *substantially* kept.[1] **Outbuildings:** Barn, stable etc good.

INCOME: **Gross Value:** £6 or 700 in good times.[2] **Tithes:** Corn and Hay – but some moduses claimed for both. **Glebe:** 46 acres – *now* lying contiguous, and all near the Rectory. **Terrier:** There is one.

SCHOOLS: **Endowed School:** None. **Subscription Day School:** ——. **Sunday School:** 40 children.

DISSENTERS: **Dissenters' School:** A small Roman Catholic one – weekly and Sunday. **Dissenting Chapels:** Roman Catholic.

POPULATION: 576 – one-third Catholic.

PARISH CLERK: William Cope. **Appointed by:** The Rector. **Salary:** None – he has Christmas gatherings.

CHURCHWARDENS: John Bagnall for the Rector. William Lyme for the Parish.

ORDERS MADE: An additional casement on each side of the Church and one in the Patron's Chancel. Iron bars of windows; straps etc of bells, hinges etc of doors, painted. The Table and Communion Rails cleaned and oiled. The walls coloured or whitewashed, ceiling repaired and whitewashed. The Tower pointed; and repaired on the W. side – the Belfry floor cleared of rubbish. An open drain all round the Church – the Gates painted. The thoroughfare of the Churchyard stopped, if possible. Both the Chancels spouted, and SE. and N. walls of the Rector's Chancel repaired and secured. The floor of the Chancel laid even, and window bars and door painted.

Revisited 27.9.1837
Everything in excellent order and repair.
  Recommended – a fixed salary of 52s. per annum for the Clerk – and *suggested* – *down-pipes* instead of overshot spouts. Walls to be

pointed in the Spring at the lower parts; and the W. and E. gables of roof of Chancel.

Revisited 28.9.1841
(1) *Recommended* – the substitution of boarded, for flagged, floors in all the pews – and also providing of a Vestry. (2) Wheels of bells repaired and braced – a new ladder for roof. (3) Spouts on N. side of Church painted – water tub removed. (4) Roof of Rector's Chancel examined and repaired. Other Chancel roof examined also. (5) The Curate having refused to replace the black cloth, removed without authority, I have brought his conduct under the notice of the Lord Bishop.
  Mem: On the 29 September I wrote to Mr Haworth, for directions about sequestration of benefice during its avoidance and appointment of a Curate with the approval of the Bishop.

[1] A/V/1/4: '. . . built'. *Eccles. Revs.*: 'Fit'. [2] *Eccles. Revs.*: Gross income £500.

ELLASTONE 17.7.1830
(A/V/1/4,p.57;A/V/1/2,p.106)

BENEFICE: Ellaston (Ecton, alias Glaston). **Nature:** Vicarage. **Ecton:** Clear value £30. Sir Thomas Fleetwood Patron. Abb. Dulacres propr. **Patron:** D Davenport Esqr. **Impropriator:** Ditto.
CHURCH: An old Gothic building; divided into two aisles of equal length, and a Chancel at the end of each – the North aisle just re-built, very handsomely – the South in a ruinous state. **Number it will contain:** The old Church 214 – additional sittings in the N. aisle 231. **Roof:** Old part, timber covered with lead; new, covered with slate. **Walls:** Stone – the new N. wall solid stone; the South very infirm. **Floor:** Of the new part, flags. **Windows:** The new ones very good, but casements wanted. **Doors:** Old – to be renewed. **Pulpit and Desk:** Oak, firm and well placed – old velvet Cushion to pulpit. **Books:** Not good. **Seats:** Those of the new aisle very neat and uniform – pews and benches. **Galleries:** A small one at the W. end of the S. aisle – low and ugly. **Organ:** A small one. **Font:** An old one, broken – to be restored. **Chapels:** None. **Benefaction Tables:** None, except a parchment writing. **Vestry:** None. **Surplices:** Two – one of them new. **Linen:** Provided – good. **Plate:** Two Silver Cups – Pewter flagon and two dishes [for offerings]. **Iron Chest for Register:** In the Church wall. **Register:** From *1540* to the present time – the oldest Vol. wants rebinding. **Porch:** There is one on the S. side, in good repair. **Vaults:** None recently. **Cleanliness:** Attended to. **Damp:** Not much visible at present. **Dimensions:** 59ft. by 32ft. 2in.
CHANCEL: 23ft. 4in. by 32ft. 2in. (for the two Chancels) [length and breadth of the two chancels the same]. **Table:** Two handsome old oak Tables – one for each Chancel. **Ornaments:** None – besides monuments. **Repaired by whom:** Mr Davenport – a new door wanted.
STEEPLE: A neat square stone tower. **State of:** Good, except the roof. **Bells:** Six – good. **Clock:** An old one – out of repair.
CHURCHYARD: **Fence:** A stone wall – wants repair in some places. **Gates:** Want repair and painting. **Drains:** Properly provided on the *North* side. **Graves:** Many too near on the South side. **Rubbish:** Much at present, owing to repairs. **Footpaths:** Many – the Church ways properly kept. **Cattle:** A poney.
DIVINE SERVICE: **On Sundays:** Two full services. **On other Days:** None regularly. **Sacrament:** Eight times a year. **Communicants:** 50 to 60. **Catechism:** Occasionally.
INCUMBENT: **Name and Residence:** Revd G Hake – the Vicarage.[1] **What duty he performs:** The whole.
PARSONAGE: Partly an old thatched building, cottage style – partly modern brick house, slated[2] roof – altogether a commodious parsonage – with good garden. **State of:** Good.[3] **Outbuildings:** Stables, coach-house etc.
INCOME: **Gross Value:** Not ascertained.[4]
SCHOOLS: **Endowed School:** None. **Subscription Day School:** National – for boys and girls, each – 100 boys, 70 girls at present. **Sunday School:** The same as above. **Lancaster School:** None.
DISSENTERS: **Dissenters' School:** ——. **Dissenting Chapels:** One chapel, and private meetings.
POPULATION: 1,300.
MISCELLANEOUS: **Monuments:** An antient one to the Fleetwoods – others to Mr Granville, [Mr] Ram etc.
PARISH CLERK: John Collier. **Appointed by:** The Vicar. **Salary:** £4 0s. 0d.
CHURCHWARDENS: Mr Thomas Smith, the Vicar. Mr Samuel Walker, the Parish.
ORDERS MADE: The state of the *South wall* to be examined and reported. Casements to be made in half the windows on each side and regularly kept open. New Prayer books for Reading and Clerk's desks – the Communion Table cleaned. The Chancel door renewed or repaired. Roof of the Tower repaired – Clock ditto. The Gates repaired and painted – the fence made good – footpaths stopped, if possible. No graves near the Church walls – nor large cattle allowed to feed. A *Vestry recommended*.

Revisited 12.9.1837
The South side of the Church has been taken down and rebuilt since my former visit – there is however much appearance of dampness about the Church.
  Ordered – (1) That two *additional casements* be opened on the North side of the Church. (2) That iron gates be placed at the W. and Chancel doors so as to admit of thorough ventilation. (3) That the walls be coloured and the ceilings washed. (4) New Prayer books for Reading and Clerk's desks. (5) The roof of the Tower examined and the Clock repaired. (6) Eave-spouts and down-pipes to the Chancel, and the earth cleared away all round and an open drain formed with flags, as has been done round the *Church*. (7) The metal spouts on the E. and N. of Chancel *painted*. (8) The trespass paths in the Churchyard stopped, and the thoroughfare stopped, if the necessary consent of the owner of the adjoining yard and fields can be obtained – locks put on the gates, except at Service time. 'Apparently *nothing done*'.

Revisited 9.9.1841
(1) Churchyard fence – near the principal gate, on S. side, repaired. (2) Base of Tower pointed on W. side – Door arch ditto ditto. (3) Window bars painted – Communion Table oiled – new Cover. (4) North windows cleaned – pannels of pews repaired and secured from decay. (5) Dampness at East end, and Communion floor, remedied, si que. (6) The gutters of the Roof cleared – copings pointed – flashings, slates – eave-spouts – down-pipes etc attended to.
(7) Drains kept open, all round.

Much appearance of slovenliness and neglect in this Church. Footpaths across the Churchyard to be stopped, if possible.

[1] *Eccles. Revs.:* Also perpetual curate of Rocester and vicar of Chilvers Coton. [2] A/V/1/4: 'tiled'. [3] *Eccles. Revs.:* 'Fit'. [4] *Eccles. Revs.:* Gross income £154.

FULFORD 15.7.1830
(A/V/1/4,p.58;A/V/1/2,p.99)

BENEFICE: Fulford. **Nature:** Perpetual Curacy, in the parish of Stone – to which it seems originally to have been a Chapel of Ease – but disputes have arisen as to the relation which it bears to the Parish Church. **Ecton:** Chapelry to Stone. Clear value £25 17s. 0d. **Patron:** Thomas Allen Esqr. Great Fenton. **Impropriator:** Ditto.
CHURCH: A neat small building, erected three years ago, by private subscription and a grant of £150 from the Society, for £1,000 – single body, pointed windows, small Chancel.[1] **Number it will contain:** 338.[2] **Accommodation for Poor:** 138. **Roof:** Deal, covered with tile. **Walls:** Brick – good. **Floor:** Quarries. **Windows:** Good, well provided with casements. **Doors:** ——. **Pulpit and Desk:** Very neat – the pulpit cushion out of repair. **Books:** Not good. **Seats:** Very neat and uniform. **Galleries:** None. **Organ:** ——. **Font:** There is one – a basin wanted. **Chapels:** None. **Benefaction Tables:** Not complete. **Vestry:** A small one – wants a casement. **Surplices:** Two – good. **Linen:** Well provided. **Plate:** Silver Cup and plated Patin. **Iron Chest for Register:** In the Vestry. **Register:** Only those in present use – (it is probable that the baptisms etc were registered at Stone till within late years). **Porch:** None. **Vaults:** ——. **Cleanliness:** Not sufficiently attended to. **Damp:** No appearance of it. **Dimensions:** 75ft. by 42ft. (including the Chancel).
CHANCEL: **Table:** Plain painted deal – no covering. **Ornaments:** None. **Repaired by whom:** The Parish, or Chapelry.
STEEPLE: A square stone tower, with battlements. **State of:** Good. **Bells:** One. **Clock:** None.
CHURCHYARD: **Fence:** On three sides hedge, repairs of which belong to the occupiers of adjoining lands – wants trimming etc next the road, a good wall. **Gates:** Good. **Drains:** Not provided properly. **Graves:** Not too near. **Rubbish:** None. **Footpaths:** ——. **Cattle:** Horses – not to be allowed.
DIVINE SERVICE: **On Sundays:** Afternoon service only, except on Sacrament Sundays. **On other Days:** None. **Sacrament:** Four times a year.

Communicants: 20. **Catechism:** Once a year in the Chapel – at other times in the School.
INCUMBENT: **Name and Residence:** Revd William Oliver. **If not resident:** At Tittensor, five miles off. **What Duty he performs:** The whole.
PARSONAGE: None.[3]
INCOME: **Gross Value:** £120. **Glebe:** 19 acres. **Surplice Fees:** £14. **Queen Anne's Bounty:** £1,200 – of which the interest is received. **Terrier:** None known of.
SCHOOLS: **Endowed School:** A small one, for 15 children, at the Oaks – £4 per annum. **Subscription Day School:** None. **Sunday School:** 60 children. **Lancaster School:** None.
DISSENTERS: **Dissenters' School:** ——. **Dissenting Chapels:** ——.
POPULATION: Not ascertained.
MISCELLANEOUS: **Parochial Library:** A small one.
PARISH CLERK: James Watson. **Appointed by:** The Minister. **Salary:** £5 0s. 0d.
CHURCHWARDENS: William Phillips.
ORDERS MADE: Iron work of windows to be painted – rain excluded from E. window. The pulpit cushion repaired; Bible rebound, new Prayer Books. The benefaction tables completed, a basin for the Font, casement in the Vestry – covering for Table – Commandments [set up]. The fence on the E., N. and W. sides of the Chapel-yard repaired and trimmed. The earth cleared away, and open drain formed, on the N. side of the Chapel. The roof to be spouted. Large Cattle not allowed to feed in the Churchyard.

Revisited 28.9.1837
Directions to the Churchwarden. (1) New books for the Reading and Clerk's desks; Vestry window repaired – iron bars painted – floors of pews repaired. (2) *Roof* and *ceiling* repaired – ridging tiles and copings secured – lead flashings; or cement, at the junction of roof with Tower. (3) Walls coloured – ceiling whitewashed – outside of Chapel, and Tower, neatly coloured (grey) in *the Spring.* (4) *Eave-spouts* and *down-pipes.* (5) Battlements of *Tower* secured; roof examined and repaired; down-pipe instead of overshot spout, which now empties itself on the roof of the Chapel. (6) Outer door of Chapel, and gates of Churchyard painted. 'Not done – for want of funds – R.D.'

Revisited 27.9.1841
(1) The floor of the bell-chamber to be repaired – litter removed. (2) The free-benches under the bell turret repaired. (3) The walls coloured – bars painted – wainscoat repaired. (4) Outer door, and casements, painted. (5) Eave spouts and pipes – open drain.
   [(1) New Prayer Book for the Clerk – baptismal font – better water-tables. (2) Copings of roof pointed all round – spouts cleared. (3) Flashings of the Tower and arch stones at each end of the middle roof, secured. (4) Flagging all round the walls, recommended.][5]

[1] Faculty dated 29.3.1825 (B/C/2/1823–6, p.327). The architect was C Winks. [2] *Eccles. Revs.:* 410. [3] *Eccles. Revs.:* 'None'. [4] *Eccles. Revs.:* 2,409. [5] These four directions are deleted.

GAYTON 4.7.1830 (A/V/1/4,p.59;A/V/1/2,p.55)

BENEFICE: Gayton. **Nature:** Perpetual Curacy. **Ecton:** Coll. Sti: Tho. Staff. Propr. £11 10s. – clear value. **Patron:** Sir William Cave Brown. **Impropriator:** John Fitzgerald Esqr.
CHURCH: A small building, consisting of Nave and Chancel – formerly there appear to have been two side aisles – supposed to have been taken down in the year 1756. **Number it will contain:** About 140. **Accommodation for Poor:** About 30. **Roof:** Oak covered with tiles – in good repair. **Walls:** Stone, faced outside with brick. **Floor:** Quarries and old tesselated pavement. **Windows:** In good order; but more casements wanted. **Doors:** Good. **Pulpit and Desk:** Desk wants some repair – the Pulpit cushion very dirty – old silk embroidery covering. **Books:** Good. **Seats:** Much out of repair; both in Church and Chancel. **Galleries:** None. **Organ:** ——. **Font:** There is one – but no proper basin. **Chapels:** None. **Benefaction Tables:** Two – one records a gift of bread – the other an endowment of £40 for teaching four poor children. **Vestry:** None. **Surplices:** One – good. **Linen:** Table Cloth and napkin – good. **Plate:** Silver Cup (out of repair) – pewter flagon and dish. **Chest for Papers:** There is one. **Iron Chest for Register:** In the Chancel. **Register:** Three Vols prior to 1813 – oldest date 1594 – mutilated. **Porch:** There is one – and a light gate at the entrance. **Vaults:** None known of. **Cleanliness:** Not sufficiently attended to. **Damp:** Much on the floor. **Dimensions:** 40ft. 4in. by 20ft.
CHANCEL: 21ft. 10in. by 13ft. 7in. **Table:** Old oak frame, with deal top – the latter so large as to prevent the table being placed in proper situation. **Ornaments:** Ancient embroidered covering to Table. **Repaired by whom:** Mr Fitzgerald – the floor is very damp, and sunk within the rails – the East window lets rain in – the Mortar on the outside of the East wall fallen off.
STEEPLE: Brick square tower – with stone surbase. **State of:** Battlements at the top want pointing – otherwise in good repair. **Bells:** Two – good. **Clock:** None.
CHURCHYARD: **Fence:** Quick hedge – kept up partly by the Parish: partly by the Impropriator – (formerly the part belonging to the Parish was kept in doles) – there is a portion of the Churchyard (formerly the site of a Parsonage house) not consecrated. **Gates:** Good. **Drains:** None. **Graves:** None near the walls – recently. **Rubbish:** None. **Footpaths:** Properly kept. **Cattle:** None – the grass is mown.
DIVINE SERVICE: **On Sundays:** Single duty – always *in the Afternoon,* except on Sacrament days. **On other Days:** None. **Sacrament:** Three times a year. **Communicants:** 10 to 15.
INCUMBENT: **Name and Residence:** Revd William Mould, East Retford, Notts.[1]
CURATE: Revd John Neale – Abbots Bromley – seven miles off [(No longer the Curate 1831.) 'Hodgkinson'.] **Licensed:** He is. **Salary:** £31 10s. 0d. One-quarter of which Mr Mould deducts for doing the duty himself when down. **If serving another church:** Abbots Bromley.
PARSONAGE: None at present – from the statement, however, of the Church wardens and others (confirmed by several Copies of the Terrier in the possession of the Churchwardens) it appears that there was a Parsonage house on what is now part of the Churchyard. It is said to have been sold, within the last 50 years – but it is not known what became of the money.[2]
INCOME: **Gross Value:** About £50. **Queen Anne's Bounty:** Interest of £1,500. **Terrier:** The Churchwarden has a Copy.
SCHOOLS: **Endowed School:** A small one, for education of four children. **Subscription Day School:** None. **Sunday School:** None. **Lancaster School:** ——.
DISSENTERS: **Dissenters' School:** ——. **Dissenting Chapels:** ——.
POPULATION: About 300.
MISCELLANEOUS: **Monuments:** An old one, in the Churchyard – supposed to be that of the founder – formerly in the Church.
PARISH CLERK: John Wyatt. **Appointed by:** The Minister. **Salary:** 52s. a year – 5s. for cleaning – and Easter dues.
CHURCHWARDENS: Mr Hugh Mellor, Mr Foster – one only acts.
ORDERS MADE: Spouts and pipes to be affixed. Open drain round the Church. Additional casements in the windows. The Reading Desk repaired – and Pulpit Cushion cleaned. The Pews put into complete repair. A basin to be provided for the Font. The Communion Cup repaired. Cleanliness better attended to. The Table altered, so as to admit of the Officiating Minister's standing *at the North side* of the Table. The floor within the Rails to be laid even and damp removed – East window guarded against admission of wet. The bricks at the Top of the Tower to be fresh pointed, and the battlements secured.

Revisited 9.9.1837
Church in very bad state both outside and inside – especially the latter.
Ordered
I. *Inside*
(1) Ceilings repaired and whitewashed; walls coloured. (2) Windows cleaned – iron bars painted. (3) Rotten straw-mats taken out of pews, and floors cleaned. (N.B. I strongly recommended *boarding* the floors.) (4) Pews varnished – hinges painted. (5) Floor of Communion space relaid – new covering for Table, and proper kneeling boards, with mats or cushions, for the Communicants. (6) Prayer Book in reading desk repaired; and the reading desk itself put into a more becoming state and position.

II. *Outside*
(1) Roof of bell-tower repaired, and belfry cleaned. (2) Chancel roof stripped and renewed – walls of Chancel stripped of Stucco, and stones chiseled. (3) Drain round the Church kept open and free from weeds.
   N.B. *New-pewing* of Church strongly recommended, and placing the reading-desk in front of Pulpit. 'Under consideration – all to be done. Mem. *Chancel floor*'.

Revisited 10.10.1841[3]
  Directions to the Churchwardens
  I. Respecting the *Church*
  (1) An increase of accommodation to be provided: (i) by erecting *a Gallery*, at the West end of the Church, *for the Schoolchildren*; (ii) by taking down the old pews, and making new ones (*of the old materials:* – the wood being well cleaned, and rubbed *with boiled linseed oil*) of *uniform size,* allowing *not less* than 18in. by 30 for each sitting. *Open benches,* similar to those lately erected, might answer the purpose as well as inclosed pews. (2) The Clergyman's, and Clerk's, desks to be new, and placed on the *West* side of the Chancel entrance. (3) *Cleanliness* and *ventilation* to be better attended to: (at present the Church is shamefully neglected and dirty) – the pews and aisles to be regularly swept out once a week – the decayed straw mats removed, and no *litters* or *sticks* suffered to lie in the entrance under the Tower.
  (N.B. I would strongly *recommend* that this entrance should be *enclosed,* and converted into a *Vestry*.)
  (4) The window bars to be painted. (5) The roof of the *Tower* to be stripped and retiled; the battlements and parapets taken down and re-built securely; the lead gutters cleaned out and kept free from obstruction; and a *conductor* (of lead, or cast iron) put up on the North side, of sufficient size to convey the water from the roof *to the ground,* instead of allowing it, as now, to be projected by over-shot spouts. (6) The broken bell-wheel to be repaired, and the weather-board replaced. (7) The roof of the Church, and of the Porch, to be repaired, where needful; the spouts painted – the open drain cleared of weeds *etc*.

II. Respecting the *Chancel*
  (1) The *internal* walls to be scraped; and fresh coloured – the floor taken up and re-laid on cinders or other dry materials. (2) The communion floor to be paved with the tesselated tiles taken out of the pews (which should have *boarded* floors). (3) The old decayed pews to be removed, or (if wanted) renewed, and the oak pannels, doors etc well rubbed with *linseed oil* (boiled).

Externally
  (1) The *roof* to be examined and repaired. (2) The *Stucco* to be either *entirely taken off* (which would be far best), or else completely renewed. If the former plan be adopted, the stones must be well *pointed,* to keep out the wet. (3) An open drain, laid with flags or quarries, all round, so as to keep the walls dry at the bottom.
  The Archdeacon will write to Mr Fitzgerald respecting the Chancel.

[1] Also perpetual curate of Stowe (Staffs.), Misterton and West Burton (both Notts.): *Eccles. Revs.* [2] *Eccles. Revs.*: 'None'. [3] Loose sheet preserved in A/V/1/3.

GRATWICH 5.7.1830 (A/V/1/4,p.60; A/V/1/2,p.41)

BENEFICE: Gratwich. **Nature:** Rectory. **Ecton:** Not mentioned – most probably however it is the same which in Ecton is called Gatewich – Pri: Tickford Propr. Clear value £17 0s. 0d. **Patron:** Lord Talbot. **Impropriator:** None.
CHURCH: A small shabby building – single body – a small doorway leading into the Chancel. **Number it will contain:** Under 100. **Accommodation for Poor:** None appropriated.[1] **Roof:** Appears in good condition. **Walls:** Brick – upright. **Floor:** Brick. **Windows:** No casements. **Doors:** Tolerably good. **Pulpit and Desk:** Steps to pulpit want repair. **Books:** Prayer book bad. **Seats:** Pretty good. **Galleries:** A small one for singers at the W. end. **Organ:** None. **Font:** There is one. **Chapels:** None. **Benefaction Tables:** ——. **Vestry:** ——. **Surplices:** Two – pretty good. **Linen:** Provided. **Plate:** Silver Cup – pewter flagon etc. **Iron Chest for Register:** In the Chancel – to be removed to the Clergyman's house. **Register:** One Vol. – from 1698. **Porch:** None. **Vaults:** None – except in the Chancel. **Cleanliness:** Attended to. **Damp:** Much on the floor.
CHANCEL: **Table:** In very bad repair – the rails ditto. **Ornaments:** None. **Repaired by whom:** The Rector – the floor much sunk – no casements.
STEEPLE: Small bell tower. **State of:** Seems good. **Bells:** One. **Clock:** None.
CHURCHYARD: **Fence:** Hedge and rails – not in good repair; the hedge wants trimming and ditch clearing out. **Gates:** Pretty good, but want painting. **Drains:** None – nor spouts. **Graves:** Several too near the walls. **Rubbish:** Much – lime, bricks, nettles etc. **Footpaths:** The Church ways not properly kept.
DIVINE SERVICE: **On Sundays:** Morning or Afternoon, alternately with Kingstone. **On other Days:** None. **Sacrament:** Five times a year. **Communicants:** 12 to 15.
INCUMBENT: **Name and Residence:** Revd Thomas Powell Browne.[2] **If not resident:** In the Parish of Stowe, about three miles from the Church. **What Duty he performs:** The whole.
PARSONAGE: A cottage, not fit for Clergyman's residence. **State of:** Not in good repair.[3] **Outbuildings:** Barn and stable.
INCOME: **Gross Value:** £130 per annum. **Tithes:** All the corn tithe – hay tithe only of one field – a modus over the rest. **Glebe:** 22 acres. **Queen Anne's Bounty:** Seven acres of land purchased by a grant. **Terrier:** There is one.
SCHOOLS: **Endowed School:** None. **Subscription Day School:** None. **Sunday School:** 15 to 20. **Lancaster School:** None.
DISSENTERS: **Dissenters' School:** None. **Dissenting Chapels:** None.
POPULATION: 130.
PARISH CLERK: Samuel Smith.
CHURCHWARDENS: Ralph Waller.
ORDERS MADE: Two casements to be made in the body of the Church – one at the W. end, for the gallery and one in the Chancel. New prayer-books to be provided. Communion-table and rails repaired. Chancel floor relaid. The hedge

repaired and trimmed – rails repaired – ditch cleared out – nettles removed, from Churchyard. Spouts, pipes, open drain, to be made. The gates painted.

'Mr Browne has recently built a House – which he hopes by exchange to make a Parsonage house; about 300 yards from his Church (Gratwich) containing on the ground floor, two sitting rooms, one 14 × 14, other 14 × 16, with kitchen and pantries, entrance 7 × 10 – bedrooms, two over parlour, one over entrance, three service rooms, with gig house – two [–] stables, cowhouses etc for £600, including fitting up and piping etc.'

Revisited 11.9.1837

Floors of Church and Chancel taken up and relaid, even. Boarded floors to the pews. Pews, pulpit etc painted. Bible repaired. Eave-spouts and down-pipes drain etc. Earth cleared away. Thoroughfare stopped. Gravel walk. Gate repaired and painted. Cupola ditto – lead restored. 'Nothing done – (R.D.).'

[1] A/V/1/4: 'None in particular'. [2] Also perpetual curate of Kingstone. [3] *Eccles. Revs.:* 'Unfit'.

HAMSTALL RIDWARE 30.9.1829
(A/V/1/4,p.61;A/V/1/2,p.12)

BENEFICE: Hamstall Ridware. **Nature:** Rectory. **Ecton:** King's books £6 1s. 0½d. – Patron Lord Leigh. **Patron:** Chandos Leigh Esqr. **Impropriator:** The Patron has part of the Tythes (qu?).
CHURCH: Handsome stone building in the early Gothic style – centre and two side aisles, separated by plain pointed arches. **Number it will contain:** 230 besides about 60 schoolchildren. **Accommodation for Poor:** 50 sittings. **Roof:** Oak, covered with lead – very handsome oak ceiling, open work. **Walls:** Stone – upright. **Floor:** Quarries and brick – some flat gravestones – even in general. **Windows:** In good repair, with casements to open. **Doors:** Good – except the bottom of the west door. **Pulpit and Desk:** In very good order, and well placed. **Books:** Bible wants rebinding. **Seats:** Oak – neat and in good repair, with a few exceptions in the floors. **Galleries:** One – occupied by the Singers, and free sittings. **Organ:** There is one – organist paid by Mr Cooper. **Font:** There is one. **Chapels:** None – but Mr Leigh claims the N. and S. Chancels. **Benefaction Tables:** One within the communion rail, records a bequest of lands in Yoxall and Hamstall, to the poor of the latter, by a former Rector, Revd Timothy Deleen. **Vestry:** There is one at the East end of the S. Chancel, small and dark, a large crack in the corner near the Communion Table. **Surplices:** Two – good. **Linen:** Table Cloth and Napkin – pretty good, but small. **Plate:** Cup and Plate, silver, a Pewter Flagon. **Chest for Papers:** There is one. **Iron Chest for Register:** At the Rectory. **Register:** Five Vols besides those now in use, earliest date 1598 – in good preservation and complete. **Porch:** In good repair. **Vaults:** None of recent date. **Cleanliness:** Attended to. **Damp:** Some appearance at the lower parts of the walls, and in the Chancels – rain comes in, over the gallery. **Dimensions:** 35ft. 9in. by 40ft. 4in. (including side aisles).
CHANCEL: 31ft. 10in. **Table:** Neat oak Table, with crimson velvet covering. **Ornaments:** None – except monuments. **Repaired by whom:** The Rector, except the N. and S. Chancels, which Mr Leigh is bound to repair. The floor in the N. chancel is out of order near the stove – Mr L. to be spoken to.
STEEPLE: Square stone tower, surmounted by handsome spire. **State of:** The coping at the top of the Tower, needs repair, also the stones near the base, much injured by Ivy, as also other parts of the Church. **Bells:** Four: new hung five years ago. **Clock:** There is one almost new.
CHURCHYARD: **Fence:** On the W. and N. a brick wall, belonging to the hall adjoining, greatly needs repair – the rest kept up by the Parish – some slight repairs wanted. **Gates:** One – in good repair. **Drains:** A surf all round, said to be in good repair. Spouting wanted along the S. side of the church. **Graves:** Many near the walls. **Rubbish:** None; but grass and weeds, allowed to grow too near the walls; and to cover the plinth. **Footpaths:** None improper – on the NE. side near the Chancel is a space enclosed by iron railing and formerly used for interment by the Riley family – now much overgrown with nettles etc – which should be cleared away. **Cattle:** Only sheep.
DIVINE SERVICE: **On Sundays:** Morning and Afternoon – sermon in the Afternoon during Summer. **On other Days:** In Passion week. **Sacrament:** Six times a year. **Communicants:** 40 to 50. **Catechism:** Occasionally at Church – generally at School.
INCUMBENT: Revd Edward Cooper – in the Rectory house.[1] **What Duty he performs:** Occasionally assists.
CURATE: **Name and Residence:** Revd Henry Cooper – [lives] with his Father. **Licensed:** Yes. **Salary:** £50.[2] **If serving another church:** None other. **Parsonage:** A very good commodious house – much improved, and enlarged, by the present Rector. **State of:** Very good.[3] **Outbuildings:** Barn, Stable, Coach-house etc.
INCOME: **Gross Value:** About £270. **Glebe:** About 30 acres. **Surplice Fees:** Uncertain. **Easter Dues and small Payments:** Mr Leigh pays a modus of £15 – Easter dues not received. **Queen Anne's Bounty:** None. **Terrier:** There is one, in the Rector's possession, who has also some other written document, explanatory of some points relative to the Benefice.
SCHOOLS: **Endowed School:** None. **Subscription Day School:** There is one supported by Mr Leigh and the Rector. **Sunday School:** 60 boys and girls together. **Lancaster School:** None.
DISSENTERS: **Dissenting Chapels:** None.
POPULATION: 455 last Census.
MISCELLANEOUS: **Monuments:** Several. **Chandeliers, etc:** None. **Parochial Library:** None.
PARISH CLERK: Samuel Tomlinson. **Appointed by:** The Rector. **Salary:** £2 10s. 0d. 12s. 6d. in addition for care of the clock.
CHURCHWARDENS: Mr Robert Lawrence, Mr Joseph Wooley.
ORDERS MADE: The Bible to be rebound. Floors of the Pews, where needful, to be repaired. Vestry

wall to be examined and secured. Floor of N. Chancel ditto. Roof over the gallery, secured from admission of wet. Spouting placed along the S. side of the roof. The Tower and walls to be repointed, and otherwise repaired. Ivy cleared away from the Tower and walls – weeds and herbage from the bottoms of the walls etc. The enclosed space near the Chancel, cleared of trees and nettles. The Churchyard fences repaired.

Revisited 26.8.1837
Much wanting attention both in the Church and Churchyard.
In the *former,* I directed – That the *Walls* should be cleaned and coloured, and ceiling whitewashed. That the steps at the South entrance taken up and relaid. That the floors of the Pews relaid where needful, especially those on the *North side.* The *Bible* repaired.
In the *latter* – That the *Ground be cleared away* to a sufficient depth all round the walls, and an open drain formed and kept clear. The *buttresses and walls* pointed and otherwise repaired. The roof of the *Porch* and wall near it repaired. The tower pointed and battlements secured. The roof adjoining the tower protected by *lead,* so as to keep out the wet. The enclosed burial place, at the NE. side of the Chancel, cleared of nettles, weeds etc and the railing removed unless kept in order by the family to whom the burying place formerly belonged. Attention, generally, to neatness, enjoined. 'Nothing done.'

Revisited 6.9.1841
(1) Much improved internally. Some pews in N. aisle need repair. (2) Outside – Tower and spire pointed – cracks under small windows of ditto filled up – heads of larger windows secured. (3) Clock face repainted. (4) Copings of roof pointed. (5) Wooden moulding under eaves on S. side repaired – lead gutters kept clear. (6) Downpipes instead of over-shot spouts (7) Water-pipe on N. side removed. Soil removed from E. end of N. aisle – soil from walls.

[1] Also rector of Yoxall. [2] *Eccles. Revs.:* £100. [3] *Eccles. Revs.:* 'Fit'.

HANBURY 18.8.1830
(A/V/1/4,p.62;A/V/1/2,p.5)

BENEFICE: Hanbury. **Nature:** Vicarage. **Ecton:** £43 15s. 2d. value in the King's Books in 1534, when it was a Rectory. It is now mentioned as a Curacy – (value not certified) – having, since that period, been made a part of the Bishopric of Lichfield and Coventry, who presents to the Cure. **Patron:** The Lord Bishop. **Impropriator:** ['John'] Smith Esqr, of Rugeley, as Lessee under the Bishop.
CHURCH: An antient Gothic structure; nave and side aisles separated by massy circular pillars and pointed arches – Chancel arch modern. **Number it will contain:** Apparently about 400.[1] **Accommodation for Poor:** 90 or 100. **Roof:** Oak, covered with lead – in sound repair. **Walls:** Stone – the North aisle rebuilt – within these few years – solid stone wall; the South wall out of the perpendicular and not solid in its structure. **Floor:** Bricks and gravestones; several of the latter: the whole however *now* tolerably even. **Windows:** Good – those on the N. side new; casements provided. **Doors:** Good – thorough ventilation N. and S. **Pulpit and Desk:** Well placed and firm; but plain and inelegant; painted yellow. **Books:** Bible wants repair. **Seats:** Pews and some open benches with backs – neat and commodious but wanting in uniformity of size and colour. **Galleries:** A small one at the W. end. **Organ:** None. **Font:** There is one. **Chapels:** None. **Benefaction Tables:** Two – which record all the charities. **Vestry:** A small one under the Tower. **Surplices:** Mr Bailye uses his own. **Linen:** Provided. **Plate:** Silver Cup and Patin – Pewter Flagon. **Iron Chest for Register:** At the Vicarage. **Register:** From 1574 – in good preservation, but somewhat mutilated – the oldest Vol. containing, among other curious entries, a record of the interment of Bishop Overton in 1609 (Bishop of Lichfield and Coventry and *Rector* of Hanbury), together with a Latin anagram on his name – there are also coats of arms prefixed to several of the names of persons buried. **Porch:** On the South side – with light-gate of wood. **Vaults:** Several – but none intended hereafter. **Cleanliness:** Well attended to. **Damp:** Not much – except towards E. and SE.
CHANCEL: **Table:** Firm but not very suitable – the Lessee has promised to provide a new Table and the Vicar a new Covering. **Ornaments:** None – except antient monuments. **Repaired by whom:** The Lessee of the Bishop – an additional casement is wanted – and the E. end wall and SE. side want supporting.
STEEPLE: An old square stone Tower. **State of:** Not good – but it has been girded with great care by iron cramps and is now thought secure. **Bells:** Six – all good but one. **Clock:** Good.
CHURCHYARD: **Fence:** Principally brick walls – that on the N. and part of the W. lately built; enclosing an additional piece of ground given by the Lessee – that on the S. is repaired in portions by the different townships. **Gates:** Good. **Drains:** Want clearing. **Graves:** Many too near. **Rubbish:** Not much. **Footpaths:** Two or three – a thoroughfare through the Churchyard – the Church ways are being put in order. **Cattle:** None.
DIVINE SERVICE: **On Sundays:** Full service morning – prayers Afternoon. **On other Days:** None. **Sacrament:** Six times a year. **Communicants:** From 50 to 60. **Catechism:** In Lent.
INCUMBENT: **Name and Residence:** Revd Dr Spry – London and Canterbury.[2]
CURATE: **Name and Residence:** Revd Hugh Bailye – Vicarage. **Licensed:** He is. **Salary:** Lately raised to £80 – and the use of the House. **If serving another church:** None – except during his residence at Lichfield, and occasionally assisting at the Chapels of Newborough and Marchington [in his Parish].
PARSONAGE: An excellent and commodious dwelling, built in 1792 by the present Curate (at that time Vicar) – brick walls, slate roof – two large parlours, kitchen and other offices on the ground floor – four good bedrooms, study and servants' rooms above. **State of:** Very good.[3] **Outbuildings:** Barn, Coach house; stables etc all good.
INCOME: **Gross Value:** Stated to be £300.[4] **Tithes:**

Endowed with all the great tythes of Newborough and the hay tithe of Fauld. **Glebe:** 60 or 70 acres. **Surplice Fees:** £5 0s. 0d. **Easter dues and small Payments:**[5] £20. **Queen Anne's Bounty:** None. **Terrier:** None known of.

SCHOOLS: **Endowed School:** £10 per annum left for the education of eight or ten children – which is incorporated with **Subscription Day School:** A National School, 60 or 70 children. **Sunday School:** The same as the weekly. **Lancaster School:** None.

DISSENTERS: **Dissenters' School:** A small Wesleyan Chapel, lately built at Draycott – and a Sunday School attached to it.

POPULATION: Of Hanbury *proper* 992 – (in 1821) of *whole Parish* 2,517; now, supposed 1,200 – now 3,000.

MISCELLANEOUS: **Monuments:** Some antient ones to the families of Villiers, Egerton, Adderley [etc].

PARISH CLERK: Aaron Bannister. **Appointed by:** The Vicar. **Salary:** £2 0s. 0d. and fees and payments for cleaning etc.

CHURCHWARDENS: John Bott Esqr for the Vicar. Mr Thomas Ford for the Parish.

ORDERS MADE: The state of the South wall, and of the roof, pillars and Arches connected with it to be examined by an experienced Architect and reported* – likewise that of the Chancel South wall and East end. The Bible to be repaired and re-bound. The unpainted Pews to be painted, by the respective occupiers, to correspond with the others. Iron work of bells – and cramps of Tower to be painted – the cracked bell recast. A more effectual open drain to be formed, of a suitable depth and width, all round the Church and Chancel. No graves [to be dug] within ten feet [of the walls].

*This report was sent to me November 18 – the Architect (Mr Johnson of Lichfield) pronounced it necessary to take down the S. wall and rebuild it, putting on, also, a new roof, with eave spouts and down-pipes – the upper part of *the Tower* likewise he considers in an insecure state and recommends spouting the North side of the roof – making a drain etc and painting the Pews.

I sent the Report to the Churchwarden (Mr Bott) the following day – with directions to have the whole of the Repairs completed within *two years* from this time – November 19, 1830.

I revisited the Church on the 25th of August 1837, and found that very few of the directions left at my former visit had been attended to. The Church and Churchyard were both in a very slovenly state.

I left with the Revd James Riddell, Vicar of Hanbury (recently appointed Rural dean of the District of Tutbury) the following directions for the Churchwardens.

(1) *Inside the Church*
The walls both of Nave and Chancel to be coloured, ceilings whitewashed – Vestry walls and ceiling ditto – Vestry chimney cured of smoking – and a casement opened in the window. The Bible repaired in the binding – a new Communion cloth – I *recommended* (but did not *order*) that the pews *should be painted uniformly* – some of them at present being painted, others not.

(2) *Outside*
The North side of the Roof to be spouted, with a down-pipe to the ground – at the NE. angle. An open drain to be formed, and kept clear, all round the Church. The Roof repaired where needful, and the Gutters cleared out. The Tower to be secured and pointed – Clock face painted. The doorway into the Chancel to be repaired. 'All done – except Chancel.'

Revisited 7.9.1841
Inside
(1) Books to be repaired – Cushion and Covering to Pulpit renewed – coverings of Clergyman's and Clerk's seats renewed. (2) Walls of Church cleaned and recoloured on S. side. (3) Floors of pews boarded – (recommended re-pewing or open benches). (4) Iron window bars painted. (5) Vestry floor boarded – walls recoloured.

Chancel
(6) New cover for Communion Table – and kneelings. (7) Walls coloured.

Tower
(8) Cracked bell recast. (9) Tower effectively repaired and secured. (10) Lead gutters of roof of ditto laid even.

Churchyard
(11) Fence on East side made good – and copings of brick wall re-placed.

[1] *Eccles. Revs.:* 570. [2] Also chancellor and canon residentiary of Lichfield cathedral: *Eccles. Revs.* [3] *Eccles. Revs.:* 'Fit.' [4] *Eccles. Revs.:* £455. [5] 'And small Payments' enclosed in brackets.

KINGSTONE[1] (A/V/1/4,p.63;A/V/1/2,p.90)

BENEFICE: Kingstone. **Nature:** Perpetual Curacy. **Ecton:** Coll. of Penkridge olim Propr. Mr Sneyd Patron. Clear yearly value £10 0s. 0d. **Patron:** Lord Talbot. **Impropriator:** Ditto.

CHURCH: A small modern building, with single body. **Number it will contain:** About 200. **Roof:** In good repair. **Walls:** Stone. **Floor:** Brick – level. **Windows:** No casements. **Doors:** Good. **Pulpit and Desk:** ——. **Books:** Pretty good. **Seats:** Good. **Galleries:** One at the W. end. **Organ:** None. **Font:** None. **Benefaction Tables:** Provided. **Vestry:** None. **Surplices:** One. **Linen:** Provided. **Plate:** Silver Cup and Patin. **Iron Chest for Register:** At the Clergyman's house. **Register:** Two Vols prior to 1812 – oldest 1628. **Porch:** There is one – but no lock on the gate. **Vaults:** None recently. **Cleanliness:** Attended to. **Damp:** Not much.

CHANCEL: **Table:** Good. **Repaired by whom:** Lord Talbot.

STEEPLE: Square brick Tower. **State of:** Pretty good. **Bells:** Three. **Clock:** None.

CHURCHYARD: **Fence:** In good repair. **Gates:** ——. **Drains:** None – nor spouts. **Cattle:** Cows.

DIVINE SERVICE: **On Sundays:** [Morning and afternoon] alternately with Gratwich. **Sacrament:** Five times a year. **Communicants:** 20 to 30.

INCUMBENT: **Name and Residence:** Revd Thomas Powell Browne.[2] **If not resident:** In Stowe Parish, adjoining. **What Duty he performs:** The whole.

PARSONAGE: None.[3]

INCOME: **Gross Value:** £48 10s. 0d. **Easter Dues and small Payments:** £10 from the Patron. **Queen Anne's Bounty:** £200 – interest paid. **Terrier:** None.
SCHOOLS: **Endowed School:** None. **Subscription Day School:** None. **Sunday School:** 40 or 50 children. **Lancaster School:** None.
DISSENTERS: **Dissenters' School:** None. **Dissenting Chapels:** None.
POPULATION: 320.
PARISH CLERK: Richard Stonier.
CHURCHWARDENS: —— Spooner.
ORDERS MADE: Three casements, at least, to be made. A font to be provided. A lock put on the Porch Gate. Spouts, pipes and drains.

Visited 11.9.1837
Directions to Churchwarden. (1) A new gate to the Porch and roof repaired. (2) Grass etc removed from the walls – and open space laid with gravel etc. (3) Eave-spouts and down-pipes. (4) Buttresses repaired – walls pointed etc. (5) Windows repaired – bars painted. (6) Walls and ceilings repaired and coloured. (7) Brick floors of pews taken up, and boards put instead. (8) Bible rebound or new – new surplice. (9) Roof and floor of belfry repaired – weatherboards put up.

[1] A/V/1/2: 'Not personally visited, owing to the badness of the roads and want of time – enquiries made of Mr Browne the Incumbent, when I visited Gratwich'. [2] Also rector of Gratwich. [3] *Eccles. Revs.:* 'None'.

LEIGH 14.7.1830 (A/V/1/4, p.64; A/V/1/2, p.94)

BENEFICE: Leigh. **Nature:** Rectory. **Ecton:** King's Books £14 0s. 5d. Abb. Burton 66s. 8d. **Patron:** Lord Bagot. **Impropriator:** None.
CHURCH: Has been a remarkably handsome Gothic structure; nave, side aisles, transept and chancel – the tower over the transept; pointed Arches and fluted pillars. **Number it will contain:** About 350 or 400.[1] **Accommodation for Poor:** 30 or 40. **Roof:** Oak covered with lead – in good state. **Walls:** Stone – much out of the perpendicular, especially on North side; as also the pillars and arches on that side. **Floor:** Quarries and flat stones – much sunk in some places. **Windows:** Good – but not provided with casements. **Doors:** Good. **Pulpit and Desk:** In good condition and well placed – purple cloth ornaments. **Books:** Much out of repair. Seats: Oak – not uniform; the free seats and those in the Chancel much out of repair. **Galleries:** One at W. end – one on N. side. **Organ:** None. **Font:** A very old one, of stone, lined with lead. **Chapels:** The transept seems to have been divided into two chapels, or chancels, North and South – one still retains the name of the Ashenhurst Chancel, but now belongs to Mr Evans of Derby – the other is called 'Wood's aisle', or Chancel. **Vestry:** None – recommended. **Surplices:** A new one is to be ordered. **Linen:** Provided. **Plate:** Silver Flagon, Chalice and Patin. **Iron Chest for Register:** At the Rectory. **Register:** From 1541 to present time – in good preservation. **Porch:** One on the South side – no light gate. **Vaults:** None for the last 40 years (many before that time) – at which time the Rector put a stop to the practice of burying inside the Church, from the mischief done to the Pillars and arches. **Damp:** Much on the floor – especially on South side. **Dimensions:** 56ft. by 41ft. 6in. Transept. 70ft. 6in. by 19ft. 6in.
CHANCEL: 37ft. 3in. by 18ft. 8in. **Table:** Neat oak table, with green cloth covering. **Ornaments:** Painted glass. **Repaired by whom:** The Rector; who has lately had the roof repaired and walls strengthened – the latter are much out of perpendicular still, but said to be safe – the floor is very uneven.
STEEPLE: Square stone Tower, with battlements. **State of:** Good. **Bells:** Five – one of them new – all good. **Clock:** In good repair.
CHURCHYARD: **Fence:** Partly kept by the Rector – partly by the Parish – partly Mr Evans as proprietor of the Ashenhurst estate; on the side next the Rectory there is no sufficient fence. **Gates:** Good. **Drains:** None – much wanted. **Graves:** None very near. **Rubbish:** None. **Footpaths:** No trespass paths – the others properly kept. **Cattle:** None *now*.
DIVINE SERVICE: **On Sundays:** Full service morning – prayers afternoon. **On other Days:** None. **Sacrament:** Six times a year. **Catechism:** In Lent.
INCUMBENT: **Name and Residence:** Lord Bishop of Oxford.[2]
CURATE: **Name and Residence:** Revd James Beaven – in the Rectory. **Licensed:** Not yet – only just appointed. **Salary:** £150 and the house. **If serving another church:** No other.
PARSONAGE: A spacious, old house – brick walls, tiled roof – two sitting rooms; kitchen etc on ground floor – five bedrooms and dressing room on first floor – five attics – handsome oak staircase and wainscoting to parlours. **State of:** Very good – lately put into thorough repair.[3] **Outbuildings:** Stable, Coach house, Cow-house etc all new.
INCOME: **Gross Value:** About £700.[4] **Glebe:** 58 acres. **Easter Dues and small Payments:**[5] Collected. **Terrier:** There is one.
SCHOOLS: **Endowed School:** There is one – £60 or 70 per annum – free to all the Parishioners. **Sunday School:** There is. **Lancaster School:** None.
DISSENTERS: **Dissenters' School:** ——. **Dissenting Chapels:** A Wesleyan Chapel.
POPULATION: About 1,000.
MISCELLANEOUS: **Monuments:** Several – belonging to the Ashenhurst and Whitehall families and others.[6]
PARISH CLERK: Samuel Atkins. **Appointed by:** The Rector. **Salary:** Not stated.
CHURCHWARDENS: Mr Edward Blurton for the Rector. Mr John Carter for the Parish.
ORDERS MADE: The floor of the Church to be laid even – that of the Chancel relaid. The Pews, and free benches, in the body of the Church: and N. and S. Chancels, to be put into proper repair. Three Casements to be made on each side of the body of the Church and one in each Chancel. Light iron gates to be placed at the North and South entrances [– 'not done on S.' –]. New books to be provided for the Reading and Clerk's desks. An open drain to be formed all round the Church. The fence, on the Rector's side; to be made good. No graves to be allowed within ten

feet. The North wall, together with the Pillars and Arches on the N. side, to be examined by an Architect, and reported. A Vestry *recommended*.

Revisited 11.9.1837
Roof to be examined and repaired. Spouts and down-pipes made fit to carry off the wet. Windows repaired – iron bars painted. Pews and floors repaired. Roof of Woods aisle repaired – rubbish removed.

[1] *Eccles. Revs.*: 600. [2] Also dean of Canterbury and rector of Blithfield: *Eccles. Revs.* [3] *Eccles. Revs.*: 'Fit.' [4] *Eccles. Revs.*: gross value £811. [5] A/V/1/4: 'And small Payments' enclosed in brackets. [6] Altered from 'Several, in the Ashenhurst aisle (or Chancel).'

MAYFIELD 17.7.1830
(A/V/1/4,p.65;A/V/1/2,p.109)

BENEFICE: Church Mayfield (alias Mathfield). **Nature:** Vicarage. **Ecton:** Pri: Tutbury Propr. Clear value £47 0s. 0d. **Patron:** Dr Greaves (Ecton. Mrs Turner). **Impropriator:** Mr Bill of Farley has one-half of the Tithes, the Vicar one-half.
CHURCH: An antient, handsome Saxon structure – nave and side aisles separated by circular pillars and arches – Chancel arch and windows pointed. **Number it will contain:** About 300 in pews. **Accommodation for Poor:** Some benches for adults and children. **Roof:** Oak covered with lead – good. **Walls:** Stone – good. **Floor:** Flags – even. **Windows:** Pretty good – but an additional window much wanted on the N. side, and two more casements. **Doors:** Want repair. **Pulpit and Desk:** Good and well placed – velvet Cushion. **Books:** Bible wants repair. **Seats:** Very handsome carved oak. **Galleries:** One for the singers and others, at the W. end. **Organ:** None. **Font:** There is. **Chapels:** None. **Benefaction Tables:** Not complete – some benefactions lost. **Vestry:** None. **Surplices:** Three – one new. **Linen:** Provided. **Plate:** Silver Cup – pewter flagon and Patin. **Iron Chest for Register:** In the Clerk's seat. **Register:** Not seen – the Clergyman did not attend. **Porch:** A very good one on the S. side. **Vaults:** None lately – several formerly. **Cleanliness:** Attended to. **Damp:** Much on the N. wall. **Dimensions:** 53ft. 5in. by 36ft. 3in.
CHANCEL: 40ft. by 17ft. 11in. **Table:** Wants repair and cleaning. **Ornaments:** None. **Repaired by whom:** Mr Bill of Farley.
STEEPLE: Square stone tower, roofed with lead. **State of:** Good – excepting the weatherboards and floor of belfry. **Bells:** Three – good. **Clock:** None.
CHURCHYARD: **Fence:** Stone wall and hedge – the latter wants trimming. **Gates:** Good. **Drains:** Not provided. **Graves:** Some too near. **Rubbish:** None. **Footpaths:** There are trespass paths – to be prevented, if possible. **Cattle:** A horse.
DIVINE SERVICE: **On Sundays:** Full service Morning – prayers afternoon. **On other Days:** None ordinarily. **Sacrament:** Four times a year. **Communicants:** 20 to 40. **Catechism:** Before confirmation.
INCUMBENT: **Name and Residence:** Revd Paul Belcher. **If not resident:** At Ashbourn – about two miles off. **What Duty he performs:** The whole.
PARSONAGE: A good, large, brick house; tiled roof. **State of:** Good.[2] **Outbuildings:** Barns, stables etc in good repair.
INCOME: **Gross Value:** £3 or 400.[3] **Tithes:** All the small tithes, one-half of the large. **Terrier:** There is one.
SCHOOLS: **Endowed School:** None. **Subscription Day School:** A small Infant School. **Sunday School:** A small one – not well attended to.
DISSENTERS: **Dissenters' School:** One. **Dissenting Chapels:** Two.
POPULATION: From 1,800 to 2,000.[4]
PARISH CLERK: Thomas James. **Appointed by:** The Vicar. **Salary:** £2 2s. 0d. – too small.
CHURCHWARDENS: Mr Thomas Smith for the Vicar. Mr S Jackson for the Parish.
ORDERS MADE: An additional window to be put in on the North side of the Church – and two more casements towards the West end. No new graves to be made inside the Church. The Bible repaired – benefaction tables completed – Communion table repaired and cleaned, rails fixed and cleaned. The roof, walls and door of the *Chancel* to be repaired – the floor taken up and relaid – iron bars of windows painted; the walls externally pointed and made good – ivy removed. Trees removed from the North side of the Church, and the grass and weeds etc from the East end – Ivy removed from the North side. The hedge trimmed – earth cleared away round the Church walls – open drain formed, spouts and pipes affixed. No graves within ten feet of Church walls – nor large cattle to feed. The footpath stopped if possible. Light Gates at the Porch entrance recommended – also a Vestry, and an increase of the Clerk's Salary.

Revisited 12.9.1837
Everything in excellent order – almost all my former directions carried into effect – nothing necessary but – (1) To repair Bible. (2) To varnish old oak pews. (3) To complete the Benefaction table. (4) To have metal spout on N. side of Chancel painted and the old chimney pipes removed. (5) To provide a *Vestry*, either under the Tower, or in some more convenient position. 'Qu? *Chancel*. Mullions of windows.'

[1] Also rector of Heather (Leics.): *Eccles. Revs.* [2] *Eccles. Revs.*: 'Fit.' [3] *Eccles. Revs.*: Gross income £151. [4] *Eccles. Revs.*: 915.

MARCHINGTON 18.8.1830
(A/V/1/4,p.66;A/V/1/2,p.7)

BENEFICE: Marchington. **Nature:** Perpetual Curacy – under Hanbury to which it is properly a Chapelry. **Ecton:** £8 clear value. **Patron:** The Vicar of Hanbury. **Impropriator:** Supposed, the Bishop, as Rector of the *Parish;* but from advantage taken of recent *inclosures* it appears that the inhabitants of Marchington neither pay great nor small tythes.
CHURCH: A plain building – rebuilt 70 or 80 years ago – single body and roof – no Chancel. **Number it will contain:** About 200. **Accommodation for Poor:** All the seats free. **Roof:** Good. **Walls:** Brick; with stone surbase, window frames and

quoins. **Floor:** Flags and some bricks – not even and much worn. **Windows:** Only one on the N. side; three blocked up – those on S. good but casements not properly opened. **Doors:** Good. **Pulpit and Desk:** Not very firm; but in other respects good – a faded cushion to pulpit. **Books:** Very much out of repair. **Seats:** Neat and uniform – but brick floors, many sunk and damp. **Galleries:** One at the W. end. **Organ:** None. **Font:** There is one – basin wanted. **Chapels:** None. **Benefaction Tables:** Two large ones recording several benefactions – some in land, rental £34 19s. 5d. yearly – others in money, £3 7s. 0d. yearly. **Vestry:** None. **Surplices:** One – not very good. **Linen:** Provided. **Plate:** Silver Cup, plated Patin, Pewter flagon. **Iron Chest for Register:** At the Parsonage. **Register:** From 1672 – the latter Vols not regularly filled up. **Porch:** None. **Vaults:** Some. **Cleanliness:** Not well attended to – nor ventilation. **Damp:** Some appearance on the floors of pews and towards E. end.

CHANCEL: **Table:** Good and firm – faded covering and cushion of crimson cloth. **Ornaments:** None. **Repaired by whom:** All repairs done by the inhabitants of the Township – who complain heavily of having to contribute also to Hanbury Church, and the new Church in the Forest.[1]

STEEPLE: A small brick tower, with octagonal cupola above. **State of:** Good. **Bells:** Four – good. **Clock:** A new one.

CHURCHYARD: **Fence:** Hedge on N. and S. sides; not neatly kept – paling on W. – posts and rails on E. – the two latter kept by the Parish. **Gates:** Good. **Drains:** None – nor spouts. **Graves:** Some too near – the Churchyard very wet – graves often full of water. **Rubbish:** None. **Footpaths:** A thoroughfare – said to be necessary. **Cattle:** The Curate's horse.

DIVINE SERVICE: **On Sundays:** Once, alternately with Newborough. **On other Days:** None. **Sacrament:** Four times a year. **Communicants:** 25 to 30. **Catechism:** In Lent.

INCUMBENT: **Name and Residence:** Revd Hugh Bennett – in the Parsonage.[2] **What duty he performs:** The whole.

PARSONAGE: A brick building, erected in 1811 – not substantially built – four rooms on ground floor, eight bedrooms above and one attic chamber. The present Curate advanced £200 – the Governors of Queen Anne's bounty granted £300 in addition to £400 granted before. **State of:** The timbers of roof not good.[3] **Outbuildings:** Stable, cowhouse etc.

INCOME: **Gross Value:** Not ascertain – supposed about £100. **Glebe:** 22 acres. **Easter Dues and small Payments:** None. **Queen Anne's Bounty:** £27 remaining from the grant before alluded to. **Terrier:** None.

SCHOOLS: **Endowed School:** £10 chargeable on land in the Parish – to which £10 is added by subscriptions and the Parish – 30 children taught free, on the national plan. **Subscription Day School:** None besides the preceding. **Sunday School:** About 50 children. **Lancaster School:** None.

DISSENTERS: **Dissenters' School:** None. **Dissenting Chapels:** None.

POPULATION: About 800.

MISCELLANEOUS: **Monuments:** An antient one (1591) to *Walter Vernon*.

PARISH CLERK: Samuel Bagshaw. **Appointed by:** The Minister. **Salary:** £2 0s. 0d. and other sums for cleaning etc.

CHURCHWARDENS: Mr John Owen for Marchington. Mr Benjamin Hickling for Woodlands.

ORDERS MADE: An additional window to be thrown out on the N. side, towards the top – with a casement. Attention to be paid to *ventilation*. The floor to be laid even and *raised* – the floors of the Pews *boarded*. The Bible to be rebound or a new one provided – new Prayer Book – and the Clerks repaired. A suitable basin for the Font. The roof to be spouted etc and an open drain formed – also a *surf* to drain the Chapel yard. No graves to be allowed within ten feet.

Recommend for consideration. The expediency of putting up a Gallery along the N. side. The practicability of stopping the thoroughfare of the Chapel yard not mentioned.

25.8.1837
Revisited this Church, in company with Revd James Riddell, the Rural Dean.

Found the very same defects, increased by lapse of time, which I noticed and desired to be remedied on my first visit – the Church disgracefully dirty, damp, and bearing every appearance of neglect – the Churchyard in a very slovenly state – hedges untrimmed, fences ruinous etc.

I left the following directions, which the Rural dean promised to have carried into effect.

Inside – The roof to be examined, and repaired where needful. The walls (internally) repaired and coloured. The windows put into thorough repair. A new window thrown out on the N. side of the Church. The Pews cleaned out, and kept free from dust and damp. The stairs leading to the Gallery, and the pannels etc of the Gallery, repaired. The Bible and Clerk's Prayer Book repaired and rebound.

Outside – The Light Gates at the W. entrance of the Churchyard, and the railing on the same side, repaired and painted. The hedges all round trimmed and kept neat; nettles removed etc. The Church spouted all round, and down-pipes put up. The outside of the Church, and Bell-tower, coloured – a grey stone colour. 'Partly done – Marchington Woodlands.'

Revisited 6.9.1841
Much improved internally. (1) Bible and Reading desk to be repaired – new Prayer Book for Clerk – Service book for Communion Table. (2) I strongly recommended a *new floor* along the middle aisle – and boarded floors to pews. (3) Spouts and down-pipes – open drain round the Church. (4) Fences renewed and kept in order. (5) New lich-gates – gates locked – thoroughfare stopped.

[1] Christ Church, Needwood. [2] Also perpetual curate of Newborough (Staffs.) and vicar of Elmley Castle (Worcs.): *Eccles. Revs.*: [3] *Eccles. Revs.*: 'Fit'.

NEWBOROUGH 6.7.1830
(A/V/1/4,p.67;A/V/1/2,p.6)

BENEFICE: Newborough. **Nature:** Chapel of Ease to Hanbury. **Ecton:** £5 clear value. **Patron:** The Vicar of Hanbury. **Impropriator:** Ditto – the Vicarage being endowed with the *great* tythes of Newborough.
CHURCH: A small modern building – plain and neat – single body. **Number it will contain:** 216 in pews.[1] **Accommodation for Poor:** About 40 sittings in the Gallery – and some benches for children. **Roof:** Oak covered with tile – in sound repair. **Walls:** Brick – firm and upright. **Floor:** Quarries; even, but rather damp. **Windows:** Good – well provided with casements. **Doors:** Good. **Pulpit and Desk:** Very neat and well-placed: crimson cloth cushion. **Books:** Prayer-book bad; Bible and Clerk's Prayer Book want repair. **Seats:** Very neat and in good condition; but wanting in uniformity. **Galleries:** A small one at the W. end, for the Organ. **Organ:** There is one. **Font:** There is. **Chapels:** None. **Benefaction Tables:** None. **Vestry:** None. **Surplices:** One – good. **Linen:** Suitable. **Silver Cup and Patin** – Pewter flagon. **Iron Chest for Register:** At Marchington. **Register:** Five Vols, from 1601 to 1812 – not in good state – the Vols in present use are not regularly filled up, nor transmitted to Lichfield. **Porch:** None. **Vaults:** ——. **Cleanliness:** Attended to. **Damp:** Some on the floor – occasioned by the late excessive rains. **Dimensions:** 49ft. 11in. by 24ft.
CHANCEL: There is no chancel. **Table:** Neat – oak. **Ornaments:** None.
STEEPLE: A square brick tower. **State of:** Good. **Bells:** Two. **Clock:** None.
CHURCHYARD: **Fence:** Out of repair; the yard much trespassed upon from adjoining garden and cottages. **Gates:** Good. **Drains:** None. **Graves:** No burials in the Chapel yard. **Cattle:** None.
DIVINE SERVICE: **On Sundays:** Morning and Afternoon alternately [with Marchington] – prayers and sermon. **On other Days:** None. **Sacrament:** Four times a year. **Communicants:** 30.
INCUMBENT: **Name and Residence:** Revd Hugh Bennett.[2] **If not resident:** At Marchington – two or three miles off. **What Duty he performs:** The whole, alternately with Marchington.
PARSONAGE: None.[3]
INCOME: **Gross Value:** Not ascertained; the income stated to arise greatly from land, partly from a payment by the Vicar – the Curate was prevented by illness from meeting me.[4]
SCHOOLS: **Endowed School:** There is one, supported by land at Moreton – value £10 a year. **Subscription Day School:** None; but there is a Girls' School at Holly Bush, supported by Mrs Hall. **Sunday School:** 30 children. **Lancaster School:** None.
DISSENTERS: **Dissenters' School:** ——. **Dissenting Chapels:** ——.
POPULATION: 8 or 900 (in 1821, 744).
PARISH CLERK: James Lloyd. **Appointed by:** The Curate. **Salary:** £2 2s. 0d.
CHURCHWARDENS: Mr Isaac Mousley – chosen[5] by the inhabitants of the chapelry.
ORDERS MADE: A new Prayer Book to be provided for the Reading desk – the Clerk's Prayer Book and Bible in reading desk rebound. A benefaction table to be set up and a table of the Ten Commandments. The fence of the Churchyard to be put into complete repair; and all trespasses forbidden. Spouts to be placed round the roofs, and pipes affixed. The Ivy prevented from being injurious to the windows etc of the Chapel.
   Mem: An enlargement of the Chapel and Chapel yard, and a consecration of the latter so as to allow of burials, is *much needed* – the population being large, and the distance from the Mother Church (to which at present all the dead are carried) three miles, through very bad roads.

Revisited 26.8.1837
This Church has recently been enlarged and much improved;[6] both externally and internally – partly by means of a grant from the Diocesan Church-building Society, but chiefly at the expense of Mr Hall, of Holly Bush. It is expected that the woodwork in the inside will be completed, and the Chapel reopened, in the course of a few weeks. Mr Hall intends also to have the Churchyard cleared and consecrated – and, if possible, to have the houses removed which have, by a most shameful encroachment, been built upon it. Everything being in a state of progress, I had nothing to suggest except the expediency of putting up spouts, and keeping an open space all round the walls.

Revisited 6.9.1841
Nothing wanted in this Church – (beautifully repaired and restored since my last visit) except spouts and pipes – and Churchyard consecrated and freed from encroachments.
   N.B. Resident Curate *much wanted*.

[1] *Eccles. Revs.:* 289. [2] Also perpetual curate of Marchington (Staffs.) and vicar of Elmley Castle (Worcs.): *Eccles. Revs.* [3] *Eccles. Revs.:* 'None'. [4] *Eccles. Revs.:* £91. [5] 'Appointed' deleted. [6] Faculty granted 12.5.1835 (B/C/2/1832–6, p.485) for the extension of the church eastwards and the extension of the W. gallery.

ROCESTER 17.7.1830
(A/V/1/4,p.68;A/V/1/2,p.107)

BENEFICE: Rocester (alias Rocettur, Ecton). **Nature:** Perpetual Curacy – formerly a Vicarage, with several Chapels in the neighbourhood attached to it. **Ecton:** Vicarage, Clear value £4 6s. 8d. – Mon. Rocettur Impr. **Patron:** – Bainbrigg Esqr. **Impropriator:** Different individuals have the great Tythes.
CHURCH: A small building, rebuilt seven years ago – single body, flat ceiling – bow-window at the East end. **Number it will contain:** 450.[2] **Accommodation for Poor:** 270. **Roof:** Oak covered with slate – not in very good condition. **Walls:** Solid stone – firm and good. **Floor:** Flags. **Windows:** Good – but no casements on the N. side – two wanted. **Doors:** Good. **Pulpit and Desk:** Good – handsome crimson velvet Cushion and hangings. **Books:** Bible bad. **Seats:** Neat and in good state, except some of the floors on N. side. **Galleries:** At the W. end, and partially along the N. and S. sides. **Organ:** None. **Font:** There is one

– no basin. **Chapels:** None. **Benefaction Tables:** There are – some benefactions have been lost. **Vestry:** There is one – a closet wanted for the Surplices etc. **Surplices:** Two – good. **Linen:** Provided. **Plate:** Pewter flagon and old Silver Cup – very indifferent. **Chest for Papers:** There is one. **Iron Chest for Register:** In the Vestry Wall. **Register:** From 1568 to the present time. **Porch:** None. **Vaults:** One made last year, without the Minister's knowledge. **Cleanliness:** Not well attended to. **Damp:** Not much appearance. **Dimensions:** 50ft. 4in. (exclusive of the Bow) by 45ft. 9in.

CHANCEL: **Table:** Good and firm. **Ornaments:** None. **Repaired by whom:** The Parish – the windows want cleaning and repairs.

STEEPLE: Square stone Tower. **State of:** Good. **Bells:** Five. **Clock:** There is one.

CHURCHYARD: **Fence:** Brick wall, and hedge – the latter wants attention. **Gates:** Good. **Drains:** Provided – a pipe wanted at the W. end. **Graves:** None too near. **Rubbish:** Weeds etc in abundance. **Footpaths:** A thoroughfare to a Manufactory, which leads close past the East end of the Church, very objectionable. **Cattle:** Horses.

DIVINE SERVICE: **On Sundays:** Usually in the Afternoon only – sometimes Morning also. **On other Days:** None. **Sacrament:** Eight or ten times a year. **Communicants:** 50. **Catechism:** In the Church, occasionally.

INCUMBENT: **Name and Residence:** Revd G Hake, Ellaston, two or three miles off.[3] **What Duty he performs:** The whole.

PARSONAGE: None.[4]

INCOME: **Gross Value:** Not much exceeding £50 per annum – the benefice has been much despoiled of its rights – the only payments (exclusive of Fees) are £3 6s. 8d. paid out of an estate in the Parish, and £50 from Queen Anne's Bounty. **Queen Anne's Bounty:** The present Incumbent has never yet obtained possession of the Churchyard, which is claimed as *private property* – by purchase. **Terrier:** There is a Copy, dated 1751 – which clearly establishes the Clergyman's right to the Churchyard, as his freehold – it states various payments as then *lost*.

SCHOOLS: **Endowed School:** None. **Subscription Day School:** None. **Sunday School:** 120 or 130 children.

DISSENTERS: **Dissenting Chapels:** One – and some meetings.

POPULATION: 1,000.

PARISH CLERK: James Thompson. **Appointed by:** The Minister. **Salary:** £5 0s. 0d. including various duties.

CHURCHWARDENS: Mr Thomas Smith for the Minister. Mr William Arnold for the Parish.

ORDERS MADE: The roof to be examined and repaired – two casements made on the North side of the Church – and all the casements regularly opened. A new Prayer Book provided for the Reading Desk [Qu? *Bible* – see Art. 15]. The floors of the Pews on the North side repaired. A proper basin for the Font, and closet in the Vestry. A new Flagon for the Sacramental Wine. The Covering of the Table renewed and a cover provided for it. The Chancel windows cleaned, and repaired so as to exclude the wet. The hedge on the East side of the Churchyard repaired – and the thoroughfare stopped if possible; or else the road carried to a greater distance from the Church. A Pipe, or Trunk spout, to be placed at the W. end of the Church. The Churchyard to be kept free from weeds and large Cattle. No interments to be made within the Church without the express permission of the Minister.

Revisited 12.9.1837

Much out of order still – the Churchwarden however promises immediate and effective attention to the following *Directions*. (1) *Two large casements* to be opened on *North* side of the Church – and casements regularly opened. (2) New prayer-book for the Clerk's desk, and new altar service – also new covering for Table. (3) The roofs carefully examined and repaired – water-courses kept clear etc. (4) The walls (inside) coloured and ceilings whitewashed. (5) Ditto in the Vestry – and the chimney cured of smoking. (6) Ditto in the *Chancel* – and the cracks filled up etc. (7) Windows cleaned – and repaired; iron bars painted etc.

Outside – (8) Nettles and bushes removed from S. and SW. sides of Church. (9) Down-pipe at NW. end of the Church, near the door. (10) The thoroughfare of Churchyard stopped if possible – otherwise an iron fence to guard the East end of the Church. (11) No heavy cattle in Churchyard. 'Nothing done – apparently.'

[1] *Eccles. Revs.* gives Mrs Bainbrigge as patron and impropriator. [2] *Eccles. Revs.:* 652. [3] Also vicar of Ellastone and Chilvers Coton: *Eccles. Revs.* [4] *Eccles. Revs.:* 'None'.

ROLLESTON 17.11.1829
(A/V/1/4,p.69;A/V/1/2,p.3)

BENEFICE: Rolleston. **Nature:** Rectory. **Ecton:** £13 19s. 7d. King's Books – (priori de Tutbury 40s. pro duabus partibus decim: terr: dominical: in Rolston). **Patron:** Sir Oswald Moseley, Bart. **Impropriator:** Sir Oswald claims a modus over about 100 acres – the remainder of the Tythes are in the Rector.

CHURCH: An ancient Gothic building – with a centre and one side aisle – spacious Chancel. **Number it will contain:** About 500.[1] **Accommodation for Poor:** 60 in pews, and in the gallery. **Roof:** Oak covered with lead. **Walls:** Stone – upright in general, with exception of part of the S. wall. **Floor:** Brick – even. **Windows:** Good – three open casements. **Doors:** Good. **Pulpit and Desk:** Very neat, and well situated. Velvet cushion to pulpit. **Books:** Very handsome, and in good order. **Seats:** Oak varnished – board floors. **Galleries:** One for the Singers. **Organ:** None. **Font:** A handsome old fashioned stone font. **Chapels:** None. **Benefaction Tables:** Several, which record all the charities. **Vestry:** A small one, not in very good order – suffers from damp. **Surplices:** Two – one of them wants repair. **Linen:** Good. **Plate:** Two pewter flagons, silver Cup and Paten. **Chest for Papers:** There is one. **Iron Chest for Register:** At the Rectory. **Register:** Four vols besides those in present use – the oldest date appears to be 1589 – the earlier volumes mutilated. **Porch:** There is one on the South side: formerly one on the North, which was taken down some years ago and a handsome entrance made in its stead. **Vaults:** Within the Communion rail, and in other parts of the Church. **Cleanliness:** Attended to. **Damp:** A little: at the bottom of the walls and in the Vestry. **Dimensions:** 54ft. by 25ft., side aisle 17ft. 6in. wide.

CHANCEL: 23ft. long. 19ft. 4in. wide. **Table:** Oak – handsomely covered. **Ornaments:** Commandments – Lord's Prayer – King's Arms. **Repaired by whom:** The Rector repairs the walls, roof and windows; the parish, the floor and communion rails. The whole in good repair.

STEEPLE: Square tower: with spire above. **State of:** Very good: recently pointed and repaired. **Bells:** Five. In good order. **Clock:** There is one: in good order.

CHURCHYARD: **Fence:** Kept by the Parish: a quick hedge, rails, and school-house on the East and South: on the West, handsome iron palisade belonging to Sir Oswald. On the N. next the road, a low stone wall. The fence on the S. and E. wants repair. **Gates:** Pretty good. **Drains:** None at present – ordered. **Graves:** Not near the walls. **Rubbish:** Some – ordered to be removed. **Footpaths:** None that can be prevented – the boys attending the school tread the grass down very much and otherwise injure the appearance of the Churchyard – ordered that they do not make a playground of it. **Cattle:** Chiefly sheep: occasionally a horse turned in.

DIVINE SERVICE: **On Sundays:** Full service in the Morning – prayers the Afternoon. **On other Days:** During Lent. **Sacrament:** Four times a year. **Communicants:** 40 to 60. **Catechism:** In the Sunday school.

INCUMBENT: **Name and Residence:** Revd John Peploe Moseley, Rectory. **What Duty he performs:** The whole usually.

PARSONAGE: A roomy commodious building, brick, rough cast, the front old fashioned – a large handsome dining room, and drawing room, built not long since, behind. **State of:** Very good.[2] **Outbuildings:** Stable, Coach-house, cowshed etc, a *farmyard* thoroughly furnished – buildings in good repair.

INCOME: **Gross Value:** About £900.[3] **Tithes:** £250. **Glebe:** About 130 acres, which lets for 50s. per acre. **Surplice Fees:** About £50. **Easter Dues and small Payments:**[4] Collected. **Queen Anne's Bounty:** None. **Terrier:** The Rector has a copy.

SCHOOLS: **Endowed School:** There is one supported by charitable bequests which have been left at different times, especially by members of the Caldwell family, as recorded on their monuments in the Chancel. **Subscription Day School:** None – the endowed school is free to the whole parish. **Sunday School:** About 70, boys and girls. **Lancaster School:** None.

DISSENTERS: **Dissenters School:** None. **Dissenting Chapels:** ——.

POPULATION: 869 in 1821.

MISCELLANEOUS: **Monuments:** Several – belonging to the Moseley family, and others. **Chandeliers, etc:** None. **Parochial Library:** There is one – not much used.

PARISH CLERK: Charles Taylor. **Appointed by:** The Rector. **Salary:** £5.

CHURCHWARDENS: Joseph Holbrook, John Mason. Joseph Davis for a township in the Parish.

ORDERS MADE: The South wall of the Church, between the Porch and Chancel end, to be examined and repaired – the stonework made good, where deficient, pointed etc. A surface drain to be carried all round the Church. The paling on the south side of the Churchyard put in repair; and the ditch adjoining cleared out; and kept free from soil, rubbish etc. The schoolboys not to be allowed to play in the churchyard nor injure the headstones etc.

Revisited 25.8.1837

In the *interior* of the Church nothing wanted, but additional casements, which I desired to be made.

Externally – The battlements of *the Tower* to be effectually secured, etc. The Gutters of the *roof* to be cleared out – from want of which wet has penetrated to the ceiling. The buttresses all round the Church pointed, under-built where needful, and otherwise repaired. The South wall under-built and otherwise repaired. An open drain formed all round the walls. A light gate placed at the North door, so as to admit of a thorough ventilation with the South door. The thoroughfare of the Churchyard to be stopped – and a new road formed along the *East* side, behind *a new fence* which is to be carried along that side and the South side of the Churchyard – so as to admit of the schoolboys going to the School without trespassing on the Churchyard. The Gates leading to the Church to be kept *locked,* except at times of divine service. '*All done, excellently.*'

Revisited 7.9.1841

Church generally in excellent order – nothing required except repairs to Churching pew and the free seats at the W. end. Flashings of roof next tower secured. Copings pointed.

[1] *Eccles. Revs.:* 400. [2] *Eccles. Revs.:* 'Fit.' [3] *Eccles. Revs.:* Gross income £711. [4] 'And small Payments' enclosed in brackets.

STOWE 28.9.1829 (A/V/1/4,p.70;A/V/1/2, p.53)

BENEFICE: Stowe. **Nature:** Perpetual Curacy. **Ecton:** £14 3s. 4d. Clear value. Pri. Sti. Tho. Staff. Propr. **Patron:** John Browne Esqr of Stretton in the fields. **Impropriator:** John Fitzgerald Esqr.

CHURCH: An ancient building, consisting of nave and chancel, the latter higher and longer than the former. The windows pointed: the arch which separates the Nave from the Chancel, handsome Saxon – formerly a Saxon arch to a side entrance, now converted into a window. **Number it will contain:** 300 in all. **Accommodation for Poor:** Only four Pews, capable of holding about 30 persons – three of these appropriated in the year 1795 out of a charitable bequest belonging to the Parish. These are a few benches for children. **Roof:** Oak, covered with slate – in good repair. **Walls:** Stone covered with thick coat of plaister – firm and upright. **Floor:** Quarries and brick – good and even. **Windows:** In indifferent condition – want cleaning and another casement

129

to open. **Doors:** Good. **Pulpit and Desk:** Want fixing more securely. **Books:** Bible wants re-binding. Clerk's Prayer Book very bad. **Seats:** Pews, oak – regular and good – floors boarded, in general good – some of the floors need repair. **Galleries:** One at the W. end of the nave – comfortably pewed – a few forms. **Organ:** None. **Font:** There is one. **Chapels:** None attached to the Church – there used to be a Chapel on the Chartley Estate – now in ruins. **Benefaction Tables:** Two – which record all the Charities. **Vestry:** None. **Surplices:** One – in good condition. **Linen:** Table cloth and napkin – in tolerable condition. **Plate:** Handsome silver Flagon, Cup and Paten, kept in the Chancel, in the Register chest. **Chest for Papers:** There are two – one locked and no keys; another contains parish indentures. **Iron Chest for Register:** There is one – kept in the Chancel. **Register:** Four Vols (besides those now in use) hitherto kept at the Clerk's house. The oldest dated about 1570 – the two earliest volumes, not quite entire – the two last complete. **Porch:** None. **Vaults:** None of modern date. **Cleanliness:** Not well attended to. **Damp:** A good deal, at the lower part of the walls, and floors of the Pews – partly from rain, beating in at the windows – but chiefly from want of drains, outside. **Dimensions:** 41ft. by 22ft.

CHANCEL: 46ft. 7in. by 17ft. 10in. **Table:** Old oak, quite plain – no covering. **Ornaments:** None – tables of Commandments, Lord's Prayer etc are at the E. end of the Nave. The whole chancel is in a shameful state of damp and neglect. The floor very uneven, wet and dirty – The roof (oak covered with tile) not very good. **Repaired by whom:** The roof, walls and windows by J Fitzgerald Esq as Impropriator – no substantial repairs seem to have been made lately.

STEEPLE: Handsome, square stone tower. **State of:** In good repair – but some new *pointing*, wanted [– and weatherboards]. **Bells:** Five – said to be good, except the wheels, which want repair. **Clock:** There is one, in good order; but the works open inside to persons, coming up to the gallery.

CHURCHYARD: **Fence:** Partly stone – partly hedges – the former kept up by the Parish – the latter by the occupier of the adjoining ground – in pretty good state, *generally*. **Gates:** In good repair. **Drains:** None – much wanted. **Graves:** Several close to the wall, on the S. side. **Rubbish:** Some – ordered to be removed. **Footpaths:** None, except public ways. **Cattle:** Cows, belonging to the landlord of the public house opposite to the Churchyard, who rents the herbage of the Minister – said to do injury to the graves.

DIVINE SERVICE: **On Sundays:** One service only – Morning and Afternoon alternately: half past ten and half past two. **On other Days:** None except Good Friday, and Christmas Day. **Sacrament:** Four times a year. **Communicants:** 12 to 15. **Catechism:** Not in the Church.

INCUMBENT: **Name and Residence:** Revd William Mould, East Retford, Notts.[1] **If not resident:** Not – during four months of the year, he resides at Abbots Bromley, during which period **What Duty he performs:** he does the whole duty.

CURATE: **Name and Residence:** Revd John Hand [now Revd J Hodgkinson 1831]. **If not resident:** Resides at Bramshall (6 miles off). **Licensed:** Yes. **Salary:** £40 per annum. **If serving another church:** Bramshall.

PARSONAGE: None.[2]

INCOME: **Gross Value:** About £50 a year. **Tithes:** None. **Glebe:** None. **Surplice Fees:** £2 or 3. **Easter Dues and small Payments:** No Easter dues. The Lessee pays £20 a year out of the Tythes – the late Lord Ferrars used to give £15. The present Earl discontinues it. **Queen Anne's Bounty:** £1,000 granted – but no investment has as yet been obtained for it. **Terrier:** None known of.

SCHOOLS: **Endowed School:** There is one – supported partly by Lord Ferrers, partly by payment out of the poors land. The Master lives at *Hixon*, and very seldom attends the school at Stowe. **Subscription Day School:** None. **Sunday School:** A small one, taught at Hixon. **Lancaster School:** None.

DISSENTERS: **Dissenters' School:** A Sunday school, taught by the Wesleyans, at Hixon. **Dissenting Chapels:** A small Methodist chapel at Hixon.

POPULATION: 1,285 in 1821 – now probably much increased.

MISCELLANEOUS: **Monuments:** One ancient one, belonging to the Ferrers family in the Chancel – not well preserved. **Chandeliers, etc:** None. **Parochial Library:** None.

PARISH CLERK: John Gretton. **Appointed by:** The Incumbent. **Salary:** None – but he receives 3d. from each sitting at Christmas, for Sunday duty, and cleaning the Church.

CHURCHWARDENS: George Tavernor and George Betson.

ORDERS MADE: A second casement to be made, opposite that, on the N. side of the nave. The windows to be cleaned; and the lead repaired, where needful. The Pulpit and desk, to be made more firm and secure. The Bible to be rebound, and a new Prayer Book procured for the Clerk. The floors of the Pews repaired, where necessary.

Also the Register books, to be kept, in future, in the Iron chest; and the chest itself either to be placed in a situation more free from damp,[3] within the Church, or kept at some house ir. the Parish. The Plate also taken better care of.

More attention paid to *cleanliness;* and means used, both internally and externally, to preserve the Church from damp. An *open drain* to be made outside the walls, all round, to the depth of the Church floor; and the spouts along the Chancel roof, to incline in the opposite direction, so as to carry off the wet, on the Chancel end. The whole Chancel, to be put into, and kept in, proper repair. Mr Fitzgerald and Lord Ferrers to be applied to for that purpose.

Recommended: that stoves be used in the Church in Winter. The Tower to be pointed afresh – rubbish and weeds, removed from the Churchyard. The wheels of the bells repaired – a partition to be put up to protect the Clock. The fence in one or two places, repaired in the Churchyard.

N.B. The whole state of the Church and Parish, suffering grievously, from want of a resident Minister – the Church accommodation sadly inadequate – not one-fourth of the Parishioners can attend.

Revisited 16.10.1837
Directions to Churchwardens – (1) *Roofs* of Church and Chancel examined and repaired. (2) *Down-pipe* at *East* end of Church. (3) *Windows of Bell-chamber* guarded by lattice work of wood or wire; and holes in walls stopped. (4) *Windows* of Church mended and frames cemented outside. (5) Walls coloured, ceilings whitewashed. (6) Outside of walls pointed where needful – and buttresses repaired. (7) Bible and prayer book in the reading desk repaired and reading desk lengthened. 'All in progress. *More room wanted* – Pop. 1,400 – Church holds 300.'

Visited 10.10.1841[4]
Directions to the Churchwardens.

I. *Inside the Church*
(1) The pannels and floors of the Pews to be carefully looked over, and repaired, where needful, at the expense of the respective occupiers. (2) Water tables to be made for the windows, so as to carry the wet *outside* – the iron bars of the windows painted – the casement in the window on the North side of the Gallery, to be secured. (3) A proper baptismal Font, of *Stone*, to be provided. (4) The Communion Table to be cleaned and well rubbed with boiled linseed oil. (5) The Register Chest to be raised from the floor, and set on bricks, or a wooden frame, as a preservative from damp. (6) The Communion Plate *not* to be kept *in the Church*. (7) The leaves of the Prayer-book, in the Clergyman's desk, to be smoothed down.

II. *In the Tower etc*
(1) The lead gutters on the roof to be laid even and kept free from obstruction; the flashings properly secured and pointed. (2) The wheel of one of the bells to be repaired and fresh braced. (3) The Clock weight to be brought down, if possible, nearer the North Corner of the West Entrance, so as to be out of the way of the inner door leading into the Church. If this cannot be done, effectual precaution against danger, in case of its falling, to be used. (4) The wet from the Tower to be conveyed by a *down-pipe* to the ground, and carried off in a drain of sufficient depth and fall.

III. *Outside* the Church
(1) The roof to be carefully examined and repaired; the Spouts painted. (2) The open drain, round the Church, to be laid with flags, or tiles, so as to carry the wet from the bottom of the walls, and to be kept free from grass, weeds etc.

IV. The *Chancel*
(1) The roof *to be stripped* and retiled; the timbers examined and repaired where needful. (2) The spouts painted. (3) The walls repaired and pointed, with good mortar or cement, along the bottom. (4) The buttress at the SE. corner under-built. (5) The tomb-stones removed from the East wall, and placed at a distance of three or four feet from it.

[1] Also perpetual curate of Gayton (Staffs), Misterton and West Burton (Notts): *Eccles. Revs.* [2] *Eccles. Revs.*: 'None.' [3] A/V/1/4: '. . . in a drier and more secure place.
[4] Loose sheet preserved in A/V/1/3.

TATENHILL 13.7.1829
(A/V/1/4,p.71;A/V/1/2,p.8)

BENEFICE: Tatenhill – a village three miles from Burton. **Nature:** Rectory. **Ecton:** King's Books 26 1s. 8d. – (annexed to the Deanery of Lichfield by Act of Parliament 4 and 5 Annae Reginae). **Patron:** Dean of Lichfield.
CHURCH: A plain Gothic building, with nave and chancel – no side aisle. **Number it will contain:** Scarcely 300 in all.[1] **Accommodation for Poor:** Sittings for not more than 100 including the benches in the chancel. **Roof:** Timber covered with blue slate – in good repair. **Walls:** Stone – firm, solid and in good repair. **Floor:** Brick (except where there are flat tombstones) not very even. **Windows:** Whole and in very good state. **Doors:** Very sound and good. **Pulpit and Desk:** Old fashioned, and not very convenient – no covering to reading Desk – old velvet cushion to pulpit. **Books:** Prayer book good – Bible wants rebinding. Clerk's Prayer Book the same. **Seats:** Oak – with boarded floor. **Galleries:** None. **Organ:** A small hand organ, standing within the communion rails. **Font:** An old-fashioned stone one, near the West end. **Chapels:** None. **Benefaction Tables:** One small brass plate, recording the only benefaction to the poor. **Vestry:** None. **Surplices:** Two – new and very good. **Linen:** A Table cloth and one napkin – pretty good. **Plate:** Not very good – a small silver cup and paten. **Chest for Papers:** An old Oak chest, in the Chancel. **Iron Chest for Register:** Provided. **Register:** Seven Vols – the first beginning 1563 – in good preservation. **Porch:** None. **Vaults:** None made since 1823. **Cleanliness:** Attended to. **Damp:** There is some appearance of it (– stated however to have much diminished, since the surf was made outside). **Dimensions:** 60ft. long. 24ft. 9in. wide.
CHANCEL: 44ft. 6in. long. 19ft. 8in. wide. Length of whole 104ft. 6in. **Table:** Old fashioned oak, in pretty good repair – but very insufficiently covered with an old green cloth – the rails very loose and insufficient. **Ornaments:** None – no table of Commandments. The roof timber covered with slate – a flat ceiling. **Repaired by whom:** The Dean of Lichfield. The communion floor should be *raised,* and covered with matting or carpet – new rails wanted – also cloth for table.
STEEPLE: Square tower of stone – upper part of brick. **State of:** In good repair. **Bells:** Three in good state – belfry ditto. **Clock:** New one – in good state.
CHURCHYARD: **Fence:** That next the road, posts and rails – the other three sides quick hedge, except the part, bounded by the Rectory house, and about 33 feet, adjoining a house, on the opposite side, which is very insufficiently fenced with paling, within which are pigs.[2] **Gates:** Two – one wants renewing. **Drains:** A surf surrounding the church, into which the wet from the roof is conducted by perpendicular spouts. **Graves:** None near the walls. **Rubbish:** Some accumulation of earth and stones – ordered to be removed. **Foot-**

paths: Two leading to the Church [properly kept] – one across the South side of the Churchyard, said to be an ancient footway, to the Market town (I presume, Burton). **Cattle:** A poney belonging to the tenant of the Rectory, and sheep.

DIVINE SERVICE: **On Sundays:** Full service morning – Prayers afternoon. **On other Days:** None except on Good Friday and Christmas Day. **Sacrament:** Five times in the year (i.e. at the Festivals, and Michaelmas). **Communicants:** From 16 to 18. **Catechism:** Not at the Church, taught at the Sunday school.

INCUMBENT: **Name and Residence:** Dean of Lichfield —— Lichfield. **If not resident:** Not. **What Duty he performs:** ——.

CURATE: **Name and Residence:** Revd Hugh Jones [now Revd H Cooper, 1830]. **If not resident:** Resides at Burton [he is]. **Licensed:** Yes. **Salary:** £90 – a gratuity of £10 additional, given by the present Rector. **If serving another church:** Not ordinarily – though occasionally assisting at his Church in Burton.

PARSONAGE: Large, roomy; but old fashioned – built of brick – two large parlours, on the ground floor, besides a good kitchen. Five good bedrooms, besides good attics. **State of:** In good substantial repair. **Outbuildings:** Stable, Coach-house, Barn and other household and husbandry offices.

INCOME: **Gross Value:** Said to be upwards of £2,000 a year. **Glebe:** 122 acres – besides 21 acres of forest allotment. **Surplice Fees:** About £3 per annum. **Easter Dues and small Payments:** None. **Queen Anne's Bounty:** None. **Terrier:** In the possession of the Dean of Lichfield.

SCHOOLS: **Endowed School:** None. **Subscription Day School:** Upon the National plan, containing about 60 children, boys and girls together. **Sunday School:** About 60. **Lancaster School:** None.

POPULATION: 500[3] at the last return, including the townships of Dunstall and Callingwood.

MISCELLANEOUS: **Monuments:** Three. **Chandeliers, etc:** None. **Parochial Library:** None.

PARISH CLERK: William Gething. **Appointed by:** The Dean of Lichfield. **Salary:** Five Pounds.

CHURCHWARDENS: Mr Atkin for Tatenhill. Mr CP Johnson for Dunstall.

ORDERS MADE: Bible and Clerk's Prayer book to be rebound, and repaired. Accumulation of soil outside the Church to be removed, and the ground all round the church, to be kept clear of weeds, and sloped, so as to let the wet run off, towards the Churchyard. The paling said to belong to – Brown, proprietor of the house on the south side of the Churchyard, to be repaired at his expense, if by law the repair belongs to him.[4] The fence next the road to be repaired, and the smaller gate to be repaired or renewed. The rails at the communion table, repaired.

The Dean of Lichfield however to be consulted as to the expediency of raising the floor of the Communion-space, making *new rails;* and also providing a respectable covering of Velvet or cloth, for the Table. The Churchwardens were recommended also to provide a suitable covering of some kind for the *reading desk;* and a new cushion for the Pulpit.

Having visited this Church in the Summer of 1836, I left the revisitation, in 1837, to the Rural dean, who reported to me as follows, in a statement sent 18.11.1837.

I visited Tatenhill September 14; and I left the following observations with the Churchwardens.

'The *interior* of this Church is quite a pattern for country Churches. It is beautiful and nicely kept, and when the new painted window above the Altar is put in, the whole will be complete. As to the *exterior,* I think the following directions necessary for the guidance of the Churchwardens.

(1) The horizontal wooden spouts North and South of the Church and Chancel to be carefully examined, repaired where needful, and fresh painted. (2) The herbage removed from the base of the walls, the walls pointed especially on the South side, at bottom, and an open drain of brick or tile, three feet wide, made round the Church. (3) The soil levelled round the Church walls, and not left in heaps, as at present is the case. (4) The old Burial place south of the Church, which is surrounded with iron railings, should be laid open to the Churchyard, the railings removed, and the nettles and rubbish cleared away. (5) The Churchyard fence next the road repaired. (6) The Churchyard cleared of nettles.

With respect to the upper part of the Tower, which is in an unsafe state, it should be taken down and rebuilt as soon as possible: and as I am informed by the churchwardens of Barton under Needwood that that parish is ready to contribute its proportion of the expense* I trust I shall shortly have the satisfaction of hearing that the work has been commenced.'

*In making this statement, the Churchwarden afterwards told me that he was *incorrect,* the Barton people being by no means willing to pay their quota, which I believe is only £18. James Riddell, Rural Dean. 'Qu? Tower.'

Revisited 7.9.1841

Tower has been thoroughly repaired. All in good order – no directions needful; except to lock the gates and stop the thoroughfare.

[1] *Eccles. Revs.*: 200. [2] A/V/1/4: '... within which is a pigstye – apparently an encroachment'. [3] *Eccles. Revs.*: 620. [4] A/V/1/4: '... made more becoming – the pigs removed or screened from public view'.

TUTBURY 17.11.1829
(A/V/1/4,p.72;A/V/1/2,p.4)

BENEFICE: Tutbury. **Nature:** Vicarage. **Ecton:** £20 clear yearly value – living discharged. **Patron:** Vicar of Bakewell in Derbyshire (by exchange with the Duke of Devonshire for Buxton). **Impropriator:** Robert Stone Esqr, Needwood House, by purchase from the Duke of Devonshire.

CHURCH: A remarkably fine, noble Saxon structure, though mutilated and otherwise injured by time. The Saxon arch at the West entrance, one of the finest in the kingdom – large [massy] circular pillars and arches, on each side of the centre aisle – two side aisles one just built,[1] upon an old foundation, the whole new pewed and put in complete repair. **Number it will contain:** About

1,000. **Accommodation for Poor:** Upwards of 500. **Roof:** Baltic timber covered with lead – in good repair. **Walls:** Stone – upright, with the exception of W. end of S. wall. **Floor:** Flags in centre aisle and chancel – the rest quarries [– chiefly new]. **Windows:** Good – five casements – two more to be made. **Doors:** Very good. **Pulpit and Desk:** New and handsome. **Books:** Bible wants rebinding. **Seats:** All new – boarded floors. **Galleries:** Two – all the sittings in them free, that at the West for the singers. **Organ:** None. **Font:** There is one, not in very good order. **Chapels:** None. **Vestry:** A new one – small but convenient. **Surplices:** Two – good. **Linen:** Table cloth and napkin – good. **Plate:** Silver cup, pewter flagon – plated cup and dish at the Vicarage. **Iron Chest for Register:** In the Vestry. **Register:** Two vols prior to 1813. **Porch:** There was one formerly on the S. side – [which was] removed [some time ago] and a window put in its place. **Vaults:** Several in the Chancel. **Cleanliness:** Attended to – all new at present. **Damp:** No appearance. **Dimensions:** 94ft. by 62, including the Chancel, or more properly exclusive of the Chancel, which seems to have been destroyed.

CHANCEL: **Table:** Deal – neatly painted, handsome purple velvet covering. **Ornaments:** None at present. **Repaired by whom:** The lay Rector (who has, since my visit, put in a neat window,[2] corresponding with that at the W. end).

STEEPLE: Square Tower – low and not very handsome, pinnacles wanting. **State of:** Wants repointing, which is to be done. **Bells:** Five good. **Clock:** There is one.

CHURCHYARD: **Fence:** Belongs to the Parish – of various materials – kept in tolerable repair. **Gates:** Good. **Drains:** A surf carried recently all round the Church, below the depth of the Church floor. **Graves:** None too near the Church now – some removed in repairing the Church. **Rubbish:** At present difficult to judge from repairs going forward. **Footpaths:** One [trespass path] from the Clerk's house – [since] stopped up. **Cattle:** Sheep.

DIVINE SERVICE: **On Sundays:** Two full services. **On other Days:** A weekly lecture. **Sacrament:** Every six weeks. **Communicants:** 60 to 80. **Catechism:** In the school.

INCUMBENT: **Name and Residence:** Revd G Robinson, Vicarage. **What Duty he performs:** The whole.

PARSONAGE: A small, unsubstantial and inconvenient building erected by the late Vicar, close to the Churchyard, instead of the former one, which stood farther back towards the street. It was built by contract; and is very slight. **State of:** Very unsound.[3] **Outbuildings:** None.

INCOME: **Gross Value:** £130. **Glebe:** 70 acres of forest land. **Easter Dues and small payments:** The Impropriator pays £6 8s. 0d. yearly. **Queen Anne's Bounty:** A farm at Newborough, purchased by money from the Bounty; lets for £25 a year. **Terrier:** A copy at the end of one of the vols of the Register.

SCHOOLS: **Endowed School:** There is one – £60 or £70 per annum. **Subscription Day School:** An Infant school. **Sunday School:** Upwards of 200 children. **Lancaster School:** None.

DISSENTERS: **Dissenters' School:** Sunday school – 130 children. **Dissenting Chapels:** Four.

POPULATION: 1,444 last Census.

MISCELLANEOUS: **Monuments:** Some. **Chandeliers, etc:** None. **Parochial Library:** Sunday school library.

PARISH CLERK: Joseph Mackin. **Appointed by:** The Vicar. **Salary:** None – query, should one be assigned him? He has small payments amounting to £4 1s. 0d. per annum.

CHURCHWARDENS: Mr John Brown. Mr W Cox.

ORDERS MADE: None necessary, the church having just been put into complete repair; and an additional aisle and gallery erected: the soil cleared away to a considerable depth, and surf made (as ordered by me in June), at an expense of about £1,500 raised by subscription. The road into, and through the Churchyard, has also been much improved, and other improvements are going on, in the Church and Churchyard.

15.3.1830
Received a letter from 'a True Churchman' complaining that the West window was still unfinished – as also the road through the Churchyard – answered to the Churchwarden, directing immediate attention to the subject.

29.6.1830
At the Visitation at Cheadle I was informed by the Vicar that the West window was now handsomely completed, and a corresponding one put in at the East end by the Lay Impropriator – also that the road through the Churchyard was completed (or in progress – I forget which).[4]

August 1831
Visited the Church and found all in excellent order.

25.8.1837
Everything, externally and internally, in excellent order – except some weeds, ivy etc beginning to encroach on the W. wall – and grass, thistles and nettles not sufficiently cleared away from the bottom of the walls and other parts of the Churchyard.

9.5.1838
Rural dean reported *nothing* done – water comes in at windows – and frame of third bell nearly down.
   Recommend *keeping* things in good repair.

Revisited 7.9.1841
(1) Books to be repaired – Covering of Communion Table dyed afresh – and brown holland covering provided. (2) East window frosted. (3) Skirting of pews boxed to prevent dry-rot. (4) Water tables to windows. (5) Cracks in ceiling over N. Gallery and W. window stopped.

[1] A/V/1/4: '. . . the N. aisle lately rebuilt.' [2] A/V/1/4: '. . . a handsome East window . . .' [3] *Eccles. Revs.:* 'Fit.' [4] A/V/1/4: '. . . was nearly completed.'

UTTOXETER 14.7.1830
(A/V/1/4,p.73;A/V/1/2,p.92)

BENEFICE: Uttoxeter. **Nature:** Vicarage. **Ecton:** Living discharged – Clear value £48 3s. 4d. **Patron:** The Dean and Canons of Windsor. **Impropriator:** The Lessee of the Patrons.
CHURCH: A handsome Gothic building; rebuilt (except the Tower) in 1828/9 – nave and side aisles and small Chancel. **Number it will contain:** 1,449. **Accommodation for Poor:** 420. **Roof:** Red deal covered with slate. **Walls:** Stone. **Floor:** Flags. **Windows:** Good – well provided with casements. **Doors:** Good. **Pulpit and Desk:** Of handsome materials, but clumsy execution, and not well placed – reading desk and clerk's do much too low. **Books:** Good. **Seats:** Ditto. **Galleries:** On three sides. **Organ:** There is one. **Font:** ——. **Chapels:** None. **Benefaction Tables:** Sufficient. **Vestry:** There is one. **Surplices:** Three – good. **Linen:** Provided. **Plate:** Silver Flagon – two Cups – a Patin – two Dishes. **Chest for Papers:** There is one. **Iron Chest for Register:** In the Vestry. **Register:** Several Vols from 1596 to the present time – in very good preservation. **Porch:** None. **Vaults:** None since the rebuilding of the Church, except three in the Chancel, entrances to which [are] outside the Church. **Cleanliness:** Attended to. **Damp:** Much on the Walls – especially at the E. end and Vestry. **Dimensions:** 98ft. 9in. by 58ft. 3in.
CHANCEL: Included in the above – the Chancel very short. **Table:** Handsome oak – firm – crimson covering. **Ornaments:** None. **Repaired by whom:** The Patrons by their Lessee.
STEEPLE: Square stone tower (antient) surmounted with a Spire. **State of:** Far from good – apparently insecure. **Bells:** Six – of which five belong to the Parish – one to the Impropriator. **Clock:** There is one, with chimes.
CHURCHYARD: **Fence:** Partly iron paling – partly brick wall – partly hedge – the latter, on the side of the Vicarage garden and one below it, wants trimming and repair – ditch clearing out etc. **Gates:** Good. **Drains:** Provided. **Graves:** Not too near. **Rubbish:** Some near the Vicar's garden. **Footpaths:** No trespass paths now – the thoroughfare having been recently stopped – the Church ways properly kept – there is however a private entrance, which seems an encroachment. **Cattle:** None.
DIVINE SERVICE: **On Sundays:** Two full services. **On other Days:** Prayers on Wednesday and Friday. **Sacrament:** Monthly. **Communicants:** 50. **Catechism:** In the School.
INCUMBENT: **Name and Residence:** Revd Clement Broughton. **If not resident:** In the Parish. **What Duty he performs:** Half.
CURATE: **Name and Residence:** Revd John Dashwood, Vicarage. **Licensed:** He is. **Salary:** £50 – together with the Vicarage, Garden and Churchyard. **If serving another church:** None.
PARSONAGE: A good commodious brick house – three parlours, kitchen and offices on ground floor – six bedrooms. **State of:** Good – lately put into complete repair.[1]
INCOME: **Gross Value:** £150 or £160. **Glebe:** About 40 acres. **Surplice Fees:** £25. **Easter Dues and small Payments:** Collected – £20 per annum from Dean of Windsor. **Queen Anne's Bounty:** £800 – laid out in purchase of Glebe. **Terrier:** There is a Copy – 1693.
SCHOOLS: **Endowed School:** There is one – the Master appointed by Trinity College, Cambridge – £13 6s. 8d. annual payment, charged upon land. **Subscription Day School:** A National School, lately built – 100 children – room for 200. **Sunday School:** None at present – intended. **Lancaster School:** None.
DISSENTERS: **Dissenters' School:** Two Sunday Schools. **Dissenting Chapels:** Three – Quaker, Calvinist, Methodist.
POPULATION: Upwards of 5,000.
MISCELLANEOUS: **Monuments:** Several – some antient.
PARISH CLERK: Robert Smith. **Appointed by:** The Vicar. **Salary:** £3 7s. 6d. and fees.
CHURCHWARDENS: Mr Thomas Blade for the Vicar. Mr Michael Cluley for the Parish.
ORDERS MADE: Light iron gates to be placed at the N. and S. doors – for ventilation. The Reading, and Clerk's, desks to be raised – at least 1½ feet. The ten Commandments to be set up. The tower and spire to be examined by an Architect – and his Report laid before the Archdeacon. The hedge adjoining the Vicarage garden to be repaired – and rubbish cleared away. The private doorway into the Churchyard to be stopped. The Architect to be consulted as to the cause of dampness at the E. end of the Church, and on the Vestry wall. An increase of the Salaries of Clerk and Sexton *recommended*.

Revisited 12.9.1837
Everything in admirable order. No directions needful except – (1) To provide a suitable baptismal font, under the direction of the Vicar as to its situation. (2) To have the warm-air apparatus put in order. (3) To have the iron rails round the Church painted and the Vestry walls ditto.

[1] *Eccles. Revs.:* 'Fit.'

YOXALL 19.9.1829 (A/V/1/4,p.74;A/V/1/2,p.11)

BENEFICE: Yoxall. **Nature:** Rectory. **Ecton:** King's Books £17 6s. 8d. – the Earl of Uxbridge is stated to be the Patron. **Patron:** Chandos Leigh Esqr. **Impropriator:** None.
CHURCH: Handsome Gothic building – two side aisles separated from body by pointed arches – Chancel. **Number it will contain:** 730 exclusive of 254 sittings for children.[1] **Accommodation for Poor:** 150. **Roof:** Handsome oak, open carved work inside – roof oak, covered partly with tiles, partly wooden shingles, partly lead.[2] **Walls:** Stone – that on the South side, not in a good state. **Floor:** Quarries – even. **Windows:** In good repair – five open casements. **Doors:** Double – very good. **Pulpit and Desk:** Oak – handsome, with velvet cushion and coverings. **Books:** Prayer book and Clerk's book, both out of repair – Bible good except in one part, which is to be repaired. **Seats:** Oak: boarded floors – in good repair. **Galleries:** There are three. **Organ:** There is one. **Font:** Is one. **Chapels:** None. **Benefaction Tables:**

Two – which record all the Charities. **Vestry:** There is one – quarries on the floor, want repair. **Surplices:** Two – good. **Linen:** Table Cloth and two napkins – want repair greatly. **Plate:** Silver Flagon Cup and Paten. **Chest for Papers:** There is one. **Iron Chest for Register:** At the Rectory. **Register:** Five vols besides those in present use[3] – oldest date 1645. **Porch:** One on the South side – in bad condition. **Vaults:** None except that of the Arden family within the Communion rails. **Cleanliness:** Tolerably attended to – except the windows.[4] **Damp:** Some appearance of it, on the walls, windows and floor. **Dimensions:** 60ft. by 50ft.

CHANCEL: 34ft. by 18ft. **Table:** Old fashioned oak table, in good order, and neatly covered. **Ornaments:** None except monuments. The floor and walls need some repairs – the floor within the Communion rail [over the Arden vault] is sinking. **Repaired by whom:** The Rector.

STEEPLE: Square, stone [tower] with four pinnacles. **State of:** Good. **Bells:** Six bells in good repair – new hung in 1813. **Clock:** There is one.

CHURCHYARD: **Fence:** Partly wall (brick or stone) partly hedge, rails, houses. In one part where a house has been pulled down the Churchyard is open – other parts need repair very much [– but about to be improved]. **Gates:** Principal gate bad – none of the entrances in good state. **Drains:** None. **Graves:** Many close to the wall. **Rubbish:** Some. **Footpaths:** Several public ones.[5] **Cattle:** None – except a poney.

DIVINE SERVICE: **On Sundays:** Morning and Evening – full services. **On other Days:** None. **Sacrament:** Eight times a year. **Catechism:** At the school.

INCUMBENT: **Name and Residence:** Revd E Cooper – Hamstall.[6] **If not resident:** Not. **What Duty he performs:** None at present.

CURATE: **Name and Residence:** Revd John Riland, in the Rectory. **Licensed:** He is. **Salary:** £100. **If serving another church:** None.

PARSONAGE: An old rambling brick building – rooms low and cold – many parts in an infirm condition – the east end very insecure and dangerous, and greatly needing to be rebuilt. **State of:** Very indifferent.[7] **Outbuildings:** Stable, Coach-house, [etc]. Barn converted into a school.

INCOME: **Gross Value.**[8] **Tithes:** Great and small. **Glebe:** Ten acres. **Surplice Fees:** Uncertain. **Easter Dues and small Payments:** There are. **Queen Anne's Bounty:** None. **Terrier:** There is a Copy in the possession of the Churchwarden containing an accurate account of Tythes, Glebe, Buildings belonging to the Rectory etc.

SCHOOLS: **Endowed School:** There is one endowment arising from land, and a house – the present National School incorporated with it. **Subscription Day School:** None. **Lancaster School:** None.

DISSENTERS: **Dissenters' School:** None. **Dissenting Chapels:** A Catholic chapel, and a small Methodist Chapel.[9]

POPULATION: About 1,700.

MISCELLANEOUS: **Monuments:** Several in the Chancel, chiefly to the Arden family – one to the memory of Mr Thomas Taylor, a benefactor to the Parish. **Chandeliers, etc:** Lamps suspended from the ceiling. **Parochial Library:** There is one at the school.

PARISH CLERK: John Teswell. **Appointed by:** The Rector. **Salary:** £4 per annum – exclusive of Easter dues. He complains that he is not sufficiently paid.

CHURCHWARDENS: Mr Michael Poysor, Joseph Jackson.

ORDERS MADE: Books to be repaired or renewed. Damp to be removed, by means of an open drain, all round the walls. Chancel floor repaired – Vestry floor ditto. Table linen renewed. Windows secured against rain. Walls inside to be new washed [or coloured]. The wall on the S. side to be examined by an Architect, and its state reported to me. The shingles on the N. side of the roof over the main body of the Church, stripped and re-tiled. The walls all round repointed and repaired, where needful. Buttresses repaired both in the body and chancel. The Porch either repaired or removed. The Fence repaired or renewed. The Churchyard cleared of weeds and overgrown herbage. New gates erected.

Revisited 26.8.1837

In consequence of my former visit, a new fence and gates have been put up, the North roof tiled and the walls pointed etc – the S. wall and buttresses strengthened. Still the Church, internally, is very far from being in a neat or becoming state.

I desired that the *roof* of the Church and Chancel might be carefully examined and repaired. The *walls* repaired and coloured. The *windows* new rodded and leaded. The pannels of the *Pews* repaired where needful, especially in the *Chancel*. More attention paid to *Cleanliness* and *ventilation* – the latter by means of a light gate at the North entrance, corresponding to that at the *South*. The *gutters of the roofs* cleared. The *drain*, round the Church, completed with bricks or tiles, and kept open. The thoroughfare of the Churchyard stopped, if possible, and the *doors* and the windows of the houses which are built on the North side of the Churchyard, taken away. 'Partially done – nothing in Chancel. Mem. thoroughfare. Light Gate on N. side.'

Revisited 6.9.1841

Very much improved.

Inside – (1) Broken basin disused – water poured into Font. (2) Bible and Prayer Book repaired. (3) Pannels in Rectory servants pew repaired.

Outside – (4) Lead work in roof, and gutters, examined and repaired. (5) Down-pipes – coping stones pointed all round roof. (6) New flag at W. entrance, inside. (7) Key stone of Arch above Vestry door secured. (8) Weeds removed from Vestry wall. (9) Tiling and copings of Chancel roof repaired – iron bars of windows painted.

Churchyard – (1) Coping of brick wall adjoining Rectory garden, secured. (2) Thoroughfare of Churchyard stopped – gates locked (– Mr Wills will then make new entrance to Rectory). (3) Church lands surveyed – and full rent obtained and properly applied.

[1] *Eccles. Revs.:* 800. [2] In A/V/1/4 the shingles are mentioned last, with the words 'the latter bad'. [3] A/V/1/4: 'Five Vols prior to 1813 . . .' [4] A/V/1/4: 'Not very well observed.' [5] A/V/1/4: 'Several trespass paths. [6] Also rector of Hamstall Ridware. [7] *Eccles. Revs.:* 'Fit.' [8] *Eccles. Revs.:* Gross income £100. [9] A/V/1/4: . . . both small.'

I trust that the contemplated improvement of fencing the Churchyard with a brick wall on the sides now exposed may speedily be carried into effect.

[1] Loose sheet preserved in A/V/1/3.

OAKAMOOR 28.9.1837
(A/V/1/4,p.75; not in A/V/1/2)

BENEFICE: Oakamoor. **Nature:** Chapel of ease to Cheadle. **Patron:** Rector of Cheadle.
CHURCH: **Number it will contain:** 470. **Accommodation for Poor:** 304. **Roof:** Timber covered with slate – handsome open ceiling. **Walls:** Brick. **Floor:** Quarries. **Windows:** Good – water-tables wanting. **Linen:** Provided. **Plate:** Provided. **Iron Chest for Register:** Ordered.
INCOME[1]
SCHOOLS: **Subscription Day School:** Under the Chapel – containing 60 or 70 in the week – about 130 or 140 on Sundays.
ORDERS MADE: 28.9.1837
An iron fence to be provided, so as to separate the Chapel yard from the playground of the school – the *nuisances removed* lower down etc. Windows mended – and down-pipes, which have been injured by the children of the school. Roof of bell-chamber properly protected – water-courses of roof of Chapel kept in order. Water-tables to windows, inside the Chapel. A Register Chest – new ladder for bell-tower.

Revisited 28.9.1841
Directions to Churchwardens – (1) Walls coloured, internally, a neat stone colour, and ceilings whitewashed. (2) Small lead pipes provided for water-tables, to prevent the wet from streaming down the walls inside. (3) Buttresses at N. and S. angles of Tower repaired at base. (4) Iron Register Chest provided, as required by Act of Parliament.

[1] Gross benefice income £57, no glebe house, according to *Eccles. Revs.*

FENTON 17.9.1841
(A/V/1/4,p.76; not in A/V/1/2)

BENEFICE: Fenton.
ORDERS MADE: Directions to Churchwardens –
(1) Church insured against fire. (2) Additional casements provided – water-tables made.
(3) Ladder for ascent of Tower inside. Roof of Church examined and repaired. Mouths of pipes guarded against obstruction.

STRETTON 7.9.1841 (A/V/1/4,p.77; not in A/V/1/2)

BENEFICE: Stretton Chapel.
ORDERS MADE: The Chapel being new – no orders needful.

CHRIST CHURCH, STAFFORD[1]

Visited October 12th
Nothing further seems needful in the way of direction, except to urge the importance of carefully watching the roof, spouts, and pipes, with a view of *preventing* mischief.

APPENDIX I

CHURCHWARDENS' EXPENDITURE ON CHURCH FABRICS

The following tables are an attempt to illustrate the range of expenditure in parishes of different sizes. A complete analysis of expenditure on church fabrics is impossible. In many cases the accounts give the recipients' names but not the details of work carried out. In other cases it is not clear whether work was being carried out on the church, churchyard walks or churchyard walls. Furthermore, on occasion a parishioner might pay directly for repairs, which would therefore not appear in the churchwardens' accounts. In addition it is impossible to show in the tables and notes all small payments for work on the fabric. The tables give first the churchwardens' total annual expenditure. This includes payments other than for the fabric, for example the clerk's salary, visitation fees and in some cases the destruction of vermin. Work on the fabric is, however, the main variable factor in the expenditure, and fluctuations in the total usually reflect greater or lesser expenditure on the fabric. The notes indicate the main objects of expenditure on the fabric. In three of the parishes, Alstonefield, Barton-under-Needwood and Leigh, a number of tradesmen regularly carried out work and payments to these men have been analysed separately. In view of Hodson's great concern for adequate drainage a detailed account of expenditure on the provision of soughs at Stowe is printed.

ALSTONEFIELD[a]

	Total Expenditure	Payments to main tradesmen			
		Ralph Wooddisse[b] *joiner*	James Austin *blacksmith*	Mr Roose[c] *glazier*	Ralph Fearn *plasterer*
	£ s. d.	£ s. d.	£ s. d.	£ s. d.	£ s. d.
1824–5	413 17 7½[d]	189 19 8			3 18 6
1825–6	182 5 4[e]	1 6 10	3 2 3	13 0 10	
1826–7	65 12 8	8 6	9 0	18 15 6	2 0
1827–8	50 18 8	11 7 4[f]	1 0 0		
1828–9	46 2 6	2 6 0	6 8	1 12 0[g]	5 6[h]
1829–30	30 12 3	10 5 6[i]	(8 0)[j]	(5 6)[k]	
1830–1	29 6 2		1 12 0	3 6 9	1 6 6
1831–2	54 18 4½	24 19 2½[l]	2 3 6	1 4 0	2 0
1832–3	24 11 8	1 16 11½	9 7	11 0	4 6
1833–4	32 2 6	12 5 0½	2 3	13 0	
1834–5	16 7 4½				8 0
1835–6	18 13 1				7 6
1836–7	29 7 11[m]	2 5 10½	1 6		
1837–8	26 2 6½	2 1 2	1 2		
1838–9	45 1 8½	1 1 4½			
1839–40	22 9 4		3 6	2 14 6	11 0
1840–1	22 12 3	10 6	1 6	4 13 6[n]	
1841–2	25 6 5	1 18 3[o]	2 2	4 1 11	
1842–3	18 0 3			12 6	12 6[p]
1843–4	16 16 4			6 6	
1844–5	26 1 7	3 0 0	4 0	1 0 6	2 12 6
1845–6	43 12 1	4 0 10		8 3 3	6 6
1846–7	17 5 3	13 6			

a SRO, D922/36.
b Wooddisse, Austin and probably Fearn were of Alstonefield.
c In 1833–4, Mrs Roose; from 1839 onwards, 'Mr Roose' or 'Joseph Roose'.
d Of this, £210 was raised by church rate and £130 12s. from the sale of lead. £103 9s. was paid to plasterers and £31 2s. 10½d. to Isaac Billinge, a mason from Fawfieldhead, in the parish of Alstonefield.
e £210 was raised by church rate, partly to pay off the previous year's deficiency. £26 5s. 3d. was paid to Isaac Billinge, £21 12s. 3d. to Mr Lamb for painting, and £63 7s. 10½d. to Mr Bestwick, 'as per Bill', for an unspecified purpose.
f Including £5 15s. for new church gates.
g For repairing lead gutters and the windows.

h For plastering the windows.
i Including £6 6s. for a Communion table and £3 2s. 6d. for painting, lettering and varnishing.
j 'Blacksmiths bill'; not named.
k 'Glaziers bill'; not named.
l 'Timber and work done to the first floor of the Steeple, Clock Case, belfry door, etc. etc.'
m Including £6 10s. 8d. to 'Mr Potter' (perhaps the Lichfield architect).
n For lead pipes and glazing.
o For painting and repairing pews, etc.
p For painting, etc.

LEIGH[a]

		Payments to main tradesmen			
	Total Expenditure	William Perkin, from 1838 Joseph Perkin *joiners*	William Mellor, from 1834 James Beardmore *blacksmiths*	Peter Harvey *plumber & glazier*	John Chell *plasterer & painter; also paid for miscellaneous work*
	£ s. d.	£ s. d.	£ s. d.	£ s. d.	£ s. d.
1829	48 5 4	10 19 3	12 5	13 15 8	1 8
1830	142 9 1[b]	37 11 4	2 13 5	19 8 –	7 6 8
1831	68 0 4	16 16 6	4 7	14 5 11	8 6
1832	58 17 8[c]	10 12 –	13 7	2 6	5 6
1833	45 2 8½	9 6 3	4 –	4 17 8	3 14 0
1834	50 15 8[d]	14 14 0	11 –	1 3 6	2 3
1835	42 5 8[e]	1 0 11	14 3	1 19 2	
1836	39 2 7	1 16 0	1 0 8	5 16 11	3 4
1837	26 10 9		1 0 7		
1838	60 19 8	1 17 3	3 12 5	22 17 –	6 – –
1839	58 13 4[f]	10 0	7 5	7 19 1	14 –
1840	28 6 1[g]	7 –	18 10		
1841	40 12 3[h]			3 14 4	5 –
1842	42 12 0½[i]	8 7 8½	1 11 8	2 8 6	
1843	30 3 4	1 1 0	2 6 7	1 3 2	
1844[j]	27 7 4	3 1 8	4 5	16 –	

a SRO, D795/16. This volume is in poor state; the edges of the pages are worn and the last column of figures is frequently missing. A dash indicates that the amount of shillings and pence is missing.
b Including £8 10s. for stone and carriage, and £2 10s. for lime and carriage, the purpose not stated but perhaps for the buttresses; £2 13s. 4d. paid to Philip Johnson and – Holmes for repairing the buttresses; £8 8s. 6d. paid to Johnson, George Armishaw and Thomas Atterbury for unspecified work in the church; and £1 4s. 6d. for 'Matts and making for the Altar'. See above p. xxviii.
c Including £2 9s. 9d. to John Dumolo (of Uttoxeter) for painting and varnishing the altar rails, and £6 18s. 5d. paid to – Hatfield for a pair of iron gates for the porch and for cast iron spouts.

d   Including £2 18s. 2d. to John Dumolo for painting the chancel.
e   Including £12 –s. –d. for a pulpit cloth, etc.
f   Including £23 10s. –d. to Messrs. Porter and Keats (of Uttoxeter) for four stoves and –s. –d. to John Dumolo for glazing the windows.
g   Including some expenditure on the school.
h   Including £2 10s. for carpeting for the altar.
i   Including £1 13s. for piping for the stove in the chancel, 8s. for pointing the tower, and 6s. for four days fencing in the churchyard.
j   In 1845 £500 was paid to Mr Johnson towards repairs. It was paid by a loan at 4 per cent on the security of the church rates.

BARTON-UNDER-NEEDWOOD[a]

Payments to main tradesmen

	Total Expenditure[b]	William Sanders[c] joiner	William Shipton (from 1832 Mrs Shipton) blacksmith	William Riley blacksmith	– Whiting (from 1832 Mrs Whiting) plumber & glazier
	£ s. d.	£ s. d.	£ s. d.	£ s. d.	£ s. d.
1826–7	47 10 10[d]		2 16 10		
1827–8	146 4 3½		17 8	1 2 5	24 17 2
1828–9	92 2 7			6 11	
1829–30	53 5 6½		2 0 0	14 6	
1830–1	66 18 9	1 0 0			1 9 2
1831–2	53 16 8½[e]		8 10		
1832–3	57 0 1		12 10	4 0	4 10 5
1833–4	78 1 7[f]	14 11 0		3 4 11	15 0
1834–5	45 17 8½				
1835–6	87 13 5[g]	11 15 4[i]		12 5[h]	7 0 6[h]
1836–7	46 13 6¼	2 11 4½	2 9		3 0
1837–8	44 3 5½[i]			1 5 5	
1838–9	40 11 7½[j]			1 1 0	
1839–40	35 5 6[k]				
1840–1	88 4 2½[l]	3 7 4			
1841–2	60 17 6[m]				

a   SRO, D1137/4/1.
b   During the years 1826–42 (except 1829–30 and 1839–40) the chapelry paid £174 18s. 10d. to the churchwardens of Tatenhill for the general expenses of the mother-church. In addition it paid £9 7s. 6d. in 1830–1 as its share of the cost of building the wall of Tatenhill churchyard and £7 in 1841–2 as its share of the cost of a new churchyard fence there. Sums paid to Tatenhill are included in the total expenditure.
c   Sanders, Shipton, Riley and Whiting were all of Barton-under-Needwood.
d   Including £2 10s. 0d. spent on repairs to the organ.
e   Including £13 17s. 0d. on building the Barton-under-Needwood churchyard wall.
f   Including £3 10s. 0d. paid to James Brunt, of Burton-upon-Trent, for new pinnacles for the tower, and £7 to – Banister 'for printing Commandments and Donations'.

g Between 1832 and 1835 Edward Ironmonger, joiner, of Barton, received £10 15s. 7d.
h The payments to Riley and Sanders, together with £5 1s. 6d. of the payment to Whiting, were for work carried out 1832–4. £48 5s. 11d. of the total was for work in 1832–4
i £23 of the total was paid for work carried out 1836–7.
j £4 0s. 6d. paid to John Mathews for colouring and repairing in the church and £5 19s. 9d. paid to James Derry for painting the skylights.
k Including 12s. 3d. paid to James Derry.
l Including £3 13s. 8d. paid to John Mathews and £6 6s. 10d. paid to James Derry.
m Including £6 15s. 4½d. paid to James Derry. Between 1834 and 1842 John Brown, joiner, a Barton man, received £24 19s. 11½d.

SEIGHFORD[a]

	Total Expenditure	Main items of expenditure on the fabric
	£ s. d.	
1827–8	20 14 11	
1828–9	17 10 2	
1829–30	23 9 5	Including 500 tiles for £1 5s. and 200 bricks for 6s.; also four new churchyard gates for £3 18s.
1830–1	34 18 7	
1831–2	22 8 3½	Including a new spout for the steeple £1 12s. 1½d.
1832–3	14 9 10	
1833–4	25 19 6½	Including £2 2s. 6d. to Mr Trubshaw for stone for the belfry steps, 12s. for its carriage; also £2 1s. 7d. paid to a glazier and £2 10s. for tiles.
1834–5	21 3 4	Including £3 15s. for tiles.
1835–6	16 17 10	Including £1 10s. 6d. for tiles.
1836–7	17 11 11	
1837–8	12 15 5	Including 6s. 9d. for mats for the chancel.
1838–9	20 13 11½	
1839–40	76 11 6	Including £30 on account to Mr Williams (perhaps a builder from Stafford)
1840–1	38 17 7½	
1841–2	79 18 –	
1842–3	36 – 11	

a SRO, D731/11.

STOWE[a]

	Total Expenditure	Main items of expenditure on the fabric
	£ s. d.	
1828–9	19 7 10½	
1829–30	37 10 4½	
1830–1	25 16 5	
1831–2	27 14 7	Including 3s. 4d. for a gutter around the walls; for the cost of laying a sough, see the detailed account below.
1832–3	15 9 0½	
1833–4	11 6 5	
1834–5	18 4 3½	
1835–6	11 12 2	
1836–7	15 17 11	
1837–8	30 3 2½	Including £3 3s. for whitewashing and cleaning the church and repairing the walls; also £2 9s. on the 'pulpit pillow and clothing'.
1838–9	18 8 0	Including £3 9s. 6d. for glazing.
1839–40	32 10 9	Including £6 9s. 6d. for new gallery stairs etc.
1840–1	24 7 0¼	Including £6 15s. 9¼d. to a glazier.
1841–2	43 5 1	Including £3 6s. 10½d. for a casement and other work on the windows, £1 4s. 6d. for pointing the church walls, mending the slating etc, £5 7s. 6d. to Thomas Trubshaw for a stone font, £5 2s. 2d. for colouring, and 104 lb sheet lead.
1842–3	26 8 11	Including repairs to slating, pointing etc.
1843–4	25 7 6½	Including £3 6s. 8d. for lead on the tower.

a SRO, D14/A/PC/2.

STOWE

The accounts of the churchwardens of Stowe for making soughs in the churchyard.

			£	s.	d.
Novr	19	To Joseph Dix for 9½ days work		16	10
		To Joseph Ballance 6½ Do		11	8
		To John Gretton 6½ Do		10	0
	18	To Beer and Ale for the workmen			4
	19	To Do Do Do			6½
	21	To Beer and Ale 9d. Bread Cheese and Beer		1	9
	22	To Beer and Ale 5d. Tobacco 1½d.			6½
		To Horse and Cart 1 day drawing Brickends		5	0
	23	To Brickends and Carriage		2	0
	24	To Beer and Ale 9d. Beer 6d.		1	3
	25	To Ale and Beer			9
	26	To Brickends and Carriage		2	6
		To Ale and Beer			9
	27	To Brickends and Carriage		2	0
		To John Dix 6 days		11	0
		To Chell 6 days		10	0
	28	To Sharpening Picks			6
		To Ale and Beer			5
	29	To Ale and Beer 6d. Ale 6d.		1	0
		To Carriage of Tiles and Brickends		2	6
	30	To Beer 3d. Beer 6d.			9
Decr	2	To Carriage of Tiles and Brickends		2	6
		To Beer and Ale			6½
		To Carriage of Tiles and Brickends		3	6
		To Chell 5 days		8	4
		To Ballance 2 days		3	4
		To William Middleton 4 days		4	0
	3	To Joseph Dix 6 days		11	0
		To John Dix 6 days		11	0
		To John Gretton 3 days		4	6
		To William Bridgwood 2½ days		3	0
		To Ale for the Men		1	0
		To Sharpening 5 Picks			5
		To John Dix for use of tools			6
		To Caskett 8d. barrow 1s.		1	8
		To 1350 Tiles at 36s.	2	8	5
		Total for Soughing the Church yard	9	5	9½

APPENDIX II

EXAMPLES OF HODSON'S ORDERS AND THE RESPONSE TO THEM

The documents published in this appendix are examples of the actual letters sent by Hodson to the churchwardens and preserved among parish records and of replies sent to Hodson from the parishes. They are (a) Hodson's orders in the Cheadle vestry minute-book, together with the decisions of the vestry; (b) the reply of the vestry meeting of Lapley and Wheaton Aston to Hodson's orders of 1830, preserved loose in the volume A/V/1/2; (c) Hodson's orders to the church-wardens of Kinver, 1841 and 1847, preserved among the parish records, SRO, D1197/3/4.

(a) CHEADLE

Meeting held, 12 Aug 1830, 'for the purpose of taking into consideration the purport of a Letter received by the Churchwardens from the Archdeacon of which the following is a copy.'

'Directions to the Church Wardens.

1. A Light iron Gate to be placed at the entrance of the South Porch, in stead of the present outer door so as to admit of the inner door being kept open in fine weather – for the proper ventilation of the Church. 2. Two Additional Casements to be made on each side of the Church in the lower windows. 3. The sealing and walls of the Belfry to be repaired and whitewashed. The Organ Gallary to be kept clean. 4. The pews, and floor of the pews, to be repaired where needful – especially on the South Side. 5. The Covering of the Communion Table to be repaired or renewed – the Bible in the Reading Desk be bound.
6. The Earth to be removed, by degrees, from the North side of the church, till a clear open Space, Six feet wide, and as deep (at the least) as the Level of the church floor within, has been obtained, this Space to be laid with flags, bricks, or tiles, so as to preserve the lower part of the wall free from damp and other injury. 7. The water tub to be removed from the North side of the church and all *Trespass* footpaths into, or through, the churchyard to be stopped up as also the door leading to the Garden on the North Side of the churchyard.

George Hoder [sic]
Archdeacon of Stafford

Rectory, July 16, 1830. To the Church Wardens of Cheadle parish.
Gentlemen, I send you the directions which I have found necessary to give relative to the State of your Parish Church. In addition, I feel it my duty strongly to press upon your Consideration the Propriety of promoting a *suitable Vestry* for the use of the Officiating Minister. You will be so good as to report to me your attention to these matters at the Spring Visitation. I am, Gentlemen, Your etc. etc., George Hoder [sic].

1. It being the unanimous opinion of this meeting that the outer door of the South Porch cannot be dispensed with particularly during the Winter, and that the Casements now ordered to be put in the lower part of the Church renders an iron gate unnecessary, 2. Ordered that one Casement be put on each side of the lower part of the Church. 3. Ordered that the Ceiling and Walls of the Belfry be repaired and whitewashed. 4. —— 5. Ordered that the present Covering of the Communion Table be dyed blue. 6. It appearing that the soil on the North side of the Church cannot with propriety be removed, ordered that the said side of the Church be spouted with two descending Spouts, and the water conveyed away therefrom. 7. Ordered that the door leading to the Garden be removed, and the space walled up – The other roads through the Churchyard are considered of absolute necessity to the safety of the Public. The present Vestry to be widened, and the Clock Weights partitioned off.

(b) LAPLEY AND WHEATON ASTON

The inhabitants of Lapley, respecting the repairs of Wheaton Aston Chapel. June 1830. To the Very Reverend the Archdeacon of Stafford, We the undersigned Inhabitants of Wheaton Aston, at a Vestry Meeting held this 28th Day of June 1830 in conformity with a requisition from the Archdeacon of Stafford, in order to take into our serious consideration the state of the Chapel of ease for the Protestant Church of the parish of Lapley, and after a very minute examination both of the interior and exterior of the premises by us, We do not contemplate any necessity for taking down the present Chapel as we consider it being of sufficient size quite adequate to the number of the population but allow that the building wants to undergo some necessary repairs, and that the Chapel should have the whole of the old pews taken down and new ones built upon an approved plan by a proper Architect. There would be a considerable number more pews than what there are at present, consequently the interior accommodation for the Inhabitants of this Chapelry would be considerably increased. We further consider it necessary that the Gallery should be put in complete repair together with the Bell Tower etc. etc. likewise to have the Communion Table properly railed off, the Desk repaired, Books and Surplice provided. We also do recommend a railing and fencing round the Chapel as it would secure it from considerable damage to which it has hitherto been exposed. And it would be regarded with a considerable greater degree of Solemnity, decorum and reverence to divine worship absolutely required.

But under our present distressed circumstances which have gradually been increasing for within the last few years from the consequent general depressed state of Agriculture from which alone our means are derived, We are with feelings of extreme sorrow obliged to acknowledge that what we shall be able to raise by voluntary contribution or parochial rate will amount to very little, for it is with great difficulty we can support our poor, hoping you will take it into your most serious consideration and will think the afore mentioned repairs requisite and sufficient, and remain Your most Obedient and humble Servants, Thomas Astley Smith, Churchwarden, Charles Bayley, Samuel Reynold, Edward Ward, Thomas Childs, John Addison, Thomas Shotton, Thomas Hitchcox, Charles Parker, A Biddle, George Healey, Samuel S Therwin, John Starkey.

(c) KINVER

Brewood, Nov. 3, 1841

Gentlemen, I send you a Copy of the instructions given to you by the Archdeacon at his recent inspection of the Church at Kinver, and which he has desired me to forward. I remain, Gentlemen, Your obedient servant, AB Haden.

1. Water Tables to be affixed to the Church windows, and the Books in reading desks to be repaired. 2. The lead flashings and battlements of the Tower to be well pointed *in the Spring*: the gutters to be cleaned out. 3. The roof of the Church to be examined and repaired where needful: the gutters frequently cleared of weeds, and laid even where sunk: the east wall of the middle aisle to be pointed externally. 4. A new Spout to be fixed at the South east angle of the Church: and the copings of the East gable to be secured and pointed. 5. The whole of the South wall to be carefully examined by a competent Surveyor, especially towards the East end of it, with a view to ascertaining its stability; the requisite repairs and precautions against future danger, to be applied forthwith. 6. The walls of the Churchyard to be repaired and underbuilt where needful, and the gates to be painted. 7. Additional burial ground to be obtained as soon as practicable, and *if possible* on the *south* side of the Church.

N.B. I strongly recommend the adoption of vigorous measures for erecting a Chapel of ease at the lower part of the Town.

G Hodson, Archdeacon of Stafford

To the Church Wardens of the Parish of *Kinfare*

Wombourn Vicarage, Wolverhampton, May 3, 1847.

Gentlemen,

I am desired by the Archdeacon to forward to you the following Copy of Remarks, that I have received from him. I am, Gentlemen, Yours faithfully, John Hughes, Rural Dean of Trysull

Kinfare, visited April 21, 1847

In excellent order, inside and out, with the single exception of the *Foley* Chancel, the Roof of which needs some repairs. The Church yard is kept remarkably neat. Mem: A National School, and Chapel of Ease, at the lower part of the Town, much wanted. George Hodson, Archdeacon of Stafford

APPENDIX III

THE VISITATION OF ALREWAS

Correspondence between Hodson and Robert Wyatt, the agent of the earl of Lichfield, respecting Alrewas church and churchyard, preserved among records of the earls of Lichfield, SRO 615/P.

Hodson's visitation was carried out as chancellor of Lichfield cathedral and prebendary of Alrewas. The earl of Lichfield was Hodson's tenant, leasing the prebendal tithes, and was responsible as lessee for the maintenance of the chancel. As one of the major landowners in the parish, he could also take a leading part in encouraging united action by the parishioners for the upkeep of the churchyard wall.

The earl's seat, Shugborough, was in Hodson's parish of Colwich, and each letter begins with discussion of the Colwich charities, here omitted.

. . . allow me to trouble you, further, on the subject of *Arlewas* [sic] *Church and Vicarage*. I went over last week to inspect the state of the Church and Chancel. On the repairs etc required in the former I have given the necessary directions to Mr Mottram, the Church-warden. With respect to the Chancel, I found a few particulars out of order, to which you will kindly allow me to request your attention on behalf of Lord Lichfield, in his Lordships twofold capacity of Proprietor, and Lessee of the Prebendary.

1. The *windows*, both in Lord L's and the Rector's Chancels, need some reparations, which should be attended to before winter. I understand the occupiers of pews in the *Turton* (or South) Chancel complain of the cold air coming in at the apertures in the window near them.
2. I observe a *large crack* in the East end wall of the Rector's Chancel, which should be looked into. There is an *appearance* of insecurity in the whole of the East end, and a hideous deformity caused by the *brick battlement* at the top, which I should be very glad to see removed.
3. The *Spout, over the Chancel door* on the South side, is much out of repair, and suffers the water from the roof to fall on the ground and accumulate, to the inconvenience of the Vicar and others entering in thereat.
4. The *posts and rails* which form the fence round the chief part of the Church-yard are in a sadly ruinous and disgraceful state. I understand an offer was very liberally made, some years ago, by Mr Wyatt on behalf of (the then) Lord Anson to furnish his Lordship's tenants with materials for building a brick wall, to the extent of their liability, in lieu of the post and rails, on condition of their finding the labour. This offer was then declined, but I have some reason to think that, if now repeated, it would meet with a better reception, and perhaps lead to a similar measure on the part of the other proprietors and occupiers of land in the Parish.

To the foregoing observations on matters connected with the Church and Church-yard I beg to add that the present Vicar is very naturally anxious to effect an exchange of glebe for land belonging to Lord Lichfield *adjoining the*

Vicarage – I take the liberty of strongly recommending his wishes on this head to the favourable consideration of his Lordship, being convinced that such an exchange would [. . .] essentially to the comfort and advantage of the Vicar of Arlewas [*sic*], whose premises are, at present, most awkwardly hemmed in by land and occupiers of land not subject to his control.

With many apologies for this lengthened communication I remain, Dear Sir, your very faithful Servant,

George Hodson

Lichfield, Dec. 10, 1833

Ranton Abbey, Dec. 18, 1833

. . . In respect to Alrewas Church Chancels I have given Mr Charles Haywood directions, and hope he will very soon have the repairs completed to your satisfaction. To the best of my recollection when the late Mr Mott endeavoured to get a more substantial fence round the church yard of Alrewas, I proposed that if the landowners would concur in substituting a wall for a rail and post fence, that the then Lord Anson would furnish his tenants with materials if they would pay for the workmanship; this proposition was in the express condition that the other landowners would cause their portions of a wall to be built, and that the whole extent of fence now repairable by Lord Lichfield's tenants should be connected, which is now in detached lengths – Lord Lichfield will have no objection to such an arrangement at this time. His Lordship has previously allowed me to confer with the Vicar on the best means of effecting the exchange which the Vicar was anxious to obtain. In regard to the Prebendal Tithe Barn Lord Lichfield is quite willing to join the Prebendary in making it legally part of the Vicarage Glebe.

Lord and Lady Lichfield will be at Shugborough for Christmas. I am, Reverend Sir, Your most obedient Servant, Robert H Wyatt.

INDEX OF VISITATION RETURNS

Abbots Bromley 104
Aldridge 1
Alstonefield 75
Alton 105
Ashley 39
Audley 40

Bagnall 77
Barlaston 42
Barr, Great 1
Barton under Needwood 107
Betley 42
Biddulph 76
Blithfield 108
Blore 109
Bloxwich 2
Blurton 44
Blymhill 43
Bradley 45
Bradley in the Moors 109
Bramshall 110
Brierley Hill 3
Bucknall 77
Burslem, St John the Baptist 78
Burslem, St Paul 79
Burton upon Trent, Holy Trinity 112
Burton upon Trent, St Modwen 111
Bushbury 4
Butterton 79

Castle Church 46
Cauldon 81
Caverswall 80
Cheadle 112
Chebsey 47
Checkley 113
Cheddleton 82
Cheswardine 48
Chilcote 6
Christchurch, Needwood 114
Church Eaton 49
Clifton Campville 4
Cobridge 104
Colton 50
Coseley 22
Cotton 82
Croxden 115

Darlaston 7
Dilhorne 83
Draycott in the Moors 116
Drayton Bassett 8

Elford 9
Elkstone 84
Ellastone 117
Ellenhall 51
Endon 85
Enville 10
Ettingshall 75

Fazeley 11
Fenton 136
Forton 36
Fulford 118

Gayton 119
Gornal, Lower 12
Gornal, Upper 75
Gratwich 120
Grindon 86

Hamstall Ridware 121
Hanbury 122
Handsworth 12
Hanford 37
Hanley 87
Harlaston 13
Haughton 37
Hilderstone 51
Himley 14
Hopwas 75
Horton 87

Ilam 88
Ingestre 38
Ipstones 89

Keele 52
Kingsley 90
Kingstone 123
Kingswinford 16
Kinver 15

Lane End 91
Lapley 53
Leek 92
Leigh 124
Longnor 92
Longton 104

149

Madeley 54
Maer 55
Marchington 125
Marston 56
Mayfield 125
Meerbrook 93
Milwich 56
Mucklestone 58

Newborough 126
Newcastle under Lyme, St George 60
Newcastle under Lyme, St Giles 59
Newchapel 94
Norbury 59
Norton in the Moors 95

Oakamoor 135
Onecote 95

Patshull 18
Pattingham 17
Penn 18
Perry Barr 36

Quarnford 96
Quatt 19

Ranton 61
Rocester 127
Rolleston 128
Rushall 20
Rushton Spencer 97

Sandon 62
Sedgley 21
Seighford 63
Sheen 98
Shelton 104
Shenstone 22
Sheriff Hales 67
Stafford, Christ Church 136
Stafford, St Mary 64
Standon 66

Stoke upon Trent 98
Stone, Christ Church 75
Stone, St Michael 68
Stonnall 24
Stowe 129
Stretton 136
Swynnerton 68

Talke 99
Tamworth 24
Tatenhill 131
Thorpe Constantine 26
Tixall 69
Trentham 70
Trysull 26
Tunstall 104
Tutbury 132

Uttoxeter 133

Walsall, St Matthew 27
Walsall, St Paul 28
Walsall, St Peter 75
Walsall Wood 75
Warslow 100
Waterfall 101
Wednesbury 29
West Bromwich, All Saints 30
West Bromwich, Christ Church 31
Weston under Lizard 71
Weston upon Trent 72
Wetley Rocks 103
Wetton 102
Whitmore 73
Wigginton 32
Wilnecote 33
Wolstanton 102
Wolverhampton, St Paul 75
Wombourn 34
Woodcote 67
Woore 74
Wordsley 75
Worfield 35
Wychnor 31

Yoxall 134

Printed in England for Her Majesty's Stationery Office
by Hobbs the Printers of Southampton
(936) Dd0504281 K6 9/80 G327